Quantitative Marketing and Marketing Management

Adamantios Diamantopoulos
Wolfgang Fritz · Lutz Hildebrandt (Eds.)

Quantitative Marketing and Marketing Management

Marketing Models and Methods in Theory and Practice

With contributions by
András Bauer, Hans Baumgartner, Albert C. Bemmaor, Markus Blut, Yasemin Boztuğ,
Philipp Broeckelmann, Reinhold Decker, Adamantios Diamantopoulos, Claus Ebster,
Wolfgang Fritz, Christoph Fuchs, Dominic Gastes, Hubert Gatignon, Wolfgang Gaul,
Nicolas Glady, Andrea Gröppel-Klein, Reinhard Grohs, Nadine Hennigs,
Lutz Hildebrandt, Hartmut Holzmüller, Christian Homburg, Daniel Hoppe,
Harald Hruschka, Michael Kempe, Karsten Kieckhäfer, Daniel Klapper,
Martin Klarmann, Tetyana Kosyakova, Manfred Krafft, Gilles Laurent,
Peter S. H. Leeflang, Michael Löffler, Bettina Lorenz, Ariel Mitev, Rajan Nataraajan,
Martin Natter, Thomas Otter, Ana-Marija Ozimec, Marcel Paulssen,
Alessandro M. Peluso, Kalyan Raman, Heribert Reisinger, Thomas Reutterer,
Cam Rungie, Henrik Sattler, Christian Schlereth, Steffen Schmidt, Oliver Schnittka,
Nadja Silberhorn, Günter Silberer, Bernd Skiera, Thomas Stefan Spengler,
Markus Stolper, Thomas Suwelack, Dirk Temme, Dirk Totzek, Franziska Völckner,
Thomas Volling, Klaus-Peter Wiedmann, Thomas Wüstefeld, German Zenetti

Dedicated to
o. Univ.-Prof. Dipl.-Ing. Dr. Dr. h. c. Udo Wagner

Editors

Prof. DDr. Adamantios Diamantopoulos
University of Vienna
Vienna, Austria
http://international-marketing.univie.ac.at

Prof. Dr. Lutz Hildebrandt
Humboldt University of Berlin
Berlin, Germany
http://www.wiwi.hu-berlin.de/professuren/bwl/
marketing

Prof. Dr. Wolfgang Fritz
Technische Universität Braunschweig
Braunschweig, Germany
https://www.tu-braunschweig.de/marketing

ISBN 978-3-8349-3060-6
DOI 10.1007/978-3-8349-3722-3

ISBN 978-3-8349-3722-3 (eBook)

The Deutsche Nationalbibliothek lists this publication in the Deutsche Nationalbibliografie; detailed bibliographic data are available in the Internet at http://dnb.d-nb.de.

Springer Gabler

Editorial office: Barbara Roscher | Walburga Himmel
Cover design: KünkelLopka GmbH, Heidelberg

Printed on acid-free paper

Springer Gabler is a brand of Springer DE. Springer DE is part of Springer Science+Business Media.
www.springer-gabler.de

o. Univ.-Prof. Dipl.-Ing. Dr. Dr. h. c. Udo Wagner

Preface and Overview

On July 19, 2012, Udo Wagner, Chair of Marketing at the University of Vienna, will be 60 years of age. This event marks a period of more than 30 years during which Udo Wagner has influenced the development of marketing science through many important contributions. As close marketing colleagues in Vienna and as his friends, we have therefore decided to publish a *Festschrift* entitled *"Quantitative Marketing and Marketing Management"* aimed at honoring Udo Wagner's work and person.

Many of his friends, colleagues and former academic students in Europe and overseas supported our project by writing a chapter exclusively for this *Festschrift* thus dedicating it to Udo Wagner. These contributions are classified according to his major research fields namely: (1) marketing models and marketing research methods, (2) consumer behavior and retailing, and (3) marketing management.

Part 1
Marketing Models and Marketing Research Methods

After a short introduction highlighting the stations of Udo Wagner's life and his most important contributions to marketing science, the *Festschrift* begins in **Part 1** with the article **"Implementing the Pareto/NBD Model: A User-Friendly Approach"** by **Albert C. Bemmaor, Nicolas Glady, and Daniel Hoppe**. The paper addresses an issue that has been qualified as "challenging" in the literature, that is, estimating the parameters of the well-known Pareto/NBD model. The authors propose a maximum likelihood method to compute the model parameters and illustrate it with two data sets that have been previously used in the literature. The proposed procedure leads to the same parameter estimates as previously published approaches and can be implemented in a user-friendly fashion using a spreadsheet.

The chapter **"The Consistency Adjustment Problem of AHP Pairwise Comparison Matrices"** by **Dominic Gastes and Wolfgang Gaul** is dedicated to some important issues surrounding the application of the Analytical Hierarchy Process (AHP) method, that is, the creation of pairwise comparison matrices, the examination of their consistencies, and the derivation of weights for the underlying objective functions. The authors conduct a simulation study showing, among other things, the negative effects of increasing inconsistencies on the derived weights. These findings underline the importance of controlling for consistencies and the consequences of subsequent adjustments of comparison matrices in AHP applications.

Lutz Hildebrandt, Dirk Temme, and Marcel Paulssen show in their contribution **"Choice Modeling and SEM"** how two dominant methodological approaches in quantitative marketing research of the last decades can be integrated. Combining the strengths of covariance structure analysis to control for measurement errors and the ability to predict choice behavior via the Multinomial Logit (MNL) model creates a powerful hybrid approach – the Integrated Choice and Latent Variable (ICLV) model – for marketing research. The authors document the basic features of this approach and present an example which illustrates how the ICLV model can be used to explain travel mode choice.

The important key informant and common method problems in survey research are taken up by **Christian Homburg, Martin Klarmann, and Dirk Totzek** in their article **"Using Multi-Informant Designs to Address Key Informant and Common Method Bias"**. The authors focus on the question how researchers can rely on multi-informant designs in order to limit the threats of key informant and common method bias on the validity and reliability of survey research. In particular, they show how researchers can effectively design studies that employ multiple informants and how multi-informant data can be aggregated in order to obtain more accurate results than can be obtained with single informant studies.

Harald Hruschka gives in his paper **"Using Artificial Neural Nets for Flexible Aggregate Market Response Modeling"** an overview of the state of research on aggregate market response modeling by means of multilayer perceptrons (MLPs), the most widespread type of artificial neural nets. As the author shows, MLPs are not limited to fixed parametric functional forms, but offer flexible approaches for modeling market response functions of marketing instruments.

In their paper **"Supporting Strategic Product Portfolio Planning by Market Simulation"**, **Karsten Kieckhäfer, Thomas Volling, and Thomas Stefan Spengler** propose a decision support for the strategic planning of the future powertrain and vehicle portfolio in the automotive industry. They use a hybrid market simulation approach for a simultaneous consideration of aggregated system and individual consumer behavior. This non-traditional simulation model allows for estimating the development of market shares of various powertrains in different vehicle size classes subject to the vehicle portfolio offered and to assumptions about consumer behavior and market environment.

Peter S. H. Leeflang and Alessandro M. Peluso discuss in their contribution **"Knowledge Generation in Marketing"** how knowledge can be acquired in marketing. In particular, they argue that generalizations offered by meta-analyses are very useful for managers in order to improve their decision making. To support their argument, the authors perform an empirical study on subjective estimations of price, advertising, and price promotion elasticities.

In their contribution **"Implications of Linear Versus Dummy Coding for Pooling of Information in Hierarchical Models"**, **Thomas Otter and Tetyana Kosyakova** address the topic of how to pool information more effectively across respondents in problems that involve a large number of (a priori) categorical attributes. The authors illustrate the problem contrasting linear versus categorical coding. Their findings are relevant to the analysis of hierarchical models particularly in the context of conjoint choice experiments.

Ana-Marija Ozimec, Martin Natter, and Thomas Reutterer take up in their contribution **"Visual Decision Making Styles and Geographical Information Systems"** a relatively new perspective of marketing, that is, the support of managerial decision making by using data visualization aids, in particular Geographical Information Systems (GIS). Using an online experiment, the way in which different GIS representations influence marketing analysts' decision making styles is investigated.

The paper **"Analyzing Sequences in Marketing Research"** by **Günter Silberer** emphasizes that sequences of discrete events and states researched in sociology and psychology are largely neglected in marketing research. Nonetheless, sequences are typical attributes of market behavior. Against this background, the author addresses the questions of which sequences could be of particular interest to marketing science and practice and how they could be researched empirically.

Christian Schlereth and Bernd Skiera present in their contribution **"DISE: Dynamic Intelligent Survey Engine"** an extendable, web-based survey engine (DISE) that supports the construction of technically sophisticated surveys and limits the effort that researchers must invest to develop new preference methods (e.g., in conjoint analysis settings). The authors discuss the overall architecture and implementation of DISE and outline how it can be employed in surveys, using an illustrative example.

Part 2
Consumer Behavior and Retailing

Part 2 of the *Festschrift* begins with the chapter **"The Effect of Attitude Toward Money on Financial Trouble and Compulsive Buying - Studying Hungarian Consumers in Debt During the Financial Crisis"** by **András Bauer and Ariel Mitev**. The aim of this study is to develop a deeper understanding of the different dimensions of attitude toward money and financial trouble in the light of the economic crisis in 2008/09. Furthermore, it is analyzed whether compulsive buying would moderate the relationships between these constructs. The research is based on a large scale empirical study that has been carried out in Hungary.

"Repetitive Purchase Behavior" is the subject of **Hans Baumgartner**'s contribution to the *Festschrift*. Eight different types of purchase behavior are distinguished in the model of the purchase cube proposed by the author. One of these types is repetitive purchase behavior, characterized by functional purchases that are made deliberately rather than spontaneously and are relatively low in purchase involvement. The author discusses the concept of repetitive purchase behavior and briefly reviews prior research that has investigated repetitive purchases from various perspectives.

Yasemin Boztuğ, Lutz Hildebrandt, and Nadja Silberhorn concentrate in their study **"Investigating Cross-Category Brand Loyal Purchase Behavior in FMCG"** on the widely neglected aspects of cross-category relationships of national brands and on consumers' brand choice decisions across several product categories. Their measure of brand loyalty is the Share of Category Requirements (SCR) to capture the relative share of category purchases that individual households give to each brand they buy. The authors use scanner panel and corresponding survey data for the empirical analysis. The scanner panel data contain households' repeated FMCG purchase information of purchases in different kinds of store types within a limited geographic region. From an analysis of brand loyalty patterns different consumer segments result. An ex-post analysis based on general attitudes and other consumer characteristics reveals distinguishing factors between the consumer segments.

In the next article entitled **"Validation of Brand Relationship Types Using Advanced Clustering Methods"**, **Wolfgang Fritz, Michael Kempe, and Bettina Lorenz** reanalyze the data of an existing study on consumer-brand relationships conducted in Germany. Based on a mixture clustering approach, the new analysis supports in principle the former findings indicating the existence of four generic types of consumer-brand relationships. Furthermore, as the findings suggest, advanced methods of cluster analysis do not improve the solution provided by traditional clustering in each case.

Christoph Fuchs and Adamantios Diamantopoulos introduce in their paper **"Positioning Bases' Influence on Product Similarity Perceptions: An Open Sort Task Approach"** the communication of similar types of positioning bases as a means for creating similarity perceptions. They use an open sort task employing real products and advertisements in order to empirically test their hypotheses. The study demonstrates that consumers classify products in terms of similarity based on their underlying positioning bases as anchored in advertisements. It also shows that consumers do not use concrete positioning bases more often as a basis for classification than abstract positioning bases.

The study **"The Influence of Location-Aware Mobile Marketing Messages on Consumers' Buying Behavior"** by **Andrea Gröppel-Klein and Philipp Broeckelmann** reports the findings of two experiments involving location-aware mobile marketing messages (LA-MMM). The findings suggest that LA-MMM have only a limited influence on consumers' approach behavior towards stores, store choice and buying behavior. Therefore, LA-MMM is not an effective way to increase sales of a particular brand in the short term and should only be used in conjunction with other marketing tools and promotions.

Daniel Klapper and German Zenetti demonstrate in their paper **"Combining Micro and Macro Data to Study Retailer Pricing in the Presence of State Dependence"** how firms can use store-level scanner data in combination with tracking data to estimate the impact of state dependence on consumer purchase behavior and determine the resulting effect on pricing decisions. The authors show how pricing and profitability are affected if a retailer does or does not anticipate state dependence in predicting consumer purchase behavior.

The identification of cross-cultural mattering drivers of customer service satisfaction in after sales business is the topic of the paper **"Service Satisfaction With Premium Durables: A Cross-Cultural Investigation"** by **Michael Löffler and Reinhold Decker**. This study contrasts individualistic with collectivistic cultural contexts and empirically substantiates nonlinearity of satisfaction triggers. The findings show that individualistic and collectivistic cultural backgrounds reveal significant differences regarding important triggers of service satisfaction, whereas brand sympathy over-proportionally triggers service satisfaction across cultures.

While many studies have been devoted to brand loyalty, very few have compared brand loyalty with loyalty to specific product attributes, such as a certain pack size or price level. In their paper **"Brand Loyalty vs. Loyalty to Product Attributes"** **Cam Rungie and Gilles Laurent** propose the Polarization Index as a more valid measure of behavioral loyalty than common measures and show on the example of detergents how to use this measure to compare loyalty across different attributes and different levels of a given attribute.

Part 3
Marketing Management

Part 3 of the *Festschrift* is opened by the chapter **"Market Shaping Orientation and Firm Performance"**. In this study, **Markus Blut, Hartmut Holzmüller, and Markus Stolper** discuss two approaches to the market orientation of the firm. The first is characterized as a 'market driven'- the second as a 'market shaping'-approach. The authors develop new measures for the latter construct and empirically test its antecedents and consequences also considering moderator variables affecting the market shaping orientation–performance linkage.

In their paper **"Sponsorship of Televised Sport Events - An Analysis of Mediating Effects on Sponsor Image"**, **Reinhard Grohs and Heribert Reisinger** propose that event image, event-sponsor fit and sponsorship exposure mediate the effect of interest in the sponsored event on sponsor image in two ways. First, high interest in the sponsored event increases perceived event image which, in turn, benefits sponsor image. Second, high event interest increases spectatorship of the event, and hence exposure to the sponsors of the event. High sponsorship exposure positively impacts perceived event-sponsor fit and sponsor image. Empirical tests relating to two large televised sport events confirm the proposed hypotheses.

In his "thought piece" entitled **"The Countenance of Marketing: A View From the 21st Century Ivory Tower"**, **Rajan Nataraajan** reflects on what truly matters to marketing in this century. Based upon a careful scan of the "going on" in the world, he first offers a configuration that may aid in research ideas generation and then culls out broad areas worthy of academic enquiry by marketers (e.g., e-commerce, green marketing, health care, altruism, evolutionary psychology, and government).

Kalyan Raman and Hubert Gatignon show in their study **"Profiting From Uncertainty"** that market response uncertainty can be judiciously harnessed in determining the optimal advertising budget and spending pattern to improve the expected profitability of a firm. Using stochastic optimal control, the authors derive the optimal feedback advertising policy to accomplish this objective, and they establish that the optimal advertising policy increases profitability at a rate directly proportional to the error variance.

"An Empirical Analysis of Brand Image Transfer in Multiple Sports Sponsorships" is the focus of the contribution of **Henrik Sattler, Oliver Schnittka, and Franziska Völckner.** Their study is the first to analyze image transfer effects within multiple sponsorships. Specifically, image transfer effects are investigated (1) from the sponsee (e.g., FIFA World Cup) to the sponsoring brands, and (2) between the sponsoring brands, as well as the influence of the fit between the participating entities and brand familiarity on these transfer effects. The findings indicate that a familiar sponsoring brand primarily benefits from the sponsee, whereas an unfamiliar sponsoring brand mainly benefits from a connection with a familiar sponsoring brand.

In their paper **"Effects of Money-Back and Low-Price Guarantees on Consumer Behavior - State of the Art and Future Research Perspectives"**, **Thomas Suwelack and Manfred Krafft** present a literature review of 28 money-back guarantees (MBGs) and 30 low-price guarantees (LPGs) studies. While both a behavioral and an economic research stream exist, the focus of this review is on the effects of MBGs and LPGs on consumer behavior. This literature review subsequently provides some avenues for future MBG and LPG research and offers implications for retailing practice.

Klaus-Peter Wiedmann, Nadine Hennigs, Steffen Schmidt, and Thomas Wüstefeld outline in their study **"The Perceived Value of Brand Heritage and Brand Luxury - Managing the Effect on Brand Strength"** a multidimensional framework for analyzing the consequences of brand heritage and brand luxury for consumers. Based on a structural modeling approach, the most important effects of the perceived luxury and heritage of a brand on consumers' perceived brand value in terms of the economic, functional, affective, and social evaluation of a brand are identified empirically as well as is the impact on brand strength.

Part 4
Business Administration in Vienna

The paper **"Studying Business Administration in Vienna - The Perception of Alternative Educational Institutions by Freshmen Now and Then"** by **Claus Ebster and Heribert Reisinger** does not fit clearly into the three major parts of this *Festschrift*. However, it is an interesting and relevant piece of research relating directly to the University of Vienna to which Udo Wagner has been affiliated for more than 20 years. For this reason, we have exclusively created a separate **part 4** for this article.

Ebster and Reisinger present a study carried out to aid the positioning and targeting of the Center for Business Studies at the University of Vienna, an institution shaped by the leadership of Udo Wagner. It does not only reveal the general image students have of business education at the University of Vienna and its main competitor, the Vienna University of Economics and Business, but is also a replication of similar research carried out by Udo Wagner and colleagues in 1996. This study thus allows for a longitudinal analysis of students' perceptions of their alma mater through a comparison of now and then.

Acknowledgements

The editors warmly thank all the authors for their contributions to this *Festschrift* in honor of Udo Wagner. We all congratulate Udo Wagner on his 60th birthday and wish him all the best for his personal and professional future.

We also thank all persons who gave us the support needed to accomplish our editorial work. We are very grateful for the help of Jessica Fleer, Wencke Gülow, Michael Kempe, Marie Schulte, and especially of Stefanie Sohn from the Institute of Marketing, Technische Universität Braunschweig, for all the work associated with coordinating the editing activities, formatting, and proofreading of each article. For their informal help at the University of Vienna we thank Maria Kiss and Heribert Reisinger very much.

Many thanks go also to the companies who supported this *Festschrift* by a kind sponsorship – GfK Austria, Vienna, Management Consult Dr. Eisele & Dr. Noll, Mannheim, Germany, and Otto Beisheim Group, Düsseldorf, Germany. Finally, we warmly thank Barabara Roscher who did not hesitate to add this *Festschrift* to the publisher's program of the Gabler Verlag, Wiesbaden, Germany.

The authors and the editors would be delighted if this collection of studies could serve as a source of inspiration as well as enjoyment for Udo Wagner.

Adamantios Diamantopoulos, Wolfgang Fritz, and Lutz Hildebrandt

Vienna, Braunschweig, and Berlin   July 2012

Otto Beisheim Group   **management consult**
Dr. Eisele & Dr. Noll GmbH

Table of Contents

Introduction

Part 1
Marketing Models and Marketing Research Methods

Part 2
Consumer Behavior and Retailing

Part 3
Marketing Management

Part 4
Business Administration in Vienna

Part 5
Udo Wagner

List of Authors

Bauer, András, PhD from the Hungarian Academy of Sciences; Professor of Marketing and Head of the Marketing Department at Corvinus University of Budapest, Hungary.

Baumgartner, Hans, PhD from Stanford University, Stanford, California, USA; Smeal Professor of Marketing, Smeal College of Business at Pennsylvania State University, State College, Pennsylvania, USA.

Bemmaor, Albert C., PhD from Purdue University, West Lafayette, Indiana, USA; Professor of Marketing at ESSEC Business School, Cergy-Pontoise, France.

Blut, Markus, PhD from the University of Münster, Germany; Juniorprofessor of Marketing at Technische Universität Dortmund, Germany.

Boztuğ, Yasemin, PhD from Humboldt University of Berlin, Germany; Professor of Marketing and Consumer Research at the Georg-August-University Göttingen, Germany.

Broeckelmann, Philipp, PhD from Saarland University, Saarbrücken, Germany; Consultant at t+d innovation + marketing consultants GmbH, Berlin, Germany.

Decker, Reinhold, PhD from the University of Karlsruhe, Germany; Professor of Marketing, Chair of Business Administration and Marketing at the University of Bielefeld, Germany.

Diamantopoulos, Adamantios, PhD from University of Strathclyde and DLitt from Loughborough University, UK; Professor of Marketing, Chair of International Marketing at the University of Vienna, Austria.

Ebster, Claus, PhD from the University of Vienna; Associate Professor at the University of Vienna, Austria.

Fritz, Wolfgang, PhD from the University of Mannheim, Germany; Professor of Marketing and of the Institute of Marketing at Technische Universität Braunschweig, Germany; Honorary Professor at the University of Vienna, Austria.

Fuchs, Christoph, PhD from University of Vienna, Austria; Assistant Professor at the Department of Marketing, Rotterdam School of Management, Erasmus University, Rotterdam, The Netherlands.

Gastes, Dominic, PhD from the University of Karlsruhe, Germany; Product Manager TruLaser Tube, TRUMPF Werkzeugmaschinen GmbH & Co. KG, Ditzingen, Germany.

Gatignon, Hubert, PhD from the University of California, Los Angeles, California, USA; The Claude Janssen Chaired Professor of Business Administration and Professor of Marketing at INSEAD, Fontainebleau, France.

Gaul, Wolfgang, PhD from the University of Bonn, Germany; Professor of Marketing, Institute of Decision Theory and Operations Research, Karlsruhe Institute of Technology (KIT), Karlsruhe, Germany.

Glady, Nicolas, PhD from K.U. Leuven, The Netherlands; Assistant Professor of Marketing at ESSEC Business School, Cergy-Pontoise, France.

Gröppel-Klein, Andrea, PhD from the University of Paderborn, Germany; Professor of Marketing, Chair of Business Administration and Marketing, Director of the Institute of Consumer Research and Behavior Research, Saarland University, Saarbrücken, Germany.

Grohs, Reinhard, PhD from the University of Vienna, Austria; Assistant Professor at the Department of Strategic Management, Marketing, and Tourism, Innsbruck University, School of Management, Innsbruck, Austria.

Hennigs, Nadine, PhD from Leibniz University Hannover; Assistant Professor at the Institute of Marketing and Management, Leibniz University Hannover, Germany.

Hildebrandt, Lutz, PhD from Technische Universität Berlin; Professor of Marketing, Director of the Institute of Marketing at Humboldt University of Berlin, Germany; Honorary Professor at the University of Vienna, Austria.

Holzmüller, Hartmut, PhD from Vienna University of Economics and Business, Vienna, Austria, Professor of Marketing, Chair of Marketing at Technische Universität Dortmund, Germany.

Homburg, Christian, PhD from the University of Karlsruhe (TH), Germany; Honorary Doctorates from Copenhagen Business School, Copenhagen, Denmark, and Technische Universität Bergakademie Freiberg, Germany; Professor of Marketing, Chair of the Marketing Department, Director of the Institute of Market-oriented Management at the University of Mannheim, Germany.

Hoppe, Daniel, PhD from the University of Vienna, Austria; Project Leader at The Boston Consulting Group, São Paulo, Brazil.

Hruschka, Harald, PhD from Vienna University of Economics and Business, Vienna, Austria; Professor of Marketing, Chair of Marketing at the Institute of Business Administration, University of Regensburg, Germany.

Kempe, Michael, PhD from Technische Universität Braunschweig; Assistant Professor at the Institute of Marketing, Technische Universität Braunschweig, Germany.

Kieckhäfer, Karsten, Research and Teaching Assistant at the Institute of Automotive Management and Industrial Production, Technische Universität Braunschweig, Germany.

Klapper, Daniel, PhD from Humboldt University of Berlin; Professor of Marketing, Director of the Institute of Marketing at Humboldt University Berlin, Germany.

Klarmann, Martin, PhD from the University of Mannheim, Germany; Professor of Marketing, Institute of Decision Theory and Operations Research, Karlsruhe Institute of Technology (KIT), Karlsruhe, Germany.

Kosyakova, Tetyana, Research Associate at the Chair of Services Marketing, Goethe University Frankfurt, Germany.

Krafft, Manfred, PhD from the University of Kiel; Professor of Marketing, Director of the Institute of Marketing, University of Münster, Germany.

Laurent, Gilles, PhD from Massachusetts Institute of Technology (MIT), Cambridge, Massachusetts, USA; Professor of Marketing at École des Hautes Études Commerciales (HEC) Paris, Jouy-en-Josas, France.

Leeflang, Peter S. H., PhD from Erasmus University, Rotterdam, The Netherlands; Frank M. Bass Professor of Marketing, University of Groningen, The Netherlands; Research Professor at Aston Bussiness School, Birmingham, United Kingdom; BAT Chair in Marketing at LUISS Guido Carli University Rome, Italy.

Löffler, Michael, Head of Customer Relations, Dr. Ing. h. c. F. Porsche AG, Stuttgart, Germany.

Lorenz, Bettina, PhD from Technische Universität Braunschweig, Germany; Research Consultant and Knowledge Manager at Volkswagen Consulting, Volkswagen AG, Wolfsburg, Germany.

Mitev, Ariel, PhD from Corvinus University of Budapest; Assistant Professor at the Marketing Department, Corvinus University of Budapest, Hungary.

Nataraajan, Rajan, PhD from Drexel University, Philadelphia, Pennsylvania, USA; Professor of Marketing and Director of Consumer Economics, Department of Economics, Auburn University, Auburn, Alabama, USA.

Natter, Martin, PhD from Vienna University of Economics and Business Vienna, Austria; Professor of Marketing, Strothoff-Chair of Retailing, Goethe University Frankfurt, Germany.

Otter, Thomas, PhD from Vienna University of Economics and Business, Vienna, Austria; Professor of Marketing, Chair of Services Marketing, Goethe University Frankfurt, Germany.

Ozimec, Ana-Marija, PhD from Goethe University Frankfurt; Research Assistant at the Strothoff-Chair of Retailing at Goethe University Frankfurt, Germany.

Paulssen, Marcel, PhD from Technische Universität Berlin, Germany; Professor of Marketing, HEC Geneva, University of Geneva, Switzerland.

Peluso, Alessandro M., PhD from the University of Salento, Lecce, Italy; Adjunct Professor of Marketing, Department of Business and Management, LUISS Guido Carli University, Rome, Italy.

Raman, Kalyan, PhD from the University of Texas at Dallas, USA; Professor in the Medill IMC Department, Courtesy Professor of Marketing in the Kellogg School of Management at Northwestern University, Evanston, Illinois, and Associate Faculty in the Center for Complex Systems at the University of Michigan, Ann Arbor, USA.

Reisinger, Heribert, PhD from the University of Vienna; Associate Professor at the University of Vienna, Austria.

Reutterer, Thomas, PhD from Vienna University of Economics and Business; Professor of Marketing and Head of the Institute for Service Marketing and Tourism, Vienna University of Economics and Business, Austria.

Rungie, Cam, PhD from the University of South Australia; Senior Lecturer at the School of Marketing, Division of Business, University of South Australia, Adelaide, South Australia.

Sattler, Henrik, PhD from the University of Kiel, Germany; Professor of Marketing and Management and Director of the Institute of Marketing and Media, University of Hamburg, Germany.

Schlereth, Christian, PhD from Goethe University Frankfurt; Assistant Professor of Marketing and Electronic Services at Goethe University of Frankfurt, Germany.

Schmidt, Steffen, PhD from Leibniz University Hannover; Research Assistant at the Institute of Marketing and Management, Leibniz University Hannover, Hannover, Germany.

Schnittka, Oliver, PhD from the University of Hamburg; Research Assistant at the Institute of Marketing and Media, University of Hamburg, Germany.

Silberhorn, Nadja, PhD from Humboldt University of Berlin; Senior Research Consultant, FactWorks GmbH, Berlin, Germany.

Silberer, Günter, PhD from the University of Mannheim, Germany; Emeritus Professor of Marketing and Consumer Research at the Georg-August-University Göttingen, Germany.

Skiera, Bernd, PhD from the University of Kiel, Germany; Professor of Electronic Commerce, Director of the Department of Marketing, Goethe University Frankfurt, Germany.

Spengler, Thomas Stefan, PhD from the University of Karlsruhe (TH); Professor of Production and Logistics and Director of the Institute of Automotive Management and Industrial Production at Technische Universität Braunschweig; Vice President for Research and Technology Transfer of Technische Universität Braunschweig, Germany.

Stolper, Markus, PhD from Technische Universität Dortmund, Germany; Head of Strategic Corporate Development at ARDEX GmbH, Witten, Germany.

Suwelack, Thomas, Doctoral Student at the Institute of Marketing, University of Münster, Germany.

Temme, Dirk, PhD from Humboldt University of Berlin; Professor and Chair of Methods of Economic and Social Research, Schumpeter School of Business and Economics, Bergische Universität Wuppertal, Germany.

Totzek, Dirk, PhD from the University of Mannheim; Assistant Professor of Empirical Research Methods, Department of Marketing I, University of Mannheim, Germany.

Völckner, Franziska, PhD from the University of Hamburg, Germany; Professor of Marketing, Director of the Seminar of Marketing and Brand Management, University of Cologne, Germany.

Volling, Thomas, PhD from Technische Universität Braunschweig; Assistant Professor at the Institute of Automotive Management and Industrial Production at Technische Universität Braunschweig, Germany.

Wiedmann, Klaus-Peter, PhD from the University of Mannheim, Germany; Professor of Marketing and Management and Director of the Institute of Marketing and Management at Leibniz University Hannover, Germany.

Wüstefeld, Thomas, PhD from Leibniz University Hannover; Research Assistant at the Institute of Marketing and Management, Leibniz University Hannover, Germany.

Zenetti, German, Doctoral Student and Research Assistant at the Chair of Consumer Goods, Goethe University Frankfurt, Germany.

Introduction

1   In Honor of Udo Wagner, Professor at the University of Vienna, Austria

Adamantios Diamantopoulos, University of Vienna, Austria

Wolfgang Fritz, Technische Universität Braunschweig, Germany, and University of Vienna, Austria

Lutz Hildebrandt, Humboldt University of Berlin, Germany, and University of Vienna, Austria

1.1   Education and Academic Career

Udo Wagner was born on the 19th of July, 1952 in Klagenfurt, the capital of Kärnten in Austria. He went to school in Vienna from 1959 to 1970. After the school-leaving exam at the 2nd Bundesrealgymnasium XIX (Secondary High School), he studied Technical Mathematics at the Vienna University of Technology (1970-1976) which he completed with a Diploma (Master degree). He started his academic career in 1976 as a research assistant and was later employed as an assistant professor in the Institute of Business Management at the Vienna University of Economics and Business (1976-1988). He received his Doctorate in Econometrics in 1984 from the Vienna University of Technology, followed by the completion of his habilitation in 1991 at the Vienna University of Economics and Business. He received the Venia docendi (official Austrian teaching qualification) in the field of „Quantitative Business Administration and Operations Research".

Already before completing his habilitation, Udo Wagner held noteworthy guest professorships. The way led him in 1987 to the Marketing Chair of the Ecole Supérieure des Sciences Economiques et Commerciales (ESSEC) in Cergy-Pontoise and to the Institute d'Administration des Entreprises (IAE) at the Université de Droit, d'Economie et des Sciences d'Aix-Marseilles, Aix-en-Provence (France). In 1989 and from 1990 to 1991, he was visiting and assistant professor respectively in the Marketing Institute of the Graduate School of Management at Purdue University in West Lafayette, Indiana (USA). He also obtained a fixed-term professorship for Quantitative Marketing in the Institute of Decision Theory at the University of Karlsruhe (Germany) from which he received an offer for a chaired professorship one year later. Nevertheless, he decided instead, to join the Vienna University of Economics and Business at which he was appointed Associate Professor for Business Administration with focus on Marketing and International Management in 1991. In the same year, he accepted an offer from the University of Vienna as Full Professor of Business Administration and holder of the Chair of Marketing. From 1992 to 2004, he was Head of the Institute of Business Administration and from 2004 to 2006 Dean of the Faculty of Business, Economics, and Statistics. From 1994 to 1999, he was also academic director of the "International Economic Relations" program at the University of Applied Sciences in Eisenstadt. Further visiting professorships took him to the Babes-Bolyai University in Cluj-Napoca (Romania) in 2006 and to the National Chiao Tung University, Hsinchu (Taiwan) and Université Paris Dauphine (France) in 2007.

During 2005-2011, Udo Wagner was Vice-President "Development" of the European Marketing Academy (EMAC). In 2011, he became the President-elect and in 2012 the President of EMAC for the term from 2012 to 2014. Furthermore, he has been a member of the Board of Directors of the Korean Academy of Marketing Science since 2006 (which renamed itself as Korean Scholars of Marketing Science in 2011).

1.2   Global Scholarly Activities

The various visiting professorships which Udo Wagner has had in France, the USA, Romania, and in Taiwan already distinguish him as a globally-oriented marketing scientist. This also applies for his memberships in numerous international academic associations and institutes such as the Academy of Marketing Science (AMS) and the INFORMS Society of Marketing Science (ISMS). Besides an extensive activity in Editorial Boards or as Editor of leading journals (e.g., *International Journal of Research in Marketing; Journal of Business Research; Marketing ZFP-Journal of Research and Management; OR Spectrum*), a long-standing reviewer activity for both highly respected journals (e.g., *Journal of Marketing; Journal of Marketing Research; European Journal of Operational Research; Management Science*) and for major foundations (e.g., National Science Foundation; Austrian Science Fund (FWF); Schmalenbach Award), he has been intensely involved in international conferences. In addition to his long-standing commitment to EMAC conferences since 1994, Udo Wagner has been repeatedly involved in the conferences of the German Society for Operations Research (GOR) where he acted as the chair of the section "Marketing" from 2003 to 2005. This activity spectrum has been considerably extended in recent years, as illustrated in his role as Conference Co-Chair of the Global Marketing Conference in Shanghai (2008) and Seoul (2012) as well as Conference Chair of the Fourth German-French-Austrian (GFA) Conference on Quantitative Marketing in Vienna (2010).

The strong international orientation of Udo Wagner also becomes apparent in the number and diversity of his conference presentations. Two thirds of his ca. 120 presentations have taken place in 17 countries beyond Austria. He has also presented his research at several universities in the USA (Stanford University, University of Southern California, University of Illinois at Urbana Champaign, Purdue University), Canada (University of Alberta), Korea (Hannam University, Daejeon; Sungshin Women's University, Seoul; Yonsei University, Seoul; Dongguk University, Seoul; Kyunghee University, Seoul), Taiwan (National Chiao Tung University, Hsinchu), China (Cheung Kong Graduate School of Business, Beijing; Jiao Tong University, Shanghai), France (ESSEC, Cergy Pontoise; INSEAD, Fontainbleau; Université Paris Val de Marne, Paris; Université Montpellier; Université Nantes), Italy (Educational Institute of South Tirol, Merano), Switzerland (University of St. Gallen), Denmark (Odense University), the Netherlands (Amsterdam School of Business; Erasmus University of Rotterdam; Tilburg University), Russia (Finance Academy under the Government of the Russian Federation, Moscow) and Germany (universities of Berlin, Bielefeld, Bonn, Braunschweig, Freiburg, Heidelberg, Karlsruhe, Köln, Mannheim, Oldenburg, Regensburg, Saarbrücken).

1.3   Honors and Awards

For his scientific achievements, Udo Wagner has received several honors and awards. He was honored in Austria in 1989 with the Senator Wilhelm Wilfing Award of the Vienna University of Economics and Business; in 1993 and 1997 with the University Award of the Viennese economy; in 1995 with the Order of Merit of the state capital of Burgenland Eisenstadt; in 2000 with the Komturkreuz of the federal state Burgenland; and in 2007 with the distinction "Top Publication 2007" of the Vienna University of Economics and Business. In Germany, one of his early articles published in 1978 in the *Zeitschrift für Betriebswirtschaft/ Journal of Business Economics*, was recognized as a "Milestone of Business Administration" (Albach 1991). Furthermore, Udo Wagner was awarded an honorary doctorate (Dr. h.c.) at the Technische Universität Braunschweig in 2006. In 2007 and 2008, the Korean Academy of Marketing Science honored Udo Wagner with two Excellence Service Awards; in 2008 he received also with the Premier Award the Best Paper Award of the *Journal of the Korean Academy of Marketing Science*. In 2009 he also received the Best Paper Award of the German Academic Association for Business Research (VHB). In 2011, the European Marketing Academy appointed Udo Wagner to an "EMAC Fellow".

1.4   Contributions to Marketing Science

The research achievements of Udo Wagner are reflected in an extensive list of publications with more than 200 titles (see part 5 of this *Festschrift*). According to the JOURQUAL ranking of the German Academic Association for Business Research (VHB), five of his articles count among the top category A + and further 24 among the categories A and B. The five top publications were published in the worldwide leading journals *Marketing Science* and *Journal of Marketing Research* over the period from 1979 to 2008. This fact alone makes clear the quality of Udo Wagner's research achievement in international terms. Closer to home, according to the Handelsblatt Ranking of business administration researchers in 2009, Udo Wagner is listed in the Top-Ten of all German-speaking marketing academics.

1.4.1   Research Foci

The main field of Udo Wagner's scientific activity is quantitative business administration. The focus of interest is on empirical market research and market modeling, the application of quantitative procedures and methods of Operations Research in management and marketing as well as on the applications of statistics and econometrics in these fields. However, his research interests go far beyond methodological perspectives. Udo Wagner has researched important substantive issues relating to consumer behavior, such as brand choice and the influence of children on the purchase decision of adults. Furthermore, questions about the effect of marketing instruments have repeatedly figured in his research and deal, among other things, with the effects of pricing policy and promotion, brand presentation, new shop concepts in retailing, product relaunches as well as product placement and sponsoring. Topics such as e-commerce, strategic marketing, marketing ethics and corporate social responsibility further highlight Udo Wagner's interest in important fundamental questions in business administration and management. This also becomes apparent in his contribution to the conception of business administration as a normative science, co-authored with Erich Loitlsberger. Such a broad level of fundamental reflection is unusual for a marketing scientist.

1.4.2   Marketing Models

Udo Wagner has made important contributions in the mathematical modeling of consumer behavior from the beginning of his research work. Already in his doctoral thesis in 1984, entitled „*Full Stochastic Models of Buying Behavior and their Application in the Analysis of Real Markets*" he addressed himself to a field of research which, due to its technical and mathematical complexity, was open only to a few business researchers. In subsequent years, he systematically extended the level of knowledge in this area through regular contributions in leading scientific journals. These include, among others, two publications in *Marketing Science* and *European Journal of Operational Research* in 1986 and 1987 respectively.

His contributions to stochastic models of consumer behavior now provide the basis of modern, quantitatively-oriented marketing research monographs (cf., e.g., Decker, R./Wagner, R., 2002, pp. 382, 384, 386, 404-412) and have received international recognition in research. As Reinhold Decker, professor at the University of Bielefeld, put it:

„Particularly the multivariate Polya-Model of the analysis of brand choice and purchase frequency decisions, which was published by Udo Wagner in 1986 in the renowned journal Marketing Science, signals a milestone in the mathematical modeling of consumer behavior. Although the integrated modeling of brand choice and purchase frequency has been subject of publications in internationally renowned journals during the subsequent years, in my opinion, there is hardly any other approach that reached the methodical elegance of the Polya-Model."

Given his academic background, Udo Wagner could be classified as a mathematician. Mathematicians who successfully teach and research in business or economics, are often viewed with suspicion by colleagues who research only "qualitatively" and therefore do not understand anything about mathematics. This suspicion results from the assumption that the mathematically-oriented colleague, due to limited talent, could hardly have succeeded in the field of mathematics and therefore chose the (mathematically) less demanding terrain of business or economics! To pre-empt this suspicion, Udo Wagner did something exceptional for a marketing scientist, namely he published the following article in a leading journal of mathematics!

"A Maximum Entropy Method for Inverting Laplace Transforms of Probability Density Functions", in: *Biometrika 82 (4), 1995, 887-892* (with A. Geyer).

The journal *Biometrika* is one of the famous Oxford journals in the category "Mathematics & Physical Sciences". As professional colleagues of mathematics confirmed, such a publication would have also considerably increased Udo Wagner's chance for an offer of a professorship in mathematics. Nevertheless, we are very pleased that Udo Wagner did not undertake serious steps in this direction!

1.4.3 Marketing Management

Despite the highly quantitative-formal research focus, Udo Wagner has not lost sight of applying his findings to marketing management. Thus, several of his papers lead directly to the solution of practical marketing problems, such as pricing, marketing mix planning, success factors in sponsorships and shop concepts in retailing. The publication of five case study books on Austrian marketing cases further demonstrates his interest in issues of marketing practice.

Udo Wagner's research achievements help disprove one unfortunately wide-spread conception in economic and social sciences' theory. Inspired by Niklas Luhmann's sociology of science that conceptualizes science as a self-referential social system (Luhmann 1993), the disciples of this doctrine establish an irreconcilable difference between science and practice. Under this perspective, management science and management practice represent disconnected communication systems or closed social constructions with finally incompatible cultures, whereby the scientific system treats exclusively problems arising from itself and not from a practical perspective. By the continuous work on the problems created by itself, the scientific system thus reproduces itself and hence drifts away from practice more and more. According to this point of view, a practical application of scientific knowledge cannot exist (Kieser 2002; Kieser/Nicolai 2005, p. 276).

Udo Wagner's research offers clear evidence that the gloomy scenario mentioned above does not correspond to reality. An example is the article (published in *Marketing Science* in 2008) entitled: „*Planning New Tariffs at Tele.ring – The Application and Impact of an Integrated Segmentation, Targeting and Positioning Tool*" (with M. Natter/A. Mild/A. Taudes) which made it to the finals during "*2006 Practice Prize Competition*" initiated by INFORMS Society for Marketing Science (ISMS). The article shows how a methodological complex approach of quantitative marketing research can be applied in practice in order to improve, for example, the pricing of the Austrian mobile communications company Tele.ring in an extremely intensive competitive environment. The jury's justification for the final entry of this article was: "*For Outstanding Implementation of Marketing Science Concepts and Methods*" (INFORMS 2006).

This example shows that a quantitative research approach can indeed generate helpful advice for marketing practice and helps dispel doubts about the "relevance" of marketing science.

1.5   Looking to the Future

Udo Wagner has been contributing to the development of the quantitative business administration and marketing science for more than 30 years and shows no signs of stopping doing in the years to come.

Despite his established scientific reputation, Udo Wagner has always been an open-minded, helpful, and modest person. His open-mindedness finds its expression in also supporting doctoral and habilitation studies which are based on very different research paradigms than that characterizing quantitative business research. Moreover, he is always willing to help and provide guidance and advice to both students and colleagues alike. Regarding his modesty, Udo Wagner does not showcase his research achievements for the purpose of grandstanding and self-marketing. A marketing professor who does not market himself is an extraordinary colleague indeed!

We wish Udo Wagner all the best for the future both personally and professionally and feel privileged to have him as a colleague and friend.

Literature

[1] Albach, H. (Ed.) (1991): Meilensteine der Betriebswirtschaftslehre. 60 Jahre Zeitschrift für Betriebswirtschaft/ Journal of Business Economics, Wiesbaden: Gabler; pp. 110-121: „Empirische Befunde zum Verhältnis zwischen Marktführer und Zweitmarke. Von Manfred Nenning, Edgar Topritzhofer und Udo Wagner", Wiederabdruck aus ZfB/ JBE, Vol. 48, (1978), pp. 1025-1036.

[2] Decker, R./Wagner, R. (2002): Marketingforschung. Methoden und Modelle zur Bestimmung des Käuferverhaltens, München: Redline Wirtschaft.

[3] Kieser, A. (2002): On Communication Barriers Between Management Science, Consultancies and Business Organizations, in: Clark, T. & Fincham, R. (Eds.): Critical Consulting: New Perspectives on the Management Advice Industry, Oxford, UK: Blackwell, pp. 206-227.

[4] Kieser, A./Nicolai, A. T. (2005): Success Factor Research – Overcoming the Trade-Off Between Rigor and Relevance?, in: Journal of Management Inquiry, Vol. 14, 3, pp. 275-279.

[5] Luhmann, N. (1993): Theoretische und praktische Probleme der anwendungsbezogenen Sozialwissenschaften, in: Luhmann, N. (Ed.): Soziologische Aufklärung, Bd. 3, 3rd ed., Opladen: Westdeutscher Verlag, pp. 321-334.

Marketing Models and
Marketing Research Methods

1 Implementing the Pareto/NBD Model: A User-Friendly Approach

Albert C. Bemmaor, ESSEC Business School, Cergy-Pontoise, France

Nicolas Glady, ESSEC Business School, Cergy-Pontoise, France

Daniel Hoppe, The Boston Consulting Group, Brazil

Abstract

The paper addresses an issue that has been qualified as "challenging" in the literature, i.e., estimating the parameters of the well-known Pareto/NBD model. Previous researchers have circumvented the apparent difficulty by bringing slight variations to the model. These changes turn out to be less innocuous than initially thought. The study proposes an alternative method to compute the parameters of the Pareto/NBD model with maximum likelihood. The method relies on the evaluation of a single one-dimensional integral. It is illustrated with two data sets that have been used in the literature. The procedure leads to the same parameter estimates as the previously published ones. It can be implemented in a spreadsheet.

Keywords

Customer-Base Analysis, Probability Models, Maximum Likelihood.

1.1   Introduction

Models for customer-base analysis have been the subject of much research over the past decade. These models can be used for a variety of purposes such as customer targeting, customer valuation or pricing segmentation. Perhaps, the most influential effort so far has been the Pareto/NBD model (Schmittlein/Morrison/Colombo 1987). The Negative Binomial Distribution (NBD) describes transaction behavior while customers are alive and the Pareto distribution represents customer lifetimes. The model applies to the non-contractual setting, i.e. when customer defection times are not observed. Since its publication, it has generated a number of applications and extensions (e.g., Abe 2009; Fader/Hardie/Lee 2005a; Ho/ Park/Zhou 2006; Krafft 2002; Ma/Liu 2007; Reinartz/Kumar 2000). However, despite the repeated calls for higher relevance of academic research to practice, to our knowledge, these applications have been restricted to academic circles (Bemmaor/Franses 2005, Reibstein/Day/Wind 2009). Recent work has supported the use of the traditional Recency/Frequency/Monetary Value (RFM) for individual-level predictions (Wubben/ v. Wangenheim 2008). A possible reason for the limited impact of the Pareto/NBD model has been the apparent difficulty encountered with the estimation of its parameters. Fader/Hardie/Lee (2005b, p. 275) state: "The Pareto/NBD is a powerful model for customer base analysis but its empirical application can be challenging, especially in terms of parameter estimation." This argument has motivated slight variations in the customer lifetime model for spreadsheet applications and further extensions (e.g., Batislam/Denizel/Filiztekin 2007, 2008; Fader/Hardie/Lee 2005b; Hoppe/Wagner 2007; van Oest/Knox 2011; Wagner/Hoppe 2008). These changes turn out to be less innocuous than initially thought (Jerath/Fader/Hardie 2011). At this stage, it remains unclear whether this additional work has received greater echo than the previous effort.

This chapter aims to cope with the issue of parameter estimation for the Pareto/NBD model by implementing it in a spreadsheet without a tweak to its formulation. The estimation method is maximum likelihood. The proposed procedure consists of assessing the likelihood function by computing a single one-dimensional integral. We illustrate the method with two data sets, including the well-known CDNOW data, and show that it gives the same estimates as the previously obtained ones. The next section describes the assumptions and implications of the Pareto/NBD model and its special cases. Section 1.3 presents the estimation method, the data sets and the results. Section 1.4 is the conclusion.

1.2   The Pareto/NBD Model

1.2.1   Assumptions and Implications

The model relies on five assumptions:

- The variation of a customer's lifetime τ is consistent with an exponential distribution with parameter μ (mean = $1 / \mu$);

- μ varies across customers according to a gamma distribution with shape parameter s and scale parameter β (mean = s / β);

- While active, a customer makes transactions which are distributed Poisson with mean λ per unit time;

- λ varies across customers according to a gamma distribution with shape parameter r and scale parameter α (mean = r / α);

- λ and μ are independently distributed across customers.

It results that the distribution of customer lifetimes is a Pareto distribution with the following cumulative distribution function:

$$F(\tau \mid s, \beta) = 1 - (1 + \tau / \beta)^{-s}, \tau > 0, s, \beta > 0. \tag{1.1}$$

Let x_i be the number of repeat purchases made by a customer i over the observation period $(0, T_i]$ that starts on the date of his/her first purchase. The distribution of the number of repeat transactions for a randomly picked customer i while he/she is alive is a NBD:

$$P(x_i \mid T_i) = \{\Gamma(r + x_i)/[\Gamma(r)x_i!]\} [\alpha /(\alpha + T_i)]^r [T_i /(\alpha + T_i)]^{x_i}, x_i = 0, 1, 2,.., r, \alpha > 0. \tag{1.2}$$

Let t_{xi} be the time to the last repeat purchase for customer i $(0 \le t_{xi} < T_i)$. When x_i equals 0, t_{xi} is equal to 0. Schmittlein/Morrison/Colombo (1987) derive (i) the conditional probability that an individual customer i is alive at time T_i given x_i, t_{xi} and his/her individual-level parameters μ and λ (equation 1.A1), (ii) the conditional probability that a randomly picked customer i is alive at T_i given x_i, t_{xi} and the aggregate-level parameters s, β, r and α (equation 1.A3), (iii) the mean and variance of the number of transactions for a randomly picked customer i over the period $(0, T_i]$: $E(x_i \mid s, \beta, r, \alpha, T_i)$ and $V(x_i \mid s, \beta, r, \alpha, T_i)$ respectively (equations 17 and 19 in their paper), and (iv) the conditional expectation of the number of future transactions x_i^* over the subsequent time period $(T_i, T_i + T^*]$ given x_i, t_{xi}, T_i and the parameter values: $E(x_i^* \mid s, \beta, r, \alpha, x_i, t_{xi}, T_i, T^*)$ – see equation (22). The conditional variance of the number of future transactions for a randomly picked customer i with vector (x_i, t_{xi}, T_i) over the time period $(T_i, T_i + T^*]$ is such as:

$V(x_i^* \mid s, \beta, r, \alpha, x_i, t_{xi}, T_i, T^*) = P(\tau > T_i \mid s, \beta, r, \alpha, x_i, t_{xi}, T_i) \, E(x_i^{*2} \mid s, \beta^*, r^*, \alpha^*, T^*)$

$- E^2(x_i^* \mid s, \beta, r, \alpha, x_i, t_{xi}, T_i, T^*)$ 　　　　　　　　　　　　　　　　　　　　　　　　　(1.3)

where $\beta^* = \beta + T_i$, $r^* = r + x_i$, $\alpha^* = \alpha + T_i$ and $E(x_i^{*2} \mid s, \beta^*, r^*, \alpha^*, T^*) = V(x_i^* \mid s, \beta^*, r^*, \alpha^*, T^*)$ $+ E^2(x_i^* \mid s, \beta^*, r^*, \alpha^*, T^*)$.

The mean and variance of the number of transactions for a randomly picked customer i over the period (0, T] where T ≥ maximum (T$_i$) are given by:

$E(x_i \mid s, \beta, r, \alpha, T) = E[E(x_i \mid s, \beta, r, \alpha, T_i)]$ 　　　　　　　　　　　　　　　　　　　(1.4)

and

$V(x_i \mid s, \beta, r, \alpha, T) = V[E(x_i \mid s, \beta, r, \alpha, T_i)] + E[V(x_i \mid s, \beta, r, \alpha, T_i)]$ 　　　　　　　(1.5)

respectively. The mean and variance of the number of transactions over the period (T, T + T*] can be derived from $E(x_i^* \mid s, \beta, r, \alpha, x_i, t_{xi}, T_i, T^*)$ and $V(x_i^* \mid s, \beta, r, \alpha, x_i, t_{xi}, T_i, T^*)$ (equation 1.3) in a similar fashion.

The predictions of the model are relatively straightforward to compute once the parameters s, β, r and α have been estimated.

1.2.2　　The Special Cases

When the shape parameter s approaches 0, the mean of μ of tends to 0 and the customers' lifetimes become infinite: the Pareto/NBD reduces to the simple NBD (equation 1.2). When s tends to ∞, the coefficient of variation of the gamma distribution $1 / \sqrt{s}$ approaches 0 and the gamma distribution shrinks towards a mass point at its mean s / β: the Pareto distribution gets close to an exponential distribution with parameter μ = s / β. The customers become more homogeneous in their mean lifetimes.

Overall, depending on the value of the parameter s, the Pareto/NBD can approach either the NBD model or the Exponential/NBD model. In most cases, we expect it to lie in-between these two extremes when attrition occurs.

1.3   The Estimating Equation, the Data and the Results

1.3.1   The Estimating Equation

For customer i with vector (x_i, t_{xi}, T_i), the individual-level likelihood function is such as (Fader, Hardie and Lee 2005a):

$$L(\mu, \lambda \mid x_i, t_{xi}, T_i) \ = \lambda^{x_i} e^{-(\mu + \lambda)T_i} + \lambda^{x_i} \mu \int_{t_{xi}}^{T_i} e^{-(\mu + \lambda)\tau} \, d\tau$$

$$= \lambda^{x_i} e^{-(\mu + \lambda)T_i} + \lambda^{x_i} \mu \left[1 /(\mu + \lambda)\right] \left[e^{-(\mu + \lambda)t_{xi}} - e^{-(\mu + \lambda)T_i}\right] \tag{1.6}$$

Integrating out λ and μ, we find that:

$$L(s, \beta, r, \alpha \mid x_i, t_{xi}, T_i) = (r)_{xi} \left[\alpha /(\alpha + T_i)\right]^r \left[1 /(\alpha + T_i)^{xi}\right] \left[\beta /(\beta + T_i)\right]^s + (r)_{xi} \, \alpha^r \, s\beta^s \int_{t_{xi}}^{T_i} (y + \alpha)^{-(r + xi)} (y$$

$$+ \beta)^{-(s + 1)} \, dy \tag{1.7}$$

where $(r)_{xi} = \Gamma(r + x_i)/\Gamma(r)$ is the Pochhammer's symbol (Abramowitz and Stegun 1972, p. 256). A closed-form expression of the integral in equation (1.7) is given in equation (1.A2). When the size of a cohort equals N, the sample log-likelihood function is such as:

$$LL = \Sigma_{i=1}^{N} \ln L(s, \beta, r, \alpha \mid x_i, t_{xi}, T_i). \tag{1.8}$$

Equation (1.8) can be maximized with Solver, a standard numerical optimization tool. To evaluate the integral in equation (1.7), we use the dqags subroutine that is available in Quadpack, an open-source package for numerical integration (Piessens et al. 1983). We insert the subroutine in a dynamic link library for computation in a spreadsheet.

1.3.2   The Data and the Results

Table 1.1 provides a description of two data sets.

1.3.2.1   CDNOW

The CDNOW data set consists of the number of repeat transactions made by a cohort of 2,357 new customers of music CDs. The length of the observation period is 78 weeks. We focus on the initial 39 weeks for the estimation of the parameters. The customers made their first purchase (ever) during the first quarter of 1997. Fader/Hardie/Lee (2005a, 2005b) and Abe (2009) among others analyze the CDNOW data set.

1.3.2.2   Grocery Retailer

The data includes the repeat transactions at a Turkish store made by two cohorts of 5,479 and 6,276 new loyalty card-holders respectively (Batislam/Denizel/Filiztekin 2007). The first transaction occurred between July 28, 2001 and October 27, 2001 for Cohort 1 and between October 27, 2001 and January 26, 2002 for Cohort 2. The length of the observation period is 91 weeks starting on July 28, 2001. In each week, either the customer visited the store (coded as a one) or he/she did not (coded as a zero). The maximum number of store visits is equal to the number of weeks in the period. For Cohort 1, we estimate the Pareto/NBD over two periods: the first 52 weeks and the first 78 weeks of the observation period. For Cohort 2, we use a single estimation period: the first 52 weeks of the observation period.

Table 1.1   Data Description[a]

Data set, Cohort number	Business description	Observation period	Length of the observation period (in weeks)	Cohort Size	Length of the estimation period (in weeks)	Number of trans-actions in the esti-mation period	Average T_i
CDNOW	Electronic commerce (music CDs)	January 1, 1997 - June 30, 1998	78	2,357	39	2,457	32.716
Grocery retailer, Cohort 1	-	July 28, 2001 - April 25, 2003	91	5,479	52	18,019	44.035
Grocery retailer", Cohort 1	-	July 28, 2001 - April 25, 2003"	91"	5,479"	78	28,840	70.035
Grocery retailer", Cohort 2	-	Oct' 27, 2001 - April 25, 2003	78	6,276	52	14,585	44.845

[a] We do not take account of the validation period which is equal to the length of the observation period minus the length of the estimation period.

For both data sets, we obtain the same maximum likelihood parameter estimates as the previously published ones (**Table 1.2**). (We carried additional comparisons on other data sets and obtained similar results.)

Table 1.2   Maximum Likelihood Parameter Estimates

Data set, Cohort number	Length of the estimation period (in weeks)	r	α	s	β	LL[a]
CDNOW	39	0.553	10.578	0.606	11.669	-9,594.98
Grocery retailer, Cohort 1	52	0.488	4.063	1.429	42.444	-48,870.35
Grocery retailer", Cohort 1	78	0.482	4.383	0.572	17.604	-67,925.77
Grocery retailer", Cohort 2	52	0.405	4.450	0.763	15.582	-43,329.11

[a] LL = Maximum of the log-likelihood.

1.4   Conclusion

The study addresses an issue that has been qualified as "challenging" in the literature, i.e., estimating the parameters of the well-known Pareto/NBD model. Previous researchers have circumvented the apparent difficulty by bringing slight variations to the model. These changes turn out to be less innocuous than initially thought. The study proposes an alternative method to compute the parameters of the Pareto/NBD model with maximum likelihood. The method relies on the evaluation of a single one-dimensional integral. It is illustrated with two data sets. The procedure leads to the same parameter estimates as the previously published ones. It can be implemented in a spreadsheet.

We hope this investigation will encourage researchers to devise ways to implement relatively complex models in a user-friendly environment for a larger impact.

Acknowledgments

The authors are grateful to Emine Persentili Batislam and Alpay Filiztekin for providing them with data. A spreadsheet is available at: http://bit.ly/qPumbz.

Appendix

Likelihood Equations and Conditional Probabilities for a Customer to Be Active

Let $L(\lambda \mid x_i, \tau > T_i)$ be the likelihood function for customer i who made x_i repeat transactions over the period $(0, T_i]$ and is still active at time T_i. The conditional probability that customer i is active at time T_i given x_i, t_{xi} and the individual-level parameters μ and λ, is such as (Fader/Hardie 2005, equation 31):

$$P(\tau > T_i \mid \mu, \lambda, x_i, t_{xi}) = L(\lambda \mid x_i, \tau > T_i) \, P(\tau > T_i \mid \mu)/ L(\mu, \lambda \mid x_i, t_{xi}, T_i)$$

$$= \lambda^{xi} \, e^{-(\mu + \lambda)T_i} / L(\mu, \lambda \mid x_i, t_{xi}, T_i) \tag{1.A1}$$

where $L(\mu, \lambda \mid x_i, t_{xi}, T_i)$ is given in equation (1.6). Equation (1.7) can be expressed in the following fashion:

$$L(s, \beta, r, \alpha \mid x_i, t_{xi}, T_i) = (r)_{xi} \, [\alpha /(\alpha + T_i)]^r \, [1 /(\alpha + T_i)^{xi}] \, [\beta /(\beta + T_i)]^s + \tag{1.A2}$$

$$(r)_{xi} \, \alpha^r \, \beta^s \, [(\alpha + t_{xi})^{-(r + xi)} \, (\beta + t_{xi})^{-s} \, {}_2F_1(r + x_i, 1; 1 - s; (\beta + t_{xi})/(\alpha + t_{xi})) -$$

$$(\alpha + T_i)^{-(r + xi)} \, (\beta + T_i)^{-s} \, {}_2F_1(r + x_i, 1; 1 - s; (\beta + T_i)/(\alpha + T_i))], \, \alpha > \beta,$$

where ${}_2F_1()$ denotes a Gauss hypergeometric function (Abramowitz/Stegun 1972, pp. 556-566). When α is less than β, we replace α by β (and inversely) inside the brackets in the second term of the right-hand side of the equation. Equivalently, equation (1.A2) can be written as equation (1.A1) in Fader/Hardie/Lee (2005a, p. 428).

The conditional probability that a randomly picked customer i is active at time T_i given x_i, t_{xi} and the aggregate-level parameters s, β, r and α, is such as:

$$P(\tau > T_i \mid s, \beta, r, \alpha, x_i, t_{xi}) = L(r, \alpha \mid \tau > T_i) \, P(\tau > T_i \mid s, \beta)/ L(s, \beta, r, \alpha \mid x_i, t_{xi}, T_i)$$

$$= (r)_{xi} \, [\alpha /(\alpha + T_i)]^r \, [1 /(\alpha + T_i)^{xi}] \, [\beta /(\beta + T_i)]^s / L(s, \beta, r, \alpha \mid x_i, t_{xi}, T_i). \tag{1.A3}$$

Literature

[1]   Abe, M. (2009): Counting Your Customers One by One: A Hierarchical Bayes Extension to the Pareto/NBD Model, in: Marketing Science, Vol. 28, 3, pp. 541-553.

[2]   Abramowitz, M./Stegun, I. A. (eds.) (1972): Handbook of Mathematical Functions, New York: Dover Publications.

[3]   Batislam, E. P./Denizel, M./Filiztekin, A. (2007): Empirical Validation and Comparison of Models for Customer Base Analysis, in: International Journal of Research in Marketing, Vol. 24, 3, pp. 201-229.

[4]   Batislam, E. P./Denizel, M./Filiztekin, A. (2008): Formal Response to "Erratum on the MBG/NBD Model ", in: International Journal of Research in Marketing, Vol. 25, 3, p. 227.

[5]   Bemmaor, A. C./Franses, P. H. (2005): Editorial - The Diffusion of Marketing Science in the Practitioners' Community: Opening the Black Box, in: Applied Stochastic Models in Business and Industry, Vol. 21, 4/5, pp. 289-301.

[6]   Fader, P. S./Hardie, B. G. S. (2005): A Note on Deriving the Pareto/NBD Model and Related Expressions. http://www.brucehardie.com/notes/009/.

[7]   Fader, P. S./Hardie, B. G. S./Lee, K. L. (2005a): RFM and CLV: Using Iso-Value Curves for Customer Base Analysis,. in: Journal of Marketing Research, Vol. 42, 4, pp. 415-430.

[8]   Fader, P. S./Hardie, B. G. S./Lee, K. L. (2005b): Counting Your Customers the Easy Way: An Alternative to the Pareto/NBD Model, in: Marketing Science, Vol. 24, 2, pp. 275-284.

[9]   Ho, T.-H./Park, Y.-H./Zhou, Y.-P. (2006): Incorporating Satisfaction into Customer Value Analysis: Optimal Investment in Lifetime Value, in: Marketing Science, Vol. 25, 3, pp. 260-277.

[10] Hoppe, D./Wagner, U. (2007): Customer Base Analysis: The Case for a Central Variant of the Betageometric/NBD Model, in: Marketing - Journal of Research and Management, Vol. 3, 2, pp. 75-90.

[11] Jerath, K./Fader, P. S./Hardie, B. G. S. (2011): New Perspectives on Customer "Death" Using a Generalization of the Pareto/NBD Model, in: Marketing Science, posted in Articles in Advance on June 6, 2011.

[12] Krafft, M. (2002): Kundenbindung und Kundenwert, Heidelberg: Physica-Verlag.

[13] Ma, S.-H./Liu, J.-L. (2007): The MCMC Approach for Solving the Pareto/NBD Model and Possible Extensions, in: Third International Conference on Natural Computation (ICNC 2007), pp. 505-512.

[14] Piessens, R./deDoncker-Kapenga, E./Überhuber, C. W./Kahaner, D. K. (1983): Quadpack: A Subroutine Package for Automatic Integration, New York: Springer Verlag.

[15] Reibstein, D. J./Day, G./Wind, J. (2009): Guest Editorial: Is Marketing Academia Losing Its Way? in: Journal of Marketing, Vol. 73, 4, pp. 1-3.

[16] Reinartz, W. J./Kumar, V. (2000): On the Profitability of Long-Life Customers in a Non-contractual Setting: An Empirical Investigation and Implications for Marketing, in: Journal of Marketing, Vol. 64, 4, pp. 17-35.

[17] Schmittlein, D. C./Morrison, D. G./Colombo, R. (1987): Counting Your Customers: Who Are They and What Will They Do Next? in: Management Science, Vol. 33, 1, pp. 1-24.

[18] Van Oest, R./Knox, G. (2011): Extending the BG/NBD: A Simple Model of Purchases and Complaints, in: International Journal of Research in Marketing, Vol. 28, 1, pp. 30-37.

[19] Wagner, U./Hoppe, D. (2008): Erratum on the MBG/NBD Model, in: International Journal of Research in Marketing, Vol. 25, 3, pp. 225-226.

[20] Wübben, M./v. Wangenheim, F. (2008): Instant Customer Base Analysis: Managerial Heuristics Often "Get it Right", in: Journal of Marketing, Vol. 72, 2, pp. 82-93.

2 The Consistency Adjustment Problem of AHP Pairwise Comparison Matrices

Dominic Gastes, TRUMPF Werkzeugmaschinen GmbH & Co. KG, Germany

Wolfgang Gaul, Karlsruhe Institute of Technology (KIT), Germany

Abstract

The Analytic Hierarchy Process (AHP) is an often applied and well researched method in the area of multiattribute decision making. One of the main recurring tasks in AHP situations is the creation of pairwise comparison matrices, the examination of their consistencies, and the derivation of weights for the underlying objective functions.

The importance of controlling these consistencies and the consequences of subsequent adjustments of comparison matrices are sometimes unvalued issues in AHP applications. We conduct a simulation study to show that increasing inconsistencies caused by superimposed stochastic error-terms on consistent starting pairwise comparison AHP data result in decreasing correlations between the corresponding weights of the error-perturbed matrices and those of the consistent starting data and demonstrate that the weights derived from adjusted matrices do not show the improvements expected.

Keywords

Analytic Hierarchy Process, Consistency Improvement, Pairwise Comparison Matrices.

2.1   Introduction

The Analytic Hierarchy Process (AHP) is a technique which supports decision makers in multiattribute decision making situations. Recent overviews (Vaidya/Kumar (2006); Ho (2008); Ho et al. (2010)) show that the AHP is utilized in many different areas like Education, Engineering, Management or Manufacturing, and also in Marketing (Scholz et al. (2010)). Generally, it can be used for solving ranking and selection problems w.r.t. a finite set of alternatives in multiattribute decision situations. Additionally, it can be integrated in other methods, e.g., QFD (Quality Function Deployment), Project Portfolio Analysis, or SWOT (Strengths-Weaknesses-Opportunities-Threats) Analysis. Diffusion and universality of the AHP approach is also indicated by the number of articles in different journals in which applications are discussed from theoretical and practical points of view (see **Figure 2.1**).

Figure 2.1   Number of Articles by Journals Related to the Query "Analytic Hierarchy Process" in the ScienceDirect Database (1980 - 2011)

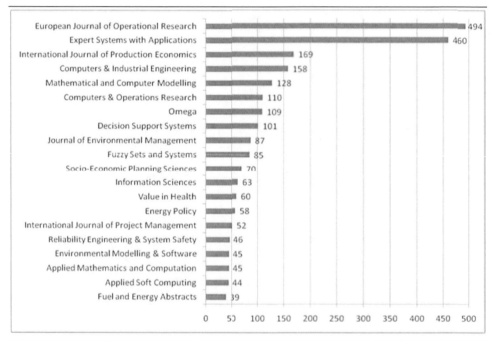

One principle of the AHP methodology is decomposition of complex multiattribute problems into hierarchically ordered sub-problems. Decision makers can then conduct evaluations by simple pairwise comparisons between elements within sub-problems w.r.t. higher level attributes. Resulting pairwise comparison matrices can be checked w.r.t. the consistency of these sub-problem evaluations.

Applications show that decision makers are seldom able to state all pairwise comparisons in a perfectly consistent manner, which may have different reasons, e.g., limitations of the scale used, inaccuracies caused by a lack of concentration or uncertainties about the judgment task. But, consistency, which is required according to restrictions that AHP has to fulfill, is necessary for successfully deriving reasonable weights from comparison matrices. Thus, improving not sufficiently consistent comparison matrices is an important topic in AHP applications and theory (see, e.g., Zeshui/Cuiping (1999); Saaty (2003); Mamat/Daniel (2007); Cao et al. (2008); Lin et al. (2008); Bozoki et al. (2010); Gaul/Gastes (2010)).

The remainder of this paper is organized as follows: The next section provides the mathematical background of measuring consistency and different consistency improvement techniques. After that, a simulation study, conducted to analyze which method performs best, will be presented. In the last section the results derived will be discussed and conclusions will be drawn.

2.2 Consistency: Measurement and Adjustment

2.2.1 Background

An entry a_{ij} of a comparison matrix A represents a relative preference of an element i over an element j. For a sub-problem containing n elements a $n \times n$ matrix with the following characteristics can be constructed:

$$A = \begin{pmatrix} a_{11} & \cdots & a_{1n} \\ \vdots & \ddots & \vdots \\ a_{n1} & \cdots & a_{nn} \end{pmatrix} \qquad (2.1)$$

under the assumptions

$$a_{ij} \in S = \left\{ \tfrac{1}{9}, \tfrac{1}{8}, \ldots, 1, \ldots, 8, 9 \right\} \ \forall \ i,j \ \text{(Saaty Scale)} \qquad (2.2)$$

$$a_{ij} \times a_{ji} = 1 \ \forall \ i,j \ \text{(reciprocity)} \qquad (2.3)$$

$$a_{ij} = a_{ik} \times a_{kj} \ \forall \ i,j,k \ \text{(consistency)} \qquad (2.4)$$

The priority weights of the n elements can be calculated by solving the eigenvalue problem:

$$Aw(A) = \lambda_{max}(A)w(A) \qquad (2.5)$$

The normalized eigenvector $w(A) = (w_1 (A),..., w_n (A))^T$, which is assigned to the principal eigenvalue $\lambda_{max} (A)$ of matrix A, represents the priority weights of the decision maker for the n elements. If assumption (2.2), (2.3), and (2.4) hold $\lambda_{max} (A)$ is equal to the number of elements n and for all entries $a_{ij} = \frac{w_i(A)}{w_j(A)}$ is valid (see Saaty (1980)).

Assumption (2.4) is often violated in empirical decision situations but, as Saaty (2003) has argued, small violations of the consistency constraint can be ignored, because the derived priority vectors change only slightly compared to the weight vectors derived from consistent matrices. To measure the degree of inconsistency of comparison matrices, a Consistency Index

$$CI (A) = \frac{\lambda_{max} (A) - n}{n - 1} \tag{2.6}$$

was developed. To make this measure comparable for different sized matrices the CI-value was related to an average Random Index $RI(n)$ of randomly chosen reciprocal matrices of size n × n, constructed via entries the values of which were taken from the Saaty scale S (see (2.2)). The Consistency Ratio is given as:

$$CR(A) = \frac{CI(A)}{RI(n)} \tag{2.7}$$

Matrix A is called "consistent", if $CR(A)=0$, "α-consistent", if $0 < CR(A) \leq \alpha$, and "inconsistent" if $CR(A) > \alpha$ for $\alpha \in (0, \infty)$. Usually, a value of $\alpha=0{,}1$ is chosen, which was suggested on the basis of statistical experiments (see Vargas (1982)).

2.2.2   Consistency Adjustment Approaches

In applications comparison matrices are often not α-consistent on a sufficient level of α. In this situation consistency should be adjusted, for which several methods can be used. One can distinguish between manual adjustments and automated adjustments.

Manual adjustments, more precisely, reassessments of potentially all comparisons can be very time consuming and one cannot be sure that α-consistency is reached with certainty. In order to make reassessment tasks more effective, different suggestions have been made how to select entries which should be reassessed first and how to make recommendations which alternative new values for these entries will improve consistency best (see, e.g., Harker (1987a); Harker (1987b); Saaty (2003); Lia/Ma (2007); Bozoki et al. (2010)). Automated consistency adjustment approaches improve the consistency of not sufficiently consistent comparison matrices without manual reassessment. In the following three approaches will be presented:

1. The first approach changes single entries of inconsistent comparison matrices successively. It is based on the modification of that entry x_{ij} of a comparison matrix X, which has the greatest corresponding deviation

$$d_{ij} = x_{ij} \frac{w_j (X)}{w_i(X)}$$

from the value 1. This method of selecting an entry for adjustment is also used in the Expert Choice AHP Software (see Saaty(2003)). The new matrix, which improves the consistency of X, can be calculated by constructing first an intermediate matrix $\dot{X}$ as a copy of X with the following modifications: $\dot{x}_{ii} = \dot{x}_{jj} = 2$ and $\dot{x}_{ij} = \dot{x}_{ji} = 0$.

Then, x_{ij} is replaced by $x_{ij} = \frac{w_i(\dot{X})}{w_j(\dot{X})}$ (and $x_{ji} = \frac{w_j(\dot{X})}{w_i(\dot{X})}$)

where $w(\dot{X})$ is the principal eigenvector of $\dot{X}$ (see Harker 1987b). This procedure can be repeated until an at least α-consistent matrix has been found. For all adjusted entries of X the Saaty scale restriction (2.2) may be violated after the adjustments. We call this procedure Maximum Deviation Approach (MDA).

2. A second approach is based on the idea of what the authors (Cao et al. (2008)) have called exponential smoothening. It can change more than one entry of a not α-consistent matrix X simultaneously. In $k = 1, ..., K$ iteration steps a deviation matrix $D^{(k)} = X^{(k)} \ominus W^{(k)T}$ (with $X^{(1)} = X$) is constructed which is the Hadamard product ($\ominus$, elementwise multiplication of matrix entries) of $X^{(k)}$ and a consistent matrix

$$W^{(k)} = \left(\frac{w_i(X^k)}{w_j(X^k)} \right)$$

where $w(X^k)$ is the principal eigenvector of $X^{(k)}$. For calculating matrix $X^{(k+1)} = X^k \cdot \dot{D}^k$ ($\cdot$, standard matrix multiplication) with improved consistency, a modified deviation matrix $\dot{D}^{(k)}$ is constructed via a convex combination of the deviation matrix $D^{(k)}$ and a zero deviation matrix D_1, which is a $n \times n$ matrix all elements of which have the value 1 ($D_1 = (1)$). Then $\dot{D}^{(k)} = \gamma D^{(k)} \oplus (1 - \gamma) D_1$ ($\oplus$, elementwise summation of matrix entries). Parameter $\gamma \in (0, 1]$ influences the convergence of the algorithm and should be set near to one (see Cao et al. (2008)). Again, the Saaty scale restriction (2.2) may be violated after adjustments. We call this approach Exponential Smoothening Technique (EST).

3. Our third approach is implemented with the help of a particle swarm optimization algorithm (see Kennedy/Eberhart (1995)). A basic principle of this approach is the minimization of the dissimilarity between a given inconsistent matrix X and an α-consistent matrix Y. Thus, the algorithm finds a "best fitting" comparison matrix Y, w.r.t. the given matrix X, as solution of the following minimization problem:

$$min: \left\{ \Sigma_{ij} (x_{ij} - y_{ij})^2 \right\} \tag{2.8}$$

subject to

$$y_{ij} \in S \left\{ \frac{1}{9}, \frac{1}{8}, ..., 1, ..., 8, 9 \right\} \text{ (Saaty Scale)} \tag{2.9}$$

$$y_{ij} \times y_{ji} = 1 \ \forall \ i, j \text{ (reciprocity)} \tag{2.10}$$

$$CR(Y) \leq 0,1 \tag{2.11}$$

This minimization problem leads to an α-consistent solution, which preserves as much information of the given matrix as possible and, additionally, constraint (1.9) ensures that only values of the Saaty scale are used. The latter feature is an advantage, if a decision maker wants to prove the solution after adjustments, because, if (s)he would be faced with values from outside of the Saaty scale, (s)he may be confused, due to the fact, that in the foregoing evaluation task, these values were not allowed. We call this approach Particle Swarm Optimization (PSO).

2.3   Simulation Study

To find out which of the automated adjustment approaches works best, we conducted a simulation study. Therefore we selected randomly $l = 1,... ,L$ different consistent matrices, with only Saaty scale values, and constructed $m = 1,... ,M$ perturbed matrices for each consistent matrix by multiplication with a stochastic error term matrix. After that we adjusted the perturbed matrices to $\alpha = 0$, 1-consistency with each of the three approaches and analyzed the results w.r.t. different performance measures.

2.3.1   Correlation as Performance Measure for Consistency Adjustments

Main objective of matrix adjustments in the AHP paired comparison situation is the construction of an improved matrix with a desired α-consistency level, while preserving most of the original comparison information.

One measure for this is the mean squared error of matrix entries. This measure is concerned with the (dis-)similarity between given, not α-consistent matrices and improved matrices. Another measure to assess the performance of consistency improvement methods is the correlation between the weights derived from the different matrices. This measure is important, because within the AHP approach the derived weights are used for calculating additive objective functions. Thus, the derived weights influence the overall evaluation of alternatives in the underlying AHP situations directly.

We employed the Pearson correlation coefficient (ρ) as a performance measure to analyze the results (see, e.g., Carmone et al. (1997); Zanakis et al. (1998)). For comparison matrices A, B and corresponding weight vectors $w(A)$, $w(B)$ this measure is

$$\rho\big(w(A), w(B)\big) = \frac{\sum_{i=1}^{n}\big(w_i(A)-\frac{1}{n}\big)(w_i(B)-\frac{1}{n})}{\sqrt{\sum_{i=1}^{n}(w_i(A)-\frac{1}{n})^2 \ \sum_{i=1}^{n}(w_i(B)-\frac{1}{n})^2}} \qquad (2.12)$$

2.3.2 Simulating Inconsistency of Comparison Matrices

Starting with consistent and Saaty scale conform 5 x 5 matrices $A^{(l)}$, $l = 1,..., L$, each matrix is elementwise multiplied ($\odot$) with stochastic error terms of error matrices $E_m^{(l)}$:

$$E_m^{(l)} = (\epsilon_{ij}), \epsilon \sim LogN(1, \sigma^2), \epsilon_{ij} = \frac{1}{\epsilon_{ji}}, m = 1, ..., M$$

$$\sigma^2 \epsilon \ [0.25, 0.5, 0.75, 1, 1.25, 1.5, 1.75, 2]$$

Figure 2.2   Average CR $\left(X_m^{(l)}\right)$ and Average Correlation Between Underlying (A) and Perturbed (X) Matrices Dependent on Error Term Variance

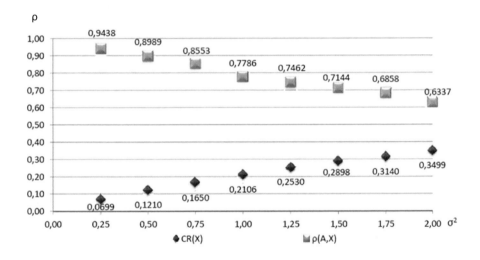

With $L = 100$ and $M = 10$ we got as a result 8000 matrices of the form $\tilde{A}_m^{(l)} = A^{(l)} \odot E_m^{(l)}$ for $l = 1, ..., 100$; $m = 1, ..., 10$. Then the matrices $\tilde{A}_m^{(l)}$ have been adjusted to Saaty scale values according to

$$x_{ij} = \arg\min_{s \in S} = \left\{ |\tilde{a}_{ij} - s| \right\}$$

which resulted in 8000 matrices $X_m^{(l)}$. The created perturbed matrices $X_m^{(l)}$ are very similar to observable reported AHP comparison matrices and show expected characteristics w.r.t. Consistency Ratio and correlations between weight vectors. With increasing variance σ^2 the average Consistency Ratio is increasing and the correlation between weights is decreasing (see **Figure 2.2**).

2.3.3   Simulation Results

Starting from the underlying consistent matrices and after having created the corresponding perturbed matrices, we improved the consistency of the perturbed matrices, if $CR\left(X_m^{(l)}\right) > 0.1$, until the corresponding adjusted matrices $Y_m^{(l)}$ fulfill the α-consistency condition: $CR\left(Y_m^{(l)}\right) \leq 0.1$.

Figure 2.3   Average Correlations Between Perturbed and Adjusted Data

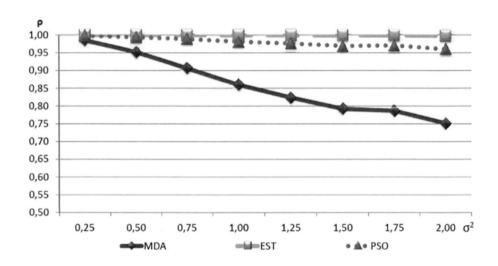

The average correlations between the weight vectors derived from perturbed and adjusted matrices show, that EST produces highest values while MDA has least average correlations (see **Figure 2.3**).

However, the correlations between the weight vectors from the underlying consistent matrices and the corresponding adjusted matrices demonstrate that recovery of the underlying consistent matrices by consistency adjustment approaches seems not to be possible. **Figure 2.4** depicts that the adjustment approaches checked cannot improve the average correlation between underlying "true" weights and weights derived from adjusted matrices where MDA has the least convincing results.

Figure 2.4 Average Correlations Between Underlying and Adjusted Data

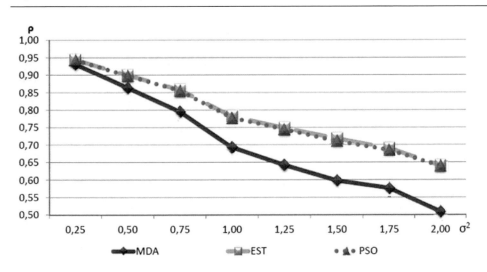

2.4 Conclusions

In AHP related research the problem of transitivity and consistency, as a measure for rationality of the stated preferences, has been discussed by many authors. Practical experiences have shown that comparison matrices of decision makers are often not α-consistent and that reassessments of comparison matrices are very time consuming, thus, automated consistency adjustment approaches have emerged and have been utilized in applications.

But, as far as we know, the question, how good these approaches are w.r.t. the correlation between weight vectors derived from underlying "true" matrices and adjusted α-consistent matrices has not been investigated. We show that adjustment approaches seem not to be able to improve these correlations as expected.

It may be an important topic for future research to understand, why decision makers do not state sufficiently consistent preferences and to control consistency right from the beginning of pairwise comparisons tasks. This should be done without forcing decision makers to erroneous preference statements just because they have to fulfill consistency constraints. One objective may be, to find processes of preference interrogation, which result in more consistent comparison matrices than traditional questioning.

Literature

[1]   Bozoki, S./Fülöp, J./Poesz, A. (2010): On pairwise comparison matrices that can be made consistent by the modification of a few elements, Central European Journal of Operations Research Vol. 19, 2, pp. 157–175.

[2]   Cao, D./Leung, L./Law, J. (2008): Modifying inconsistent comparison matrix in analytic hierarchy process: A heuristic approach, Decision Support Systems Vol. 44, 4, pp. 944–953.

[3]   Carmone, F. J./Kara, A./Zanakis, S. H. (1997): A monte carlo investigation of incomplete pairwise comparison matrices in ahp, European Journal of Operational Research Vol. 102, 3, pp. 538–553.

[4]   Gaul, W./Gastes, D. (2010): Missing values and the consistency problem concerning ahp data, in H. Locarek-Junge & C. Weihs, eds., 'Proc. 11th Conference of the International Federation of Classification Societies (IFCS-09)', Springer, pp. 228–230.

[5]   Harker, P. T. (1987a): Alternative modes of questioning in the analytic hierarchy process, Mathematical Modelling Vol. 9, 3-5, pp. 353–360.

[6]   Harker, P. T. (1987b): Shortening the comparison process in the ahp, Mathematical Modelling 8, pp. 139–141.

[7]   Ho, W. (2008): Integrated analytic hierarchy process and its applications – a literature review, European Journal of Operational Research Vol. 186, 1, pp. 211–228.

[8]   Ho, W./Xu, X./Dey, P. K. (2010): Multi-criteria decision making approaches for supplier evaluation and selection: A literature review, European Journal of Operational Research Vol. 202, 1, pp. 16–24.

[9]   Kennedy, J./Eberhart, R. (1995): Particle swarm optimization', in 'Proceedings of the IEEE International Conference on Neural Networks, Perth, Australia.

[10] Lia, H.-L./Ma, L.-C. (2007): Detecting and adjusting ordinal and cardinal inconsistencies through a graphical and optimal approach in ahp models, Computers & Operations Research Vol. 34, 3, pp. 780–798.

[11] Lin, C.-C./Wang, W.-C./Yu, W.-D. (2008): Improving ahp for construction with an adaptive ahp approach (a3), Automatation in Construction Vol. 17, 2, pp. 180–187.

[12] Mamat, N./Daniel, J. (2007): Statistical analyses on time complexity and rank consistency between singular value decomposition and the duality approach in ahp: A case study of faculty member selection, Mathematical and Computer Modelling Vol. 46, 7-8, pp. 1099–1106.

[13] Saaty, T. L. (1980): The Analytic Hierarchy Process, McGraw-Hill.

[14] Saaty, T. L. (2003): Decision-making with the ahp: Why is the principal eigenvector necessary, European Journal of Operational Research Vol. 145, 1, pp. 85–91.

[15] Scholz, S./Meissner, M./Decker, R. (2010): Measuring consumer preferences for complex products: A compositional approach based on paired comparisons, Journal of Marketing Research Vol. 47, 4, pp. 685–698.

[16] Vaidya, O. S./Kumar, S. (2006): Analytic hierarchy process: An overview of applications, European Journal of Operational Research Vol. 169, 1, pp. 1–29.

[17] Vargas, L. (1982): Reciprocal matrices with random coefficients, Mathematical Modelling Vol. 3, 1, pp. 69–81.

[18] Zanakis, S. H./Solomon, A./Wishart, N./Dublish, S. (1998): Multi- attribute decision making: A simulation comparison of select methods, European Journal of Operational Research Vol. 107, 3, pp. 507–529.

[19] Zeshui, X./Cuiping, W. (1999): A consistency improving method in the analytic hierarchy process, European Journal of Operational Research Vol. 116, 2, pp. 443–449.

3 Choice Modeling and SEM

Integrating Two Popular Modeling Approaches in Empirical Marketing Research[1]

Lutz Hildebrandt, Humboldt University of Berlin, Germany and University of Vienna, Austria

Dirk Temme, Schumpeter School of Business and Economics - Bergische Universität Wuppertal, Germany

Marcel Paulssen, Univerity of Geneva – HEC Geneva, Switzerland

---

[1] This research was supported by the Deutsche Forschungsgemeinschaft through the SFB 649 "Economic Risk".

Abstract

The paper shows how two dominant methodological approaches in quantitative marketing research of the last decades can be integrated. Combining the strengths of covariance structure analysis to control for measurement errors and the ability to predict choice behavior via the Multinomial Logit (MNL) model creates a powerful hybrid approach – the Integrated Choice and Latent variable (ICLV) model – for marketing research. We document the basic features of this approach and present an example which illustrates how the ICLV model can be used to explain travel mode choice. The hybrid modeling framework provides several advantages: (1) it gives a more realistic and comprehensive representation of the choice process taking place in the consumer's "black box"; (2) it provides greater explanatory power; (3) it helps to remedy the biasing effect of neglecting important latent variables to explain choice behavior, thus allowing for a more accurate assessment of how marketing influences customers' choice behavior.

Keywords

Hybrid Choice Models, Integrated Choice and Latent Variable Models, Structural Equation Modeling, Mplus.

3.1   Overview

For several decades two approaches have dominated empirical research in quantitative marketing. In consumer-oriented psychological studies, the structural equation approach (e.g., LISREL, AMOS) has been the sine qua non to control for measurement errors in surveys testing consumer behavior theories with unobserved psychological constructs. Using covariance data, this approach mainly has its advantages in the testing of complex structural (causal) hypotheses and the development of behavioral science theories while simultaneously establishing the construct measures' reliability and validity (see e.g., Bagozzi, 1998; Hildebrandt/Temme 2006). The prediction of individual behavior in the structural equation approach, however, is only possible by using some auxiliary techniques and cumbersome technical programming in the existing software tools. Therefore, quantitative researchers in the 'Marketing Science' tradition preferred the Multinomial Logit Model (MNL) to predict individual choice behavior of customers and the impact of marketing efforts. Since the publication of the seminal paper by Guadagni/Little (1983), the dominant application of the MNL model has been the prediction of brand choice using (scanner) panel data. Here, choice behavior is almost exclusively explained by observed data collected at the point of sale (e.g., price, display) and/or some behavioral indicators derived from a customer's brand choice history in the data (e.g., loyalty). Brand choice in the MNL approach is based on the concept of utilities which shape the brand preferences of the individual consumers. Utility in turn is regarded as mainly a function of tangible and intangible brand characteristics. Assuming utility maximizing consumers, brand choice probabilities can be derived from the estimated parameters of the discrete choice model. Thus, the MNL approach and its different variants has become a powerful tool for predicting brand choice. However, since the MNL approach neglects psychological constructs relevant in the marketing context (e.g., attitudes) and assumes error-free explanatory variables, it is less suitable for theory testing.

The MNL approach is very flexible and the models for brand choice decisions based on random utility theory can be applied to all kinds of choice data (e.g., choice-based conjoint analysis), although it might be most appropriate for scanner panel data. Scanner panel data covers information on objective brand attributes and specific marketing-mix variables as well as the individual buying decision. Here, the MNL model is a valuable tool to predict the impact of managerial decisions, for example, on prices and discounts. Over the last decades, this basic MNL model has been extended in several ways in order to overcome some of its methodological limitations (e.g., IIA property). However, extensions which allow for the inclusion of important latent variables reflecting the psychological states of the customers have almost completely been neglected in most choice modeling articles, although Ben-Akiva et al. (2002a) suggested major routes to extend the traditional MNL model in this direction.

This article is concerned with the issue of incorporating latent variables, e.g., attitudinal factors or brand reputation, into multinomial choice models which in turn should allow for better predictions of brand choice behavior and brand value. To be more specific, we pursue the following goal: Based on the Hybrid Choice Framework first proposed by Ben-

Akiva et al. (1999) and used in marketing studies such as those from Ashok, Dillon/Yuan (2002), Deleart/Stremersch (2005), Bodopati/Drolet (2005) and Temme/Paulssen/Dannewald (2008), we show how to merge the multinomial choice model with a structural equation model to incorporate latent variables as additional predictors of choice. Based on sound behavioral theories, such an approach should help to improve the predictive power of discrete choice models and should contribute to a more realistic model of the choice process.

The remaining part of the paper is structured as follows: First, we present the general structure of ICLV models and discuss recent trends in the estimation of such models. Second, we use data from an earlier study on travel mode choice for daily commutes in Germany (Temme, Paulssen/Dannewald, 2007, 2008) to illustrate the application of ICLV models. We conclude by summarizing the main results and by providing avenues for further research.

3.2 Integrated Choice and Latent Variable Models in the Hybrid Choice Framework

3.2.1 The General Model

The hybrid choice framework extends the standard discrete choice model (e.g., classical Multinomial Logit model) by (1) allowing for flexible error structures such as the mixed logit kernel, (2) jointly analyzing revealed and stated preferences, (3) assuming latent classes which represent distinct market segments with, for example, specific tastes or choice sets and (4) including latent variables like attitudes or perceptions as explanatory variables in the utility function (Walker/Ben-Akiva, 2002). Following Bolduc/Ben-Akiva/Walker/Michaud (2005), we refer to the latter extension as the integrated choice and latent variable (ICLV) model. The ICLV model integrates two subcomponents: a multinomial discrete choice model and a structural equation model (see **Figure 3.1** for an overview of the structure of ICLV models). Each component consists of a structural and a measurement part. In the discrete choice model, alternatives' utilities (U) are functions of observed (x) and latent (η) characteristics of the choice options and decision makers (structural part of the discrete choice model). Since utilities are not observed, a single nominal variable u indicates whether a certain alternative from a given choice set has been chosen or not (measurement part of the discrete choice model). Since the structural model of the discrete choice component contains unobserved explanatory variables η, each of these latent variables is linked to a factor model with multiple manifest indicators y (measurement part of the structural equation model). The additional information provided by these indicators contributes both to model identification and efficiency of model estimation (Ben-Akiva et al., 1999). Furthermore, the structural equation model is rather flexible in that it allows for both simultaneous relationships between the latent variables and MIMIC-type models (Jöreskog/Goldberger, 1975), where observed exogenous variables (e.g., socio-demographic variables) impact the latent variables. In the literature on hybrid choice models, two broad categories of latent variables characterizing the decision makers are distinguished (Walker, 2001): Attitudes reflect the individuals' idiosyncratic needs, values, goals or tastes which shape their preferences for the attributes of the different options. Perceptions on the other hand represent the individuals' beliefs as to the levels of attributes the different options offer.

Figure 3.1 Integrated Choice and Latent Variable Model

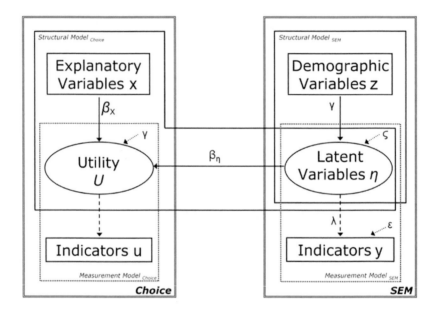

Adapted from Walker/Ben-Akiva (2002)

3.2.2   Model Specification

The specification of the ICLV model will now be discussed in more detail. For alternative treatments of this model refer, for example, to Ashok, Dillon/Yuan (2002), Walker/Ben-Akiva (2002) and Bolduc/Ben-Akiva/Walker/Michaud (2005). The description of the structural equation part follows the common LISREL notation (e.g., Bollen, 1989) and thus slightly departs from accounts in the discrete choice literature (e.g., Walker/ Ben-Akiva, 2002).

Discrete Choice Model: The random utility component is based on the assumption that a decision maker n ($n = 1,\ldots, N$), faced with a finite set C_n of mutually exclusive alternatives i ($i = 1,\ldots, I_n$), chooses the option i which provides the greatest utility U_{ni}. Each alternative's utility is described as a function of explanatory variables building the systematic part of the utility, $V(\cdot)$, and disturbances, v_{ni}, representing the stochastic utility component:

$$U_{ni} = V\left(x_{ni}, \eta_{ni}; \beta\right) + v_{ni}, \tag{3.1}$$

where x_{ni} is a ($K \times 1$) vector of observed variables and η_{ni} is a ($M \times 1$) vector of latent variables. These variables represent either (latent) characteristics of the decision maker (x_{sn}, η_{sn}) or (latent) attributes of the alternatives (x_{zni}, η_{zni}). The importance of the explanatory variables to the utility of the options is reflected in the (($K+M$) $\times 1$) vector β. By assuming, for example, that each v_{ni} is independently, identically distributed (i.i.d.) extreme value, the widely used Multinomial Logit (MNL) model results (e.g., Ben-Akiva/Lerman, 1985):

$$P\left(u_{ni} = 1 \mid x_{ni}, \eta_{ni}; \beta\right) = \frac{e^{V\left(x_{ni}, \eta_{ni}; \beta\right)}}{\sum_{j \in C_n} e^{V\left(x_{nj}, \eta_{nj}; \beta\right)}}. \tag{3.2}$$

As is common practice in choice modeling, the representative utility $V(\cdot)$ is specified to be linear in parameters:

$$V_{ni} = \beta'_x x_{ni} + \beta'_\eta \eta_{ni}, \tag{3.3}$$

where β_x and β_η are ($K \times 1$) and ($M \times 1$) vectors, respectively. In the traditional discrete choice model the latent variables η either do not enter the utility function or are represented by single-indicators.

Structural Equation Model: Model identification typically requires that the unobserved ηs are operationalized by multiple manifest variables, y.[2] In the simplest case, a linear factor model is appropriate to describe the mapping of the indicators onto the latent variables, leading to the following measurement equation:

$$y_{ni} = \Lambda \eta_{ni} + \varepsilon_{ni}, \tag{3.4}$$

where y_{ni} is a ($P \times 1$) vector, Λ is a ($P \times M$) matrix of factor loadings and ε_{ni} is a ($P \times 1$) vector of measurement errors which are i.i.d. multivariate normal.

---

[2] For restricted types of the extended choice model without additional indicators see, for instance, Elrod (1991) and Elrod and Keane (1995).

Our structural model for the latent variables integrates alternative formulations by Ashok, Dillon/Yuan (2002) and Walker/Ben-Akiva (2002) by allowing for interrelationships among the latent variables as well as the influence of observed explanatory variables x_{ni} on the latent variables:

$$\boldsymbol{\eta}_{ni} = \mathbf{B}\boldsymbol{\eta}_{ni} + \boldsymbol{\Gamma}\mathbf{x}_{ni} + \boldsymbol{\zeta}_{ni},$$ (3.5)

where the $(M \times M)$ matrix $\mathbf{B}$ and the $(M \times L)$ matrix $\boldsymbol{\Gamma}$ contain unknown regression coefficients. For simplicity, it is assumed that the same set of observed exogenous variables x as in the random utility equation (3.1) enters the structural model for the latent variables. Of course, different variable sets can be defined for both equations. The $(M \times 1)$ vector $\boldsymbol{\zeta}_{ni}$ represents random disturbances assumed to be i.i.d. multivariate normal.

Likelihood Function: Since all information about the latent variables is contained in the multiple observed indicators, the joint probability of the choice and latent variable indicators conditioned on the exogenous variables is considered. Assuming that the random errors v, ε and ζ are independent, integrating over the joint distribution of the latent variables leads to the following multidimensional integral:[3]

$$P(u_i = 1, \mathbf{y} \mid \mathbf{x}, \boldsymbol{\theta}) = \int_{R_\eta} P_u(u_i = 1 \mid \mathbf{x}, \boldsymbol{\eta}; \boldsymbol{\beta}, \boldsymbol{\Sigma}_v) f_y(\mathbf{y} \mid \boldsymbol{\eta}; \boldsymbol{\Lambda}, \boldsymbol{\Sigma}_\varepsilon) f_\eta(\boldsymbol{\eta} \mid \mathbf{x}; \mathbf{B}, \boldsymbol{\Gamma}, \boldsymbol{\Sigma}_\zeta) d\eta,$$ (3.6)

where $\boldsymbol{\theta}$ represents the model parameters, P_u denotes the probability function of observing the choice of a specific alternative (3.2), the density function f_y for the latent variable indicators relates to the measurement model (3.4), and the density function f_η for the latent variables corresponds to the structural model (3.5). $\boldsymbol{\Sigma}_v$, $\boldsymbol{\Sigma}_\varepsilon$ and $\boldsymbol{\Sigma}_\zeta$ indicate covariance matrices for the residuals. R_η denotes that integration is over the range space of the vector of latent variables that have a direct impact on the choice decision.

If maximum likelihood techniques are applied to estimate the parameter vector $\boldsymbol{\theta}$ in (3.6), for any particular individual we obtain the following likelihood function:

$$L = \prod_{i \in C_n} P(u_i = 1, \mathbf{y} \mid \mathbf{x}, \boldsymbol{\theta})^{u_i}$$

$$= \int_{R_\eta} \prod_{i \in C_n} P(u_i = 1 \mid \mathbf{x}, \boldsymbol{\eta}; \boldsymbol{\beta}, \boldsymbol{\Sigma}_v)^{u_i} f_y(\mathbf{y} \mid \boldsymbol{\eta}; \boldsymbol{\Lambda}, \boldsymbol{\Sigma}_\varepsilon) f_\eta(\boldsymbol{\eta} \mid \mathbf{x}; \mathbf{B}, \boldsymbol{\Gamma}, \boldsymbol{\Sigma}_\zeta) d\eta,$$ (3.7)

where $u_i = 1$ if the decision maker chooses i and zero otherwise.

---

[3] The index denoting the individual decision-maker has been dropped for notational simplicity.

3.2.3 Estimation Approaches

Besides directly entering manifest indicators of psychological factors in the discrete choice equations as if they were error-free variables, the sequential approach is the easiest way to implement the estimation of an ICLV model (e.g., Ashok, Dillon/Yuan, 2002). First, factor scores based on a separate estimation of the latent variable part of the ICLV model are derived (Eqs. (3.4) and (3.5)). Second, computed factor scores substitute the latent variables in the discrete choice model (Eq. (3.3)) as additional exogenous variables x_{ni}. This two-step limited information estimation is straightforward using standard software for both discrete choice (e.g., SAS, NLOGIT, or STATA) and SEM (e.g., LISREL, AMOS, or EQS) analysis. However, since the factor scores are confounded by measurement error, the approach is deficient in the sense that it leads to inconsistent and biased estimates for the random utility part (e.g., Walker/Ben-Akiva, 2002). A more sophisticated sequential estimation approach which leads to consistent but not fully efficient estimators requires that the choice probability is integrated over the distribution of factors (Morikawa/Ben-Akiva/McFadden, 2002). Still, this approach likewise does not allow for estimating more elaborated behavioral theories (e.g., direct and indirect effects for multiple layers of latent variables impacting the decision maker's utilities).

Full information estimation on the other hand is rather involved due to the multidimensional integral in Eq. (3.6). For a limited number of latent variables (typically at most three) entering the utility function, numerical integration methods like Gaussian quadrature are feasible (e.g., Ashok, Dillon/Yuan, 2002). With an increasing number of latent variables, the computational complexity rises exponentially. This issue is further compounded if the restrictive assumptions of the classical Multinomial Logit model (i.e., independence from irrelevant alternatives (IIA) property) are relaxed by imposing the flexible error structure of a logit mixture kernel. Hence, in the case of more than three latent variables and/or a mixed logit discrete choice model, other techniques such as maximum simulated likelihood or Bayesian estimation are found to be more appropriate for ICLV models. The latter estimation technique appears to be preferable especially in situations with a large number of latent variables and extensive choice sets which induce correlated errors in the utility function (e.g., Bolduc/Alvarez-Daziano, 2010).

Also, via the introduction of latent classes, consumer heterogeneity can increasingly be accommodated. For example, with the finite mixture approach, segment-specific coefficients for a limited number of more or less homogeneous consumer segments, that are unobservable for the researcher, are estimated (Dillon et al., 1994). In the case of a discretely distributed heterogeneity, a model that accounts for latent classes, e.g., the finite mixture logit model (Chintagunta, Jain/Vilcassim, 1991; Kamakura/Russell, 1989), can be integrated into the hybrid choice model (Walker, 2001).

Until recently, researchers conducting full information estimation of an ICLV model had to develop their own custom-coded routines in flexible software like GAUSS (e.g, Ashok, Dillon/Yuan, 2002) or FORTRAN (e.g., Bolduc/Giroux, 2005). Meanwhile, more convenient options have become available. For example, simulated maximum likelihood estimation of

ICLV models might be performed using the latest version of BIOGEME (Bierlaire, 2003) or the software program GLLAMM running in STATA (Skrondal/Rabe-Hesketh, 2004). WINBUGS on the other hand offers a comparatively easy tool for Bayesian estimation (e.g, Walker/Ben-Akiva, 2002).

Having seen considerable advancement of the ICLV framework both in terms of models and estimation in the last ten years or so, the development has almost exclusively been driven by methodologically inclined researchers in the area of discrete choice modeling. Therefore, it was only recently that Mplus (Muthén/Muthén, 1998-2011) – arguably the most sophisticated commercial software for structural equation analysis – was detected to be able to accommodate the estimation of ICLV models (Temme/Paulssen/Dannewald, 2007; 2008). Besides offering the full flexibility of structural equation modeling software to specify complex structures of latent variable relationships, both numerical and Monte Carlo integration are available for simultaneously estimating a Multinomial Logit model with latent predictors (for a detailed description of the estimation with Mplus as well as an example input file, see Temme, Paulssen/Dannewald (2008)). Simulation evidence reveals that Mplus' estimation of ICLV models performs reasonably well at sample sizes of 500 and provides excellent results for sample sizes of 1,000 or larger (Temme/Paulssen/Dannewald, 2008). In principle, Mplus is also able to estimate a finite mixture MNL model using its latent class approach. A disadvantage of Mplus is that it so far has not allowed for specifying a mixed logit kernel.

In the following, the application of an ICLV model is illustrated by an empirical example on travel mode choice.

3.3   Empirical Application of an ICLV Model

In 2002 the Deutsche Bahn (DB), the former German national railway and now a leading passenger/logistics company in Germany, introduced a new pricing system for passenger transportation. A key feature of the pricing system was to abolish a customer card that gave a 50% price discount for travel in Germany for one year. The new customer card only allowed for a general 25% price discount. A 55% discount would only be offered if the passenger reserved his train seat seven days in advance. Since reserving seats in advance is common for flights, the management of DB did not anticipate any problems when the new pricing system was introduced. Even though the total discount that a customer could attain increased by 5% to 55%, the new pricing system was not accepted at all. Customers, especially those that choose the train for daily commutes, were switching to other transport modes resulting in an estimated loss in revenues of about 130 million euros in the first quarter of 2003 (Schmid, 2003). After several organizational changes, the "old" customer card was re-introduced, though at a considerably higher fee. This example underscores two points relevant to the empirical study to be presented in this section. First, obviously the customers of the DB highly valued a soft criteria implicitly offered as part of the old customer card - the flexibility to freely choose trains on short notice. Customers were not willing to sacrifice flexibility even though they could possibly receive a higher discount.

Second, traditional travel mode choice models considering only observable individual characteristics of the decision maker, such as income, employment status, gender, number of children as well as the observable attributes of the travel mode choice alternatives such as travel time, travel cost and availability, might fall short of providing an adequate representation of the decision making process (Vredin Johansson, Heldt/Johansson, 2006).

Against this background, an ICLV model enriched by a hierarchical latent variable structure was developed to explain commuter-mode choice decisions. Such a model is responsive to the recent call for including unobservable or latent variables, such as preferences for convenience, flexibility or safety, into models of mode choice (e.g., McFadden, 1986; Ashok, Dillon/Yuan, 2002; Morikawa, Ben-Akiva/McFadden, 2002) and additionally considers how commuters' value orientations might shape their attitudes towards mode choice. The following sections will briefly present the study's hypotheses, model, data, selected results as well as its main implications (for a more extensive description of the study see Temme, Paulssen/Dannewald (2008)).

3.3.1   Hypotheses

The ICLV model on commuters' mode choice decisions is based on an individual's value orientation, attitudes toward travel mode choice and socio-demographics as well as alternative-specific attributes of the traffic mode options often used in traditional discrete choice models (see **Figure 3.2**).

The inclusion of personal value orientations was inspired by previous studies which indicated that values might play a role in travel mode choice (Bamberg, 1996; Bamberg/Kühnel, 1998; Choo/Mokhtarian, 2004; Lanzendorf, 2002). None of those studies have, however, developed and tested a model on how values impact actual transport mode choice. In line with empirical studies supporting a completely mediated impact of values on behavior (intentions, preferences) through the so-called value-attitude hierarchy (e.g., McCarthy/Shrum, 1994; Thøgersen/Grunert-Beckmann, 1997), we propose a direct effect of values on attitudes only (Proposition P1). Attitudes towards mode choice, in turn, are supposed to impact travel mode choice. Following recent research by Vredin Johansson, Heldt/Johansson (2005; 2006) we consider attitudes such as convenience and flexibility as latent predictors of mode choice in our model (Proposition P2). Differences in people's demographic characteristics such as age, gender and income give rise to distinct life circumstances (e.g., in terms of socialization, social roles, life stage and expectations) which also affect the salience of certain values (Schwartz, 2003). For example, with increasing age, the ability to cope with change wanes and security values might become more relevant. Therefore, we propose that socio-demographics such as age, income and gender influence personal value orientations (Proposition P3). Both theoretical arguments (Ben-Akiva et al. 2002b) and empirical evidence (Vredin Johansson/Heldt/Johansson, 2006) suggest that a commuter's socio-demographic characteristics affect his/her attitudes toward mode choice (e.g., the relevance of flexibility of a transport mode depends on having children or not; Proposition P4). As in more traditional travel mode choice models, we use individual socio-demographic characteristics such as age, gender and income (Proposition P5) as well as modal attributes such as travel time (Proposition P6) as further explanatory variables of mode choice behavior (e.g., Vredin Johansson/Heldt/Johansson, 2006).

Figure 3.2 Structural Hypotheses of the Transportation Choice Study

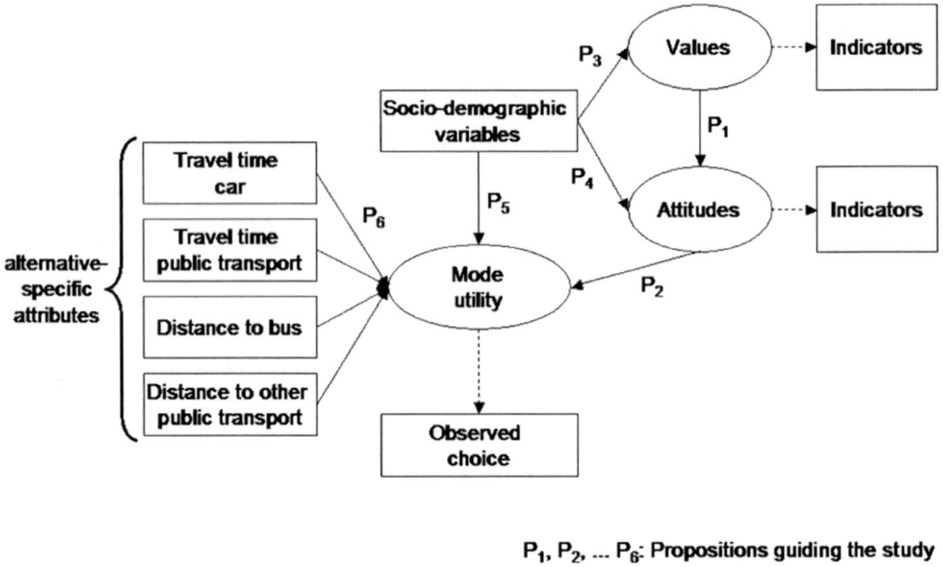

P_1, P_2, ... P_6: Propositions guiding the study

3.3.2   Data and Methods

Survey data resulted from interviewing a representative sample of 902 German consumers between 14 and 75 years of age drawn from a consumer panel of a major international market research company. Since for 43% of the respondents daily trips to work/education did not apply (e.g., they were homemakers, unemployed or retired) or alternative travel modes did not exist (e.g., they did not possess a driver's license or had no car in the household), the final sample reduced to N = 519 respondents. Whereas the majority of these respondents almost exclusively used the car for their daily commute (n = 412), 50 persons relied on public transport only and 57 persons combined car and public transport.

The interviews had the following structure: Respondents were first asked demographic questions needed for quota sampling. Second, information about personal mobility was gathered by posing questions about the possession of a driver's license, of seasonal tickets for public transport alternatives (bus, tram, integrated public transport system, railroad) and of cars. Third, the distance to the nearest stations of various public transport alternatives (if available) and the time needed for daily trips to work with public transport, as well as with the car, had to be estimated. Since many car drivers do not know the cost per driven kilometer, nor do they possess adequate knowledge about prices of public transportation alternatives, the respondents were not asked about the estimated cost of the different transport modes in order to avoid a large portion of biased or missing values for these variables. Fourth, indicators of the three attitudes towards transport modes for daily trips to work - flexibility, comfort/convenience and safety, were evaluated including the perceived importance of these choice criteria. Fifth, respondents were requested to reveal their mode choice for their daily trips to work or education. Respondents had to indicate whether they predominantly used car, public transport or a combination of both. Finally, commuters' value orientations were measured with the Portraits Value Questionnaire (PVQ) from Schwartz et al. (2001). Respondents had to indicate their perceived similarity to person descriptions (portraits); gender-matched with the respondent on six-point rating scales ranging from very unalike to very much alike (Schwartz et al., 2001).

3.3.3   Results

Following the widely adopted two-step approach to structural equation modeling (Anderson/Gerbing, 1988), confirmatory factor analysis was used to assess the reliability and validity of the reflective measurement models for the attitude and value constructs. Although established scales for measuring personal values (Schwartz et al. 2001) were used, one indicator had to be eliminated for power and security, respectively. Concerning attitudes, the scale for safety turned out to be the most problematic; probably because it consisted of a mixture of personal safety and traffic safety criteria. As a pragmatic solution, the item indicating the importance of possessing the means of transport was kept. While robust WLSMV estimation with Mplus (Muthén/Muthén, 1998-2007) lead to an acceptable level of overall fit for the final confirmatory factor model, some scales showed only moderate levels of reliability and validity.

In the following, we focus on the multinomial discrete choice part of the ICLV model. The MNL model contains both observed variables describing the choice alternatives (e.g., travel time) and the commuters (e.g., age) as well as individual attitudes towards mode choice (e.g., flexibility). The utilities of the three mode choice alternatives (public transport only (PTO), car + public transport (CPT) and car only (CO)) are given by:

$$U_{PTO} = \beta_{0,PTO} + \beta_1 TT_{PT,PTO} + \beta_3 DB + \beta_5 DOPT + \beta_7 AGE + \beta_8 GEND + \beta_9 INC$$
$$+ \beta_{13} FLEX + \beta_{14} CC + \beta_{15} SAFE + v_{PTO},$$
$$U_{CPT} = \beta_{0,CPT} + \beta_1 TT_{PT,CPT} + \beta_2 TT_{C,CPT} + \beta_4 DB + \beta_6 DOPT + \beta_{10} AGE + \beta_{11} GEND + \beta_{12} INC$$
$$+ \beta_{16} FLEX + \beta_{17} CC + \beta_{18} SAFE + v_{CPT},$$
$$U_{CO} = \beta_2 TT_{C,CO} + v_{CO}.$$

with observed variables: TTPT, = travel time public transport, TTC,· = travel time car, DB = distance to nearest bus stop, DOPT = distance to other public transport, AGE = age, GEND = gender and INC = net monthly income; and latent variables: FLEX = flexibility, CC = convenience/comfort and SAFE = safety. For identification purposes, the alternative-specific constant (i.e., $\beta_{0,CO}$) as well as the coefficients of the socio-demographic variables and the latent variables are set to zero for mode car only.

The estimation of both the traditional MNL model and the ICLV model was performed by the software Mplus. McFadden's pseudo R^2 for the ICLV model including latent variables is 11.5%. Compared to a R^2 of 7% for a MNL model which only contains observed variables, explanatory power increases by more than 60% (see **Table 3.1**); both the information criteria and a significant chi-square difference test point in the same direction. Though pseudo R^2 for the ICLV model might still be considered rather low, given the fact that in contrast to many other studies, our analysis does not focus on commutes in a specific area (e.g., Train, 1978) or between specific cities (e.g., Vredin Johansson/Heldt/Johansson, 2006), this result can be considered reasonable. Our sample was drawn from areas across Germany, thus commuters' mode choices occurred under very different circumstances (e.g., concerning the quality and safety of public transport systems). This substantial heterogeneity is likely to considerably reduce the explanatory power of our model.

Table 3.1   The Results of the Transportation Study

Robust ML parameter estimates for the traditional and ICLV model – Discrete choice part					
Explanatory variable/ parameter	Traditional MNL model			ICLV MNL model	
	Estimate	t-statistic		Estimate	t-statistic
Flexibility1	—	—		−0.44***	−2.81
Flexibility2	—	—		−0.39**	−2.09
Conv./Comf.1	—	—		0.61**	2.06
Conv./Comf.2	—	—		0.54*	1.85
Safety1	—	—		−0.57***	−2.98
Safety2	—	—		−0.19	−1.02
Travel time PT1,2	−1.16***	−2.64		−1.24***	−2.64
Travel time car2,3	−1.62***	−2.64		−1.51**	−2.31
Distance bus1	−0.09	−0.72		−0.10	−0.74
Distance bus2	−0.03	−0.71		−0.03	−0.58
Distance other PT1	−0.12**	−2.46		−0.11**	−2.34

Robust ML parameter estimates for the traditional and ICLV model – Discrete choice part				
Distance other PT2	–0.13**	–2.13	–0.13**	–2.11
Age1	–0.00	–0.13	–0.00	–0.24
Age2	0.00	0.06	–0.00	–0.34
Gender1	0.06	0.19	0.12	0.36
Gender2	–0.41	–1.35	–0.40	–1.26
Income1	–0.11**	–1.99	–0.03	–0.44
Income2	–0.08	–1.53	–0.02	–0.33
Mode constant1	–0.72	–1.00	–0.89	–1.10
Mode constant2	–0.62	–1.00	–0.64	–0.96
LL	–11,766		–11,752	
McFadden's R^2	7%		11.5%	
AIC	23,741		23,724	
BICadj	23,853		23,843	

Notes: Variable subscripts denote travel modes: 1 = public transport only, 2 = car + public transport (PT), 3 = car only.
Travel time by public transport differs for modes 1 and 2; travel time by car differs for modes 2 and 3.
Coding of the gender variable: 0 = male, 1 = female.
A constants-only model was used to determine McFadden's pseudo R^2.
*** $p < 0.01$, ** $p < 0.05$, * $p < 0.10$

The estimated coefficients for the ICLV model lend empirical support for Proposition 2, in that all three attitudes show significant effects on mode choice. The desire for flexibility significantly increases the propensity to avoid any means of public transport and to exclusively use the car for daily work trips. In turn, importance of a convenient and comfortable commute increases the probability of choosing public transport. If a commuter finds it important to own the means of transport – a proxy variable for personal safety – this decreases the probability of using public transport either alone or in combination with the car (the latter effect, however, is not significant). In additional analyses, personal value orientations turn out to influence mode choice only indirectly by significantly impacting attitudes towards mode choice. Thus, Proposition 1 is likewise supported. Compared to the model without latent variables, coefficients for the observed alternative-specific variables as well as the commuters' socio-demographics remain rather stable. A noteworthy exception is the vanishing effect of income on avoiding public transport in the ICLV model. The impact of income is absorbed by the attitudinal variables, especially the desire for flexibility. In turn, our results show that income has a strong effect on flexibility.

Thus, income determines transport mode through its strong positive effect on the desire for flexibility.

To sum up, our results support the contention that attitudes and also values as more remote causes are important determinants in mode choice. The general theoretical conclusion of this study is that future models of choice can be made more powerful by including the attitudes and personality variables of the decision makers.

3.4   Summary and Outlook

In this article we have shown how structural equation models can be merged with the multinomial choice framework. Such an integrated discrete choice and latent variable (ICLV) model provides a powerful technique for analyzing marketing data, more thorough understanding choice behavior and better predicting choice.

The ICLV approach allows for the enrichment of the former "black box" of consumers' choice processes in discrete choice models by relevant theoretical constructs from consumer psychology using well developed and validated measurement models for these latent variables. Furthermore, the approach allows for the specification of complex relationships between these constructs in line with the underlying behavioral theory. Of course, all methodological advances in discrete choice modeling such as logit mixture models are available.

From the perspective of applied researchers, estimation might still be a bottleneck. Although we have seen promising software developments in the recent past (e.g., BIOGEME), researchers, especially those more familiar with structural equation than with discrete choice modeling, will suffer from considerable "entry barriers" to the ICLV approach. As shown in this paper, the SEM software Mplus can be used to estimate an ICLV model including a classical multinomial logit model in the discrete choice part. Although further extending this model to a finite mixture discrete choice model is possible with the latent class approach implemented in Mplus, allowing for more flexible error structures in the utility equations is urgently needed in order to provide state-of-the-art estimation techniques.

Literature

[1] Anderson, J. C./Gerbing, D. W. (1988): Structural equation modeling in practice: A review and recommended two-step approach, in: Psychological Bulletin, Vol. 103, 3, pp. 411–423.

[2] Ashok, K./Dillon, W. R./Yuan, S. (2002): Extending Discrete Choice Models to Incorporate Attitudinal and Other Latent Variables, in: Journal of Marketing Research, Vol. 39, 1, pp. 31-46.

[3] Bagozzi, R. P. (1998): A Prospectus for Theory Construction in Marketing: Revisited and Revised, in: Hildebrandt, L./Homburg, C. (eds.): Die Kausalanalyse, Stuttgart: Schäffer-Poeschel, pp. 47-81.

[4] Bamberg, S. (1996): Allgemeine oder spezifische Einstellungen bei der Erklärung umweltschonenden Verhaltens? [General or specific attitudes as predictors of environmentally friendly behavior?], in: Zeitschrift für Sozialpsychologie, Vol. 27, 1, pp. 47–60. (in German)

[5] Bamberg, S./Kühnel, S. (1998): Überzeugungssysteme in einem zweistufigen Modell rationaler Handlungen [Systems of conviction in a two-stage model of rational behavior], in: Zeitschrift für Soziologie, Vol. 27, 4, pp. 256–270. (in German)

[6] Ben-Akiva, M./Lerman, S. R. (1985): Discrete choice analysis: Theory and application to travel demand, Cambridge: MIT Press.

[7] Ben-Akiva, M./McFadden, D./Gärling, T./Gopinath, D./Walker, J. L./Bolduc, D./Börsch-Supan, A./Delquié, P./Larichev, O./Morikawa, T./Polydoropoulou, A./Rao, V. (1999): Extended Framework for Modeling Choice Behavior, in: Marketing Letters, Vol. 10, 3, pp. 187-203.

[8] Ben-Akiva, M./McFadden, D./Train, K./Walker, J. L./Bhat, C./Bierlaire, M./Bolduc, D./Börsch-Supan, A./Brownstone, D./Bunch, D. S./Daly, A./de Palma, A./Gopinath, D./Karlstrom, A./Munizaga, M. A. (2002a): Hybrid Choice Models: Progress and Challenges, in: Marketing Letters, Vol. 13, 3, pp. 163-175.

[9] Ben-Akiva, M./Walker, J./Bernardino, A. T./Gopinath, D. A./Morikawa, T./Polydoropoulou, A. (2002b): Integration of choice and latent variable models, in: Hani S. Mahmassani (ed.): In perpetual motion: Travel behaviour research opportunities and application challenges, Oxford: Elsevier Science Ltd., pp. 431–470.

[10] Bierlaire, M. (2003): BIOGEME: A Free Package for the Estimation of Discrete Choice Models, Proceedings of the 3rd Swiss Transportation Research Conference, Ascona, Switzerland.

[11] Bodopati, A. V./Drolet, A. (2005): A Hybrid Choice Model That Uses Actual and Ordered Attribute Value Information, in: Journal of Marketing Research, Vol. 42, 3, pp. 256-265.

[12] Bolduc, D./Giroux, A. (2005): The Integrated Choice and Latent Variable (ICLV) Model: Handout to accompany the estimation software, Département d'économique, Université Laval.

[13] Bolduc, D./Ben-Akiva, M./Walker, J. L./Michaud, A. (2005): Hybrid Choice Models with Logit Kernel: Applicability to Large Scale Models, in: Lee-Gosselin, M./Doherty, S.T. (eds.), Integrated Land-Use and Transportation Models: Behavioral Foundations, Amsterdam: Elsevier, pp. 275-302.

[14] Bolduc, D./Alvarez Daziano, R. (2010): On Estimation of Hybrid Choice Models, in: Hess, S./Daly, A. (eds.): Choice Modeling: The State-of-the-Art and the State-of-Practice, Bingley, UK: Emerald, pp. 259-288.

[15] Bollen, K. A. (1989): Structural Equations with Latent Variables. New-York: Wiley-Interscience

[16] Chintagunta, P. K./Jain, D. C./Vilcassim, N. J. (1991): Investigating heterogeneity in brand preferences in logit models for panel data, Journal of Marketing Research, Vol. 28, 4, pp. 417-428.

[17] Choo, S./Mokhtarian, P. L. (2004): What type of vehicle do people drive? The role of attitude and lifestyle in influencing vehicle type choice, in: Transportation Research Part A: Policy and Practice, Vol. 38, 3, pp. 201–222.

[18] Dellaert, G. C./Stremersch, S. (2005): Marketing Mass-Customized Products: Striking a Balance Between Utility and Complexity, in: Journal of Marketing Research, Vol. 42, 2, pp. 219-227.

[19] Dillon, W. R./ Böckenholt, U./Smith de Borrero, M./Bozdogan, H./de Sarbo, W./Gupta, S./Kamakura, W./Kumar, A./Ramaswamy, B./Zenor, M. (1994): Issues in the Estimation and Application of Latent Structure Models of Choice, in: Marketing Letters, Vol. 5, 4, pp. 323-334.

[20] Guadagni, P. M./Little, J. D. C. (1983): A Logit Model of Brand Choice Calibrated on Scanner Data, in: Marketing Science, Vol. 2, 3, pp. 203-238.

[21] Hildebrandt, L./Temme, D. (2006): Probleme der Validierung mit Strukturgleichungsmodellen [Problems in validation with structural equation models], in: Die Betriebswirtschaft, Vol. 66, 6, pp. 618-639. (in German)

[22] Jöreskog K. G./Goldberger, A. S. (1975): Estimation of a Model with Multiple Indicators and Multiple Causes of a Single Latent Variable, in: Journal of the American Statistical Association , Vol. 70, 351, pp. 631-639.

[23] Kamakura, W./Russell, G. J. (1989): A probabilistic choice model for market segmentation and elasticity structure, in: Journal of Marketing Research, Vol. 26, 4, pp. 379-390.

[24] Lanzendorf, M. (2002): Mobility styles and behaviour – Application of a lifestyle approach to leisure travel, in: Transportation Research Record, Vol. 1807, pp. 163–173.

[25] McCarthy, J. A./Shrum, L. J. (1994): The recycling of solid wastes: Personal value orientation, and attitudes about recycling as antecedents of recycling behavior, in: Journal of Business Research, Vol. 30, 1, pp. 53–62.

[26] McFadden, D. L. (1986): The choice theory approach to marketing research, in: Marketing Science, Vol. 5, 4, pp. 275–297.

[27] Morikawa, T./Ben-Akiva, M./McFadden, D. L. (2002): Discrete Choice Models Incorporating Revealed Preferences and Psychometric Data, in: Franses, P. H./Montgomery, A. L. (eds.): Econometric Models in Marketing, pp. 29-55.

[28] Muthén, L. K./Muthén, B. O. (1998–2007): Mplus User's Guide. 5th ed., Los Angeles: Muthén & Muthén.

[29] Muthén, L. K./Muthén, B. O. (1998–2011): Mplus User's Guide. 6th ed., Los Angeles: Muthén & Muthén.

[30] Schmid, K.-P. (2003): Begrenzt einsatzfähig [Limited fitness for use], in: Die Zeit, Vol. 21. (in German)

[31] Schwartz, S. H. (2003): A proposal for measuring value orientations across nations, in: European Social Survey: The questionnaire development package of the European Social Survey, Chapter 7, pp. 259–319.

[32] Schwartz, S. H./Melech, G./Lehmann, A./Burgess, S./Harris, M./Owens, V. (2001): Extending the cross-cultural validity of the theory of basic human values with a different method of measurement, in: Journal of Cross Cultural Psychology, Vol. 32, 5, pp. 519–542.

[33] Skrondal, A./Rabe-Hesketh, S. (2004): Generalized latent variable modeling, Boca Raton: Chapman & Hall.

[34] Temme, D./Paulssen, M./Dannewald T. (2007): Integrating Latent Variables in Discrete Choice Models – How Higher-Order Values and Attitudes Determine Consumer Choice, Discussion Paper No. 65, SFB 649 Economic Risk, Humboldt University Berlin.

[35] Temme, D./Paulssen, M./Dannewald T. (2008): Incorporating Latent Variables into Discrete Choice Models – A Simultaneous Estimation Approach Using SEM Software, in: BuR – Business Research, Vol. 1, 2, pp. 220-237.

[36] Thøgersen, J./Grunert-Beckmann, S. C. (1997): Values and attitude formation towards emerging attitude objects: From recycling to general waste minimizing behavior, in: Advances in Consumer Research, Vol. 24, pp. 182–189.

[37] Train, K. E. (1978): A validation test of a disaggregate mode choice model: Transportation Research Part A: Policy and Practice, Vol. 12, 2, pp. 167–174.

[38] Vredin Johansson, M./Heldt, T./Johansson, P. (2005): Latent variables in a travel mode choice model: Attitudinal and behavioural indicator variables, Working Paper 2005:5, Uppsala University.

[39] Vredin Johansson, M./Heldt, T./Johansson, P. (2006): The effects of attitudes and personality traits on mode choice, in: Transportation Research Part A: Policy and Practice, Vol. 40, 6, pp. 507–525.

[40] Walker, J. L. (2001): Extended Discrete Choice Models: Integrated Framework, Flexible Error Structures, and Latent Variables, Ph.D. thesis, Massachusetts Institute of Technology.

[41] Walker, J./Ben-Akiva, M. (2002): Generalized random utility model, in: Mathematical Social Sciences, Vol. 43, 2, pp. 303–343.

4 Using Multi-Informant Designs to Address Key Informant and Common Method Bias

Christian Homburg, University of Mannheim, Germany

Martin Klarmann, Karlsruhe Institute of Technology (KIT), Germany

Dirk Totzek, University of Mannheim, Germany

Abstract

The important key informant and common method problems in survey research are taken up in this article. The authors focus on the question how researchers can rely on multi-informant designs in order to limit the threats of key informant and common method bias on the validity and reliability of survey research. In particular, they show how researchers can effectively design studies that employ multiple informants and how multi-informant data can be aggregated in order to obtain more accurate results than can be obtained with single informant studies.

Keywords

Organizational Survey Research, Survey Designs, Common Method Bias, Key Informant Bias.

4.1   Introduction

A major part of empirical marketing and management research is based on survey data. Surveys are notably used to collect data on consumer attitudes and preferences. As a result, quantitative models and tools for marketing decision making can be developed and, for example, combined with sales data (e.g., Natter et al. 2008). Surveys are also used to assess internal, firm-related phenomena such as a firm's strategic orientation or a firm's marketing mix decisions. For example, there is a large body of work assessing the firm's market orientation (Kirca, Jayachandran, and Bearden 2005) or the firm's current customer relationship management practices (Reinartz/Krafft/Hoyer 2004) with survey data.

However, survey research has been frequently challenged (Rindfleisch et al. 2008, p. 261). This especially holds for research addressing firm-related phenomena with surveys directed towards key informants. Two major concerns have been put forward:

1. The accuracy of the informants' responses has been questioned (e.g., Kumar/Stern/Anderson 1993; Starbuck/Mezias 1996). In particular, the questions emerged whether single key informants are (1) capable to judge complex organizational phenomena and (2) systematically biased in their responses. As a result, the accuracy of the data largely depends on the ability of the informants to correctly answer the survey questions.

2. It has been stressed that inferences about causal relationships between two variables of interest may be artifacts because the variables were collected in the same survey (Podsakoff et al. 2003). For example, surveys frequently assess both performance variables and strategic or operational marketing decisions to identify causal relationships.

These two critiques have been labeled as *key informant bias* and *common method bias*. Both biases threaten the reliability and validity of empirical research based on survey data. Addressing this critique, multi-source and multi-informant designs have been suggested as an adequate way to assess firm-related phenomena (Podsakoff et al. 2003; van Bruggen/Lilien/Kacker 2002).

In this article, we focus the question how researchers can rely on multi-informant designs in order to limit the threats of key informant and common method bias. In particular, we address how researchers can effectively design studies that rely on multiple informants and how multi-informant data can be aggregated in order to obtain more accurate results than can be obtained by single informant studies.

We do not explicitly address the questions of when and how to rely on multiple sources of data (e.g., survey data and secondary data) or on longitudinal data (Rindfleisch et al. 2008). However, many rationales how multi-informant designs should enhance the reliability and validity of key informant survey data also apply to these contexts.

In the following, we first discuss the theoretical foundations and the major sources of key informant and common method bias. We then introduce different types of multi-informant designs and discuss how to use them appropriately in order to reduce the risk of a key informant bias, a common method bias, or both. We also discuss how the reliability and validity of multi-informant data can be assessed and how multi-informant data should be analyzed. Finally, we give recommendations for research practice.

4.2 Key Informant and Common Method Bias

4.2.1 Conceptual Background

Many empirical survey studies in marketing and management research observe phenomena at the business unit or firm level and try to identify success factors for marketing or management decision making. For example, the head of the marketing department is asked to evaluate the firm's actual market orientation or the innovativeness of the product portfolio. Then, he or she is asked to evaluate the firm's market-related or financial performance.

However, when particular members (e.g., employees of a firm) judge organizational phenomena, a *key informant bias* can occur. A key informant bias is a bias in the variance and covariance structure of data that can be attributed to the fact that one single key informant is used for data collection. Key informants are subjects who are asked to evaluate phenomena of a social entity, for example, a group of people, a business unit, or a firm (van Bruggen/Lilien/Kacker 2002, p. 469). The general question is whether the key informant's judgment is accurate.

Formally, a key informant's response to a particular variable x consists of the true value t_x, a systematic measurement error i_x, and a random measurement error e_x (Churchill 1979; van Bruggen/Lilien/Kacker 2002):

$$x = t_x + i_x + e_x$$

A key informant bias is reflected in a systematic measurement error i_x that is caused by particular informant characteristics. Major potential sources of a key informant bias are (e.g., van Bruggen/Lilien/Kacker 2002; Podsakoff et al. 2003):

- *The informant's position and functional affiliation*: A particular functional culture or the informant's hierarchical level in the firm can shape the informant's view on firm-related phenomena (Phillips 1981).

- *The informant's knowledge and experience*: The informant may not be knowledgeable to judge particular phenomena (e.g., the effectiveness of particular marketing activities or aspects of organizational culture). This can occur because the informant does not have access to the underlying data necessary to correctly answer the question, may be inadequate to judge phenomena outside his or her own job, or the informant has only recently joined the firm.

- *The informant's self-interest and a self-serving bias*: Informants may try to give socially desirable answers or to give answers that produce desirable results in the context of the study (Podsakoff et al. 2003, p. 881). For example, sales reps may evaluate their sales effectiveness too positively or higher-level managers may evaluate their leadership style too positively (compared with their employees' perceptions).

- *The informant's general perspective on the phenomenon*: This especially occurs in a marketing context when informants of a supplying firm are asked to evaluate their customers' attitudes or behaviors or when they have to evaluate the nature of buyer-seller relationships. Key informants may not know what their customers actually think or might have a different perspective on the relationship (John/Reve 1982; Vosgerau/Anderson/Ross 2008).

- *The informant's bounded rationality and human judgment biases*: The subjective perceptions of informants may be biased because of their bounded rationality and general cognitive biases. Behavioral decision theory has identified a high number of judgment biases that affect human judgment (e.g., Bazerman/Moore 2009; Tversky/Kahneman 1974). When there is space for subjective interpretation of a question, there is a higher risk of a systematic error due to subjectivity.

The random measurement error e_x can also reflect non systematic judgment errors of a key informant which are caused by the ambiguous nature of the question or the difficulty of the judgment task.

A *common method bias* can be defined as a bias in the variance and covariance structure of data caused by the fact that the independent and dependent variables of a model come from the same source of data, for example, the same survey (Podsakoff/Organ 1986). Thus, common method bias is a more general phenomenon than key informant bias: It is not exclusively related to situations when key informants are surveyed. However, a key informant bias can lead to a common method bias when analyzing relationships between two or more variables which were assessed by the same key informant.

There are several sources of a common method bias related to informant characteristics, item characteristics, characteristics of the item context (e.g., the design of the questionnaire), and effects of the general measurement context, i.e., the study context (see for an extensive list Podsakoff et al. 2003, p. 882). Informant characteristics basically relate to the sources of key informant bias. A common method bias can notably occur because informants have implicit assumptions about the relationships that are addressed between the variables in a particular survey. As a result, informants answer according to these implicit theories (Chandon/Morwitz/Reinartz 2005; Feldman/Lynch 1988).

In addition, Halo effects and general response tendencies can cause a common method bias (Baumgartner/Steenkamp 2001; Lance/LaPointe/ Fisicaro 1994).

As examples for the role of item characteristics and the item context, the use of common scale formats and of the same anchors for all items in a survey can cause common method bias. In a similar vein, the order of items can lead to common method bias (Podsakoff et al. 2003). For example, when assessing variables in the same order as hypothesized, causal relations between these variables may be an empirical artifact.

Formally, a common method bias (m_y) can be included into the measurement of an additional variable y as follows:

$$y = t_y + i_y + m_y + e_y \qquad \text{with } m_y = f(x)$$

Assuming that the random measurement errors are uncorrelated with the systematic errors and with the true values t_x and t_y; and that the true values and systematic errors are uncorrelated, the correlation between the two variables x and y is:

$$r_{x,y} = \frac{Cov(t_x, t_y) + Cov(i_x, i_y) + Cov(t_x, m_y) + Cov(i_x, m_y)}{\sqrt{Var(t_x) + Var(i_x) + Var(e_x)} \cdot \sqrt{Var(t_y) + Var(i_y) + Var(m_y) + Var(e_y)}}$$

As a result, the correlation between the two variables x and y does not only depend on the two true scores t_x and t_y, but is also affected by systematic and random measurement errors related to x and y. The following consequences for $r_{x,y}$ occur (van Bruggen/Lilien/Kacker 2002):

■ The observed correlation r between x and y decreases as random measurement errors of x and y increase.

■ The covariance between the two systematic error components i_x and i_y affects $r_{x,y}$ depending on the direction and magnitude of this covariance. The correlation $r_{x,y}$ is biased when there are differences between the systematic errors of the individual informants. When the systematic errors i_x and i_y as well as the common method bias m_y are identical for all individuals, the corresponding variance and covariance terms are Zero. As a result, $r_{x,y}$ is not systematically biased. For example, if all informants systematically rate their firm's performance relative to the performance of their major competitors too high, the level of all responses is shifted in an upward direction without affecting estimated correlations between the two variables.

■ If the systematic errors are uncorrelated, they affect the correlation between two variables in the same way as a random measurement error.

The distinction between a systematic measurement error and random measurement error relates to the distinction between measurement reliability and validity that has been put forward by Churchill (1979). Thus, the *reliability* of key informant data is generally enhanced by minimizing the effects of random measurement errors. The *validity* of key informant data is enhanced by reducing systematic measurement errors.

4.2.2   Empirical Evidence

Prior work has analyzed whether and to what extent the use of key informants produces systematic errors and measurement errors. In addition, a relatively small body of research has focused on the existence and level of common method variance in survey data. More specifically, there are two major areas of research: (1) research on the general level of common method variance in survey data and on the effect of common method variance on the estimated relationships between two variables and (2) research addressing the accuracy of key informant data. **Table 4.1** summarizes selected studies.

With respect to the general level of common method variance, simulation studies show that inferences about the relationships between to variables can indeed be biased (e.g., Cote/Buckley 1988; Evans 1985; Williams/Brown 1994). Furthermore, Chandon/Morwitz/Reinartz (2005) show that informants' responses to several phenomena are driven by their implicit assumptions on relationships between these phenomena.

Table 4.1   Selected Studies on the Reliability and Validity of Key Informant Data (Adapted from Klarmann 2008, pp. 127)

Authors (Year)	Key Informants	Variables	Selected Results
Selected studies on the validity and reliability of key informant responses			
Mezias/Starbuck (2003)	Executive MBA-students, senior level managers	Sales, sales volatility, success of quality improvements	Evaluations of MBA-students with respect to sales and evaluations of managers with respect to quality improvements are substantially different from objective data
Sathe (1978)	Employees at different hierarchical levels of an insurance company	Centralization, specialization, formalization	Subjective evaluations of the firm's centralization, specialization, and formalization show fairly low correlations with organizational measures (between .14 and .17)
Venkatraman/ Ratmanujam (1987)	Senior level managers	Sales/profitability growth, ROI relative to competitors	High consistency between subjective assessments and objective performance data (correlations between .40 and .50)
Wall et al. (2004)	Three samples of senior level managers	Firm performance and productivity relative to competitors	Correlations between subjective performance measures and objective data are relatively strong (between .40 and .60)

Selected studies comparing the responses of different key informants and of key informants over time			
Conant/Mokwa/ Varadarajan (1990)	Marketing directors in the health industry	Miles and Snow (1978)-Typology	Test-retest-correlations between different items are between .50 and .82 (Mean: .63)
Golden (1992)	CEOs	Miles and Snow (1978)-Typology	In retrospect, 58% of the managers indicate a different strategy type than two years ago
Hambrick (1981)	Managers at three hierarchical levels, expert panel	Miles and Snow (1978)-Typology	Evaluations of CEOs are highly correlated with evaluations of expert panel (. 84); on lower hierarchical levels, correlations are lower
Selected studies on the relative importance of method variance			
Cote/Buckley (1987)	Meta-Analysis	Different classes of constructs in different research areas	Average method variance is 26,3% (15% in marketing); average true variance is 41,7% (64,4% in marketing)
Doty/Glick (1998)	Meta-Analysis	-	Method variance accounts for 32% (Mean) of the observed variance; average true variance accounts for 46%; correlational bias between two constructs is about 26% (Median)
Phillips (1981)	CEOs and other key informants	Product portfolio, channel power	Less than 50% of the observed variance relates to the true measurement; substantial differences between constructs
Williams/ Cote/Buckley (1989)	Meta-Analysis	-	Method variance accounts for 25% of the observed variance (Median); true variance accounts for 48% (Median)

The proportion of common method variance compared to the variance that can be attributed to the true variable scores is an ongoing "topic of debate" (Rindfleisch et al. 2008, p. 263). Some studies stress that it is very substantial and that common method variance accounts for more than 50% of the observed variance (e.g., Phillips 1981). Other studies show that method variance accounts for lower proportions (e.g., Cote/Buckley 1987; Crampton/Wagner 1994; Harrison/McLaughlin/Coalter 1996). Furthermore, Doty/Glick (1998) show that method variance does not affect the estimated relationships between two variables in a way that inferences about theoretical relationships between the variables have to be challenged.

Research on the accuracy of key informant data is more elaborated. Researchers have analyzed whether the key informants' subjective ratings correspond to objective data available for the same variables. In general, findings are relatively mixed with respect to the convergence between subjective assessments and objective data. Whereas some studies indicate fairly low correlations between the subjective assessments and objective data (e.g., Sathe

1978) other authors show that correlations are substantial: For example, Wall et al. (2004) show that there are correlations of .40 up to .60 between the managers' assessments of firm performance and the objective data (see also Venkatraman/Ratmanujam 1987).

Another stream of research on the accuracy of key informant data has compared responses of different key informants and responses over time. The findings are mixed with respect to the convergence across key informants and over time. Whereas Golden (1992) indicates a substantial bias when comparing managers' evaluations over time, Co-nant/Mokwa/Varadarajan (1990) show a fairly high test-retest correlation for key inform-ants' responses.

In summary, prior research shows that there is indeed a risk of a key informant bias and common method bias. However, results do not indicate that key informant data has gener-ally to be dismissed and shows that the risk of biased findings is context-specific. In par-ticular, the key question is whether these biases alter inferences on relationships between two or more variables.

4.2.3   Criteria to Evaluate the Risk of Key Informant and Common Method Bias

As outlined in the last chapter, the risk of key informant bias and common method bias for the validity of inferences on relationships between variables is context-specific. Based on prior work and on an empirical study (Homburg/Klarmann 2009), the following criteria and exemplary questions can be used to evaluate the risk of key informant bias and com-mon method bias when conducting survey studies with key informants. The more of these criteria are fulfilled, the higher the risk that key informant and common method bias affect the relationships under consideration:

■ *Key informant's self interest*: Do the informants have a high interest to put themselves in a good position with respect to the variables of interest (e.g., socially responsible behav-ior)? Do key informants have a high interest that particular relationships between vari-ables emerge (e.g., that their management decisions increase performance)?

■ *Key informant competency*: Do informants have access to the necessary data to answer the questions as precise as possible (e.g., CRM-databases or accounting information) or not? Do informants frequently deal with the issues under consideration, i.e., are these issues familiar to them, or not?

■ *Construct operationalization*: Do the constructs relate to commonly accepted criteria or performance indicators or are there no commonly accepted criteria for operationaliza-tion? Are the constructs very general in nature and address global phenomena?

■ *Construct domain*: Do the constructs relate to traits and behaviors of particular persons? Do the constructs relate to organizational phenomena which cannot be affected by the informant? Do the constructs relate to environmental phenomena?

■ *Relations between constructs*: Do informants associate particular constructs as belonging to other higher-order phenomena? Are there popular theories on the relationships between constructs (e.g., higher customer satisfaction is always better)? Does the informant's position lead to a particular implicit theory between constructs (e.g., accountants believe that marketing expenses are costs rather than investments)?

When there is a high risk of key informant bias and common method bias, multi-informant studies are suggested as an effective means to reduce this risk. Multi-informant studies can thus establish and enhance the reliability and validity of survey data. We discuss these issues in the next chapters.

4.3 Conducting Multi-Informant Studies

4.3.1 Types of Designs

There are several types of multi-informant designs. Depending on the specific risks which might be present in a particular research project, researches have to choose the appropriate design. Multi-informant designs can be classified according to the following two criteria:

1. Informants are clearly distinguishable or not (Kenny/Kashy/Cook 2006). The question here is whether informants can be identified and classified according to grouping criteria across the different units of analysis (e.g., business units, firms). With respect to survey studies in marketing and management research, this notably relates to the informants' functional affiliation or hierarchical level in a business unit or firm.

2. All informants respond to all questions of a survey or particular questions are attributed to particular informants. This criterion addresses the question whether different informants are asked to evaluate different or the same phenomena. The latter case also refers to situations when several subjective individual evaluations are supposed to form a global evaluation. For example, individual evaluations of job satisfaction can be aggregated to an overall employee satisfaction score for a particular firm.

According to these two dimensions, four different types of multi-informant designs emerge. Each type of design has specific implications with respect to the existence and the minimization of a key informant bias and/or a common method bias.

In order to limit a risk of common method bias, particular constructs of a dependence structure should be assessed with different informants (Podsakoff et al. 2003). In this case, researchers can target specific informants to assess particular variables or randomly choose them. It is reasonable to choose informants who are considered as most knowledgeable to respond to the specific question (see also Kumar/Stern/Anderson 1993). For example, the head of the accounting department should be able to evaluate financial performance as he or she has access to the corresponding data. As a result, such a procedure should reduce both systematic measurement error and random measurement error as key informants have access to the corresponding objective data.

When informants respond to all questions of a survey, there generally is risk of common method bias. However, such multi-informant designs can increase the reliability and validity of the measurement:

- When (a random set of) several informants is used, random measurement error should be lower. The design aims at making the measurement more precise.

- When several distinguishable informants who presumably have different perspectives on the same phenomenon are chosen, systematic measurement error should be reduced. Such a design can be labeled as *validation design*. This implies that researchers know that key informant bias is caused by criteria that differentiate informants (van Bruggen/Lilien/Kacker 2002). For example, when it is reasonable to expect that functional affiliation shapes responses to particular organizational phenomena (such as organizational culture), it is important to select informants from different functional units or departments to account for this bias.

Ideally, a multi-informant design would assess different constructs with different informants which are considered most knowledgeable for the specific issue under consideration. In addition, researchers would assess each construct with more than one informant. The problem is that data collection is very sophisticated, time consuming, and usually expensive (see also Rindfleisch et al. 2008). As a result, in research practice, researchers frequently target one key informant first who answers all survey questions. Then, other informants from the same or other departments additionally evaluate a limited number of constructs. Then, ratings are compared in order to check whether the key informant's responses are generally reliable and valid.

In a similar vein, several studies use secondary data to validate the key informant's ratings of firm performance. Depending on the degree to which multi-informant or secondary data is available for the entire sample, additional data is either used for model estimation (e.g., Reinartz/Krafft/Hoyer 2004) or for a reliability and validity check of the key informant data (e.g., Homburg/Droll/Totzek 2008). In the following chapter, we elaborate more on the process of collecting multi-informant data.

4.3.2 Data Collection Procedure

- When collecting multi-informant data, the first question is how many informants researchers want to recruit for each unit of analysis. The optimal number of informants depends on trading the benefits of reducing random measurement and systematic error against the costs of getting additional responses (van Bruggen/Lilien/Kacker 2002). It also depends on the research topic, i.e., the type of variable researchers want to assess.

- The literature generally advocates a number of two to five informants per unit of analysis. However, as response rates in marketing and management surveys are declining (e.g., Baruch/Holtom 2008), this is an increasingly difficult number to obtain in multi-informant studies. In particular, non-response is critical when different variables of interest are assessed with different informants: Both informants are needed to get usable data.

- Notably when several informants have to respond to all questions of a survey, informants may be reluctant to respond as they suspect that their responses are "cross-checked" with responses of their colleagues. In addition, multi-informant designs imply that responses are not fully anonymous in order to match the data during the research process. This may additionally reduce an informant's willingness to participate or it might systematically change his or her response behavior (Podsakoff et al. 2003, p. 887).

- When researching organizational phenomena, a reasonable number of informants would be two or three. In this case, researchers assume that there is one true value of the variable at the level of the organization. In order to reduce random measurement error, using three informants is a reasonable approach (Libby/Blashfield 1978). However, many procedures to evaluate the quality of multi-informant data (with respect to reliability and validity) are already applicable with two informants per unit of analysis.

- When researchers assess subjective judgments at the informant level and then aim at aggregating these subjective judgments (e.g., attitudes, job satisfaction) to an overall score (e.g., employee satisfaction), five or more responses are needed to get a reasonable aggregate. This holds as there are individual-level differences with respect to the true values of the variable – in addition to potential systematic and random measurement errors.

- Once the ideal number of informants is fixed, the question emerges how informants can be recruited. The current practice is to identify first one adequate informant (e.g., by relying on data bases or commercial providers) and then ask this informant to indicate further informants. This procedure basically relies on snowball sampling (Goodman 1961).

4.4   Assessing the Quality of Multi-Informant Data

As outlined in chapter 4.3.1, multi-informant designs aim at establishing and enhancing the reliability and validity of key informant data. **Figure 4.1** provides an overview of the most frequently used methods to assess the quality of multi-informant data. These methods apply when data on the same variables is obtained from two or more informants. In the following, we briefly discuss these methods (chapter 4.4.1) and then indicate a recommended procedure (chapter 4.4.2). A more detailed and formal discussion of the particular measures is provided by Homburg/Klarmann (2009).

4.4.1   Overview of Key Methods

The general idea of evaluating the quality of multiple responses for one particular variable is that a high consistency of the data of multiple informants serves as a predictor of high reliability. To identify the degree of systematic error and thus to also evaluate the validity of multi-informant data, it is mandatory that informants are clearly distinguishable, for example with respect to their hierarchical level of functional affiliation. Furthermore, the applicability of the specific methods to analyze the quality of multi-informant data depends on the scale format of the observed variables (**Figure 4.1**).

To assess the consistency of several informants' responses, the distinction between the measurement of consensus (agreement) and the measurement of reliability is highly relevant (James/Demaree/Wolf 1993; Kozlowski/Hattrup 1992; Schmidt/Hunter 1989). Consensus checks determine the level of *absolute* agreement between the informants: "[T]he degree to which ratings from individuals are interchangeable: that is, agreement reflects the degree to which raters provide essentially the same rating" (Bliese 2000, p. 351).

When nominal data is obtained, a very simple approach is to count the number of identical responses. (Cohen's) Kappa accounts for the fact that even when answers of several informants are totally random, there is certain number of identical responses (e.g., Cohen 1960). However, there are no commonly accepted cutoff criteria for both measures.

When data is (quasi-)metric, the standard deviation of a particular informant's response to the average response of the unit of analysis can be computed (Kozlowski/Hattrup 1992; Schmidt/Hunter 1989). However, this standard deviation depends on the number of informants per unit and on the scale format. The most commonly used consistency check is the $rWG_{(J)}$ agreement index (James/Demaree/Wolf 1984), which relates the variance of the informants' responses to an expected variance of random responses. This index is standardized and the literature suggests cutoff criteria. In particular, Brown/Hauenstein (2005, p. 178) suggest that an agreement below .60 is not acceptable, that values between .60 and .69 (between .70 and .79) indicate a weak (moderate) agreement, and that values above .80 indicate a strong agreement.

Reliability checks verify the *relative* consistency of the informants' responses: "Interrater reliability represents the degree to which the ratings of different judges are proportional when expressed as deviations from their means" (Tinsley/Weiss 1975, p. 359). The intraclass correlation coefficient (ICC, e.g., Shrout and Fleiss 1979) —more specifically ICC(1) (e.g., Bliese 2000) – is an appropriate and the most commonly used reliability measure when informants are not distinguishable (e.g., data from several members of one team).

The validity of multi-informant data can be assessed when informants are distinguishable (**Figure 4.1**). The most common method is the multi-trait multi-method (MTMM) approach that is based on the seminal work of Campbell/Fiske (1959). The idea is to rely on data using multiple methods (i.e., informants) and multiple traits (i.e., constructs) to assess systematic error in survey ratings. In particular, MTMM-correlation matrices can be analyzed with confirmatory factor analysis and a number of different approaches to assess the degree of systematic error have emerged (Bagozzi/Yi 1991, Podsakoff et al. 2003). The MTMM approach allows for the integration of the different data sources in a structural equation model with latent variables and the relationships between the constructs of interest can be estimated while controlling for systematic error (Doty/Glick 1998). However, the resulting models are complex: Problems of model identification and estimation can occur (Podsakoff et al. 2003). Based on our experience, a confirmatory MTMM analysis usually requires a sample of 250 units of analysis, with three informants for each units of analysis.

A general concern regarding the outlined analyses is their applicability to either formative or reflective measurement approaches (e.g., Jarvis/MacKenzie/Podsakoff 2003). On that score, the most stringent assumptions apply to methods of confirmatory MTMM analysis: They can only be applied for reflective measures.

Other methods generally do not require a particular measurement model; notably when the quality of the informant data is determined separately for each indicator of a construct. For methods which implicitly assume a reflective measurement, certain assumptions are necessary to guarantee the quality assessment at the construct level. This notably holds for the agreement index $rWG_{(J)}$ (James/Demaree/Wolf 1984, p. 88; LeBreton/James/Lindell 2005, pp. 129). As a result, the quality of multiple responses for formative constructs has to be checked at the level of the single indicators.

Figure 4.1   Overview of Methods to Evaluate the Quality of Multi-Informant Data

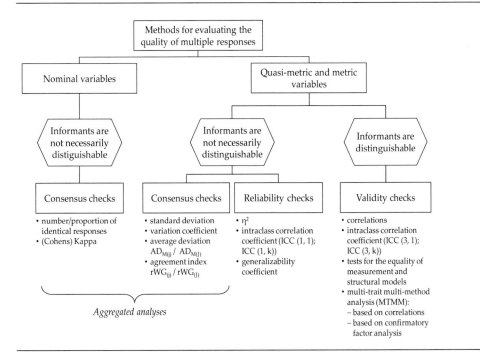

4.4.2   Recommended Procedure

Given the wide array of different methods to assess the quality of multi informant data (**Figure 4.1**), the question arises which of the methods should be used in order to properly analyze data from multi-informant studies. Similar to Kumar/Stern/Anderson (1993), we recommend a combination of several methods.

First, a confirmatory factor analysis of the observed variables should be accomplished for each construct based on the data of all informants – independent of their affiliation to particular units of analysis. As a result, unreliable construct indicators can already be excluded at an early stage of the analysis. If the informants are distinguishable on the basis of systematic criteria, it should then be reviewed whether measurement invariance is given across the corresponding groups of informants (e.g., Vandenberg/Lance 2000). Subsequently, the use of a method to assess validity is recommended. The choice of the appropriate method is determined by the research context and the available sample size.

The reliability of the informants' responses should always be assessed. First, a meaningful consensus check should be conducted (generally $rWG_{(J)}$ or $AD_{M(J)}$) for each unit of analysis (Klarmann 2008; p. 154; LeBreton and Santer 2008). Then, an interclass correlation coefficient should be computed. In general, it is recommended to perform the corresponding analyses for the indicators as well as for the constructs (Glick 1985, p. 608).

When the number of informants per unit of analysis is rather low (lower than five informants), it is useful to assess the general quality of the data by mostly relying on consensus checks (Bliese 1998, p. 369). However, reliability should also be checked in order to substantiate the subsequent decisions, notably related to the aggregation of data (chapter 4.5.3).

4.5   Analysis of Multi-Informant Data

4.5.1   Choice of the Level of Analysis

A key question when dealing with multi-informant designs is the level of analysis of the data: Should responses of different informants be aggregated for each unit of analysis or not? When the informants' responses refer to the same phenomenon (e.g., the characteristics of a firm) a disaggregated analysis usually does not make sense – unless it is sought to analyze differences in the perceptions of the informants.

Another situation arises when informants provide subjective individual evaluations, i.e., self-reports, but the analysis aims at evaluating and comparing the data at the level of the unit of analysis (e.g., an analysis of employee satisfaction per company). By means of the ICC (1,1), which was presented in chapter 4.4.1, it can be checked whether an aggregation of data is useful in such cases.

An analysis at the aggregate level is regarded as justified if the ICC (1,1) is positive and significantly different from zero (Dixon/Cunningham 2006, p. 95; Klein et al. 2000, p. 518) and/or its value is .20 or higher (e.g., Homburg/ Fürst 2005, p. 101). The reasoning is that such ICC (1,1)-values indicate significant differences between the units of analysis.

If the informant data is not aggregated, the ICC (1,1) provides information whether an analysis on the level of the informants violates the assumption of independent observations. Heck (2001, p. 99) suggests that ICC (1,1)-values of .05 and smaller predict a non-existence of differences between units of analysis. Otherwise, a multi-level analysis has to be considered analyzing both the informant and the unit of analysis (Wieseke 2008).

4.5.2   Identification of the Final Sample

The identification of the final sample refers to two major issues: First, it is important to decide which informants are used to form the aggregate evaluations. This is notably important when several distinguishable informants have been surveyed and validity checks (chapter 4.4.1) show that there is a systematic measurement error related to the use of different informants. In this case, those informants should be used that have the highest construct-specific and the lowest informant type-specific variance for each construct. For example, when organizational culture has been assessed by using informants from different functional units, the situation can arise that responses of the informants of one particular department are systematically biased across all firms. In such a case, all informants from this particular department are disregarded from further analysis. If this decision cannot be based on variance components, conceptual considerations should lead the selection of the informants (e.g., the familiarity of the respondents with the topic, their work experience, their hierarchical level, and the functional affiliation in the firm).

Second, when an aggregated analysis is performed with multi-informant data, units of analysis can be dropped from further analysis when the underlying informants have provided too inconsistent answers. This is reasonable as aggregation is problematic for these units. In any case, a unit of analysis should only be removed from the sample if the data shows no acceptable consistency with respect to *all* core constructs. Otherwise, the final sample size could be heavily reduced. In this respect, as information gets lost, the removal of cases from the sample has negative effects as well. However, if all units of analysis are used in the final sample, researchers should include the degree of consistency in the model when analyzing dependence structures (LeBreton/Senter 2008, pp. 837).

4.5.3 Data Aggregation

If the data should be analyzed at an aggregate level, researchers have to decide *how* to aggregate. An excellent overview of the available aggregation methods is provided by van Bruggen/Lilien/Kacker (2002). When comparing different aggregation methods, their study shows that a simple average is a quite effective form of aggregation.

However, various weighted forms of averages across informants are (slightly) more effective. Effective weighting factors are among others (van Bruggen/Lilien/Kacker 2002): the informants' confidence in their own assessments, the self-assessment of competence as well as the deviation of the informant's response from the average value for the unit of analysis. Since these methods can be easily implemented, they should be used in multi-informant research. However, it is important to note that these types of aggregation are only meaningful when the reliability and the validity of the underlying multi-informant data have been checked (chapter 4.4.2).

4.6 Conclusion and Recommendations

This chapter highlights that using key informants in the context of survey studies bears a risk of key informant and common method bias. This is important as a large part of marketing and management research draws on survey data. In addition, surveys are frequently the only way to observe particular organizational phenomena. The use of multi-informant designs is a solution of this conflict. However, several problems are connected with the implementation of multi-informant designs. In this chapter, we have indicated some of the major problems that occur when conducting multi-informant studies. Regarding the substantial investments of time and money related to multi-informant studies, our recommendations might contribute that these efforts pay off even more in the future. The major recommendations are as follows:

- Do not generally question single-informant studies, but carefully assess the risk of key informant and common method bias in your specific research context.

- When single informant data is particularly susceptible to key informant and common method bias, use a multi-informant design. An extensive pretest of the survey helps to identify such risks.

- Choose the appropriate multi-informant design according to the research-specific risks of key informant and common method bias.

- When determining the number of informants, consider the nature of the constructs and potential problems of non-response. In this respect, the benefits of surveying more than two or three informants for each unit of analysis have to be critically examined.

- Conduct a confirmatory factor analysis to assure similar factor structures for all informants.

■ Use a combination of consensus and reliability checks. In addition to the threshold values in the literature, refer to comparable values from previous research projects. If less than five informants are surveyed for each unit of analysis, consensus and reliability checks are crucial for evaluating the quality of multi-informant data.

■ If the need for aggregating the data does not arise due to conceptual considerations, use the ICC (1,1) for decision making.

■ In case of systematic differences between the data provided by various informants, use the most reliable informants for further analysis. If necessary, exclude units of analysis from the final sample if the data shows no acceptable consistency with respect to *all* core constructs.

■ For aggregating data across informants use the methods recommended by van Bruggen/Lilien/Kacker (2002), if possible.

Literature

[1]   Bagozzi, R. P./Yi, Y. (1991): Multitrait-multimethod matrices in consumer research. Journal of Consumer Research, Vol. 17, 4, pp. 426-439.

[2]   Baruch, Y./Holtom, B. C. (2008): Survey response rate levels and trends in organizational research. Human Relations, Vol. 61, 8, pp. 1139-1160.

[3]   Baumgartner, H./Steenkamp, J.-B. (2001): Response styles in marketing research: a cross-national investigation. Journal of Marketing Research, Vol. 38, 2, pp. 143-156.

[4]   Bazerman, M. H./Moore, D. A. (2009): Judgment in managerial decision making, 7th ed. Hoboken, NJ: Wiley.

[5]   Bliese, P. D. (1998): Group size, ICC values, and group-level correlations: a simulation. Organizational Research Methods, Vol. 1, 4, pp. 355-373.

[6]   Bliese, P. D. (2000): Within-group agreement, non-independence, and reliability: implications for data aggregation and analysis. In: Klein, K. J., & Kozlowski, S. W. (eds.). Multilevel theory, research, and methods in organizations. San Francisco, CA: Jossey-Bass, pp. 349-381.

[7]   Brown, R. D./Hauenstein, N. M. A. (2005): Interrater agreement reconsidered: an alternative to the rwg indices. Organizational Research Methods, Vol. 8, 2, pp. 165-184.

[8]   Campbell, D. T./Fiske, D. W. (1959): Convergent and discriminant validation by the multitrait-multimethod matrix. Psychological Bulletin, Vol. 56, 2, pp. 81-105.

[9]   Chandon, P./Morwitz, V. G./Reinartz, W. J. (2005): Do intentions really predict behavior? Self-generated validity effects in survey research. Journal of Marketing, Vol. 69, April, pp. 1-14.

[10] Churchill, G. A. (1979): A paradigm for developing better measures of marketing constructs. Journal of Marketing Research, Vol. 16, 1, pp. 64-73.

[11] Cohen, J. (1960): A coefficient of agreement for nominal scales. Educational and Psychological Measurement, Vol. 20, 1, pp. 37-46.

[12] Conant, J. S./Mokwa, M. P./Varadarajan, P. R. (1990): Strategic types, distinctive marketing competencies and organizational Performance: a multiple measures-based study. Strategic Management Journal, Vol. 11, 5, pp. 365-383.

[13] Cote, J. A./Buckley, M. R. (1987): Estimating trait, method, and error variance: generalizing across 70 construct validation studies. Journal of Marketing Research, Vol. 24, 3, pp. 315-318.

[14] Cote, J. A./Buckley, M. R. (1988): Measurement error and theory testing in consumer research: An illustration of the importance of construct validation. Journal of Consumer Research, Vol. 14, 1, pp. 579-582.

[15] Crampton, S. M./Wagner, J. A. (1994): Percept-percept inflation in microorganizational research: an investigation of prevalence and effect. Journal of Applied Psychology, Vol. 79, 1, pp. 67-76.

[16] Dixon, M./Cunningham, G. B. (2006): Data aggregation in multilevel analysis: a review of conceptual and statistical issues. Measurement in Physical Education and Exercise Science, Vol. 10, 2, pp. 85-107.

[17] Doty, D. H./Glick, W. H. (1998): Common methods bias: Does common methods variance really bias results. Organizational Research Methods, Vol. 1, 4, pp. 374-406.

[18] Evans, M. G. (1985): A Monte Carlo study of the effects of correlated method variance in moderated multiple regression analysis. Organizational Behavior and Human Decision Processes, Vol. 36, 3, pp. 305-323.

[19] Feldman, J. M./Lynch, J. G. (1988): Self-generated validity and other effects of measurement on belief, attitude, intention, and behavior. Journal of Applied Psychology, Vol. 73, 3, pp. 421-435.

[20] Glick, W. H. (1985): Conceptualizing and measuring organizational and psychological climate: pitfalls in multilevel research. Academy of Management Review, Vol. 10, 3, pp. 601-616.

[21] Golden, B. R. (1992): The past is the past – Or is it? The use of retrospective accounts as indicators of past strategy. Academy of Management Journal, Vol. 35, 4, pp. 848-860.

[22] Goodman, L. A. (1961): Snowball sampling. The Annals of Mathematical Statistics, 32, pp. 148-170.

[23] Hambrick, D. C. (1981): Strategic awareness within top management teams. Strategic Management Journal, Vol. 2, 3, pp. 263-279.

[24] Harrison, D. A./McLaughlin, M. E./Coalter, T. M. (1996): Context, cognition, and common method variance: psychometric and verbal protocol evidence. Organizational Behavior and Human Decision Processes, Vol. 68, 3, pp. 246-261.

[25] Heck, R. H. (2001): Multilevel modeling with SEM. In: Marcoulides, G. A., & Schumacker, R. E. (eds.). New developments and techniques in Structural Equation Modeling. 2nd ed. Mahwah, NJ: Lawrence Erlbaum, pp. 89-128.

[26] Homburg, Ch./Fürst, A. (2005): How organizational complaint handling drives customer loyalty: an analysis of the mechanistic and the organic Approach. Journal of Marketing, Vol. 69, 3, pp. 95-114.

[27] Homburg, Ch./Klarmann, M. (2009): Multi Informant-Designs in der empirischen betriebswirtschaftlichen Forschung, Die Betriebswirtschaft, Vol. 69, 2, pp. 147-171.

[28] Homburg, Ch./Droll, M./Totzek, D: (2008): Customer prioritization: Does it pay off, and how should it be implemented? Journal of Marketing, Vol. 72, 5, pp. 110-130.

[29] James, L. R./Demaree, R. G./Wolf, G: (1984): Estimating within-group interrater reliability with and without response bias. Journal of Applied Psychology, Vol. 69, 1, pp. 85-98.

[30] James, L. R./Demaree, R. G./Wolf, G. (1993): rwg: an assessment of within-group interrater agreement. Journal of Applied Psychology, Vol. 78, 2, pp. 306-309.

[31] Jarvis, C. B./MacKenzie, S. B./Podsakoff, P. M. (2003): A critical review of construct indicators and measurement model misspecification in marketing and consumer research. Journal of Consumer Research, Vol. 30, September, pp. 199-218.

[32] John, G./Reve, T. (1982): The reliability and validity of key informant data from dyadic relationships in marketing channels. Journal of Marketing Research, Vol. 19, 4, pp. 517-524.

[33] Kenny, D. A./Kashy, D. A./Cook, W. L. (2006): Dyadic data analysis. New York: Guilford Press.

[34] Kirca, A. H., Jayachandran, S./Bearden, W. O. (2005): Market orientation: a meta-analytic review and assessment of its antecedents and impact on performance. Journal of Marketing, Vol. 69, 2, pp. 24-41.

[35] Klarmann, M. (2008): Methodische Problemfelder der Erfolgsfaktorenforschung: Bestandsaufnahme und empirische Analysen, Wiesbaden: Gabler.

[36] Klein, K. J./Bliese, P. D./Kozlowski, S. W./Dansereau, F./Gavin, M. B./Griffin, M. A./Hofmann, D. A./James, L. R./Yammarino, F. J./Bligh, M. C. (2000): Multilevel analysis techniques: commonalities, differences, and continuing questions. In: Klein, K. J., & Kozlowski, S. W. (eds.). Multilevel theory, research, and methods in organizations. San Francisco, CA: Jossey Bass, pp. 512-553.

[37] Kozlowski, S. W./Hattrup, K. (1992): A disagreement about within-group agreement: disentangling issues of consistency versus consensus. Journal of Applied Psychology, Vol. 77, 2, pp. 161-167.

[38] Kumar, N./Stern, L. W./Anderson, J. C. (1993): Conducting interorganizational research using key informants. Academy of Management Journal, Vol. 36, 6, pp. 1633-1651.

[39] Lance, C. E./LaPointe, J. A./Fisicaro, S. A. (1994): Tests of three causal models of halo rater error. Organizational Behavior and Human Decision Processes, Vol. 57, 1, pp. 83-96.

[40] LeBreton, J. M./Senter, J. (2008): Answers to 20 questions about interrater reliability and interrater agreement. Organizational Research Methods, Vol. 11, 4, pp. 815-852.

[41] LeBreton, J. M./James, L. R./Lindell, M. K. (2005): Recent issues regarding rWG, r*WG, rWG(J), and r*WG(J). Organizational Research Methods, Vol. 8, 1, pp. 128-138.

[42] Libby, R./Blashfield, R. K. (1978): Performance of a composite as a function of the number of judges. Organizational Behavior and Human Performance, Vol. 21, 2, pp. 121-129.

[43] Mezias, J. M./Starbuck, W. H. (2003): Studying the accuracy of managers' perceptions: a research odyssey. British Journal of Management, Vol. 14, 1, pp. 3-17.

[44] Miles, R. E./Snow, C. C. (1978): Organizational strategy, structure, and process. New York: McGraw-Hill.

[45] Natter, M./Mild, A./Wagner, U./Taudes, A. (2008): Planning new tariffs at tele.ring: the application and impact of an integrated segmentation, targeting, and positioning tool. Marketing Science, Vol. 27, 4, pp. 600-609.

[46] Phillips, L. W. (1981): Assessing measurement error in key informant reports: a methodological note on organizational analysis in marketing. Journal of Marketing Research, Vol. 18, 4, pp. 395-415.

[47] Podsakoff, P. M./Organ, D. W. (1986): Self-reports in organizational research: problems and prospects. Journal of Management, Vol. 12, 4, pp. 531-544.

[48] Podsakoff, P. M./MacKenzie, S. B./Lee, J.-Y./Podsakoff, N. P. (2003): Common method biases in behavioral research: a critical review of the literature and recommended remedies. Journal of Applied Psychology, Vol. 88, 5, pp. 879-903.

[49] Reinartz, W./Krafft, M./Hoyer, W. D. (2004): The customer relationship management process: measurement and impact on performance. Journal of Marketing Research, Vol. 41, 3, pp. 293-305.

[50] Rindfleisch, A./Malter, A. J./Ganesan, S./Moorman, C. (2008): Cross-sectional versus longitudinal survey research: concepts, findings, and guidelines. Journal of Marketing Research, Vol. 45, June, pp. 261-279.

[51] Sathe, V. (1978): Institutional versus questionnaire measures of organizational structure. Academy of Management Journal, Vol. 21, 2, pp. 227-238.

[52] Schmidt, F. L./Hunter, J. E. (1989): Interrater reliability coefficients cannot be computed when only one stimulus is rated. Journal of Applied Psychology, Vol. 74, 2, pp. 368-370.

[53] Shrout, P. E./Fleiss, J. L. (1979): Intraclass correlations: uses in assessing rater reliability. Psychological Bulletin, Vol. 86, 2, pp. 420-428.

[54] Starbuck, W. H./Mezias, J. M. (1996): Opening Pandora 's Box: studying the accuracy of managers' perceptions. Journal of Organizational Behavior, Vol. 17, 2, pp. 99-117.

[55] Tinsley, H. E. A./Weiss, D. J. (1975): Interrater reliability and agreement of subjective judgements. Journal of Counseling Psychology, Vol. 22, 4, pp. 358-374.

[56] Tversky, A./Kahneman, D. (1974): Judgment under uncertainty: heuristics and biases. Science, Vol. 185, September, pp. 1124-1131.

[57] Van Bruggen, G. H./Lilien, G. L./Kacker, M. (2002): Informants in organizational marketing research: why use multiple informants and how to aggregate responses. Journal of Marketing Research, Vol. 39, 4, pp. 469-478.

[58] Vandenberg, R. J./Lance, C. E. (2000): A review and synthesis of the measurement invariance literature: suggestions, practices, and recommendations for organizational research. Organizational Research Methods, Vol. 3, 1, pp. 4-70.

[59] Venkatraman, N./Ratmanujam, V. (1987): Measurement of business economic performance: an examination of method convergence. Journal of Management, Vol. 13, 1, pp. 109-122.

[60] Vosgerau, J./Anderson, E./Ross, W. T. (2008): Can inaccurate perceptions in business-to-business (b2b) relationships be beneficial? Marketing Science, Vol. 72, 2, pp. 205-224.

[61] Wall, T. D./Michie, J./Patterson, M./Wood, S. J./Sheehan, M./Clegg, C. W./West, M. (2004): On the validity of subjective measures of company performance. Personnel Psychology, Vol. 57, 1, pp. 95-118.

[62] Wieseke, J. (2008): Mehrebenenmodelle. In: Herrmann, A., Homburg, Ch., & Klarmann, M. (eds.). Handbuch Marktforschung. 3rd ed. Wiesbaden: Gabler, pp. 499-519.

[63] Williams, L. J./Brown, B. K. (1994): Method variance in organizational behavior and human resources research: effects on correlations, path coefficients, and hypothesis testing. Organizational Behavior and Human Decision Processes, Vol. 57, 2, pp. 185-209.

[64] Williams, L. J./Cote, J. A./Buckley, M. R. (1989): Lack of method variance in self-reported affect and perceptions at work: reality or artifact. Journal of Applied Psychology, Vol. 74, 3, pp. 462-468.

5 Using Artificial Neural Nets for Flexible Aggregate Market Response Modeling

Harald Hruschka, University of Regensburg, Germany

Abstract

The author gives an overview of the state of research on aggregate market response modeling by means of multilayer perceptrons (MLPs), the most widespread type of artificial neural nets. As the author shows, MLPs are not limited to fixed parametric functional forms, but offer flexible approaches for modeling market response functions of marketing instruments.

Keywords

Market Response Models, Flexible Models, Artificial Neural Nets.

5.1   Introduction

In this paper I give an overview of the state of research on aggregate market response modeling by means of multilayer perceptrons (MLPs) which are the most widespread type of artificial neural nets (see Krycha and Wagner 1999 for applications of neural nets in management science in general). To the best of my knowledge all papers about applications of neural nets to aggregate market response modeling use MLPs. As MLPs are not limited to fixed parametric functional forms, they are flexible modeling approaches. I do not treat other flexible modeling techniques, which, e.g., are based on splines or kernels (relevant publications are Kalyanam/Shively 1998; Hruschka 2000; van Heerde et al. 2001; Hruschka 2001b; Steiner et al. 2007; Brezger/Steiner 2008).

Variables of aggregate market response models are summed or averaged across persons, households or organizations in a certain state, region, etc. I will only look at two response variables, namely sales and market share. As independent variables of market response models we typically find marketing variables for the brand whose sales or market share constitute the dependent variable as well as marketing variables for other brands. To these independent variables other market or environmental variables may be added (see Hanssens et al. 2001; Hruschka 1996).

Till the mid 1990s practically without exception authors of studies on aggregate marketing response modeling assumed fixed parametric functional forms (like the very popular multiplicative function, e.g., Bemmaor and Wagner 2002). With respect to German speaking countries this fact can be seen from the collection of papers in Nenning et al. (1981). Hanssens et al. (2001) began to consider flexible approaches in the second edition of their eminent book on aggregate market response modeling (see Hanssens et al. 1990 for the first edition).

I introduce basic concepts, explain components and mention mathematical results about approximation properties of MLPs in section 5.2. In section 5.3 I deal with different estimation approaches. Among these approaches I emphasize stochastic back propagation for which I give a pseudo algorithmic description. Then I present the most important approaches to evaluate the performance of MLPs, i.e., error measures, information criteria and posterior model probabilities. In section 5.5 I explain two possible ways to interpret MLPs which are based on marginal effects and elasticities, respectively. Then I provide an overview of studies which use MLPs to model aggregate market response and discuss two of these studies in more detail. In the concluding section I summarize empirical evidence on the statistical performance of MLPs relative to parametric models and indicate what MLPs imply for marketing decision making.

5.2   Multilayer Perceptron

A MLP with one hidden layer consists of input units, hidden units and output units. Hidden units, which are not observable, are computed as nonlinear transformation of a linear combination of values of independent variables. Values of output units (sales or market shares in our case) result as linear combination of values of hidden units and values of independent variables.

MLPs with H hidden units can be written as follows with $i = 1, \cdots, I$ denoting the index of observations:

$$y_{ik} = \begin{cases} f^{(2)}\left(a_{ki}^{(2)}\right) \\ f^{(2)}\left(a_{ki}^{(2)}\right), a_{1i}^{(2)} \end{cases} \tag{5.1}$$

$$a_{ki}^{(2)} = w_{0k}^{(2)} + \sum_{h=1}^{H} w_{hk}^{(2)} z_{hi} + \sum_{p=1}^{P} w_{pk}^{(L)} x_{pi} \; for \; k = 1, K \tag{5.2}$$

$$z_{hi} = f^{(1)}\left(a_{hi}^{(1)}\right) \tag{5.3}$$

$$a_{hi}^{(1)} = w_{0h}^{(1)} + \sum_{p=1}^{P} w_{ph}^{(1)} x_{pi} \; for \; h = 1, H \tag{5.4}$$

Each activation function $f^{(2)}$ of output units transforms either one potential $a_{ki}^{(2)}$ or two potentials $(a_{ki}^{(2)}, a_{1i}^{(2)})$ into a value of the response variable k. Each potential $a_{ki}^{(2)}$ is a linear function of both hidden units with coefficients $w_{hk}^{(2)}$ and $w_{0k}^{(2)}$ symbolizing H coefficients of hidden units z_{hi} and a constant term, respectively.

Each potential also depends linearly on independent variables with coefficients $w_{pk}^{(L)}$. These coefficients measure linear effects of independent variables on response variable k. Because of coefficients $w_{pk}^{(L)}$ the MLP nests the related, less flexible linear model. On the other hand coefficients $w_{hk}^{(2)}$ of the MLP reproduce nonlinear effects of independent variables which work in addition to the linear effects.

Often the identity function $ID(\alpha) = \alpha$ is used as activation function $f(a_{ki}^{(2)})$, in other words each response variable is set equal to the potential. As alternative, sometimes the logistic function (see expression (5.5)) serves as activation function $f(a_{ki}^{(2)})$, after the response variable has been transformed to the unit interval.

Each activation function $f^{(1)}$ transforms a potential $a_{hi}^{(1)}$ into the value of the corresponding hidden unit. Each potential is a linear function of independent variables with coefficients $w_{ph}^{(1)}$, which link independent variables to hidden unit h, and a constant term $w_{0h}^{(1)}$.

As I show in section 5.6 most applications of MLPs for aggregate market response modeling specify $f^{(1)}$ as logistic function, only few studies use the tangens hyberbolicus. Both the logistic and the tangens hyperbolicus are S-shaped. The logistic function σ, which returns values which lie in the unit interval, is:

$$\sigma(\alpha) = 1/(1 + exp(-\alpha)) \tag{5.5}$$

Given a sufficient number of hidden units with S-shaped activation functions MLPs approximate any continuous multivariate function and its derivatives with desired accuracy (Cybenko 1989; Hornik et al. 1989; Ripley 1993). MLPs are capable to discover interactions, thresholds and concave relationships of independent variables. Mathematical proofs by Hornik et al. (1989) and Barron (1993) demonstrate better approximation properties of MLPs in comparison to other flexible methods which are based on polynomial expansions, splines or kernels.

Just like in the case of conventional regression models one could use market shares directly as output variables of a MLP. But such an approach may lead to implausible estimation results. The sum of estimated market shares across brands as a rule will be different from one. Moreover and more problematic, estimated market shares of individual brands may be negative or greater than one.

Attraction models do not suffer from these problems (Cooper/Nakanishi 1988). In attraction models the market share ms_{li} of each brand l is defined as ratio of its attraction A_{li} and the sum of attractions A_{ki} ($k = 1, \cdots, K$) across all brands of a product category in period i with each attraction restricted to be positive:

$$ms_{li} = A_{li} / \sum_{k=1}^{K} A_{ki} \text{ for } l = 1, \cdots, K \tag{5.6}$$

By means of the log ratio transformation of market shares $log(ms_{li}/ms_{1i})$ taking brand 1 as reference one obtains a system of $K - 1$ loglinear equations (McGuire et al. 1977):

$$y_{li} \equiv log\left(\frac{ms_{li}}{ms_{1i}}\right) = log(A_{li}) - log(A_{1i}) \text{ for } l = 2, \cdots, K \tag{5.7}$$

Hruschka (2001a) specifies in his model ANNAM (Artificial Neural Net Attraction Model) logs of attractions as linear combinations of hidden units. That is why ANNAM is more flexible than conventional attraction models, for which logs of attraction are constrained to be linear combinations of independent variables.

5.3   Model Estimation

To avoid numeric problems due to independent variables with strongly different value ranges, it is customary to either compute z-transforms or to transform into a smaller interval $[\tilde{x}^{min}, \tilde{x}^{max}]$, e.g., $[0.1, 0.9]$, before estimation:

$$\tilde{x}_{pi} = \begin{cases} (x_{pi} - \tilde{x}_p)/s_p \\ \tilde{x}^{min} + (\tilde{x}^{max} - \tilde{x}^{min})(x_{pi} - x_p^{min})/(x_p^{max} - x_p^{min}) \end{cases} \tag{5.8}$$

$\tilde{x}_{pi}, s_p$ denote arithmetic mean and standard deviation of independent variable p, x_p^{max}, x_p^{min} its maximum and minimum, respectively.

Almost all studies using MLP for aggregate market response modeling determine coefficients by minimizing the sum of squared errors (SSE) by means of a variant of backpropagation (BP). The paper of Hruschka (2006) constitutes an exception by using a Markov chain Monte Carlo (MCMC) technique which samples coefficients from their posterior distribution.

The sum of squared errors is defined as:

$$SSE = \sum_i \sum_k E_{ki} \text{ with } E_{ki} = (\hat{y}_{ki} - y_{ki})^2 \tag{5.9}$$

y_{ki} denotes the observed value i of response variable k, $\hat{y}_{ki}$ the respective value estimated by the MLP. In stochastic or online backpropagation (SBP) gradients are computed for randomly selected observations and coefficients are updated based on these gradients. Random selection of observations reduces the risk of getting trapped in a local minimum. In offline backpropagation coefficients are updated using gradients which are computed based on all observations in the estimation sample (Bishop 1995).

In backpropagation gradients are determined as products of error terms and values of either hidden units or independent variables. Gradients of coefficients linking hidden units to output units and independent variables to output units can be written as:

$$grad\left(w_{hk}^{(2)}\right) = \delta_{ki}^{(2)} z_{hi}, grad(w_{pk}^{(L)}) = \delta_{ki}^{(2)} x_{pi} \tag{5.10}$$

Error terms of output units are defined as:

$$\delta_{ki}^{(2)} \equiv \frac{\partial E_{ki}}{\partial \alpha_{ki}^{(2)}} = f^{(2)'}\left(a_{ki}^{(2)}\right) \frac{\partial E_{ki}}{\partial \hat{y}_{ki}} \tag{5.11}$$

As **Table 5.1** shows, expressions for error terms of output units depend on the form of their activation function.

Table 5.1   Error Terms of Output Units

Activation function	Error term
Identity function	$2(\hat{y}_{ki} - y_{ki})$
ANNAM	$2(-2\delta_{k1} + 1)(\hat{y}_{ki} - y_{ki})$
Logistic function	$2\hat{y}_{ki}(1 - \hat{y}_{ki})(\hat{y}_{ki} - y_{ki})$

Kronecker $\delta_{k1} = 1$ if $k = 1$, else $\delta_{k1} = 0$

Gradients of coefficients linking independent variables and hidden units result as:

$$grad(w_{ph}^{(1)}) = \delta_{hi}^{(1)} x_{pi} \tag{5.12}$$

Backpropagation of previously computed error terms of output units leads to the following error term of a hidden unit h with logistic activation function:

$$\delta_{hi}^{(1)} = \sigma\left(a_{hi}^{(1)}\right)\left(1 - \sigma\left(a_{hi}^{(1)}\right)\right)\Sigma_k w_{hk}^{(2)} \delta_{ki}^{(2)} \tag{5.13}$$

The algorithm described by the following pseudocode differs from basic SBP by the momentum term $0 < \theta < 1$, which accounts for changes of coefficients in the previous iteration $t - 1$ (symbolized by $\Delta w_{hk}^{(2)}(t - 1), \Delta w_{pk}^{(L)}(t - 1), \Delta w_{ph}^{(1)}(t - 1)$). The momentum term prevents oscillation of coefficients and speeds up estimation of gradients by preferring equal signs of coefficients during iterations. Coefficient updating is based on a constant learning rate $0 \le \eta \ge 1$.

The pseudocode is as follows:

1. Set $t = 0$ and $c = 0$ and randomly initialize coefficients in the interval $[-0.1; 0.1]$.

2. Set $t = t + 1$ and $c = c + 1$ and randomly select an observation i.

3. Compute gradients according to expressions (5.10) and (5.12).

4. Update coefficients by adding:

$$\Delta w_{hk}^{(2)}(t) = \eta \, grad(w_{hk}^{(2)}) + \theta \Delta w_{hk}^{(2)}(t - 1) \text{ for } h = 0, H \text{ and } k = 1, K$$

$$\Delta w_{pk}^{(L)}(t) = \eta \, grad(w_{pk}^{(L)}) + \theta \Delta w_{pk}^{(L)}(t - 1) \text{ for } p = 1, P \text{ and } k = 1, K$$

$$\Delta w_{ph}^{(1)}(t) = \eta \, grad\left(w_{ph}^{(1)}\right) + \theta \Delta w_{ph}^{(1)}(t - 1) \text{ for } p = 0, P \text{ and } h = 1, H$$

to their respective value from iteration $t - 1$.

5. If $c < I$ go to 2.

6. If changes of coefficients are small across the last I iterations, stop; otherwise set $c = 0$ *and go to* 2.

Obviously gradient descent may be replaced by faster nonlinear optimization techniques such as scaled conjugate gradient descent (Møller 1993), BFGS (Saito/Nakano 1997) or Levenberg-Marquardt (Bishop 1995). The problem that these techniques often provide local minima can be alleviated by random restarts or hybrid procedures. The latter start by a stochastic method like SBP and continue by a nonlinear optimization technique (see, e.g., Hruschka 2001a).

Hruschka (2006) develops a MCMC technique for heterogeneous MLPs with a metric response variable. Heterogenous MLPs are characterized by coefficients which vary across units (e.g., stores, regions, etc.), but are restricted to be broadly similar by introducing a multivariate normal prior. Coefficients determined this way are expected to be less noisy and less unstable compared to estimates of separate unit specific MLPs. The MCMC technique in Hruschka (2006) consists of several iterations of which each one encompasses the following four steps:

1. a Metropolis-Hastings algorithm which samples unit specific coefficients (Chib/Greenberg, 1995 and 1996; Gelman et al., 1995), but keeps only samples which satisfy monotonicity restrictions.

2. a Gibbs sampler which draws the error precision (i.e. the inverse of the error variance) from the conditional Gamma distribution whose parameters depend on the sum of squared errors and number of observations.

3. a Gibbs sampler which draws from the conditional multivariate normal distribution of mean coefficients given unit specific coefficients and their covariance matrix.

4. a Gibbs sampler which draws from the conditional inverted Wishart distribution of the covariance matrix of coefficients given unit specific and mean coefficients.

5.4 Evaluating Model Performance

Squared errors or absolute errors constitute two possible starting points for evaluating the performance of MLPs. Sum of squared errors (SSE), mean squared error ($MSE = SSE/I$), root mean squared error ($RMSE = \sqrt{MSE}$) start from squared errors. Mean absolute error ($MAE = \sum_i |\hat{y}_{ki} - y_{ki}|/I$) and mean absolute percentage error ($MAPE = 100/I \sum_i |\hat{y}_{ki} - y_{ki}|/\hat{y}_{ki}$) are based on absolute errors and less sensitive with respect to large values.

Each of the performance measures mentioned so far leads to an overly optimistic evaluation if it is determined for the same data which were used for estimation. The more complex a model is, the worse this problem typically becomes. Randomly dividing the whole data set into two parts, using one part for estimation and the other part, a holdout sample, for computation of a performance measure provides a possible solution. Unfortunately this procedure leads to results which turn out to be too pessimistic (Ripley 1993).

In an alternative method, K-fold cross-validation, the whole data set is randomly divided into K exhaustive and disjoint subsets. A performance measure is computed for each subset based on coefficients estimated from data of the remaining $K-1$ subsets. Finally, the model is evaluated by averaging performance measures across subsets. Bishop (1995) and Ripley (1993) recommend to set K to an integer between 5 and 10. Leaving-one-out, i.e. predicting the response of each observation by a model which is estimated using the remaining $I-1$ observations, seems to be appropriate for small data sets (Bishop 1993).

Information criteria evaluate a model's performance by considering both its fit and its complexity. Complexity is measured by degrees of freedom df of a model. Information criteria prefer a less complex model among several alternative models if these models attain the same fit. Three information criteria which are often used to evaluate MLPs are given in **Table 5.2** (Akaike 1974; Schwartz 1979; Amemiya 1980).

Table 5.2   Information Criteria

Information criteria
$AIC = 2\,log(MSE) + 2df/I$
$BIC = 2\,log(MSE) + df\,log(I)/I$
$PC = MSE(1 + df/I)$

In most publications researchers have set the degrees of freedom of a MLP equal to the number of its coefficients. But Ingrassia/Morlini (2005) show that degrees of freedom of a MLP with one hidden layer correspond to the number of hidden neurons plus one if the MLP includes a constant term. In other words, most researchers working with MLPs may have overestimated their complexity. This result of Ingrassia and Morlini also could explain why cross-validation often leads to a higher number of hidden units compared to information criteria.

Performance of MLPs may be also evaluated by posterior model probabilities which are often used in Bayesian statistics. Posterior model probabilities penalize models for complexity, i.e. all else being equal the more complex model receives a lower value.

Under the assumption of equal a priori model probabilities the posterior probability of a model m' is related to marginal model densities $p(y|m)$ in the following way:

$$p(y|m') = p(y|m')/\sum_m p(y|m) \qquad (5.14)$$

Marginal model densities can be obtained by the harmonic mean estimator of Gelfand and Dey (1994) which uses MCMC draws.

5.5   Model Interpretation

To see whether the effect of an independent variable is positive or negative (i.e., whether responses increase or decrease with higher values of an independent variable) one only has to look at the sign of its coefficient if a model is linear or linearizable. Such a simple interpretation of models can also be achieved for MLPs which do not include coefficients $w_{pk}^{(L)}$ by allowing only positive values of coefficients $w_{hk}^{(2)}$ which link hidden units to output values (see Hruschka 2006 for a more general approach which imposes monotonicity restrictions on MLPs).

Of course, interpretation of a MLP turns out to be more involved if appropriate restrictions on coefficients are not imposed. In the following I consider MLPs with logistic activation functions for hidden units. The expression of the marginal effect of independent variable p on response variable k contains $z_{hi}(1 - z_{hi})$ which is always positive and equals the first derivative of the logistic function:

$$\frac{\partial y_{ik}}{\partial x_{pi}} = \Sigma_{h=1}^{H} w_{hk}^{(2)} \, z_{hi}(1 - z_{hi}) w_{ph}^{(1)} \tag{5.15}$$

In the case of a MLP with one hidden unit, the marginal effect of independent variable p is positive, if the coefficients $w_{ph}^{(1)}$ which connect independent variable p to the hidden unit and the coefficients $w_{1k}^{(2)}$ which connect hidden unit to the response variable have the same sign. If these two coefficients have different signs, the marginal effect is negative.

Interpretation of MLPs with more hidden units without appropriate restrictions on coefficients becomes more complicated. In their case partial dependence plots may be used to recognize nonlinear effects of independent variables. The response variable or its potential estimated by the MLP are plotted against the value range of an independent variable for one or several fixed constellations of the other independent variables (see, e.g., Hruschka 2001a, Hruschka et al. 2004).

Marginal partial dependence plots are based on marginal averages of a response variable, its potential or its elasticity. Such values are obtained by averaging across observations. That is why such values reflect the effect of an independent variable across its value range after accounting for the average effects of the other independent variables (Hastie et al. 2002, for a marketing application see Hruschka 2006).

Elasticities are relative measures which compare the relative change of a dependent variable to the relative change of the respective independent variable. The point elasticity of an independent variable x_{pi} with respect to response variable k may be defined in two equivalent ways as:

$$el(x_{pi}) \equiv \frac{\partial \hat{y}_{ik}}{\partial x_{pi}} \frac{x_{pi}}{\hat{y}_{ki}} \equiv \frac{\partial log(\hat{y}_{ik})}{\partial log(x_{pi})} \tag{5.16}$$

Table 5.3 contains expressions of point elasticities for different types of MLPs, which represent generalizations of well-known expressions for conventional models. They consist of coefficient $w_{pk}^{(L)}$ of the linear component and a nonlinear term Z_{pi} which is a weighted sum of marginal effects of the (usually transformed) independent variable on hidden units.

Usually MLPs have transformed independent variables as inputs and one has to multiply by the first derivative of the transformed with regard to the original independent variable $\frac{\partial \tilde{x}_{pi}}{\partial x_{pi}}$ to obtain the elasticity (e.g., by $1/s_p$ and $(\tilde{x}^{max} - \tilde{x}^{max})/(x_p^{max} - x_p^{min})$ for the two transformations shown in expression (5.8)).

Table 5.3   Point Elasticities for Different MLPs

MLP Type	$el(x_{ip})$
Linear output	$\frac{x_{pi}}{\hat{y}_{ki}}(w_{pk}^{(L)} + Z_{pi})\frac{\partial \tilde{x}_{pi}}{\partial x_{pi}}$
Linear output, response variable and independent variables	$(w_{pk}^{(L)} + Z_{pi})\frac{\partial \tilde{x}_{pi}}{\partial x_{pi}}$
Log transformed ANNAM	$(1 - \widehat{m}s_{ki})(w_{pk}^{(L)} + Z_{pi})\frac{\partial \tilde{x}_{pi}}{\partial x_{pi}}$
Logistic output	$(1 - \hat{y}_{ki})(w_{pk}^{(L)} + Z_{pi})\frac{\partial \tilde{x}_{pi}}{\partial x_{pi}}$

$$Z_{pi} = \sum_{h=1}^{H} w_{hk}^{(2)} z_{hi}(1 - z_{hi})w_{ph}^{(1)}$$

5.6   Empirical Studies

Table 5.4 gives an overview of studies which use MLPs to model aggregate market response. All of these studies include a comparison to conventional regression models. **Table 5.4** characterizes studies by performance measures and performance relative to conventional aggregate market response models, independent variables and observations (number of brands, stores and time periods).

Readers should easily see that most studies give evidence to superior performance of MLP models.

In the following I discuss the studies of Hruschka (2001a) and Hruschka (2006) in more detail. Hruschka (2001a) estimates various ANNAM models with different numbers (between zero and four) of brand-specific hidden units. The model with no hidden unit equals a conventional attraction model. Estimation data consist of 104 weekly observations of store-level data on market shares, current retail prices and features for four brands of a certain FMCG category.

ANNAM with one brand-specific hidden unit for two of these four brands performs best in terms of approximate posterior model probabilities. Contrary to the conventional attraction model this model reproduces threshold effects of prices, i.e. higher market share changes if prices are below or above a certain level. For one of the two brands with a hidden unit ANNAM implies a weaker price effect except at very low prices.

For the other of these two brands ANNAM indicates higher price effects at very high prices and lower price effects over the remaining price range.

Hruschka (2006) compares the heterogeneous MLP to the heterogeneous multiplicative model using store level data on sales and retail prices of the nine leading brands of a FMCG category. These data were acquired in 81 stores and comprise 62,878 observations in total.

In a preliminary study the heterogeneous multiplicative model attained a much better performance than several other heterogeneous parametric models with linear, exponential, semi-log, logistic, and asymmetric logistic functional forms. In terms of posterior model probabilities the heterogeneous MLP turns out to heavily outperform the heterogeneous multiplicative model. This result demonstrates that consideration of flexibility may be beneficial even if heterogeneity is accounted for.

Hruschka (2006) plots sales against prices of brands for three different competitive price constellations (high, medium, low) based on coefficients averaged across stores (see **Figure 5.1** which does not include brand 5 for which curves are almost identical for the MLP and the multiplicative model). Especially at high competitive prices the MLP and the multiplicative model differ very much with the MLP expecting higher sales compared to the multiplicative model.

Prices of competitive brands do not affect sales of brand 9 which explains that we only have one curve for each model for this brand. Sales of brand 9 are higher according to the MLP except at very own high prices at which sales decreases are more pronounced.

Curves indicate (very) large differences between the MLP and the multiplicative model for the other seven brands at high competitive prices. In the case of brands 6 and 7 price effects according to the MLP are stronger in comparison to the multiplicative model.

At medium competitive prices the MLP expects higher sales for brands 2, 3, 4, 7, and 8 given that own prices are not too high. In the case of brands 2 and 5 the MLP implies stronger price effects at medium competitive prices. Sales of brands 2, 3, 4 and 8 are smaller at low prices according to the MLP.

Table 5.4   Studies Using MLPs to Model Aggregate Market Response

Study	Performance measures used	Performance relative to conventional models	Independent variables	Observations
Ainscough/ Aronson (1999)	MSE	++	price, feature display, coupons lagged sales	1 brand 6 stores 96 weeks
Gruca et al. (1998)	MAPE	0	price, feature display, lagged market share or	7 and 4 brands 58 and 156 weeks
Hruschka (1993)	MSE MAD	++	Price (lagged) advertising	1 brand 60 months
Hruschka (2001a)	BIC	++	price, feature	4 brands 104 weeks
Hruschka (2006)	posterior probability	++	price	9 brands 81 stores 61 - 88 weeks
Lim/Kirikoshi (2005)	MAPE	++	number, duration costs of sales calls, advertising product samples	1 brand 21 months
Natter/Hruschka (1997, 1998)	PC	+	price, lagged market share, trend	7 brands 21 stores 73 weeks
Pantelidaki/ Bunn (2005)	MAPE	++	price (reduction) feature, display weighted number of SKUs, lagged sales	7 brands 104 weeks
van Wezel/Baets (1995)	RMSE	+	price, advertising share, distribution	5 brands 51 bi-months
Wierenga/Kluyt-mans (1996)	RMSE	++	relative price price, advertising share, distribution, trend	5 brands 51 bi-months

++, +, and 0 indicate that MLPs perform much better,
better and about the same as conventional models, respectively

In the following we look at absolute own price elasticities for total sales, i.e., sales summed across all 81 stores of the retailer. These elasticities are averaged across all observations. **Figure 5.2** contains 95 % credible intervals of elasticities for all brands except brand 5 for which the two models produce almost identical results.

The multiplicative model implies that elasticities decrease very slightly at higher prices. Elasticities differ between the multiplicative model and the MLP over most of the observed price range with the exception of brand 9. Elasticities inferred from the MLP tend to follow a bell-shaped curve which can be clearly seen for brands 3, 7 and 8. The incomplete bell shape for brands 2, 4 and 6 can be traced back to the lack of observations at low prices, for brand 9 it is due to the lack of observations at higher prices.

5.7 Conclusions

Estimation of MLPs involves more effort compared to parametric regression models. On the other hand, MLPs perform much better than conventional models as the clear majority of relevant studies (seven of ten studies shown in **Table 5.4**) demonstrate. This fact lends support to the suspicion that parametric approaches are overly restrictive.

MLPs differ from conventional models not only with respect to statistical performance. MLPs often also lead to elasticities which clearly differ from elasticities which more conventional models imply. This fact has consequences for marketing decision making. Decision makers which use conventional marketing response models could inadvertently waive profit opportunities.

Hruschka (2001a) provides an example. He determines optimal prices both for the conventional attraction model and its best performing MLP counterpart assuming fictitious play of competitors. He obtains higher optimal prices based on the MLP model. This result, of course, is in accordance with the lower absolute price elasticities which the MLP model implies. For prices set on the basis of this MLP profits increase by 10.7 % and 15.61 % for two of the four investigated brands.

Figure 5.1   Sales Response Curves

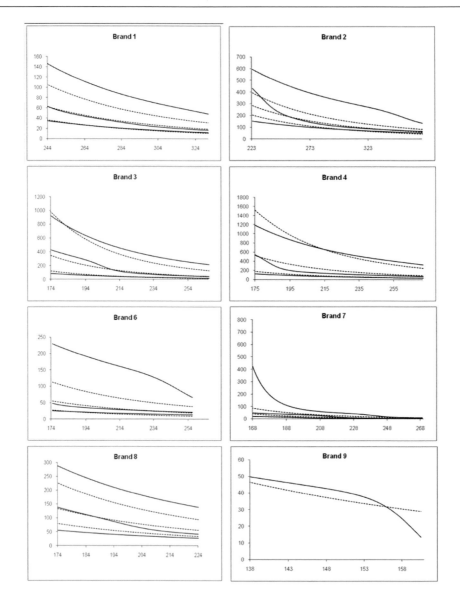

Top, middle and bottom curves for high, medium and low prices of competitors, respectively MLP (solid curves), multiplicative model (dotted curves).

Figure 5.2   Price Elasticity Curves

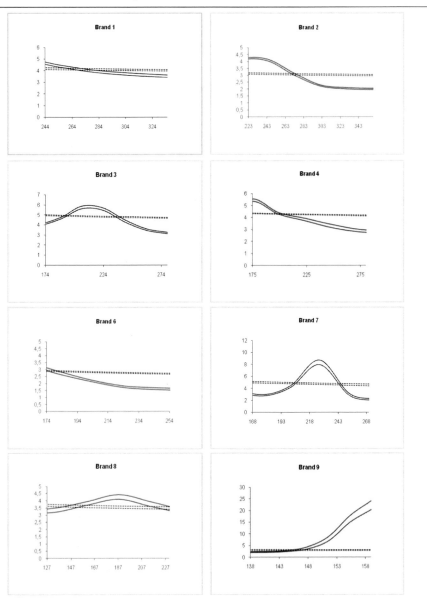

Top, middle and bottom curves for high, medium and low prices of competitors,
respectively MLP (solid curves), multiplicative model (dotted curves).

Literature

[1] Ainscough, T. L./Aronson, J. E. (1999): An empirical investigation and comparison of neural networks and regression for scanner data analysis. Journal of Retailing and Consumer Services, Vol. 6, 4, pp. 205-217.

[2] Akaike, H. (1974): A new look at statistical model identification, IEEE Transactions on Automatic Control, Vol. 19, pp. 716-727.

[3] Amemiya, T. (1980): Selection of regressors. International Economic Review, Vol. 21, pp. 331-354.

[4] Barron, A.R. (1993): Universal approximation bounds for superpositions of a sigmoidal function. IEEE Transactions on Information Theory 39, pp. 930-945.

[5] Bemmaor, A. C./Wagner, U. (2002): Estimating market-level multiplicative models of promotion effects with linearly aggregated data - A parametric approach, in: Franses, P. H. and Montgomery, A. L., Econometric Models in Marketing. Elsevier Science, (Advances in Econometrics, 16), pp. 165-189.

[6] Bishop, C.M. (1995): Neural networks for pattern recognition. Clarendon Press, Oxford, UK.

[7] Brezger, A./Steiner, W. (2008): Monotonic regression based on Bayesian P-splines: An application to estimating price response functions from store-level scanner data. Journal of Business & Economic Statistics, Vol. 26, 1, pp. 90-104.

[8] Chib, S./Greenberg, E. (1995): Understanding the Metropolis-Hastings algorithm, The American Statistician, Vol. 49, pp. 327-335.

[9] Chib, S./Greenberg, E. (1996): Markov chain Monte Carlo simulation methods in econometrics. Econometric Theory, Vol. 12, pp. 409-431.

[10] Cooper, L.G./Nakanishi, M. (1988): Market-share analysis. Kluwer, Boston.

[11] Cybenko, G. (1989): Continuous value neural networks with two hidden layers are sufficient. Mathematics of Control, Signal and Systems, Vol. 2, pp. 303-314.

[12] Gelman, A./Carlin, J.B./Stern, H.S./Rubin, D.B. (1995): Bayesian data analysis. Chapman and Hall, London.

[13] Greene, W.H. (2003): Econometric analysis. 5th edition, Prentice Hall, Upper Saddle River, NJ.

[14] Gruca, T.S./Klemz, B.R./Petersen, E.A. (1998): Mining sales data using a neural network model of market response. SIGKDD Explorations, Vol. 1, 1, pp. 39-43.

[15] Hanssens, D.M./Parsons, L.J./Schultz, R.L. (1990): Market response models. Kluwer Academic Publishers, Boston, MA.

[16] Hanssens, D.M./Parsons, L.J./Schultz, R.L. (2001): Market response models. Econometric and Time Series Analysis, 2nd edition, Kluwer Academic Publishers, Boston, MA.

[17] Hastie, T./Tibshirani, R./Friedman, J. (2002): The elements of statistical learning. Springer, New York.

[18] Van Heerde, H./Leeflang, P.S.H./Wittink, D.R. (2001): Semiparametric analysis to estimate the deal effect curve. Journal of Marketing Research, Vol. 38, pp. 197-216.

[19] Hornik, K./Stinchcombe, M./White, H. (1989): Multilayer feedforward networks are universal approximators. Neural Networks, Vol. 3, pp. 359-366.

[20] Hruschka, H. (1993): Determining market response functions by neural network modeling. A comparison to econometric techniques. European Journal of Operations Research, Vol. 66, pp. 27-35.

[21] Hruschka, H. (1996): Marketing-Entscheidungen. Verlag Vahlen, München.

[22] Hruschka, H. (2000): Specification, estimation and empirical corroboration of Gutenberg's kinked demand curve. in: Albach, H., Brockhoff, K., Eymann, E., Jungen, P., Steven, M., Luhmer, A. (eds.): Theory of the firm. Erich Gutenberg's foundations and further developments. Springer, Berlin, pp. 153-168.

[23] Hruschka, H. (2001a): An artificial neural net attraction model (ANNAM) to analyze market share effects of marketing instruments. Schmalenbach Business Review - zfbf, Vol. 53, pp. 27-40.

[24] Hruschka, H. (2001b): Semi-parametrische Marktanteilsmodellierung. Zeitschrift für Betriebswirtschaft, pp. 571-589.

[25] Hruschka, H. (2006): Relevance of functional flexibility for heterogeneous sales response models: A comparison of parametric and seminonparametric models. European J. Oper. Res., Vol. 174, pp. 1009-1020.

[26] Ingrassia, S./Morlini, I. (2005): Neural network modeling for small datasets. Technometrics, Vol. 47, pp. 297-311.

[27] Kalyanam, K./Shively, Th.S. (1998): Estimating irregular pricing effects: a stochastic spline regression approach, Journal of Marketing Research, Vol. 35, pp. 16-29.

[28] Krycha, K. A./Wagner, U. (1999): Applications of artificial neural networks in management science: A survey. Journal of Retailing and Consumer Services, Vol. 6, pp. 185-203.

[29] Lim, C.W./Kirikoshi, T. (2005): Predicting the effects of physician-directed promotion on prescription yield and sales uptake using neural networks. Journal Targeting, Measurement and Analysis for Marketing, Vol. 13, pp. 156-167.

[30] McGuire, T.W./Weiss, D.L./Houston, F.S. (1977): Consistent multiplicative market share models. Greenwood, B.A., Bellinger, D.N. (eds.): Contemporary Marketing Thought. AMA, Chicago, pp. 129-134.

[31] Møller, M. (1993): A scaled conjugated gradient algorithm for fast supervised learning. Neural Networks, Vol. 6, pp. 525-533.

[32] Natter, M./Hruschka, H. (1997): Ankerpreise als Erwartungen oder dynamische latente Variablen in Marktreaktionsmodellen. Zeitschrift für betriebswirtschaftliche Forschung, Vol. 49, pp. 747-764.

[33] Natter, M./Hruschka, H. (1998): Using artificial neural nets to specify and estimate aggregate reference price models. Aurifeille, J.-M., C. Deissenberg, (eds.): Bio-Mimetic Approaches in Management Science, Kluwer, Dordrecht, Netherlands, pp. 101-118.

[34] Nenning, M./Topritzhofer, E./Wagner, U. (1981): Empirische Marktmodellierung, Physica- Verlag, Würzburg/Wien.

[35] Pantelidaki, S./Bunn, D. (2005): Development of a multifunctional sales response model with the diagnostic aid of artifical neural networks. Journal of Forecasting, Vol. 24, pp. 505-521.

[36] Ripley, B.D. (1993): Statistical aspects of neural networks. Barndorff-Nielsen, O.E., J.L. Jensen, W.S. Kendall(eds.): Networks and chaos - Statistical and probabilistic aspects. Chapman & Hall, London, pp. 40-123.

[37] Saito, K./Nakano, R. (1997): Partial BFGS update and efficient step-length calculation for three-layer neural networks. Neural Computation, Vol. 9, pp. 123-141.

[38] Schwarz, G. (1979): Estimating the dimension of a model. Annals of Statistics, Vol. 6, pp. 461-464.

[39] Steiner, W./Brezger, A./Belitz, C. (2007): Flexible estimation of price response functions using retail scanner data. Journal of Retailing and Consumer Services, Vol. 14, 6, pp. 383-393.

[40] Van Wezel, M.C./Baets, W.R.J. (1995): Predicting market responses with a neural network: the case of fast moving consumer goods. Marketing Intelligence & Planning, Vol. 13, 7, pp. 23-30.

[41] Wierenga, B./Kluytmans, J. (1996): Prediction with neural nets in marketing times series data. Management Report Series no. 258, Erasmus Universiteit Rotterdam.

6 Supporting Strategic Product Portfolio Planning by Market Simulation

The Case of the Future Powertrain Portfolio in the Automotive Industry

Karsten Kieckhäfer, Technische Universität Braunschweig, Germany

Thomas Volling, Technische Universität Braunschweig, Germany

Thomas Stefan Spengler, Technische Universität Braunschweig, Germany

Abstract

In this paper, the authors propose a decision support for the strategic planning of the future powertrain and vehicle portfolio in the automotive industry. They use a hybrid market simulation approach for a simultaneous consideration of aggregated system and individual consumer behavior. This non-traditional simulation model allows for estimating the development of market shares of various powertrains in different vehicle size classes subject to the vehicle portfolio offered and to assumptions about consumer behavior and market environment.

Keywords

Agend-Based Simulation, System Dynamics, Strategic Portfolio Planning, Market Simulation, Alternative Powertrains.

6.1   Introduction

All over the world, automobile manufacturers are increasingly obligated to reduce the greenhouse gas (GHG) emissions, in particular carbon dioxide (CO_2), and thus the fuel consumption of their vehicle fleets. This is due to the high contribution of the transportation sector to the worldwide GHG emissions, one major driver of climate change. In the European Union (EU) for example, the transportation sector accounts for approximately 20 percent of the CO_2 emissions (UNFCCC 2011). The largest share of these emissions is caused by road traffic (IPCC 2007), which will be the fastest growing sector in the future (OECD/IEA 2008). For this reason, policy has issued regulations to enforce emission reduction from passenger cars in several countries. In the most cases these regulations aim at limiting average fleet emissions respectively fuel consumption. Well-known examples are the CO_2 regulations in the EU and the Corporate Average Fuel Economy (CAFE) regulations in the United States (EU 2010; NHTSA 2011). In the state of California automobile manufacturers are additionally obligated to produce and sell zero emission vehicles that do not cause any local emissions during operation (CARB 2010). In all cases non-compliance is sanctioned with civil penalties. It can be observed that the regulatory requirements and the corresponding sanctions will become even stricter in the future.

Due to these trends in CO_2 regulation automobile manufacturers are forced to adjust their vehicle portfolio offered to the market, as the requirements can hardly be met with the current product offer. High civil penalties will be the consequence (e. g. Walther et al. 2010) threatening automobile manufacturers' competitiveness. This threat is additionally increased by the scarcity of crude oil, which leads to rising fuel prices and thus higher costs from the consumer's perspective for conventionally powered vehicles.

To adjust the vehicle portfolio and thus to remain competitive, automobile manufacturers can generally choose between three basic options (Kieckhäfer et al. 2009; Walther et al. 2010): improve the fuel efficiency of vehicles with a conventional gasoline or diesel powertrain, offer a higher share of small vehicles with low fuel consumption or integrate vehicles with an alternative powertrain (e. g. partly or fully electric vehicles) in their vehicle portfolio. A combination of all three options seems to be promising, resulting in a high variety of strategic powertrain and vehicle portfolio options and thus challenging decisions about the future product portfolio. More specifically, decisions have to be made about the powertrains to be offered in a specific vehicle model in a specific market at a certain point in time. In this context, it has to be considered that most of the alternative powertrains are still in the stage of research and development. They are more expensive and an appropriate service station network is missing. Nevertheless, they have to compete with the advanced conventional powertrains. High uncertainties about the market success are the consequence. Due to this complex and dynamic character, portfolio decisions cannot be made intuitively or based on simplified assumptions. In fact, with regard to the introduction of alternative powertrains there is a need for a decision support for the strategic product portfolio planning in the automotive industry.

Against this background, we propose a decision support for the strategic planning of the future powertrain and vehicle portfolio in the automotive industry. It is based on a market simulation for estimating the development of the market shares of conventionally and alternatively powered vehicles. To support strategic portfolio planning the vehicle portfolio supplied to the market can be defined exogenously by assigning powertrains to different vehicle size classes. In addition to vehicle supply, we model powertrain technology and service station development as well as consumer choice. From a methodological point of view our contribution lies in a hybrid simulation approach that allows for a simultaneous consideration of aggregated system and individual consumer behavior. Nonlinear ordinary differential equations are applied to simulate the dynamic developments of the powertrain technologies and the service station network on an aggregated level. Both developments are dependent on consumer demand. To model demand, a detailed approach is used integrating discrete choice modeling with agent-based simulation. This allows for simulating individual consumer choices from the wide range of powertrains and size classes. Choice probabilities are modeled dynamically and consumer specifically. They are dependent on changing vehicle characteristics resulting from the aggregated model behavior, consumer characteristics and consumer specific choice sets. These in turn are generated based on transition probabilities for powertrain technologies and size classes.

The remainder of the paper is structured as follows. In Section 6.2 we analyze challenges in planning the future powertrain and vehicle portfolio in the automotive industry. The potential of using market simulation to support strategic product portfolio planning as well as existing approaches to model the automotive market are discussed in Section 6.3. Based on these findings, we develop a hybrid simulation model of the automotive market in Section 6.4. Concluding remarks are given in Section 6.5.

6.2 Planning the Future Powertrain Portfolio in the Automotive Industry

6.2.1 Strategic Product Portfolio Planning in the Automotive Industry

In general, a product portfolio is defined as the sum of all products offered to the market. It can be described by its breadth and depth. The breadth of a product portfolio is determined by the number of product lines offered (group of related products), whereas the number of related products (product variants) in one product line defines the depth of a product portfolio. The major task of strategic product portfolio planning is to synchronize the product offers with market demand over time.

With regard to the automotive industry strategic product portfolio planning decisions focus on the coverage of market segments with product lines (Diez 1990; Schneider 2006). To this end, especially the following criteria are used: regions (e. g. Europe), body styles (e. g. limousine) and size classes (e. g. small) (Niederländer 2000). If the region is used as the segmentation criteria, a market segment is usually referred to as a market. In turn, a market segment that indicates a specific combination of body style and size class is called a segment. With regard to strategic product portfolio planning one specific product line is defined in such a way that is exactly the counterpart of a single segment. In the following, we will use the more common denomination vehicle model (e. g. Volkswagen Golf VI, limousine) instead of product line (Schneider 2006). Powertrains respectively engines are not considered on this strategic level. They play a major role in planning the variants of each vehicle model. Note that this classification is in contrast to existing classifications from product variety management, where the powertrain/engine and the body style are used to define variants of different vehicle models that are based on the same platform (Pil and Holweg 2004; Watanabe and Ane 2004). This is due to the fact that strategic product portfolio planning requires an aggregated level of detail in the product definition as well as comparability between the product offering and the market segments. Both of which are not adequately addressed by the conventional classification. In addition to that, body style and size class can be considered as the two most important purchase decision factors (Schneider 2008). Thus, within strategic product portfolio planning automobile manufacturers have to decide about offering vehicle models with a specific body style and a specific size class in a specific market at a certain point in time. The product portfolio is then the result of "an expedient combination of interdependent decisions on product offers across markets and segments" (Raasch et al. 2007, 273).

Strategic product portfolio decisions in the automotive industry are mainly based on a so called cycle plan and long-range product plan respectively (Adelt 2003; Grube 2003; Hill et al. 2007). In this plan all vehicle models of the current and potential future product portfolios of one manufacturer are considered. Furthermore, all important milestones (e. g. start of development, start of production) in the life-cycle of the vehicle models are regarded (Raasch et al. 2007). To prepare a portfolio decision, alternative cycle plans are generated and then evaluated by means of financial performance indicators (Adelt 2003; Raasch et al. 2007). In this context, the success of a product portfolio decision especially depends on the correct assessment of the future market development of the different segments. Forecasting these developments is very challenging: First, the expected total market volume has to be approximated. Afterwards, the shares of the body styles and size classes of this market volume have to be estimated. By taking into account competition, sales volumes for every vehicle model of a manufacturer can be deduced, which have a direct influence on the financial performance indicators (Adelt 2003; Hill et al. 2007).

6.2.2 Strategic Product Portfolio Planning With Alternative Powertrains on the Rise

As a consequence of the introduction of alternative powertrains automobile manufacturers have to integrate powertrain decisions into strategic product portfolio planning. As long as only conventional powertrains are offered to the market, no further differentiation of the market segments becomes necessary, which is especially due the almost similar characteristics of the powertrain technologies. Thus, considering the powertrains within mid-term variant planning is sufficient. However, with alternative powertrains on the rise the number of powertrain technologies increases. In addition, these technologies have different characteristics and different areas of application than the conventional ones. Thus, offering every powertrain available in each vehicle model does not seem to be appropriate. The suitability of one powertrain and thus the market success is especially dependent on the time of introduction, the size class of the vehicle model to be powered, and the provided cruising range. Considering their relative advantages in terms of technological performance and price, conventional as well as (plug-in) hybrid electric powertrains seem to be promising in the short to medium term. In the long run, fully electric powertrains (battery or fuel cell) will become more important with increasing technological progress. This trend could be reinforced by the limited potential of conventional powertrains with regard to energy efficiency. Furthermore, battery electric powertrains are better suited for short driving distances and the operation of small cars. In contrast, conventional as well as (plug-in) hybrid and fuel cell electric powertrains offer advantages for long driving distances and the operation of medium and larger cars respectively (Anon 2010). Overall, with regard to strategic product portfolio planning additional decisions have to be made on the powertrains to be offered in a specific vehicle model in a specific market at a certain point in time.

With an increasing number of powertrains, especially forecasting the development of market shares to support strategic product portfolio decisions becomes even more challenging for automobile manufacturers. Additional complexity arises from the fact that this development is influenced by various factors (Kieckhäfer et al. 2009; Struben/Sterman 2008; Walther et al. 2010): On the one hand, it is dependent on the direct interaction of supply and demand. Here, the individual consumer preferences for the various competing powertrains as well as the actual product portfolio offered to the market are important. On the other hand, the market shares of the different powertrains are dependent on highly uncertain developments in the market environment. With regard to the introduction of alternative powertrains especially the development of the service station network, the technological and economic characteristics of the powertrains (e. g. energy density and costs of the battery system) as well as the energy prices play a major role. Also, changes in the legal environment have an influence on manufacturer and consumer behavior and thus on the development of the market shares. In addition to these manifold influencing factors, consumers. Consumers have to be aware of the new technologies and perceive them as a real alternative before considering the purchase of an alternative powertrain (Struben/Sterman 2008; Walther et al. 2010).

Due to the high complexity of this task there is a need for a model-based approach for estimating the development of the market shares of the various powertrains to support strategic product portfolio planning in the automotive industry. In particular, a decision support is required that allows for evaluating the effects of different vehicle portfolios as well as of different assumptions about consumer behavior and the market environment on the development of the market shares.

6.2.3   Requirements on a Decision Support

The requirements on the decision support are fourfold: First, the tool has to allow for specifying vehicle models to be offered to the market on the aggregation level of combinations of size class, body style and powertrain. The definition of the time of introduction of these models as well as their characteristics (e. g. price, cruising range) that influence purchase decisions is important. Second, to describe the consumer choice between the manifold vehicle models offered to the market, consumer demand has to be modeled appropriately. In this context, the consideration of the competitive situation between conventional and alternative powertrains is required. Furthermore, the individual consumer characteristics and preferences as well as their awareness of the alternative powertrains have to be taken into account. Third, the interaction between supply and demand has to be embedded in the market environment. To this end, modeling the technology and service station network development as well as considering further influencing factors like energy prices and regulatory requirements on an aggregated level becomes necessary. Fourth, the decision support has to incorporate the uncertainty in the development of various influencing factors.

To sum up, supporting strategic product portfolio planning with regard to the introduction of alternative powertrains requires an evaluation of different vehicle portfolio options by means of the development of the market shares. To this end, an appropriate modeling of the socio-economic system "automotive market" has to be carried out, including supply and demand as well as the market environment (Kieckhäfer et al. 2009). For this reason, we suggest an approach called "market simulation". In the following, this approach is embedded in the literature by defining the term "market simulation" and discussing existing approaches to model the automotive market.

6.3 Market Simulation to Support Strategic Portfolio Planning

6.3.1 Fundamentals of Market Simulation

Following Eliashberg and Lilien (2003, 4) and Lilien et al. (1992, 6) marketing models can be subdivided into measurement models, decision-making models and theory-buliding models. These models can be either verbal or mathematical (Lilien et al. 1992). To define the term "market simulation" we concentrate on mathematical measurement models and decision-making models.

Measurement models serve for measuring "the 'demand' for a product as a function of various independent variables" (Eliashberg/Lilien 2003, 4). "Demand" can either be measured on an individual (disaggregated) or a market (aggregated) level, including dependent variables like sales volumes or market shares, but also consumer's preference (Eliashberg/Lilien 2003). Note that the latter variable is often the basis for estimating the first two (Cooper 2003). As independent variables marketing mix variables that can be controlled by a company as well as variables that describe competitive and environmental influences are considered (Eliashberg/Lilien 2003). Decision-making models have a broader scope than measurement models. Beyond purely estimating the demand for a product they are utilized to support marketing mix decisions. To this end, decision-making models comprise measurement models that serve as their fundament. Here, the interactions between supply and demand as well as the competitive and environmental influences on the market behavior are modeled. To allow for a decision support, marketing mix interventions as well as their impact on consumer response and on the achievement of company goals are regarded. By applying methods like mathematical optimization, optimal control, or simulation, expedient recommendations are derived, e. g. with regard to the optimal design of a product portfolio (Eliashberg/Lilien 2003).

Against this background, we define a market simulation as an approach to simulate the consumer response to companies' marketing mix decisions as well as to the competitive and environmental influences. Thereby, the response is based on a mathematical measurement model that comprises sub-models of supply, demand and the market environment. By evaluating the impact of different product portfolios on "demand" and other company objectives recommendations concerning strategic product portfolio decisions can be derived. This way, the market simulation can be used as a decision support for strategic product portfolio planning.

With regard to strategic portfolio planning especially the application of a dynamic simulation model that describes "a system as it evolves over time" (Law/Kelton 2000, 5) bears great potential. This potential is threefold (Wiedmann/Löffler 1989): First, the underlying system can be modeled close to reality. This is due to the possibility of considering the manifold system elements respectively variables as well as the interdependencies between them, which are partially non-linear and delayed.

Second, based on the realistic model of the system structure the dynamic and complex system behavior over time can be analyzed in detail. Furthermore, the impact of a multitude of system interventions on system behavior can be tested. Third, this leads to a better decision support with regard to strategic product portfolio planning. Based on the comprehensive understanding of the underlying system and its behavior, recommendations concerning the strategic design of product portfolios can be derived. In this context, it has to be regarded that the achievement of point estimates for the dependent variables plays a subordinate role. Rather, the explication of the mechanisms leading to the estimates is in focus (Gilbert/Troitzsch 2005).

6.3.2   Review of Existing Approaches

With regard to the automotive market there exists a huge variety of approaches that can be considered as a "market simulation" following the definition provided. These approaches can be divided into three major groups.

The first group comprises demand models that have been applied to forecast the consumer demand. Typically, the demand in terms of sales or market shares is measured on a level of vehicle models, variants or powertrains. The most common approach is to use conjoint (Teichert/Shehu 2010) or discrete choice models (Train 2009) to simulate the individual consumer choice from the range of alternatives offered to the market at a certain point in time (e. g. Achtnicht et al. 2008; Berry et al. 2004; Brownstone et al. 2000; Bunch et al. 1993; Train/Winston 2007). These models use vehicle attributes like purchase price, brand or fuel consumption as independent variables. In some cases choice models are combined with diffusion models (Mahajan et al. 2003) to consider the development of the demand for new products over time (e. g. Eggert 2003; Urban et al. 1996). Thereby, the diffusion models are either based on differential equations (Bass 1969) or on probabilistic flow processes (Urban et al. 1990). All models can be considered as pure measurement models, whereby environmental influences on demand are only, if at all, analyzed to a minor extent, especially with regard to their temporal development. Most models regard the choice between different alternative powertrains from a macro-economic point of view. There are only a few models that incorporate the manufacturers' perspective and thus can be used to support manufacturers' product portfolio planning. In turn, these models usually do not consider the huge variety of alternative powertrains.

The second group of approaches includes simulation models that are founded on systems theory. Most of the models are based on system dynamics (Forrester 1961, Sterman 2000) to simulate the aggregated and endogenous system behavior over time. Forecasting consumer demand is not in focus primarily. On the one side, these models have been developed to measure the emission reduction potential of improved conventionally and alternatively powered vehicles on the market level (e. g. BenDor/Ford 2006; Bosshardt et al. 2008; Walther et al. 2010). On the other side, the interdependencies between the development of powertrain technologies and/or product offering, the development of service station networks and the diffusion of alternative powertrains are analyzed (e. g. Janssen et al. 2006;

Meyer/Winebrake 2009; Struben/Sterman 2008; Walther et al. 2010). Often, influencing factors of the market environment like regulatory measures serve as the independent variables. To describe the vehicle respectively powertrain choice on an aggregated level different approaches are suggested. One typical approach is to use a discrete choice model that describes the purchase probabilities of an average consumer for the different powertrains and combine it with a diffusion model to regard innovative technologies. Thus, even if not intended primarily, the system dynamics models allow forecasting consumer demand on an aggregated level. Consumer demand is usually measured in terms of market shares of the different powertrains. Only Walther et al. (2010, 243-244) consider combinations of powertrains and size classes. This way, simulating the consumer response to different vehicle portfolios becomes possible.

In contrast to the system dynamic based approaches, De Haan et al. (2009, 1088-1089) and Mueller and De Haan (2009, 1074-1077) present a static agent based microsimulation model (Gilbert/Troitzsch 2005) that can also be assigned to the class of system models. Here, the individual purchase decision processes of the agents are modeled in detail comprising the phase of the choice set formation as well as the phase of the vehicle choice itself. The choice set formation is based on a stationary Markov process (Massy et al. 1970) and the vehicle choice on a discrete choice model. Manifold vehicle models as well as a detailed consumer population are considered. However, alternative powertrains, influencing factors of the market environment as well as product portfolio decisions are largely neglected.

The last group of approaches comprises simulation models that can be described as scenario models to forecast the market development of different powertrains, sometimes in combination with different size classes (e. g. Book et al. 2009; Friedrich 2010). As compared to the system models these models regard even more influencing factors from the market environment. Scenarios result from the combination of specific values for each influencing factor. The values itself are given exogenously. The modeling of consumer behavior is less theoretically founded with respect to the other approaches discussed. Scenario models are often used by consulting groups. Information about the modeling assumptions is hard to obtain and the review of the models becomes nearly impossible.

6.3.3   Potentials and Limitations of Existing Approaches

With regard to the required decision support none of the previously presented approaches meets all of the requirements stated in 6.2.3. The potential of the demand models lies especially in simulating individual consumer demand for a wide range of vehicle models on a disaggregated level; either statically or dynamically (cf. **Table 6.1**). However, supporting strategic product portfolio decisions based on pure demand models has its limitations, especially with regard to the introduction of alternative powertrains. This is due to the missing consideration of the endogenous system behavior, for example in terms of the interdependencies between demand, technology and service station development. The same holds true for the static microsimulation approach, whose strength lies in the consideration of individual consumers with heterogeneous preferences as agents as well as the possibility to define a highly differentiated vehicle portfolio. The potentials and limitations of the system dynamics based modeling approaches are almost contrary. The endogenous system behavior and the diffusion processes of alternative powertrains can be taken into account appropriately. However, modeling demand based on individual and heterogeneous consumer preferences is nearly impossible. This is due to the high aggregation level of system dynamics models, which is also the reason why portfolio decisions can only, if at all, be considered to a small extent. Modeling a complete product portfolio with system dynamics is at least very difficult. With regard to both groups of modeling approaches considering the manifold uncertain developments in the market environment and their influence on consumer demand can be judged as possible. However, these influences have been largely neglected up to now. In this context, using different scenarios to define the market environment like it is done in scenario models has a high potential.

Overall, to support strategic product portfolio planning by market simulation, the integration of the demand and the system modeling approaches seems to be promising. This allows for considering the interdependencies between the individual consumer behavior on a disaggregated level and the system behavior on an aggregated level. Thus, the influence of different vehicle portfolios as well as the environmental influences on the demand for conventionally and alternatively powered vehicles can be measured appropriately. By additionally taking into account different scenarios to describe uncertain developments in the market environment, it becomes possible to also benefit from the strength of the scenario models. This requires a new and non-traditional simulation approach, which integrates not only the different perspectives but also various methods. The following section deals with the development of such a non-traditional, hybrid simulation model for estimating the development of market shares of conventionally and alternatively powered vehicles.

Table 6.1   Comparison of Existing Approaches to Model the Automotive Market

Requirements: Consideration of	Demand Models		System Models		Scenario Models*
	Static	Dynamic	Static	Dynamic	
... a sufficiently differentiated vehicle portfolio (more than just on the level of powertrains)	✓	✓	✓	(✓)	(✓)
... strategic portfolio decisions with regard to the introduction of alternative powertrains				(✓)	
... individual consumer behavior	✓	✓	✓		
... diffusion processes		✓		✓	(✓)
... endogenous system behavior				✓	
... scenarios of uncertain developments in the market environment	(✓)	(✓)	(✓)	(✓)	✓

* Difficult to judge

6.4   A Hybrid Simulation Model of the Automotive Market

6.4.1   Framework

The framework for the decision support comprises three sub-modules to allow for simulating the development of the market shares of the various powertrains subject to the vehicle portfolio offered to the market and the scenario of the market environment (cf. **Figure 6.1**): a manufacturer module to model the supply side in terms of the product portfolio offered to the market, a consumer module to model individual new car buyers with heterogeneous characteristics and preferences, and an environment module to model the endogenous developments in the market environment as well as the different scenarios.

The manufacturer and the consumer module aim at describing the interaction between the product offering and the purchase decisions of the new car buyers on a disaggregated level. To this end, consumers in a specific market are divided into different consumer segments. Each consumer segment is defined by socio-economic respectively socio-demographic characteristics influencing the consumer behavior. To model the actual consumer behavior, a purchase decision rule is used that describes the process of choosing one vehicle model from the vehicle portfolio offered to the market. The vehicle models in the portfolio are specified by means of their powertrain and size class. To reduce complexity, body styles are not regarded in the first step. Each vehicle model is specified by means of attributes, which have an influence on the purchase decisions (e. g. purchase price, energy costs, cruising range). To compute the market shares of the various combinations of powertrain and size class on a market level, the individual purchase decisions are aggregated. Different competitors are not taken into account.

The market share estimates are utilized to model the development of the market environment and thus to simulate the system behavior on an aggregated level. For instance, the vehicle stock is computed as an input for simulating the evolution of the service station network. Furthermore, the market share estimates are used to model technological improvement. Based on this improvement process the values of the attributes describing the vehicle models that are offered to the market are updated. For example, the cruising range of a battery electric vehicle is adjusted due to improvements with regard to the energy density of the traction battery, which is in turn based on the amount of batteries produced. The structure of the vehicle portfolio offered to the market can be adjusted by exogenously defining new combinations of powertrain and size class and their time of introduction. This way, assessing the impact of different vehicle portfolios on the development of the market shares becomes possible. To allow for considering uncertainties in the development of the market environment and their influence on the market shares, different scenarios are regarded. These scenarios comprise possible combinations of specific values of influencing factors like energy prices or regulatory measures, which are defined exogenously.

Figure 6.1   Framework of the Automotive Market Simulation

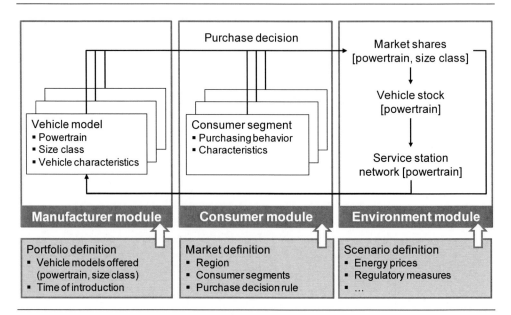

Based on this framework it becomes possible to consider the interdependencies between the individual consumer behavior and the aggregated system behavior of the market environment. In the next step, the manufacturer, consumer and market environment module have to be specified by taking into account the methods and modeling approaches presented in 6.3.2. As noted above, this results in a hybrid simulation approach. Thereby, we face the challenges to model a disaggregated demand model and an aggregated system model as well as to integrate these two contrary perspectives.

6.4.2   Model Development

■ Disaggregated demand model

To describe the individual consumer behavior an agent-based and discrete event simulation approach is used. The consumers are modeled as agents, which carry out purchase decisions during a simulation run based on a predefined purchase decision rule.

To this end, it is required to initialize the agents as well as the vehicle portfolio offered to the market at the start of the simulation. The consumers are divided into consumer segments. Every consumer segment is described by a group of agents, whereas one agent represents a certain number of consumers of the regarded market. The agents are characterized by means of socio-economic and socio-demographic attributes (e. g. age, environmental awareness, kilometers travelled).

Furthermore, decision rules for carrying out the purchase decision are predefined. To define the product portfolio offered to the market, vehicle models are added to the simulation models as objects. These models differ in terms of powertrain and size class. In addition, vehicle characteristics that influence the purchase decision (e. g. purchase price, cruising range) are specified. To initialize the simulation, one specific vehicle model is assigned to every agent randomly. This is done by taking into account the actual powertrain and size class split of the current vehicle fleet that is operated in the considered market. Thus, at the start of the simulation every agent owns one vehicle. So the number of vehicles in stock is determined by the number of agents.

While the simulation is running, the agents turn into new car buyers. To this end, the time of purchase has to determined first. This is done by defining the holding period of a vehicle, which is modeled as an exponentially distributed random variable. Due to the fact that the holding period reflects the whole vehicle lifetime, a used vehicle market is not considered. Every agent has to replace the current vehicle at a certain point in time and passes a multistage purchase decision process following Mueller and De Haan (2009, 1076-1077). In the first step of this process, an agent specific choice set is specified. To this end, the choice set size and composition are determined. The determination of the choice set size is based on a discrete probability distribution that describes the likelihood that a certain number of vehicle models is evaluated during the purchase decision. To compose the choice set of an agent, vehicle models from the product portfolio offered to the market are selected. The selection process is modeled as a stationary Markov process, which is based on transition matrices for the attributes size class and powertrain. These matrices describe the likelihoods that an agent evaluates a vehicle model with a specific size class and powertrain given the powertrain and size class of the current model. Due to the fact that the selection of alternative powertrains is less likely in the beginning, diffusion processes are regarded. In the second step of the purchase decision process, the actual purchase decision is modeled. To this end, discrete choice theory is utilized to describe the selection of one specific vehicle model from the choice set by the consumer. First, the utility for every vehicle model in the choice set is computed. This utility is a deterministic and linear in the parameters function of the vehicle characteristics and the characteristics of the consumer/agent. Afterwards, the purchase probabilities for the vehicle models in the choice set are determined. Here, a nested logit model is used, whose parameters were estimated for Germany by Achtnicht et al. (2008, 9-12). The nests are built with regard to the different powertrains. Based on the estimated purchase probabilities the purchase decision of the agent is simulated by means of random wheel selection.

Overall, this modeling approach allows simulating the purchase decision process in detail and heterogeneously across agents. The individual purchase decision of an agent is dependent on the agent's characteristics and preference, the vehicle portfolio offered to the market as well as the current vehicle model and the resulting choice set composition.

■ Aggregated system model

To describe the aggregated system behavior, a system dynamics based modeling approach is utilized. The developments in the market environment as well as the development of technological and economic vehicle characteristics are modeled with nonlinear ordinary differential equations following Walther et al. (2010, 245-249). During a simulation run, these equations are solved with the help of numerical integration methods.

In the approach adopted, the system behavior is especially determined by endogenously modeling the service station network development as well as learning and experience curve effects with regard to technologies of the alternative powertrains. Furthermore, exogenous definitions of the energy price development and the application of regulatory measures are considered. With regard to the development of the service station network it is assumed that the number of service stations for an alternative powertrain develops with a delay and in co-evolution with the vehicle stock until saturation. The more vehicles are powered by a specific powertrain the higher is the demand for a certain energy carrier and the more service stations are required. In addition to the number of vehicles in stock, the cruising range of the vehicle models, the kilometers travelled as well as the refueling/charging time are considered to determine the required number of service stations (Struben/Sterman 2008). With regard to the powertrain technologies especially the endogenous adjustment processes of the production costs and the energy density of the traction battery are modeled. The energy density follows a logistic growth curve until a technical maximum is reached. The development is dependent on the cumulated experience (Wissema 1982). The costs per kilowatt hour battery capacity follow a standard experience curve and decrease with increasing amount of battery capacity produced (Henderson 1984). The amount of battery capacity produced is directly dependent on the vehicle sales.

The exogenously predefined as well as the endogenously determined aggregated developments in the market environment serve as the basis for specifying the technological and economic vehicle characteristics during simulation runtime. For instance, the purchase price of a battery electric vehicle is modeled in dependence on the battery costs, the cruising range in dependence on the energy density and the service station availability in dependence on the number of service stations installed.

■ Model integration

On the one hand, the integration of the models is realized by means of the vehicle portfolio offered to the market. On the other hand, it is based on the sales and stock figures resulting from the purchase decisions of the agents. In the beginning, the agents choose their new vehicle model from the vehicle portfolio that is initialized at the start of the simulation run. During runtime, purchase decisions take place at discrete points in time, which results in a recalculation of the vehicle sales and stock figures. The sales and stock figures are then transferred to the system model (cf. **Figure 6.2**). Here, the information is used to time-continuously simulate the developments in the market environment as well as the development of the vehicle characteristics. For instance, the battery capacity installed in the sold battery electric vehicles is computed in the agent model. This value is then used to approximate the cumulative experience in the system model to simulate the energy density development of the traction batteries. In turn, the information generated in the system model is used to adjust the characteristics of the vehicle models the agents can choose from. This adjustment takes place at certain points in time. It is to be defined exogenously before the start of a simulation run (e. g. once a year). Additionally, the composition of the vehicle portfolio offered to the market can be changed at these points in time. To this end, the corresponding information about the introduction of new vehicle models (e. g. time of introduction, size class, powertrain) has to be predefined. After this adjustment procedure, the agents can purchase vehicle models from the new product portfolio leading to new sales and stock figures that again influence the aggregated system behavior.

Figure 6.2   Functionality of the Hybrid Simulation Model

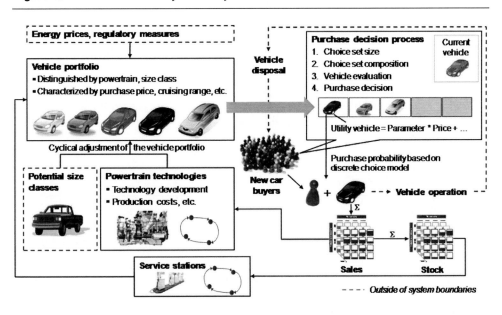

To allow for running simulation experiments and thus to support strategic product portfolio planning, the presented hybrid simulation model of the automotive market is implemented in the software AnyLogic 6.6 from XJ Technologies. This software supports the integration of the agent based and the system dynamics model (Borshchev and Filippov 2004). It is based on the Java development environment Eclipse and thus allows for object-oriented modeling. In part, predefined model elements can be used. Nevertheless, complex functions like the detailed purchase decision process of the agents or the model integration have to be implemented directly in the source code. Based on this implementation, single simulation runs as well as comprehensive sensitivity analyses and Monte Carlo experiments can be executed. Furthermore, Java applets can be generated. Thus, the simulation model can be run independently from the development environment.

6.4.3   Illustrative Example

To illustrate the appropriateness of the presented hybrid simulation approach to support strategic product portfolio planning, we apply the model exemplarily. The illustrative example is based on publicly available data sources for the German market. At the start of the simulation 41,000 agents are initialized taking into account information about the vehicle stock and the vehicle owners from the German Federal Motor Transport Authority (Kraftfahrt-Bundesamt). The agents are assigned to six consumer segments that are segmented demographically: younger than 30 years, 30 to 39 years, 40 to 49 years, 50 to 59 years, 60 to 69 years and older than 69 years. The parameters of the discrete choice model are based on Achtnicht et al. (2008, 11-12), the probability distribution and transition matrices to compose the choice set on Mueller/De Haan (2006, 19-21) and Peters/ De Haan (2006, 13). The vehicle portfolio comprises of up to nine models. Gasoline, diesel and battery electric powertrains are considered. These powertrains are offered in the size classes small, compact and middle. Additionally, the vehicle models are characterized by means of the attributes purchase price, energy costs, cruising range, service station availability, engine power and CO_2 emissions. The initial values of the attributes are approximated based on information about the number of newly registered vehicles from the German Federal Motor Transport Authority as well as information about vehicle characteristics from manufacturers' catalogs and from Walther et al. (2010, 281). With regard to the battery electric vehicles a lithium ion battery serves as the energy storage device.

To simulate and analyze the market share development of the different powertrains, we set up four different simulation experiments. Thereby, each simulation experiment comprises of 50 simulation runs with different seed values of the random number generator. All simulation runs begin in 2009 and end in 2030. The first experiment can be considered as the base run, whereby the following assumptions are made: At the start of the simulation period no battery electric vehicles are offered to the market. They are introduced in the small class in 2012, in the compact class in 2014 and in the middle class in 2016. The consumer awareness of these battery electric vehicles is assumed to be high, which is regarded in the transition matrices. Furthermore, the service station availability is normalized to the current availability of service stations for gasoline and diesel powered vehicles. For battery electric vehicles this availability is set to 35 percent at the start of the simulation. The energy prices for gasoline, diesel and electricity as well as the allocation of the agents to the consumer segments are assumed to be constant during the simulation run. Regulatory measures are not considered. To define further simulation experiments, the parameter values have to be changed. This can be done with regard to the portfolio definition, the market definition or the scenario definition (cf. 6.4.1). The parameter values can be changed separately or simultaneously. In our example, we change the values for the introduction time (experiment 2: portfolio definition), the energy price development (experiment 3: scenario definition) and the consumer awareness (experiment 4: market definition) separately (cf. **Table 6.2**). In the second experiment, all battery electric vehicles are introduced in 2012. In the third experiment, the prices for conventional fuels rise continuously. In the fourth experiment, the consumer awareness of battery electric vehicles is assumed to be very high.

This means, that it is equally likely that a battery electric vehicle or a diesel powered vehicle (a gasoline powered vehicle) is part of the choice set of an agent, who has previously used a gasoline powered vehicle (a diesel powered vehicle).

Table 6.2   Definition of Simulation Experiments

Simulation experiment	Introduction of battery electric vehicles	Prices of conventional fuels	Awareness of battery electric vehicles
1: Base run	2012, 2014, 2016*	constant	high
2: Portfolio definition	**all 2012**	constant	high
3: Scenario definition	2012, 2014, 2016*	**increasing**	high
4: Market definition	2012, 2014, 2016*	constant	**very high**

* 2012: small, 2014: compact, 2016: medium

In **Figure 6.3** exemplary simulation results are illustrated. In particular, the average values of the estimated market shares of the powertrains of the 50 simulation runs are shown with regard to the different simulation experiments. The standard deviation is negligibly small. In the diagram on the top, it can be seen that the model is able to reproduce the market shares of gasoline and diesel powered vehicles that have been realized in Germany in 2010 and 2011. Furthermore, the impact of the introduction of battery electric vehicles in 2012, 2014 and 2016 is illustrated for the base run. Especially, the introduction of the battery electric vehicle in the compact class leads to a considerable market share gain, which is due to the high consumer awareness of compact cars. However, only a slow growth of the market shares of the battery electric vehicles can be noticed in the long run. The reason for this lies in the high level of competitiveness of the gasoline and diesel powered vehicles.

To analyze the impact of the parameter variation on the development of the market shares, simulation results of the second to fourth experiment are shown in the diagram on the bottom of **Figure 6.3**. Here, the relative changes of the market shares of the battery electric vehicles with regard to the base run are illustrated. Overall, it should be noticed that the results are sensitive with regard to the parameter variations, both in terms of the level and the development of the market shares. The early introduction of all battery vehicles in 2012 has the lowest influence. In contrast, the increasing fuel prices as well as the very high consumer awareness of battery electric vehicles have a big impact on the market shares. Whereas the rising fuel prices leads to a continuously increasing competitiveness of the battery electric vehicles, the very high consumer awareness enhances the likelihood that a battery electric vehicle is part of an agent's choice set right from the beginning.

Figure 6.3   Simulation Results: Market Share Development of Powertrains

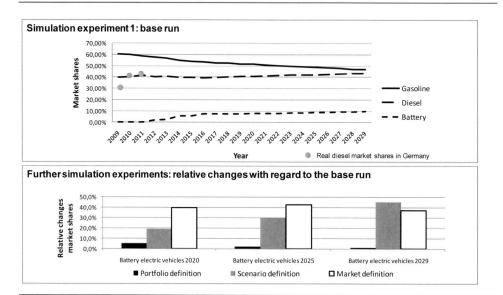

6.5   Conclusion

In this contribution we present a non-traditional, hybrid simulation model of the automotive market to support strategic product portfolio planning with regard to the introduction of alternative powertrains. Individual consumer behavior as well as aggregated system behavior is considered. The hybrid simulation model allows for estimating the development of market shares of various powertrains in different vehicle size classes subject to the vehicle portfolio offered to the market and assumptions about consumer behavior and the market environment.

Based on a literature review we show that the introduction of alternative powertrains leads to new challenges in strategic product portfolio planning. In contrast to the past, automobile manufacturers have to integrate powertrain decisions already into strategic product portfolio planning. To this end, manufacturers have to forecast the market share developments of conventionally and alternatively powered vehicles accurately. Different potential vehicle portfolios as well as the uncertain developments in the market environment have to be taken into account. In this context, a model-based approach is essential due to the high complexity of this task.

We introduce market simulation as an appropriate model-based approach to support the introduction of alternative powertrains. In general, this method allows simulating the consumer response to companies' marketing mix decisions as well as to the competitive and environmental influences. With regard to the automotive market different modeling approaches exists that can be considered as a market simulation. However, none of these approaches meets all of the requirements on a decision support for the strategic product portfolio planning in the automotive industry. This is due to the fact that the models have been developed either to measure individual consumer demand for vehicles on a disaggregated level or to analyze system behavior with regard to the introduction of alternative powertrains on an aggregated level.

For this reason, we develop a non-traditional, hybrid simulation model that integrates an agent based model to consider individual consumer behavior and a system dynamics model to consider aggregated system behavior. By applying this model to an illustrative example, we show that the model meets all of the requirements on a decision support for the strategic product portfolio planning with regard to the introduction of alternative powertrains. The market share developments of the various powertrains can be simulated subject to the vehicle portfolio offered to the market as well as assumptions about consumer behavior and the market environment. First results show that the model is able to sufficiently reproduce the market shares of conventional powertrains of the last few years. The development of the market shares of the battery electric vehicles is sensitive to the assumptions made about the vehicle portfolio, the consumer behavior and the market environment.

Based on the illustrative example well-founded statements about the market development cannot be made so far. The same holds for the derivation of recommendations. To this end, more comprehensive simulation experiments have to be run taking into account realistic scenarios of the market environment and more product portfolio options. The latter requires the consideration of partly electrified powertrains like hybrid or plug-in hybrid powertrains as well as the consideration of more differentiated size classes. This in turn requires the improvement of the data base, for instance with respect to the transition matrices. For this reason, the presented hybrid simulation model is currently being extended to consider party electrified powertrains. Furthermore, the data base is being improved and extended to allow for simulating the market share development of the various powertrains in the EU5 countries (UK, France, Germany, Spain and Italy). The model will be applied to a case study to validate the model behavior comprehensively and to show applicability of the decision support with regard to the strategic product portfolio planning. Additionally, recommendations will be derived concerning the introduction of alternative powertrains in the automotive industry.

Acknowledgement

This research project is partially funded by the German Federal Ministry of Education and Research (BMBF). The authors would like to acknowledge the support of the BMBF for funding the research project "STROM – Strategic options of the automobile industry for the migration towards sustainable powertrains in established and emergent markets" under the reference 01UN1006A. The authors would also like to acknowledge the support of the Volkswagen AG for providing additional funding, data and expert knowledge.

Literature

[1] Achtnicht, M./Bühler, G./Hermeling, C. (2008): Impact of service station networks on purchase decisions of alternative-fuel vehicles, ZEW Discussion Paper No. 08-088. Mannheim: Zentrum für Europäische Wirtschaftsforschung GmbH.

[2] Adelt, B. (2003): Überlegungen zur Weiterentwicklung der Unternehmensplanung bei Volkswagen. Horváth, P./Gleich, R. (Hrsg.): Neugestaltung der Unternehmensplanung: Innovative Konzepte und erfolgreiche Praxislösungen, pp. 451-467. Stuttgart: Schäffer-Poeschel.

[3] Anon (2010): A portfolio of power-trains for Europe: A fact-based analysis: the role of battery electric vehicles, plug-in hybrids, and fuel cell electric vehicles. Available: http://www.zeroemissionvehicles.eu/.

[4] Bass, F. M. (1969): A new product growth for model consumer durables. Management Science, Vol. 15, 5, pp. 215-227.

[5] BenDor, T./Ford, A. (2006): Simulating a combination of feebates and scrappage incentives to reduce automobile emissions. Energy, Vol. 31, 8, pp. 1197-1214.

[6] Berry, S./Levinsohn, J./Pakes, A. (2004): Differentiated products demand systems from a combination of micro and macro data: The new car market. Journal of Political Economy, Vol. 112, 1, pp. 68-105.

[7] Book, M./Groll, M./Mosquet, X./Rizoulis, D./Sticher, G. (2009): The Comeback of the electric car? How real, how soon, and what must happen next. Available: http://www.bcg.com/documents/file15404.pdf.

[8] Borshchev, A./Filippov, A. (2004): From system dynamics and discrete event to practical agent based modeling: reasons, techniques, tools, in: Kennedy, M./Winch, G. W./Langer, R. S./Rowe, J. I./Janni, J. M. (Eds.): Proceedings of the 22nd International Conference of the System Dynamics Society. Oxford.

[9] Bosshardt M./Ulli-Beer, S./Gassmann, F./Wokaun, A. (2008): The effect of multi-incentive policies on the competition of drivetrain technologies. Dangerfield, B. C. (Ed): Proceedings of the 26th International Conference of the System Dynamics Society. Athens.

[10] Brownstone, D./Bunch, D./Train K. E. (2000): Joint mixed logit models of stated and revealed preferences for alternative fuel vehicles. Tranportation Research B, Vol. 34, 5, pp. 315-338.

[11] Bunch, D. S./Bradely, M./Golob, T. F./Kitamura, R./Occhiuzzo, G. P. (1993): Demand for clean-fuel vehicles in California: A discrete-choice stated preference pilot project. Transportation Research A, Vol. 27, 3, pp. 237-253.

[12] CARB (2010): Low-Emission Vehicle Program. Available: http://www.arb.ca.gov/msprog/levprog/levprog.htm.

[13] Cooper, L. G. (2003): Market-Share Models. Eliashberg, J./Lilien, G. J. (Eds.): Handbook in Operations Research and Management Science: Marketing, pp. 259-314. Amsterdam: North-Holland.

[14] De Haan, P./Mueller, M. G./Scholz, R. W. (2009): How much do incentives affect car purchase? Agent-based microsimulation of consumer choice of new cars: Part I: Forecasting effects of feebates based on energy-efficiency. Energy Policy, Vol. 37, 3, pp. 1083-1094.

[15] Diez, W. (1990): Modellzyklen als produktpolitisches Entscheidungsproblem: Erfahrungen und Perspektiven in der deutschen Automobilindustrie. Schmalenbachs Zeitschrift für betriebswirtschaftliche Forschung (Zfbf), Vol. 42, 3, pp. 263-275.

[16] Eggert, W. (2003): Nachfragemodellierung und -prognose zur Unterstützung der langfristigen Absatzplanung am Beispiel der deutschen Automobilindustrie, Dissertation. Karlsruhe: Universität Karlsruhe.

[17] Eliashberg, J./Lilien, G. L. (2003): Mathematical marketing models: some historical perspectives and future projections. Eliashberg, J./Lilien, G. J. (Eds.): Handbook in Operations Research and Management Science: Marketing, pp. 3-23. Amsterdam: North-Holland.

[18] EU (2010): Reducing CO2 emissions from passenger cars. Available: http://ec.europa.eu/clima/policies/transport/vehicles/cars_en.htm.

[19] Forrester, J. W. (1961): Industrial dynamics. Cambridge: MIT Press.

[20] Friedrich, H. E. (2010): Market shares of various powertrains: scenarios till 2030. ATZ autotechnology, Vol. 10, 4, pp. 47-51.

[21] Gilbert, N./Troitzsch, K. G. (2005): Simulation for the social scientist, 2nd edition. Maidenhead: open University Press.

[22] Grube, R. (2003): Das global führende Automobilunternehmen DaimlerChrysler: Strategieentwicklung und deren konsequente Umsetzung. Hungenberg, H./Meffert, J. (Hrsg.): Handbuch Strategisches Management, pp. 89-104. Wiesbaden: Gabler.

[23] Henderson, B. D. (1984): The application and misapplication of the experience curve. Journal of Business Strategy, Vol. 4, 3, pp. 3-9.

[24] Hill, K./Edwards, M./Szakaly, S. (2007): How automakers plan their products: A primer for policy makers on automotive industry business planning. Available: http://www.cargroup.org/documents/ProductDevelopmentFinalReport7-30.a_000.pdf.

[25] IPCC (2007): IPCC Fourth Assessment Report: Climate Change 2007. Available: http://www.ipcc.ch/publications_and_data/publications_and_data_reports.shtml.

[26] Janssen, A./Lienin, S. F./Gassmann, F./Wokaun, A. (2006): Model aided policy development for the market penetration of natural gas vehicles in Switzerland. Transportation Research A, Vol. 40, 4, pp. 316-333.

[27] Kieckhäfer, K./Walther, G./Axmann, J./Spengler, T. (2009): Integrating Agent-based Simulation and System Dynamics to support product strategy decisions in the automotive industry. Rossetti, M. D./Hill, R. R./Johansson, B./Dunkin, A./Ingalls R. G. (Eds.): Proceedings of the 2009 Winter Simulation Conference, pp. 1433-1443. Austin, Texas.

[28] Law, A. M./Kelton, W. D. (2000): Simulation modeling and analysis, 3rd edition. Singapore: McGraw-Hill.

[29] Lilien, G. L./Kotler, P./Moorthy, K. S. (1992): Marketing Models. Englewood Cliffs, New Jersey: Prentice-Hall.

[30] Mahajan, V./Muller, E./Bass, F. M. (2003): New-product diffusion models. Eliashberg, J./Lilien, G. J. (Eds.): Handbook in Operations Research and Management Science: Marketing, pp. 3-23. Amsterdam: North-Holland.

[31] Massy, W. F./Montgomery, D. B./Morrison, D. G. (1970): Stochastic models of buying behavior. Cambridge: MIT Press.

[32] Meyer, P. E./Winebrake, J. J. (2009): Modeling technology diffusion of complementary goods: the case of hydrogen vehicles and refueling infrastructure. Technovation, Vol. 29, 2, pp. 77-91.

[33] Mueller, M. G./de Haan, P. (2006): Autokaufentscheid: Treue zur Marke, zum Fahrzeugsegment, zur Treibstoffart und zum Getriebetyp: Deskriptive Auswertung von Transaktionsdaten. Berichte zum Schweizer Autokaufverhalten Nr. 10. Zürich: ETH Zürich.

[34] Mueller, M. G./De Haan, P. (2009): How much do incentives affect car purchase? Agent-based microsimulation of consumer choice of new cars: Part I: Model structure, simulation of bounded rationality, and model validation. Energy Policy, Vol. 37, 3, pp. 1072-1082.

[35] Niederländer, F. (2000): Dynamik in der internationalen Produktpolitik von Automobilherstellern. Wiesbaden: Gabler.

[36] NHTSA (2011): CAFE - Fuel Economy. Available: http://www.nhtsa.gov/fuel-economy.

[37] OECD/IEA (2008): Word Energy Outlook 2008, Paris: International Energy Agency 2008.

[38] Peters, A./de Haan, P. (2006): Der Autokäufer: seine Charakteristika und Präferenzen: Ergebnisbericht im Rahmen des Projekts „Entscheidungsfaktoren beim Kauf treibstoff-effizienter Neuwagen". Berichte zum Schweizer Autokaufverhalten Nr. 11. Zürich: ETH Zürich.

[39] Pil, F. K./Holweg, M. (2004): Linking product variety to order-fulfillment strategies. Interfaces, Vol. 34, 5, 394-403.

[40] Raasch, C./Schneider, A. S./Friedl, G. (2007): Strategic portfolio planning in industries with long R&D cycles and interrelated product offerings: a practical approach to optimization. International Journal of Technology intelligence and Planning, Vol. 3, 3, pp. 271-291.

[41] Schneider, A. (2006): Die strategische Planung der Produktportfolios bei Automobilherstellern: Konzeption eines Instruments zur Bewertung des Cycle-Plans. Baden-Baden: Nomos.

[42] Sterman, J. (2000): Business dynamics: systems thinking and modeling for a complex world. Boston: Irwin/McGraw-Hill.

[43] Struben, J./Sterman J. D. (2008): Transition challenges for alternative fuel vehicle and transportation systems. Environment and Planning B: Planning and Design, Vol. 35, 6, pp. 1070-1097.

[44] Teichert, T./Shehu, E. (2010): Investigating research streams of conjoint analysis: a bibliometric study. Business Research, Vol. 3, 1, pp. 49-68.

[45] Train, K. E. (2009): Discrete choice methods with simulation, 2nd edition. Cambridge: Cambridge University Press.

[46] Train, K. E./Winston, C. (2007): Vehicle choice behavior and the declining market share of U.S. automakers. International Economy Review, Vol. 48, 4, pp. 1469-1496.

[47] UNFCCC (2011): Greenhouse Gas Inventory Data. Available: http://unfccc.int/ghg_data/items/3800.php.

[48] Urban, G. L./Hauser, J. R./Roberts, J. R. (1990): Prelaunch forecasting of new automobiles. Management Science, Vol. 36, 4, pp. 401-421.

[49] Urban, G. L./Weinberg, B. D./Hauser, J. R. (1996): Premarket forecasting of really-new products. Journal of Marketing, Vol. 60, 1, pp. 47-60.

[50] Walther, G./Wansart, J./Kieckhäfer, K./Schnieder, E./Spengler, T. S. (2010): Impact assessment in the automotive industry: mandatory market introduction of alternative powertrain technologies. System Dynamics Review, Vol. 26, 3, pp. 239-261.

[51] Watanabe, C./Ane, B. K. (2004): Constructing a virtuous cycle of manufacturing agility: concurrent roles of modularity in improving agility and reducing lead time. Technovation, Vol. 24, 7, pp. 573-583.

[52] Wiedmann, K.-P./Löffler, R. (1989): Portfolio-Simulationen und Portfolio-Planspiele als Unterstützungssysteme der strategischen Früherkennung. Raffée, H./Wiedmann, K.-P. (Eds.): Strategisches Marketing, 2nd edition, pp. 419-462. Stuttgart: Poeschel.

[53] Wissema, J. G. (1982): Trends in technology forecasting. R&D Management, Vol. 12, 1, pp. 27-36.

7   Knowledge Generation in Marketing

Peter S. H. Leeflang, University of Groningen, The Netherlands, and Aston Business School, United Kingdom, and LUISS Guido Carli University Rome, Italy

Alessandro M. Peluso, LUISS Guido Carli University Rome, Italy

Abstract

In the present chapter, we briefly discuss how knowledge generation in marketing can be accomplished. In particular, we argue that generalizations offered by meta-analyses are very useful for managers in their decision making. To support this argument, we perform an empirical study on subjective estimations of price elasticities, advertising elasticities, and price promotion elasticities, showing that actual and future managers (i.e., master and PhD students) usually underestimate the effects of price changes, overestimate the impact of advertising, and heavily underestimate that of price promotions. We also demonstrate that subjective estimations improve after being confronted with the outcomes of meta-analyses.

Keywords

Marketing Knowledge, Meta-Analysis, Price Elasticity, Advertising Elasticity, Price Promotion Elasticity.

7.1   Introduction

The past six decades have seen tremendous developments in the generation of marketing knowledge. In this chapter we discuss components of marketing knowledge, known as marketing science. The term "marketing science" was appropriated in the early 1980s by researchers who favor quantitative and analytical approaches. Udo Wagner has contributed to the development of marketing science in a visible manner through his publications, supervision of PhD students, master students and the presentations of his research at many conferences such as the annual conference of the European Marketing Academy (EMAC) and Marketing Science Conferences.

In this paper we start to discuss briefly how knowledge generation in marketing can be accomplished. We will then concentrate on a number of specific outcomes that results from meta-analyses. We demonstrate that this knowledge is highly useful to assist managers and future managers in their decision-making in marketing. We do this through the discussion of outcomes of several surveys that we performed among managers, PhD students and regular master students to measure price and advertising elasticities. We found that each of these groups of respondents underestimate the effects of regular and promotional prices on sales. In contrast, the effects of advertising on sales are overestimated. We also demonstrate that (future) managers can improve their decision-marking through learning from the knowledge generated in marketing.

7.2   Knowledge Generation in Marketing[4]

Decision making in marketing should be based on knowledge about customers, and, more broadly, about market phenomena. In the past six decades, much of this knowledge has been generated, also known as marketing science. Marketing knowledge contains the following components:

- specific knowledge about marketing phenomena
- generalizations and
- models and methods.

7.2.1   Specific Knowledge

First, knowledge about marketing phenomena can be generated through *specific studies*. Consider for example studies that decompose the sales promotion bump into own, cross-brand, and cross-period effects (van Heerde, Leeflang, and Wittink 2004), as well as cross-category effects (Leeflang et al. 2008; Leeflang and Parreño Selva 2012).

---

[4] This text is partly based on Leeflang (2011).

Another example is the successful application of a segmentation, targeting and positioning tool, which provides managers with information on their target markets, customer preferences, competitors' strengths, and customer segments. Natter et al. (2008) developed such a tool for a mobile phone organization selling contracts and cell phones in the Austrian market. Many other examples appear in textbooks, such as those by Kotler and Keller (2006) or the *Handbook of Marketing* (Weitz and Wensley 2002).

Although most specific knowledge refers to companies that provide products and services to (final) customers, we are far from what Hermann Simon (1994) sarcastically called "coffee marketing science." The number of formal applications in business-to-business (B2B) areas is growing in absolute terms—though it remains relatively low, considering the substantial percentage of firms that perform B2B marketing activities. Studies now consider contracts between firms (Bolton, Lemon, and Verhoef 2008), network externalities (Goldenberg, Libai, and Muller 2010), dyadic relationships between firms such as partner selection (Wuyts and Geyskens 2005; Wuyts, Verhoef, and Prins 2009), vertical marketing systems (Wuyts et al. 2004), channel pass-through (Nijs et al. 2010), and cooperation versus competition between manufacturers and retailers (e.g., Ailawadi, Kopalle, and Neslin, 2005; Villas-Boas and Zhao, 2005).

Specific topics that have not yet received (much) attention include empirical studies of sponsoring, investments in experience marketing (Tynan and McKechnie 2009), and opportunities for social media effects. Other topics that lack sufficient knowledge as of yet are the best practices for marketing planning procedures and the composition of marketing plans, though well-known handbooks offer some exceptions (e.g., Greenley 1986; Hiebig and Cooper 2003).

7.2.2 Generalized Knowledge

Generalized knowledge about market phenomena can be generated by: a. finding regularities, b. using panel data, c. meta-analysis, and d. simulation.

■ Regularities

Finding regularities is the first source that is considered to generate knowledge. This form of knowledge creation has been strongly advocated by Ehrenberg (1972, 1988, 1995). Udo Wagner has contributed much to the generation of this knowledge through the development and application of "multivariate polya models" of brand choice and purchase incidences (Wagner and Taudes 1986) and the development and application of binominal/Dirichlet and multinominal/Dirichlet models on preferences scores (Bemmaor and Wagner 2000).

■ Panel data

Generalized knowledge also derives from studies that cover many circumstances (usually with multiple cross-sectional units, such as brands, markets, or countries) and relatively long time periods. Often panel data aids in this purpose.

For example, Deleersnyder et al. (2009) investigate the cyclical sensitivity of advertising expenditures in 37 countries in four key media forms (magazines, newspapers, radio, and television). For 85 country–media combinations, these authors use 25 years of data to explain differences between cyclical sensitivity over media and countries. And they show that advertising is considerably more sensitive to business-cycle fluctuations than is the economy as a whole. Countries in which advertising behaves more cyclically exhibit slower growth in their advertising industry. Furthermore, private labels are growing in countries characterized by more cyclical spending. Another finding shows that stock price performance is lower for companies that exhibit procyclical advertising spending patterns.

Other examples of this type of knowledge generation include Nijs et al. (2001), Steenkamp et al. (2005), and Lamey et al. (2007).

■ Meta-analyses

Meta-analyses offer statistical assessments of the results from several individual studies to generalize their findings (Wold 1986), as exemplified by Bijmolt, Van Heerde, and Pieters (2005), and Kremer et al. (2008). Krycha and Wagner (1999) performed a meta-analyses with respect to the methods used and the results achieved applying artificial neural networks. For many other examples, see Hanssens (2009).

■ Simulation experiments

Generalized knowledge also can be obtained through simulation experiments, as used by Andrews et al. (2008), who investigate whether and how heterogeneity in marketing mix effects, both between and within segments of stores, affects model fit, forecasts, and the accuracy of marketing mix elasticities. Contrary to expectations, accommodating store-level heterogeneity does not improve the accuracy of marketing mix elasticities relative to a homogeneous (SCAN*PRO) model. Improvements in fit and forecasting accuracy are also fairly modest. In another simulation study, Andrews, Currim, and Leeflang (2011) show that demand models with various heterogeneity specifications and using consumer panel data and store-level data, do not produce more accurate sales response predictions than does a homogeneous demand model applied to store-level data.

■ More about generalizations

Although most generalizations refer to frequently bought consumer products, more and more publications feature empirical generalizations in B2B marketing settings (see Hanssens 2009). Yet there are few formal generalizations about the marketing of services, though some examples can be found in Muller, Peres, and Mahajan (2009) and in the literature on retailing (see the special issue of the *Journal of Retailing*, 85(1), 2009).

Thus, there is still substantial room for generating empirical generalizations in areas such as B2B, services, and the relations of performance measures, including commitment, loyalty, satisfaction, and financial metrics (cf., Gupta and Zeithaml 2006). Corporate social responsibility and financial metrics (van Diepen, Donkers, and Franses 2009; Hung and Wyer, 2009; Lusch and Webster 2010; Sen and Bhattacharya 2001), international marketing strategies (Burgess and Steenkamp 2006), the effects of advertising content (Aribarg, Pieters, and Wedel 2010; Pieters, Wedel, and Batra 2010), non-price promotions, co-branding (Helmig, Huber, and Leeflang 2008), and the effects of frontline employees represent additional key topics (Di Mascio 2010).

An area that demands both specific and generalized knowledge is customer-to-customer (C2C) marketing. To the best of our knowledge, there is hardly any extant knowledge about transactions on sites such as eBay or in second-hand markets or garage sales. Another interesting research area, still in development, is the modeling of WoM (Van Eck, Jager, and Leeflang 2012).

Finally, we want to highlight the potential for generalizations of consumer behavior. The first decade of model building for marketing centered on the numerical specification of models with substantial behavioral detail, modeled at the individual customer demand level. Behavior results from a complex interaction of model components. For example, Amstutz (1967) explicitly models variables such as perceived need, awareness, attitudes, perceived brand image, and so on. Farley and Ring (1970) even tried to calibrate Howard and Sheth's (1969) customer behavior model, though without much success. Yet it remains remarkable that the numerical specification of general, formalized customer behavior models has received so little attention, even as attention has shifted to the various partial models that shed some light on customer behavior. The popularity of experimentation among behavioral scientists may explain this trend.

7.2.3   Models and Methods

In this sub-section we concentrate on developments in "marketing science-type" models. For extensive reviews of these models, see for example monographs by Blattberg, Kim, and Neslin (2008); Leeflang et al. (2000); Lilien, Rangaswamy, and De Bruyn (2007); and Wieringa (2008), as well as review articles by Bijmolt et al. (2010); Leeflang et al. (2009); Leeflang and Hunneman (2010); Leeflang and Wittink (2000), and Wierenga, Van Bruggen, and Staelin (1999). Finally, we refer readers to the special *IJRM* issue on "Marketing Modeling on the Threshold of the 21st Century" (Vol. 17, no 2-3).

Early model building in marketing started by applying organizational (OR) and marketing science (MS) methods to a marketing framework. Less well known is that early demand equations were based on an *economic theory* of customer behavior.

The modeling of optimal marketing behavior in different types of oligopolistic markets (Lambin, Naert, and Bultez 1975), which simultaneously consider demand and supply relations, offers another example of early research based on economic theory. This fundamental approach has been worked out in more detail and in different directions by Plat and Leeflang (1988), Leeflang and Wittink (1992, 1996, 2001), and Horvath et al. (2005). A current revival thus seems to emphasize models based on economic theory (e.g., structural models; Chintagunta et al. 2006).

Early model building paid substantial attention to stochastic customer behavior models, such as Markov (Leeflang 1974; Leeflang and Koerts 1974), learning (Leeflang and Boonstra 1982; Lilien 1974a, 1974b; Wierenga 1974, 1978), Bernoulli (Wierenga 1974) and purchase incidence models, including Poisson-type purchase models (Ehrenberg 1959, 1972). Wagner and Taudes (1987) reviewed these stochastic models of consumer behavior. Thus another recent revival centers on stochastic customer behavior models that modify Markov models (e.g., hidden Markov models; Netzer, Lattin, and Srinivasan 2008) and the frequent use of Poisson processes (Van Nierop et al. 2011).

The developments and/or application of statistical methods and tools also contribute to advance marketing knowledge. As an example we mention a study developed a statistical testing sequence that allows for the endogenous determination of potential market changes due to competitive entries in existing markets (Kornelis, Dekimpe, and Leeflang 2008). Other examples include the introduction and use of dynamic linear models in marketing (Ataman, Mela, and Van Heerde 2007, 2008; Van Heerde, Mela, and Manchanda 2004), spatial models (Bronnenberg and Mahajan 2001; Van Dijk et al. 2004), semi-parametric estimation (Rust 1988; Van Heerde, Leeflang, and Wittink 2001), and the "revival" of Kalman filtering (Osinga, Leeflang, and Wieringa 2010; Osinga et al. 2011).

Of the many promising research avenues we mention the modeling of the choice behavior of multiple agents and the use of agent-based modeling and social simulation. Examples of models that consider multiple agents are the studies of intra-household behavioral interactions (Yang et al. 2010; Aribarg, Arara, and Kang 2010), interactions between physicians and patients in the choice of new drugs (Ding and Eliashberg 2008), and extended interactions between manufacturers and retailers (Ailawadi et al. 2005; Villas-Boas and Zhao 2005).

Goldenberg et al. (2007) use an agent-based approach to simulate the effects of negative news about the firm and/or its products on the net present value of a firm. Combinations of empirical data and simulated data also offer key opportunities to study (individual) customer behavior in the future (Van Eck, Jager, and Leeflang 2011).

The development of models and methods to support decision making is not without problems though, and several issues demand more adequate answers. First, vast numbers of firms do not make data-driven marketing decisions, often because of their limited capacities (e.g., time, money, capabilities) to collect data about relevant metrics. Nor do most firms estimate relations between the metrics they have. Subjective estimation methods thus would be useful tools in these cases. The development of relatively simple methods to establish relations between marketing efforts and marketing performance measures for these firms would be widely welcomed.

Second, even firms that can collect appropriate data face problems. Well-known modeling issues include error-in-variables, (unobserved) heterogeneity, and endogeneity (Shugan 2006). Despite commendable progress in challenging endogeneity problems (Gupta and Park 2009; Kuskov and Villas-Boas 2008; Petrin and Train 2010), many solutions remain complicated and model specific.

Third, marketing model building usually centers more on the specification and calibration of the demand side rather than the supply side. More recently, the simultaneity of demand and supply relations has received greater attention in so-called structural models (Dubé et al. 2002; Chintagunta et al. 2006; see also commentaries in *Marketing Science*, vol. 25, no. 6), which "rely on economic and/or marketing theories of consumer or firm behavior to derive the econometric specification that can be taken to data" (Chintagunta et al. 2006, 604).

Consider, for example, Draganska and Jain (2004), who estimate market equilibrium models; Kim et al. (2010), who assess user demand for competing products; Liu's (2010) investigation of alternative pricing strategies; and Musalem et al.'s (2010) effort to measure the effects of out-of-stock situations. These models attempt to optimize the behavior of agents, manufacturers, wholesalers, retailers, and customers. Structural models therefore offer excellent opportunities, at least in principle, to (1) test behavioral assumptions, (2) investigate alternative strategies through policy simulations, and (3) eliminate or reduce endogeneity problems. As outlined previously, this approach is not really new, and Chintagunta et al. (2006) demand that we recognize the drawbacks of structural models, such as their strong identification of mostly parametric assumptions, because otherwise no optimal behavior can be determined. Furthermore, builders of structural marketing models must rely on insufficiently developed theories.

Given shortcomings, a comparison between structural and reduced-form models offers an interesting research area. Skiera (2010) has compared both models (to improve pricing decisions) and concluded that each has unique characteristics and offers promise for different areas of application. An even more profound analysis may lead to a better evaluation of the advantages of structural models compared with reduced-form equations.

Finally, we emphasize the many opportunities to advance our knowledge in the interdisciplinary marketing discipline using theories developed in other sciences, such as economics and psychology. Even flashbacks to theories and models that were developed decades ago may be useful tools in this respect.

In what follows we elaborate on knowledge generation through meta-analyses. In a MSI-monograph, Hanssens (2009) collected many outcomes on, e.g., price elasticities, advertising elasticities, and price promotion elasticities that are based on meta-analyses. We briefly discuss outcomes in the following section.

7.3   Empirical Generalizations About Price and Advertising Impact

7.3.1   Pricing

In the past decades, at least two meta-analyses have generalized knowledge about price-to-sales elasticities for consumer packaged goods. In an influential meta-analytical study, Tellis (1988) summarized price elasticity research findings until 1986. This generalizations are based on 367 price elasticities. The average price-to-sales elasticity that has been found by Tellis is -1.76.

Bijmolt, Van Heerde, and Pieters (2005) updated Tellis' (1988) generalizations. Their meta-analysis includes 1851 price elasticities covering the period 1961 to 2004. The overall mean elasticity in their meta-analysis is -2.62. The distribution is strongly peaked; 50% of the observations are between -3 and -1 and 81% are between -4 and 0. Furthermore, 2.2% of the price elasticities are positive.

7.3.2   Advertising

There are a number of meta-analyses that report average sales-to-advertising elasticities. Sethuraman and Tellis (1991) performed a meta-analysis of over 262 brand level elasticities and found an average sales-to-advertising elasticity of .1. It is higher for new products than for established products and higher for durables than non-durables. In a recent study, Sethuraman, Tellis, and Briesch (2011) find an average short term elasticity of .12. This study is based on 751 short term direct-to-consumer brand advertising elasticities

Lodish et al. (1995) found slightly higher average TV advertising to sales elasticity: .11 for established consumer products in more than 200 real world TV advertising tests conducted by IRI. However, a high variability in effects are around those elasticities. Some tests had elasticities over .5 and others were even negative.

7.3.3   Price Promotions

Price promotions lead to strong temporary sales increases for the promoted brands. The average price promotion elasticity is -3.63, meaning that 1% in promotional price discount leads to a 3.63% increase in sales (Van Heerde 2009). Hence price promotion elasticities are larger in absolute size than regular price elasticities.

Table 7.1 summarizes the estimated values of the parameters of interest, based on the outcomes of the meta-analyses.

Table 7.1	Parameter Estimates Based on Meta-Analyses	
(Regular) Price	**Advertising**	**Price Promotion**
-2.62	.12	-3.63

7.4   Subjective Estimation

The elasticities we discussed in the preceding section are based on objective data. The knowledge which generated through these meta-analyses could be used for decision-making in marketing. There are a large number of situations in which parameterization on the basis of objective data is impossible. If objective data do not suffice to obtain reliable parameter estimates, all is not lost. Decision markers always make-be it often implicitly-judgments about (response) parameters. In what follows we will confront these judgments with the estimated values of response parameter based on the outcomes of meta-analyses.

7.4.1   Method

We collected data on three samples. These are samples of master students (116 observations), PhD students (36 observations), and managers (60 observations). These data are obtained through questionnaires in which individual participants had to specify the impact on sales of L'Oreal shampoo at different:

- regular prices

- advertising expenditures, and

- promotional prices.

- Appendix A includes the questionnaire.

Regression analysis was run on each sample and on the pooled dataset, using the Ordinary Least Squares with Dummy Variables (OLSDV) approach, to estimate elasticities based on multiplicative analytical models with the following structure:

$$Sales_{ij} = \alpha_k \times (Price_{ij})^{\beta_k} e^{u_{ij}} \tag{7.1}$$

where k indicates the subsample (k = 1, 2, 3, for the three subsamples), i refers to the respondent and j to a particular price that has been considered in this experiment (10% decrease, 20% decrease, 10% increase, 20% decrease), and u_{ij} is a disturbance term. Hence we estimate equations such as (7.1) using subjective data.

a. Regular price

Table 7.2 includes the estimated constant price elasticities for the different samples of respondents and a number of statistical outcomes.

From **Table 7.2** we conclude that:

■ all three subsamples underestimate the effects of price changes, where

■ the PhD students are more closer to the average price parameters estimates based on the
   outcomes of meta-analyses (compare Table 7.1); the elasticities of the three subsamples
   are significantly different given the F-value of the Chow test.

Table 7.2   Estimated Price Elasticities Based on Subjective Data

Sample	Obs.	Elasticity (Std. error)	R^2	R^2 adj.	Std. error of estimate	F-value
Managers	60	-.653 (.095)	.448	.439	.12	47.14
PhD students	36	-1.127 (.103)	.778	.772	.09	119.45
Students	116	-.577 (.042)	.621	.618	.07	186.97
Pooled data	212	-.692 (.042)	a	a	.10	118593.94

Chow test: $F(2, 206) = 12.81$, Critical F-value $= F(2, 206) = 3.04$ ($\alpha = .05$).

When estimating parameters with OLSDV, the values of R^2 and R^2 adj. are not correct,
and for that reason we do not show the values of these statistics.

b. Advertising

The advertising elasticities are obtained in a similar way as the (regular) price elasticities
through a multiplicative demand equation with a similar structure as equation (7.1). **Table
7.3** summarizes main findings and statistics.

Hence we conclude that participants usually <u>over</u>estimate the effect of advertising. The
value of the Chow test indicates that the estimates of advertising elasticities are in the same
order of magnitude for all groups.

Table 7.3 Estimated Advertising Elasticities Based on Subjective Data

Sample	Obs.	Elasticity (Std. error)	R^2	R^2 adj.	Std. error of estimate	F-value
Managers	60	.478 (.074)	.417	.407	.09	41.52
PhD students	36	.692 (.079)	.695	.686	.08	77.44
Students	174	.467 (.028)	.618	.616	.13	278.74
Pooled data	270	.477 (.024)	a	a	.12	106217.88

Chow test: $F(2, 264) = 1.64$, Critical F-value $= F(2, 264) = 3.03$ ($\alpha = .05$).

When estimating parameters with OLSDV, the values of R^2 and R^2 adj. are not given.

c. Price promotions

Again we collected data on three samples of master students (87 observations), PhD students (27 observations), and managers (45 observations).

Table 7.4 Estimated Sales Promotion Elasticities Based on Subjective Data

Sample	Obs.	Elasticity (Std. error)	R^2	R^2 adj.	Std. error of estimate	F-value
Managers	45	-.365 (.071)	.380	.366	.12	26.38
PhD students	27	-.486 (.098)	.496	.476	.13	24.64
Students	87	-.324 (.050)	.329	.321	.12	41.71
Pooled data	159	-.363 (.038)	a	a	.12	61827.74

Chow test: $F(2, 153) = 1.19$, Critical F-value $= F(2, 153) = 3.06$ ($\alpha = .05$).

When estimating parameters with OLSDV, the values of R^2 and R^2 adj. are not given.

These data regarded individual perceptions of sales changes as a function of a temporary price cut. Regression analysis was run on each sample and on the pooled dataset to estimate the effect of temporary price cuts on sales. Again we used a multiplicative demand equation such as (7.1). **Table 7.4** includes the price promotional elasticities for the three samples and the pooled data.

The value of the Chow test reveals that the data over the three subsamples can be pooled. Hence we observe a substantial deviation from the estimated elasticities and the average estimated value of sales promotion elasticities from the meta-analyses (see **Table 7.1**: estimated value = -3.63). This value is ten times as large as the perceived effectiveness of sales promotions as estimated by the participants in our samples. Also the absolute values of the sales promotion elasticities are smaller than those of the estimated (regular) price elasticities.

7.5   Learning Effects

In this section we will answer the question whether "the sensitivity" for sensitivities (as measured by elasticities) can be improved through teaching. More specially, if we confront people with the generated knowledge about elasticities will that influence their subjective estimates of the effects of Marketing effects on sales?

This question is answered by asking the master students to fill in the questionnaire again after they have been confronted during their master course on marketing management with outcomes of the meta-analyses on:

■ price elasticities,

■ advertising elasticities, and

■ sales promotion elasticities (price promotions).

In this course they were (at that time) not confronted with the outcomes of generalizations about the effects of price promotions. Table 7.5 shows a comparison of the elasticities which have been obtained before and after confrontation of the students with the outcomes of the meta-analyses.

Table 7.5   Estimated Elasticities Before and After Learning Experiences (Master Students)

Condition	Price elasticity	Advertising elasticity	Sales promotion elasticity
Before confrontation with outcomes of meta-analyses	-.577 (.042)	.467 (.028)	-.324 (.050)
After confrontation with outcomes of meta-analyses (post-learning)	-.900 (.050)	.378 (.015)	-.319 (.029)
Chow test:	$F(1, 408) = 15.04$, Critical F-value = $F(1, 408) = 3.86$ ($\alpha = .05$)	$F(1, 614) = 8.83$, Critical F-value = $F(1, 614) = 3.86$ ($\alpha = .05$)	$F(1, 290) = 0.1$, Critical F-value = $F(1, 290) = 3.87$ ($\alpha = .05$)

By pooling the data that refer to prior and after the learning experiment and performing Chow test we conclude that:

1. The estimates for the (regular) price elasticities are significantly different and are closer (higher in absolute value) to the average price-to-sales elasticities that have been found in the meta-analyses.

2. The advertising elasticities are significantly lower after the learning experiment and closer to the meta-analytic finding.

3. There is no significant difference between the sales promotion price parameters that have been estimated using the data from both samples.

Hence we conclude that confronting (future) managers with generalizations which are found in marketing may assist them in improving their feeling for sensitivities which ultimately must lead to better decision making in marketing. This decision making is based on knowledge generated in marketing.

7.6   Summary and Conclusions

In this contribution we briefly discussed different ways to generate knowledge in marketing. We spent some attention to the generation of estimates of a number of elasticities of frequently bought consumer goods.

We also determined corresponding elasticities on the basis of subjective estimates of sales conditional on different values for price, advertising and price promotions. We asked managers, PhD students and master students to specify their demand estimates under different conditions. We confronted the master students a number of weeks that we performed the first survey with the outcomes of average price and advertising-to-sales elasticities. After a number of weeks we asked these students to participate again in our survey. We find that the knowledge to which they have been confronted influence their demand estimates in such a way that the estimated parameters that are based on these demand estimates are significantly closer to the "true" elasticities. Hence we conclude that knowledge generation in marketing may contribute to better decision making. We thank in this way Udo Wagner for his contributions to the generation of knowledge in marketing.

Appendix

Table 7.6   Product Group: Shampoo – L'OREAL – Price per Bottle € 3.60

Regular price	Questions What is the increase or decrease of the demand in percentages?
* Assume the price of this brand will decrease with 10 percent:	_____
The same with a decrease of 20 percent	_____
The same with an increase of 10 percent	_____
The same with an increase of 20 percent	_____
Advertisements	
* The expenses for advertisements increase with 10%	_____
The same with an increase of 20%	_____
The same with an increase of 50%	_____
The same with a decrease of 10%	_____
The same with a decrease of 20%	_____
The same with a decrease of 50%	_____
This all with regard to the demand of the brand within a year	
Price promotions	
* A temporary price cut will be given	
Of 10 percent	_____
Of 20 percent	_____
Of 50 percent	_____

Literature

[1] Ailawadi, K. L./Kopalle, P. K./Neslin, S.A. (2005): Predicting competitive response to a major policy change: combining game-theoretic and empirical analyses. Marketing Science, Vol. 24, 1, pp. 12-24.

[2] Amstutz, A. E. (1967): Computer simulations of competitive marketing response. Cambridge: MIT Press.

[3] Andrews, R. L./Currim, I. S./Leeflang, P. S. H. (2011): A comparison of sales response predictions from demand models applied to store-level vs. panel data. Journal of Business and Economic Statistics, Vol. 29, 2, pp. 319-326.

[4] Andrews, R. L./Currim, I. S./Leeflang, P. S. H./Lim, J. (2008): Estimating the SCAN*PRO Model of stores sales: HB, FM or Just OLS? International Journal of Research in Marketing, Vol. 25, 1, pp. 22-33.

[5] Aribarg, A./Arara, N./Kang, M.Y. (2010): Predicting joined choice using individual data. Marketing Science, Vol. 29, 1, pp. 139-157.

[6] Aribarg, A./Pieters, R./Wedel, M. (2010): Raising the BAR: Bias adjustment of recognition tests in advertising. Journal of Marketing Research, Vol. 47, 3, pp. 387-400.

[7] Ataman, M. B./Mela, C. F./Van Heerde, H. J. (2007): Consumer packaged goods in France: national brands, regional chains, and local branding. Journal of Marketing Research, Vol. 44, 1, pp. 14-20.

[8] Ataman, M. B./Mela, C. F./Van Heerde, H. J. (2008): Building brands. Marketing Science, Vol. 27, 6, pp. 1036-1054.

[9] Bemmaor, A. C./Wagner, U. (2000): A multiple-item model of paired comparisons: separating chance from latent preference. Journal of Marketing Research, Vol. 37, 4, pp. 514-524.

[10] Bijmolt, T. H. A./Leeflang, P. S. H./Block, F./Eisenbeiss, M./Hardie, B. G. S./Lemmens, A./Saffert, P. (2010): Analytics for customer engagement. Journal of Service Research, Vol. 13, 3, pp. 341-356.

[11] Bijmolt, T. H. A./Van Heerde, H. J./Pieters, R. G. M. (2005): New empirical generalizations on the determinants of price elasticity. Journal of Marketing Research, Vol. 42, 2, pp. 141-156.

[12] Blattberg, R. C./Kim, B. D./Neslin, S. A. (2008): Database marketing: analyzing and managing customers. New York: Springer.

[13] Bolton, R. M./Lemon, K. M./Verhoef, P. C. (2008): Expanding business-to-business customer relationships: modeling the customer's upgrade decision. Journal of Marketing, Vol. 72, 1, pp. 46-64.

[14] Bronnenberg, B. J./Mahajan, V. (2001): Unobserved retailer behavior in multimarket data: joint spatial dependence in market shares and promotion variables. Marketing Science, Vol. 20, 3, pp. 284-300.

[15] Burgess, S. M., & Steenkamp, J. E. M. (2006). Marketing renaissance: how research in emerging markets advances marketing science and practice. International Journal of Research in Marketing, 23(4), 337-356.

[16] Chintagunta, P./Erdem, T./Rossi, P. E./Wedel, M. (2006): Structural modeling in marketing: review and assessment. Marketing Science, Vol. 25, 6, pp. 604-616.

[17] Deleersnyder, B./Dekimpe, M. G./Steenkamp, J. E. M./Leeflang, P. S. H. (2009): The role of national culture in advertising sensitivity to business cycles: an investigation across continents. Journal of Marketing Research, Vol. 46, 5, pp. 623-636.

[18] Di Mascio, R. (2010): The service models of frontline employees. Journal of Marketing, Vol. 74, 4, pp. 63-80.

[19] Ding, M./Eliashberg, J. (2008): A dynamic competitive forecasting model incorporating dyadic decision making. Management Science, Vol. 54, 4, pp. 820-834.

[20] Draganska, M./Jain, D. (2004): A likelihood approach to estimating market equilibrium models. Management Science, Vol. 50, 5, pp. 605-616.

[21] Dubé, J./Chintagunta, P./Petrin, A./Bronnenberg, B./Goettler, R./Seetharaman, P. B./Sudhir, K./Thomadsen, R./Zhao, Y. (2002): Structural application of the discrete choice model. Marketing Letters, Vol. 13, 3, pp. 207-220.

[22] Ehrenberg, A. S. C. (1959): The pattern of consumer purchases. Applied Statistics, Vol. 8, 1, pp. 26-41.

[23] Ehrenberg, A. S. C. (1972): Repeat-buying: theory and applications. Amsterdam: North-Holland Pub. Co.

[24] Ehrenberg, A. S. C. (1988): Repeat-Buying: facts, theory and applications (2nd edition). London: Oxford University Press.

[25] Ehrenberg, A. S. C. (1995): Empirical generalizations, theory and method. Marketing Science, Vol. 14, 3, pp. 195-196.

[26] Farley, J. U./Ring, L.W. (1970): An empirical test of the Howard-Sheth Model of buying behavior. Journal of Marketing Research, Vol. 7, 4, pp. 427-438.

[27] Goldenberg, J./Libai, B./Moldovan, S./Muller, E. (2007): The NPV of bad news. International Journal of Research in Marketing, Vol. 24, 3, pp. 186-200.

[28] Goldenberg, J./Libai, B./Muller, E. (2010): The chilling effects of network externalities. International Journal of Research in Marketing, Vol. 27, 1, pp. 4-15.

[29] Greenley, G. E. (1986): The strategic and operational planning of marketing. Maidenhead: McGraw-Hill Book Company.

[30] Gupta, S./Park, S. (2009): Simulated maximum likelihood estimator for the random coefficient Logit model using aggregate data. Journal of Marketing Research, Vol. 46, 4, pp. 531-542.

[31] Gupta, S./Zeithaml, V. (2006): Customer metrics and their impact on financial performance. Marketing Science, Vol. 25, 6, pp. 718-739.

[32] Hanssens, D. M. (2009): Empirical generalizations about marketing impact. Cambridge: Marketing Science Institute.

[33] Helmig, B./Huber, J. A./Leeflang, P. S. H. (2008): Co-branding: the state-of-the-art. Schmalenbach Business Review, Vol. 60, October, pp. 359-377.

[34] Hiebig, R. G./Cooper, S.W. (2003): The successful marketing plan (3rd edition). New York: McGraw-Hill.

[35] Horvath, C./Leeflang, P. S. H./Wieringa, J. E./Wittink, D.R. (2005): Competitive reaction- and feedback effects based on VARX models of pooled store data. International Journal of Research in Marketing, Vol. 22, 4, pp. 415-426.

[36] Howard, J. A./Sheth, J. N. (1969): The theory of buyer behavior, New York: Wiley.

[37] Hung, I. W./Wyer, R.S. (2009): Differences in perspective and the influence of charitable appeals: when imagining oneself as the victim is not beneficial. Journal of Marketing Research, Vol. 46, 3, pp. 421-434.

[38] Kim, Y./Telang, R./Vogt, W. B./Krishnan, R. (2010): An empirical analysis of mobile voice service and SMS: a structural model. Management Science, Vol. 56, 2, pp. 234-252.

[39] Kornelis, M./Dekimpe, M. G./Leeflang, P. S. H. (2008): Does competitive entry structurally change key marketing metrics. International Journal of Research in Marketing, Vol. 25, 3, pp. 173-182.

[40] Kotler, P./Keller, K. (2006): Marketing Management., Upper Saddle River (NJ): Pearson Education.

[41] Kremer, S. T. M./Bijmolt, T. H. A./Leeflang, P. S. H./Wieringa, J. E. (2008): Generalizations on the effectiveness of pharmaceutical promotional expenditures. International Journal of Research in Marketing, Vol. 25, 4, pp. 234-246.

[42] Krycha, K. A./Wagner, U. (1999): Applications of artificial neural networks in management science: a survey. Journal of Retailing and Consumer Services, Vol. 6, pp. 185-203.

[43] Kuskov, E./Villas-Boas, J. M. (2008): Endogeneity and individual consumer choice. Journal of Marketing Research, Vol. 45, 6, pp. 702-714.

[44] Lambin, J. J./Naert, P. A./Bultez, A. V. (1975): Optimal marketing behavior in oligopoly. European Economic Review, Vol. 6, 2, pp. 105-128.

[45] Lamey, L./Deleersnyder, B./Dekimpe, M. G./Steenkamp, J. E. M. (2007): How business cycles contribute to private-label success: evidence from the United States and Europe. Journal of Marketing, Vol. 71, 1, pp. 1-15.

[46] Leeflang, P. S. H. (1974): Mathematical models in marketing. Leiden: H.E. Stenfert Kroese.

[47] Leeflang, P. S. H (2011): Paving the way for "distinguished marketing". International Journal of Research in Marketing, Vol. 28, 2, pp. 76-88.

[48] Leeflang, P. S. H./Bijmolt, T. H. A./Van Doorn, J./Hanssens, D. M./Van Heerde, H. J./Verhoef, P. C./Wieringa, J. E. (2009): Creating lift versus building the base: current trends in marketing dynamics. International Journal of Research in Marketing, Vol. 26, 1, pp. 13-20.

[49] Leeflang, P. S. H./Boonstra, A. (1982): Some comments on the development and application of linear learning models. Marketing Science, Vol. 28, 11, pp. 1233-1246.

[50] Leeflang, P. S. H./Hunneman, A. (2010): Modeling market response: trends and developments. Marketing - Journal of Research and Management, Vol. 6, 1, pp. 71-80.

[51] Leeflang, P. S. H./Koerts, J. (1974): Some applications of mathematical response models in marketing, based on Markovian consumer behavior model. Conference proceedings: ESOMAR-seminar, Amsterdam, the Netherlands, pp. 287-319.

[52] Leeflang, P. S. H./Parreño Selva, J. (2012): Cross-category demand effects of price promotions. Journal of the Academy of Marketing Science, forthcoming.

[53] Leeflang, P. S. H./Parreño Selva, J./Van Dijk, A./Wittink, D. R. (2008): Decomposing the sales promotion bump accounting for cross-category effects. International Journal of Research in Marketing, Vol. 25, 3, pp. 201-214.

[54] Leeflang, P. S. H./Wittink, D. R. (1992): Diagnosing competitive reactions using (aggregated) scanner data. International Journal of Research in Marketing, Vol. 9, 1, pp. 39-57.

[55] Leeflang, P. S. H./Wittink, D. R. (1996): Competitive reactions versus consumer response: do managers overreact? International Journal of Research in Marketing, Vol. 13, 2, pp. 103-119.

[56] Leeflang, P. S. H./Wittink, D. R. (2000): Building models for marketing decisions: past, present and future. International Journal of Research in Marketing, Vol. 17, 2/3, pp. 105-126.

[57] Leeflang, P. S. H./Wittink, D. R. (2001): Explaining competitive reaction effects. International Journal of Research in Marketing, Vol. 18, 1/2, pp. 119-137.

[58] Leeflang, P. S. H./Wittink, D. R./Wedel, M./Naert, P. A. (2000): Building models for marketing decisions. Boston: Kluwer Academic Publishers.

[59] Lilien, G. L. (1974a): A modified linear learning model of buying behavior. Marketing Science, Vol. 20, 7, pp. 1027-1036.

[60] Lilien, G. L. (1974b): Application of a modified linear learning model of buying behavior. Journal of Marketing Research, Vol. 11, 3, pp. 279-285.

[61] Lilien, G. L./Rangaswamy, A./De Bruyn, A. (2007): Principles of marketing engineering. Bloomington: Trafford Publishing.

[62] Liu, H. (2010): Dynamics of pricing in the video game console market: skimming or penetration? Journal of Marketing Research, Vol. 47, 3, pp. 428-443.

[63] Lodish, L. M./Abraham, M./Kalmenson, S./Livelsberger, J./Lubetkin, B./Richardson, B./Stevens, M.E. (1995): How T.V. advertising works: a meta-analysis of 389 real world split cable T.V. advertising experiments. Journal of Marketing Research, Vol. 32, 2, pp. 125-139.

[64] Lusch, R.F./Webster, C. (2010): Marketing's responsibility for the value of the firm. Marketing Science Institute, Working paper.

[65] Muller, E./Peres, R./Mahajan, V. (2009): Innovation diffusion and new product growth. Cambridge: Marketing Science Institute.

[66] Musalem, A./Olivares, M./Bradlow, E. T./Terwiesch, C./Corsten, D. (2010): Structural estimation of the effect of out-of-stocks. Management Science, Vol. 56, 7, pp. 1180-1197.

[67] Natter, M./Mild, A./Wagner, U./Taudes, A. (2008): Planning new tariffs at Tele.Ring: the application and impact of an integrated segmentation, targeting, and positioning tool. Marketing Science, Vol. 27, 4, pp. 600-609.

[68] Netzer, O./Lattin, J. M./Srinivasan, V. (2008): A hidden Markov model of customer relationship dynamics. Marketing Science, Vol. 27, 2, pp. 185-204.

[69] Nijs, V. R./Dekimpe, M. G./Hanssens, D.M./Steenkamp, J. E. M. (2001): The category-demand effects of price promotions. Marketing Science, Vol. 20, 1, pp. 1-22.

[70] Nijs, V. R./Misra, K./Anderson, E. T./Hansen, K./Krishnamurthi, L. (2010): Channel pass-through of trade promotions. Marketing Science, Vol. 29, 2, pp. 250-267.

[71] Osinga, E. C./Leeflang P. S. H./Srinivasan, S./Wieringa, J. E. (2011): Why do firms invest in consumer advertising with limited sales response? A shareholder perspective. Journal of Marketing, Vol. 75, 1, pp. 109-124.

[72] Osinga, E. C./Leeflang, P. S. H./Wieringa, J. E. (2010): Early marketing matters: a time-varying parameter approach to persistence modeling. Journal of Marketing Research, Vol. 47, 1, pp. 173-185.

[73] Petrin, A./Train, K. (2010): A control function approach to endogeneity in consumer choice models. Journal of Marketing Research, Vol. 47, 1, pp. 3-13.

[74] Pieters, R./Wedel, M./Batra, R. (2010): The shopping power of advertising: measures and effects of visual complexity. Journal of Marketing, Vol. 74, 5, pp. 48-60.

[75] Plat, F. W./Leeflang, P. S. H. (1988): Decomposing sales elasticities on segmented markets. International Journal of Research in Marketing, Vol. 5, 4, pp. 303-315.

[76] Rust, T. R. (1988): Flexible regression. Journal of Marketing Research, Vol. 25, 1, pp. 10-24.

[77] Sen, S./Bhattacharya, C. B. (2001): Does doing good always lead to doing better? Consumer reactions to corporate social responsibility. Journal of Marketing Research, Vol. 38, 2, pp. 225-243.

[78] Sethuraman, R./Tellis, G. J. (1991): An analysis of the tradeoff between advertising and price discounting. Journal of Marketing Research, Vol. 28, 2, pp. 160-174.

[79] Sethuraman, R./Tellis, G. J./Briesch, R.A. (2011): How well does advertising work? Generalizations from meta-analysis of brand advertising elasticities. Journal of Marketing Research, Vol. 48, 3, pp. 457-471.

[80] Shugan, S. M. (2006): Editorial: errors in the variables, unobserved heterogeneity, and other ways of hiding statistical error. Marketing Science, Vol. 25, 3, pp. 203-216.

[81] Simon, H. (1994): Marketing science's pilgrimage to the ivory tower. In Laurent, G., Lilien, G.L., & Pras, B. (eds.), Research Tradition in Marketing, pp. 27-43.

[82] Skiera, B. (2010): Differences in the ability of structural and reduced-form models to improve pricing decisions. Marketing - Journal of Research and Marketing, Vol. 6, 1, pp. 91-99.

[83] Steenkamp, J. E. M./Nijs, V. R./Hanssens, D. M./Dekimpe, M. G. (2005): Competitive reactions to advertising and promotion attacks. Marketing Science, Vol. 24, 1, pp. 35-54.

[84] Tellis, G. J. (1988): The price elasticity of selective demand: a meta-analysis of econometric models of sales. Journal of Marketing Research, Vol. 25, 4, pp. 331-341.

[85] Tynan, C./McKechnie, S. (2009): Experience marketing: a review and reassessment. Journal of Marketing Management, Vol. 25, 5/6, pp. 501-517.

[86] Van Diepen, M./Donkers, B./Franses, P. H. (2009): Does irritation induced by charitable direct mailings reduce donations? International Journal of Research in Marketing, Vol. 26, 3, pp. 180-188.

[87] Van Dijk, A./Van Heerde, H. J./Leeflang, P. S. H./Wittink, D. R. (2004): Similarity-based spatial models to estimate shelf space elasticities. Quantitative Marketing and Economics, Vol. 2, 3, pp. 257-277.

[88] Van Eck, P. S./Jager, W./Leeflang, P. S. H. (2011): Opinion leaders' role in innovation diffusion: a simulation study. Journal of Product Innovation Management, Vol. 28, 2, pp. 187-203.

[89] Van Eck, P. S./Jager, W./Leeflang, P. S. H. (2012): Word of mouth: the complexity of the process. Working paper, Faculty of Economics and Business, Department of Marketing, University of Groningen, the Netherlands.

[90] Van Heerde, H. J. (2009): Price promotion elasticity. In Hanssens, D. (ed.), Empirical Generalizations about Marketing Impact, Cambridge: Marketing Science Institute, pp. 69-76.

[91] Van Heerde, H. J./Leeflang, P. S. H./Wittink, D. R. (2001): Semiparametric analysis to estimate the deal effect curve. Journal of Marketing Research, Vol. 38, 2, pp. 197-215.

[92] Van Heerde, H. J./Leeflang, P. S. H./Wittink, D. R. (2004): Decomposing the sales promotion bump with store data. Marketing Science, Vol. 23, 3, pp. 317-334.

[93] Van Heerde, H. J./Mela, C. F./Manchanda, P. (2004): The dynamic effect of innovation on market structure. Journal of Marketing Research, Vol. 41, 2, pp. 166-183.

[94] Van Nierop, J. E. M./Leeflang, P. S. H./Teerling, M. L./Huizingh, K. R. E. (2011): The impact of the introduction and use of informational website on offline customer buying behavior. International Journal of Research in Marketing, Vol. 28, 2, pp. 155-165.

[95] Villas-Boas, J. M./Zhao, Y. (2005): Retailer, manufacturers, and individual consumers: modeling the supply side in the ketchup marketplace. Journal of Marketing Research, Vol. 42, 1, pp. 83-95.

[96] Wagner, U./Taudes, A. (1986): A multivariate Polya model of brand choice and purchase incidence. Marketing Science, Vol. 5, 3, pp. 219-244.

[97] Wagner, U./Taudes, A. (1987): Stochastic models of consumer behaviour. European Journal of Operational Research, Vol. 29, 1, pp. 1-23.

[98] Weitz, B. A./Wensley, R. (2002): Handbook of marketing. Teller Road: Sage.

[99] Wierenga, B. (1974): An investigation of brand choice processes. Rotterdam: University Press.

[100] Wierenga, B. (1978): A least squares estimation method for the linear learning model. Journal of Marketing Research, Vol. 15, 1, pp. 145-153.

[101] Wierenga, B. (2008): Handbook of marketing decision models. New York: Springer.

[102] Wierenga, B./Van Bruggen, G. H./Staelin, R. (1999): The success of marketing management support systems. Marketing Science, Vol. 18, 3, pp. 196-207.

[103] Wold, F. M. (1986): Meta-analysis: quantitative methods for research synthesis. Teller Road: Sage.

[104] Wuyts, S./Geyskens, I. (2005): The formation of buyer-supplier relationship: detailed contract drafting and close partner selection. Journal of Marketing, Vol. 69, 4, pp. 103-117.

[105] Wuyts, S./Stremersch, S./Van den Bulte, C./Franses, P. H. (2004): Vertical marketing systems for complex products: a triadic perspective. Journal of Marketing Research, Vol. 41, 4, pp. 479-487.

[106] Wuyts, S./Verhoef, P. C./Prins, R. (2009): Partner selection in B2B information service markets. International Journal of Research in Marketing, Vol. 26, 1, pp. 41-51.

[107] Yang, S./Zhao, Y./Erdem, T./Zhao, Y. (2010): Modeling the intrahousehold behavioral interaction. Journal of Marketing Research, Vol. 47, 3, pp. 470-484.

8   Implications of Linear Versus Dummy Coding for Pooling of Information in Hierarchical Models

Thomas Otter, Goethe University Frankfurt, Germany

Tetyana Kosyakova, Goethe University Frankfurt, Germany

Abstract

Hierarchical models have become a workhorse tool in applied marketing research, particularly in the context of conjoint choice experiments. The industry has been pushing for ever more complex studies and 50+ random effects in a study are very common today. At the same time, respondent time and motivation is scarce as ever. Consequently, inference about high dimensional random effects critically depends on efficient pooling of information across respondents. In this paper we show how restrictions on the functional form of effects translate into more efficient pooling of information across respondents, compared to flexible functional forms achieved through categorical coding. We develop our argument contrasting the most restrictive functional form, i.e. linearity to categorical coding and then generalize to simple ordinal constraints. We close with suggestions on how to improve the pooling of information when definite functional form assumptions cannot be justified a priori, for example in studies that measure preferences over large sets of brands.

Keywords

Hierarchical Models, Conjoint Choice Experiments, Categorical Coding, Pooling of Information.

8.1   Introduction

Market researchers and their clients often are reluctant to formally assess prior knowledge. Many if not most research clients prefer 'the data to speak' without the constraining influence of prior assumptions[5]. Choice experiments that involve attributes with large numbers of levels represented by categorical coding such as effects- or dummy coding exemplify the idea of letting 'the data speak'. Estimation of the implied high dimensional models is greatly facilitated by hierarchical models (e.g. Allenby/Rossi 1998). In fact, given the constraints on respondent time and attention, individual level fixed effects estimation of such high dimensional models is infeasible in practice. Hierarchical models compensate the lack of likelihood information about, say, a specific dummy coefficient from a particular respondent with an (informative) hierarchical prior that is obtained by pooling likelihood information across respondents. The hierarchical prior will be more informative the more similar respondents are in the population. The overall similarity between respondents is inversely related to the amount of heterogeneity in a population.

A useful measure of the amount of heterogeneity in the univariate case is the variance of the unobserved parameter across respondents. The multivariate generalization of this measure is the determinant of the variance-covariance matrix of unobserved parameters across respondents.[6] Comparing between multivariate distributions of heterogeneity one could be of smaller 'volume' than the other as measured by the determinant of the variance covariance matrix because of two reasons: i) the variances are small and ii) (stochastic) dependence between random effects in the population as indicated e.g. by large bivariate correlations. In the limit of vanishing variances, reason one leads to fixed effects estimation based on pooling responses from all respondents, which is unlikely to be empirically relevant in marketing. The second point as a reason for a low volume heterogeneity distribution, i.e. a small amount of heterogeneity is more interesting.

Consider the simple case of a brand-price trade off conjoint with three inside brands A, B and C and an unspecified outside alternative at the price of zero. The goal is to measure preferences for A, B, C and price sensitivity relative to the outside alternative. If preferences are independently distributed in the population, the only way to learn about an individual's preferences for say brand B is through the likelihood information about the corresponding parameter supplied by this individual. However, the more dependent preferences are in the population, e.g. individuals with relatively larger preference for A (relative to the outside good) have relatively smaller preference for B, the more likelihood information about preferences for A relative to the outside good helps to simultaneously pinpoint this individual's preferences for B relative to the outside good and vice versa.

---

[5] At the same time clients are very critical of results that are counterintuitive or lack face validity and many researchers spend large amounts of their time and expertise on 'fine-tuning' results from data that did not 'speak' in line with apparently available subjective prior knowledge.

[6] We note that this measure does not per se require multivariate normality of the distribution of heterogeneity. However, when this distribution is multivariate normal it is a sufficient measure.

A structural motivation for dependence among coefficients associated with levels of a categorical attribute in a population are shared restrictions on the functional form relating the levels of categorical attributes to each other. Consider the example where the data generating mechanism consists of a population of linear functions characterized by different slope coefficients (Equation (8.1)). Each function is associated with an individual i in the population and manifests how levels $j = 1,..., J$ of an attribute x such as e.g. price translate into utility for this respondent.

$$u_i\left(x_j\right) = \gamma_{ij} = x_j\beta_i \qquad (8.1)$$

Categorical coding of a fixed number J of x- levels gives rise to a multivariate distribution of random effects. Equation (8.2) shows how the collection of categorical effects $\{\{\gamma_{ij}\}\}$ where $i = 1, ..., N$ indexes individuals and $j = 1, ..., J$ indexes levels of a metric attribute, are related through the linear function in Equation (8.1). The right hand side demonstrates that, at the true values of the random coefficients, all rows and columns are perfectly linearly dependent. Therefore, the $J \times J$ correlation matrix summarizing the distribution of $\{\gamma_i\}$ in the population has all pairwise correlations equal to 1.

$$\begin{pmatrix} 1 & \cdots & j & \cdots & J \\ \gamma_{11} & \cdots & \gamma_{1j} & \cdots & \gamma_{1J} \\ \vdots & \cdots & \vdots & \cdots & \vdots \\ \gamma_{i1} & \cdots & \gamma_{ij} & \cdots & \gamma_{iJ} \\ \vdots & \cdots & \vdots & \cdots & \vdots \\ \vdots & \cdots & \vdots & \cdots & \vdots \\ \gamma_{N1} & \cdots & \gamma_{Nj} & \cdots & \gamma_{NJ} \end{pmatrix} = \begin{pmatrix} x_1 & \cdots & x_j & \cdots & x_J \\ x_1\beta_1 & \cdots & x_j\beta_1 & \cdots & x_J\beta_1 \\ \vdots & \cdots & \vdots & \cdots & \vdots \\ x_1\beta_i & \cdots & x_j\beta_i & \cdots & x_J\beta_i \\ \vdots & \cdots & \vdots & \cdots & \vdots \\ \vdots & \cdots & \vdots & \cdots & \vdots \\ x_1\beta_N & \cdots & x_j\beta_N & \cdots & x_J\beta_N \end{pmatrix} \qquad (8.2)$$

This example illustrates how a shared functional form translates into structural dependence between the coefficients associated with the categorical representation of an attribute. The example can be generalized in different directions. First, the representative or average response function could be arbitrarily non-linear. If all individuals share the same arbitrary functional form, correlations between the random effects associated with the categorical representation of the attribute are again equal to 1. Second, individuals might share only some features of the representative functional form introducing less than perfect dependence among coefficients in the population. Third, the shared aspect might relate to more qualitative features of the functional form that relates attribute levels to each other.

For example, individuals in a population may share similar rank orderings of levels of an a priori truly categorical attribute. Generally, if a population of individuals is similar with respect to how levels of an a priori categorical attribute relate to each other, the coefficients associated with the categorical representation of an attribute will be dependently distributed in the population.

The objective of this paper is to investigate how much information is lost in a hierarchical setting when there is a shared functional form but the analyst decides to stay agnostic and resorts to categorical coding. We use linear functions as our primary example and then generalize to (shared) rank orderings. We investigate the performance of categorical coding in terms of recovering the representative utility function and the dependence structure in the population. We find that coding a linear attribute categorically recovers the representative utility function well but fails to recover the dependence structure of utilities, especially when there are many categories and the individual level likelihoods are less informative. The utilities are estimated to be more independent than they are. This causes the pooling of information across individual to be less effective when the shared functional form is ignored. In turn, this translates into relatively worse holdout predictions and estimates of optimal actions. Finally, we investigate the case of rank ordered attributes and find again that simple categorical coding fails to recover the dependence structure among utilities.

Our paper generalizes the discussion about the merits and pitfalls of choosing flexible functional forms in the fixed effects case to random effects in a hierarchical setting (e.g. Gertheiss/Tutz 2009, Labowitz 1970, Mayer 1970, 1971). Our contribution is to highlight how shared functional forms cause dependence between categorically coded effects in the population that may be poorly recovered based on simple categorical coding. Failure to recover the dependence structure translates into inefficient and therefore ineffective pooling of information across individuals.

The remainder of this paper is organized as follows. First, we lay out the data generating mechanism based on shared linearity and its categorical approximation. Then we discuss the set up of our illustrative simulations. It follows a discussion of recovery of the functional form and the implied dependence structure in the absence of functional form assumptions, i.e. using categorical coding. Finally, we show how a shared rank order of categorical effects causes dependence among categorical coefficients that may not be recovered without functional form assumptions. We close with remarks about how to improve pooling of information in studies that involve a priori categorical attributes with many levels such as found in industry grade choice experiments to study brand-price trade offs.

8.2   Data Generation and Categorical Approximation

We consider the simple model that consists of only one metric explanatory variable, e.g. price. We assume a linear utility function such that the utility of alternative m in choice set j for individual i is:

$$u_{ijm} = x_{jm}\beta_i + \varepsilon_{ijm} \tag{8.3}$$

Here x_{jm} is the covariate value that defines alternative m in choice set j, β_i is unobserved and ε_{ijm} is an extreme value distributed error term. Error terms are assumed to be iid distributed across alternatives, choice sets and individuals. The unobserved $\{\beta_i\}$ are assumed to be independently distributed across individuals. Without loss of generality we assume a normal distribution.

As a flexible alternative to the linear coding that generates the data we use dummy coding. Dummy coding represents the observed levels of covariate x as separate categories. If there are k levels of the covariate in the data set, as a rule, k-1 dummy variables are formed. The k_{th} variable is redundant because it can be expressed as a linear combination of other dummy variables. The omitted value of x serves as a reference point or baseline such that parameter estimates for the dummy variables can be interpreted as expected utility differences between the baseline and the other x-values, respectively. Therefore, it is important to keep track of the baseline choice for interpretation. When the predictor values exhibit ordinality, some researchers prefer to choose the smallest or the largest value to be the reference point, whereas others prefer the category that is roughly the midrange (Hardy 1993). In the following, we define the baseline category to correspond to the smallest level of x in the data set, e.g. the smallest price.

8.3   Simulation Design

In our simulation we generate multinomial choices based on utilities in Equation (8.3). We use choice sets with three alternatives each that are differentiated by their 'price' levels. We look at choices by 200 simulated heterogeneous individuals. The heterogeneity distribution of the data generating linear coefficient is $N{\sim}(-2,1)$. We vary the amount of likelihood information from each individual by varying the number of choices by each individual. We investigate 2, 6, and 13 choices per individual. The conditions with 2 and 6 choices are sparse relative to current industry and academic practice. However, our simulation looks at one attribute only.

To illustrate the effect of increasing the number of attribute levels we increase the number of price levels in our design from seven {1, 2, 3, 4, 5, 6, 7} to thirteen {1, 1.5, 2, 2.5, ... , 7}, and finally to the 25 levels in the set {1, 1.25, 1.5, 1.75, 2, ... , 7}. The price levels in the three designs are represented by 6, 12, and 24 dummy coefficients, respectively.

At the implied parameters (see Equation (8.2)) our categorical representations therefore exactly correspond to the data generating linear model. Any difference in inference from the linear model and its categorical representation therefore is due to differential efficiency.[7] We document how functionally flexible dummy coding decreases efficiency because the dependence structure between dummy coefficients in the hierarchical prior may not be well recovered. Finally, we investigate a shared rank ordering of attribute levels as data generating mechanism and show again that the implied dependence structure in the preferences for attribute levels may not be well recovered using functionally unrestricted dummy coding.

All estimation is carried out using the routine rhierMnlRwMixture and standard diffuse subjective priors. The routine rhierMnlRwMixture is part of the R package bayesm (Rossi/Allenby/McCulloch 2005) and offers an efficient implementation of MCMC for fully Bayesian estimation of the mixed logit model.

8.4   Results

We organize the presentation of results as follows. First, we discuss the recovery of the representative utility function. Then we illustrate how dummy coding may fail at recovering the structural dependence between coefficients. Finally, we document the implications for predictions and the choice of optimal actions. As an example for choosing an optimal action we search for prices that maximize static, monopolistic profits.

Figure 8.1 summarizes the recovery of the representative, i.e. the average utility function across simulation conditions.

The number of calibration choices, i.e. the amount of individual level likelihood information increases from left to right. The number of dummy coefficients increases from the first row (6) to the second (12), and finally, the third row (24). As the amount of individual level likelihood information decreases and the dimensionality of the categorically coded price attribute increases, dummy coding recovers the representative utility function relatively worse. However, even in the most challenging condition with only two calibration choices and 24 dummy coefficients, the correlation between estimated mean utilities and true utilities is 0.89 and regressing estimated utilities on true utilities yields a constant of 1.80 and a slope coefficient of 1.07. These results suggest that inference about the representative utility function is relatively robust to ignoring the functional relationship between attribute levels.

---

[7] The categorical representation is certainly consistent as the number of observations per individual increases. It is not entirely clear if dummy coding yields consistent results for a fixed small number of observations per individual when the number of individuals increases without bounds. We leave this question for future research.

Figure 8.1   Recovery of Average Utilities

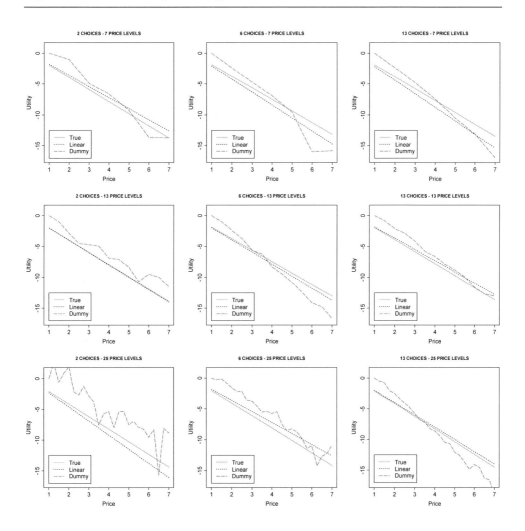

Next we illustrate the recovery of the structural dependence between dummy coefficients. We assess the recovery of dependence by computing the estimated correlations between dummy coefficients in the hierarchical prior distribution. **Table 8.1** and **Table 8.2** report posterior means for the condition with 7 price levels (6 dummy coefficients) and two and 13 calibration choices, respectively. Recall that the data generating correlations between dummy coefficients are all equal to 1 (see Equation (8.2)). **Table 8.1** shows that the correlations between expected utilities at the price of 2 and expected utilities at larger prices are poorly recovered. All estimates are slightly negative. Correlations between expected utilities that are further from the baseline are better recovered, i.e. are much closer to 1. When we increase the amount of likelihood information at the individual level from two choice observations to 13 choice observations per individual for model calibration (**Table 8.2**), all estimated correlations come closer to 1 and especially the correlations between expected utilities at the price of 2 and expected utilities at larger prices are estimated much closer to their true value.

Table 8.1   Correlation Matrix of Dummy Estimates - 7 Price Levels and
2 Calibration Choices

	2	3	4	5	6	7
2	1.00					
3	-0.16	1.00				
4	-0.12	0.77	1.00			
5	-0.16	0.82	0.80	1.00		
6	-0.13	0.83	0.86	0.87	1.00	
7	-0.17	0.85	0.83	0.89	0.92	1.00

Table 8.2   Correlation Matrix of Dummy Estimates - 7 Price Levels and
13 Calibration Choices

	2	3	4	5	6	7
2	1.00					
3	0.82	1.00				
4	0.79	0.92	1.00			
5	0.81	0.92	0.96	1.00		
6	0.82	0.92	0.96	0.96	1.00	
7	0.81	0.93	0.96	0.97	0.98	1.00

Table 8.3   Correlation Matrix of Dummy Estimates – 13 Price Levels and 6 Calibration Choices

	1.5	2	2.5	3	3.5	4	4.5	5	5.5	6	6.5	7
1.5	1.00											
2	0.13	1.00										
2.5	-0.08	0.13	1.00									
3	-0.07	0.18	0.65	1.00								
3.5	0.02	0.27	0.57	0.75	1.00							
4	-0.03	0.12	0.75	0.71	0.71	1.00						
4.5	-0.06	0.21	0.74	0.79	0.76	0.85	1.00					
5	-0.01	0.19	0.76	0.77	0.74	0.89	0.91	1.00				
5.5	-0.00	0.14	0.77	0.74	0.70	0.89	0.88	0.95	1.00			
6	-0.03	0.14	0.79	0.75	0.73	0.92	0.91	0.95	0.96	1.00		
6.5	-0.03	0.15	0.79	0.77	0.75	0.93	0.92	0.96	0.96	0.97	1.00	
7	-0.01	0.16	0.78	0.77	0.74	0.91	0.90	0.96	0.97	0.97	0.97	1.00

Table 8.4   Correlation Matrix of Dummy Estimates – 13 Price Levels and 13 Calibration Choices

	1.5	2	2.5	3	3.5	4	4.5	5	5.5	6	6.5	7
1.5	1.00											
2	0.27	1.00										
2.5	0.26	0.50	1.00									
3	0.29	0.55	0.63	1.00								
3.5	0.19	0.52	0.66	0.81	1.00							
4	0.21	0.54	0.65	0.81	0.90	1.00						
4.5	0.26	0.56	0.67	0.84	0.90	0.91	1.00					
5	0.24	0.53	0.63	0.84	0.90	0.91	0.93	1.00				
5.5	0.22	0.55	0.62	0.83	0.90	0.92	0.93	0.94	1.00			
6	0.21	0.53	0.67	0.84	0.92	0.92	0.93	0.94	0.93	1.00		
6.5	0.25	0.56	0.64	0.85	0.91	0.92	0.94	0.95	0.95	0.95	1.00	
7	0.22	0.56	0.66	0.85	0.91	0.93	0.95	0.94	0.95	0.95	0.95	1.00

Table 8.5   Correlation Matrix of Dummy Estimates - 25 Price Levels and 6 Calibration Choices

	1.25	1.5	1.75	2	2.25	2.5	2.75	3	3.25	3.5	3.75	4
1.25	1.00											
1.5	0.39	1.00										
1.75	0.23	0.03	1.00									
2	0.25	0.31	0.10	1.00								
2.25	0.19	0.29	0.01	0.22	1.00							
2.5	0.24	0.24	0.08	0.23	0.18	1.00						
2.75	0.03	-0.10	0.28	0.10	-0.13	0.03	1.00					
3	0.32	0.31	0.04	0.30	0.35	0.22	-0.19	1.00				
3.25	0.27	0.27	0.18	0.25	0.11	0.16	0.13	0.16	1.00			
3.5	0.16	0.09	0.23	0.04	-0.04	-0.00	0.12	-0.01	0.05	1.00		
3.75	-0.29	-0.40	0.14	-0.35	-0.25	-0.19	0.22	-0.41	-0.17	0.07	1.00	
4	-0.16	-0.15	-0.02	-0.24	-0.01	-0.15	-0.00	-0.15	-0.02	-0.07	0.08	1.00
4.25	0.09	0.18	0.10	0.13	0.03	0.12	-0.03	0.13	-0.03	0.11	0.01	-0.23
4.5	-0.10	-0.14	0.18	0.02	-0.06	-0.04	0.16	-0.17	-0.01	0.10	0.32	-0.11
4.75	-0.37	-0.35	-0.02	-0.29	-0.34	-0.29	0.19	-0.40	-0.13	0.01	0.40	0.22
4	-0.43	-0.43	-0.06	-0.41	-0.32	-0.34	0.01	-0.44	-0.31	0.03	0.46	0.25
5.25	0.03	0.04	0.03	0.15	-0.08	-0.04	0.09	0.01	0.03	0.04	0.03	-0.11
5.5	-0.35	-0.17	-0.14	-0.25	-0.17	-0.24	-0.02	-0.29	-0.16	-0.05	0.31	0.13
5.75	-0.42	-0.40	-0.05	-0.42	-0.35	-0.31	0.09	-0.55	-0.26	0.03	0.55	0.18
6	-0.45	-0.38	-0.10	-0.36	-0.25	-0.30	0.04	-0.40	-0.27	0.01	0.47	0.17
6.25	-0.54	-0.51	-0.13	-0.48	-0.38	-0.37	0.04	-0.53	-0.35	-0.06	0.54	0.26
6.5	-0.48	-0.47	-0.14	-0.46	-0.39	-0.39	0.01	-0.51	-0.31	-0.09	0.48	0.21
6.75	-0.32	-0.41	-0.02	-0.21	-0.42	-0.28	0.10	-0.32	-0.19	-0.01	0.29	0.13
7	-0.24	-0.19	-0.05	-0.21	-0.19	-0.21	0.10	-0.27	-0.08	0.02	0.35	0.10

	4.25	4.5	4.75	5	5.25	5.5	5.75	6	6.25	6.5	6.75	7
4.25	1.00											
4.5	0.18	1.00										
4.75	-0.14	0.11	1.00									
4	-0.11	0.14	0.52	1.00								
5.25	0.10	0.11	0.03	-0.01	1.00							
5.5	0.05	0.17	0.40	0.40	0.10	1.00						
5.75	-0.10	0.21	0.56	0.63	0.02	0.46	1.00					
6	-0.07	0.23	0.44	0.57	0.03	0.48	0.63	1.00				
6.25	-0.14	0.16	0.63	0.72	-0.03	0.53	0.74	0.66	1.00			
6.5	-0.15	0.12	0.58	0.67	-0.01	0.48	0.74	0.61	0.81	1.00		
6.75	-0.13	0.08	0.48	0.49	0.04	0.30	0.45	0.37	0.52	0.55	1.00	
7	-0.03	0.14	0.36	0.34	0.05	0.27	0.39	0.27	0.39	0.36	0.24	1.00

Table 8.3 to **Table 8.5** report estimates of dependence among expected utilities in the population when the dimensionality of the categorically coded price attribute is increased to 13 levels and to 25 levels, however, keeping the range of the price attribute constant. It is clear from these tables that increasing the number of categories exacerbates the problem of underestimating the degree of dependence among expected utilities. When the number of categories increases, the ordering of neighboring categories becomes harder to distinguish based on small samples of individual level choices; and any individual's responses contain little information about all parameters when the number or individual level choices

is limited. As a consequence, the way information is pooled across individuals becomes more important. However, pooling is only efficient and effective if the dependence between expected utilities is estimated correctly.

Table 8.6   Determinants of Correlation Matrices – Mean and Standard Deviation

	2 Calibration Choices	6 Calibration Choices	13 Calibration Choices
7 Price Levels	1.10e-02	3.77e-05	1.25e-05
	(3.45e-02)	(2.09e-04)	(1.98e-05)
13 Price Levels	9.97e-04	1.30e-08	4.58e-08
	(1.70e-03)	(4.15e-07)	(1.46e-06)
25 Price Levels	4.63e-10	3.60e-11	4.71e-15
	(2.78e-09)	(4.46e-10)	(1.87e-13)

To conserve space we do not report all 9 correlation matrices from our simulation but summarize the recovery of dependence via their determinants. **Table 8.6** reports posterior means and standard deviations of the determinant of the correlation matrix for each cell in our simulation. Recall that the data generating utilities are collinear in the population (Equation (8.2)). Therefore the data generating determinants, i.e. the true values equal zero. We can see that dummy coding comes closer to recovering the true dependence structure the more individual level likelihood information is available, i.e. moving from left to right in **Table 8.6**. The comparison across dummy attributes with different numbers of levels, i.e. across the rows in **Table 8.6** seems to suggest that dependence is better recovered when the number of categorically coded attributes increases. However, this is an artefact of the diffuse subjective Inverse Wishart prior used for the covariance matrix in the HB model. The default value for the shape or degrees of freedom parameter in rhierMnlRwMixture equals the dimensionality of the random effects vector plus three. Two hypothetical prior observations in addition to the number that corresponds to a prior covariance matrix with full rank contribute less prior information about the prior dependence structure when the dimensionality of the random effects vector increases.

Next we illustrate how ineffective pooling of information affects predictions and the choice of optimal actions. We measure predictive performance using hit rates and predictive likelihoods. In each of the nine data generating settings of our simulation we randomly create one holdout choice per respondent that is not used for model calibration. The prices differentiating the alternatives in the holdout set are drawn without replacement from the same set that was used to create the calibration choices. E.g. when there are only 7 price levels in the calibration sets, the holdout sets are restricted to the same 7 levels too. This way, a predictive comparison between linear and dummy coding is always possible. Using the posterior distributions from the models fitted, we compute predicted choice probabilities for each of the three alternatives in each holdout choice set for each respondent.

When the actual choice by the simulated respondent in that set corresponds to the maximum of the predicted choice probabilities we declare this observation a hit. The hit rate is the relative frequency of hits in a cell of our simulation.

The hit rate is a practically important measure because it corresponds to decision rules used in practice. However, the hit rate neither distinguishes between barely and certainly hitting the observed choice nor between barely and certainly missing it. Therefore we additionally report quasi predictive log-likelihoods. Quasi predictive log-likelihoods are defined as the sum of the log of the predicted probabilities of observed choices. These are 'quasi' because the expectation over the posterior that yields predicted probabilities is taken independently for each simulated individual. The adjective 'quasi' signals that posterior dependence between predicted probabilities due to posterior uncertainty about the parameters in the hierarchical prior distribution is ignored. However, the measure reflects that decisions depend on correct predictions of the corresponding individual choice probabilities.

Table 8.7   Predictive Performance: Hit Rates (Quasi Predictive Log-Likelihoods)

	2 Calibration Choices		6 Calibration Choices		13 Calibration Choices	
	Linear	Dummy	Linear	Dummy	Linear	Dummy
7 Price Levels	0.875 (-87.771)	0.865 (-120.141)	0.895 (-69.927)	0.885 (-82.144)	0.900 (-59.359)	0.900 (-64.637)
13 Price Levels	0.840 (-87.623)	0.820 (-115.031)	0.845 (-78.665)	0.850 (-87.367)	0.870 (-62.323)	0.855 (-63.726)
25 Price Levels	0.815 (-106.017)	0.765 (-154.744)	0.845 (-100.229)	0.815 (-118.037)	0.860 (-71.914)	0.835 (-84.391)

Table 8.7 summarizes the predictive performance of the data generating linear model relative to functionally flexible dummy coding across the nine data generating settings in our simulation. Going from left to right in **Table 8.7**, the amount of individual level likelihood information increases. Going down the rows, the number of dummy coefficients increases from 6 to 12, and finally to 24. We find that the data generating linear coding consistently outperforms functionally flexible dummy coding predictively. The predictive advantage from knowing, and a priori imposing, the data generating functional form diminishes from left to right in **Table 8.7**, i.e. when the amount of individual level likelihood information increases. The predictive advantage increases when the number of dummy coefficients increases moving down the rows of **Table 8.7**.

Predictive differences between models are important but may be negligible if two models imply the same optimal action. As an example for the choice of an optimal action we compute prices that statically maximize monopolistic profits. We look at a choice set of three alternatives and fix the prices of two options that together constitute the fixed outside good from the point of view of our monopolistic target option.

One fixed alternative is offered at the (low) price of 2 and the other fixed alternative is offered at the (high) price of 6. We compute the price that maximizes the profits π for our target option (Equation (8.4)) varying marginal costs c on a grid from .5 to 7.

$$\pi = \sum_{i=1}^{N} MS_i(p-c) \tag{8.4}$$

MS_i in Equation (8.4) is the predicted probability of individual i choosing our target brand from the set at a price equal to p. We compute market shares for the grid of prices implied by the respective categorical representation of the price attribute and then evaluate profits for each price over the grid of marginal costs to determine the profit maximizing price (-category).

Figure 8.2 summarizes profit maximizing prices for two data generating settings in our simulation. We show the true profit maximizing prices as a function of marginal costs and data generating parameters, profit maximizing prices as implied by the posterior from estimating the data generating linear model and finally profit maximizing prices implied by the posterior from estimating the functionally flexible model with dummy coded categories. We display the results from the design with 7 price levels on the left and those from the design with 25 price levels on the right. In both cases the posteriors are estimated from 6 calibration choices per individual. In the case of 7 price levels we find that dummy coding tends to effectively overestimate price sensitivity as the implied profit maximizing prices tend to be below the true profit maximizing prices and below the prices obtained using the linear functional form in estimation. In the scenario with 25 price levels we find that both the linear and the categorical model effectively underestimate the price sensitivity for small prices and overestimate price sensitivity for larger prices. However, the price path implied by the linear model comes closer to the true price path as a function of marginal costs.

Figure 8.2   Optimal Price Prediction

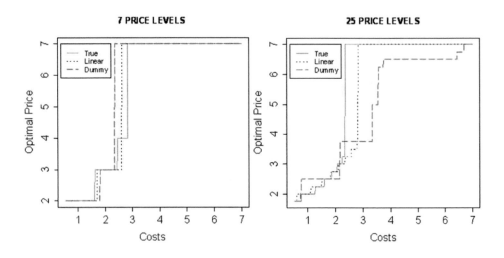

8.4.1   Ordinal Constraints

Ordinal constraints on parameters of a categorically coded attribute are used successfully in marketing and other disciplines such as e.g. psychology (Myung 2005 [17], Johnson 1999 [11], Srinivasan 1973 [20], Allenby, Arora, Ginter 1995 [2]). Ordinal constraints are an example of non-parametric prior knowledge and constrain the posterior in a region that, if supported by the data, translates into improved inference and predictions. An aspect of ordinal constraints that has not received much attention yet, however, is that if a population of individuals shares the same constraints then the parameters of categorically coded attributes will be dependently distributed across individuals in that population. A larger parameter value for a lower ranked level implies that parameters for higher ranked levels are at least large enough to preserve the rank ordering. Across individuals these relationships imply some degree of positive dependence.

We illustrate this argument using sums of exponentiated normal variables to generate ordered coefficients for an attribute with k levels:

$$\beta_{1i} = \exp(\beta_{1i}^{*});$$
$$\beta_{2i} = \beta_{1i} + \exp(\beta_{2i}^{*});$$

...

$$\beta_{pi} = \beta_{(p-1)i} + \exp(\beta_{pi}^{*}).$$

In our illustration the unrestricted β^* increments are independently drawn from N(0, 0.01I) for a seven level attribute. The true correlations of ordered $\beta 2i, ..., \beta 7i$ generated such are reported in **Table 8.8**[8]. The table shows that adjacent utilities are highly correlated, as the distance between βs defined by the ranking increases, the correlation decreases. The closer utilities are to the baseline, the lower are correlation values. When we estimate utilities under the data generating ordinal constraint, we recover the dependence between utilities in the population very well (see **Table 8.9**).

Table 8.8   Correlation Matrix of True Utilities under Ordinal Constraints – 7 Price Levels and 6 Calibration Choices

	2	3	4	5	6	7
2	1.00					
3	0.73	1.00				
4	0.56	0.81	1.00			
5	0.52	0.72	0.90	1.00		
6	0.48	0.65	0.80	0.89	1.00	
7	0.43	0.58	0.73	0.84	0.91	1.00

Table 8.9   Correlation Matrix of Order-Restricted Dummy Estimates – 7 Price Levels and 6 Calibration Choices

	2	3	4	5	6	7
2	1.00					
3	0.77	1.00				
4	0.70	0.87	1.00			
5	0.61	0.79	0.93	1.00		
6	0.60	0.70	0.84	0.90	1.00	
7	0.51	0.62	0.72	0.87	0.94	1.00

[8] β_{1i} was chosen as the base line level.

However, fitting an HB model with unrestricted dummy coefficients essentially misses the data generating dependence structure (see **Table 8.10**). All estimated correlations are very small relative to the data generating correlations. Simple dummy coding without functional restrictions therefore again results in inefficient pooling of information across individuals.[9]

Table 8.10   Correlation Matrix of Unrestricted Dummy Estimates – 7 Price Levels and 6 Calibration Choices

	2	3	4	5	6	7
2	1.00					
3	0.21	1.00				
4	0.05	-0.01	1.00			
5	-0.07	0.24	0.03	1.00		
6	0.06	0.09	0.08	0.07	1.00	
7	-0.08	-0.09	0.04	-0.02	0.06	1.00

8.5   Discussion

In this paper we generalized the discussion about the merits and pitfalls of choosing flexible functional forms in the fixed effects case to random effects in a hierarchical setting (e.g. Gertheiss/Tutz 2009, Labowitz 1970, Mayer 1970, 1971). We showed how shared functional forms cause dependence between categorically coded effects in the population that may be poorly recovered based on simple categorical coding. Failure to recover the dependence structure translates into inefficient and therefore ineffective pooling of information across individuals decreasing predictive performance. Inefficient pooling of information also introduces biases in the estimates of optimal actions such as the profit maximizing price level.

We illustrated our argument contrasting linear coding to unrestricted dummy coding when the data is generated from linear coding. We then showed how shared qualitative aspects, such as ordinal constraints, give rise to dependently distributed utilities in the population. Independent from our discussion in this paper, it has been noted that ordinal constraints can substantively improve small sample fixed effects inferences (e.g. Allenby/Arora/Ginter 1995). The observations in this paper additionally suggest substantive gains in efficiency from ordinal constraints through better pooling of information in hierarchical models. To date, this potential is only partially leveraged because applications are restricted to homogenous orderings that are known a priori.

---

[9] It should be noted however that in this instance of generating ordered coefficients, the HB model coupled with unrestricted dummy coding also suffers from misspecifying the marginal hierarchical prior distributions which are Log-Normal and not Normal.

Attributes with potentially very many levels such as e.g. 'brand' in some product categories do not follow a prior ordering for individual respondents. At the individual level, estimating the unknown ordering offers limited improvements over estimating categorical coefficients because the posterior distribution of categorical effects and estimated orderings become more concentrated at a similar rate as more data from that individual becomes available. However, in instances where segments of respondents share the same unobserved ordering of attribute levels, estimating the distribution of these orderings promises to result in much more effective pooling of information across respondents for attributes with many levels in hierarchical models. We are currently developing MCMC algorithms that treat orderings of (a priori) categorical attribute levels as random effects the population distribution of which is estimated.

In general, the topic of how to more effectively pool information across respondents in problems that involve large (a priori) categorical attributes seems to be an area that deserves more research attention. In this paper we illustrated the problem contrasting linear versus categorical coding but of course do not imply that linear coding is a solution to the practical problem posed by large, a priori categorical attributes. Other potential solutions include adaptively parsimonious priors as proposed by Frühwirth-Schnatter/Tüchler (2008) and Elrod/Häubl/Tipps (2012).

Literature

[1]   Albert, J. H./Chib, S. (2001): Sequential Ordinal Modelling with Applications to Survival Data, in: Biometrics Vol. 57, 3, pp. 829-836.

[2]   Allenby, G. M./Arora, N./Ginter, J. L. (1995): Incorporating Prior Knowledge into the Design and Analysis of Conjoint Studies, in: Journal of Marketing Research Vol 32, 2, pp. 152-162.

[3]   Allenby, G. M./Rossi, P.E. (1998): Marketing Models of Consumer Heterogeneity, in: Journal of Econometrics Vol. 89, 1-2, pp. 57-78.

[4]   Armstrong, B./Sloan, M. (1989): Ordinal Regression Models for Epidemiologic Data, in: American Journal of Epidemiology Vol. 129, 1, pp. 191-204.

[5]   Cox, C. (1995): Location-scale Cumulative Odds Models for Ordinal Data: A Generalized Nonlinear Model Approach, in: Statistics in Medicine Vol. 14, 11, pp. 1191-1203.

[6]   Elrod, T./Häubl, G./Tipps, S. (2012): Parsimonious Structural Equation Models for Repeated Measures Data, With Applications to the Study of Consumer Preferences, in: Psychometrika, forthcoming.

[7]   Gertheiss, J./Tutz, G. (2009): Penalized Regression with Ordinal Predictors, in: International Statistical Review Vol. 77, 3, pp. 345-365.

[8]   Frühwirth-Schnatter, S./Tüchler, R. (2008): Bayesian Parsimonious Covariance Estimation for Hierarchical Linear Mixed Models, in: Statistics and Computing Vol. 18, 1, pp. 1-13.

[9]   Hardy, M. A. (1993): Regression with Dummy Variables. Sage University Paper Series on Quantitative Applications in the Social Sciences, 07-093, Sage, Newbury Park.

[10] Hastings, W. K. (1970): Monte Carlo Sampling Methods using Markov Chains and Their Applications, in: Biometrika Vol. 57, 1, pp. 97-109.

[11] Johnson, R. (1999): The Joys and Sorrows of Implementing HB Methods for Conjoint Analysis, in: Johnson R. Research Paper Series, (Sequim, WA: Sawtooth Software, Inc.).

[12] Labowitz, S. (1970): The Assignment of Numbers to Rank Order Categories, in: American Sociological Review Vol. 35, 3, pp. 515-524.

[13] Lenk, P. J./DeSarbo, W. S./Green, P. E./Young, M. R. (1996): Hierarchical Bayes Conjoint Analysis: Recovery of Partworth Heterogeneity from Reduced Experimental designs, in: Marketing Science, Vol. 15, 2, pp. 173-191.

[14] Mayer, L. S. (1970): Comment on 'the Assignment of Numbers to Rank Order Categories'", in: American Sociological Review Vol. 36, 3, pp. 916-917.

[15] Mayer, L. S. (1971): A Note on Treating Ordinal Data as Interval Data, in: American Sociological Review Vol. 36, 3, pp. 519-520.

[16] McCullagh, P. (1980): Regression Model for Ordinal Data, in: Journal of the Royal Statistical Society B, Vol. 42, 2, pp. 109-127.

[17] Myung, J. I./Karabatsos, G./Iverson, G.J. (2005): A Bayesian Approach to Testing Decision Making Axioms, in: Journal of Mathematical Psychology, Vol. 49, 3, pp. 205-225.

[18] Peterson, B./Harrell, F. E. (1990): Partial Proportional Odds Models for Ordinal Response Variables, in: Applied Statistics Vol. 39, 2, pp. 205-217.

[19] Rossi, P. E./Allenby, G./McCulloch, R. (2005): Bayesian Statistics and Marketing - Repr. - Chichester: Wiley.

[20] Srinivasan, V./Shocker, A. D. (1973): Linear Programming Techniques for Multidimensional Analysis of Preferences, in: Psychometrika, Vol. 38, 3, pp. 337-369.

[21] Walter, S. D./Feinstein, A. R./Wells, C. K. (1987): Coding Ordinal Independent Variables in Multiple Regression Analysis, in: American Journal of Epidemiology Vol. 125, 2, pp. 319-323.

9 Visual Decision Making Styles and Geographical Information Systems

Ana-Marija Ozimec, Goethe University Frankfurt, Germany

Martin Natter, Goethe University Frankfurt, Germany

Thomas Reutterer, Vienna University of Economics and Business, Austria

Abstract

Data visualization aids have become popular tools to assist managerial decision making in marketing. For example, Geographical Information Systems (GIS) are often used to identify suitable retail locations, regional distributions for advertising campaigns, or targeting of direct marketing activities. GIS-based visualizations facilitate the assessment of store locations and help planners to select the most promising options. The selection of the best alternative requires a "visual optimization" which is typically supported by GIS–thematic maps. In an online experiment, we investigate the way how different GIS-based data representations influence marketing analysts' decision making styles. Our results show that GIS-maps are a relevant part of the task environment and that the type of map visualization influences the activated decision processes. The invoked decision process is also shown to depend on the way symbol overload is handled by GIS-maps. We further find that analysts' decision processes vary under time pressure and also relate to personal characteristics.

Keywords

Geographical Information Systems (GIS), GIS-Thematic Maps, Data Visualization, Visual Decision Making, Decision Heuristics, Multi-Criteria Choice Tasks.

9.1   Introduction

Marketing decision makers are increasingly overloaded with potentially relevant data from various sources of the marketing environment. Even though a large amount of mathematical models to support marketing decisions have been proposed in the relevant literature (e.g., Leeflang/ Wittink 2000; Wierenga/Van Bruggen 2000), it often remains difficult to communicate them to the decision maker. In recent decades, a variety of visual decision aids have been developed to facilitate the interpretation of results. For example, Cornelius/Wagner/Natter (2010) provide a state-of-the-art review of alternative graphical formats to represent competitive market structures. Besides visualizations of model outcomes where customer perceptions and/or preferences are displayed as maps (Natter et al. 2008), Geographical Information Systems (GIS) have become a widely used tool in marketing practice for visualizing, analyzing, and organizing managerially relevant geospatial marketing data. GIS are routinely used by retailers or by direct marketers to support strategic and tactical decisions with respect to managing pricing and promotions (Jank/Kannan 2005), targeted advertising (Parker 2004) and direct marketing campaigns (Steenburgh et al. 2003) or retail site selection (Ter Hofstede et al. 2002).

In contrast to an algorithmic solution of the underlying decision making problem offered by mathematical decision models, it is a specific property of such visual decision aids that at some stage of the decision-making process the human decision maker is required to perform some kind of "visual optimization" (in terms of selecting what appears to be the best alternative). GIS traditionally accommodate this by supporting the decision maker with different thematic maps for representing quantitative data, such as choropleth maps, proportional symbol maps, diagram maps or cartograms. Each of these thematic maps can be interpreted as a specific information visualization style that attempts to represent the underlying data in a manner compatible with the psychology of decision makers (Hoch/Schkade 1996; Van Bruggen et al. 1998).

Since this match between a map-based representation and the cognitive capabilities of human decision makers appears to be highly contingent on the characteristics of the decision problem (DeSanctis 1984; Benbasat/Dexter 1985), we need to better understand the relationships between decision task, map-based information visualization and decision performance. Past research has not evaluated the effectiveness of different thematic maps across varying task environments. Indeed, only a few studies have compared graphical formats (e.g. Cleveland/McGill 1984; Hutchinson et al. 2010). Moreover, research has often addressed only the outcome of decision making, such as decision quality, confidence, and satisfaction, without examining the decision processes (e.g., Lucas/Nielsen 1980; Dickson et al. 1986; Ozimec et al. 2010) that link information to decision outcomes. Hence, we still have little knowledge about how human information processing is affected by different data visualization formats for the same underlying data. Such knowledge, however, is vital for efforts to improve existing mapping approaches, to guide the design of new thematic maps, and to create guidelines for usage of GIS-maps. This becomes particularly relevant when decision problems involve the evaluation of multiple decision criteria, which is typically the case in marketing. There are good reasons to doubt that decision makers – especially if they have to make decisions under time pressure – evaluate the complete set of available information in detail but rather rely on some simplified decision making styles (see Etizioni 1989; Gigerenzer/Goldstein 1996; Gigerenzer/Selten 2001). In this paper, we investigate how alternative GIS-map representations of spatial data and decision maker attributes such as spatial ability, GIS-experience, and gender affect the adoption of certain decision making styles.

We next summarize the related literature, describe our research questions within a previously developed conceptual framework, and outline the experimental setting of our empirical approach, where respondents had to solve a series of multi-criteria site selection tasks. Finally, we discuss the results and draw conclusions.

9.2   Literature Review

A substantial body of literature on human decision-making behavior has emphasized the importance of congruence between a decision task's nature and the way in which the information is represented. Research into different mental representations derived by problem-solvers for structurally similar problems (so-called "problem isomorphs") suggests that decision makers perform significantly better when their problem-solving processes are compatible with the problem representation (Hayes/Simon 1977).

Studies on the role of various tabular displays in consumers' decision behavior have demonstrated that the format used to present information affects decision outcomes (e.g., Biehal/Chakravarti 1982; Painton/Gentry 1985). Bettman/Kakkar (1977) and Bettman/Zins (1979) have shown that the information presentation format may actually change the employed decision strategy. Jarvenpaa (1989) extends these previous findings by investigating their validity in the domain of graphical information visualizations. Her results suggest that the visual information representation format influences both the time needed to arrive at a decision and the cognitive costs perceived by the decision maker to evaluate the complete task environment, which lead to different selection or acquisition strategies of the task relevant information.

In the context of GIS-based marketing decision making several spatial components need to be inspected simultaneously and to be combined with each other. Vessey (1991) has shown that the performance of such tasks significantly depends on the match or "cognitive fit" between the decision task and the problem representation, i.e., the way of presenting the problem-related information to the decision maker. In the vein of this conceptual understanding, Ozimec/Natter/Reutterer (2010) provided some insights about the relative decision performance of GIS-thematic map types for representing geospatial data. However, in that research the focus is on the impact of different visualization types on effectiveness and efficiency metrics, but not on the study how the choice of a particular thematic map type can affect the congruence between the visual information representation and the decision maker's mental representation of the decision task.

According to Vessey's (1991) cognitive fit theory, such incongruence leads to higher cognitive effort, which in turn might affect the problem solving process and the decision outcomes.

A potentially rewarding approach to explain such contingent decision behavior builds on the tradeoff-relationship between decision accuracy and the cognitive effort required to solve the decision task (Payne et al. 1993). This framework posits that the decision strategy chosen by the decision maker represents a compromise between the goals of being as accurate as possible and conserving limited cognitive resources. In line with Vessey's (1991) arguments this implies that the "cognitive fit" of a visual decision aid facilitates the decision process and fosters decision accuracy. According to the findings by Creyer et al. (1990), decision makers are willing to put more efforts and to invest more time in the information acquisition and the evaluation of alternatives, if the goal is to maximize decision accuracy rather than to minimize efforts. On the other hand, with increasing opportunity costs decision makers tend to minimize time and efforts and revert to well-established, simple heuristics (Rieskamp/Hoffrage 2008; Etzioni 1989; Wierenga 2011). There are numerous indications in the literature on human decision making that such simple heuristics may work better than more complex decision making strategies for various types of tasks.

Gigerenzer and colleagues (e.g., Gigerenzer/Goldstein 1996) advocate the "fast-and-frugal" approach to decision making and propose a number of heuristics, which are compatible with the probabilistic mental models of human inference (Gigerenzer/Hoffrage/Kleinbolting 1991) and Simon's (1956) concept of "bounded rationality". One of the most prominent heuristics under the bounded rationality paradigm is the satisficing rule; i.e., looking for "good enough" solutions that approximate the accuracy of optimal algorithms rather than placing extensive demand on the cognitive system of the decision maker. The set of the most popular fast-and-frugal heuristics include the recognition principle, the "take-the-best" (TTB) heuristic, and elimination heuristics. The recognition principle states that in a decision made under uncertainty, the only one alternative among a set of alternatives is chosen which is recognized by the decision maker (Goldstein/Gigerenzer 2002). Under the regime of the TTB heuristic the search process is assumed to be extended in the case when more than one of the alternatives are recognized and thus do not provide enough discriminatory information to arrive at an unambiguous decision. This is accomplished by sequentially looking for the "best" information cue along a list of potentially relevant decision criteria, which are subjectively ranked by the decision maker in descending order of their apparent validity, until a cue is identified that discriminates one alternative over the others (Gigerenzer/Goldstein, 1996). Similar to the non-compensatory decision rule accommodated in the TTB heuristic, various elimination heuristics in the spirit of the seminal Elimination by Aspects (EBA) model of probabilistic choice introduced by Tversky (1969) also assume human decision makers to categorize the decision environment by a sequential search process to select and order information cues..

Even though previous research provides evidence of the astonishingly high efficiency of such fast-and-frugal heuristics vis-à-vis more complex decision strategies (e.g., Czerlinski et al. 1999; Goldstein et al. 2001), there are also doubts, whether decision makers indeed use these heuristics in their pure form in real-world decision environments.

For example, Newell/Shanks (2003) and Newell et al. (2003) report from experiments that even though the majority of participants adopted some kind of frugal decision strategies there was also a significant proportion of participants who accumulated more information than it was expected under the TTB stopping rule. Notwithstanding their impressive performance observed in laboratory settings, these findings suggest that the empirical validity of the above mentioned decision heuristics are highly contingent on the specific task environment. Furthermore, and even more important, it seems to be very likely that decision makers employ them, if at all, in some modified versions, which remains to be further investigated by additional, context-specific empirical investigations.

In the next section, we present our research approach to study the use of decision making styles and their relative decision performance in the context of GIS-thematic maps for visualizing managerially relevant geospatial marketing data.

9.3   Research Approach

Our research seeks to provide a better understanding on which decision strategies are invoked by alternative GIS-thematic maps. In this respect, we extend the previous research by Ozimec et al. (2010) by focusing on the impact of data visualization formats on the choice of decision making styles. **Figure 9.1** presents a conceptual outline of our research framework. A fundamental property of spatial marketing decision making assisted by GIS-thematic maps is that the latter aim at representing the most important aspects of the task relevant environment in an as accurate as possible manner. This is accomplished by an abstraction of reality using some kind of symbolizations (e.g., circles, bars, area distortions and color shading) to visualize the underlying managerially relevant spatial information.

Depending on the employed symbolization strategy different types of GIS-thematic maps accrue. In this research, we consider four mapping approaches that are commonly used in marketing practice. As an illustration, **Figure 9.2** provides examples of these basic GIS–thematic maps.

Figure 9.1   Outline of Our Research Framework

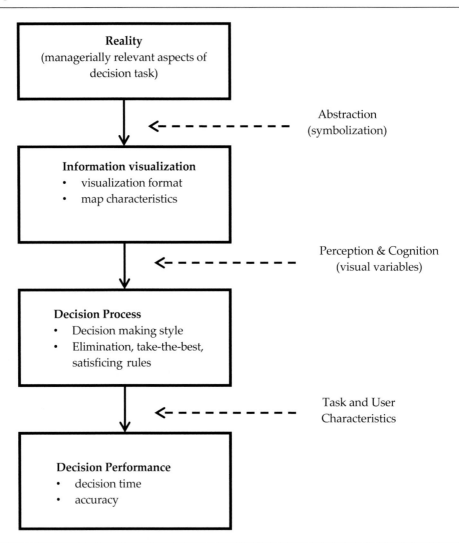

A choropleth map (**Figure 9.2** a) portrays the distribution of a quantitative spatial variable of interest across geographic areas, such as administrative or ZIP-code regions, by using color-coding or shadings that are proportional to the values to be represented (Tyner 1992). A cartogram is a map in which a thematic mapping variable (e.g., purchasing power) is substituted for land area. Cartograms allow the presentation of two spatial variables within a single map without overloading the overall representation. It attempts to accomplish this by rescaling the area of each geographic region according to the relative magnitude of one of the two variables and color-coding the other (see **Figure 9.2** b).

A proportional symbol map (**Figure 9.2** c) is a type of thematic map in which symbols like circles or squares are drawn at the central point of each geographic area such that their magnitudes reflect the respective values of the represented spatial variable (Tyner 1992). A diagram map (**Figure 9.2** d) attempts to place a set of diagrams, such as bar or pie charts, on the map inside a structure that is divided by territory. In contrast to choropleth maps and cartograms, proportional symbol maps and diagram maps are potentially affected by symbol overload, which becomes apparent when the symbols (or diagrams) to be plotted in smaller geographic areas on the map overlap. For symbol overload handling GIS typically allow two possibilities for proportional symbol map (symbol squeezing and symbol overlap) and three possibilities for diagram map (symbol overlap, symbol dislocation, and symbol squeezing).

According to Bertin's (1983) "sign system", a universally recognized concept used to examine the cartographic transcription of geographic information, the syntax of the language of symbolizations used in the above described GIS–thematic maps for representing spatial information arises from the perceptual properties of human vision. Bertin (1983) identifies six elementary visual (also denoted as "retinal") variables, each of them invoking different perceptual processes that allow human decision makers to infer the apparent scale property (and hence the meaning or relative magnitude) of the visually represented spatial data. In the context of our research it is important to notice that the above introduced GIS-thematic maps make use of different visual variables, namely, "value" in the case of choropleth maps and cartograms as well as "size" in the case of proportional symbol and diagram maps. Furthermore, as Gestalt Theory (Wertheimer 1923) and Guided Search Theory (Wolfe 1994) suggest, human vision and, as a consequence, the cognitive effort required by the decision maker to solve a decision task is also likely to be affected by the way symbol overload is handled in proportional symbol and diagram maps (for a more in-depth discussion see Ozimec et al. 2010).

The discussion in the last paragraph leads us to the crucial research question, to what extent the respective visualization format used in GIS-thematic maps affects the decision process or the decision making style employed by decision makers to arrive at a solution for the same underlying task relevant data, respectively. Regarding decision performance, it becomes apparent to further investigate whether the adoption of specific decision making styles affects the probability of choosing the correct solution for the decision task. In our experimental study reported in the next section we provide answers to both of these questions.

Figure 9.2 Illustrative Examples of GIS-Thematic Maps
(Source: Ozimec et al. 2010)

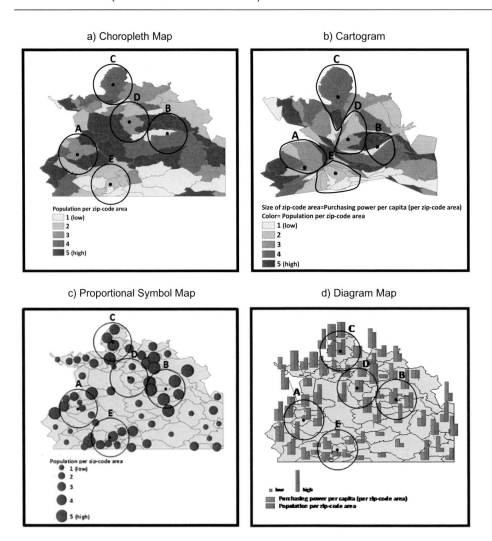

In addition, we examine whether personal background characteristics of the decision makers exert an influence on the used decision heuristic. In particular, cognitive skills tend to have a strong impact on decision making. It has been shown that solving spatial tasks and working with maps require good spatial ability (Golledge/Stimson 1997). Experience with decision tools (e.g., GIS-thematic maps) can also influence the choice of a decision heuristic, because experienced analysts are equipped with knowledge about the strengths and weaknesses of alternative visual representations and could be able to counterbalance these effects by choosing an appropriate decision heuristic. According to human decision making literature, also gender could influence information processing (for example, see Meyers/Levy 1988; Hunt/Einstein 1981). Therefore, it seems to be important to control for user attributes (spatial ability, GIS-experience and gender) when information processing based on GIS-maps is assessed. Finally, we test the influence of time pressure on the choice of a specific decision heuristic.

9.4   Experimental Study

9.4.1   Study Design and Identification of Decision Making Styles

To examine each of the questions raised in the previous section, we conducted an online experiment using the above described GIS-map types for displaying quantitative geospatial data. In addition to the four basic GIS-map types (choropleth maps, proportional symbol maps, diagram maps and cartograms), the consideration of available overload handling alternatives resulted in a total of seven alternative visualization formats (each format assigned to one group).

Each respondent within a group had to solve a six-criterion (average purchasing power, population, traffic access, target group share, parking space availability, and competitive intensity per ZIP-code area) site selection task, either with or without time pressure. For the situation with time pressure, the maximum available time budget was fixed on the median of the problem solving time of participants who participated in the no-time-pressure experimental group. Notice that because of the different GIS-map characteristics for representing these six variables, we had to display different numbers of maps within each map type (choropleth map and proportional symbol map: 6 maps, cartogram: 3 maps, and diagram map: 2 maps). The respondents were randomly assigned to the experimental groups. After a brief introduction and one learning task to familiarize the respondents with the usage of the relevant basic GIS-map type, the respondents were instructed to indicate the most attractive out of five candidate store locations. Furthermore, they were instructed to base their decision only on the information shown in the maps provided.

Before running the major experiment we conducted a qualitative pretest study, where 20 participants were asked to explain which decision processes they used for solving the described tasks for different map types. This study served us to identify the decision making styles typically employed by decision makers. A careful analysis of the responses resulted in the following three decision strategies predominantly used by the participants:

1. *Parallel processing*: The decision makers made decisions on the basis of browsing over all available maps trying to process most of the relevant information available. This decision strategy can be assumed to require much cognitive effort and being rather time consuming.

2. *Selective processing*: They selected the most promising alternative (e.g., location A) on the first map and then revised this preliminary solution only when an information cue provided on the following maps suggested another alternative to be the "better" solution. This decision strategy can be considered as a frugal type of decision heuristic in a sense that it shows major characteristics of both the satisficing rule and the TTB heuristic as discussed in the literature review.

3. *Deselective processing*: The participants unselected the least promising solutions on the first map and then proceeded with a further elimination of the remaining alternatives according to their potential on the following maps. This decision strategy seems to come very close to the elimination heuristic discussed above.

Based on the findings from our pre-test, in our main experiment, we asked the participants to indicate the decision strategy that best described their problem solving process directly after performing the site selection task. We also controlled for the spatial ability of respondents (Ekstrom et al. 1976), GIS-experience (using a 7-point rating scale) and gender.

9.4.2   Results

The online experiment took place in May and June 2009. A total of 1,349 respondents with an average age of 30.4 years participated in our study. The sample consisted of 41% female respondents. 34.9 % of the participants were GIS-experts, 19.4% were employed in the area of site location planning, 45.5% were students, and 8.6% were classified as "others". In our sample, selective processing (40.7%) was indicated the most frequently adopted decision making style, followed by deselective processing (37.8%) and parallel processing (21.5%).

With respect to our first research question, we find that the GIS-visualization format is a relevant part of the task environment, and changes in map type can lead to changes in the decision strategies used. In our experiment, on average, 45.2% of respondents chose the optimal location in our site selection task.

With respect to decision performance we find that the choice of site locations depends on the decision process used. This is an important finding, because it provides evidence that visualization not only triggers the activation of certain decision making styles but also influences the probability of choosing the right (or wrong) site location. More specifically, we find that the respondents who use selective processing have chosen the optimal solution most frequently (50%), followed by deselective processing (44%) and parallel processing (33%), the differences between process groups being highly significant ($p < .01$).

In the following, we report our core findings regarding the remaining research questions by discussing the drivers of the three alternative decision making styles.

1. *Parallel processing:* Our results show that choropleth maps tend to cause parallel processing. This seems to make sense, because color symbolization permits automatic processing without actively looking at each location. Diagram maps, in contrast, which handle symbol overload by allowing for overlaps do not seem to be suitable for parallel processing. Respondents with high spatial ability are unlikely to pursue parallel processing. Further, we found that female decision makers are relying less on parallel processing.

2. *Selective processing:* We find that the way symbol overload is handled critically influences the way analysts process the decision task. Our results indicate that situations of overload avoidance by symbol squeezing (available options in proportional symbol maps and diagram maps) support the activation of selective processing. The proportional symbol map with dislocation, in contrast, leads to a reduced probability of selective processing. While analysts with higher spatial ability show a higher probability, experienced GIS users and female analysts are more reluctant using selective processing. Especially under time pressure, selective processing does not seem to occur very likely.

3. *Deselective processing:* Proportional symbol maps and diagram maps (for the cases of overlap and dislocation) show a significantly higher probability of invoking deselective processing as compared to cartograms and choropleth maps. Analysts with higher spatial ability are found to avoid deselective processing, whereas experienced GIS-users and female analysts are more prone to deselective processing.

9.5   Conclusions

We study whether alternative GIS-visualization formats favor the activation of specific decision processes. The results of our study support the notion that changes in a presentation format (e.g., GIS-thematic maps) can actually lead to different decision processes when the same task (e.g., retail site selection) has to be solved. Our results suggest that choropleth maps favour parallel processing, whereas proportional symbol and diagram maps activate deselective processing. In instances where symbol overload is avoided by squeezing, proportional symbol and diagram maps increase the probability of using selective processing. Thus, our results clearly show that decision processes are sensitive to the way symbol overload is handled.

Regarding the potential influence of personal background characteristics, we found that spatial ability, GIS-experience and gender systematically relate to the activated decision making styles. Our findings indicate that analysts with high spatial ability prefer selective processing (the process with the highest probability of choosing the optimal solution), a factor that can easily be considered when hiring new GIS marketing analysts. Beside these personal characteristics time pressure favors the use of deselective processing.

Our results demonstrate that the use of different decision making styles actually influences decision quality (in our case the choice of the optimal site location). In this study, we asked respondents after performing their task about the type of decision process they used. It would be interesting and managerially relevant to experimentally test whether respondents are actually able to follow specific heuristic guidelines for improving their marketing decisions or whether these processes are rather automated.

Literature

[1]   Benbasat, I./Dexter, A. S. (1985): An Experimental Evaluation of Graphical and Color-Enhanced Information Presentation. Management Science, Vol. 31, 11, pp. 1348-1364.

[2]   Bertin, J. (1983): Semiology of Graphics: Diagrams, Networks, Maps. Madison: University of Wisconsin Press.

[3]   Bettman J. R./Kakkar, P. (1977): Effects of Information Presentation Format on Consumer Information Acquisition Strategies. Journal of Consumer Research, Vol. 3, 3, pp. 233-240.

[4]   Bettman J. R./Zins, M. A. (1979): Information Format and Choice Task Effects in Decision Making. Journal of Consumer Research, Vol. 6, 9, pp. 141-1 53.

[5]   Biehal, B./Chakravarti, D. (1982): Information-Presentation Format and Learning Goals as Determinants of Consumers' Memory Retrieval and Choice Processes. Journal Consumer Research, Vol. 8, 3, pp. 431-441.

[6]   Cleveland, W. S./McGill, R. (1984): Graphical Perception: Theory, Experimentation, and Application to the Development of Graphical Methods. Journal of the American Statistical Association, Vol. 79, 387, pp. 531-554.

[7]   Cornelius, B./Wagner, U./Natter, M. (2010): Managerial Applicability of Graphical Formats to Support Positioning Decisions. Journal für Betriebswirtschaft, Vol. 60, 3, pp. 167-201.

[8]   Czerlinski,J./Gigerenzer, G./Goldstein,D. G. (1999): How good are simple heuristics? In G. Gigerenzer, P. M. Todd, & The ABC Research Group (Eds.), Simple heuristics that make us smart (pp. 97–118). New York: Oxford University Press.

[9]   DeSanctis, G. (1984): Computer Graphics as Decision Aids: Direction for Research. Decision Science, Vol. 5, 4, pp. 463-487.

[10] Dickson, G. W./DeSanctis, G./McBride D. J. (1986): Understanding the Effectiveness ofcomputer Graphics for Decision Support: A Cumulative Experimental Approach. Cornm. ACM, Vol. 29, 1, pp. 40-47.

[11] Einstein, G. O./Hunt, R. R. 1980: Levels of Processing and Organization: Additive Effects of Individual-Item and Relational Processing. Journal of Experimental Psychology: Human Learning and Memory, Vol. 6, pp. 588-598.

[12] Ekstrom, R. B./French, J.W./Harmann, H. H. (1976): Manual for kit of factor-referenced cognitive tests. Princeton, N.J: Educational Testing Service.

[13] Etizioni, A. (1989): Humble Decision Making. Harvard Business Review, Vol. 67, pp. 122-125.

[14] Gigerenzer, G./Hoffrage, U./Kleinbolting, H. (1991): Probabilistic mental models: A Brunswikian theory of confidence. Psychological Review, Vol. 98, pp. 506–528 .

[15] Gigerenzer, G./Goldstein,D. G. (1996): Reasoning the fast and frugal way: Models of bounded rationality. Psychological Review, Vol. 103, pp. 650–669.

[16] Gigerenzer, G./Selten, R. (2001): Rethinking rationality. In G. Gigerenzer & R. Selten (Eds.), Bounded rationality: The adaptive toolbox (pp. 1–13). Cambridge, MA: MIT Press.

[17] Goldstein, D. A./Gigerenzer ,G./Hogarth, R. M./Kacelnik ,A./Kareev,Y./Klein, G./Martignon, L./Payne,J. W./Schlag,K. H. (2001): Group report: Why and when do simple heuristics work?. In G. Gigerenzer & R. Selten (Eds.), Bounded rationality: The adaptive toolbox (pp. 173–190). Cambridge, MA: MIT Press.

[18] Goldstein, D. G./Gigerenzer,G. (2002): Models of ecological rationality: The recognition heuristic. Psychological Review, Vol. 109, pp. 75–90.

[19] Golledge, R. G./Stimson, R. J. (1997): Spatial Behavior: A Geographical Perspective. NY: The Guilford Press.

[20] Hayes, J. R./Simon, H. A. (1977): Psychological Differences Among Problem Isomorphs. In D. B. Pisoni & G. R. Potts (Ed), Cognitive theory. Hillsdale, NJ:Lawrence Erlbaum Associates.

[21] Hoch, S. J./Schkade D.A. (1996): A Psychological Approach to Decision Support Systems. Management Science, Vol. 42, 1, pp. 51-64.

[22] Hutchinson, J. W./Alba, J.W./Eisenstein, E.M. (2010): Heuristics and Biases in Data-Based Decision Making: Effects of Experience, Training, and Graphical Data Displays. Journal of Marketing Research, Vol. 47, 4, pp. 627-642.

[23] Jarvenpaa, S. (1989): The Effect of Task Demands and Graphical Format on Information Processing Strategies. Management Science, 35(3), pp. 285-303.

[24] Jank, W./Kannan, P. K. (2005): Understanding Geographical Markets of Online Firms Using Spatial Models of Customer Choice. Marketing Science, Vol. 24, 4, pp. 623-634.

[25] Leeflang, P.S.H./Wittink, D. R. (2000): Building models for marketing decisions: Past, present and future. International Journal of Research in Marketing, Vol. 17, 2-3, pp. 105-126.

[26] Lucas, H. C./Nielsen, N. R. (1980): The Impact of the Mode of Information Presentation on Learning and Performance. Management Science, Vol. 26, 10, pp. 982-993.

[27] Meyers-Levy, J. (1988): Influence of Sex Roles on Judgment. Journal of Consumer Research, Vol. 14, pp. 522-530.

[28] Natter, M./Mild, A./Wagner, U./Taudes, A. (2008): Planning new tariffs at tele.ring – the application and impact of an integrated segmentation, targeting and positioning tool. Marketing Science, Vol. 27, July-August, pp. 600-609.

[29] Newell, B. R./Shanks D. R. (2003): Take the Best or Look at the Rest? Factors Influencing 'One-Reason' Decision Making," Journal of Experimental Psychology: Learning, Memory, & Cognition, Vol. 29, 1, pp. 53–65.

[30] Newell, B. R./Weston, N. J./Shanks, D. R. (2003): Empirical Tests of a Fast-and-Frugal Heuristic: Not Everyone 'Takes-the-Best. Organizational Behavior & Human Decision Processes, Vol. 91, 1, pp. 82–96.

[31] Ozimec, A.-M./Natter, M./Reutterer, T. (2010): GIS-Based Marketing Decisions: Effects of Alternative Visualizations on Decision Quality. Journal of Marketing, Vol. 74, 6, pp. 94-110.

[32] Painton, S./Gentry, J. W. (1985): Another Look at the Impact of Information Presentation. Journal of Consumer Research, Vol. 12, 9, pp. 240-244.

[33] Parker, P. (2004): Google Focuses Local Ad Targeting. ClickZ, April 15. Available as http://www.clickz.com.

[34] Payne, J. W./Bettman, J. R./Johnson E. J. (1993): The Adaptive Decision Maker. Cambridge, UK: Cambridge University Press.

[35] Rieskamp, J./Hoffrage, U. (1999): When Do People Use Simple Heuristics and How Can We Tell? In Simple Heuristics That Make Us Smart, Gerd Gigerenzer, Peter M. Todd, and The ABC Research Group, eds. New York: Oxford University Press, pp. 141–68.

[36] Simon, H. A. (1956): Rational choice and the structure of environments. Psychological Review, Vol. 63, pp. 129–138.

[37] Steenburgh, T. J./Ainslie, A./Engebretson, P. H. (2003): Massively Categorical Variables: Revealing the Information in ZIP Codes. Marketing Science, Vol. 22, 1, pp. 40-57.

[38] Ter Hofstede, F./Wedel, M./Steenkamp, J. E. M. (2002): Indentifying Spatial Segments in International Markets. Marketing Science, Vol. 21, 2, pp. 160-177.

[39] Tversky, A. (1969): Elimination by Aspect: A Theory of Choice. Psychological Review, Vol. 79, pp. 281-299.

[40] Tyner, J. (1992): Introduction to Thematic Cartography. New Jersey: Prentice Hall.

[41] Vessey, I. (1991): Cognitive Fit: A Theory-Based Analysis of the Graphs Versus Tables Literature. Decision Sciences, Vol. 22, 2, pp. 219-240.

[42] Van Bruggen, G. H./Smidts, A./Wierenga, B. (1998): Improving Decision Making by Means of a Marketing Decision Support System. Management Science, Vol. 44, 5, pp. 645-658.

[43] Wertheimer, M. (1923): Untersuchungen zur Lehre von der Gestalt II. Ín Psychologische Forschung, 4, 301-350. Translation published in Ellis, Willis, D. (1938). A source book of Gestalt psychology (pp. 71-88). London: Routledge & Kegan Paul. [available at http://psy.ed.asu.edu/~classics/Wertheimer/Forms/forms.htm]

[44] Wierenga, B./Van Bruggen, G. H. (2000): Marketing Management Support Systems. Principles, Tools and Implementation. Boston, MA: Kluwer Academic Publishers.

[45] Wierenga, B. (2011): Mangerial decision making in marketing: The next research frontier. International Journal of Research in Marketing, Vol. 28, 2, pp. 89-101.

[46] Wolfe, J. M. (1994): Visual search in continuous, naturalistic stimuli. Vision Research, Vol. 34, pp. 1187-1195.

10 Analyzing Sequences in Marketing Research

Günter Silberer, Georg-August-University Göttingen, Germany

Abstract

In this paper, the author emphasizes that sequences of discrete events and states researched in sociology and psychology are largely neglected in marketing research. Nonetheless, sequences are typical attributes of market behavior. Against this background, the author addresses the questions of which sequences could be of particular interest to marketing science and practice and how they could be researched empirically.

Keywords

Sequence Analysis, Market Behavior, Buying Sequences, Marketing Sequences, Customer Behavior, Uni- and Multidimensional Sequences.

10.1   Introduction

Former research concerning dynamic aspects of market behavior was focused on phenomena like the development of sales figures, prices, and advertising expenses. However, sequences of discrete events and states researched in sociology and psychology are neglected in marketing research. There are several reasons for this: The high effort in measuring such sequences, the lack of text book literature dealing with sequence analysis, and the lack of scientific interest to build theories which try to explain sequences in market behavior. Nonetheless, sequences are typical attributes of market behavior and for that reason it is worth every effort. The question as to whether analyzing sequences in market behavior is worthwhile should be answered later when appropriate research has emerged.

Looking at the research gap just outlined, we pursue the following questions in this article: Which sequences could be of particular interest to marketing science and practice? What does analyzing sequences mean in regard to data collection and data processing? Which studies have already dealt with sequences in market behavior? Which methodology did they use? And what can be recommended for future research in market related sequences?

10.2   Sequences in Market Behavior

Sequences of states and events in market behavior are numerous. These sequences can be found at the supplier side as well as at the demand side. Even the regulation measures can be seen as sequences influencing the market behavior.

1. Sequences in market dynamics

Market dynamics can be found in market structures and market behaviors. As for market forms, it can happen, for example, that a monopoly develops into a duopoly, a duopoly into an oligopoly, and an oligopoly into a polypoly on the supply side as well as on the demand side. Changes in market behavior that manifest themselves in intensity and character of the dominant competition also constitute sequences. Advertising competition may be followed by pricing competition and quality competition by service competition. Developments in the other direction are equally conceivable.

The market life cycle model also differentiates between states such as launch, growth, maturity, and degeneration. If such phases are defined by the development of market volume or sum of sales, we are dealing with a development analysis. And if the phases are defined by states such as predominant forms of competition or events, e.g. predominant selling and buying strategies, we are dealing with an analysis of sequences.

2. Sequences in supplier behavior

Looking at the behavior of single companies sequences also exist. Long-term sequences can be expected in the field of market strategies, whereas short-term sequences are rather be found in the field of operative marketing measures.

A sequence of strategic market orientations can be seen, for example, in the change from mass market marketing to market segmentation or in the change from single brand strategy to brand family strategy. Event sequences emerge in operative marketing, e.g. product innovations, new advertising campaigns or changing service offers. Marketing mix sequences are found in analyzing the change regarding the suppliers´ combination of product, pricing, channel choice, and advertising or promotion.

3.   Sequences in buyer behavior

According to the buying decision process, sequences exist, for example, concerning the engagement and roles of deciders and influencers in the buying center, the use of information sources, the change in the evoked set of relevant product and services, and the different commitments made. Looking at buying histories sequences of interest are, for example, the brands bought, the shops visited or the transfers of money and services (cf. Agrawal & Srikant 1995, Diller et al. 2007). Changes in the family life cycle of single consumers or consumer segments are also worth mentioning here.

4.   Sequences in supplier-buyer-interaction processes

Sequences in the supplier-buyer-interaction also exist. A change may be the transition from formal to informal communication, from interaction using old media to interaction using new or interactive media or from media-based interaction to personal or face-to-face interaction and vice versa. Describing the individual contacts between suppliers and buyers in more detail, not only the channels have to be specified, but also the content of communication and the type of interaction – symmetric or asymmetric interaction, for example.

10.3   Seven Steps of Analyzing Sequences

Comprehensive sequence analysis includes seven steps (see also Kruskal 1983, Abbott 1995, Abbot/Tsay 2000 describing some of them): 1. Defining relevant states or events, 2. Defining a sequence, 3. Operationalization and recording the events, 4. Analyzing single sequences, 5. Comparing sequence (mainly similarities and dissimilarities) and searching for sequence patterns or clusters, 6. Explaining sequences and 7. Predicting the effects of sequences.

1.   Defining relevant states or events

Kruskal (1983 p. 231) wrote that the "variables selected" should not only be relevant to the topic, they should also cover "all important aspects of the topic". A selection of events or states can be restricted, e.g. to those that exhibit a minimum frequency or those, who are of high practical relevance for a supplier. And if a theory makes statements about the predictive value of special events or states, it may suffice to only consider the elements addressed in the theory.

2. Defining and describing a sequence

The definition of what is to be understood by a "sequence" may also be crucial. Generally, a sequence is understood as a succession of events or states. Abbott (1995 p. 94f.) defines it as follows: "By sequence I mean and ordered list of elements", and goes to comment: "The elements of sequence are events, drawn from a set of all possible events…, the universe of events."

Considering sequences more closely can help to specify the type of the sequence. If only certain elements of a sequence are of interest and these elements are interspersed with other elements, it is referred to as an "open sequence". Uninterrupted sequences can be termed "chains" or "strings". If only special parts of a sequence or a string are of interest, they are called "subsequences" resp. "substrings". Therefore, analyzing sequences also includes clarifying whether open or closed sequences are meant and whether they are complete sequences or subsequences.

Comparing time based sequences and DNA sequences it shows that sequence analysis also has to make clear, if a chronological arrangement is meant or something different. In this paper we will only deal with chronological sequences typical for sequences in market behavior.

3. Operationalization and recording the events

In principle, the interesting events or states can be operationalized as one-dimensional, two-dimensional or multi-dimensional elements (cf. Abbott/Tsay 2000 p. 9f.). The fact that the majority of sequence analyses conducted in different scientific areas deal with one-dimensional elements can be attributed to the lack of software and computing capacities in past times which are needed to compute multi-dimensional sequences (cf. Abbott/Tsay 2000 p. 10).

Recording the chronological order of elements knows different options and can also lead to special problems. By researching behavioral sequences, the survey, observation, and registration come into question. Purchase sequences, for example, can be measured by questioning buyers at home, by observing shoppers in the store, and by using scanner checkout data and their fusion with personal customer data. The interview methodology implies a correct remembering of the buying history. Correct remembering may be impossible, e.g. when the involvement of the person is too low and their shopping history too long ago.

4. Analyzing single sequences

The analysis of single sequences can refer to complete sequences, sometimes called "global analysis", or refer to parts or sections of the sequences, sometimes called "local analysis" (cf. Sackett 1979 p. 644; Abbott 1995 p. 104f.). A comprehensive analysis will pursue both directions or use both methods. Complete sequences can be characterized by properties like their length, the number of included elements, the frequency of particular elements, including particular subsequences and substrings contained in one sequence or in a group of sequences.

Frequent subsequences and frequent substrings can also be seen as "homogenous portions" of sequences (Kruskal 1983 p. 227). Local analysis is typical for looking at subsequences and substrings itself, including their position in the whole sequence. The same is true when particular substrings are seen as transitions and when transition probabilities are calculated (cf. Abbott 1995 p. 98). When changes in transition probabilities (Netzer et al. 2007) are also of interest local analyses and global analyses are intertwined, i.e. they go hand in hand.

5. Comparing sequence similarity and dissimilarity and searching for sequence patterns or clusters

All sequence analyses done in past studies mainly look at similarity and dissimilarity of sequences. Most of them calculate dissimilarity following the Levensthein (1966) proposal to calculate the minimum effort which is necessary when a sequence – called "source sequence"- has to be transformed into the sequence to be compared with – the "target sequence" (Levensthein 1966, Kruskal 1983 p. 209, Biemann 2009 pp. 193-196). Levensthein proposed to focus at three possible transformations and to calculate the sum of the necessary transformation steps, seen as total transformation costs and seen as an appropriate scale of similarity or dissimilarity. The proposed three transformations to be used in the so-called "matching process" are: insertion, deletion, and substitution of an element (Levensthein 1966). This method of calculating similarity or dissimilarity of sequences can be used even when the sequences differ in length. This is very important because most sequences in market behavior and other areas of behavior differ in length. According to the importance of the three kinds of transformation - insertion, deletion, and substitution - they can be weighted in the same or in a different manner. The researcher has to decide which weight is given to each transformation category.

Comparing sequences and calculating similarity and dissimilarity can also take into account the number of common subsequences or the "longest common subsequence" (so Kruskal 1983 p. 226). In doing so, is has to be clear that the position of these subsequences in the whole sequence is disregarded.

Complexity of comparing sequences arises when the elements are multidimensional. This is the case, for example, when sequences of advertising contacts include elements which are not only described by the media used but also by the duration and the intensity of the contacts. The same is true when customer contact sequences include elements which are measured by the channel used, the interaction type and the importance of the contact as perceived by the customer. In such cases the researcher who uses the Levensthein-Metric has not only decide the weight he attributes to the three transition costs - insertion, deletion, and substitution – but also the weight he attributes to the different dimensions of the single elements.

For all large number of sequences, research can try to find clusters or patterns (Abbott 1995 p. 107, Sackett 1979 p. 644f., van Hooff 1982 p. 366, Biemann 2009 pp. 195-197). If cluster analysis is done and if sequence clusters could be identified, they can be described by sequence characteristics and by other variables such as characteristics of the subjects like values, attitudes, interests, media use, etc.

Looking at sequence clusters or sequence patterns it should be kept in mind, that the results depend not only on the sequences included or analyzed but also on the calculation of distances between the sequences, the selected algorithm in identifying clusters, and on the definition of a good cluster solution.

6. Explaining sequences or sequence patterns

Comprehensive sequences analyses include the search for causes or determinants of sequences and sequence patterns. According to Netzer et al. (2007 p. 7) this involves finding the "motor patterns" or the "drivers of the dynamics" (van Hooff 1982 p. 366). However, it will make a difference if total sequences have to be explained or solely parts of it, e.g. particular subsequences or "change points" (Netzer et al. 2007 p. 7) as changes in transition probabilities. Explaining sequences or sequence patterns depends not only on available data but also on the theoretical background or framework underlying the recording and interpreting potential "drivers of the dynamics" (cf. Steinmann 2011 pp. 38-51).

7. Predicting effects of sequences or sequence patterns

Last but not least, a comprehensive sequence analysis also tries to find out the consequences or effects of sequences and sequence patterns (cf. Steinmann 2011 pp. 53-64). Looking at buying sequences including indications of brand loyalty or brand change, marketing practitioners and marketing scientists may be interested in satisfaction and the future need for variety. Looking at sequences of advertising contacts they may be interested in buying intentions as a main advertising impact. Predicting potential effects of sequences also has two options concerning the use of explaining variables: looking at the whole sequence and looking at selected parts of the sequence such as particular subsequences. It will also depend on the available data and the theoretical framework chosen if the prediction of sequence effects succeeds.

10.4   Sequence Analysis in Recent Marketing Research

The design, the methodology, and the results of sequence analyses conducted in the past research concerning market behavior can show us different directions and some more details of existing sequences and of sequence analyses already performed. We start with research in uni-dimensional sequences and continue with multi-dimensional sequence analysis.

10.4.1   Uni-Dimensional Sequence Analysis of Marketing Behavior

1. Developments in corporate cooperation

Stark/Vedres (2004, 2006) investigated the developments of corporate cooperation and the corresponding network structures in Hungary during the transition for planned to market economy (1987 – 2001). After determining the network types, the sequences of such types were reconstructed for the selected companies. Clustering 1,696 network histories they found 12 development patterns or "typical sequences" (2004 p. 20). The results of an analysis of variance, Stark/Vedres (2006) confirm the assumption that companies integrated in a network are more capable of passing orders on to network partners and less prone to financial bottlenecks. The same goes for the assumption that integrated companies can reconstruct their capacities better and recognize new opportunities more rapidly (p. 26).

2. Contact sequences in retailing

Silberer et al. (2006, 2007) recorded 132 contact sequences in retailing electronic products. The contacts were restricted to one purchase process including the post-purchase phase. The buyers were divided into two segments – one segment with long sequences and one segment with short sequences. Clustering the sequences in both segments showed different sequence patterns. These patterns were first described by the sequences with minimal distances to the cluster centroid and second by purchase intentions, purchase time, purchased goods and socio-demographic variables.

3. Shopping paths of store visitors

Larson et al. (2005) recorded the movement of shopping carts using a "Radio Frequency Identification (RFID) System" assuming convergence of carts movements and visitors shopping paths. They built three segments: short, medium and long pathways. Due to the great number of sequences and the limited capacity in data processing they used only percentiles or points for identification of typical shopping paths in these three segments. Clustering the sequences for each of the three segments Larson et al. found different sequence patterns and typical paths in all segments. The common assumption that most shoppers tend to move around in a counter-clockwise direction is not confirmed by these results.

Silberer et al. (2007a) observed store visitors in a German supermarket and recorded shopping paths and the approach to products offered. The observation focused on the real behavior of individual shoppers. Both shopping paths and approach behavior sequences were analyzed separately by cluster analysis and sequence clustering. Identification of sequence patterns in both areas allowed a cross tabulation of both patterns. A multi-dimensional sequence analysis was not performed because of the lack of appropriate software at that time. Interviewing the observed shoppers leaving the store and asking them about their household size, store loyalty, number of planned purchases, and shopping satisfaction allowed the researchers to describe the moving and approaching clusters not only by typical sequences but also by these additional variables.

4. Visiting websites and online shops

Engelhardt (2004, 2006) examined the behavioral dynamics of online shops using as click sequences and eye movements. Click streams and the sequence of areas of interests fixed by the eyes of 127 users were analyzed in detail. That was carried out in a lab experiment to examine the influence of motivation and website structure on online shop visiting. In a first step, selected subsequences and their frequency were analyzed. Transition matrices showed expected differences in the experimental conditions (2006 p. 312-322). Engelhardt (2006 p. 322-355) was also interested to show the most frequent "longest common subsequences" in these conditions. In a second step, the click sequences and eye movements were clustered to find out existing patterns. Four click clusters and eye movement clusters were identified and attributed to the experimental conditions.

In order to find navigation patterns, Hay et al. (2004) analyzed server files which were obtained for a telecommunication provider and a university faculty of economics. The telecommunication site comprised 492 pages, the faculty site 228 pages. The number of files included in the final analysis was 271. To evaluate two different methods of comparing sequences Hay et al. (2004) realized both sequence alignment and association distance measuring. The association distance measuring is a method which discounts the sequence character (p. 152-154). Comparing the results of the cluster analyses based on sequence alignment and the results based on association distance measure show similar patterns. They also show that the "sequence clusters" based on sequence alignment are more selective and better to interpret or explain (p. 159f.).

5. Purchase sequences and brand loyalty

Using customer data from a financial service provider, Prinzie/van den Poel (2006) analyzed contract histories as sequences. The aim was to find out whether a regression with sequence data predicts provider change better than regression without sequence data. In a first step, sequence clustering was preformed and patterns of provider loyalty or disloyalty were identified. In a second step two regression models were constructed. Both models included five identical independent variables: time to the next contract possibility, invoiced amount in the recent month, number of services not yet used, time since the first contract, and additional time frame. Though, only one of both models included the sequence cluster affiliation as another dependent variable (p. 522). The results of both regressions reveal that the model including the sequence cluster affiliation predicts provider change better than the other model (p. 522f.).

Another study by Prinzie/van den Poel (2007) examines sequences for household appliances to investigate how the data can be used to predict the next purchase. In doing so, they test four variations of a discrete choice model which only partially considers the purchase sequence and only partially the duration of the purchasing sequence. The selected product groups comprised washing machines and driers, cleaning equipment, telephones, TV, and audio devices. The results support the model that is not only based on influential covariates but also on the time since the last purchase (p. 40). But one cannot rule out that this influence comes from the fact that some devices used were outdated, defective, and difficult to repair.

6. Summary

First studies dealing with one-dimensional sequences show a broad variety of research areas and research interests. Identifying sequence clusters and sequence patterns in several studies underscores the variety of sequences in market behavior. The research done also includes first steps in explaining sequences as well as in predicting the effects of sequences. The predictive value of sequence analysis results is enhanced when other variables are included. Some studies also show the researchers' interest in an integrated look at more than one dimension of the behavior by cross tabulating separated "one-dimensional sequences".

10.4.2   Multi-Dimensional Sequence Analysis of Market Behavior

A significant and important step forward in analyzing sequences is the ability to perform multi-dimensional sequence analyses. Joh et al. (2001a,b, 2002a,b) developed a computer program for multi-dimensional sequence analysis where the necessary calculation time can be kept within reasonable limits because not all subsequences and all dimensions of the elements have to be compared. The shortest distances are determined first with regard to the uni-dimensional sequences followed by a comparison of these distances for the different dimensions (Joh et al. 2002a pp. 391-393). In an early study of 71 three-dimensional mobility sequences, Joh et al. (2002a) demonstrate that the comparison of these sequences took 63 hours in the complete comparison and only "about one minute" in the curtailed comparison (p. 398).

1. Multi-dimensional vacation sequences

Using the data of a large vacationer panel stemming from 1991 to 1994, Bargemann et al. (2002) analyzed 1,163 vacation sequences. The sequences extracted by the panel protocols contained symbols for every day of the year such as D for domestic vacation and H for vacation at home. Therefore the single vacations in the multi-dimensional vacation sequences could be characterized by four dimensions, namely duration, frequency, destination and seasonal position (p. 329f.). In order to limit the necessary calculation time, basic vacation patterns were identified first by means of a subsample. In a second step these types of sequences then were used as input for clustering the rest of the sample (p. 330). By doing so, eight vacation patterns were identified and they were described by the sequences which were typical for each cluster (p. 330-333).

2. Multi-dimensional sequences in mobility behavior

Using the procedure and software developed by Joh et al. (2001a,b, 2002a,b), Schlich (2003) examined daily mobility behavior. Four dimensions were recorded: destination, transport method, distance, and starting time. 361 residents of two cities had to record their mobility behavior for 42 days (giving 15,162 daily entries).

To limit the data processing time Schlich (2003 p. 12) took only the data of one day per person. Clustering these 361 daily mobility sequences, the author found five mobility clusters (pp. 15-19).

3. Multi-dimensional customer contact sequences

Interested in multi-channel-marketing and multi-channel-customers, Steinmann/Silberer (2008a, 2008b, 2011) and Steinmann (2011) investigated multi-dimensional customer contact sequences for a tour operator. In doing so, all contacts in all decision and transaction phases were recorded by interviews with 131 travellers. The phases were: prior to booking, whilst booking, after booking and before vacation, during vacation and after vacation. Three contact dimensions were of interest: the contact points (channels), the contact functions and the importance of the contacts. In the multi-channel system several contact points were important, mainly travel agencies, catalogues and websites. Contact functions included information, consultation, and complaints. Contact importance was measured as the importance perceived by the customers.

Applying the similarity measure and the software developed by Joh et al. (2001a,b, 2002a,b), the distances between the sequences were calculated and the clustering done. The results show four sequence clusters or sequence patterns. They are described or characterized by variables such as selected substring frequencies, transition probabilities, and association measures concerning open subsequences (Steinmann 2011 pp. 244-261). The study also deals with the determinants and effects of the contact sequences, effects of the belonging to sequence clusters included. This is done in the light of different relevant theories such as motivation theory, attitude theory, media richness theory, and the concept of adaptive decision making (Steinmann 2011 pp. 38-51). Results concerning potential determinants indicate an influence of both personal and situational factors which include age, sex, income, motives, experience with the operator and variety of offers, price level, and private communication (word of mouth) (pp. 97-103, 195-206). Customer satisfaction, perceived risk, confidence, and loyalty were seen as possible consequences of sequences. The comparison of the sequence clusters also shows most of the expected differences (pp. 216-222).

Using the same research design, Steinmann/Silberer (2008a, 2008b) and Steinmann (2011) also investigated the multi-dimensional contact sequences with and electronic retailer. They also found four clusters (Steinmann 2011 pp. 230-244) and described them in the same way. The results again underscore the influence of customer age, customer motivation and complexity of technical products offered. They also show customer loyalty to be an effect of contact sequence patterns (pp. 186-195, 211-216).

4. Two-dimensional click sequences

Hay et al. (2003, 2004) analyzed web surfing as two-dimensional sequences in contacting web pages. The first dimension was the page contacted and the second dimension was the time of contacting a page - so called "page impression". In order to restrict data processing time, they selected only page impressions with specific impression times (p. 56). The open sequences then were analyzed by sequence clustering.

By doing so, six clusters were identified and described by frequent subsequences (pp. 57-59). Due to the fact that extremely long sequences were not suitable to describe the surf patterns, the typical sequences were also transformed into shorter versions using symbols for the elements representing subsequences.

5. Multi-dimensional shopping behavior

Silberer et al. (2008) were interested in analyzing shopping behavior as multi-dimensional sequence. Therefore shopping behavior was operationalized as store navigation, shelf-related approach behavior and product-related approach behavior. The data was collected by observing 160 shoppers in a store for electronic products. Data preparation had to ensure all three sequences – store navigation sequences, shelf approaching sequences, and product approaching sequences – show the correct temporal fit and the same length.

Calculating the distances between the three-dimensional sequences all three dimensions were given equal weights. In clustering all sequences three shopping patterns were identified. Characterizing these patterns relies on descriptions using sequences quite similar to the computed centroid sequences (so called "centroid proxies").

6. Summary

The analysis of multi-dimensional sequences constitutes an important advancement in market behavior research. First steps in comparing and clustering multi-dimensional sequences as presented above demonstrate an additional diagnostic value of the results. The first studies dealing with multi-dimensional sequences also show a broad variety of dynamic patterns in market behavior.

10.5 Analyzing Sequences in Future Marketing Research

Further advancement of analyzing sequences in market behavior is to be expected by the following research directions:

1. Broadening the research topic analyzing multi-dimensional sequences concerning the development of markets regarded as a whole, the marketing measures of suppliers and the shopping baskets of customers.

2. Intensifying the efforts in explaining the structure of multi-dimensional sequences and sequence patterns by using relevant theories of supplier and buyer behavior. Explaining parts of these sequences by foregoing parts looking for "internal causes" should be combined by looking for "external causes" as variables not identical with the elements of a sequence. For example, single shopping baskets and subsequences of shopping baskets should not only be explained by preceding subsequences but also by personal variables like interests, intentions, and attitudes, as well as by situational buying conditions.

3. Intensifying the efforts in analyzing the effects of sequences or sequence patterns. It can be distinguished between "extrapolation of sequences" as a prediction of next elements to exist in the future and the prediction of effects not identical with the elements of the sequence. For example, the prediction of shopping satisfaction should not only look at preceding sequences or subsequences in shopping behavior but also at variables like former shopping experiences and shopping satisfaction.

4. Studying the methodology of sequence analysis itself, especially the impact which special options exert on the results of the study. It has to be assumed that the results of a sequence analysis not only reflects the reality, but also the method used, mainly the selected distance measure, the weights given to the dimensions of the elements, and the selected cluster algorithms. The impact of simplification rules used in calculating sequence distances to restrict the duration of data processing should find a special interest.

In doing so, research of market behavior will proceed substantially in diagnostic value and in advancing relevant theories. Research focusing on the "historical depth" of market behavior and of the "drivers" of this behavior implies more efforts than classical research. But future research will show – as former research has also shown - that "sequence matters".

Literature

[1] Abbott, A. (1995): Sequence Analysis: New Methods for Old Ideas, in: Annual Review of Sociology, Vol. 21 (1995), pp. 93-113.

[2] Abbott, A./Tsay, A. (2000): Sequence Analysis and Optimal Matching Methods in Sociology: Review and Prospect, in: Sociological Methods Research, Vol. 29 (2000), 1, pp. 3-33.

[3] Agrawal, R./Srikant, R. (1995): Mining Sequential Patterns, in: Proceedings of the 11th International Conference on Data Engineering (ICDE), ed. Ba Philip S. Yu & Arbee L. P. Chen, Taipei, March 6-10, 1995, pp. 3-14.

[4] Bargemann, B./Joh, C.-H./Timmermans, H. (2002): A Typology of Tourist Vacation Behavior Using a Sequence Alignment Method, in: Annals of Tourism Research, Vol. 29, 2, pp. 320-337.

[5] Biemann, T. (2009): Sequenzdatenanalyse, in: Albers, Sönke, Klapper, Daniel, Konradt, Udo, Walter, Achim & Wolf Jürgen (Eds.). (2009). Methodik der empirischen Forschung, 3. Auflage, Gabler: Wiesbaden, pp. 191-203.

[6] Diller, H./Bauer, T./Scheffler, C. (2007): Sequenzanalysen als Methoden einer dynamischen Kundenanalyse, Arbeitspapier Nr. 152, Universität Erlangen-Nürnberg, Lehrstuhl für Marketing.

[7] Engelhardt, J.-F. (2004): Kundenlauf in elektronischen Shops – Typologisierung und Analyse des Erlebens und des Blick-, Click- und Kaufverhaltens, Dissertation an der Wirtschaftswissenschaftlichen Fakultät der Georg-August-Universität Göttingen.

[8] Engelhardt, J.-F. (2006): Kundenlauf in elektronischen Shops – Typologisierung und Analyse des Erlebens und des Blick-, Click- und Kaufverhaltens, Hamburg: Dr. Kovac.

[9] Hay, B./Wets, G./Vanhoof, K. (2003): Web Usage Mining by Means of Multidimensional Sequence Alignment Methods, in: Proceedings of the 4th Internationals Workshop on Mining Web Data, Edmonton, Canada, July 2005, pp. 50-65.

[10] Hay, B./Wets, G./Vanhoof, K. (2004): Mining Navigation Patterns Using a Sequence Alignment Method, in: Knowledge and Information Systems, Vol. 6, pp. 150-163.

[11] Joh, C.-H./Arentze, T./Timmermans, H. (2001a): A Position-Sensitive Sequence-Alignment Method Illustrated for Space-Time Activity-Diary Data, in: Environment and Planning A, Vol. 33, pp. 313-338.

[12] Joh, C.-H./Arentze, T./Timmermans, H. (2001b): Multidimensional Sequence Alignment for Activity-Travel Pattern Analysis – A Comparison of Dynamic Programming and genetic Algorithms, in: Geographical Analysis, Vol. 33, 3, pp. 247-270.

[13] Joh, C.-H./Arentze, T./Hofman, F./Timmermans, H. (2002a): Activity Pattern Similarity: A Multidimensional Alignment Method, in: Transportation Research B, Vol. 36, 5, pp. 385-403.

[14] Joh, C.-H./Arentze, T. A./Timmermans, H. J. P. (2002b): DANA: Dissimilarity Analysis of Activity-travel Patterns, Urban Planning Group, Faculty of Architecture, Building and Planning, Eindhoven University of Technology, The Netherlands.

[15] Kruskal, J. B. (1983): An Overview of Sequence Comparison: Time Warps, String Edits, and Macromolecules, in: SIAM Review (Society for Industrial and Applied Mathematics), Vol. 25, 2, pp. 201-237.

[16] Larson, J. S./Bradlow, E. T./Fader, P. S. (2005): An Exploratory Look at Supermarket Shopping Paths, in: International Journal of Research in Marketing, Vol. 22, pp. 395-414.

[17] Levenshtein, V. I. (1966): Binary Codes Capable of Correcting Deletions, Insertions, and Reversals, in: Soviet Physics – Doklady, Vol. 10, 8, pp. 707-710.

[18] Netzer, O./Lattin, J. M./Srinivasan, V. (2007): A Hidden Markov Model of Customer Relationship Dynamics, Research Paper No 1904 (R), Stanford Research Paper Series, Graduate School of Business.

[19] Prinzie, A./Van den Poel, D. (2006): Investigating Purchasing-Sequence Patterns for Financial Services Using Markov, MTD and MTDg Models, in: European Journal of Operational Research, Vol. 170, 3, pp. 710-734.

[20] Prinzie, A./Van den Poel, D. (2007): Predicting Home-Appliance Acquisition Sequences: Markov/Markov for Discrimination and Survival Analysis for Modeling Sequential Information in NPTB Models, in: Decision Support Systems, Vol. 44, 1, pp. 28-45.

[21] Sackett, G. P. (1979): The Lag Sequential Analysis of Contingency and Cyclicity in Behavioral Interaction Research, in: Osofsky, G. D. (Ed.). The Handbook of Infant Development, New York: Wiley, pp. 623-649.

[22] Schlich, R. (2003): Homogenous Groups of Travellers, Paper presented at the 10th International Conference on Travel Behaviour Research, Luzern 10.-15. August 2003.

[23] Silberer, G./Steinmann, S./Mau, G. (2006): Customer Contact Sequences as a Basis for Customer Segmentation, in: Retailing 2006: Strategic Challenges in the New Millennium, Special Conference Series Volume XI 2006, ed. by J. R. Evans, Hempstead/NY: Academy of Marketing Science, pp. 232-237.

[24] Silberer, G./Steinmann, S./Mau, G. (2007): Clustering Customer Contact Sequences in Retailing, in: Conference Proceedings of the 14th International Conference on Research in the Distributive Trades 2007, ed. by Zentes, Joachim, Morschett, Dirk & Schramm-Klein, Hanna, pp. 1531-1554.

[25] Silberer, G./Büttner, O./Gorbach, A. (2007a): Exploring Shopping Paths and Attention Behavior at the Point of Sale, in: Marketing Theory and Practice in an Inter-functional World, Volume XIII 2007, ed. by Carol. W. DeMoranville, Academy of Marketing Science, pp. 288-292.

[26] Silberer, G./Steinmann, S./Gürocak, H. (2008): Die mehrdimensionale Analyse des Kundenlaufverhaltens in einem Elektrofachmarkt, unveröffentlichter Bericht, Institut für Marketing und Handel, Georg-August-Universität Göttingen.

[27] Stark, D./Vedres, Balázs (2004): Social Times of Network Spaces: Network Sequences and Foreign Investment in Hungary, Paper presented at the 99th Annual Meeting of the American Sociological Association, San Francisco, Aug. 14-17, 2004.

[28] Stark, D./Vedres, B. (2006): Social Times of Network Spaces: Network Sequences and Foreign Investment in Hungary, in: American Journal of Sociology, Vol. 111, 5, pp. 1367-1411.

[29] Steinmann, S. (2011): Kundenkontakte und Kundenkontaktsequenzen im Multi Channel Marketing, Wiesbaden: Gabler & Springer.

[30] Steinmann, S./Silberer, Günter (2008a): Clustering Multidimensional Customer Contact Sequences, paper submitted to the 37th EMAC Conference 2008: Marketing Landscapes: A Pause for Thought, University of Brighton, 27-30 May 2008.

[31] Steinmann, S./Silberer, G. (2008b): Multidimensional Customer Contact Sequences - A New Approach for Customer Segmentation, Paper submitted to the 2008 AMA Summer Marketing Educators' Conference, San Diego, CA, 8 - 11 August 2008, in: AMA Educators' Proceedings, Vol. 19, ed. by James R. Brown & Rajiv P. Dant, Enhancing Knowledge Development in Marketing, pp. 240-247.

[32] Steinmann, S./Silberer, G. (2011): Analyzing Multidimensional Customer Sequences with a Multi-State Markov Model: Results of an Empirical Study in Retailing, in: S. M. Noble & C. H. Noble (eds.) Marketing 2011: Delivering Value in Turbulent Times, 2011 AMA Educators' Proceedings, Vol. 22, Chicago, Il.

[33] Van Hooff, J. A. R. A. M. (1982): Categories and Sequences of Behaviour: Methods of Description and Analysis, in: Scherer, K. R. & Ekman, P. (Eds.). Handbook of Methods in Nonverbal Behavior Research, Cambridge: Cambridge University Press, pp. 362-439.

11 DISE: Dynamic Intelligent Survey Engine

Christian Schlereth, Goethe University Frankfurt, Germany

Bernd Skiera, Goethe University Frankfurt, Germany

Abstract

Knowledge about consumers' preferences is of utmost importance for many marketing decisions, but transactional data are frequently unavailable. Therefore, marketing researchers have developed ground-breaking methods that build upon stated preference data to measure consumers' preferences; these methods include self-explicated methods, rating-based conjoint analysis, and choice-based conjoint analysis. This article describes DISE (Dynamic Intelligent Survey Engine), which aims to enhance research involving the measurement of consumer preferences. DISE is an extendable, web-based survey engine that supports the construction of technically sophisticated surveys and that limits the effort that researchers must invest to develop new preference methods. We discuss the overall architecture of DISE, discuss how to implement and include new data collection methods, and finally outline how these new methods can be employed in surveys, using an illustrative example. We conclude this article with an invitation to researchers to join in the development of DISE.

Keywords

Web-Based Survey, Survey Platform, Conjoint Analysis, Preference Measurement.

11.1   Introduction

Knowledge about consumers' preferences and the resulting utilities is of utmost important for many marketing decisions, but transactional data (i.e., revealed preference data) are frequently unavailable, for example, in the case of a new product introduction (Wertenbroch/Skiera 2002). Therefore, marketing researchers have developed ground-breaking methods that build upon stated preference data to measure consumers' prefer-ences. For example, marketing researchers have developed methods in the area of conjoint measurement, specifically rating-based conjoint analysis (Green/Rao 1971) and choice-based conjoint analysis (Louviere & Woodworth 1983), which are currently widely used in marketing as well as in other areas such as environmental and health economics. Other examples include multi-dimensional scaling (Green/Carmone/Smith 1989) or self-explicated methods (Srinivasan/Park 1997).

While the methods to measure preferences certainly differ, there is relatively solid agree-ment about the steps, as outlined in **Figure 11.1**, that any article should cover to have a strong chance of becoming published in a top academic journal:

Figure 11.1   Process for Developing New Methods to Measure Preferences

Research in this field, however, is difficult because the costs of conducting research are usually very high. Although Step 1 is "easy" to achieve because it "just" requires having a good idea, Steps 2-5 usually require knowledge from different fields and substantial finan-cial resources.

In particular, Step 2 requires the development of web-based software for the new method because "paper-and-pencil" surveys do not allow for an individual adaptation of the survey and frequently require additional costs for the collection of data. Given the sophistication of the software for existing preference methods, software for new preference methods must fulfill very high standards for graphical user interfaces and response times. In addition, the software for new preference methods also requires a large number of standard functionali-ties, such as the implementation of relatively simple questions (e.g., "what is your age") with validation checks and error messages (e.g., is age a numerical value between 1 and 120), quota-management (e.g., 50% of the responses from men, 50% of the responses from women), and the opportunity to randomly assign different versions of a survey to respond-ents and compatibility with survey panels.

These functionalities must have the same "look and feel" as the new method, to increase the quality of the responses.

Step 3 benefits from representative samples of at least 500 respondents per study (e.g., 50 respondents for a pretest, 3 versions of a survey with 150 respondents each), which currently can be easily collected via specialized survey panels. However, at approximately 8 € per respondent, the total cost for two studies with at least 500 respondents each culminates in approximately 8.000 € (=2*500*8€), which can be a relatively large amount, especially for junior researchers. At present, Step 4 requires having extensive knowledge of statistical methods such as Hierarchical Bayesian Methods, which demand a substantial amount of time to be properly implemented. Step 5 typically involves knowledge about optimization techniques, which are less known to Marketing academics.

Given these relatively high requirements and the risks involved in the development of such methods, it is not surprising to find that most existing research in marketing concentrates on Step 4, the development of models to analyze data. New stated preference measurement methods were primarily developed by senior researchers (e.g., Paul Green, Wharton; Seenu Srinivasan, Stanford) and at institutions that are well-known for having large research budgets (e.g., MIT and its senior researchers such as John Hauser and Glen Urban).

This article describes DISE (Dynamic Intelligent Survey Engine). The major concept in DISE is to enhance the research involving the measurement of consumer preferences. It supports Steps 1-3 outlined in **Figure 11.1** and limits the effort that researchers must invest to develop new preference methods. DISE has already been instrumental in developing new methods for the measurement of consumer preferences and has been used since 2007 by more than 30 companies, professors, Ph.D. students, and post-docs across more than 10 European universities.

In the remainder of this paper, we first present the basic concept of DISE and then, we detail its implementation. Next, we discuss the overall architecture, discuss how to implement and include new data collection methods, and finally outline how these new methods can be employed in surveys. We outline the use of DISE in an illustrative example of a self-explicated approach, which was recently proposed by Netzer & Srinivasan (2011). We finally conclude this article with an invitation to researchers to join in the development of DISE.

11.2   Basic Concept of Survey-Platform DISE

DISE is web-based software built with the basic goal of providing researchers with a powerful environment to develop new methods for measuring consumer preferences. DISE was intended to be as flexible as possible in the creation of surveys while avoiding being restricted to the technical capabilities of commercial survey platforms. As such, DISE supports steps 1-3 of **Figure 11.1** and offers an acceptable range of new and advanced data collection methods, as follows:

- Ranking-, Rating-, and Choice-Based Conjoint Analysis (Green/Rao 1971; Louviere/Woodworth 1983; Schlereth, Skiera/Wolk 2010)

- Mouselab (Johnson et al. 1989)

- Best-Worst Discrete Choice Experiment for Cases 1, 2, and 3 (Flynn et al. 2007; Louviere et al. 2008; Louviere/Islam 2008)

- Self-Explicated Approach (SEA, such as the constant sum method, see Srinivasan/Park 1997)

- Adaptive Self-Explicated Approach for Multiattribute Preference Meas-urement (ASEMAP, see Netzer/Srinivasan 2011)

- Improved Adaptive Self-Explicated Approach for Multiattribute Preference Measurement (IASEMAP, see Schaaf et al. 2011)

- Dual Response (Brazell et al. 2006)

- Reduced Dual Response (Schlereth/Skiera 2011)

In addition to these augmented stated preference methods, DISE also contains all of the basic functionalities that are required for creating and distributing high-quality surveys. These functionalities include the following:

- All of the basic data collection methods, such as constant sum, textboxes, radio buttons, or spectrums, which are used together with advanced data collection methods.

- Definition of quotas for the sampling of respondents.

- Multilingual user interface.

- Ability to conditionally show questions depending on previous responses.

- Ability to create different versions of a survey and to assign respondents randomly to one of the versions.

- Ability to integrate survey panel providers.

Because of its architecture and implementation, DISE can be easily extended to include completely new preference methods or modifications of existing preference methods.

11.3   Realization of DISE

11.3.1   Architecture

Figure 11.2 presents the architecture of DISE, which builds upon the service-oriented architecture of IBM (Arsanjani et al. 2007). The basic concept behind using a service-oriented architecture for DISE is to create a set of principles and methodologies for designing and developing data collection methods and surveys in the form of interoperable services. This architecture reduces the complexity (Berbner et al. 2005), which DISE realizes by loosely coupling services and decoupling them from the underlying technologies. This strategy results in all of the services being autonomous, reusable, and semantically coherent software components that encapsulate the business functionality of each data collection method. As a result, each data collection method is a separate component. The functionality of each component is then accessible through well-defined interfaces. Therefore, services can be exchanged, maintained, and improved separately from each other.

Figure 11.2   Architecture of DISE

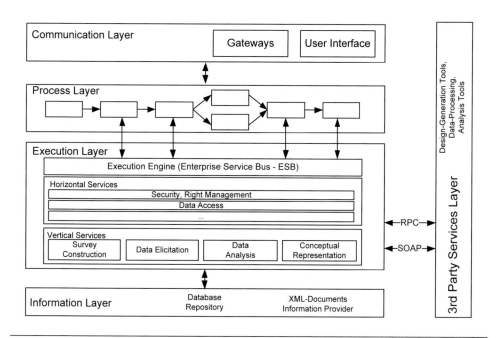

DISE distinguishes three types of users: first, the developer, i.e., the person who implements new data collection methods and adds them to DISE; second, the researcher, i.e., the person who employs the data collection methods in their survey; and third, the respondent, i.e., the person who answers the questions in a survey.

The "Communication Layer" generates a multi-lingual and web-based user interface for the researcher and respondents and serves as a gateway for the researcher to access the results. A strict separation between the application logic for the respondent when entering information and for viewing the survey allows the appearance of the survey to be adapted to the company's corporate design.

The "Process Layer" ensures that the services are executed in the correct order. Use cases specify this order. The "Process Layer" accesses the services of the "Execution Layer" via standardized interfaces. The services of the "Execution Layer" are divided into "vertical services" and "horizontal services". Vertical services handle the business logic of specific survey processes (e.g., the execution of choice-based conjoint analysis), and horizontal services provide generic functions, such as database access or the provision of security solutions.

The "Information Layer" provides the required databases and applications in the form of proprietary software components (such as DLLs). Finally, the "3rd-party Service Layer" enables the integration of third party software so that outsourcing services to experts in different areas is easily accomplished. For example, the generation of optimal choice designs for choice-based conjoint studies must be based on sophisticated mathematical and statistical knowledge (Street, Burgess/Louviere 2005; Yu, Goos/Vandebroek 2011). Implementing insights from the literature could be too cumbersome and time-consuming, if the new data collection method is not intended to provide a contribution to the literature, because well-tested soft-ware, such as Sawtooth or NGene, already exists.

11.3.2   Implementation

DISE is written in C# and ASP.net (Microsoft .Net 4.0 framework). These languages rely on the extensive functional .NET Framework, which supports XML processing within web services. Additionally, to clearly separate the look of the survey from its functionality, DISE utilizes the .Net Master Page concept, which enables a strict separation of the layout from the appearance of the website and provides native support to specify a survey in different languages.

DISE uses XML-techniques to create a survey. XML is the abbreviation for Extensible Markup Language (XML) and is a set of rules for encoding documents in a machine-readable, but also human–readable, format. XML emphasizes simplicity, generality, and usability.

DISE distinguish two types of XML-files. First, an XSD-schema file contains a meta-specification of all of the data collection methods that are implemented by the developers. This document contains instructions on the specification of all of the data collection methods. Developers use this specification to outline for researchers the possibilities for configuring these methods. The second file is the survey-XML. This file is developed by the researcher and specifies the sequence of questions that the respondents receive in a survey.

Figure 11.3 illustrates the use of XSD-Schema and XML in the context of a choice-based con-joint analysis. The XSD schema divides survey pages into two classes: the ComposablePages and the PredefinedPages. PredefinedPages are predefined survey processes such as choice-based conjoint analysis or self-explicated methods that extend over one or more survey pages. These pages contain various types of questions (e.g., formation of rankings or choice sets) or even evaluation services, which allows for instant execution of additional methods to analyze the collected data. For example, an evaluation service could dynamically analyze a respondent's answer in a survey and automatically adjust the subsequent choice sets in a choice-based conjoint analysis. Survey pages can combine all of the data collection methods in the ComposablePages.

Figure 11.3   Use of XSD-Schema and XML for Specification of Surveys

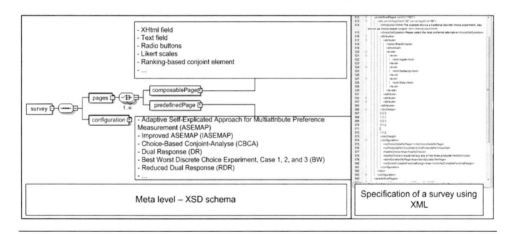

In DISE, researchers directly specify a survey in XML. Even though this specification might seem complicated and not user friendly, most researchers who used DISE for their own studies recognize that this approach substantially speeds up the creation of a survey. The reason for this speed-up is that the researcher gains flexibility, especially when changing and rearranging large parts of the survey. In addition, it is simple to create different versions of the survey or to reuse large parts of it in other surveys, and the specification. The whole survey creation is supported by the rich functionalities of common XML-editors; linking the survey-XML-file to the DISE-XSD-schema file within the XML-editor simplifies the creation because the XML-editor will then automatically propose the possible data collection methods and configuration settings to the researcher.

11.3.3   Integration of Additional Preference Methods

The architecture of DISE was designed to make it easy to integrate new data collection methods. Technically, this integration is possible through the use of well-defined design patterns, which are a set of guidelines and reusable solutions to well-known problems in software engineering. DISE especially makes use of the Composite Pattern (Gamma et al. 2005), as shown in **Figure 11.4**. This pattern treats all of the data collection methods uniformly and connects them with the Enterprise Server Bus (see **Figure 11.2**) through interfaces, which are the same for all of the methods.

A developer who aims to extend DISE with a new data collection method must implement a set of common functions (see **Table 11.1**). For example, for a data collection method that belongs to the class of Predefined Pages, the set of common functions consists of those listed in **Table 11.1**. To reduce the implementation effort for new data collection methods, DISE provides a rich library of functionalities that are frequently used (e.g., calculation of arithmetic means, matrix operations, or regression operations).

Figure 11.4   Link Between Data Collection Methods from PredefinedPages and ComposablePages

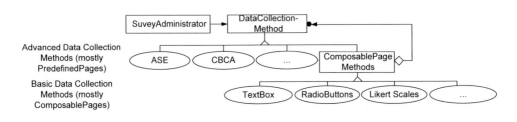

After implementing a new data collection method, developers add its specification to the XSD-schema-file in such a way that the new data collection method will be accessible to the researcher. Whenever this new method is used, DISE delegates the actual execution to its respective software components and controls its execution (e.g., the interpretation of a correctly configured data collection method).

Table 11.1   Most Important Functions That Must Be Implemented in Any Data Collection Method

public abstract PollElements Type;	Design-time: To specify the type of data collection method, such that it can be linked to the entries in the XSD-schema-file
public abstract string BuildTable();	Design-time: Creates all required database entries when a new survey-XML-file is uploaded
public abstract void BuildControls(…);	Execution of the data collection method: Renders all questions on a survey page
public abstract int Progress(…);	Execution of the data collection method: Calculates the progress percentage that should be shown to a respondent at the current state of the survey
public abstract bool IsValid(…);	Execution of the data collection method: Tests whether the responses are meaningful and fulfill a set of specified rules (e.g., that a number between 1900 and 2011 was entered as a response to the question: "What's your year of birth?")
public abstract string Update(…);	Execution of the data collection method: Reads all responses and stores them into the database
public abstract void Estimate(…);	After execution of the data collection method: Optional function that is called after completing the data collection method

11.3.4   XML-Example of Choice-Based Conjoint Analysis

Choice-based conjoint analysis (Louviere et al. 2000; Fritz/Schlereth/Figge 2011; Schlereth/Skiera 2012) is currently an important data collection method for measuring customer preferences in a variety of disciplines, such as marketing, psychology, or health care. Choice-based conjoint analysis has a firm foundation in sociology and behavioral research and explains actual purchasing behavior very well (Swait/Andrews 2003).

The respondents repeatedly choose their preferred alternative in a choice set (see **Figure 11.5** for an example of a choice set), which is modeled on real decision-making situations. A choice set consists of several alternatives, which are described by their attributes and levels. Thus, in every choice set, trade-off decisions must be made between different attractive combinations of attribute levels, which in turn allows for conclusions to be made about the preferences of the respondents.

Figure 11.5   Example of Choice Set

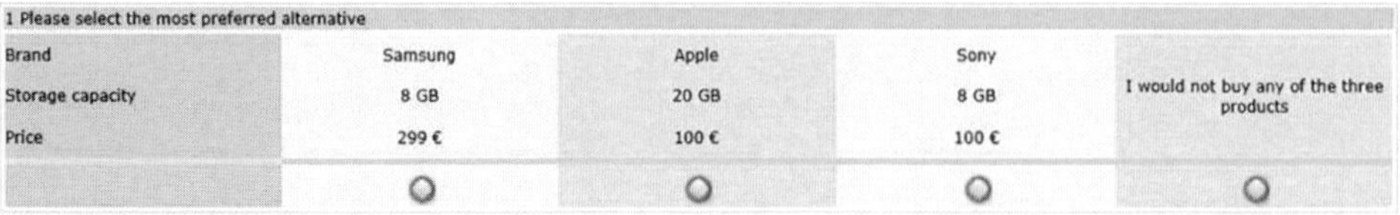

1 Please select the most preferred alternative			
Brand	Samsung	Apple	Sony	
Storage capacity	8 GB	20 GB	8 GB	I would not buy any of the three products
Price	299 €	100 €	100 €	
	○	○	○	○

Subsequently, we outline how to implement a choice-based conjoint experiment, which contains 9 choice sets, in DISE. The XML-code shown in **Table 11.2** is taken from the DISE demonstration survey (http://www.dise-online.net/demo.aspx). First, the researcher specifies the type of data collection method and indicates the range in the percent of progress that is indicated to a respondent. Then, the researcher provides an introduction, which should explain the subsequent task to the respondent.

The specification of choice sets consists of three steps. First, all of the attributes and levels must be specified. These specifications can contain formatted text and even pictures. Second, the researcher includes the choice design that should be employed in this study. These designs can be generated easily with software such as NGENE or Sawtooth or with well-defined methods such of those of Street, Burgess/Louviere (2005). Including the design by simply pasting the respective matrix is convenient because DISE combines the design and the attributes as well as the levels and creates the respective choice sets. Finally, the researcher must add some simple configurations, such as how many choice sets per page should be shown, how many alternatives form a choice set, and whether a no-choice option should be included.

Table 11.2 XML-Code of a Choice-Based Conjoint Analysis

``xml
<predefinedPages>
  <cbc percentageStart="25" percentageEnd="90">
    <introductionXhtml>This example shows a traditional discrete choice-experiment, also known as choice-based con-joint.</introductionXhtml>
    <choiceSetQuestion>Please select the most preferred alterna-tive</choiceSetQuestion>
    <attributes><attribute>
      <name>Brand</name>
      <levels><level>
        <text>Apple</text>
      </level><level>
        <text>Samsung</text>
      </level><level>
        <text>Sony</text>
      </level></levels>
    </attribute><attribute>
      <name>Storage capacity</name>
      <isNominal/>
      <levels><level>
        <text>20 GB</text>
      </level><level>
        <text>8 GB</text>
      </level><level>
        <text>1 GB</text>
      </level></levels>
    </attribute>
    <attribute>
      <name>Price</name>
      <levels><level>
        <text>100 €</text>
      </level><level>
        <text>120 €</text>
      </level><level>
        <text>299 €</text>
      </level></levels>
    </attribute></attributes>
    <cbcDesign>
    2,2,3;
    1,1,1;
    3,2,1;
    3,1,2;
    2,3,2;
    3,1,3;
    3,1,2;
    2,2,1;
``
	Type of the question (here choiceSet)
	Some introduction text
	
	Here is the question
	
	Description of the attributes and all their levels
	
	Design used in the choice-based conjoint study

```
        1,1,3;
        1,3,2;
        2,3,1;
        3,1,3;
        3,2,1;                                    How many choices-sets
        3,3,2;                                    should be shown per page?
        2,1,3;                                    How many alternatives has
        3,1,1;                                    a choice set?
        2,2,3;                                    Also show a no-choice
        1,1,2;                                    option?
      </cbcDesign>                                Text of no-choice option
      <configuration>
        <noChoiceSetsPerPage>1</noChoiceSetsPerPage>
                                                  End
        <noProductsPerChoiceSet>3</noProductsPerChoiceSet>

        <hasNoChoice>true</hasNoChoice>

        <textNoChoice>I would not buy any of the three prod-
ucts</textNoChoice>
      </configuration>
    </cbc>
  </predefinedPages>
```

11.4 Demonstration of DISE

11.4.1 Access and Sample Survey

A demonstration of the advanced data collection methods can be accessed at the following site: http://www.dise-online.net/demo.aspx. The questionnaire used in this demonstration also contains all of the basic data collection methods (e.g., constant sum, textboxes, radio buttons, and spectrums), which are typically used together with these advanced methods.

DISE is available at www.dise-online.net. Here, researchers can login and create their own surveys. If you are interested in a test-account, please contact the first author, Christian Schlereth (schlereth@wiwi.uni-frankfurt.de). DISE supports integration with survey panel providers, and more than 50,000 respondents have already participated in studies that use DISE. Thus, DISE has proven that it fulfills all of the requirements that professional software must fulfill, including the requirement that involves handling more than 100 respondents per hour.

11.4.2 Illustration: Adaptive Self-Explicated Approach for Multiattribute Preference Measurement

Self-explicated approaches offer a popular preference measurement method that is compositional in nature (e.g., Scholz/Meissner/Decker 2010). Respondents directly evaluate the desirability of each attribute level (stage 1) and the importance of the attributes (stage 2). The combination of both evaluations determines the utilities for the products. Because self-explicated approaches impose less of a cognitive burden than conjoint analysis when the number of attributes is high, self-explicated approaches are standard methods for complex products (Park/Ding/Rao 2008).

Recently, Netzer/Srinivasan (2011) published a new preference method called Adaptive Self-Explicated Approach for Multiattribute Preference Measurement (ASEMAP), which differs from existing approaches because two steps are used for the evaluation of an attribute's importance. Netzer/Srinivasan (2011) focus on stage 2 of the evaluation process and propose a method for managing a high number of attributes and avoiding the weaknesses of the rating and constant-sum methods. In stage 1, they ask respondents to evaluate all of the levels of each attribute on an 11-point rating scale. In stage 2, respondents first rank the attributes and then divide 100 points, multiple times, across several two-paired attributes. The combination of the ranking method with constant-sum paired comparisons removes the assumption of equal differences in the importance weights between the ranks.

Netzer/Srinivasan (2011) had to develop software to implement their new method for measuring preferences. This development process was cumbersome and delayed the research progress. The same method is currently also accessible in DISE, and its implementation was relatively easy. The specification is similar to the specification in a choice-based conjoint analysis (see Section 11.4). **Figure 11.6** demonstrates the usage of ASEMAP in a simplified example of Triple Play offering (i.e., an offer by telecommunication companies, which combines Internet, telephone, and IP-TV services). First, a researcher specifies all of the attributes and their levels in the XML-file and then adds some simple configuration settings (1). A design is not required because the result will be created adaptively, using the observations from previous questions. Then, the researcher uploads the survey-XML-file to DISE and sets up all of the required databases and web-pages (2). Thereby, DISE uses the XSD schema to analyze whether the survey specification is valid and well-formed to ensure that it is executed correctly.

During data collection, respondents are asked in several sequential steps to evaluate the product characteristics using double-bounded Likert scales (3), a ranking (4), and pairwise comparisons (5). In real-time, DISE estimates and stores the parameters of the utility function of the respondent in the database (6). These estimates then allow for the importance weights of the product attributes to be determined and presented (7).

Figure 11.6   Development of New Preference Methods
                    (Here, The Adaptive Self-Explicated Approach: ASEMAP)

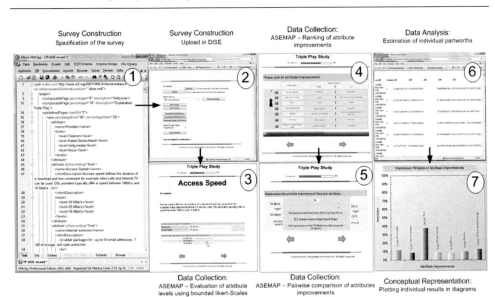

11.5   Future of Survey-Platform DISE

Because the data quality of any analysis strongly depends on the quality of the collected data and thereby on the data collection process, we would like to work towards developing new or improved survey-based data collection methods. All of the currently offered data collection methods in DISE are summarized at the following site: http://www.dise-online.net/demo.aspx.

We intend to continuously extend the functionality of DISE. Possible extensions could be (but are not limited to) the following:

■ Development of an innovative new data collection method or improvement of an existing method (see, for example, Individually Adjusted Choice-Based Conjoint, pro-posed by Gensler et al. 2011)

■ Integration of new adaptive design techniques (see, for example, Polyhedral Methods for Adaptive Choice-Based Conjoint Analysis, proposed by Toubia/Hauser/Simester 2004)

■ Real-time data-analysis for the individual adaptation of a survey (see, for example, Reduced Dual Response, proposed by Schlereth/Skiera 2011).

- Integration of decision aids in discrete choice experiments (e.g., integration of a bill amount calculator for metered pricing plans). The motivation for this extension is that the comparison of alternatives in a discrete choice experiment is sometimes very difficult. In this case, decision aids that are accessible at any time during the survey could not only help the respondents to better compare the alternatives but also better deliver important information about respondents' certainty in their choices, which could allow the estimation of utility functions to have a higher validity (see, e.g., Schlereth 2010).

In addition, we invite other researchers to participate in the development of DISE. One example of this participation could be that we offer our knowledge and routines for Step 2 ("soft-ware-based implementation") of **Figure 11.1** as well as Step 5 ("optimization"; see, for example, Schlereth/Stepanchuk/Skiera 2010). Then, researchers could concentrate on Step 1 ("development of a new idea") and Step 4 ("analysis of data"). Performing Step 3 and writing the paper would be accomplished together. Thus, the idea is to leverage our investment into the development of DISE with new ideas for measuring consumer preferences.

Literature

[1]   Arsanjani, A./Zhang, L.-J./Ellis, M./Allam, A./Channabasavaiah, K. (2007): Design an SOA Solu-
      tion Using a Reference Architecture, https://www.ibm.com/developerworks/library/ar-archtemp/.

[2]   Berbner, R./Grollius, T./Repp, N./Heckmann, O./Ortner, E./Steinmetz, R. (2005): An Approach for
      the Management of Service-oriented Architecture (SoA) based Application Systems, Paper pre-
      sented to the Enterprise Modelling and Information Systems Architectures (EMISA), Klagenfurt,
      Austria, 2005.

[3]   Brazell, J. D./Diener, C. G./Karniouchina, E./Moore, W. L./Séverin, V./Uldry, P.-F. (2006): The No-
      Choice Option and Dual Response Choice Designs, Marketing Letters, Vol. 17, 4, pp. 255-268.

[4]   Flynn, T. N./Louviere, J. J./Peters, T. J./Coast, J. (2007): Best-Worst Scaling: What it can do for
      Health Care Research and How to do it, Journal of Health Economics, Vol. 26, 1, pp. 171-189.

[5]   Fritz, M./Schlereth, C./Figge, S. (2011): Empirical Evaluation of Fair-Use Flat Rate Strategies for
      Mobile Internet," Business & Information Systems Engineering, Vol. 3, 5, pp. 269-277.

[6]   Gamma, E./Helm, R./Johnson, R./Vlissides, J. M./Larman, C. (2005): Design Patterns: Elements of
      Reusable Object-Oriented Software, Boston: Addison Wesley.

[7]   Gensler, S./Hinz, O./Skiera, B./Theysohn, S. (2011): Willingness-to-Pay Estimation with Choice-
      Based Conjoint-Analysis: Addressing Extreme Response Behavior with Individually Adapted De-
      signs, Working Paper.

[8]   Green, P. E./Carmone, F. J./Smith, S. M. (1989): Multidimensional Scaling, Concepts and Applica-
      tions.

[9]   Green, P. E./Rao, V. (1971): Conjoint Measurement for Quantifying Judgemental Data," Journal of
      Marketing Research, Vol. 8, pp. 355-363.

[10] Johnson, E. J./Payne, J. W./Schkade, D. A./Bettman, J. R. (1989): Monitoring Information Processing
      and Decisions: The Mouselab System," Fuqua School of Business, Technical Report.

[11] Louviere, J./Islam, T. (2008): A Comparison of Importance Weights and Willingness-to-pay
      Measures Derived from Choice-based Conjoint, Constant Sum Scales and Best-worst Scaling,"
      Journal of Business Research, Vol. 61, pp. 903-911.

[12] Louviere, J./Street, D./Burgess, L./Wasi, N./Islam, T./Marley, A. A. J. (2008): Modeling the Choices
      of Individual Decision-Makers by Combining Efficient Choice Experiment Designs with Extra
      Preference Information, Journal of Choice Modelling, Vol. 1, 1, pp. 128-163.

[13] Louviere, J. J./Woodworth, G. (1983): Design and Analysis of Simulated Consumer Choice or
      Allocation Experiments: An Approach Based on Aggregated Data, Journal of Marketing Research,
      Vol. 20, 4, pp. 350-367.

[14] Netzer, O./Srinivasan, S. (2011): Adaptive Self-Explication of Multi Attribute Preferences, Journal
      of Marketing Research, Vol. 48, 1, pp. 140-156.

[15] Park, Y. H./Ding, M./Rao, V. (2008): Eliciting Preference for Complex Products: A Web-Based
      Upgrading Method," Journal of Marketing Research, Vol. 45, 5, pp. 562-574.

[16] Schaaf, R./Schlereth, C./Skiera, B./Eckert, J. (2011): A Comparison of Six Self-Explicated Approach-
      es, Working Paper.

[17] Schlereth, C. (2010): Optimale Preisgestaltung von internetbasierten Diensten, Hamburg: Verlag
      Dr. Kovač.

[18] Schlereth, C./Skiera, B. (2011): Reduced Dual Response, University of Frankfurt, Working Paper.

[19] Schlereth, C./Skiera, B. (2012): Measurement of Consumer Preferences for Bucket Pricing Plans
      with Different Service Attributes, International Journal of Research in Marketing, forthcoming.

[20] Schlereth, C./Skiera, B./Wolk, A. (2010): Augmented Methods of Ranking-Based and Choice-Based
      Conjoint Analysis to Estimate Willingness to Pay for Services under Two-Part Tariffs, Goethe
      University Frankfurt, Working Paper.

[21] Schlereth, C./Skiera, B./Wolk, A. (2011): Measuring Consumers' Preferences for Metered Pricing of
      Services, Journal of Service Research, Vol. 14, 4, pp. 443-459.

[22] Scholz, S. W./Meissner, M./Decker, R. (2010): Measuring Consumer Preferences for Complex Products: A Compositional Approach Based on Paired Comparisons, Journal of Marketing Research, Vol. 47, 4, pp. 685-698.

[23] Srinivasan, V./Park, C. S. (1997): Surprising Robustness of the Self-Explicated Approach to Customer Preference Structure Measurement," JMR, Vol. 34, 2, pp. 286-291.

[24] Street, D. J./Burgess, L./Louviere, J. J. (2005): Quick and Easy Choice Sets: Constructing Optimal and Nearly Optimal Stated Choice Experiments, International Journal of Marketing Research, Vol. 22, 4, pp. 459-470.

[25] Toubia, O./Hauser, J. R./Simester, D. I. (2004): Polyhedral Methods for Adaptive Choicebased Conjoint Analysis, Journal of Marketing Research, Vol. 41, 1, pp. 116-131.

[26] Wertenbroch, K./Skiera, B. (2002): Measuring Consumer Willingness to Pay at the Point of Purchase," Journal of Marketing Research, Vol. 39, 2, pp. 228-241.

[27] Yu, J./Goos, P./Vandebroek, M. (2011): Individually Adapted Sequential Bayesian Conjoint-Choice Designs in the Presence of Consumer Heterogeneity, International Journal of Research in Marketing, Vol. 28, 4, pp. 378-388.

Consumer Behavior and Retailing

1 The Effect of Attitude Toward Money on Financial Trouble and Compulsive Buying

Studying Hungarian Consumers in Debt During the Financial Crisis

András Bauer, Corvinus University of Budapest, Hungary

Ariel Mitev, Corvinus University of Budapest, Hungary

Abstract

This study contributes to our understanding of different aspects of consumer behavior and its potential ties to economic crisis.

Compulsive buying has attracted the attention of several researchers in the consumer behavior domain dealing with both antecedents and consequences. However we know relatively little about whether and how compulsive buying is connected to the economic crisis. This event could magnify or change consumer tendencies and would allow us to tie attitudes to actual (or predicted) behavior. Our aim is to discover to develop a deeper understanding between the different dimensions of attitude toward money and financial trouble. Further we are interested whether compulsive buying would moderate this effect. We measure the dimensions of financial attitude on a scale developed by Yamauchi and Templer (1982) and use the Faber and Quinn scale (1992) for measuring compulsive buying.

Our research is based on a large scale empirical study that has been carried out in 2009 in Hungary. 1000 respondents, carrying one of housing, mortgage or personal loans, aged 18-59 created the sample. Hypothesis testing was done by structural equation modeling.

Keywords

Consumer Behavior, SEM, Financial Behavior.

1.1 Consumer Behavior in Hungary During the Economic Crisis

Hungarian households went on a buying spree during the last decade. Data from 2008 show that households preferred consumption and housing investment against savings (Berhlendi 2007). That is partly reflected in the fact that in households' wealth real estate represents a much higher proportion than financial wealth compared internationally by Vadas (2007).

Figure 1.1   Households' Debt Service Burden in Proportion to Disposable Income And Changes in the Exchange Rate of the Swiss Franc

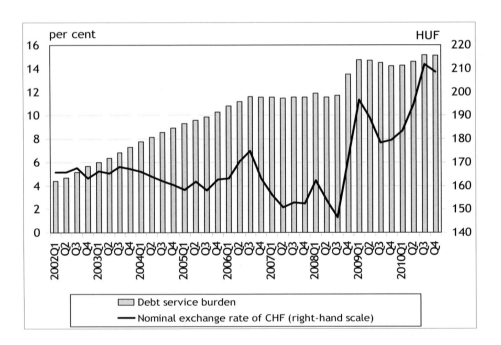

Source: Stability report, Hungarian National Bank, April 2011

The fact that the high loan supply led to low saving rates has led to an instable situation even before the financial crisis. This was partly supported by the analysis of Gáspár and Varga (2011) showing that more than half of the households have taken loans beyond their capabilities (monthly loan payments reached more than 40 % of the household net income).

The second major problem for the debtors is created by the increase of their installments due to the exchange rate fluctuations (most Hungarians have taken Swiss Franc or Euro denominated loans, in a time when the national currency was relatively strong). This resulted in delays in loan repayments that reached 12,4 % in 2009 according to the Hungarian Financial Overseer Body. A further explanation is provided by **Figure 1.1**.

1.2 Defining Compulsive Buying

Consumer societies often face phenomena that can be classified out of the ordinary. The concept of compulsive buying originates in clinical psychology and based on this insight Quinn and Faber defined it as "chronic, repetitive purchasing that becomes a primary response to negative events or feelings" (O'Guinn/Faber 1989, 155). Due to its nature only a small proportion of the population is considered to have compulsive buying habits.

This low proportion however has often been challenged by recent research in consumer behavior and believes to be more widespread. Further researchers considered compulsive buying more and everyday phenomenon and less extreme than previously thought. (d'Astous 1990; Manolis/Roberts 2008). Based on this **Table 1.1** elaborates on different perspectives in marketing research.

Table 1.1   Different Definitions of Compulsive Buying

Author	Definition
O'Guinn/Faber (1989)	"chronic, repetitive purchasing that becomes a primary response to negative events or feelings"
Edwards (1992, 7)	'an abnormal form of shopping and spending in which the afflicted consumer has an overpowering, uncontrollable, chronic and repetitive urge to shop and spend as a means of alleviating negative feelings of stress and anxiety'
Mittal et al. (2008)	a chronic tendency to spend beyond one's needs and means
Ridgway et al. (2008)	Compulsive buying is defined as a consumer's tendency to be preoccupied with buying that is revealed through repetitive buying and a lack of impulse control over buying.

Source: Collected by the authors

One can state that compulsive buying is dealt with differently from a psychiatric perspective than from a marketing research one. In our research we do not want to address the issue of chronicness in psychiatric terms, we only aim at the measurement the tendency of compulsiveness. In other words we are more interested in the tendency than in typology of illness.

Depending on the research aspects (**Table 1.1**) the original definition of O'Guinn and Faber (1992) underwent different several changes. It is an important conceptual question whether we include the consequences of compulsive buying in its definition (e.g. Mittal et al. 2008). In principle one could be a compulsive buyer without carrying its negative financial consequences and this person would not look problematic to the outside world. According to Chaker (2003) there is a large number of consumers that suffer from compulsive buying disorder still cannot be considered ill in a psychiatric sense. These consumers will experience similar consequences as others considered to be ill in a psychiatric sense, whether these experiences are social or emotional. Due to their sufficient financial background however, they will not have to bear the negative financial consequences.

1.2.1   The Spread of Compulsive Buying and the Consumer Society

Researchers of consumer behavior started to study compulsive buying in the middle of the 1980ies as a potential problem field. In 1992 the proportion of compulsive buyers was estimated by Faber and Quinn between 2 to 8 % of the U.S. population Later however other researchers felt this number as an underestimation, and quoted a growing tendency in the most developed countries (Muller és Zwaan 2004). The main reason behind the growth of compulsive buying can be the materialistic consumer culture we live in (Belk 1985; Palan et al. 2011). Further, other researches have shed light to the fact that the desire to become part of the consumer society can clearly be seen in less developed societies as well (Droge/Mackoy 1995).

As it is demonstrated by Schulze (1992) consumer in the modern age are more involved in the pursuit of everyday new experiences, rather than in satisfying their elementary, basic needs. This pursuit is full of frustrations where only newer and newer experiences offer a temporary solution. This argument finds resonance by Baumann (2005), who argues that in a consumer society the freedom of choice defines social standing and a saving lifestyle is only rewarded if it serves the promise of future consumption.

Neuner at al. (2005) found a growing tendency in the previous East Germany, where the tendency to compulsive buying has increased much faster than in the Western part, probably due to the recent exposure to consumer culture. We have quite limited results about compulsive behavior in Hungary – where the situation could be similar to East Germany -, the problem has only been addressed in the addictology domain by Kelemen (2009), but no empirical data are available.

1.2.2   The Characteristics of the Compulsive Buyer

The early wisdom that compulsive buyers were mainly women was supported by a stream of popular books at the turn of 1980-1990 (Kelemen 2009). This myth has been later challenged by Koran et al. (2006) and several further researchers. According to them compulsive buying does not show any dependence on education, social or family status, or whether consumers are urban or rural.

Compulsive buyers depend on shopping activities and need continuous engagement. (Faber/Christenson 1996). Shopping is a stable element of their lifestyle and this way they can reach their emotional goals easier. Further, they experience stronger and volatile emotions than other consumers and their self-esteem strongly depends on their behavior. (DeSarbo/Edwards 1996). Christenson et al. (1994) listed feelings associated with compulsive behavior, such as joy, anticipation, thrill that can easily lead to guilt, depression or dissatisfaction. Latter can make consumers vulnerable and easily disappointed.

Compulsive buyers tend to be more anxious, depressive, tense and have a stronger tendency to feel guilt (Faber/O'Guinn 1992; Christenson et al. 1994; O'Guinn/Faber 1989). Compared with other customers they are also more accommodating and less stable and conscientious than other consumers (Mowen/Spears 1999), have a high need for stimulation and arousal (Faber et al. 1987), and appreciate promotional offers more than other consumers (d'Astous/Jacob 2002). Finally, compulsive buyers have a higher need to escape reality than other consumers, as they have negative and painful self-awareness and hold themselves to almost impossible standards (Kyrios et al. 2004).

Compulsive buyers often experience emotional lows before shopping, which can only be lifted temporarily during the buying process. This joy however is quite short-lived and can be easily followed by depression again. (Saraneva/Sääksjarvi 2008). Consumers are motivated to go shopping when they feel down (negative emotion), feel uplifted while shopping (positive emotion), but then feel depressed after the shopping activity is over (negative emotion).

1.3   The Structural Model and the Measurements

We set the research objectives to explore how do the saving and spending dimensions of the attitude toward money effect financial trouble. A further question was whether this effect is direct or is indirectly moderated by compulsive buying. **Figure 1.2** shows the structural model and the hypotheses. Further we explain the constructs, their measurement, and the hypothesized relationships. All items are measured on a 5 point Likert scale (where 1 = Totally disagree, and 5 = Totally agree).

Figure 1.2   The Structural Model and Hypotheses

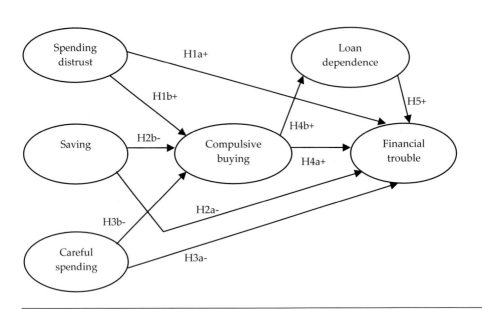

1.3.1   Financial Trouble

The financial trouble dimension became quite important in our research due to the fact that Hungarian households' savings rate is very low and therefore they react to any negative effects very sensitively. Financial trouble can mean monthly problems, e.g. related to monthly basic payments or loan installments. Based on the literature and expert interviews and consumer focus groups we developed and tested our own scale.

1.3.2   Money Attitude Scale (MAS)

People can have quite different relationship towards money where Sigmund Freud in 1908 provided the first explanation comparing money to feces (Kelemen 2009). Accoridng to Krueger (1986, 3): "Money is probably the most emotionally meaningful object in contemporary life: only food and sex are its close competitors as common carriers".

Attitude toward money is a complex, multidimensional construct that can extract both positive (such as love, quality and freedom) and negative feelings (such as distrust, failure and unability) from people. The economic (rational) value is by far surpassed by its emotional and psychological one (Medina et al. 1996). Yamauchi/Templar (1982) developed their own scale based on the multidimensional nature or attitude toward money.

Money is the common language of consumer culture. Attitude toward money expands its influence over every area of life, let it be savings, spending, work performance, ideology, charity, or attitude toward the environment. Because money is an organic part of people's life, it plays a determining role in emotional sense, as well. (Phau/Woo 2008).

Money has been regarded as the common language of consumer culture. Money attitudes have impacted all areas of a person's life which include saving habits, spending, workplace performance, political ideology, charitable giving and attitude towards the environment.

Compulsive buyers tend to suffer from lower self-esteem, and show lack of esteem compared with "ordinary" customers, and perceive money as a symbolic mean to increase self-esteem.

Yamauchi/Templer (1982) have identified four dimensions of money attitude which consist of power prestige, retention-time, distrust and anxiety. Out of the four dimensions we incorporated the (spending) distrust and retention-time constructs into our analysis, dividing the latter into two further factors.

1.3.3   Spending Distrust

Customers are often suspicious and doubtful about money, they often hesitate. This maybe due to insecurity and the drive that they want to economize and get the best value out of money. We postulate that the more someone is unsecure about spending money the higher financial trouble s/he may face.

Yamauchi/Templer (1982) linked distrust to paranoia and to other clinical symptoms. Roberts/Jones (2001) however felt that spending distrust is more a kind of price sensitivity since its direction is toward products and services. Further they stated that those who care about prices will become less compulsive in buying. This negative relationship however was not supported either by Phau/Woo (2008), or by Roberts/Sepulveda (1999). In addition, Lejoyeux et al. (2011) and Norum (2008) found positive relationship between the two constructs (**Table 1.2**).

The idea of attaching a "price sensitivity" label to "distrust" dimension by Roberts/Jones (2001) is completely the opposite approach to Yamauchi/Templer's conception (1982). As the judgment about the distrust dimension is by no means unified, this dimension needs further revision.

Table 1.2　　　　The Relationship Between Spending Distrust and Compulsive Buying

Relationship	Measurement scale	Authors	Country	Sample
Not found	Yamauchi/Templer (1982)	Phau/Woo (2008)	Australia (Perth)	n = 415 18-29 years old, at a major shopping mall
Not found	Yamauchi/Templer (1982)	Roberts/Sepulveda (1999)	Mexico (Monterrey)	n = 274 18-67 years old, acquaintances of students
Negative	Yamauchi/Templer (1982)	Roberts/Jones (2001)	USA (a private university in Texas)	n = 406, 17-21 years old students
Positive	Yamauchi/Templer (1982)	Lejoyeux et al. (2011)	France (Paris)	n = 203, medical students
Positive	Yamauchi/Templer (1982)	Norum (2008)	USA (Midwestern University)	n = 4429, 18-27 years old students

Source: Authors collection

Contrary to Roberts/Jones we emphasize the psychological notion that compulsive buyers are unsecure and feel redemptive about the spent money as it was reported by (Saraneva/Sääksjarvi 2008). Losing control makes them feel puzzled and disturbed, e.g. the new product or solution did not change their negative thinking (Christenson et al. 1994; Dittmar et al. 2007; Faber et al. 1987). As a reaction compulsive shoppers try to return products (Corbett 2000). The negative emotions created by unsuccessful shopping events make consumers to repeat shopping again. We postulate that the higher spending distrust the more likely compulsive buying is. Psychological insights lead us to the following hypotheses:

H1a: Spending distrust has a positive effect on financial trouble.
H1b: Spending distrust has a positive effect on compulsive buying.

1.3.4　　　The Two Constructs of the Retention-Time Dimension

The retention-time dimension of the MAS describes individuals who are scoring high on this dimension, as someone who places a great value on the process of preparation to carefully plan and closely monitor their financial future (Roberts/Sepulveda 1999; Yamauchi/Templer 1982).

Further, they are having high self-esteem In contrast, individuals with low scores are low on self esteem and tend to be very-present oriented rather than future oriented. Consequently, there is little concern for the careful management of their funds.

When we compare research studies focusing on the linkage of the retention-time dimension to compulsive shopping, results show a great variety that may create methodological concerns. While Roberts/Sepuvelda (1999), and Li et al. (2009) found a negative relationship between the two constructs, Phau/Woo (2008) and Lejoyeux et al. (2011) did not find any, but Hanley/Wilhelm (1992) found a positive relationship (albeit the latter have used the Furnham (1984) scale that has somewhat different content). Common wisdom may suggest a negative relationship stating the more someone cares more about finances the lower is the propensity of compulsive buying. Differences are usually explained by different culture. Phau/Woo (2008) regard Australia (where the research has taken place) as a melting pot, Li et al. (2009) regard the time orientation in China as a long-term phenomenon that would lead to more careful financial behavior.

Table 1.3   Relationship Between Retention-Time and Compulsive Buying

Relationship	Research scales	Authors	Country	Sample
Not found	Yamauchi/Templer (1982)	Phau/Woo (2008)	Australia (Perth)	n =415 18-29 years old at a major shopping complex
Not found	Yamauchi/Templer (1982)	Lejoyeux et al. (2011)	France (Paris)	n = 203 Medical students
Negative	Yamauchi/Templer (1982)	Li et al. (2009)	China (Tianjin/Ningbo)	n = 303, 18-23 years old students
Negative	Yamauchi/Templer (1982)	Roberts/Sepulveda (1999)	Mexico (Monterrey)	n = 274, 18-67 years old, acquaintances of students
Positive	Furnham (1984)	Hanley/Wilhelm (1992)	USA (several cities)	43 self-reported compulsive spenders, 100 'normal' consumers

Source: Authors collection

The variety of results in **Table 1.3** shed light the multidimensionality of the retention-time dimension. We believe that the psychological foundations and the nature of saving and spending are different, and this multidimensionality hasn't yet been researched adequately. Our explorative factor analysis shows that the retention-time dimension consists of not one, but two factors. One factor contains the saving dimension measured by items such as regular (monthly) saving capability and having financial reserves. The second factor relates to careful spending. While saving is related to long-term finances, spending is rather short-term.

As an explanation we cite Loewenstein (1996) in which he argues that "much human action is based on visceral or transient responses that go against long-term self-interest". Schelling (1984) argues that one person has two selves and that leads to different weighting of certain attributes often in different times. Individuals have different preferences when deciding about a future action or about an immediate one. Loewenstein (1996) calls them the "want self" and the "should self" having a constant fight. Latter should theoretically dominate the long-term decisions, but due the immediate rewards the want-self dominates the instant decision. The saving and careful spending relate to this dichotomy and that leads to different financial strategies.

- Saving

While the effect of saving on getting into financial trouble is relatively straightforward (i.e lowers the propensity), the effect on compulsive buying needs more explanation. Expanding on the mainstream literature findings (**Table 1.3**) we propose the negative effect (i.e. saving lowers the propensity of compulsive buying).

> **H2a:** Saving has a negative effect on financial trouble.
> **H2b:** Saving has a negative effect on compulsive buying.

- Careful spending

We believe that the more carefully someone spends, the less s/he will face financial trouble. However, careful spending refers to the everyday spending which can be easily overwritten by short-term rewards (Loewenstein, 1996). Compulsive buying can be also characterized as a malfunction in impulse control (Kellett/Bolton 2009) which is a sign of the inconsiderate spending decisions. The absence of due consideration and the disregards of financial considerations are two main factors which have been identified for impulsive buying (Dittmar/Drury 2000; Verplanken/Herabadi 2001). To sum it up, compulsive buying is less likely when someone is spending carefully and the same is true on getting into financial trouble.

> **H3a:** Careful spending has a negative effect on financial trouble.
> **H3b:** Careful spending has a negative influence on compulsive buying.

1.3.5   Compulsive Buying

In their original study Faber/O'Guinn (1992) developed a measurement scale for compulsive buying that mainly served the purpose to clinically screen and diagnose psychiatric patients. Since then the scale has found wide acceptance in consumer research based on a certain income level. This creates a problem that consumers with higher income who can afford buying compulsively cannot be identified due to the nature of the scale items. (Ridgway et al. 2008). While these consumers possess higher income they are still subject of suffering from the emotional or social consequences of compulsive buying. Another measurement question is raised by multidimensionality.

Ridgway et al. (2008) found a two-factor solution, similar to Roberts/Sepulveda (1999), who emphasized the potential impact of culture on the original dimensions. The Faber/O'Guinn scale was originally developed for U.S. customers, and some items cannot be interpreted in a Hungarian context (e.g. Hungarians do not write checks). To overcome this issue we applied an explorative factor analysis/found – similar to the authors cited above – a two-factor solution.

Compulsive buying can have both financial (e.g. extreme load dependence), or emotional negative consequences (e.g. Edwards 1993). We postulate that consumers who buy compulsively can face higher financial trouble/can depend more on loans.

> **H4a:** Compulsive buying has a positive effect on financial trouble.
> **H4b:** Compulsive buying has a positive effect on loan dependence.

1.3.6   Loan Dependence

Financial consequences of compulsive buying are usually measured by credit card usage (Faber/O'Guinn 1988; 1992; Phau/Woo 2008; Ridgway et al. 2008). Consumers buying compulsively usually generate higher debts.

In the Western economies access to credit is easy, which can lead to lapses in self-control and financial bankruptcy. The „culture of indebtedness" (Lea et al. 1995) has become a major risk factor leading to compulsive buying in the whole society. (Lunt/Livingstone 1992), and owning credit card is an invitation to dance for compulsive buyers. Compulsive buyers have chronically larger credit card balances (Ritzer 1995), and the stronger compulsiveness is the higher proportion of available income is spent (Black et al. 2001).

In Hungary credit card usage is much lower than in the U.S. and even below the European average. Overspending can take several other forms of different load products (revolving credit, personal loans, mortgage loans etc.). Consumers often mix-up credit and charge cards and do not understand the fact of overspending. Since Faber/O'Quinn (1992) pointed out that having negative balances is more important that having credit cards, we measured load dependence by the frequency of loan applications. Since compulsive buyers face a lack of self- control at the moment of transaction (Phau és Woo 2008), this can lead to negative financial consequences.

> **H5:** Loan dependence has a positive influence on financial trouble.

1.4   Research Strategy

During the fall of 2009 we carried out a survey research among consumers having loans (housing, mortgage or personal loans) aged 18-59. To generate the sample we used a random walk quota-based technique. Quotas were representative to sex, age, education, settlement type, region and loan types (**Table 1.4**). The surveys were carried out by a research company.

Table 1.4   Sample Characteristics (n = 1000)

Gender		Settlement	
Male	50,4%	Capital town	15,0%
Female	49,6%	Major towns	25,0%
		Other towns	30,0%
		Village	30,0%
Age		**Per capital net income (HUF)**	
18-29	18,0%	-50.000	25,6%
30-39	36,0%	50.001-80.000	33,2%
40-49	26,0%	80.001-110.000	23,4%
50-59	20,0%	110.001-	17,8%
Education			
Elementary school	12,1%		
Trade school	37,2%		
High school	32,6%		
University/college	18,1%		

1.5 Results

We tested our theory by a two-step method, first with fit and construct validity of the measurement model. In the second step we tested the structural theory (Hair et al. 2006).

1.5.1 Measurement Model: Confirmatory Factor Analysis

Confirmatory factor analysis (CFA) was conducted to verify the reliability and validity of the constructs. In the CFA, we assumed that every possible pair of latent factors was correlated and one variable belonged to one construct only. Results are reported in the **Table 1.5** and in Attachment A. Convergent validity was controlled by standardized factor loadings being higher than .5.

To achieve convergent validity we used two composite measures; CR (composite reliability) and AVE (average variance extracted), where CR has to be higher than .7 and AVE higher than .5 (Hair et al., 2006). From the AVE measures only spending distrust is below this level (**Table 1.5**).

Table 1.5   Validity Measures and Correlations of the Constructs (CFA)

	Construct	CR	AVE	1	2	3	4	5	6
1	Spending distrust	0,741	0,491	1,000	0,054	0,038	0,230	0,097	0,212
2	Saving	0,897	0,686	0,233***	1,000	0,057	0,090	0,004	0,053
3	Careful spending	0,833	0,713	0,195***	0,239***	1,000	0,066	0,079	0,031
4	Compulsive buying	0,822	0,607	0,480***	0,300***	-0,228***	1,000	0,345	0,201
5	Loan de-pendence	0,776	0,634	0,311***	0,064	-0,281***	0,587***	1,000	0,198
6	Financial trouble	0,885	0,720	0,460***	-0,230***	-0,176***	0,448***	0,445***	1,000

CR = composite reliability; AVE = average variance extracted

Note: Values below the diagonal are interconstruct correlation estimates. Values above the diagonal are squared interconstruct correlations (SIC). *** Correlation is significant at the $p < 0.001$ level (two-tailed).

Since discriminant validity measures the extent to which a construct is truly distinct from other constructs Hair (2006) argued that all construct average variance extracted (AVE) estimates should be larger than the corresponding squared interconstruct. We refer to **Table 1.5** that this criterion is met.

Nomological validity is tested by examining whether the correlations between the constructs in the measurement model make sense. The construct correlations are used to assess this which is reasonable in our case.

Thus, there is sufficient statistical evidence to support the existence of the six factors and that the selected measures are reasonable indicators of their corresponding factors.

1.5.2   Structural Model: Hypothesis Testing

Hypotheses were tested by a structural equation (SEM). A SEM fit statistics are good, they fulfill the requirements by Hair et al. (2006)[1]. A χ^2 = 335,33 (df = 107; p = 0,000); RMSEA = 0,046; SRMR = 0,046; GFI = 0.962; AGFI = 0.945; CFI = 0,973. The overall fit is good and the model can be used to hypotheses testing.

Figure 1.3 shows that most of the hypotheses can be accepted. Two dimensions (spending distrust and saving) of the money-attitude construct have the hypothesized direct effect on financial trouble (H1a and H2a). The higher is the spending distrust the bigger is the financial trouble, and the more someone retains (saves) money the less he has financial trouble. The third construct, careful spending, has no direct effect on financial trouble, so we reject H3a. An indirect effect however does exist, careful spending has an indirect effect (see Attachment B for direct and indirect effects.)

Spending distrust and careful spending have the hypothesized effect on financial trouble, so H1b and H3b are accepted. Higher spending distrust leads to a higher level of compulsive buying, at the same time the more carefully someone spends the lower is the propensity of compulsive buying, as a short term stress reduction mechanism.

The positive relationship between saving and compulsive buying was somewhat surprising and H2b was rejected. We explain this in a way that compulsive buying can be found by individuals who can afford the spending (Ridgway et al. 2008) and cover buying sprees from their reserves.

In a recession people are more willing to save as a safety measure (Faragó 2003; Katona 1975). During the 1970-71 recession in the U.S. saving rates were higher than before or after the crisis. While this seemed intuitively wrong, Katona (1974) argued that in a recession the wish to save is higher and proportional to the seriousness of the crisis. However due to multiple possible motivations for saving it is hard to offer one single explanation (Faragó 2003).

Compulsive buying effect financial trouble in the hypothesized positive way, and this support the acceptance of H4a and H4b. The stronger compulsive buying is, the higher is the propensity of loan dependence and financial trouble. Loan dependence has a positive effect on financial trouble (H5). At the same time compulsive buying exercises an indirect effect on financial trouble through loan dependence. The effect of compulsive buying on financial trouble can be lowered by the fact that some consumers can afford buying compulsively. So the other part of consumers – those who cannot afford compulsive buying, but still do – can have higher financial difficulties due to the crisis.

---

[1] Hair et al. (2006) defined the following criteria when the sample size is higher than 250 and the number of observed variables are between 12 and 30, the expected significant value of χ CFI > 0,92; SRMR ≤ 0,08; RMSEA ≤ 0,07.

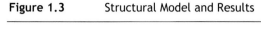

Figure 1.3   Structural Model and Results

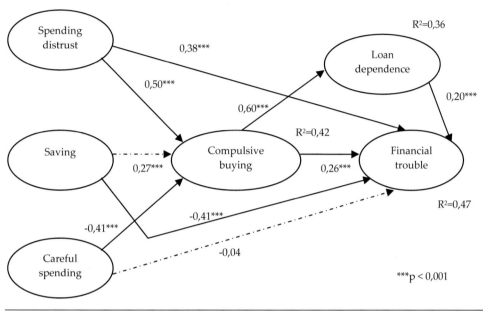

Note: All coefficients are standardized. Dotted line represents relationship that is hypothesized but not supported.

1.6   Summary

It is of great importance how financial decisions or the perceive effect influence the financial situation of individuals, especially in a recession. We have shown how the different dimensions of money attitude (spending distrust, saving, careful spending influence financial trouble in a direct or indirect way.

The research contributed to the understanding of compulsive buying among individuals in Hungary having accumulated loans. We used compulsive buying as a mediating variable due to the fact that a great part of population has accumulated debts at the time of taking the loans.

A further contribution of our research is the realization that saving and compulsive buying can coexist that supports the findings of Ridgway et al. (2008) that some buyers can afford buying compulsively.

The research indicates that some constructs need further measurement development, including the money attitude scale, compulsive buying or loan dependence. For the retention-time dimension in the future one should more focus on the different psychological nature of saving and spending, described by the problem of the double self (Bazerman et al. 1998).

Appendix A

Table 1.6   Model Items and Their Standardized Factor Weights (CFA)

Construct	Statements	Stand. factor load.	Mean	Var.
Spending distrust	I argue and complain about the cost of things I buy.	0,598	2,90	1,44
	I hesitate to spend money even on necessities.	0,760	2,82	1,33
	I automatically say "I can't afford it", whether I can or not.	0,734	2,48	1,28
Saving	I do financial planning for the future.	0,847	2,52	1,43
	I save to prepare for my old age.	0,711	2,49	1,49
	I have money available in the event of another economic depression.	0,881	2,18	1,36
	I put money aside on a regular basis for the future.	0,863	2,17	1,27
Careful spending	I keep track of my money.	0,857	4,05	1,00
	I follow a careful financial budget.	0,832	3,98	1,01
Compulsive buying	Bought things even though I couldn't afford them.	0,812	1,91	1,20
	Felt others would be horrified if they knew of my spending habits.	0,763	1,81	1,18
	Felt anxious or nervous on days I did not go shopping.	0,761	1,69	1,11
Loan dependence	I often buy products on credit.	0,791	1,95	1,17
	I buy almost everything on credit.	0,802	1,88	1,16
Financial trouble	I had problems with monthly payments.	0,799	2,23	1,35
	Last year I had often longer financial trouble.	0,872	2,19	1,35
	I could not pay my loan instalment because of other expenditures.	0,872	1,82	1,21

Appendix B

Table 1.7   Standardized Direct and Indirect Effects

Construct		Construct	Direct effect	Indirect effect	Total effect
Spending distrust	→	Compulsive buying	0,500	0	0,500
Spending distrust	→	Loan dependence	0	0,299	0,299
Spending distrust	→	Financial trouble	0,380	0,190	0,570
Saving	→	Compulsive buying	0,267	0	0,267
Saving	→	Loan dependence	0	0,160	0,160
Saving	→	Financial trouble	-0,405	0,101	-0,304
Careful spending	→	Compulsive buying	-0,408	0	-0,408
Careful spending	→	Loan dependence	0	-0,244	-0,244
Careful spending	→	Financial trouble	-0,043	-0,154	-0,198
Careful spending	→	Loan dependence	0,597	0	0,597
Loan dependence	→	Financial trouble	0,262	0,117	0,379
Loan dependence	→	Financial trouble	0,196	0	0,196

Literature

[1]   Bauman, Z. (2005): From the work ethic to the aesthetic of consumption. In Bauman, Z. Work, Consumerism and the New Poor. Second Edition. New York: Open University Press, pp. 23–42.

[2]   Bazerman, M. H./Tenbrunsel, A. E./Wade-Benzoni, K. (1998): Negotiating with yourself and losing: Making decisions with competing internal preferences. Academy of Management Review, Vol. 23, 2, pp. 225-241.

[3]   Belk, R. W. (1985): Materialism: Trait aspects of living in the material world. Journal of Consumer Research, Vol. 12, 3, pp. 265–280.

[4]   Bethlendi, A. (2007): A hitelpiac szerepe a hazai háztartások fogyasztási és megtakarítási döntéseiben. Közgazdasági Szemle, Vol. 54, December, pp. 1041–1065.

[5]   Black, D. W./Monahan, P./Schlosser, S./Repertinger, S. (2001): Compulsive buying severity: An analysis of compulsive buying results in 44 subjects. Journal of Nervous and Mental Disease, Vol. 189, pp. 123–126.

[6]   Chaker, A. M. (2003): Hello, I'm a shopaholic! There's a move afoot to make compulsive shopping a diagnosable mental disorder: But should it be? Wall Street Journal (January 14).

[7]   Christenson, G.A./Faber, R.J./de Zwaan, M./Raymond, N. C./Specker, S. M./Ekern, M. D./Mackenzie, T. B./Crosby, R. D./Crow, S. J./Eckert, E. D./Mussell, M. P./Mitchell, J. E. (1994): Compulsive buying: descriptive characteristics and psychiatric comorbidity. Journal of Clinical Psychiatry, Vol. 55, pp. 5-11.

[8]   Corbett, G. (2000): Women, body image and shopping for clothes. In Baker, A. (Ed.). Serious Shopping. London: Free Association Books, pp. 114-133.

[9]   d'Astous, A. (1990): An inquiry into the compulsive side of 'normal' consumers. Journal of Consumer Policy, Vol. 13, 1, pp. 15–31.

[10] d'Astous, A./Jacob, I. (2002): Understanding consumer reactions to premium-based promotional offers. European Journal of Marketing, Vol. 36, 11/12, pp. 1270-1286.

[11] DeSarbo, W./Edwards, E. (1996): Typologies of compulsive buying behavior: A constrained clusterwise regression approach. Journal of Consumer Psychology, Vol. 5, 3, pp. 231–262.

[12] Dittmar, H./Drury, J. (2000): Self image—is it in the bag? A qualitative comparison between 'ordinary' and 'excessive' consumers. Journal of Economic Psychology, Vol. 21, pp. 109–142.

[13] Dittmar, H./Long, K./Bond, R. (2007): When a better self is only a button click away: associations between materialistic values, emotional and identity-related buying motives, and compulsive buying tendency online. Journal of Social and Clinical Psychology, Vol. 26, 3, pp. 334-361.

[14] Droge, C./Mackoy, R. D. (1995): The consumption culture versus environmentalism: Bridging value systems with environmental marketing. In Ellen, P. S. & Kaufman, P. (eds.) Proceedings of the 1995 Marketing and Public Policy Conference. Georgia State University Press: Atlanta, pp. 227–232.

[15] Edwards, E. A. (1992): The Measurement and Modeling of Compulsive Consumer Buying Behavior. Ph.D. dissertation, University of Michigan.

[16] Edwards, E. A. (1993): Development of a new scale for measuring compulsive buying behavior. Financial Counseling and Planning, Vol. 4, pp. 67–84.

[17] Faber, R. J./Christenson, G. A. (1996): In the mood to buy: Differences in the mood states experienced by compulsive buyers and other consumers. Psychology and Marketing, Vol. 13, pp. 803–820.

[18] Faber, R. J./O'Guinn, T. C./Krych, R. (1987): Compulsive consumption. In Anderson, P. & Wallendorf, M. (Eds). Advances in Consumer Research. Provo: Association for Consumer Research, Vol. 14, pp. 132-135.

[19] Faber, R. J./O'Guinn, T. C. (1988): Compulsive consumption and credit abuse. Journal of Consumer Policy, Vol. 11, pp. 97-109.

[20] Faber, R. J./O'Guinn, T. C. (1992): A Clinical Screener for Compulsive Buying. Journal of Consumer Research, Vol. 19, December, pp. 459–469.

[21] Faragó, K. (2003): Etikai kérdések a gazdaságpszichológiában. In Hunyadi Gy. (ed.). Gazdaságpszichológia. Osiris: Budapest. pp. 716-761.

[22] Furnham, A. (1984): Many sides of the coin: The psychology of money usage. Personal and Individual Differences, Vol. 5, pp. 501 -509.

[23] Gáspár K./Varga Zs. (2011): A bajban lévő lakáshitelesek elemzése mikroszimulációs modellezéssel. Közgazdasági Szemle, Vol. 58, June, pp. 529–542.

[24] Hair, J. F./Black, W. C./Babin, B. J./Anderson, R. E./Tatham, R. L. (2006): Multivariate Data Analysis. Sixth Edition. Upper Saddle River: Pearson Education.

[25] Hanley, A./Wilhelm, M. S. (1992): Compulsive buying: An exploration into self-esteem and money attitudes. Journal of Economic Psychology, Vol. 13, pp. 5-18.

[26] Kellett, S./Bolton, J. V. (2009): Compulsive Buying: A Cognitive–Behavioural Model. Clinical Psychology and Psychotherapy, Vol. 16, pp. 83–99.

[27] Koran, L./Faber, R. J./Aboujaoude, E./Large, M. D./Serpe, R. T. (2006): Estimated prevalence of compulsive buying behavior in the United States. American Journal of Psychiatry, Vol. 163, 1, pp. 1806–1812.

[28] Krueger, D. W. (1986): Money, success and success phobia. In: Krueger, D.W. (ed.). The Last Taboo: Money as Symbol and Reality in Psychotherapy and Psychoanalysis. New York: Brunner/Mazel, pp. 3-16.

[29] Kyrios, M./Frost, R. O./Steketee, G. (2004): Cognitions in compulsive buying and acquisition. Cognitive Therapy and Research, Vol. 28, pp. 241-258.

[30] Lea, S. E. G./Webley, P./Walker, C. M. (1995): Psychological factors in consumer debt: Money management, economic socialisation and credit usage. Journal of Economic Psychology, Vol. 16, pp. 681–701.

[31] Lejoyeux, M./Richoux-Benhaim, C./Betizeau, A./Lequen, V. /Lohnhardt, H. (2011): Money attitude, self-esteem, and compulsive buying in a population of medical students. Front Psychiatry,Vol. 2, 13.

[32] Li, D./Jiang, Y./An, S./Shen, Z./Jin, W. (2009): The influence of money attitudes on young Chinese consumers' compulsive buying. Young Consumers, Vol. 10, 2, pp. 98-109.

[33] Loewenstein, G. (1996): Out of control: Visceral influences on behavior. Organizational Behavior and Human Decision Processes, Vol. 65, pp. 272-292.

[34] Medina, J. F./Saegert, J./Gresham, A. (1996): Comparison of Mexican-American and Anglo-American attitudes toward money. The Journal of Consumer Affairs, Vol. 30, 1, pp. 124-146.

[35] Mittal, B./Holbrook, M. B./Beatty, S./Raghubir, P./Woodside, A. G. (2008): Consumer Behavior: How Humans Think, Feel, and Act in the Marketplace. Cincinnati: Open Mentis.

[36] Mowen, J. C./Spears, N. (1999): Understanding compulsive buying among college students: a hierarchical approach. Journal of Consumer Psychology, Vol. 8, 4, pp. 407-430.

[37] Katona, G. (1975): Psychological economics. New York: Esevier.

[38] Kelemen G. (2009): Vásárlásmánia. Lege Artis Medicinae, Vol. 19, 4/5, pp. 354-357.

[39] Lunt, P. K./Livingstone, S. M. (1992): Mass Consumption and Personal Identity. Buckingham: Open University Press.

[40] Manolis, C./Roberts, J. A. (2008): Compulsive buying: Does it matter how it's measured? Journal of Economic Psychology, Vol. 29, 4, pp. 555–576.

[41] Muller, A./de Zwaan, M. (2004): Current status of psychotherapy research on pathological buying. Verhaltenstherapie, Vol. 14, 2, pp. 112–119.

[42] Neuner, M./Raab, G./Reisch, L. A. (2005): Compulsive buying in maturing consumer societies: An empirical re-inquiry. Journal of Economic Psychology, Vol. 26, pp. 509–522.

[43] Norum, P. S. (2008): The role of time preference and credit card usage in compulsive buying behaviour. International Journal of Consumer Studies, Vol. 32, pp. 269–275.

[44] O'Guinn, T. C./Faber, R. J. (1989): Compulsive buying: A phenomenological exploration. Journal of Consumer Research, Vol. 16, 2, pp. 147–157.

[45] Palan, K. M./Morrow, P. C./Trapp, A. II/Blackburn, V. (2011): Compulsive buying behavior in college students: The mediating role of credit card misuse. Journal of Marketing Theory and Practice, Vol. 19, 1, pp. 81–96.

[46] Phau, I./Woo, C. (2008): Understanding compulsive buying tendencies among young Australians: The roles of money attitude and credit card usage. Marketing Intelligence & Planning, Vol. 26, 5, pp. 441-458.

[47] PSZÁF (2010): A bankok késedelmes kintlevőségei 2009. év végén. PSZÁF jelentés, February 11.

[48] Ridgway, N. M./Kukar-Kiney, M./Monroe, K. B. (2008): An expanded conceptualization and a new measure of compulsive buying. Journal of Consumer Research, Vol. 35, December, pp. 622-639.

[49] Ritzer, G. (1995): Expressing America: A Critique of Global Credit Card Society. Thousand Oaks: Pine Forge Press.

[50] Roberts, J. A./Jones, E. (2001): Money attitudes, credit card use, and compulsive buying among American college students. Journal of Consumer Affairs, Vol. 35, pp. 213–240.

[51] Roberts, J. A./Sepulveda, C. J. M. (1999): Money attitudes and compulsive buying: an exploratory investigation of the emerging consumer culture in Mexico. Journal of International Consumer Marketing, Vol. 11, 4, pp. 53-74.

[52] Saraneva, A./Sääksjarvi, M. (2008): Young compulsive buyers and the emotional roller-coaster in shopping. Young Consumers, Vol. 9, 2, pp. 75-89.

[53] Schelling, T. C. (1984): Choice and consequence: Perspectives of an Errant Economist. Cambridge: Harvard University Press.

[54] Schulze, G. (1992): Die Erlebnisgesellschaft. Kultursoziologie der Gegenwart. Frankfurt: Campus Verlag.

[55] Vadas, G. (2007): Wealth portfolio of Hungarian households: Urban legends and facts. Magyar Nemzeti Bank, Occasional papers 68.

[56] Verplanken, B./Herabadi, A. (2001): Individual differences in impulsive buying tendencies: Feeling and no thinking. European Journal of Personality, Vol. 15, pp. 71–83.

[57] Yamauchi, K./Templer, D. (1982): The development of a money attitude scale. Journal of Personality Assessment, Vol. 46, pp. 522-528.

2   Repetitive Purchase Behavior

Hans Baumgartner, Pennsylvania State University, United States of America

Abstract

Eight distinct types of purchase behavior are distinguished in the model of the purchase cube proposed by the author, based on the purchase motives or reasons for buying underlying a purchase. One of the purchase types is repetitive purchase behavior, which is characteristic of functional purchases that are made deliberately rather than spontaneously and are relatively low in purchase involvement. This essay discusses the concept of repetitive purchase behavior and briefly reviews prior research that has investigated repetitive purchases from various perspectives.

Keywords

Classifications of Purchase Behavior, Repetitive Purchases, Brand Loyalty, Habit.

2.1   Introduction

In several recent publications I have described a new typology of purchase behaviors called the purchase cube, which distinguishes eight distinct types of purchases (Baumgartner 2002, 2010). One of these types is repetitive purchase behavior. In this essay I would like to elaborate on this form of purchasing, which is quite common in the case of frequently purchased consumer goods, and briefly review some of the models that researchers have proposed to describe and explain repetitive purchase behavior. Professor Wagner is well-known for his work on stochastic models of consumer behavior (e.g., Wagner/Taudes 1986, 1987), which represent one major approach to thinking about repetitive purchase behavior, so this chapter would seem to be an appropriate contribution to a Festschrift honoring Professor Wagner.

2.2   The Purchase Cube: A New Typology of Purchase Behaviors

Baumgartner (2010) reviewed prior typologies of purchase behavior and found them lacking, either because they are not sufficiently comprehensive to accommodate the multitude of qualitatively distinct forms of purchasing found in practice or because they consist of a mere listing of supposedly different purchase behaviors, making it difficult to discern similarities and differences. Based on several empirical studies in which consumers were asked to classify 44 different buying behaviors expressing different purchase motives or reasons for buying things into cohesive groups (e.g., buying something out of curiosity, making a purchase based on the quality of the available products, buying something because of habit), Baumgartner (2002, 2010) proposed a new typology called the purchase cube, which distinguishes eight different purchase behaviors based on three underlying dimensions: functional vs. psycho-social purchases, low vs. high purchase involvement, and spontaneous vs. deliberate purchases. The first dimension, functional vs. psychosocial purchases, is based on whether the purchase is motivated by utilitarian or hedonic (including experiential, value-expressive, and symbolic) considerations. The second dimension, low vs. high purchase involvement, refers to how much care is devoted to buying something and how much effort is expended on the purchase. Purchase involvement is different from the importance or relevance of the product purchased, because buying a highly self-relevant product may require very little care if the consumer has purchased the product many times before. Even the riskiness of the purchase is not a strong correlate of purchase involvement, because devoting little effort to a purchase may render the purchase risky. The final dimension, deliberate vs. spontaneous purchases, indicates whether a purchase is planned or unplanned, whether or not it follows a script, whether or not it is based on prior experience, and whether or not is was driven by a previously formed intention.

Figure 2.1   The Purchase Cube: A Three-Dimensional Typology of
                      Purchase Behaviors

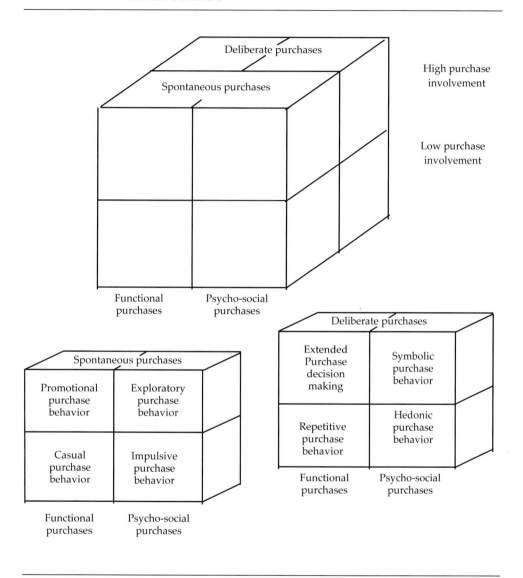

Note: Based on Baumgartner (2002)

At first sight, it might seem that high purchase involvement is confounded with the deliberateness of the purchase. However, there are deliberate purchases that are low in purchase involvement (e.g., purchases based on loyalty), just as there are spontaneous purchases that are relatively high in purchase involvement (e.g., exploratory purchases motivated by curiosity).

Cross-classifying the two poles of each of the three dimensions yields eight distinct forms of purchase behavior. The resulting scheme, known as the purchase cube, is shown in **Figure 2.1**, and a detailed description is provided in Baumgartner (2010). Here I will only briefly explain the purchase behaviors distinguished in the cube.

Starting with the spontaneous half of the purchase cube, functional purchases that are relatively high in purchase involvement are referred to as promotional purchases (e.g., buying a product because the price is good or because it's on sale), while functional purchases relatively low in purchase involvement are called casual purchases (e.g., buying a product out of convenience, mindlessly, or without thinking much about it). Conversely, psycho-social purchases that are relatively high in purchase involvement are called exploratory purchases (e.g., buying something because of a desire for variety, out of curiosity, or simply to give it a try), whereas psycho-social purchases relatively low in purchase involvement are referred to as impulsive purchases.

Continuing with the deliberate half of the purchase cube, functional purchases that are relatively high in involvement are called extended purchase decision making (e.g., making a purchase based on the performance, quality, or value of the product, buying something because the purchase solves a problem, making a purchase based on a careful comparison of the available options), while functional purchases relatively low in purchase involvement are referred to as repetitive purchase behavior (e.g., buying something out of habit, because of loyalty to the brand, or due to familiarity). Conversely, psycho-social purchases that are relatively high in purchase involvement are called symbolic purchase behavior (e.g., buying something because of social motivations such as status or social approval, or because of psychological motivations such as a desire to project a certain self-image), whereas psycho-social purchases relatively low in purchase involvement are referred to as hedonic purchases (e.g., buying something because of a desire for sensory gratification, because it's fun or because a person simply wants the product).

The model of the purchase cube is somewhat similar to the FCB grid (Ratchford 1987), which classifies purchase decisions and products along two dimensions, thinking vs. feeling and low vs. high involvement. However, involvement is conceptualized somewhat differently in the FCB grid, and the grid does not incorporate the distinction between spontaneous and deliberate buying behavior. The FCB grid was primarily developed as an advertising planning tool, and the model suggests that for low involvement, think purchases advertising should create and reinforce habits. This is broadly consistent with the placement of repetitive purchases in the model of the purchase cube, because habits are one reason why consumers buy products repetitively. In the sequel, we will focus on repetitive purchase behavior and discuss a variety of approaches that have attempted to describe and explain repeat purchases.

2.3 The Concept of Repetitive Purchase Behavior

The core purchase theme for repetitive purchases is deliberately buying something that one has repeatedly purchased in the past with a minimum of effort. As stated by Alderson (1957, p. 166), "[b]uying habits, in the sense of repetitive purchase of a given brand or customary trading at a given store, … can … be regarded as deliberately chosen routines designed to save time and energy for rational consideration of more important matters". The repeat purchase may be motivated either by the belief that the product's performance is adequate and that investing additional effort in finding a better product is not worthwhile, or by a consumer's insistence on a particular brand that he or she is loyal to. In the latter case purchase decision making is still effortless because consumers know what they want and do not have to engage in information search and alternative evaluation. Repetitive purchases are functional in the sense that the buying process does not provide hedonic or symbolic benefits. Furthermore, the emotional gratification offered by the product, if available at all, is muted because of the frequency of prior consumption experiences. Due to the repetitive nature of the task and the practice gained in previous buying situations, the consumer can make such purchases with minimal effort and conscious control (i.e., more or less automatically). However, this does not necessarily mean that repetitive purchases are non-volitional or unintentional (cf. Quellette/Wood 1998). Because consumers can draw on previous experience, repetitive purchases can be enacted quickly and with ease, but the purchase itself does not occur spontaneously and in that sense is planned and deliberate. In other words, although the purchase is not made based on a conscious decision explicitly made just before the act of buying, it is nonetheless intentional in the sense that the capricious element of spontaneous forms of buying behavior is absent.

As mentioned earlier, the model of the purchase cube was derived from an analysis of people's classification of 44 different purchase behaviors into distinct groups. Specifically, the raw data consisted of the similarities between pairs of purchase behaviors (based on the proportion of respondents who assigned each pair to the same category) and these data were then analyzed with nonmetric multidimensional scaling and average linkage clustering. Overall, repetitive purchases emerged as a cohesive category of purchase behaviors distinct from other types of purchases, but there was some evidence of two subgroups. On the one hand, consumers buy some products repetitively because they are familiar with them, have been satisfied with them in the past, have a preference for them, and are loyal to them. On the other hand, consumers also buy products repetitively because it's a routine or habit and they usually buy that product. As discussed in greater detail below, this differentiation of repeated purchase behavior into brand loyalty and habit is consistent with the recent work of Tam, Wood/Ji (2009).

2.4   Prior Marketing Research on Repeat Purchases

Research on repetitive purchase behavior (RPB) in general and brand loyalty in particular has a long tradition in marketing. Jacoby/Chestnut (1978) provided a comprehensive review of the literature from 1923 till 1976, with an emphasis on the measurement of brand loyalty. Much work on RPB has been conducted from a modeling perspective and this research will be reviewed first. Next, we will look at studies investigating brand loyalty and habitual buying from a psychological perspective. Finally, we will briefly review two other perspectives on loyalty dealing with the intergenerational transfer of loyalties and relationship-based accounts of loyalty.

2.4.1   Modeling Perspectives on RPB

The research most closely associated with modeling repetitive purchases is probably the stochastic choice literature (see Wagner/Taudes, 1987, for a review). One approach, commonly identified with Ehrenberg (e.g., Uncles, Ehrenberg/Hammond 1995), views purchase behavior as an "as-if-random" process in which previous purchases have no influence on the current purchase (so-called zero-order models). Specifically, consumers are assumed to have a certain average buying rate for the category, but individual purchases occur randomly and independently of when the last purchase was made (i.e., according to a Poisson process). In a similar way, brand choices are assumed to be based on steady probabilities of buying different brands, but the selection of a particular brand does not depend on which brand was chosen last (i.e., brand choice follows a multinomial process). Purchase behavior is considered to be habitual in the sense that consumers have a small repertoire of brands that they buy consistently with stable propensities. Both purchase rates and brand choice probabilities are allowed to vary across consumers, and the resulting integrated model of purchase incidence and brand choice predicts – based on the penetration (proportion of households that buy the product at least once during a given time period) and purchase frequency (average number of purchases per buyer in the category) for the category and the average brand in the category, as well as the market shares of individual brands – what proportion of households will buy each brand how often during any given time period, what percentage will engage in period-to-period repeat buying, how many buyers will purchase a given brand exclusively, and what other brands the buyers of a given brand will purchase as well.

The model has been applied to many fast-moving consumer goods and three interesting generalizations relevant to RPB have emerged. First, relatively few customers are completely loyal to a single brand, and exclusively loyal customers are not heavier users of the brand. For example, in the coffee category fewer than 20 percent of consumers buy a single brand in a one-year period. Second, the purchase behavior of many consumers is characterized by divided loyalty. This means that multiple brands are bought regularly, although some brands may be purchased more often than others. For example, a consumer may choose from three brands with purchase probabilities of .6, .3. and .1. Third, a brand's market share is mostly a function of how many 'loyal' buyers it has (in the sense of how many households buy it at least once during a given time period) and only secondarily of how loyal these buyers are (as measured by how often they buy the brand), although brands that are bought by fewer people also tend to have slightly lower average purchase frequencies. The latter finding is known as the double jeopardy phenomenon.

Other stochastic modeling traditions hypothesize that, in contrast to the no-purchase-feedback assumption in the Ehrenberg model, previous purchases do have an influence on brand choice. Two different approaches to modeling the influence of past purchases can be distinguished. In so-called first-order Markov models, only the last purchase occasion is assumed to affect choice probabilities. For simplicity, consider a market with only two brands, A and B, or a situation in which interest centers on whether a consumer chooses the target brand (A) or a non-target brand (B). If the probability (p) that the consumer chooses brand A at time t is independent of his or her choice at time (t-1), the process is called zero-order (the so-called Bernoulli model, a special case of the multinomial model). The parameter p in this case indicates a consumer's intrinsic preference for brand A. If the choice of A at (t-1) increases the probability that A will be chosen again at t, this is referred to as reinforcement or inertia. Mathematically, the conditional probability of choosing A at t, given a choice of A at (t-1), can be expressed as $p+R(1-p)$, where R is the reinforcement or inertia parameter ($0<=R<=1$). That is, reinforcement increases the zero-order choice probability for brand A (i.e., the intrinsic preference for brand A) by a fraction of the maximum possible increase (cf. Kahn et al. 1986). In the special case where R equals zero, reinforcement is absent and the process is zero-order. However, for R greater than 0 reinforcement is present, and when R equals 1 (i.e., when reinforcement is at its maximum value), the same brand is repurchased with probability one.

This model was first considered by Jeuland (1979), and he showed that the equilibrium choice probabilities for the Bernoulli and inertia (or reinforcement) models were exactly the same (namely p and (1-p), respectively). However, the sequencing of choices is different in the two models. Specifically, repeat purchase probabilities are higher and switching probabilities are lower in the inertia model than in the zero-order model and this leads to longer runs (i.e., instances in which the same brand is chosen repeatedly) for a given brand but fewer runs in total. Jeuland (1979) also argued that the steady-state choice probabilities (or intrinsic preferences) were an indicator of long-term loyalty and that the reinforcement or inertia parameter R assessed short-term loyalty. Givon (1984) extended Jeuland's work by developing an integrated model of repeat buying and brand switching in which a parameter VS indicates a consumer's preference for (VS>0) or avoidance of (VS<0) variety.

The variety avoidance part of the model is equivalent to Jeuland's inertia model, and the special case of VS=0 leads to the zero-order model.

In contrast to first-order Markov models, so-called learning models assume that a consumer's entire purchase history will influence the next purchase. For example, in the linear learning model first considered by Kuehn (1962), each purchase of a given brand increases the probability that the brand will be chosen again. However, the reinforcing effect of past purchases decreases exponentially and cannot exceed an upper limit Up (Up<1) even if the same brand is chosen again and again. Conversely, continued rejection of a brand cannot drop the purchase probability for the brand below a lower limit Lp (Lp>0). These phenomena are called incomplete habit formation and incomplete habit extinction. As stated by Kuehn, the model assumes that "consumers will generally not develop such strong brand loyalties (or buying habits) as to ensure either the rejection or purchase of a given brand" (p. 11). Various authors have subsequently considered extensions of the linear learning model (see Wagner/Taudes 1987).

Comparative assessments of zero-, first-, and higher-order stochastic models have not yielded very consistent results (see Bass et al., 1984, for a review). Some authors have argued that purchases of frequently-purchased, low-priced products are often consistent with a zero-order process (e.g., Bass et al. 1984), but the zero-order model certainly does not characterize the buying behavior of all consumers, and different product classes and even different brands within a product class exhibit reinforcement tendencies to varying degrees (Kahn et al. 1986). Furthermore, the same consumer may follow different choice processes in different product categories. Givon (1984) showed that variety avoiders tended to be older households, and he also hypothesized that "for functional household products where risk of low performance may be an important factor, more variety avoidance is desired" (p. 14). However, in general few generalizations are available about what factors determine the order of the choice process.

Apart from the stochastic modeling tradition, there has also been substantial interest in RPB in the discrete brand choice literature. For example, Guadagni/Little (1983) modeled brand choice as a function of brand and package size loyalty variables, which were defined as exponentially weighted averages of past purchases of a given brand or package size. They showed that customer-specific brand and size loyalties were the most important predictors of coffee purchases (compared to price and promotional influences) and that loyal buyers were less sensitive to marketing actions than switchers. Lattin (1987) proposed a similar model in which past choices influence a consumer's current choice, but by expressing the utility of a brand as a function of its attributes he was able to consider cases in which consumers seek variety for certain attributes and exhibit loyalty for others. Using data on soft drink choices, Lattin (1987) showed that most consumers were loyal to either diet or nondiet beverages but sought variety between colas and noncolas. Bawa (1990) specified a brand choice model that allows a consumer to both seek and avoid variety, depending on the length of the run of purchases of a given brand. Based on theories of exploratory behavior (see Steenkamp/Baumgartner 1992), he argued that consumers might first exhibit inertial behavior but eventually engage in variety seeking after purchasing the same brand several times. His empirical results indicated that this type of hybrid behavior (variety avoidance followed by variety seeking) was characteristic of a majority of households for facial tissue and paper towels but that variety seeking and zero-order behavior were more common for ready-to-eat cereals.

Subsequent research has tried to integrate the stochastic and discrete choice literatures and to relax limiting assumptions of both approaches. For example, Seetharaman and Chintagunta (1998) used Givon's model to represent habit-persistence (variety avoidance) and variety seeking, but they also incorporated marketing variables by expressing the choice probabilities (which represent intrinsic preference in Givon's model) as functions of price, feature, and display. Furthermore, habit persistence and variety seeking were allowed to vary across consumers, either as a function of consumer characteristics such as demographics (observed heterogeneity) or because of unexplained factors (unobserved heterogeneity). In an application to tuna purchases, they found that this market was mostly characterized by habit persistence, not variety seeking. In addition, they showed that higher-income households were more habit-prone than lower-income households and that variety seeking was more pronounced in larger households.

In a related paper, Roy et al. (1996) consider a dynamic choice model in which past purchases (specifically, the last purchase) influence current choice probabilities (similar to the specification proposed by Guadagni/Little (1983), although they allow influences beyond the past purchase). In addition, intrinsic preferences for brands and response to marketing mix variables (price, display, features) are allowed to vary for different segments of the market (unobserved heterogeneity) and the nonsystematic components of utility for different brands are not assumed to be independent. Roy et al. thus allow current choice probabilities to be a function of both purchase feedback (state dependence, the "hand of the past"), which is reflected in the impact of past choices on the systematic component of utility) and habit persistence (the influence of prior purchase propensities on current selection probabilities), which is reflected in serial correlation of the errors across purchases. In an application to catsup purchases, they show that inertia or habit persistence is minimal once the effects of state dependence and heterogeneity are accounted for.

A third modeling approach dealing with brand loyalty has been concerned with segmenting markets into groups of brand loyal and brand switching consumers, based on decompositions of brand transition matrices using latent class methods. Illustrative papers include Grover/Srinivasan (1987), Colombo/Morrison (1989), and Dekimpe et al. (1997). Since these papers are not primarily concerned with modeling purchase behavior but segmenting the market, they are not considered further here.

In summary, the modeling literature on repetitive purchase behavior is vast and only the major distinct approaches have been briefly outlined in this review. The goal of this research tradition has been to accurately describe patterns of repeated purchases of frequently bought consumer goods. Much progress has been made in this respect and increasingly sophisticated models have been developed to improve the accuracy of the predictions. However, while the models are useful in describing regularities in choice behavior and assessing the impact of past choices on current choices (i.e., choice dynamics), they provide limited insights into our understanding of why consumers engage in repeat purchase.

2.4.2 Psychological Perspectives on RPB

All psychological approaches share a focus on the mental antecedents of repeated purchases of the same brand(s) and an interest in the process through which brands are purchased repeatedly. I will distinguish between research dealing with brand loyalty and work studying the role of habit in purchase behavior.

- Brand loyalty

  Brand loyalty is usually regarded as felt commitment to a brand resulting from beliefs about a brand's superior performance (cognitive loyalty), pleasurable experiences with the brand (affective loyalty), or behavioral intentions to repurchase the brand (conative loyalty) (cf. Jacoby/Chestnut 1978; Oliver 1999). As stressed by Oliver (1999, p. 34), this commitment encourages repeated purchases of the same brand "despite situational influences and marketing efforts having the potential to cause switching behavior."

  Although the goal of attitudinal models of brand loyalty is to explain committed repurchases of a brand, it is surprising how little we know about this phenomenon. One of the earliest attempts to explain differences in the strength of brand loyalty is based on social judgment theory (Sherif/Sherif/Nebergall 1965). Jacoby (1971) argued that brands considered for purchase could be aligned along a continuum of preference and classified into one of three groups: those falling into the region of acceptance, those falling into the region of rejection, and those falling into the region of neutrality. The greater the distance between the region of acceptance on the one hand and the regions of neutrality or rejection on the other hand, the smaller the number or proportion of brands in the acceptance region, the larger the number or proportion of brands in the rejection region, and the greater the proportion of brands in the rejection region relative to the proportion of brands in the acceptance region, the stronger brand loyalty.

  Although Jacoby's (1971) study presents an interesting methodology for assessing the strength of brand loyalty, the approach does not explain why the distribution of brands along a preference continuum varies across consumers. Somebody whose region of acceptance contains only a single brand might be very brand loyal, but we still do not know what makes the consumer committed to the brand in question. A similar criticism can be levied against the work of Newman/Werbel (1973), who argue that loyalty depends on whether a certain brand was repurchased, how many brands were thought of at the outset of the decision process, and how much brand-related information seeking the consumer engaged in. Loyalty is strongest when the old brand was repurchased, the old brand was mainly thought of, and no brand-related information seeking occurred. Although this approach leads to a richer characterization of brand loyalty than approaches focused on repeat purchase, it does not provide an explanation of brand loyalty.

Dick/Basu (1994) proposed a conceptual model of customer loyalty in which loyalty depends on both a favorable attitude (relative to other choice objects) and repeat patronage. Repeat patronage in the absence of strong relative attitudes is said to indicate spurious loyalty, while the case of strong relative attitudes without repeat purchase is called latent loyalty. The reason for discrepancies between relative attitudes and repeat patronage is seen in situational influences (e.g., stockouts of the preferred brand, promotional offers by competitors) and social-normative factors (e.g., disapproval by significant others). In order to attain loyal customers, a company has to both create strong relative attitudes (which involves building strongly held attitudes and differentiating the target brand from other offerings) and manage situational and social-normative influences.

In addition to offering a conceptualization of loyalty, Dick/Basu (1994) also discuss antecedents and consequences of loyalty. They argue that accessible favorable attitudes will enhance loyalty and that accessibility may mediate the effects of attitude confidence, centrality, and clarity on loyalty. They also suggest that satisfaction and other affective states contribute to loyalty, and that switching costs and sunk costs positively influence loyalty.

In terms of consequences of loyalty, they cite evidence that loyalty decreases consumers' motivation to search for information and increases their resistance to counterpersuasion, and they suggest that loyalty may encourage positive word-of-mouth communication.

Oliver (1999) proposed a model of consumer loyalty in which commitment to a product is viewed as a function of two factors: degree of individual fortitude and extent of community/social support. Individual fortitude ranges from beliefs about the product's performance at the low end, to liking and behavioral intentions to repurchase at intermediate levels, to action inertia, defined as a commitment to overcoming obstacles that might prevent repurchase, at the high end. This factor is similar to attitude strength in previous discussions of loyalty. The novel aspect of the framework is the community/social support factor. It recognizes that the consumer's social environment may restrict access to other brands and promote the use of the target brand. The highest form of loyalty is attained in a situation of individual and social integration where "the consumer wants to be loyal, the social organization wants him or her to be loyal, and as a result, the two may become symbiotic" (Oliver 1999, p. 41).

Oliver cautions that this ultimate loyalty state may be unattainable for many providers of products because the product does not lend itself to consumer fortitude or the product cannot be embedded in a social network. In these cases, satisfaction, defined as pleasurable fulfillment and regarded as a first step in the quest for ultimate loyalty, may be a more realistic goal than loyalty.

■ Habit

A second psychological approach to understanding repetitive buying behavior, which has emerged recently based on foundational work on habits in psychology, is the literature on the habitual consumer (Wood/Neal 2009). According to this work, habits are specific behavioral responses that are elicited more or less automatically by particular contexts. For example, a consumer might stand in front of the cereal aisle of his or her favorite grocery store and habitually pick the brand of cereal he or she usually eats for breakfast. Habits are by definition a form of repetitive behavior, but Wood/Neal (2009) argue that habits differ from other repeated behaviors such as brand loyalty in that habitual acts are more rigid responses elicited by stable contexts. Although habits are not specifically guided by intentions formed for the purpose at hand, they are "the residue of past goal pursuit" (Wood/Neal 2009, p. 582). It is in this sense that habits are deliberate rather than spontaneous, because they are essentially responses that have proven rewarding in particular circumstances. Although consumers do not always display the same behavior in a given situation, Wood/Neal argue that consumers are likely to act habitually when they are under time pressure, when they are distracted, and when self-control resources are limited. All these conditions are consistent with the assumption that habits are a form of low-involvement purchase behavior, when consumers are not willing or able to devote effort and care to the purchase process, or effort and care are unnecessary because of prior experience.

Tam et al. (2009) discussed the different marketing implications for managing repeated buying behavior depending on whether repeat purchase is due to loyalty or habit. Since brand loyalty is due to favorable brand evaluations that are held with sufficient strength, the goal is to improve the favorability of consumers' attitudes toward the target brand and to bolster attitude strength (e.g., by making them more accessible) so that attitudes will be strongly related to purchase intentions and repeat purchase. In contrast, since habits trigger behavior via stable context cues without mediation by behavioral intentions, the goal is to first encourage the establishment of a habit and to subsequently ensure that the context cues that trigger repeat purchase remain stable. Of particular relevance to marketers is the so-called habit discontinuity effect. This refers to the finding that when people go through a life transition, habits are often disrupted because the context for many previously habitual behaviors changes.

For example, Wood/Tam/Guerrero Witt (2005) conducted a study with students who transferred to a new university. They showed that for students with strong exercise, newspaper reading and TV watching habits, habitual behavior persisted only when the performance context for these habits (in terms of location, presence of other people, etc.) remained relatively stable. Life transitions can thus be a challenge if habits are to be maintained, but they also offer opportune moments for marketers to encourage the establishment of new habits.

2.4.3   Other Perspectives on RPB

An interesting stream of research has investigated the intergenerational transfer of brand loyalties. The basic idea is that children inherit some of their brand preferences from their parents, either via observation or through direct communication within the family (Moschis 1985; Ward, Wackman/Wartella 1977). Moschis (1985) proposed that the extent of intergenerational transfer depended on both the type of product (e.g., parental influence may be greater for shopping goods than convenience or specialty goods and for products that are high in perceived risk) and consumer characteristics (e.g., parental influence may decline with the age of the offspring). Moore-Shay/Lutz (1988) found that daughters' self-reported brand loyalty for grocery products was similar to mothers' self-reported loyalty. Childers/Rao (1992) showed that intergenerational transfer of brand loyalty was greatest for private necessities (possibly because peers are less likely to have an influence for these types of products) and that intergenerational influence is generally greater in Thai families than in U.S. families. Visvanathan, Childers/Moore (2000) developed a measurement instrument that distinguishes between intergenerational communication and intergenerational influence and contains consumption-related preferences as a subdimension (besides consumer skills and attitudes). Finally, Moore/Wilkie/Lutz (2002) studied intergenerational influences as a source of brand equity using mother-daughter dyads. They found that the incidence of identical brand preferences exceeded chance levels for 23 of the 24 product categories studied and that some brands benefit substantially from intergenerational transfer effects. In general, this research demonstrates that social influence transmitted within families can be an important source of repetitive purchase behavior.

Another stream of research has examined brand loyalty from a relationship perspective using depth interviewing techniques (Fournier/Yao 1997). This work seeks to provide a richer characterization of brand loyalty than that afforded by modeling approaches and attitudinal accounts and attempts to answer the question why loyalty exists. In a study with eight consumers who had loyal relationships with brands of coffee, Fournier/Yao show that loyalty can have different shades of meaning (commitment and fidelity, love and passion, intimacy and self revelation) similar to different relationship forms (marriage, falling in love, best friendship) and that different loyalties are closely related to important life themes that the consumer is grappling with (control versus chaos, marginality versus significance, belonging versus independence). They also argue that criteria of usage frequency or exclusivity of use to define brand loyalty hide important brand relationships and that loyalties may not only be directed at brands but also at product categories or forms (coffee, beans), as well as processes (making coffee). Fournier/Yao ultimately recommend that a relationships perspective in which loyalty/commitment is but one of several possible brand relationship profiles (e.g., self-concept connection, nostalgic attachment, passion/love, intimacy) may provide deeper insights into consumer-brand relationships than existing loyalty conceptions.

2.5   Conclusion

In this brief essay on repetitive purchase behavior I have tried to accomplish three things. First, I have attempted to situate repeat buying within the context of other forms of purchase behavior. In the modeling area it is common to differentiate repetitive purchases from variety seeking behavior. In the model of the purchase cube, repetitive purchase behavior is most distinct from exploratory purchase behavior, because they differ on all three dimensions underlying the cube. Since exploratory purchase behavior includes variety seeking, repeat purchases and purchases motivated by variety form a natural contrast pair. However, exploratory purchase behavior is a broader concept (purchases motivated by curiosity and trial purchases also belong to this category), and it is also of interest how repetitive purchase behavior relates to other common forms of buying behavior. The model of the purchase cube shows how repetitive purchase behavior fits into the larger picture of eight qualitatively distinct types of purchases stimulated by different motives. Second, I have sought to identify the core theme underlying the notion of repetitive purchase behavior. This was done by characterizing repeat purchases in terms of the three dimensions on which the purchase cube is built – functional vs. psycho-social purchases, low vs. high purchase involvement, and spontaneous vs. deliberate purchases – and by distinguishing two subcategories of repetitive purchase behavior, loyalty and habit. Third, I have briefly reviewed the major streams of research that have studied repetitive purchase behavior. The modeling approach has studied the influence of past choices on current choices and has been very successful in accurately describing patterns of buying for repetitively purchased products, but it has provided few insights into why consumers engage in repeat buying (which, admittedly, is not the goal of this research). The psychological approach to repetitive purchase behavior is concerned with the determinants of repeated purchases of the same brand and tries to understand the mental process underlying repeat buying. Given this focus, it is surprising that this research has not resulted in widely known and accepted explanatory frameworks that can help researchers and practitioners think clearly about the phenomenon of repetitive purchase behavior. The recent research on habits is an exception and has yielded a useful model of when and how habits guide purchase behavior. Given the importance of repetitive purchase behavior in certain product categories (esp. frequently bought branded goods and services), additional research on brand loyalty and habitual buying behavior would seem to offer substantial opportunities for advancing our understanding of one important form of buying behavior.

Literature

[1]   Alderson, W. (1957): Marketing behavior and executive action: A functionalist approach to marketing theory. Homewood, IL: Richard D. Irwin.

[2]   Bass, F. M./Givon, M. M./Kalwani, M. U./Reibstein, D. J./Wright, G. P. (1984): An investigation into the order of the brand choice process. Marketing Science, Vol. 3, Fall, pp. 267-287.

[3]   Baumgartner, H. (2002): Toward a personology of the consumer. Journal of Consumer Research, Vol. 29, September, pp. 286-292.

[4]   Baumgartner, H. (2010): A review of prior classifications of purchase behavior and a proposal for a new typology. In Malhotra, N. K. (Ed.), Review of Marketing Research, Vol. 6, pp. 3-36.

[5]   Bawa, K. (1990): Modeling inertia and variety seeking tendencies in brand choice behavior. Marketing Science, Vol. 9, Summer, pp. 263-278.

[6]   Childers, T. L./Rao, A. R. (1992): The influence of familial and peer-based reference groups on consumer decisions. Journal of Consumer Research, Vol. 19, September, pp. 198-211.

[7]   Colombo, R. A./Morrison, D. G. (1989): A brand switching model with implications for marketing strategies. Marketing Science, Vol. 8, 1, pp. 89-99.

[8]   Dekimpe, M. G./Steenkamp, J.-B. E. M./Mellens, M./Vanden Abeele, P. (1997): Decline and variability in brand loyalty. International Journal of Research in Marketing, Vol. 14, 5, pp. 405-420.

[9]   Dick, A. S./Basu, K. (1994): Customer loyalty: Toward an integrated conceptual framework. Journal of the Academy of Marketing Science, Vol. 22, Winter, pp. 99-113.

[10] Fournier, S./Yao, J. L. (1997): Reviving brand loyalty: A reconceptualization within the framework of consumer-brand relationships. International Journal of Research in Marketing, Vol. 14, December, pp. 451-472.

[11] Givon, M. (1984): Variety seeking through brand switching. Marketing Science, Vol. 3, Winter, pp. 1-22.

[12] Grover, R./Srinivasan, V. (1987): A simultaneous approach to market segmentation and market structuring. Journal of Marketing Research, Vol. 24, May, pp. 139-153.

[13] Guadagni, P./Little, J. D. C. (1983): A logit model of brand choice calibrated on scanner data. Marketing Science, Vol. 2, Summer, pp. 203-238.

[14] Jacoby, J. (1971): A model of multi-brand loyalty. Journal of Advertising Research, Vol. 11, 3, pp. 25-31.

[15] Jacoby, J./Chestnut, R. W. (1978): Brand loyalty: Measurement and management. New York, NY: Wiley.

[16] Jeuland, A. P. (1979): Brand choice inertia as one aspect of the notion of brand loyalty. Management Science, Vol. 25, June, pp. 671-682.

[17] Kahn, B./Kalwani, M. U./Morrison, D. G. (1986): Measuring variety-seeking and reinforcement behaviors using panel data. Journal of Marketing Research, Vol. 23, May, pp. 89-100.

[18] Kuehn, A. A. (1962): Consumer brand choice as a learning process. Journal of Advertising Research, Vol. 2, December, pp. 10-17.

[19] Lattin, J. M. (1987): A model of balanced choice behavior. Marketing Science, Vol. 6, Winter, pp. 48-65.

[20] Moore, E. S./Wilkie, W. L./Lutz, R. J. (2002): Passing the torch: Intergenerational influences as a source of brand equity. Journal of Marketing, Vol. 66, April, pp. 17-37.

[21] Moore-Shay, E. S./Lutz, R. J. (1988): Intergenerational influences in the formation of consumer attitudes and beliefs about the marketplace: Mothers and daughters. In Houston, M. J. (Ed.), Advances in Consumer Research, 15, Provo, UT: Association for Consumer Research, pp. 461-467.

[22] Moschis, G. P. (1985): The role of family communication in consumer socialization of children and adolescents. Journal of Consumer Research, Vol. 11, March, pp. 898-913.

[23] Newman, J. W./Werbel, R. A. (1973): Multivariate analysis of brand loyalty for major household appliances. Journal of Marketing Research, Vol. 10, November, pp. 404-409.

[24] Oliver, R. L. (1999): Whence consumer loyalty? Journal of Marketing, Vol. 63, Special Issue, pp. 33-44.

[25] Quellette, J. A./Wood, W. (1998): Habit and intention in everyday life: The multiple processes by which past behavior predicts future behavior. Psychological Bulletin, Vol. 124, July, pp. 54-74.

[26] Ratchford, B. T. (1987): New insights about the FCB grid. Journal of Advertising Research, Vol. 27, August/September, pp. 24-38.

[27] Roy, R./Chintagunta, P. K./Haldar, S. (1996): A framework for investigating habits, "The hand of the past," and heterogeneity in dynamic brand choice. Marketing Science, Vol. 15, 3, pp. 280-299.

[28] Seetharaman, P. B./Chintagunta, P. (1998): A model of inertia and variety-seeking with marketing variables. International Journal of Research in Marketing, Vol. 15, February, pp. 1-17.

[29] Sherif, C. W./Sherif, M./Nebergall, R. E. (1965): Attitude and attitude change: The social judgment-involvement approach. Philadelphia, PA: W. B. Saunders.

[30] Steenkamp, J.-B. E. M./Baumgartner, H. (1992): The role of optimum stimulation level in exploratory consumer behavior. Journal of Consumer Research, Vol. 19, December, pp. 434-448.

[31] Tam, L./Wood, W./Ji, M. F. (2009): Brand loyalty is not habitual. In MacInnis, D. J., Park, C. W., & Priester, J. R. (Eds.), Handbook of Brand Relationships. Armonk, NY: M. E. Sharp, pp. 43-62.

[32] Uncles, M./Ehrenberg, A./Hammond, K. (1995): Patterns of buyer behavior: Regularities, models, and extensions. Marketing Science, Vol. 13, 3, G71-G78.

[33] Viswanathan, M./Childers, T. L./Moore, E. S. (2000): The measurement of intergenerational communication and influence on consumption: Development, validation and cross-cultural comparison of the IGEN scale. Journal of the Academy of Marketing Science, Vol. 28, 3, pp. 406-424.

[34] Wagner, U./Taudes, A. (1986): A multivariate Polya model of brand choice and purchase incidence. Marketing Science, Vol. 5, Summer, pp. 219-244.

[35] Wagner, U./Taudes, A. (1987): Stochastic models of consumer behavior. European Journal of Operational Research, Vol. 29, pp. 1-23.

[36] Ward, S./Wackman, D. B./Wartella, E. (1977): How children learn to buy: The development of consumer information processing skills. Beverly Hills, CA: Sage.

[37] Wood, W./Neal, D. T. (2009): The habitual consumer. Journal of Consumer Psychology, Vol. 19, 4, pp. 579-592.

[38] Wood, W./Tam, L./Guerrero Witt, M. (2005): Changing circumstances, disrupting habit. Journal of Personality and Social Psychology, Vol. 88, 6, pp. 918-933.

3 Investigating Cross-Category Brand Loyal Purchase Behavior in FMCG

Yasemin Boztuğ, Georg-August-University Göttingen, Germany

Lutz Hildebrandt, Humboldt University of Berlin, Germany, and University of Vienna, Austria

Nadja Silberhorn, FactWorks GmbH, Germany

Abstract

In competitive markets, customer retention is in general more efficient than trying to attract new customers. Therefore, as a resulting outcome brand loyalty is regarded as a major strategic asset that has been investigated as an important source of equity. Most analyses, however, have been conducted in one specific product category only. The aspect of cross-category related brand loyalty has been widely neglected so far. We concentrate on cross-category relationships of national brands and on how customers' brand choice decisions are related across several product categories. This knowledge is of relevance for retail managers and manufacturers who think of segment-specific promotion strategies that consider the customer segments' loyalty patterns across categories. Our measure of brand loyalty is the Share of Category Requirements (SCR) to capture the relative share of category purchases that individual households give to each brand they buy, defined to be each brand's market share among triers of the brand. We use the SCR measure as a behavioral and individual-oriented measure. We use scanner panel and corresponding survey data. The scanner panel data contains households' repeated FMCG purchase information of purchases in different kinds of store types within a limited geographic region. All the participating households were also asked to fill in a questionnaire on their values and attitudes. From an analysis of brand loyalty patterns different consumer segments result. An ex-post analysis based on general attitudes and other consumer characteristics reveals distinguishing factors between the consumer segments.

Keywords

Brand Loyalty, Cross-Category Relations, Scanner Panel Data.

3.1   Research Problem

The majority of response models in marketing research investigate the quantitative effects of marketing-mix strategies, e.g., advertising spending or pricing, on purchase probabilities, sales and market shares. Considering consumer heterogeneity, reactions to such implemented marketing strategies may vary. Additionally, such response models need to account for dependencies between choice decisions in various product categories, i.e., marketing-mix activities in a special category also may stimulate product or brand demand in other categories. Consumers include products from different categories in their decision processes. In this context, selection decisions in multiple categories are assumed to be related (Russell et al. 1997; 1999; Hruschka 1991). Additionally considering that brand manufacturers and retailers selling brands with a high rate of loyal consumers have a competitive advantage (Mellens et al. 1996), the concept of brand loyalty must not be dealt with using only isolated individual product categories.

Nevertheless, to the best of our knowledge, investigations have either neglected differences in the impact on individual consumers or at least consumer segments with diverse purchase characteristics such as loyalty, or have disregarded the cross-category relationship of choice decisions. We tie in with the research of Blattberg et al. (1976) and Wind and Frank (1969), who investigated households' brand loyalty behavior across product categories and contribute therein to combine established brand loyalty research, cross-category related choice behavior and topical panel data.

Previous studies on brand loyalty only focused on customers' brand choice behavior in one single product category (Raj 1982; Blattberg/Sen 1974), or in various but separately considered categories (Erdem/Chang 2012; Pare/Dawes 2011; Danaher et al. 2003; Bhattacharya 1997; Blattberg et al. 1976). Inspecting brand loyal behavior based on purchase transactions, researchers are faced again with the fact that consumers usually do not only buy within a single category during a shopping trip, but in more than one category simultaneously. At this point, the question whether consumers show similar loyalty behavior patterns in different product categories arises. Are consumers that exhibit brand loyalty in one product category also likely to do so in other categories? Several scenarios can be considered:

1. Consumers do not show any brand loyal behavior at all.

2. Consumers generally show brand loyal behavior, but only in one specific product category.

3. Consumers show brand loyal behavior in more than one product category, but with different loyalty patterns in each category.

4. Consumers show brand loyal behavior in more than one product category, with similar or equal loyalty patterns across- categories.

The aim of this article lies therein to classify and identify different consumer segments, based on different combinations of brand loyal behavior and category purchase relationships. Is consumer purchase behavior driven by general consumer characteristics (e.g., demographic factors or attitudes)? This question has already been focused on marketing researchers (e.g., Rao 1973) and has a long research tradition (e.g., Blattberg et al. 1976). If socio-economic characteristics discriminate between consumer loyalty segments, retailers and manufacturers would be able to easily address and positively influence those segments (Rao 1973). The greater the correlation of consumers' brand loyalty over categories, the more likely it is that one can identify a set of characteristics useful for classifying consumers for purposes such as promotion activities, media selection and market segmentation, regardless of the product category involved. On the other hand, if consumers' purchase patterns vary across product categories, or consumers do not show brand loyalty across product categories at all, product-specific characteristics and marketing activities seem to guide purchase behavior rather than consumer-specific traits.

Apart from demographic characteristics, consumers' lifestyle may play important roles in their purchase and loyalty behavior. For deriving suitable marketing strategies in general, and promotion strategies in particular, the different reactions of those consumer types towards cross-category promotions have to be taken into account. As a result, retail managers and manufacturers should think of segment-specific promotion strategies, e.g. the selective distribution of free samples and coupons (Blattberg et al. 1976) that consider the segments' loyalty patterns across categories. A free sample in only one product category might then stimulate same-brand purchases also in various other product categories. As earlier studies (e.g., Blattberg et al. 1976) have some limitations, we focus our work on three issues.

1. We do not only focus on loyal consumers as a general measure, but also take into account the fact that consumers may show loyal behavior to the same brand or to different brands across product categories.

2. We use the measure of "share of category requirements" (SCR) on an individual level to separate loyal and non-loyal consumers. The SCR is a well-established measure describing loyal behavior at the brand level.

3. We describe the different consumer segments, which resulted from an analysis of brand loyalty patterns, with an ex-post discrimination analysis based on general attitudes and other consumer characteristics to identify distinguishing factors between the consumer segments.

The paper is structured as follows: The brand loyalty concept is presented in section 3.2. In section 3.3 we briefly dwell on cross-category dependencies in purchase decisions. Both mentioned research streams are combined in section 3.4, and possible problems arising from the simultaneous consideration are pointed out. Finally, the combined approach is applied to a real data set and results are discussed.

3.2   Brand Loyalty

Our key concept brand loyalty – which we regard as having an intrinsic commitment to repeatedly purchasing a particular brand – leads to certain marketing advantages, such as reduced marketing costs (Aaker 1991), favorable word of mouth and greater resistance among loyal consumers to competitive strategies (Dick/Basu 1994). Brand-loyal consumers may be willing to pay more for a brand because they perceive some unique value in the brand that no alternative can provide (Chaudhuri/Holbrook 2001). Loyal consumers are less price sensitive with regard to the choice decision but more price sensitive to the quantity decision (Krishnamurthi/Raj 1991). The presence of a loyal customer base provides the firm with valuable time to respond to competitive actions (Aaker 1991).

While there is considerable agreement on the conceptual definition of brand loyalty, no standardized perspective to measure it has yet emerged. A systematic two-dimensional classification of brand loyalty measures is introduced and described in detail by Mellens et al. (1996). They distinguish between behavioral vs. attitudinal measures, and individual-oriented vs. brand-oriented measures, resulting in four main categories of brand loyalty measures.

Behavioral loyalty is the willingness of the average consumer to repurchase the brand and is reflected in the repeated purchases of the brand. A consumer's degree of brand loyalty is inferred from her/his observed purchase behavior (Chaudhuri/Holbrook 2001, Bhattacharya 1997; Dekimpe et al. 1997). In contrast, attitudinal loyalty refers to the level of commitment of the average consumer toward the brand and includes a degree of dispositional commitment in terms of some unique value associated with the brand (Chaudhuri/Holbrook 2001; Dekimpe et al. 1997). Most often, brand loyalty is measured according to the past purchasing patterns of consumers (Chaudhuri/Holbrook 2001). So the majority of all brand loyalty measures are behavioral (Bhattacharya 1997).

Our measure of brand loyalty is the Share of Category Requirements (SCR) (Bhattacharya 1997; Fader/Schmittlein 1993) to capture the relative share of category purchases that individual households give to each brand they buy (Stern/Hammond 2004), defined to be each brand's market share among triers of the brand. The SCR measure as we use it is a *behavioral* and *individual-oriented* measure that indicates how much the customers of each brand satisfy their product needs by purchasing a particular brand rather than buying competing alternatives (Uncles et al. 1994). We chose the SCR measure because of its simplicity and widespread use by brand managers and in academic research (e.g., Du et al. 2007; Stern/Hammond 2004; Danaher et al. 2003; Bhattacharya et al. 1996).

Although the SCR measure is generally reported at an aggregate level, several studies use it on an individual-level (e.g., Du et al. 2007):

$$SCR_{hic}(T) = \frac{\sum_{t \in T} q_{hic}(t)}{\sum_j \sum_{t \in T} q_{hjc}(t)} \tag{3.1}$$

where

$SCR_{hic}(T) =$ household h's share of category requirements for brand i in category c during time period T

$q_{hic}(t) =$ quantity of brand i purchased in category c by household h on purchase occasion t (where t is an index of all purchase occasions during time period T), and

$j =$ index for all brands in the category.

For detailed descriptions of equation (3.1) we refer to Bhattacharya et al. (1996). We ignore the purchase quantity and replace $q_{hic}(t)$ with a 0/1 variable indicating whether or not brand i was purchased in category c by household h at time t (see Russell & Kamakura 1994, Lattin & Bucklin 1989, Krishnamurthi & Raj 1988).

3.3   Cross-Category Relations

The investigation and analysis of the relations between the different items that customers place in their shopping baskets during one single purchase occasion is a central theme in marketing research when it comes to choice and purchase decisions. By means of market basket analysis customers' purchase data can be analyzed and coherences between the sold products can be detected (Boztuğ/Hildebrandt 2008; Boztuğ/Reutterer 2008; Niraj et al. 2008; Boztuğ/Silberhorn 2006; Mild/Reutterer 2003; Russell/Petersen 2000, Hruschka et al. 1999).

The examination of correlations between various product categories has a long research tradition, especially in the German-speaking research community (Hruschka 1991; Merkle 1981; Böcker 1978; 1975). The authors have mainly calculated relations between pairs of categories by association or correlation measures, and by multidimensional scaling methods representing similarities or distances between product categories.

Multi-category models are of interest to both retailers seeking to maximize store profits, and to manufacturers who sell products in multiple product categories (Fischer et al. 2010; Seetharaman et al. 2005). There are huge amounts of aggregated data available in the retail industry, and ideally case, in connection with customer card or any other loyalty programs even individual data that enable a customer-specific marketing planning. If consumers are loyal to a special manufacturer brand in general, promotional activities do not have to be category-specific.

3.4   Merging Both Topics

The contribution of this study lies therein to merge the brand loyalty concept with the aspect of cross-category related brand choice decisions, in that the focus is no longer on one but various product categories, and also on consumers' cross-category brand loyal behavior with respect to the **same** brand in several categories. So far, studies in this field have concentrated on a single product category (e.g., Kannan/Wright 1991), or on consumers' loyalty to different brands in multiple categories (e.g., Russell/Kamakura 1994).

Several issues arise when expanding the brand loyalty concept to multiple categories: Which and how many categories should be inspected? How can a brand loyal customer be defined? Does she/he need to be loyal to the same brand in multiple categories, or is loyal behavior to different brands also possible?

We suggest the following approach to address those issues:

1. First, we define several levels of brand loyalty considering behavior in multiple categories. The first group of consumers does not show any loyal behavior at all ($SCR_i \leq 0.50$ for brand i in all categories[2]). The second group shows loyal behavior in only one category ($SCR_i > 0.50$ for brand i in only one category), and purchases in more than one inspected category. Group three shows loyal behavior in more than one category ($SCR_i > 0.50$ and $SCR_j > 0.50$ for brands $i \neq j$ in at least two categories), and the last group contains all customers, who show loyal purchase behavior to the same brand in more than one category ($SCR_i > 0.50$ and $SCR_j > 0.50$ for brands $i=j$ in at least two categories).

2. In the second step, based on the results of step one, we say that cross-category purchase behavior exists for loyal customers belonging to the last two groups with loyal purchase behavior to a brand in more than one category. These are remarkably valuable customers because of their loyal behavior in general. For further analysis, loyal customers with loyalty to the same brand and those with loyalty to different brands are especially of interest. The latter are expected to be gained more easily than new customers to a brand as they already seem to exhibit a basic satisfaction level with this brand, only in another category. We thus try to investigate the characteristics of those customers, and find group-discriminating explanatory variables.

---

[2] Based on the condition that each household has to exhibit at least two different purchase dates for the accordant product category as a prerequisite for calculating the brand-specific individual SCR measure, a threshold value of 0.50 means that one purchase per brand within a category is not enough to be classified brand loyal.

3.5   Application With Real Data Set

We use scanner panel and corresponding survey data, provided by GfK Market Research. The scanner panel data contain households' repeated fast moving consumer goods (FMCG) purchase information of purchases in different store types within a limited geographic region (707,760 purchase incidences and 31 variables). As consumers can switch stores for purchasing a particular product or brand, we do not focus on a specific store but include various stores in our analyses. All the participating 4,084 households were also asked to fill in a questionnaire on their values and attitudes (353 variables).

The panel data cover 56 product categories in the food and non-food sector with 1,373 different brands. However, many of these categories had only infrequent purchases and could not be used. The average number of purchase incidences[3] per household is 173.3 with a median of 146. It becomes clear that the majority of the 4,084 households is present with only a small number of purchase incidences. 143 households have more than 400 purchase incidences per year, resulting in 7-8 products per week. Obviously, not all purchase occasions are covered in these panel data. As the analysis of brand loyalty may be biased by promotional activities, we only focus on regular price purchases.

For our analyses, choosing two category types with different turnover frequencies, we expected to find unequal results with respect to loyalty patterns and the loyalty segments' discriminating factors. So in the first step, we selected the eight most frequently purchased food product categories (instant dessert, yogurt, milk cream products, milk drinks, curd cheese, milk, frozen foods, butter) with a cumulative share of 75.7 percent of all purchases, and the eight most frequently purchased body care product categories (hand lotion, deodorant, shower gel, body lotion, bath additive, face lotion, soap, face cleansing lotion) with a cumulative share of only 7.3 percent of all purchases. Our first interest was to discover what degree of cross-category loyalty might exist in the data at all. Considering the fact that the food categories are very fast moving consumer goods compared to the body care products, the huge difference between the cumulative shares should not be given too much attention. We then left out those categories with a market share of the private label larger than 30 percent, and in the third step, concentrated on those categories that share more than one brand with at least one other category. In the end the three remaining food categories were instant dessert, yogurt and milk drinks and the three remaining body care categories were bath additive, shower gel and deodorant. There are three brand-category relationships that hold for the same brand in all three food categories (food brands D, L and P), and three brand-category relationships that hold for the same brand in all three body care categories (body care brands D, G and L).

---

[3] Each category purchase is considered a single purchase incidence, i.e., if a household makes purchases in three different categories during a single shopping trip, this results in three purchase incidences.

Further, we found brand-category relationships that hold for the same brand in two food categories (food brands F, H and O) and four brand-category relationships that hold for the same brand in two body care categories (body care brands C, E, F and M). Table 3.1 illustrates the brands' market shares within the mentioned product categories.

Table 3.1   Market Shares for Food and Body Care Categories

Categories \ Brands	Food categories			Body care categories		
	Instant dessert	Yogurt	Milk drinks	Bath additive	Deodorant	Shower gel
A	-	-	3.3	-	8.3	-
B	-	8.7	-	-	3.0	-
C	6.7	-	-	-	5.1	4.4
D	15.9	7.5	23.3	16.1	4.8	9.3
E	11.0	-	-	0.8	-	3.8
F	5.0	13.6	-	-	3.7	13.2
G	-	-	4.4	1.7	9.4	10.0
H	13.5	6.1	-	6.8	-	-
K	-	-	2.6	3.3	-	-
L	19.9	19.5	23.4	4.3	13.7	4.2
M	-	4.6	-	2.2	-	7.6
N	3.0	-	-	2.5	-	-
O	-	5.8	3.1	-	13.3	-
P	2.1	6.1	6.2	9.9	-	-
Σ	77.1	71.9	66.3	47.6	53.0	52.5

Only considering purchases in the selected product categories, we then eliminated those households with less than four purchase occasions, i.e., less than one shopping trip per quarter on average. As a prerequisite for calculating the brand-specific individual SCR measure each household had to exhibit at least two different purchase dates for the accordant product category. Otherwise we assigned a SCR measure of value zero. According to equation (3.1) without incorporating purchase quantities, we calculated each household's SCR measure for the 27 possible category-brand combinations (nine brands in each of the three categories).

In the following, all households were grouped into four segments:

- *Non-Loyal (NL):*

  $SCR_i \leq 0.50$ for any brand i in all categories

- *Brand-Loyal (BL):*

  $SCR_i > 0.50$ for any national brand i in only one category

- *Cross-Category-Different-Loyal (CCDL):*

  $SCR_i > 0.50$ and $SCR_j > 0.50$ for different national brands $i \neq j$ in at least two categories

- *Cross-Category-Same-Loyal (CCSL):*

  $SCR_i > 0.50$ and $SCR_j > 0.50$ for any national brand $i=j$ in at least two categories

After all data reduction procedures 2,326 households in the food group and 951 households in the body care group remained for classification. In case a household could be classified into different groups (e.g., *BL* for brand E in category 2 and *CCSL* for brand G in categories 1 and 3), always the "higher" group was always chosen (*CCSL* in the given example). In **Table 3.2**, we show the distribution of households in the four different loyalty groups for food and body care products. The number of CCSL (cross-category-same-loyal) households is small in both product groups. Most customers show loyal purchase behavior only in one category (BL), but not in the other categories. For body care categories, more loyal purchase behavior in one single category can be detected than for the food categories. For food categories, we have more cross-category loyal customers, who are loyal to the same or at least to different brands.

Table 3.2   Segmentation for Categories Based on SCR Measure

	Food categories		Body care categories	
	Frequency	Percent	Frequency	Percent
NL	390	16.77	183	19.24
BL	1,091	46.90	538	56.57
CCDL	606	26.05	163	17.14
CCSL	239	10.28	67	7.05
Σ	2,326	100.00	951	100.00

We then utilized 31 demographic and attitudinal variables in the dataset to discriminate between the different forms of cross-category brand loyal households. First, we conducted a factor analysis for each of the two data sets, resulting in 10 (12) factors for the food (body care) data. As displayed in **Table 3.3**, there are nine factors that are the same for both category types. Surprisingly, the factors price and quality orientation do only play a role in the body care categories.

Table 3.3   Factors Resulting From Data Reduction

	Food categories	Body care categories
Brand shopper	X	X
Conservative	X	
Convenience orientation	X	X
Environmentalist / advertising		X
Experience orientation	X	X
General demographics	X	X
Health orientation	X	X
Media involvement	X	X
Premium shopper	X	X
Price orientation		X
Quality orientation		X
Smart shopper	X	X
Traditionalist	X	X

In the second step, we conducted a discriminant analysis on all four consumer segments to uncover the drivers of different loyalty patterns. The results for the body care product categories are presented in **Table 3.4**. Here we can show, that the diagonal elements for the original and for cross-validation groups always represent the highest value compared to all other matrix elements, except for the group NL. So we are in general able to classify our households into the right segments. This is also indicated by the hit rate of 31.1% for the estimation with the body care data set. Its value is much better than a random classification, especially taking the different group sizes into account. The hit rate for cross-validation with 26.1% is a bit worse than for the original grouped cases, but still better than any random classification. The results are not as good as expected but they are still acceptable. Each of the three discriminating functions is dominated by one factor, which is either "Brand shopper", "Convenience orientation" or "Health orientation". The picture is less clear for the food categories. More than half of the factors ("Brand shopper", "Convenience orientation", "General demographics", "Premium shopper", "Smart shopper" and

"Traditionalist") have an influence on distinguishing the different loyalty types of consumers. The results of discriminate analysis for food categories are available upon request from the corresponding author. Additionally, we conducted discriminate analyses for "loyal" (only households which belong to CCSL) against all other customers (NL, BL and CCDL). The results for food and for body care product categories are very much in line with our presented results and are also available upon request.

Table 3.4 Classification Results for Consumer Segments for Body Care Products

			Predicted Group Membership				
		Group	NL	BL	CCDL	CCSL	Total
Original	Count	NL	45	56	43	39	183
		BL	103	156	121	158	538
		CCDL	25	39	60	39	163
		CCSL	12	9	11	35	67
	Percent	NL	24.6	30.6	23.5	21.3	100
		BL	19.1	29.0	22.5	29.4	100
		CCDL	15.3	23.9	36.8	23.9	100
		CCSL	17.9	13.4	16.4	52.2	100
Cross-validated	Count	NL	34	62	45	42	183
		BL	106	137	132	163	538
		CCDL	27	40	52	44	163
		CCSL	16	11	15	25	67
	Percent	NL	18.6	33.9	24.6	23.0	100
		BL	19.7	25.5	24.5	30.3	100
		CCDL	16.6	24.5	31.9	27.0	100
		CCSL	23.9	16.4	22.4	37.3	100

3.6   Summary and Outlook

The main purpose of this article was to classify and identify different consumer segments based on brand loyal purchase behavior and cross-category purchase relationships. We used scanner panel and survey data containing households' repeated fast moving consumer goods (FMCG) purchase information and information about attitudes and demographic data. After detecting four different consumer loyalty types (incorporating purchase incidence and cross-categorical information), we tried to describe those consumer segments with data from the survey. So we conducted a factor analysis based on demographic and attitudinal data to extract uncorrelated explanatory variables. Based on these factors, we applied discriminant analyses with the different loyalty segments as dependent variables gaining information about the most influencing factors to distinguish between the consumer groups.

With respect to the factors discriminating between consumer segments, there is a difference between the food and the body care categories. For the body care categories, each of the three discriminating functions is dominated by only one factor ("Health orientation", "Brand shopper"or "Convenience orientation"). Remarkably, general consumer characteristics are not appropriate to discriminate between the segments. Consumers' lifestyles perform better. On the other hand, there are no factors in the food categories case that clearly dominate the discriminating functions. These results are in line with Wind/Frank (1969), Farley (1964) and Ndubisi (2005). General consumer characteristics are not appropriate to predict brand loyal behavior. This is also known from studies concentrated on shopping behavior only in single categories, e.g., standard brand choice models. A proper classification of consumers is possible in all cases, i.e., the classification based on the discriminating factors leads to results above random classification.

As consumers' loyal behavior across product categories is exists but cannot be ascribed to consumer-specific traits, product-specific characteristics and marketing activities seem to guide purchase behavior. Nevertheless, we arrive at the conclusion that retail managers and brand manufacturers should focus on product-specific marketing strategies rather than trying to personalize marketing activities.

Literature

[1] Aaker, D. (1991): Managing Brand Equity: Capitalizing on the Value of a Brand Name. New York.

[2] Bhattacharya, C. B./Fader, P. S./Lodish, L. M./Desarbo, W. S. (1996): The Relationship Between the Marketing Mix and Share of Category Requirements, in: Marketing Letters, Vol. 7, 1, pp. 5-18.

[3] Bhattacharya, C. B. (1997): Is your brand's loyalty too much, too little, or just right?: Explaining deviations in loyalty from the Dirichlet norm, in: International Journal of Research in Marketing, Vol. 14, 5, pp. 421-435.

[4] Blattberg, R. C./Sen, S. K. (1974): Market Segmentation Using Models of Multidimensional Purchasing Behavior, in: Journal of Marketing, Vol. 38, 4, pp. 17-28.

[5] Blattberg, R. C./Peacock, P./Sen, S. K. (1976): Purchasing Strategies across Product Categories, in: Journal of Consumer Research, Vol. 3, 3, pp. 143-154.

[6] Böcker, F. (1975): Die Analyse des Kaufverbunds – Ein Ansatz zur bedarfsorientierten Warentypologie, in: Zeitschrift für betriebswirtschaftliche Forschung, Vol. 27, pp. 290-306.

[7] Böcker, F. (1978): Die Bestimmung der Kaufverbundenheit von Produkten. Schriften zum Marketing, Band 7, Berlin.

[8] Boztuğ, Y./Silberhorn, N. (2006): Modellierungsansätze in der Warenkorbanalyse im Überblick, in: Journal für Betriebswirtschaft, Vol. 56, 2, pp. 105-128.

[9] Boztuğ, Y./Hildebrandt, L. (2008): Modeling Joint Purchases with a Multivariate MNL Approach, in: Schmalenbach Business Review, Vol. 60, pp. 400-422.

[10] Boztuğ, Y./Reutterer, T. (2008): A Combined Approach for Segment-Specific Analysis of Market Basket Data, in: European Journal of Operational Research, Vol. 187, pp. 294-312.

[11] Chaudhuri, A./Holbrook, M. B. (2001): The Chain of Effects from Brand Trust and Brand Affect to Brand Performance: The Role of Brand Loyalty, in: Journal of Marketing, Vol. 65, 2, pp. 81-93.

[12] Danaher, P. J./Wilson, I. W./Davis, R. A. (2003): A Comparison of Online and Offline Consumer Brand Loyalty, in: Marketing Science, Vol. 22, 4, pp. 461-476.

[13] Dekimpe, M.G /Steenkamp, J.-B. E. M./Mellens, M./Vanden Abeele, P. (1997): Decline and variability in brand loyalty, in: International Journal of Research in Marketing, Vol. 14, 5, pp. 405-420.

[14] Dick, A. S./Basu, K. (1994): Customer Loyalty: Toward an Integrated Conceptual Framework, in: Journal of the Academy of Marketing Science, Vol. 22, 2, pp. 9-113.

[15] Du, R. Y/Kamakura, W. A./Mela, C. F. (2007): Size and Share of Customer Wallet, in: Journal of Marketing, Vol. 71, 2, pp. 94-113.

[16] Erdem, T./Chang, S. R. (2012): A cross-category and cross-country analysis of umbrella branding for national and store brands, in: Journal of the Academy of Marketing Science, Vol. 40, pp. 86-101.

[17] Fader, P. S./Schmittlein, D. C. (1993): Excess Behavioral Loyalty for High-Share Brands: Deviations from the Dirichlet Model for Repeat Purchasing, in: Journal of Marketing Research, Vol. 30, 4, pp. 478-493.

[18] Farley, J. U. (1964): "Brand Loyalty" and the Economics of Information, in: The Journal of Business, Vol. 37, 4, pp. 370-381.

[19] Fischer, M./Völckner, F./Sattler, H. (2010): How important are brands? A cross-category, cross-country study, in: Journal of Marketing Research, Vol. 47, pp. 823-839.

[20] Hruschka, H. (1991): Bestimmung der Kaufverbundenheit mit Hilfe eines probabilistischen Meßmodells, in: Zeitschrift für betriebswirtschaftliche Forschung, Vol. 43, 5, pp. 418-434.

[21] Hruschka, H./Lukanowicz, M./Buchta, C. (1999): Cross-Category Sales Promotion Effects, in: Journal of Retailing and Consumer Services, Vol. 6, 2, pp. 99-105.

[22] Kannan, P. K./Wright, G. P. (1991): Modeling and testing structured markets: a nested logit approach, in: Marketing Science, Vol. 10, 1, pp. 58-82.

[23] Krishnamurthi, L./Raj, S. P. (1988): A Model of Brand Choice and Purchase Quantity Price Sensitivities, in: Marketing Science, Vol. 7, 1, pp. 1-20.

[24] Krishnamurthi, L./Raj, S. P. (1991): An empirical analysis of the relationship between brand loyalty and consumer price elasticity, in: Marketing Science, Vol. 10, 2, pp. 172-183.

[25] Lattin, J. M./Bucklin, R. E. (1989): Reference Effects of Price and Promotion on Brand Choice Behavior, in: Journal of Marketing Research, Vol. 26, 3, pp. 299-310.

[26] Mellens, M./Dekimpe, M. G./Steenkamp, J.-B. E. M. (1996): A Review of Brand-Loyalty Measures in Marketing, in: Tijdschrift voor Economie en Management, Vol. 41, 4, pp. 507-533.

[27] Merkle, E. (1981): Die Erfassung und Nutzung von Informationen über den Sortimentsverbund in Handelsbetrieben. Schriften zum Marketing, Band 11, Berlin.

[28] Mild, A./Reutterer, T. (2003): An Improved Collaborative Filtering Approach for Predicting Cross-Category Purchases Based on Binary Market Basket Data, in: Journal of Retailing and Consumer Services, Vol. 10, 3, pp. 123-133.

[29] Ndubisi, N. O. (2005): Customer Loyalty and Antecedents: A Relational Marketing Approach in: Proceedings of the Academy of Marketing Studies, Vol. 10, 2, pp. 49-54.

[30] Niraj, R./Padmanabhan, V./Seetharaman, P. B. (2008): A cross-category model of households' incidence and quantity decisions, in: Marketing Science, Vol. 27, 2, pp. 225-235.

[31] Pare, V./Dawes, J. (2011): The persistence of excess brand loyalty over multiple years, in: Marketing Letters, to appear.

[32] Raj, S. P. (1982): The Effects of Advertising on High and Low Loyalty Consumer Segments, in: Journal of Consumer Research, Vol. 9, 1, pp. 77-89.

[33] Rao, T. R. (1973): Is Brand Loyalty a Criterion for Market Segmentation: Discriminant Analysis, in: Decision Sciences, Vol. 4, 3, S. 395-404.

[34] Russell, G. J./Kamakura, W. A. (1994): Understanding Brand Competition Using Micro and Macro Scanner Data, in: Journal of Marketing Research, Vol. 31, 2, pp. 289-303.

[35] Russell, G. J./Bell, D./Bodapati, A./Brown, C. L./Chiang, J./Gaeth, G./Gupta, S./ Manchanda, P. (1997): Perspectives on Multiple Category Choice, in: Marketing Letters,Vol. 8, 3, pp. 297-305.

[36] Russell, G. J./Ratneshwar, S./Shocker, A. D./Bell, D./Bodapati, A./Degeratu, A./Hildebrandt, L./Kim, N./Ramaswami, S./Shankar, V. H. (1999): Multiple-Category Decision-Making: Review and Synthesis, in: Marketing Letters, Vol. 10, 3, pp. 319-332.

[37] Russell, G. J./Petersen, A. (2000): Analysis of Cross Category Dependence in Market Basket Selection, in: Journal of Retailing, Vol. 76, 3, pp. 367-392.

[38] Seetharaman, P. B./Chib, S./Ainslie, A./Boatwright, P./Chan, T./Gupta, S./Mehta, N./Rao, V./Strijnev, A. (2005): Models of Multi-Category Choice Behavior, in: Marketing Letters, Vol. 16, 3/4, pp. 239-254.

[39] Stern, P./Hammond, K. (2004): The Relationship Between Customer Loyalty and Purchase Incidence, in: Marketing Letters, Vol. 15, 1, pp. 5-19.

[40] Uncles, M. D./Hammond, K. A./Ehrenberg, A. S. C./Davis, R. E. (1994): A replication study of two brand-loyalty measures., in: European Journal of Operations Research, Vol. 76, 2, pp. 378-384.

[41] Wind, Y. E./Frank, R. E. (1969): Interproduct Household Loyalty to Brands, in: Journal of Marketing Research, Vol. 6, 4, pp. 434-435.

4 Validation of Brand Relationship Types Using Advanced Clustering Methods

Wolfgang Fritz, Technische Universität Braunschweig, Germany, and University of Vienna, Austria

Michael Kempe, Technische Universität Braunschweig, Germany

Bettina Lorenz, Volkswagen Consulting, Volkswagen AG, Germany

Abstract

In this article we reanalyze the findings of an existing study on consumer-brand relationships conducted in Germany. Based on the data of more than nine hundred consumers and using advanced clustering methods, our study in principle supports the former findings indicating the existence of four generic types of consumer-brand relationships. These types are characterized as "best friendship," "unemotional purpose-based relationship," "loose contact," and "happy partnership." Furthermore, as the findings suggest, advanced methods of cluster analysis do not improve the solution provided by traditional clustering in each case.

Keywords

Brand Relationships, Cluster Analysis, Mixture Clustering.

4.1   Introduction

In recent years, the relationships between consumers and brands have gained an increasing attention in research and practice (MacInnis/Park/Priester 2009). Yet empirical studies that focus on different types of brand relationships are still relatively rare, especially in Europe. Therefore these relationship types are the central focus of this article, which examines in particular the empirical relevance of four generic types of consumer-brand relationships researched recently in Germany (Lorenz 2009; Fritz/Lorenz 2010). Furthermore, the article draws conclusions that are relevant to marketing research and marketing practice.

4.2   Current State of Research on Brand Relationships

In German-speaking Europe, Meffert (2002), Bruhn/Hennig-Thurau/Hadwich (2004) in particular take a theory-based look at the role that brands play in customer relationships in consumer goods markets. However, only few empirical studies have been carried out on this topic to date. One exception is the study called "Relationship Monitor" by the advertising agency FCB Deutschland (2002), which empirically identifies seven different consumer-brand relationships in the German marketplace, but does not provide any theoretical basis.

More recent studies have focused solely on a few specific aspects of consumer-brand relationships. For instance, a theoretical study by Jodl (2005) asks whether consumers are capable of "loving" brands, given the latter are not human beings. In contrast, Henkel/Huber (2005) transfer the brand concept to people, particularly celebreties in the media, and analyze the relationships between these persons (as brands) and other people. In other studies, Huber/Vollhardt/Vogel (2008) look at the effect of brand relationships on customer value, whereas Wenske (2008) conceptualizes the consumer-brand relationship as an unidimensional construct and outlines its implications for customer complaint management within the firm. In a recent study, Bruhn/Eichen (2010) develop a measurement model of the "brand relationship quality" construct.

A larger number of studies have been carried out in the English-speaking world (MacInnis/Park/Priester 2009). Many of these analyze important details of consumer-brand relationships, for instance, brand attachment and brand attitude strength (Park et al. 2010) as well as the transfer of brand personalities to consumers (Park/Roedder John 2010). Worth noting are also the studies by Blackston (1993), Sheth/Parvatiyar (1995), Aaker (1996), Aggarwal (2004), and Aaker/Fournier/Brasel (2004). But the most frequently cited work are the fundamental studies by Fournier (1994, 1998), who identifies a total of fifteen different types of relationships between consumers and brands (for instance, "best friendship," "secret affair," and "enslavement"). Since then, other studies about consumer-brand relationships have been carried out on the basis of Fournier's approach (Ji 2002; Kates 2000).

However, until now, studies comparable to Fournier's pioneering work, have been barely carried out in German-speaking Europe. This may be regarded as a significant research deficit, because it is an essential question whether Fournier's findings can be applied directly to the situation in Europe. Intercultural differences in consumers' brand perceptions and brand-choice behavior have long been empirically observed (Fischer/Voelckner/Sattler 2010, 831; Forquer Gupta/Winkel/Peracchio 2009; Monga/Roedder John 2009; Russell/Valenzuela 2005). Therefore it is possible that in Europe consumer-brand relationships may differ from those discovered by Fournier in the United States nearly twenty years ago. Furthermore, Fournier's research approach does not allow generalizations. She uses an idiographic research approach that relies on phenomenological interviews with three female respondents. The main objective of this particular approach is to gain deeper insights into the unique individual situation of each respondent—not to make generalizations (Jaccard/Wood 1986, 600). Fournier defended this fundamental perspective of her original study in more recent articles (Fournier 2009, 18). It is evident that brand relationships determined on such a small empirical basis and such a long time ago cannot be considered representative for all European as well as all American consumers of both genders.

Lorenz (2009) and Fritz/Lorenz (2010) have recently published a study in Germany, seeking to find generic types of consumer-brand relationships on a broad empirical base. One methodological shortcoming of this study is the rather traditional statistical approach of cluster analysis the authors used in order to determine the different types of brand relationships. In our paper, we build on these findings and extend the study by reanalyzing the empirical data using advanced and more sophisticated clustering methods. This procedure will help to better identify valid types of consumer-brand relationships representative for larger groups of consumers.

4.3 Combination of Clustering Methods

4.3.1 Four Steps of Cluster Analysis

Cluster analysis is the appropriate method in order to identify brand relationship types. In general, it is used for classification of cases or variables into groups that are internally as homogeneous and externally as heterogeneous as possible (Boßow-Thies/Clement 2009, 176). In the present study, descriptive non-overlapping methods are used, where the group membership is clearly defined. These methods can be divided into deterministic methods, where group membership is unambiguous, and probabilistic methods, which calculate a probability of belonging for every object (Jensen 2008, 339 f.; Boßow-Thies/Clement 2009, 185).

Unlike "traditional" deterministic methods, probabilistic methods of cluster analysis, like mixture models (also called mixture clustering), are based on statistical models rather than on heuristics. Additionally, mixture models take unobserved heterogeneity within the data into account (Jensen 2008, 349; Boßow-Thies/Clement 2009, Wedel/Kamakura 2003).

Following Punji/Stewart (1983, 145), Boßow-Thies/Clement (2009, 184) suggest a combination of the different clustering methods. Through different approaches of group formation the arbitrariness should be reduced. In particular, probabilistic methods can be used for the validation of deterministic methods (Boßow-Thies/Clement 2009, 184 f.; Jensen 2008, 349, 367). This extended analysis seems to be necessary because mixture clustering provides a superior estimation procedure and because deterministic clustering neglects the problem of unobserved heterogeneity within the data to a high degree (Franke/Reisinger/Hoppe 2009). An appropriate approach can be summarized as the following four steps, like they were passed in the present study:

1. Hierarchical cluster analysis: Single linkage method for the elimination of outliers, in other words cases with characteristics that are very atypical for the sample (deterministic);

2. Hierarchical cluster analysis: Ward's method for determining the number of clusters and boot partition, if unknown (deterministic);

3. Partitional clustering: K-means clustering method for optimizing the solution and for determination of a boot partition (deterministic);

4. Mixture clustering for validating the cluster solution (probabilistic).

(Kempe 2011, 153 f., Boßow-Thies/Clement 2009, 185).

4.3.2   Mixture Clustering: An Advanced Clustering Method

Mixture models assume that the distribution of objects in the different variables represent a mixture of different class-specific probability distributions due to unobserved heterogeneity. Furthermore it is assumed that the objects come from a population which is composed of a mixture of unknown latent segments, and that the origin of an object is not known in advance. Instead, a-priori probabilities, with which an object is assigned to one of these unknown segments, are used. The "true" number of clusters has to be predetermined, and therefore several cluster solutions with different numbers of clusters have to be compared in practice. In addition, besides a specified starting partition from previous deterministic cluster analysis, also random starting partitions should be used for the calculation to determine, whether there is a better solution than the predetermined (Boßow-Thies/Clement 2009, 178 ff.).

The a posteriori probabilities, by which the objects are assigned to a group, are estimated from the observed values of the associated variables. Thereby the objects are assigned to the groups in which the a posteriori probability reaches the highest value (Boßow-Thies/Clement 2009, 178 ff.).

The parameters of the distributions and its mixture proportions are in general estimated using the maximum likelihood (ML) method, and the maximization of the likelihood function is performed by the iterative expectation-maximization (EM) algorithm. This procedure is repeated until the convergence criterion is below a predefined value and the model fits best the empirical data. Since the EM algorithm, depending on the starting partition, determines different local optima, a high number of replications with different starting partitions should be calculated. In addition, the results of deterministic methods can be used as starting partitions (Boßow-Thies/Clement 2009, 178 ff.; Jensen 2008, 349 f.). The described procedure of group formation is implemented in the mixture clustering software Glimmix 3.0, which is used here.

As a result of this procedure, the researcher obtains numerous alternative models with a different number of clusters. For a given number of clusters a likelihood ratio test can be used to select the best model. More often it has to be chosen from models with different cluster numbers. Therefore, the so-called information criteria (IC) are available, which tend to be lower, the better the fit of the model and the smaller the number of parameters to be estimated are. **Table 4.1** gives an overview of the information criteria calculated by Glimmix.

Table 4.1   Information Criteria-Based Measurements

Information criterion	Abbreviation	Penalty component d
Akaike Information Criterion	AIC	$d = 2$
Modified Akaike Information Criterion	MAIC	$d = 3$
Consistent Akaike Information Criterion	CAIC	$d = \ln(N+1)$
Bayesian Information Criterion	BIC	$d = \ln(N)$

with $IC = -2\ln L + Pd$,
$\ln L$ = Log-Likelihood, P = number of parameters, d = penalty component, N = sample size

Source: Boßow-Thies/Clement 2009, 183

Moreover, the different cluster solutions can be compared using the entropy value, which is an indicator for the separation of the clusters. Values close to 1 indicate a good separation of the clusters, and values close to 0 a poor separation (Boßow-Thies/Clement 2009, 183 f.).

These measures not always provide a unique solution. In this case, the cluster solution, which is supported by the majority of the criteria, should be favorized. Furthermore, the interpretability of the solutions has to be considered (Jensen 2008, 357; Boßow-Thies/Clement 2009, 187).

4.3.3   Goodness of Clustering

After passing through the various steps and methods of cluster analysis, several competing cluster solutions may emerge. Therefore, additional fit criteria have to be used for the evaluation and selection of the final solution. Appropriate measures, which provide information of the clusters' homogeneity and heterogeneity, are the sum of squared errors, the RS-value and the F-values.

The **sum of squared errors** is calculated by the case wise squared deviation from the respective group mean value of each variable. Thus, it is a value indicating the size of the remaining heterogeneity in the clusters, also called the „Remaining within-cluster heterogeneity" (Franke/Reisinger/Hoppe 2009, 277). It reaches the highest value for the one cluster solution. Franke, Reisinger, and Hoppe (2009) label this specific value „Sum of squares total (SST)". With the RS-value (RS = Remaining sum of squares) a standardized value exists for the sum of squared errors, which makes it possible to compare clustering results from different studies with different scales.

The **RS-value** is calculated as follows:

$$RS = 1 - \frac{SSW}{SST}$$

with

SSW = Sum of squares within groups (= sum of squared errors)
SST = Sum of squares total (= sum of squared errors for the one cluster solution)

(Franke/Reisinger/Hoppe 2009, 277).

If RS is equal to 1, we have a cluster solution, in which the sum of squared errors (SSW) is 0, i.e. which is a perfectly homogeneous solution. Hence, the sum of squared errors should be as small as possible and RS close to 1. A very good value is reached already at 0.7, an acceptable value between 0.3 and 0.7. Values below 0.3 are not acceptable (Franke, Reisinger, and Hoppe 2009, 288).

Another quality measure of the clusters' homogeneity is the **F-value**. The F-values are calculated for each variable in the respective clusters. The respective F-value is calculated as follows:

$$F = \frac{V(j,g)}{V(j)}$$

with

V (j,g) = Variance of the variable j in group g
V (j) = Variance of the variable j in the whole sample

(Backhaus et al. 2006, 545).

The F-value should be lower than 1. In this case, the variance of the variable in the group is smaller than the variance of the same variable in the whole sample, which is an indicator for a good homogeneity within the respective cluster (Backhaus et al. 2006, 545). Unlike the analysis of the sum of squared errors the F-values allow a more precise identification of particular heterogeneous clusters and variables.

In addition, the **hit ratio of discriminant analysis** and significant differences based on analysis of variance are often used to validate clustering results. This approach is based on the input variables of the cluster analysis. A high hit ratio of the discriminant analysis represents a good group structure within the data, significant differences in the input variables a sufficient heterogeneity between the clusters (Bortz 2005, 583). However, the validation of cluster analysis by subordinate discriminant analysis or analysis of variance is controversial (Jensen 2008, 363; Schendera 2010, 19). In this regard, a significant separation of clusters is not seen as an evidence for the respective cluster solution, since this does not exclude the validity of other cluster solutions. Though, a non-significance of the input variables may be an indicator for an unreliable cluster solution (Schendera 2010, 20). Nevertheless, these methods can be used to compare the quality of alternative cluster solutions as it is done in our case (Lorenz 2009, 298 f.; Fritz/Lorenz 2010, 378).

4.4   Identification of Brand Relationship Types Using Traditional and Mixture Clustering Methods

4.4.1   Data Collection and Sample

For data collection, an email-supported online survey was carried out with consumers in Germany during the late summer of 2006. This type of survey sets up questionnaires on the web and sends links to email addresses, informing targeted addressees of the questionnaires. The online panel of Gesellschaft für Konsumforschung (GfK), one of the biggest market research institutes in Europe, was used to carry out the survey. The collected data were analyzed using SPSS 19.0, Glimmix 3.0, and PLS-Graph. A total of 1121 respondents took part in the survey, resulting in 986 completed questionnaires that could be included for further analysis. **Table 4.2** shows the demographic structure of the sample.

Table 4.2   Demographics of Sample

Demographics		Percentage of adjusted sample (n = 986)	Expected percentage (Basis: population)
Gender	Female	50.0% (493)	51.1% (504)
	Male	50.0% (493)	48.9% (482)
$n = 986$; χ^2 ($p = .05$; $df = 1$) = 3.84 > χ^2 (emp.) = 0.25			
Age	Under 14	0.0% (0)	N/A
	14-29	31.6% (311)	25.0% (247)
	30-49	43.4% (428)	45.0% (444)
	50-64	22.9% (226)	30.0% (296)
	over 64	2.1% (21)	N/A
$n = 986$; χ^2 ($p = .05$; $df = 4$) = 9.49 < χ^2 (emp.) = 12.06			
Education	No school-leaving certificate	1.6% (16)	7.0% (69)
	Lower secondary school	9.3% (91)	36.0% (354)
	Secondary school leaving certificate, mid-level secondary school or similar	35.5% (349)	37.0% (364)
	College/University	53.7% (528)	19.0% (187)
$n = 984$; χ^2 ($p = .05$; $df = 3$) = 7.81 < χ^2 (emp.) = 351.39			

The resulting profile corresponds to an average internet user, whose demographic profile still differs from that of the average population. The chi-square test shows that the sample is representative for the German population in terms of gender, but not in terms of age and education.

Among others, **Table 4.3** illustrates the consumer-goods categories and brands included in the study. Consumers were assigned to categories and brands at random. Each consumer only responded to questions about one brand he or she had used before.

Table 4.3　　　Consumer Goods, Brands, and Number of Respondents

Product category, brands, and number of respondents		Absolute	Percentage
Clothing	Adidas, C&A, Esprit, H&M, Levi's, Nike	116	11.76%
Banks	Deutsche Bank, Dresdner Bank, Postbank, Sparkasse, Volksbank, Raiffeisenbank	100	10.14%
Credit Cards	American Express, MasterCard, Visa	93	9.43%
Fast-Food Restaurants	Burger King, Kochlöffel, McDonald's, Nordsee, Pizza Hut, Subway	139	14.10%
Cars	Audi, BMW, Ford, Mercedes, Opel, VW	109	11.05%
Beverages	Coca-Cola, Fanta, Pepsi, Schweppes, Sprite	154	15.62%
Cosmetics	Dove, Fa, Labello, Nivea, Palmolive, Penaten	130	13.18%
Online Service Providers	AOL, Freenet, Google, T-Online, web.de, Yahoo!	145	14.71%
Total		986	100.00%

4.4.2　　Relationship Dimensions as Input Variables

In the studies by Lorenz (2009) and Fritz/Lorenz (2010), the generic types of consumer-brand relationships were developed and described by nine different relationship dimensions. These are: Interdependence, relationship duration, satisfaction, brand commitment, actual behavior, equity, brand trust, passion, and intimacy. The theoretical background as well as the conceptualization, operationalization, and empirical validation of the dimensions are demonstrated in detail in the original studies and cannot be presented here again (Lorenz 2009; Fritz/Lorenz 2010). Only a short description of the nine relationship dimensions is given in **Table 4.4**.

Table 4.4　　　Nine Dimensions of Relationships Between Consumers and Brands

Relationship dimension	Content
Interdependence	Mutual dependence between consumer and brand (see Fournier 1998) as reflected in the frequency of interaction with the brand, the scope, variety, and intensity of brand-related activities of the consumer.
Relationship duration	Absolute amount of time during which the relationship between consumer and brand exists.
Satisfaction	Result of a cognitive comparison between expected and experienced performance. In addition, satisfaction also exhibits an affective component, as in the concept of "customer delight".

Relationship dimension	Content
Brand commitment	Based on Morgan/Hunt (1994), brand commitment is understood as the consumer's desire and effort to maintain a long-term relationship with a brand.
Actual behavior	The customer's actual behavior towards the brand is composed of buying and word-of-mouth behavior.
Equity	According to Walster/Berscheid/Walster (1978), equity is defined as the perception of a balance between rewards and inputs, where rewards are defined as the difference between outcomes and inputs.
Brand trust	According to Morgan/Hunt (1994), brand trust represents the level of consumer's confidence in the brand's ability to fulfill his/her expectations.
Passion	According to Sternberg (1986), passion is an all-encompassing motivational construct that goes beyond physical attraction and includes a state of intense longing for union with the other.
Intimacy	According to Reis/Shaver (1988), intimacy occurs when a person (i.e., the consumer) reveals feelings or information to another person (i.e., the brand). Self-disclosure and the feeling that the disclosing person is understood, confirmed and cared for are important aspects of intimacy.

The following cluster analysis is based on these nine dimensions, which are included as input variables using their factor values. The analysis is not affected by the moderate correlation existing between some of the dimensions, since most clustering methods do not assume uncorrelated cluster variables (Milligan 1996, Milligan/Hirtle 2003). Accordingly, this applies if, as in our case, cluster variables represent complex constructs and the criteria for discriminant validity are met (Fritz/Lorenz 2010).

4.4.3   Identifying the Number of Relationship Types Using Traditional Cluster Analysis

At the outset, a traditional hierarchical cluster analysis is used to empirically identify relationship types in terms of relationship dimensions regarded as clustering variables (Step 1). Using the single-linkage method, we first identify outliers. The squared Euclidean distance is selected as a measure of proximity. As a result of this procedure, 37 of the 986 total cases had to be excluded from further study. Nevertheless, this is unimportant because the cases are distributed evenly among the product categories and brands under investigation. Thus, 949 cases were finally included for cluster formation.

Table 4.5 Growth of Heterogeneity and Number of Clusters

Number of clusters	Heterogeneity coefficient (Sum of squared errors)	Growth of heterogeneity
6	2699,31	145,17
5	2924,01	224,71
4	*3201,94*	*277,93*
3	3715,11	*513,16*
2	4305,96	590,85
1	6232,29	1926,33

Figure 4.1 Sum of Squared Errors and Number of Clusters

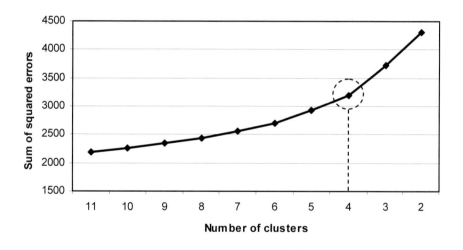

The cluster analysis then continues with the Ward procedure (Step 2). The preliminary determination of the optimal cluster number is based on the heterogeneity coefficients (sum of squared errors). When we look at their differences in **Table 4.5**, the advantage of a four clusters solution is obvious: In moving from a four clusters to a three clusters solution, the increase in the sum of squared errors nearly doubles. The graphical representation of the sum of squared errors in **Figure 4.1** also illustrates this aspect by indicating a significant elbow for the four clusters solution.

The next task is to optimize the four clusters solution using the k-means method (Step 3); this reduces the sum of squared errors by 164.76, or 5.1 percent. Multiple discriminant analyses are performed for further validation. The four clusters solution is also superior to the alternative solutions in terms of classification correctness for individual discriminant functions, as shown in **Table 4.6**

Table 4.6   Percentage of Cases Correctly Classified by Discriminant Analysis

Number of clusters	Classification correctness (hit ratio)
3 clusters solution	93.8 %
4 clusters solution	*95.2 %*
5 clusters solution	94.9 %
6 clusters solution	94.8 %

4.4.4   Identifying the Number of Relationship Types Using Mixture Models

Extending this traditional clustering approach, for example also used by Lorenz (2009) as well as by Fritz/Lorenz (2010), we finally add the advanced mixture clustering procedure in order to validate the traditional clustering solution (Step 4). Therefore, mixture clustering procedures were carried out for two up to six clusters, each replicated 200 times with different random starting partitions to find the best mixture model for each number of clusters.

Table 4.7   Findings of the Mixture Clustering Procedure

Number of clusters	Log-Likelihood	AIC	CAIC	MAIC	BIC	Entropy	df
2	-17479,25	35000,51	35170,42	35021,51	35149,42	0,896	21
3	-15727,75	31519,50	31777,19	31551,50	31745,19	0,916	32
4	*-15211,90*	*30509,80*	*30856,06*	*30552,80*	*30813,06*	*0,919*	*43*
5	-15004,31	30116,63	30551,47	30170,63	30497,47	0,898	54
6	-14818,86	29767,73	30291,15	29832,73	30226,15	0,891	65

The findings presented in **Table 4.7** support the four clusters solution. The entropy of the four clusters solution shows the highest value indicating the best separation of the clusters, and the information criteria are better for the four clusters solution than for the three or two clusters solutions. In analogy to the representation of the sum of squared errors in **Figure 4.1** an elbow is visible in the graphical representation of the information criteria for different cluster solutions in **Figure 4.2**, which indicates weaker improvements of the fit if one switches from the four to the five and the six clusters solutions.

Figure 4.2　　　Information Criteria and Number of Clusters

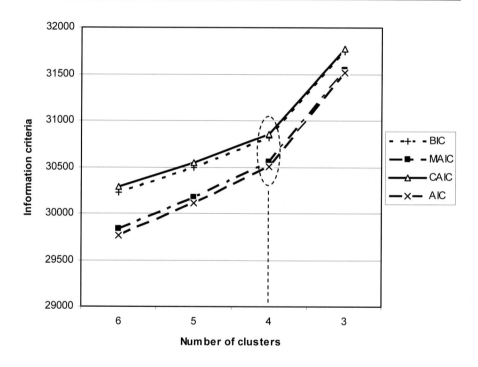

Hence, it follows that, along the nine relationship dimensions, four different clusters have been identified empirically by means of traditional and advanced clustering as well, representing four different types of relationships between consumers and brands.

4.4.5 Interpretation and Formal Comparison of the Different Clustering Solutions

First of all, to decide which of the clustering approaches leads to a better result, the criteria described in chapter 4.3.3 are employed to evaluate the four clusters solutions of both clustering approaches. The results are shown in **Table 4.8**.

Table 4.8 Comparison of Goodness of Cluster Solutions

	Sum of squared errors (SSW)	RS	Highest F-value	Average F-value	Hit ratio
k-means	3037	0.513	0.940	0.513	94.8%
Mixture clustering	3430	0.450	1.174 (!)	0.510	96.0%

RS = 1-SSW/SST, SST=6232,29

The cluster solution of the k-means algorithm fulfills all standard criteria for heterogeneity and homogeneity. All distances between the cluster centers show values between 2.2 and 5.2. The hit ratio of the discriminant analysis is very high, while all F-values within the clusters are between 0.3 and 0.9. Also RS reaches an acceptable level. All in all this indicates a sufficient degree of clusters homogeneity.

This is different for the results of the mixture clustering approach. The distances between the cluster centers also show acceptable values between 1.7 and 5.9. The average F-value within the clusters is marginally smaller and the hit ratio of the discriminant analysis is slightly higher than for the k-means solution. However, single F-values are higher than 1, indicating less homogeneity of the clustering result. This also is demonstrated by the higher sum of squared errors, which leads to a still acceptable but lower RS value than for the k-means solution. In conclusion, despite all advantages mixture clustering offers, it does not lead in any case to a more homogeneous solution than a traditional clustering approach.

Furthermore, the interpretation of the different cluster solutions is considered. Although the advanced mixture clustering supports the four clusters solution uncovered by the traditional approach in principle, it reveals some relevant differences, especially with regard to the size of the clusters resp. the four types of brand relationships as seen in **Table 4.9**.

Table 4.9   Comparison of Cluster Size

Cluster No.	Cluster (Relationship type)	Cluster size k-means	Cluster size Mixture clustering
1	Best friendship	328 (34.6%)	334 (35.2%)
2	Unemotional purpose-based relationship	257 (27.1%)	122 (12.9%)
3	Loose contact	236 (24.9%)	360 (37.9%)
4	Happy partnership	128 (13.5%)	133 (14.0%)

The key to interpret the four clusters are the mean values of the nine relationship dimensions as depicted by the profile graphs in **Figure 4.3** and **Figure 4.4**.

Figure 4.3   Profile Graphs of the Four Consumer-Brand Relationship Types Identified by the K-Means Clustering Approach

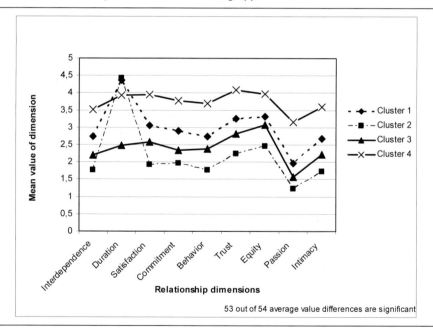

The key to interpret the four clusters are the mean values of the nine relationship dimensions as depicted by the profile graphs in Figure 4.3 and Figure 4.4.

Cluster 4, called *"happy partnership"*, is one of the smallest clusters in both clustering approaches. For this cluster all relationship dimensions are strongly developed, indicating a high level of relationship quality. A very close and trustful relationship is essential for this type, which is also characterized by passion and intimacy. Intense feelings exist between the consumer and the brand.

This shows a similarity with Fournier's "committed partnership," since that relationship is also characterized by love, intimacy, and trust (Fournier 1998, 362).

Cluster 1 is by far a larger cluster. In comparison to Cluster 4, it shows lower values in almost every relationship dimension, but the levels are still relatively high. The relationship is close-knit, long term, and consumers are satisfied with it. They feel a connection with the brand and generally trust it. Nevertheless, there is significantly less passion in this relationship than in the "happy partnership". Therefore, the consumer brand relationship is characterized as a *"best friendship"*, similar to Fournier's *"best friendships"* brand relationship (Fournier 1998, 362). In fact, however, this is the only relationship that was also discovered in the same form in Fournier's study.

Figure 4.4   Profile Graphs of the Four Consumer-Brand Relationship Types Identified by the Mixture Clustering Approach

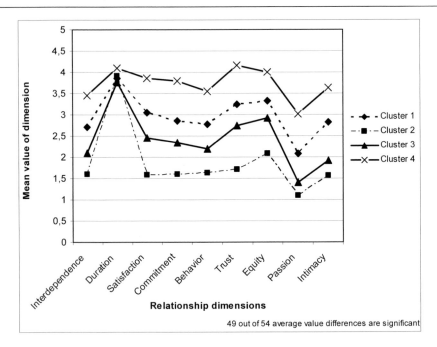

The size of Cluster 2 differs to great extent between the two clustering solutions. Whereas it is the smallest cluster of the mixture clustering approach, the size doubles when using the traditional method. Besides that it differs fundamentally from the two previously described clusters. It shows the weakest manifestations of nearly every relationship dimension. Thus, Cluster 2 indicates a low quality of relationship. This seems contradictory at first, since the relationship is also long-lasting. In fact, it is entirely possible that consumers enter into this type of brand relationship only for a specific long-term purpose, such as making the corresponding brand purchases as simple as possible or minimizing the purchasing costs. Like an interpersonal "purpose-based relationship," for instance a "marriage of convenience" or a "shared living arrangement" (Macklin 1988, 58) this type can be described as an *"unemotional purpose-based relationship"*.

The size of Cluster 3 also differs between the two clustering solutions. While it is the largest of the four clusters in the mixture clustering solution, it is much smaller in the traditional approach. Nonetheless, it describes a more superficial type of relationship. The consumer is still satisfied with the brand to some degree, but he or she does not feel a strong inner connection with it. Emotional relationship aspects, such as intimacy and passion, are also less strongly developed. Thus, the relationship type represented by Cluster 3 can be seen as a *"loose contact"*.

The interpretation of both kinds of clustering solutions clearly shows on the one hand different sizes of the four relationship types identified. But, on the other hand, it also demonstrates similar profiles of the four types. The only exception is the "duration" dimension, because in this regard the types differ less strongly for mixture than for traditional clustering. Nevertheless, the profiles of the other eight dimensions nearly show the same pattern across the four relationship types in both kinds of clustering solutions.

4.5   Consequences for Research and Practice

In her seminal studies, Fournier (1994, 1998) used three interviews with women to uncover a total of fifteen relationship types that the respondents had established with their brands in the United States. Although it is probable that the living and consumption environment in Germany is likewise shaped by a multitude of brand relationships, we were able to reproduce Fournier's findings in our study only to a limited extent. If one goes beyond Fournier's individual case studies and looks at the brand relationship types representative for larger numbers or segments of individual consumers, most of the findings are different. Based on nine relationship dimensions and using traditional and advanced clustering methods as well, our study supports empirically only the four basic types of consumer-brand relationships identified earlier (Lorenz 2009; Fritz/Lorenz 2010). These types can be described as "best friendship," "unemotional purpose-based relationship," "loose contact," and "happy partnership." The results presented in our study relativize the findings by Fournier and at the same time supplement them, since Fournier did not aim to discover generic relationship types and gave as well somewhat different descriptions for the types "unemotional purpose-based relationship" and "loose contact", and to some extent also for "happy partnership."

Most important for companies is to create and maintain favourable brand relationships, which in the context of our study means the "happy partnership" and "best friendship" relationship types. However, creating and developing these brand relationships cannot be the only objective of brand management. Another challenge is to improve the less advantageous relationships, the "unemotional purpose-based relationship" and the "loose contact," whenever the company detects such relationships with its brands. Since these two relationship types are characterized by a weaker identification with the brand, there is always a higher risk that the consumer will switch to a competitor's brand – a consequence that has to be avoided.

Overall, the present study supports the growing international understanding that firms' traditional brand management is in need of a much broader perspective. In addition to the brand, firms must also focus on the relationship between the consumer and the brand (Fournier 2009; MacInnis/Park/Priester 2009). In practice, this way of thinking has already been adopted by several companies. Henkel's web site, for example, features the slogan "A Brand like a Friend." However, many other companies are still far from implementing such a comprehensive perspective of brand management.

One limitation of our study is its character as a descriptive snapshot of the phenomena under investigation. In the future, broad empirical studies should be carried out to determine when and how consumers integrate brands into their lives, what factors influence their choice of brand relationships, how consumers develop their chosen brand relationships, reevaluate or replace them with other relationship types. Like human relationships, the relationships between consumers and brands may change over time. We agree with Fournier that there is a need to focus more extensively on the dynamics of brand relationships in the future, both in research and in practice (Fournier 2009, 15).

Furthermore, empirical follow-up studies should also use alternative methods of data collection. The well-known GfK's online panel, used in our study, seems to be more representative for the community of internet users than for the population as a whole. If clustering methods are considered for data analysis, the researcher should use the traditional and advanced approaches very carefully. As our study shows, advanced clustering methods do not lead in each case automatically to a better clustering solution as traditional methods.

Literature

[1] Aaker, D. A. (1996): Building Strong Brands, London: Simon & Schuster.

[2] Aaker, J./ Fournier S./Brasel, A. S. (2004): When Good Brands Do Bad", Journal of Consumer Research, Vol. 31, pp. 1–16.

[3] Aggarwal, P. (2004): The Effects of Brand Relationship Norms on Consumers' Attitudes and Behavior, Journal of Consumer Research, Vol. 31, pp. 87–101.

[4] Backhaus, K./Erichson, B./Plinke, W./Weiber, R. (2006): Multivariate Analysemethoden, 11th ed., Berlin: Springer.

[5] Blackston, M. (1993): Beyond Brand Personality: Building Brand Relationships, in Brand Equity and Advertising: Advertising's Role in Building Strong Brands, ed. David A. Aaker, and Alexander L. Biel, Hillsdale, NJ: Erlbaum, pp. 113–124.

[6] Bortz, J. (2005): Statistik für Human- und Sozialwissenschaftler, 6th ed., Berlin: Springer.

[7] Boßow-Thieß, S./Michel, C. (2009): Fuzzy Clustering mit Hilfe von Mixture Models, in Methodik der empirischen Forschung, 3rd. ed, ed. Sönke Albers et al., Wiesbaden: Gabler, pp. 175-190.

[8] Bruhn, M./Eichen, F. (2010): Messung und Steuerung der Markenbeziehungsqualität – Ergebnisse einer branchenübergreifenden empirischen Studie im Konsumgütermarkt, in: Aktuelle Beiträge zur Markenforschung, eds. Wolfgang Mayerhofer and Marion Secka, Wiesbaden: Gabler, pp. 27-54.

[9] Bruhn, M./Hennig-Thurau, T./Hadwich, K. (2004): Markenführung und Relationship Marketing", in Handbuch Markenführung (Band 1), 2nd ed., ed. Manfred Bruhn, Wiesbaden: Gabler, pp. 391–420.

[10] FCB Deutschland (2002): FCB Deutschland: Relationship Monitor, URL: http://www.wuv.de/daten/studien/122002/624/index.html.

[11] Fischer, M./Voelckner, F./Sattler, H. (2010): How Important are Brands? A Cross-Category, Cross-Country Study", Journal of Marketing Research, Vol. 47, October, pp. 823-839.

[12] Forquer Gupta, S./Winkel, D./Peracchio, L. (2009): Cultural Value Dimensions and Brands: Can a Global Brand Image Exist? in Handbook of Brand Relationships, ed. Deborah J. MacInnis, C. Whan Park, Joseph R. Priester, Armonk and London: Sharpe, pp. 230–246.

[13] Fournier, S. M. (1994): A Consumer-Brand Relationship Framework for Strategic Brand Management, Ann Arbor, MI.

[14] Fournier, S. M. (1998): Consumers and Their Brands: Developing Relationship Theory in Consumer Research, Journal of Consumer Research, Vol. 24, pp. 343–373.

[15] Fournier, S. M. (2009): Lessons Learned about Consumers' Relationships with Their Brands, in Handbook of Brand Relationships, ed. Deborah J. MacInnis, C. Whan Park, and Joseph R. Priester, Armonk and London: Sharpe, pp. 5–23.

[16] Franke, N/Reisinger, H./Hoppe, D. (2009), "Remaining Within-Cluster Heterogeneity: A Meta-Analysis of the 'Dark Side' of Clustering Methods", Journal of Marketing Management, 25 (3-4), 273–293.

[17] Fritz, W./Lorenz, B. (2010): Beziehungen zwischen Konsumenten und Marken – Eine empirische Analyse verschiedener Beziehungstypen, Schmalenbachs Zeitschrift für betriebswirtschaftliche Forschung (zfbf), Vol. 62, pp. 366-393.

[18] Henkel, S./Huber, F. (2005): Marke Mensch: Prominente als Marken der Medienindustrie, Wiesbaden: Gabler.

[19] Huber, F./Vollhardt, K./Vogel, J. (2008): Aufbau von Markenbeziehungen als Grundlage des Dienstleistungsmanagements, in Dienstleistungsmarken – Forum Dienstleistungsmanagement, ed. Manfred Bruhn and Bernd Stauss, Wiesbaden: Gabler, pp. 58–76.

[20] Jaccard, J./Wood, G. (1986): An Idiothetic Analysis of Attitude-Behavior Models, in Advances in Consumer Research, 13, ed. Richard J. Lutz, Provo, UT, pp. 600–605.

[21] Jensen, O. (2008): Clusteranalyse, in Handbuch Marktforschung, 3rd. ed., ed. Andreas Herrmann, Christian Homburg, and Martin Klarmann, Wiesbaden: Gabler, pp. 335-372.

[22] Ji, M. F. (2002): Children's Relationships with Brands: 'True Love' or 'One-Night Stand'?, Psychology and Marketing, Vol. 95, pp. 369–387.

[23] Jodl, F. (2005): Liebe als Beziehungsform zwischen Konsumenten und Marken, Munich: Fördergesellschaft Marketing.

[24] Kates, S. M. (2000): Out of the Closet and out of the Street! Gay Men and their Brand Relationships, Psychology and Marketing, Vol. 17, pp. 493–513.

[25] Kempe, M. (2011): Ungeplante Käufe im Internet, Wiesbaden: Gabler.

[26] Lorenz, B. (2009): Beziehungen zwischen Konsumenten und Marken. Eine empirische Untersuchung von Markenbeziehungen, Wiesbaden: Gabler.

[27] MacInnis, D. J./Park, C. W./Priester, J. R. (eds.) (2009): Handbook of Brand Relationships, Armonk and London: Sharpe.

[28] Macklin, E. D. (1988): Heterosexual Couples who Cohabit Nonmaritally, in Variant Family Forms, ed. Catherine S. Chilman, Elam W. Nunnally, and Fred M. Cox, Newbury Park, CA: Sage, pp. 56-72.

[29] Meffert, H. (2002): Relational Branding. Beziehungsorientierte Markenführung als Aufgabe des Direktmarketing, Working Paper, Universität Münster.

[30] Milligan, G. W. (1996): Clustering Validation: Results and Implications for Applied Analyses, in Clustering and Classification, ed. Phipps Arabie, Lawrence J. Hubert, and Geert de Soete, Singapore: World Scientific, pp. 341–375.

[31] Milligan, G. W./ Hirtle, S. C. (2003): Clustering and Classification Methods, in Handbook of Psychology, 2: Research Methods in Psychology, ed. John A. Schinka, Wayne F. Velicer, and Irving B. Weiner, New York: John Wiley & Sons, pp. 165–186.

[32] Monga, A. B./Roedder John, D. (2009): Understanding Cultural Differences in Brand Extension Evaluation: The Influence of Analytic versus Holistic Thinking, in Handbook of Brand Relationships, ed. Deborah J. MacInnis, C. Whan Park, and Joseph R. Priester, Armonk and London: Sharpe, pp. 247–266.

[33] Morgan, R. M./ Hunt, S. D. (1994): The Commitment–Trust Theory of Relationship Marketing, Journal of Marketing, Vol. 58, pp. 20–38.

[34] Park, C. W./ MacInnis, D. J./Priester, J./Eisingerich, A. B./Iacobucci, D. (2010): Brand Attachment and Brand Attitude Strength: Conceptual and Empirical Differentiation of Two Critical Brand Equity Drivers, Journal of Marketing, Vol. 74, pp. 1-17.

[35] Park, J. K./Roedder John, D. (2010): Got to Get You into My Life: Do Brand Personalities Rub Off on Consumers?, Journal of Consumer Research, Vol. 37, pp. 655-669.

[36] Punji, G./Stewart, D. W. (1986): Cluster Analysis in Marketing Research: Review and Suggestions for Application, Journal of Marketing Research, Vol. 20, 2, pp. 134–148.

[37] Reis, H. T./Shaver, P. (1988): Intimacy as an Interpersonal Process, in Handbook of Personal Relationships ed. Steve Duck, Chichester: Wiley, pp. 367–389.

[38] Russell, A. C./Valenzuela, A. (2005): Global Consumption: (How) Does Culture Matter? in Advances in Consumer Research, 32, ed. Geeta Menon and Akshay R. Rao, Duluth, MN, pp. 86–89.

[39] Schendera, C. (2010): Clusteranalyse mit SPSS, Munich: Oldenbourg.

[40] Sheth, J. N./Parvatiyar, A. (1995): Relationship Marketing in Consumer Markets: Antecedents and Consequences, Journal of the Academy of Marketing Science, Vol. 23, pp. 255–271.

[41] Sternberg, R. J. (1986): A Triangular Theory of Love, Psychological Review, Vol. 93, pp. 119–135.

[42] Walster, E./Berscheid, E./Walster, G. W. (1978): Equity: Theory and Research, Boston: Allyn, Bacon.

5   Positioning Bases' Influence on Product Similarity Perceptions

An Open Sort Task Approach

Christoph Fuchs, Erasmus University Rotterdam, The Netherlands

Adamantios Diamantopoulos, University of Vienna, Austria

Abstract

The goal of many product positioning strategies is to create similarity perceptions with other products in the market. Product managers often seek to reach this goal by communicating the same information as competitors (e.g., highlighting the same product feature as an existing competitor product), which however, can also generate negative side effects (e.g., "me too" perceptions). This article introduces an alternative tactic aimed at overcoming such weaknesses, namely the communication of similar types of positioning bases as a means for creating similarity perceptions. To empirically test the value of this alternative, the study here uses an open sort task employing real products and advertisements. The study demonstrates that consumers classify products in terms of similarity based on their underlying positioning bases as anchored in advertisements. The study also shows that consumers do not use concrete positioning bases more often as a basis for classification than abstract positioning bases. These findings hold in three product categories which differ along several important characteristics, and point to the importance of selection of the type positioning basis. The study discusses implications and limitations of the study as well as avenues for future research.

Keywords

Product Positioning, Product Management, Perceived Similarity, Open Sort Task, Positioning Tactics.

5.1   Introduction

Perceived similarity – the psychological proximity or nearness – of products plays an important role in business research as perceived similarity influences product evaluations, and ultimately, preference judgments and choice (e.g., Brenner, Rottenstreich/Sood, 1999; Dhar/Nowlis/Sherman, 1999). Creating (dis)similarity perceptions is particularly important for product positioning. On the one hand, becoming associated with (the strength) of a competing product, and thus creating similarity perceptions, constitutes a strategic positioning aim for many products in the marketplace (e.g., minor products, less-familiar products; newly launched products; see Alpert/Kamins, 1995; Carpenter/Nakamoto, 1989; Urban/Hulland/Weinberg, 1993). On the other hand, dissociating a product from competitors, and thus creating dissimilarity perceptions, constitutes a positioning aim of others (e.g., major – strong and established branded products; Dickson/Ginter, 1987; Punj/Moon, 2002).

Focusing specifically on the former aim, a main challenge for many managers in charge of positioning lies in the development of tactics as how to best evoke similarity perceptions with other products in consumers' minds. The most obvious tactic for this purpose is to develop a product with similar physical features like a competitor product. While this is often not feasible in practice – mainly due to corporate abilities and regulations (e.g., patents, R&D know how, corporate design styles, etc.) – a second, related tactic is to merely highlight the same product benefits or features as competitors in marketing communications (e.g., if cell phone product A promotes a specific feature such as an "MP3 player", product B would create similarity perceptions by also communicating "MP3 player"; if product A promotes a direct benefit such as being "user friendly", product B would also promote "user-friendliness", etc). Even though the latter tactic allows a little bit more flexibility than the former, both tactics are nevertheless (a) constrained in terms of feasibility (e.g., what to communicate if the product does not have a MP3 player, or the strength of product B does not lie in its user-friendliness?) and more important, (b) associated with the disadvantage of evoking a bitter after-taste in the form of undesired "me-too" perceptions. Thus, if consumers realize that one product is merely copying another, unfavorable product perceptions such as "cheap follower", "second best option", "just another copycat" can arise. In fact, it is well documented that many follower products have attitudinal disadvantages compared to pioneer products in the market (Alpert/Kamins, 1995; Carpenter/Nakamoto, 1989).

Consider an alternative tactic that may help overcome these shortcomings – that is creating similarity perceptions while at the same time maintaining a certain degree of differentiation. Managers can accomplish the goal of successfully creating similarity perceptions by communicating the same *conceptual type* of positioning information as reflected in the choice of positioning base (e.g., concrete attribute, abstract attribute, direct benefit, indirect benefit, usage, user type, etc.) rather than communicating the *specific* information used by competition.

Specifically, the present research proposes that consumers classify products as being (dis)similar based upon the generic type of positioning information conveyed by their positioning bases as communicated in product advertisements.

To test this assertion, this study investigates whether consumers classify a cell phone that is, for example, positioned on a concrete attribute like a "MP3 player" more likely together with a competing cell phone being positioned on *another* concrete attribute such as "touch display" or a "2 megapixel camera". Or whether consumers classify a cell phone that is positioned on a direct benefit such as "user friendliness" more likely together with another cell phone that is positioned on a *different* direct benefit such as "have your office in your cell phone".

The study also investigates whether or not consumers classify products employing more concrete types of positioning bases (e.g., feature-based positioning) more frequently together than products positioned on more abstract bases (e.g., user-based positioning). To address the research questions, the study employs an open sort task approach with real-world stimuli (i.e., real products and advertisements). This non-experimental study design is consistent with our basic motivation – to introduce an alternative method for creating similarity perceptions of products for practicing managers – as it offers a high degree of external validity while ensuring an acceptable level of internal validity.

The next section provides the conceptual background to the study, a presentation of the research propositions, and a description of the research design employed. Section 5.3 presents the study findings and concludes the paper by highlighting key implications and limitations as well as areas for future research.

5.2   Conceptual Background

To provide a better understanding of the product positioning concept, it is important to distinguish between the intended and the perceived positioning. The intended positioning refers to positioning information that is (aimed to be) communicated (via advertising, product packaging, sales promotions, etc.) to consumers. However, what companies (intend to) communicate is one thing; how consumers eventually perceive a product in relation to its competitors (i.e., the perceived positioning) is another (Brown/Dacin/Pratt/Whetten, 2006; Lilien/Rangaswamy, 2003; Wind, 1982). The perceived positioning comprises the associations that consumers hold for a product in relation to its competitors (see Brown et al., 2006).

5.2.1   Intended Positioning

Marketers have the possibility to communicate a nearly unlimited number of elements to position their products. In case of a wristwatch, for example, product managers may emphasize a concrete attribute such as "sapphire glas", a more abstract attribute such as "precision", or indirect benefits such as "makes you feel special". The different positioning elements are summarized into positioning bases – for automobiles, for example, product features such as "automatic gear shift", "knee airbag", "air conditioning" fall into the concrete attribute category, abstract attributes such as "design", "fuel efficiency" fall into the abstract attributes category, etc. Therefore, the intended positioning can be operationalized with the help of positioning typologies, which are classification schemes containing a variety of positioning bases (also referred to as positioning alternatives). **Table 5.1** provides an overview of the most prominent positioning bases incorporated in the positioning typologies proposed in the literature (Aaker/Shansby, 1982; Crawford, 1985; Crawford/Urban/Buzas, 1983; Myers/Shocker, 1981; Wind, 1982; see also Blankson/Kalafatis, 2004 for an excellent overview).

Table 5.1   Overview of Major Positioning Bases Tested in This Study

	Positioning Bases	Literature Extracts	Explanation	Examples
Attribute Positioning	Concrete Attribute (Feature)	Aaker/Shansby, 1982; Crawford, 1985; Park/Jaworski/ MacInnis, 1986	Directly observable features; characteristics of the product advantage; objectively measurable; frequently tangible; typically "search features" specific to the product category	Watches: sapphire glas, timer, alarm function, automatic; Cell phones: mp3-player; 2 mio. pixel camera; touch screen
	Abstract Attribute	Gutman, 1982; Olson/Reynolds, 1983; Reynolds/Gengler/ Howard, 1995	Often regarded as bundles of concrete attributes; non-tangible; frequently comparable across product categories	Watches: precision; quality; style; sporty; design
Benefit Positioning	Direct (Functional) Benefit	Crawford, 1985; Kotler, 2003; Wind, 1982	Communicate utilitarian advantages of (the usage of) a product; closer related to one's self than product attributes; not directly observable	Cell phones: "having the office in your cell phone"; Cars: more comfort
	Indirect (Experiential/ Symbolic) Benefit	Crawford, 1985; Mahajan/Wind, 2002; Keller, 1993	Communicate non-functional advantages of using or possessing the product such as positive emotions, experiences, or self-fulfillment; aim to create strong affective bonds between consumers and the	Cars: Mini "Is it love?"; Renault Modus "Have Fun" –driving fun

Positioning Bases	Literature Extracts	Explanation	Examples
		focal product; relate to what it feels like to use the product in terms of sensory pleasure, variety, and cognitive stimulation	
Personalities (Endorsement)	Crawford, 1985; Kalra/Goodstein, 1998; Keller, 1993	People you respect/appreciate, use it or say it is good; associating the product with celebrities or expert users; intention to create image congruence between personality and consumer; image transfer of endorser to product	Watches: Brad Pitt for Tag Heuer; Roger Federer for Maurice Lacroix; James Bond for Omega Seamaster;
User	Aaker/Shansby, 1982; Crawford, 1985; Keller, 1993; Kotler, 2003; Park/Jaworski/MacInnis, 1986; Wind, 1982	Is designed for a certain user type/user imagery; for users like you; can be for a certain target group in terms of psychographic (lifestyle), demographic (sex), behavioral criteria; in contrast to personalities does not refer to a specific person	IWC watches for men; Volkswagen Golf for "wild guys"
Usage (Activities)	Aaker/Shansby, 1982; Wind, 1982; Kotler, 2003; Crawford, 1985; Park/Jaworski/MacInnis, 1986	The product can be used in a certain usage situation; or the product is associated with certain activities; these activities can also reflect the personal nature of the branded product (e.g., mountaineering may reflect wildness and adventure)	Cell phones: Siemens for mountaineering; Watches: Omega for diving; Michel Herbeilein with sailing
Pioneer	Alpert/Kamins, 1995; Crawford, 1985; Carpenter/Nakamoto, 1989	The product was the first in its category; the product is the original and benefits from its pioneer advantage	Jeep "The Original"; Motorola – the Inventor of the flip phone

(Left vertical label spanning rows: Surrogate Positioning)

A closer look at the positioning bases in **Table 5.1** reveals that each of them corresponds to the conceptual hierarchical elements of the means-end concept (see Gutman, 1982; Olson/Reynolds, 1983; Vriens/ter Hofstede, 2000) and their order corresponds to their degree of abstractness (Bridges/Keller/Sood, 2000; Keller, 1993). Concrete product positioning bases (e.g., concrete attributes, abstract attributes) relate to concrete, more product-specific consumer goals (i.e., having a car with a knee airbag), whereas abstract bases (e.g., experiential benefits or user type positioning) relate more to abstract, individual consumers goals such as self-expressiveness or social approval (Ratneshwar/Barsalou/Pechmann/Moore, 2001; see also Reynolds/Gengler/Howard, 1995).

When using more abstract forms of positioning, marketers do not position products on their respective product attributes or benefits, but instead communicate something about the product that permits consumers to create associations about external aspects of a product (e.g., the energy drink Red Bull may be associated with extreme sports such as base jumping or speed skiing). In case of user positioning, for example, marketers communicate information about a typical or intended user (imagery) of the product in order to create a differential advantage. Likewise, with usage positioning marketers promote a specific usage occasion or situation, in which the product can be best used. Marketers may opt for a positioning base that highlights favorable company, instead of product, associations (e.g., Jeep, claims to be the "pioneer" or the "original" in the market). Overall, these more abstract forms of positioning do not directly point to specific product-related advantages of a product, but rather allow consumers to come up with their own interpretations how the product in question might satisfy their focal needs (Crawford, 1985).

5.2.2   Perceived Positioning

Advertising is often assumed to be the most important tool to build a product's position in the mindset of consumers (e.g., Lilien/Rangaswamy, 2003). Advertisements usually consist of an executional part and positioning part. Through the executional part, containing creative elements such as humor, styles, or graphics, the attention of the audience is captured, and directed to the positioning part of the product (Easingwood/Mahajan, 1989).

Insights into how consumers form the perceived positioning can be provided by categorization theory, which plays a central role in understanding consumer behavior phenomena in general (Ratneshwar et al., 2001). According to categorization theory, consumers structure their knowledge about specific product alternatives in categories (Gutman, 1982), and use these category structures to organize and differentiate products (Johnson/Lehmann, 1997).

Categorization, itself, is a cognitive process which "expresses the characteristic manner in which individuals organize and structure perceptual inputs deriving from the external environment" (Block et al., 1981, p. 770). Categorization is most strongly influenced by (dis)similarity perceptions (Medin/Goldstone/Gentner 1993; Ratneshwar et al., 2001; Rosch/Mervis, 1975). Thus, if consumers perceive a product to be similar to that of a competitor, they are highly likely to allocate the focal product to the same category as the focal competitor product; vice versa, if consumers perceive products to be distinct from one another, consumers are not likely to allocate them to the same category.

5.2.3   Research Propositions

Categorization theory suggests that consumers store their product knowledge in categories in their memory. Individuals are thought to form categories based on their goals at the level of benefits sought (Park/Smith, 1989; Ratneshwar/Pechmann/Shocker, 1996). These can be very abstract goals such as self-esteem, more specific goals such as having good functionality, or even concrete product-related goals such as having a certain product feature (Ratneshwar/Pechmann/Shocker, 1996). We expect that upon presentation of stimuli containing positioning bases, these respective goals become salient and are used by consumers as a basis for classifying products according to their similarity. If, for example, consumers are exposed to two different advertisements, one where a product A is associated with a specific usage situation (e.g., playing golf), and another where product B with another usage situation (e.g., mountaineering), consumers shall activate usage-related goals and hence more likely categorize these two products together. Thus, it is expected that consumers organize the products in a manner consistent with that described in **Table 5.1**. Conversely, it is expected that if two products are positioned on distinct positioning bases, consumers will, in most cases, *not* assign them to the same category.

> **P₁:** Consumers are more likely to group together products that are positioned on the same conceptual positioning base than products positioned on different bases.

Next, the study seeks to elaborate whether or not the classification performance (i.e., the extent to which consumers group products together as theoretically predicted) is better for concrete than abstract forms of positioning. In this regard, literature offers two, theoretically sound lines of argumentations – one that does predict a difference between the classification performance, and one that does not predict such a difference.

Following the first line or argumentation, concrete types of positioning bases tend to draw consumers' attention to the superiority of product-related characteristics which, in turn, lead to product-related associations that are used for similarity-based categorization. With abstract positioning bases such as user positioning, external (secondary) associations are created that only indirectly refer to the branded product. Although, in principle, various types of product information such as specific usage-based information, or benefit information can be used for creating similarity-based categories (see Martin and Stewart, 2001), extant research finds that concrete forms of information (product attributes) receive relatively more weight in similarity judgments than abstract forms of information (i.e., user positioning, indirect benefit positioning; Lefkoff-Hagius/Mason 1993). Consequently, abstract positioning bases such as usage positioning (e.g., made for "outdoor sports") should be much more open to interpretation than concrete types of positioning; the specific associations and inferences made with the usage occasion might be perceived differently by each consumer (Friedmann/Lessig, 1987). For example, for some individuals, "outdoor sports" may stand for adventure; in the eyes of others, however, it may be an indicator of reliability; for still others, such an abstract positioning may mean that using such a cell phone offers a means for self-expression and fulfilment of symbolic needs such as social approval.

Thus, products positioned on abstract bases may deliver more varied meanings to consumers (e.g., Crawford, 1985; Friedmann/Lessig, 1987) and therefore the objects are more likely to be categorized differently. In contrast, with positioning based on very concrete elements, the latitude of interpretation is likely to be much narrower and, thus, classification performance better.

The second line or argumentation, which predicts no difference between the classification performance of concrete and abstract positioning forms, is grounded in the means-end chain concept, which may partial out the above proposed effects. According to spreading activation theory, the exposure to concrete attributes, for example, can activate the next higher category in consumers' cognitive knowledge structure (Collins/Loftus, 1975, see also Cohen/Warlop, 2001). This means that consumers may automatically categorize concrete attribute information (i.e., the means) together with information at the next higher higher level(s) of abstraction such as direct consequences/direct benefits and/or psychological consequences/indirect benefits or values (i.e., the ends). For testing purposes, we rely on the first line or argumentation, which indicates an expected difference in the classification performance for abstract versus concrete bases (as directly testing a null hypotheses is problematic).

> **P2:** Consumers are more likely to group concrete conceptual positioning bases together than abstract positioning bases.

5.3   Research Design

5.3.1   Open Sort Task

To test the research propositions, the study employs an open sort task, in which subjects are provided with an array of objects (here, products), which they then sort into groups that "go together" on the basis of perceived similarity/dissimilarity (Block et al., 1981; Rosch/Mervis, 1975). Open sort task approaches are based on the general assumption that the way in which respondents categorize objects (e.g., products) externally (i.e., by doing a sort task) reflects their internal, mental representation of the objects (Fincher/Tenenberg, 2005; Hirschman/Douglas 1981). Sorting tasks are accepted as a valid and reliable method in general similarity studies (Medin/Goldstone/Gentner, 1993), consumer behavior studies (e.g., Viswanathan/Johnson/Sudman, 1999) as well as product positioning research (Hirschman/Douglas, 1981; Sujan/Bettman, 1989).

An open-sort methodology was chosen primarily because open sort tasks use free associations whereby all types of associations with regard to a product can be captured, and not only feature-specific associations (Hirschman/Douglas, 1981). Alternative procedures such as similarity judgments based on a list of attributes direct respondents to the visually salient and distinctive features (i.e., concrete attributes) of products (Creusen/Schoormans, 1997; Ratneshwar/Shocker, 1991), which however may not fully explain the similarity between a set of products/objects (Osherson/Smith/Wilkie/Lopez/Shafir, 1990). In contrast, with open sort tasks, respondents are not constrained to a particular attribute in forming their similarity perceptions; this corresponds more closely to consumers' natural formation of categories (DeSarbo/Jedidi/Johnson, 1991). In addition, frequently reported boredom and fatigue associated with conventional similarity measurement approaches that negatively impact on data quality are less likely to occur (Johnson/Lehmann/Horne, 1990). Such problems are typically encountered when consumers are asked to evaluate a great number of pairs of products, one at a time, in terms of their overall similarity (e.g., Bijmolt/Wedel/Pieters/DeSarbo, 1998).

5.3.2 Stimuli and Sampling

In a first step, in analogy to existing product positioning studies (Alden/Steenkamp/Batra, 1999; Crawford, 1985; Easingwood/Mahajan, 1989), two independent coders pre-coded 192 real print advertisements of new products from three different product categories to identify the underlying positioning bases. Only the *type* of positioning base was coded, that is, whether the positioning information belongs to feature positioning, direct benefit positioning, etc. but not its particular *content* (e.g., reliability, safety, etc.). For this purpose, an expanded version of Crawford's (1985) well-known typology incorporating the major bases of other typologies (e.g., Aaker/Shansby, 1982; Wind, 1982) was used.

Mid-class watches, compact cars, and cell phones were selected as focal product categories because (a) exploratory content analysis of 959 advertisements in various product categories revealed that a great variety of different positioning bases are used in these three categories, and (b) these product categories were deemed to be distinct in terms of several product category characteristics, including technological turbulence, product parity, and consumer involvement (Crawford, 1985; Johar/Sirgy, 1991). To empirically verify that the chosen product categories were indeed distinct in terms of these characteristics, a pilot study was conducted in which 50 consumers, varying in sex, age, and occupation were asked to rate each category on established scales. Specifically, technological turbulence was measured by four items adapted from Jaworski and Kohli (1993; alpha = 0.93), and product parity was captured by four items taken from Muncy (1996, alpha = 0.83). Furthermore, overall consumer involvement in the purchase decision was measured on a four-item scale (alpha = 0.90), while feel involvement (alpha = 0.80) and think involvement (alpha = 0.84) were respectively measured on two three-item scales borrowed from Ratchford (1987). The order of presentation of the product categories to respondents was randomized to avoid order effects.

Table 5.2 presents the result of an ANOVA showing that respondents indeed perceive these three product categories to be significantly different in terms of the aforementioned characteristics and therefore confirm their suitability for the present study.

Table 5.2   Product Category Differences: ANOVA Results

	Technology	Product Parity	Overall Involvement	Think Involvement	Feel Involvement
	Mean (Std.Dev.)	Mean (Std.Dev.)	Mean (Std.Dev.)	Mean (Std.Dev.)	Mean (Std.Dev.)
Watches	2.61 (.18) LOW	3.75 (.19) HIGH	3.41 (.22) MEDIUM	3.67 (.19) MEDIUM	4.99 (.21) HIGH
Cell Phones	5.65 (.19) HIGH	4.94 (.17) MEDIUM	3.74 (.20) MEDIUM	5.21 (.18) HIGH	3.97 (.21) MEDIUM
Compact Cars	4.60 (.20) MEDIUM	4.61 (.21) MEDIUM	5.37 (15) HIGH	5.59 (.15) HIGH	3.77 (.20) MEDIUM
F-value (2 d.f.)	78.348	15.898	41.270	40.819	11.388
p-value	0.000	0.000	0.000	0.000	0.000

[a] Items are reversely-scored.
[b] Technology and Brand Parity were measured with 7-point Likert scales; all other constructs were measured with 7-point semantic differential scales.

Out of the original pool of ads, ten ads per product category were selected, which captured either three or four of the theoretical positioning bases outlined in **Table 5.1**. The inter-coder agreement of categorizing these bases exceeded 90% and was similar to that reported by Crawford/Urban/Buzas (1983). In the few cases where the coders were unable to reach consensus, disagreements were resolved with the assistance of a third coder.

To ensure that the final positioning base categorization is not biased by similarities in the ad execution, the print advertisements were also coded according to several execution-related advertising dimensions/features listed in prevalent print advertisement coding schemes (e.g., Poels/Dewitte 2008) namely humor, inclusion of a picture of the product, colors used, prominence of visual versus textual appeals, as well as the use of direct comparative advertising. This exercise revealed minimal overlap between the groups derived based upon the positioning base categorization and those based on the aforementioned executional elements of the ads.

For the main study, a purposive sample of 109 respondents varying in age, sex, education and occupation was drawn. Forty respondents undertook the open sort task in the cell phone, thirty nine in the compact car, and thirty in the watches product category; the sample sizes are consistent with Urban/Hauser's (1993) recommendation that about thirty respondents should participate in a typical sort task. Respondents, not being familiar with the positioning literature, were exposed to ads of ten different branded products and were asked to independently sort these products into piles based on their perceived (dis)similarity. Respondents were explicitly told that the units of analysis were the products and not the ads themselves. They were further instructed to use *any* criteria for sorting; consumers' attention was purposely *not* drawn to the positioning information of the respective products.

Subjects had the option to form as many (or few) groups of products as they wanted and each group could comprise any number of products (Viswanathan, Johnson, and Sudman, 1999). In this respect, the number of products that are assigned to the same category is referred to as the breadth of the category, whereas the number of groups formed by subjects can be regarded as a measure of conceptual differentiation (Block et al., 1981; Gardner/Schoen, 1962). The results on category breadth and conceptual differentiation are summarized in Appendix.

5.4 Data Analysis Procedure

In addition to cluster analysis, which is considered as the mainstream method to analyze open sort tasks (e.g., Shaver/Schwartz/Kirson/O`Connor, 1987), three complementary analyses were conducted that together provide a more comprehensive assessment of the research propositions. For all analyses, the input data per product category consisted of a 10 x 10 similarity (co-occurrence) matrix, where the cell entries n_{ij} are the number of respondents that grouped product i together with product j for $i, j=1..10, i \neq j$. Thus, for each product category, similarity between all possible pairs of products was scored on the basis of how many respondents categorized the focal products together (Parkinson/Totterdell, 1999; Urban/Hauser, 1993).

For example, in the watches category, if two products were put together (matched) by all respondents (n = 30), their similarity was scored as 30 (maximum similarity); if none of the participants categorized the two products together, their similarity was scored as 0 (minimum similarity). A separate similarity matrix was constructed for each product category. **Table 5.3** shows the similarity matrix for watches as an illustrative example.

Table 5.3   Similarity Matrix for Watches (n=30)

		Product i									
		1	**2**	**3**	**4**	**5**	**6**	**7**	**8**	**9**	**10**
Product j	**1**		24	15	1	0	5	2	4	2	4
	2	24		20	1	1	7	4	4	4	4
	3	15	20		5	7	5	2	6	6	2
	4	1	1	5		9	4	16	6	8	13
	5	0	1	7	9		20	6	20	21	5
	6	5	7	5	4	20		6	17	19	6
	7	2	4	2	16	6	6		7	5	24
	8	4	4	6	6	20	17	7		21	6
	9	2	4	6	8	21	19	5	21		4
	10	4	4	2	13	5	6	24	6	4	
Total		57	69	68	63	89	89	72	91	90	68

5.4.1   Random Allocation

The first step of the data analysis procedure sought to investigate whether there is *a* (i.e., any) structure underlying the categorization patterns of respondents to confirm that products are *not* randomly grouped together (**Table 5.4**). For this purpose, a one-sample goodness-of-fit χ^2-test for each product category was conducted, in which the observed frequencies was the number of matches for each pair of products n_{ij}. The expected frequencies, on the other hand, were calculated by summing up the cell entries (i.e., $\sum n_{ij}$) of the lower diagonal matrix in **Table 5.3** divided by the number of cells in the matrix (a 10 x 10 matrix yields unique 45 cells), which resulted in the same expected number of matches for each pair of products. The latter corresponds to a uniform distribution of matches that would be expected to occur in the case that no rationale underlie the categorizations. The χ^2-values for each product category turned out to be highly significant, indicating that the frequencies of the matches (i.e., pairwise classifications) are not equally distributed across the different products in the focal product categories (cell phones, χ^2 (d.f. = 44 [45 cells – 1]) = 117.76, p < 0.01; compact cars, χ^2 (44) = 136.94, p < 0.01; watches χ^2 (44) = 258.90, p < 0.01, respectively).

Table 5.4   Results of the Data Analysis

Product Category	Positioning Bases	Code	Group Sizes			Test 1		Test 2	Test 3
			actual	expected	residual*	χ^2-value	p-value (8 d.f.)	psra	crsa
Watches	Abstract Attributes	1	2.9	3	0	79.9	<0.01	0.65	0.81
	Concrete/Abstract Attributes	2	3.3	3	0	38.5	<0.01	0.73	0.80
	Concrete Attributes/Benefits	3	3.3	3	0	31.1	<0.01	0.58	0.73
	Usage (Activity)	5	4.0	4	0	46.0	<0.01	0.68	0.74
	Usage (Activity)	6	4.0	4	0	33.7	<0.01	0.62	0.75
	Usage (Activity)	8	4.0	4	0	35.7	<0.01	0.64	0.75
	Usage (Activity)	9	4.0	4	0	44.0	<0.01	0.68	0.76
	Endorsement	4	3.1	3	0	24.6	<0.01	0.48	0.63
	Endorsement	7	3.4	3	0	48.8	<0.01	0.67	0.75
	Endorsement	10	3.3	3	0	48.7	<0.01	0.62	0.76
Cell Phones	Abstract Attributes	1	4.2	3	1	18.8	<0.05	0.60	0.62
	Concrete/Abstract Attributes	4	4.1	3	1	15.4	~0.05	0.54	0.60
	Concrete/Abstract Attributes	5	4.6	3	2	11.6	NS	0.54	0.53
	Direct Benefits	2	3.7	3	1	45.3	<0.01	0.60	0.70
	Direct Benefits	8	4.1	3	1	39.7	<0.01	0.69	0.70

Product Category	Positioning Bases	Code	Group Sizes				Test 1	Test 2	Test 3
	Direct Benefits/Concrete Attributes	9	4.3	3	1	10.3	NS	0.51	0.58
	Usage (Activity)	6	4.5	4	0	31.4	<0.01	0.61	0.63
	Usage (Activity)	7	4.6	4	1	22.6	<0.01	0.56	0.57
	Usage (Activity)	10	4.1	4	0	12.2	NS	0.48	0.59
	Experiential Benefit/Pioneer	3	4.3	4	0	20.0	<0.05	0.53	0.61
Compact Cars	Concrete Attributes	2	3.8	3	1	31.4	<0.01	0.62	0.67
	Concrete Attributes	5	3.8	3	1	28.3	<0.01	0.54	0.58
	Concrete Attributes	7	3.9	3	1	19.7	<0.05	0.54	0.60
	Abstract Attributes	3	3.4	2	1	27.7	<0.01	0.56	0.58
	Concrete Attributes/Benefits	6	3.3	2	1	32.1	<0.01	0.56	0.55
	Experiential Benefit	8	3.3	2	1	25.9	<0.01	0.56	0.59
	Experiential Benefit	10	3.2	2	1	34.9	<0.01	0.56	0.52
	User Type	1	3.7	3	1	24.3	<0.01	0.50	0.51
	User Type	4	3.7	3	1	7.1	NS	0.46	0.57
	User Type	9	3.5	3	1	9.3	NS	0.44	0.57

* refers to the difference (rounded) between the actual
group size and the expected group size. NS = not significant

This analysis was also conducted at the individual product level, where the observed frequencies were the cell entries for the individual product (e.g., for Product 1 [watches] n_{12} (24), n_{13} (15), etc. – see **Table 5.3**) and the expected frequencies were the average number of matches for each pair of products; the latter were derived by dividing the total number of matches by the number of products j. Thus, the expected frequencies for Product 1 is the sum of $n_{1...j}$ (57) divided by the number of products j-1 (9), which is 6.33 for each cell n_{ij} (see **Table 5.3**).

At the individual product level, the χ^2-tests were also found to be significant. For almost all products tested (25 out of 30), the χ^2-values were above 15.51 (which is the threshold value for a significant χ^2 test with 8 degrees of freedom at $p = 0.05$; see **Table 5.4**, Test 1).

Taken together, the above results reveal that the groups (categories) are not formed randomly by consumers implying that there is a rationale underlying the sorting of the products.

5.4.2   Proportion of Substantive Agreement

Having established that there is a rationale underlying consumers' product categorization, the next test was aimed at evaluating whether this rationale was indeed based on the underlying positioning bases of the specific products. For this purpose, Anderson/Gerbing`s (1991) proportion of substantive agreement (*psa*) measure was employed. This measure tests whether consumers assign products with conceptually similar/identical positioning bases to the same groups (see P_1 earlier). *Psa*-scores were calculated for each product as follows:

$$psa = \frac{\sum_{k=1}^{m-1} nc_k}{\sum_{k=1}^{m-1} N_k} \qquad\qquad (5.1)$$

where nc denotes the number of respondents who group a pair of products together as a-priori specified by the expert coders, $k = 1...m$ represents the theoretical (a-priori specified) number of products that should fall in the same category, and N represents the total number of respondents (i.e., sample size). The range for this measure is between 0 and 1, corresponding to the proportion of consumers who group pairs of products together that conceptually belong together; values greater than 0.5 are considered desirable (see Anderson and Gerbing, 1991; Lawshe, 1975).

At the product category level, the *psa* tests produced values greater than 0.5 (0.64 for watches, 0.56 for cell phones, and 0.52 for compact cars). At the individual product level, apart from very few exceptions, the majority of the respondents also indicated that products with conceptually similar positioning bases should be categorized together (see **Table 5.4**, Test 2). Thus, based on the *psa* measure, P_1 is supported.

To test P_2, *psa*-scores for each positioning basis *within* each product category were first computed and followed by z-tests for (correlated) proportions for each pair of the focal positioning bases. The pairwise comparisons of the *psa*-values for watches (i.e., attribute positioning = 0.66, usage positioning = 0.65, endorsement positioning = 0.59) reveal z-values that are smaller than 1.96 (which is the threshold value for a significant z-test at p = 0.05); thus, the *psa*-scores do not significantly differentiate across positioning bases. Similar patterns can be detected for the other two product categories – none of the pairwise comparisons reveal significant differences (*psa*-values for cell phones: attribute positioning = 0.56, direct benefit positioning = 0.60, usage positioning = 0.54; *psa*-values for compact cars: concrete attribute positioning = 0.56, abstract attribute positioning = 0.56; experiential benefit positioning = 0.56, user positioning = 0.45). Thus, P$_2$ is not supported by the results.

5.4.3   Relative Substantive Agreement

Although the *psa* index provides information on the consistency between the classifications made by respondents vis-à-vis experts, it does not indicate the extent to which respondents group products together that do *not* share the same underlying positioning base(s). To overcome this problem, a modified version of Anderson/Gerbing's (1991) substantive validity coefficient (*csv*) was used, which also takes "wrong" categorizations (i.e., classifications that are not consistent with theory as coded by experts) into account. The modified measure, which is denoted as the coefficient of relative substantive agreement (*crsa*), shows the proportion of correct matches (i.e. pairwise groupings that were made consistent with theoretical expectations) divided by the sum of correct plus the most frequent wrong matches. The *crsa* for each product in a given category is thus calculated as follows:

$$crsa = \frac{\sum_{k=1}^{m-1} nc_k}{\sum_{k=1}^{m-1} nc_k + \max \sum_{k=1}^{m-1} nw_k} \tag{5.2}$$

where *nc* and $k = 1...m$ are defined as before and *nw* denotes the number of respondents who group pairs of products together that do not share the same positioning base (and thus do not belong to the same group). For example, in the watches category (see **Table 5.3**), the products that theoretically go together with Product 1 are Product 2 and Product 3; thus, Product 1 should be matched with two (m [= 3] – 1) additional products. The number of correct pairwise classifications *nc* for Product 1 is 24 + 15. The rest of the cell entries constitute wrong classifications and are referred to as *nw*. Out of these wrong pairwise classifications (*nw*) those with the highest scores (maximum number of *nw*) for *m-1* products are selected; in this case Product 6 (*nw* = 5) and Product 8 (*nw* = 4) yield the highest (max) number *nw* scores.

Crsa-values range from 0 to 1, with values of 1 indicating that all products with the same positioning base have been classified together and none with products following a different base. Anderson and Gerbing (1991) recommend a benchmark value of 0.50 for the original substantive validity coefficient (*csv*). This value can be regarded as highly conservative for the crsa measure, given that, in this study design, the a-priori chance of attaining higher *nw* scores is substantially higher than for *nc* scores.

This is because the number of products that should *not* be grouped together (e.g., for Product 1 in the watches category these are seven) with the focal product is substantially higher than for the number of products that should conceptually fall in the same group (e.g., for Product 1 these are two).

According to the results, the aggregated *crsa*-values for each product category are also well above the .50 threshold value. More specifically, the *crsa*-values in the watches category produced the highest score with a value of 0.76; a one-sample proportions test reveals that the focal crsa value is significantly higher than the 0.5 threshold value (nc = 230, nc + nw = 304, proportion test: χ^2 [1 d.f.] = 79.03; p < 0.01). The *crsa*-value for cars came to 0.57, and for cell phones to 0.60, which are both also significantly higher than the 0.50 threshold (cars, $nc = 163$, $nc + nw = 286$; χ^2 [1] = 5.21, p = 0.01; cell phones, $nc = 269$, $nc + nw = 450$, χ^2 [1] = 16.82; p < 0.01). Finally, as shown in **Table 5.4** (Test 3), the *crsa*-values for the individual products are all also above the 0.50 threshold value, indicating that the number of correct matches is always substantially higher than the highest number of wrong matches for the same number of product pairs. In this regard, similarities in terms of ad execution (e.g., humor, colors, use of direct comparative ads, etc.) could not explain the similarities in the resulting product categorization. Taken together, the findings based on the *crsa* measure fully support P1.

Regarding P2, again a z-test for (correlated) proportions was employed to test significant differences regarding classification rates across the positioning bases within each product category. In the watches category, the crsa values are not significantly different ($z < 1.96$, n.s.) for attribute (0.75) and the two surrogate bases comprising usage (0.73) and endorsement positioning (0.69), respectively. Similar patterns can also be observed in the other two product categories: in the cell phone category, the *crsa*-values for attribute (0.60), direct benefit (0.62), and usage/experiential benefit positioning (0.57) are nearly identical. In a similar vein, concrete attribute (0.61), abstract attributes/benefit (0.55), indirect benefit (0.52), and user type positioning (0.52) do not significantly differentiate. Thus, as was the case with the psa measure, P2 is not supported.

5.4.4 Cluster Analysis

In a final step, following Parkinson and Totterdell (1999), the similarity matrices (like the one for watches in **Table 5.3**) were subjected to a series of agglomerative hierarchical cluster analyses (using the Cluster 2.11 program) to evaluate whether the resulting clusters were consistent with theoretical expectations as indicated by P2. According to this clustering procedure, a distance matrix is first calculated using the average linkage method, based on which the clustering algorithm then makes a series of binary combinations of products or groups of products (working bottom-up) which maximize both within-category similarity and between-category differences until only a single cluster remains.

The upper part of **Figure 5.1** displays the dendograms for each product category based on Cluster 2.11's integrated Tree View program. The lower part of the figure (below the dendograms) graphically illustrates the similarity between the products.

Cells that are colored black indicate lack of similarity, whereas cells in light gray show groupings that are highly similar (i.e., groupings that frequently occurred). The color intensity of the cells increases with increasing (pairwise) similarity.

As can be seen from the dendograms, the results are in accordance with the theoretical groupings of the products (based on their positioning bases) across all product categories thus providing further evidence in support of P_1.

Figure 5.1   Results of the Cluster Analysis

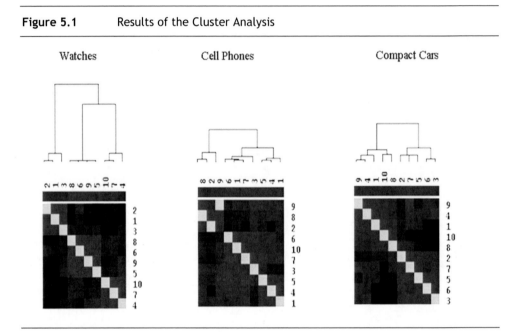

Notes:
Dendograms for each product category are shown above the figures. The branches of the dendograms correspond to the cells of the figures below, which are graphic representations of the similarity matrices of each product category. Cells held in light gray indicate high similarity, whereas dark cells indicate low similarity. The labels of the cells are outlined in **Table 5.4** in the "Code" column.

Based on the collective results of the four-stage data analysis procedure, support is found for P_1 but not for P_2.

5.5   Discussion and Conclusion

This study sheds light on how product positioning bases, as anchored in mainstream marketing literature, can be used to facilitate consumers' (dis)similarity perceptions of products. The empirical results support the assertion that managers can influence perceived similarity perceptions by selecting the underlying type of positioning basis.

The study reveals that consumers classify products as (dis)similar according to the types of positioning bases that are actually used in the advertisements of such products. Thus, the findings indicate that consumers create similarity perceptions not only based upon the (inferred) features and benefits of products (similar size, similar shape, similar price, similar product usage occasions), but also upon their communicated positioning information (i.e., positioning bases). Theoretically, the results imply that through the exposure of the positioning bases in the ads, consumers activate the respective categorical knowledge, and use this information to organize products according to (dis)similarity. The fact that the results are stable across three demonstrably different product categories positively contributes to the generalizability of the findings.

The classification performance of consumers does not appear to be materially affected by the concreteness/abstractness of the underlying positioning base. Although the psa and crsa-values were, on average, somewhat higher for concrete than for more abstract categories, the specific differences were not large enough to allow a clear support of P_2. It seems that, following the second line of argumentation, consumers are indeed able to form means-end chains which might have partialled out the predicted effect, thus making the discrimination between concrete and abstract forms of positioning not as sharp as predicted.

In-depth inspection of the individual product groupings further reveals that consumers assign products which employ a combination of different positioning bases (i.e., a "hybrid" positioning tactic) together with products that use either one of these constituent bases. For instance, products that use a combination of concrete attributes and benefits were grouped together with either products being positioned on concrete attributes or with products being positioned on benefits.

This research contributes to the positioning literature by showing that apart from its "conventional" role in forming and extending product knowledge (see, for example, Keller, 2003), product positioning plays a prominent role in consumers' product (dis)similarity perceptions as observed in their categorization behavior. Therefore, the study adds another building block to the limited literature investigating the effect of positioning bases on consumer behavior, and constitutes a first step towards the empirical consumer-based validation of positioning taxonomies anchored in numerous prominent marketing and product management textbooks (e.g., Kotler 2003; Keller, 2004, Lilien/Rangaswamy, 2003; Wind, 1982).

From a managerial perspective, the present study underscores the importance of the decision regarding which positioning bases to use, as the latter might directly affect consumers' product (dis)similarity perceptions. Product managers might have an alternative strategy at hand to associate their focal products with competitor products by selecting the same positioning bases used by competitors and/or disassociate their products from competing products by using different bases. Selecting similar positioning bases may function as a tool to associate a certain product with other products (i.e., by communicating similar type of product information) but at the same time, also create a sense of differentiation because the claims of competitors are not "directly" imitated. For example, products following a concrete attribute positioning strategy will have a higher likelihood to be grouped together, although their actual concrete attributes might not strongly overlap. The rejection of P2 may be of value to practitioners as it indicates that perceptions of (dis)similarity hold nearly equally well for abstract positioning bases, and are therefore not limited to concrete bases only.

The findings might also have implications for strategic advertising decisions. Selecting the same positioning bases as competitors may constitute an alternative to the use of (direct) comparative advertising, which is also known to have several drawbacks (see Grewal, Kavanoor/Fern/Costley/Barnes, 1997). Furthermore, the findings may be of relevance for brand extension research: the use of similar positioning bases for brand extensions may increase the "fit" between the parent brand and the extension and thus contribute the success of the extension (Aaker/Keller, 1990).

Finally, the study contributes to qualitative research methodology by introducing a structured analysis procedure comprising a series of complementary tests to statistically analyze "open sort" data (i.e., co-occurrence matrices). In addition to cluster analysis, which is considered as the mainstream technique to analyze co-occurrence matrices (see Derous/De Witte/Stroobants 2003; Shaver et al., 1987), three additional tests (i.e., χ^2, psa, crsa) were implemented that allowed a more thorough and stringent analysis of this kind of data in general. This analysis procedure should hopefully contribute to the further acceptance of open sorting as an established tool for branding and consumer behavior studies that are conceptually based on categorization theory.

5.6   Limitations and Further Research

Regarding the study's limitations, the research propositions were tested only with print advertisements. The question naturally arises whether the results remain stable when other forms of advertising (such as TV or internet-based advertisements) are considered. Similarly, an examination of the propositions in other contexts (e.g., FMCG, services) would also help establish the extent to which the findings are generalizable in different settings.

Despite the numerous advantages of open sort tasks, the latter do not generate deep insights into the concrete reasons why consumers group the focal objects together. To overcome this limitation, future studies should explore the underlying reasons for the observed categorizations in more detail. In this context, it would be particularly interesting to reveal which specific associations different types of surrogate positioning bases evoke.

In this context, similarity matrices implicitly assume that products grouped together are also "equally similar"; thus, the sorting task does not really reveal the strength of the (dis)similarity between products.

A logical extension of this research would be an explicit investigation of the relative influence of similar product positioning bases on similarity perceptions as compared to other factors such as similar product attribute or benefit cues (e.g., similar price or quality cues).

A final promising direction for future research lies in a comparative investigation of the open-sort approach and conventional (dis)similarity measurement procedures. Unfortunately, established procedures are often associated with the problem that consumers are affected by fatigue/boredom and directed to a-priori provided attributes in judging product similarity. This may, on the one hand, infiltrate the data quality, and on the other, not correspond to consumers' natural formation of similarity-based categories (see, DeSarbo/Jedidi/Johnson, 1991; Osherson et al. 1990). These issues have led Johnson/Lehmann/Horne (1990, p. 42) to conclude, "[...the apparent importance of product categorization in consumer perceptions underscores the need for research on alternative data collection procedures.]...[Product sorting tasks are very consistent with a categorization perspective and would appear to deserve considerable attention.]" Therefore, follow-up studies should contrast similarity-based measurement approaches with open sort task approaches, provide insights into particular strengths and weakness associated with each approach, and generate empirically-based guidelines on which approach to use and for what purpose.

Appendix

Conceptual Differentiation and Category Breadth

Initially, it was examined whether the average number of groups created by the study participants corresponds to the expected number of groups a-priori specified by the expert coders. Based on the theoretical similarity of the positioning bases, the formation of three groups in the watches and cell phone categories, and four groups in the compact car category respectively (see also first column in **Table 5.4**), was expected. On average, respondents formed 2.88 groups in the cell phone category (ranging from 1 to 4), with a mode of 3 groups, which corresponds to the expected number of groups as a-priori specified by expert coders. In the watches category, consumers formed, on average, 3.23 groups (ranging from 2 to 5); again the mode was 3 corresponding to the a-priori specified number of categories. For the compact car category, the average number of groups created was 3.43, ranging from 2 to 5, with a mode of 3 groups. Thus, in terms of conceptual differentiation, the results are consistent with a-priori expectations, with the exception of compact cars where respondents created, on average, fewer groups than expected.

It was further evaluated with how many other products each product was, on average, put together in a group (including the focal product), which is a measure of category breadth. **Table 5.4** (see group sizes) shows, on a per product basis, the comparison between the number of products that were actually grouped together (i.e., actual group sizes) vis-à-vis the number of products that were expected to be grouped together (i.e., expected group sizes). For example, in the watches category, the expected group size for each of the products employing usage positioning is four, since four products are positioned on the usage base (see **Table 5.4**); thus, we expect that consumers group each of these products together with three other products (with the latter ideally also employing usage positioning).

The results reveal that the actual group sizes are fully congruent with the expected group sizes in the watches category, whereas in the other two product categories the actual group sizes slightly exceed the expected ones. This indicates that respondents' categories are somewhat broader than the theoretical categories, a finding which probably reflects the smaller number of groups formed by respondents noted above. In this context, for a fixed number of elements (e.g., products), an inverse relation between conceptual differentiation (number of groups) and category breadth (number of elements within a group) exists.

Literature

[1]   Aaker, D. A./ Shansby, G. J. (1982): Positioning your product. Business Horizons, Vol. 25, 3, pp. 56-62.

[2]   Aaker, D. A./Keller, K. L. (1990): Consumer evaluation of brand extensions. Journal of Marketing, Vol. 54, pp. 27-41.

[3]   Alden, D. L./ Steenkamp, B. E. M./ Batra, R. (1999): Brand positioning through advertising in Asia, North America, and Europe: the role of global consumer culture. Journal of Marketing, Vol. 63, 1, pp. 75-87.

[4]   Alpert, F. H./Kamins, M. A. (1995): An empirical investigation of consumer memory, attitude, and perceptions toward pioneer and follower brands. Journal of Marketing, Vol. 159, 4, pp. 34-45.

[5]   Anderson, J. C./Gerbing, D. W. (1991): Predicting the performance of measures in a confirmatory factor analysis with a pretest assessment of their substantive validities. Journal of Applied Psychology, Vol. 76, 5, pp. 732-740.

[6]   Bijmolt, T. H. A./ Wedel, M./Pieters, R. G. M./DeSarbo, W. S. (1998): Judgments of brand similarity. International Journal of Research in Marketing, Vol. 15, pp. 249-268.

[7]   Blankson, C./Kalafatis, S. P. (2004): The development and validation of a scale measuring consumer/customer-derived generic typology of positioning strategies. Journal of Marketing Management, Vol. 20, pp. 5-43.

[8]   Blankson, C./Buss, D. M./Block, J. H./Gjerde, P. F. (1981): The cognitive style of breadth of categorization: longitudinal consistency of personality correlates. Journal of Personality and Social Psychology, Vol. 40, 4, pp. 770-779.

[9]   Block et al. (1981).

[10] Brenner, L./Rottenstreich, Y./Sood, S. (1999): Comparison, grouping, and preference. Psychological Science, Vol. 10, 3, pp. 225-229.

[11] Bridges, S./Keller, K. L./Sood, S. (2000): Communication strategies for brand extensions: Enhancing perceived fit by establishing explanatory links. Journal of Advertising, Vol. 29, 4, pp. 1-11.

[12] Brown, T. J./Dacin, P. A./Pratt, M. G./Whetten, D. A. (2006): Identity, intended image, construed image, and reputation: an interdisciplinary framework and suggested terminology. Journal of the Academy Marketing Science, Vol. 34, pp. 99-106.

[13] Carpenter, G. S./Nakamoto, K. (1994): Consumer preference formation and pioneering advantage. Journal of Marketing Research, Vol. 31, 3, pp. 339-50.

[14] Cohen, J. B./Warlop, L. (2001): A motivational perspective on means-end chains. In T. J. Reynolds & J. C. Olson (eds.), Understanding consumer decision making: The means-end approach to marketing and advertising strategy: Lawrence Erlbaum, 2001.

[15] Collins, A. M./Loftus, E. F. (1975): A spreading-activation theory of semantic processing. Psychological Review, Vol. 82, pp. 407-428.

[16] Crawford, M. C. (1985): A new positioning typology. Journal of Product Innovation Management, Vol. 2, 4, pp. 243-253.

[17] Crawford, M. C./Urban, D. J./Buzas, T. E. (1983): Positioning: a conceptual review and taxonomy of alternatives', Working Paper No. 354. University of Michigan.

[18] Creusen, M. E.H./Schoormans, J. P. L. (1997): The nature of differences between similarity and preference judgments: a replication with extension. International Journal of Research in Marketing, Vol. 14, pp. 81-87.

[19] Derous, E./de Witte, S./Stroobants, R. (2003): Testing the social process model on selection through expert analysis. Journal of Occupational and Organizational Psychology, Vol. 76, pp. 179-199.

[20] DeSarbo, W. S./Jedidi, K./Johnson, M. D. (1991): A new clustering methodology for the analysis of sorted or categorized stimuli. Marketing Letters, Vol. 2, pp. 267-279.

[21] Dhar, R./Nowlis, S./Sherman, S. J. (1999): Comparison effect on preference construction, Journal of Consumer Research, Vol. 26, pp. 293-306.

[22] Dickson, P. R./Ginter, S. J. (1987): Market segmentation, product differentiation, and marketing strategy. Journal of Marketing, Vol. 51, pp. 1-10.

[23] Dröge, C./Darmon, R. Y. (1987): Associative positioning through comparative advertising: attribute versus overall similarity approaches. Journal of Marketing Research, Vol. 24, pp. 377-388.

[24] Easingwood, C. J./Mahajan, V. (1989): Positioning of financial services for competitive advantage. Journal of Product of Innovation Management, Vol. 6, 3, pp. 207-219.

[25] Fincher, S./Tenenberg, J. (2005): Making sense of card sorting data. Expert Systems, Vol. 22, 3, pp. 89-93.

[26] Friedmann, R./Lessig, P. V. (1987): Psychological meaning of products and product positioning. Journal of Product Innovation Management, Vol. 4, 4, pp. 265-273.

[27] Gardner, R. W./Schoen, R. A. (1962): Differentiation and abstraction in concept formation. Psychological Monographs, 76, Whole Number 560.

[28] Grewal, D./Kavanoor, S./Fern, E. F./Costley, C./Barnes, J. (1997): Comparative versus noncomparative advertising: a meta-analysis. Journal of Marketing, Vol. 61, pp. 1-15.

[29] Gutman, J. (1982): A means-end chain model based on consumer categorization processes. Journal of Marketing, Vol. 46, 2, pp. 60-72.

[30] Hirschman, E. C./Douglas, S. P. (1981): Hierarchical cognitive content: towards a measurement methodology. Advances in Consumer Research, Vol. 8, 1, pp. 100-105.

[31] Jaworski, B. J./Kohli, A. K. (1993): Market orientation: Antecedents and consequence. Journal of Marketing, Vol. 57, pp. 53-70.

[32] Johar, J. S./Sirgy, J. M. (1991): Value-expressive versus utilitarian advertising appeals: When and why to use which appeal. Journal of Advertising, Vol. 20, pp. 23-33.

[33] Johnson, M. D./Lehmann, D. R. (1997): Consumer experience and consideration sets for brands and product categories. in Brucks, M., & MacInnis, D. (Eds), Advances in Consumer Research, Association for Consumer Research, Provo, UT, 24, pp. 295-300.

[34] Johnson, M. D./Lehmann, D. R./Horne, D. R. (1990): The effects of fatigue on judgments of interproduct similarity. International Journal of Research in Marketing, Vol. 7, pp. 35-43.

[35] Johnson, K. E./Mervis, C. B. (1997): Effects of varying levels of expertise on the basic level of categorization. Journal of Experimental Psychology: General 1997, 126, September, pp. 248-77.

[36] Kalra, A./Goodstein, R. C. (1998): The impact of advertising positioning strategies on consumer price sensitivity. Journal of Marketing Research, Vol. 35, 2, pp. 210-24.

[37] Kapferer, J.-N. (2004): The New Strategic Brand Management. London: Kogan Page.

[38] Keller, K. L. (1993): Conceptualizing, measuring, and managing customer-based brand equity. Journal of Marketing, Vol. 57, 1, pp. 1-22.

[39] Keller, K. L. (2004): Strategic Brand Management (2nd ed.) New Jersey: Prentice Hall.

[40] Kotler, P. (2003): Marketing Management (11th ed.) New Jersey: Prentice Hall.

[41] Lawshe, C. H. (1975): A quantitative approach to content validity. Personnel Psychology, Vol. 28, pp. 563-575.

[42] Lawson, R. (2002): Consumer knowledge structures: Background issues and introduction. Psychology & Marketing, Vol. 19, pp. 447-456.

[43] Lefkoff-Hagius, R./Mason, C. H. (1993): Characteristic, beneficial, and image attributes in consumer judgments of similarity and preference. Journal of Consumer Research., Vol. 20, 1, pp. 100-110.

[44] Lilien, G. L./Rangaswamy, A. (2003): Marketing engineering. New Jersey: Prentice Hall.

[45] Mahajan, V./Wind, Y. (2002): Got emotional product positioning? Marketing Management, Vol. 11, 3, pp. 36-41.

[46] Martin, I. M./Stewart, D. W. (2001): The differential impact of goal congruency on attitudes, intentions, and the transfer of brand equity. Journal of Marketing Research, Vol. 38, pp. 471-484.

[47] Medin, D. L./Goldstone, R. L./Gentner, D. (1993): Respects for similarity. Psychological Review, Vol. 100, pp. 254-278.

[48] Muncy, J. A. (1996): Measuring perceived brand parity. eds. Corfman, K. P., & Lynch, J. G. Advances in Consumer Research, 23, Association for Consumer Research, pp. 411-417.

[49] Myers, J. H.; Shocker, A. D. (1981): The nature of product-related attributes. Research in Marketing, Vol. 5, pp. 211-236.

[50] Olson, J. C./Reynolds, T. J. (1983): Understanding consumers' cognitive structures: Implications for advertising strategy. In advertising and consumer psychology. Eds. Percy, L., & Woodside, A. MA: Lexington Books.

[51] Osherson, D. N./Smith, E. E./Wilkie, O./Lopez, A./Ephraim Shafir, E. (1990): Category-based induction. Psychological Review, Vol. 97, pp. 185-200.

[52] Pan, Y./Lehmann, D. R. (1993): The influence of new brand entry on subjective brand judgments. Journal of Consumer Research, Vol. 20, pp. 76-86.

[53] Park, C. W./Smith, D. C. (1989): Product-level choice: A top-down or bottom-up process. Journal of Consumer Research, Vol. 16, December, pp. 289-299.

[54] Park, C. W./Jaworski, B. J./MacInnis, D. J. (1986): Strategic brand-concept image management. Journal of Marketing, Vol. 50, pp. 134-45.

[55] Parkinson, B./Totterdell, P. (1999): Classifying affect-regulation strategies. Cognition & Emotion, Vol. 13, 3, pp. 277-303.

[56] Pechmann, C./Ratneshwar, S. (1991): The use of comparative advertising for brand positioning: Association versus differentiation. Journal of Consumer Research, Vol. 18, 2, pp. 145-160.

[57] Poels, K./Dewitte, S. (2008): Getting a line on print ads: Pleasure and arousal reactions reveal an implicit advertising mechanism. Journal of Advertising, Vol. 37, pp. 63-74.

[58] Punj, G./Moon, J. (2002): Positioning options for achieving brand association: a psychological categorization framework. Journal of Business Research, Vol. 55, 4, pp. 275-283.

[59] Ratchford, B. (1987): New insights about the FCB grid. Journal of Advertising Research, Vol. 27, pp. 24-38.

[60] Ratneshwar, S./Pechmann, C./Shocker, A. D. (1996): Goal-derived categories and the antecedents of across-category consideration. Journal of Consumer Research, Vol. 23, pp. 240-250.

[61] Ratneshwar, S./Barsalou, L. W./Pechmann, C./Moore, M. (2001): Goal-derived categories: the role of personal and situational goals in category representations. Journal of Consumer Psychology, Vol. 10, 3, pp. 147-57.

[62] Ratneshwar, S./Shocker, A. D. (1991): Substitution in use and the role of usage context in product category structures. Journal of Marketing Research, Vol. 28, pp. 281-295.

[63] Reynolds, T. J./Gengler, C. E./Howard, D. J. (1995): A means-end analysis of brand persuasion through advertising. International Journal of Research in Marketing, Vol. 12, pp. 257-266.

[64] Rosch, E./Mervis, C. B. (1975): Family resemblances: studies in the internal structure of categories. Cognitive Psychology, Vol. 7, 4, pp. 573-603.

[65] Shaver, P./Schwartz, J./Kirson, D./O`Connor, C. (1987): Emotion knowledge: further exploration of a prototype approach. Journal of Personality and Social Psychology, Vol. 52, pp. 1061-1086.

[66] Sujan, M./Bettman, J. R. (1989): The effects of brand positioning strategies on consumers' brand and category perceptions: some insights from schema research. Journal of Marketing Research, Vol. 25, November, pp. 454-467.

[67] Urban, G. L./Hauser, J. R. (1993): Design and marketing of new products. New Jersey: Englewood Cliffs.

[68] Urban, G. L./Hulland, J. S/Weinberg, B. D. (1993): Premarket forecasting for new consumer durable goods: Modeling categorization, elimination, and consideration phenomena. Journal of Marketing, Vol. 57, pp. 47-63.

[69] Viswanathan, M./Johnson, M. D./Sudman, S. (1999): Understanding consumer usage of product magnitudes through sorting tasks. Psychology & Marketing, Vol. 16, 8, pp. 643-657.

[70] Vriens, M./Hofstede, F. ter (2000): Linking attributes, benefits, and consumer values: a powerful approach to market segmentation, brand positioning, and advertising strategy. Marketing Research, Vol. 12, pp. 5-10.

[71] Wind, Y. (1982): Product policy: Concepts, methods and strategy. Reading: Addison Wesley.

6 The Influence of Location-Aware Mobile Marketing Messages on Consumers' Buying Behavior

Andrea Gröppel-Klein, Saarland University, Germany

Philipp Broeckelmann, t+ d innovation + marketing consultants GmbH, Germany

Abstract

This study reports the findings of two experiments involving location-aware mobile marketing messages (LA-MMM). It is intended to test whether real behavioral effects can be elicited through LA-MMM received at the point of sale. In the first experiment, participants received a LA-MMM while passing the store to which the message was related; in the second experiment, they received a LA-MMM while shopping in the store itself. The messages were of different types, containing a discount coupon, drawing attention to special offers or advertising specific brands of milk and chocolate.

The findings suggest that LA-MMM have only a limited influence on consumers' approach behavior towards stores, store choice and buying behavior. LA-MMM are thus not nearly as influential on consumers as it has often been suggested. LA-MMM are by no means an effective way to increase sales of a particular brand in the short term and should only be used in conjunction with other marketing tools and promotions.

Keywords

Mobile Marketing, Location-Aware Marketing Messages, Buying Behavior, Shopper Research.

6.1   Introduction to Mobile Marketing

Today's consumers are exposed to increasing advertising pressure (Speck/Elliott 1997; Kroeber-Riel, Weinberg/Gröppel-Klein 2009). As a result, traditional TV, radio and print advertising campaigns are finding it more and more difficult to reach consumers (Ha 1996). Internet and email advertising are generally thought to be a rather distinct and effective way of reaching consumers (Wolin/Korgaonkar/Lund 2002; Martin et al. 2002). Another marketing channel that has received particular attention in recent years is mobile technology. Currently, 4.2 billion people, or 60% of the world's population, own a cellphone (Informa Telecoms & Media 2009), making this a potentially attractive channel to reach consumers directly (Barutçu 2007; Natter et al. 2008). In Japan, mobile marketing is already quite common (Okazaki 2008). Furthermore, according to Gartner research 2011, the global volume of mobile marketing is expected to grow up to more than 20 billions by 2015.

In this paper, the effectiveness of mobile marketing messages (MMM) as a means of advertising is discussed, with particular reference to location-aware MMM. First, the potential and risks of MMM are described from a supplier's perspective. After this, changes in consumer behavior as a result of MMM are investigated by means of empirical studies. Finally, the effectiveness of MMM is discussed from a consumer perspective.

6.2   Opportunities and Risks of Mobile Marketing Messages

Mobile marketing has been defined as 'using interactive wireless media to provide customers with time and location sensitive, personalized information that promotes goods, services and ideas, thereby generating value for all stakeholders' (Dickinger et al. 2004). The term 'all stakeholders' can be assumed to include both advertisers and consumers.

Location-aware mobile marketing messages (LA-MMM) are a special type of MMM that take into account the physical position of the carrier of the mobile device (Tseng et al. 2001) and his or her situational requirements (Dourish 2004; Dey 2001; Hristova and O'Hare 2004). A number of different technologies make LA-MMM possible (see Zeimpekis, Giaglis and Lekakos 2003; Tseng et al. 2001; Aalto et al. 2004). Legal restrictions of LA-MMM in the United States and the European Union with regard to opt-in and opt-out schemes are discussed in Karp (2007) and Cleff (2007, 2008).

If a consumer opts to receive MMM, it may mean that they have a positive attitude toward MMM (Bauer et al. 2005; Okazaki 2004), although their choice may be due to the novelty of the concept (Newell/Meier 2007), financial incentives (Tsang/Ho/Liang 2004) or even coincidence when consumers are not even aware that they have given their permission.

6.2.1 Opportunities of Mobile Marketing Messages

For a number of reasons, consumers are thought to gain added value from mobile marketing, as follows:

1. the personalization of messages according to their idiosyncratic needs and interests (Barnes/Scornavacca 2004; Kannan/Chang/Whinston 2001) and thus the increased usefulness and value of the content (Kim/Park/Oh 2008; Zhang/Mao 2008);

2. the location of their mobile devices and their sensitivity to space and time (Haghirian/Madlberger 2005; Leppäniemi/Karjaluoto/Salo 2004), which serves to amplify the first advantage;

3. enhanced entertainment value (Choi/Hwang/McMillan 2008; Okazaki 2008).

Rettie/Grandcolas/Deakins (2005) conducted 5,400 telephone interviews with voluntary recipients of 1 of 26 commercial mobile marketing campaigns. Rettie et al. (2005) claim that MMM can induce positive attitude changes and increase consumers' purchase intentions. However, only voluntary recipients were interviewed, who might by definition be favorably disposed toward MMM. Moreover, the study tested neither the actual buying behavior of the recipients of the MMM nor the buying intentions. In a study by Barwise/Strong (2002), 74% of participants claimed to have read most of the messages they received; however, again, no behavioral intentions or actual behavior were recorded.

6.2.2 Risks of Mobile Marketing Messages

A number of risks are also associated with MMM. It is possible that MMM, which were quite new when Barwise/Strong carried out their study in 2002, are nowadays generally viewed as 'spam'. Such a view would cause serious reactance on the part of the recipients. Reactance occurs where a threat to personal freedom results in attempts to restore that freedom, accompanied by increased attractiveness of the alternative option that was, or could be, lost (Brehm 1989). Today's consumers are bombarded daily with what they view as 'annoying' promotional messages not only on TV, on the radio and in newspapers, but also in their private electronic mailboxes (Haugtvedt et al. 1994; Petty, Haugtvedt/Smith 1995; Spira 2002). For instance, White et al. (2008) showed that overly personalized email advertisements cause reactance. An unsolicited promotional message on a mobile phone might thus be seen as an intrusion into one's privacy (Petty 2000, 2003) or as 'mobile spam' (Hinde 2003), leading to irritation and reactance (Edwards/Li/Lee 2002). Accordingly, Mahmoud/Yu (2006) and Kaasinen (2003) call for more research into consumers' actual wants and needs with regard to MMM and LA-MMM.

To sum up, although a number of researchers have drawn attention to the research gap in this field and others have discussed the 'spam' problem, the majority of published studies remain optimistic with regard to consumers' reactions towards MMM and LA-MMM: they consider them to be an efficient advertising tool. As far as we are aware, consumers' actual behavioral reactions at, or close to, the point of sale have not been tested. Our intention is therefore to find out whether the optimism regarding the potential of MMM and LA-MMM to influence consumers is justified. To obtain deeper insights in the acceptance of MMM, a qualitative pretest was conducted.

6.3   Qualitative Pretest

The field of electronic business – especially of mobile business and mobile marketing – is still emerging (Ramsey et al. 2004). Projective tests are thought to be a useful way to gain initial insights in research into fields that survey participants do not know much about (Will/Eadie/McAskill 1996). For this reason, a qualitative pretest was conducted before carrying out our main experiments, to give us an initial insight into whether MMM received in different contexts and with different types of content provoke different reactions in consumers.

Figure 6.1   Stimulus for a Projective Pretest About LA-MMM

Using a projective technique (Donoghue 2000), one of four versions of a comic strip that was positively tested for comprehension beforehand with 25 students was shown to a convenience sample of 221 participants (with n = 54-57 in each group). Projective techniques are based on the premise that participants verbalize their own feelings and thoughts through the characters shown (Rook 1988). Participants in the test were asked to respond to the presented conflict by filling in a speech balloon in the final picture. In the pictures, both the financial value and the context sensitivity of an advertisement received by text message (SMS) were manipulated. The comic strip depicted a scenario in which the text message contained either a discount coupon or a special offer, and was received either in the store in question (congruent context: bookstore) or in an unrelated store (incongruent context: supermarket). See **Figure 6.1** for an example.

Two experienced researchers working independently formed categories based on a content analysis. Discrepancies were resolved by discussion, and the results were the following six categories: anger, disinterest, skepticism, interest, desire to inspect the offers, and general liking of the MMM. The first three categories represent negative reactions, the latter three represent positive reactions. The answers given by the participants were then sorted into the six categories by two judges working independently. Agreement between the judges was 95.9% (Kendall's $W = .985$, $\chi^2 = 325.007$, $p = .000$). According to Kassarjian (1977), this value is very satisfactory.

Table 6.1   Categories and Results of the Cartoon Test on Mobile Advertising

#	Congruent context:	Yes	Yes	No	No	Sum
	Coupon:	No	Yes	No	Yes	
1	Anger	6	5	11	12	34
2	Disinterest	5	2	10	5	22
3	Skepticism	12	7	7	10	36
Sum negative		(23)	(14)	(28)	(27)	(92)
4	Interest	14	16	9	16	55
5	Check offers	15	7	16	5	43
6	Liking	5	17	2	7	31
Sum positive		(34)	(40)	(27)	(28)	(129)
Sum total		57	54	55	55	221

■ Results

There are significant differences between the four groups of participants ($\chi^2 = 39.970$, df = 15, p =.000). Disproportionately, many negative reactions are elicited in response to the cartoon stories with incongruent context/no coupon (30.4%) and incongruent context/coupon (29.3%). Congruent context/no coupon and congruent context/coupon only account for 25.0% and 15.2% respectively of all negative answers. Reversely, congruent context/no coupon and congruent context/coupon trigger more positive reactions (26.4% and 31.0%) than incongruent context/no coupon and incongruent context/coupon (20.9% and 21.7%). Across all categories, more than half (58.4%) of the participants are open-minded about mobile advertising. However, 40.2% reject mobile advertising regardless of its benefits. Overall, a preference order can be identified. Location-aware marketing messages are preferred over messages that are not customized according to the environment, and messages with a monetary incentive are preferred over purely informational messages. The location of receipt of the message appears to be slightly more important than the monetary reward.

In order to minimize negative reactions and maximize interest and liking, companies involved in mobile advertising should thus strive to include coupons in their location-aware messages.

6.4   Discussion of the Pretest and Derivation of Hypotheses

More than half of the participants (129/221 = 58.4%) showed a positive reaction to the MMM stimulus. Reactions were particularly positive where the MMM was received in the appropriate location, which should result in a more positive attitude toward the bookstore and an enhanced willingness to buy products there.

These qualitative results are relevant since, according to Staats (1996), if a stimulus elicits an emotional response, then motor and verbal approach-avoidance behavior follows. In this sense, 'approach' means that the individual reacts positively to an environment (e.g. browsing in a store), while 'avoidance' means that he or she feels an aversion to the environment and reacts by withdrawal (Mehrabian/Russell 1974; Donovan/Rossiter 1982). If a stimulus at the point of sale triggers a high level of joy and/or surprise (e.g. a visually exciting display of merchandise), approach behavior toward the stimulus is evoked (Foxall/Yani-de-Soriano 2005; Gröppel-Klein 2005).

If we apply these findings to mobile marketing, the relative novelty of receiving LA-MMM on a personal mobile device and their stimulating form (they are accompanied by an acoustic signal) would imply that LA-MMM provoke a high level of attention. If we further assume that the information or monetary incentive contained in the LA-MMM is perceived by recipients as 'interesting', the LA-MMM should stimulate their willingness to explore the environment in the direction of the message sender. Approach behavior – understood here as a distinct motion towards the window of the store or the store itself – should be the result (Mehrabian/Russell 1974).

Does the fact that consumers receive the advertising message on a mobile device rather than in a more traditional way make a difference? To answer this question, the effects of the LA-MMM will be compared with the effects of a traditional form of advertising used to draw consumers' attention to a point of sale – a 'customer stopper' (an example is shown in Figure 2 in Experiment 1). In this case we used outdoor advertising – a traditional means of guiding consumers to a commercial destination (Zineddin/Garvey/Pietrucha 2005).

Studies have shown that the visibility of outdoor advertising is very high (Donthu/Cherian/Bhargava 1993) and that there are significant effects on sales responses (Bhargava/Donthu 1999). Nevertheless, it is suggested that the attention and interest produced by a LA-MMM will be higher than that produced by a non-electronic customer stopper featuring an identical advertising slogan. This is because a mobile device 'siphons concentration, demanding attention even when it is not in use' (Plant 2000) and because a mobile device is a very personal object that people carry with them everywhere, all the time

(Bauer et al. 2005). Advertising received on a personal communication device at or near the point of sale cannot be easily avoided. Moreover (as mentioned before), the reception of a LA-MMM is normally accompanied by a ringtone – an intense stimulus with high activation potential, according to Berlyne (1960). Therefore, despite the possibility of reactance because of the LA-MMM and the high visibility of customer stoppers, our first hypothesis is as follows:

> **H1:** If consumers receive a LA-MMM, they will more frequently show distinct orientation reactions towards the emitter of the stimulus than if they are confronted with a traditional customer stopper.

Incidents, in general, are valued according to their goal relevance (Bagozzi/Baumgartner/Pieters 1998). Usually, mobile marketing informs consumers about particular offers (Kurkovsky/Harihar 2006). 'The consumer is not omniscient. He does not know where he can obtain the cheapest price for what he is looking for. Very often he does not even know what kind of commodity or service is (most) suitable [for him]' (Mises 1949). LA-MMM inform consumers about relevant offers in their immediate environment (Dey 2001; Kaasinen 2003). It follows that consumers should not treat LA-MMM like spam – especially if they offer some form of financial advantage, such as a discount coupon (De Reyck/Degraeve 2003).

In our experiment, only informative promotional messages are considered, not entertaining ones (Ducoffe 1996). Such messages should increase consumers' compliance with the message and thus their stated willingness to visit and shop at the store that is advertised when they are close to it (Hristova/O'Hare 2004; Tezinde/Smith/Murphy 2002; Heilman/Nakamoto/Rao 2002). This leads us to our second hypothesis, which has two parts:

> **H2A and H2B:** The closer a LA-MMM matches the consumers' location and the more relevant its time of receipt, the greater the consumer's (A) willingness to visit the store, and (B) willingness to buy there.

Hypotheses H1 and H2 refer to consumers' behavioral reactions to LA-MMM received outside a store. Our intention is to find out whether consumers are influenced by such LA-MMM to go toward the advertising store – in other words, whether the message distracts them from their original task. Our next hypotheses concern consumers' suggestibility when they are already inside a store as we look at the potential of LA-MMM to guide consumers toward particular products. Thus, the context in which subjects receive the message in Experiment 1 is only congruent to the location of the recipient, while the context in Experiment 2 is taken to the extreme in being both congruent to the recipient's location and the recipient's current task. Our assumption is that a congruent task and environmental context should evoke even more interest than a less congruent context.

It has long been established that promotional stimuli at the point of sale, for example displays of merchandise, result in increased sales of the advertised products (e.g. Rust 1993; Quelch/Cannon-Bonventre 1983; Woodside/Waddle 1975). However, it is not known whether LA-MMM have a similar effect. LA-MMM are not only potentially personalized messages, but they also reach the consumer on a personal device; they should therefore receive a high level of attention by recipients, as discussed in the derivation of H1. Our next hypotheses expand on this idea, placing special emphasis on consumers' behavior at the point of sale. The special features of LA-MMM lead us to our third hypothesis:

> **H3:** If consumers receive a LA-MMM within a store when they are located close to the advertised product, their stated willingness to buy the advertised product will increase.

Just as consumers' intentions to buy, their actual buying decisions are also interesting. Here, it can be argued that, above all, consumers' spontaneous and habitualized buying decisions can be altered by LA-MMM.

Certain factors promote spontaneous buying decisions at the point of sale. These factors include visual merchandising concepts (Gröppel-Klein 2005) or items on sale (McGoldrick, Betts and Keeling 1999). Spontaneous buying decisions can, for instance, be evoked by special offers that are seen at the point of sale. The impulse to buy spontaneously is characterized by a strong and intense urge to buy, an inner conflict over whether to buy or not, yet at the same time a disregard for the consequences (Rook 1987).

Habitual buying decisions can be characterized as quasi-automatic buying behavior, where consumers' information processing at the point of sale is restricted to situational information such as price and availability (Hoyer 1984). When confronted with a LA-MMM, consumers' regular, routine buying behavior might be interrupted. The information contained in the LA-MMM might make the consumer buy a different product from the one that they had intended to buy.

The experiments presented concentrate on products that consumers usually buy either on impulse or habitually. Purchases that are cognitively driven are ignored because we believe that simple LA-MMM will not significantly influence such decisions. The LA-MMM used in our experiment are stimuli that contain situational information about the products at the point of sale, including price information. Moreover, participants received them unexpectedly. Therefore we believe that the LA-MMM might alter habitual and spontaneous buying decisions (Barnes 2002) by drawing shoppers' attention to the advertised products. This leads to hypotheses 4 and 5:

> **H4 and H5:** If consumers receive a LA-MMM at the point of sale for products in categories that are generally bought (H4) impulsively or (H5) habitually, the number of actual sales of the product advertised should increase.

6.5   Experiment 1

■ Methodology

Experiment 1 tests the first and second hypotheses. Participants in Experiment 1 were recruited a few days before the experiment and asked for their mobile phone numbers in case
the experiment had to be postponed. The experiment itself took place on a university campus where there were a few stores. A convenience student sample totaling 163 people
(93 females, 70 males, M_{age} = 24.4, SD = 4.2) participated. Subjects were asked to walk on
their own to a grocer's located approximately 200 yards from the starting point on the campus, where they performed an orientation task involving finding a number of products
from a shopping list. They were instructed emphatically to shop for their own needs if they
wished to and to take as much time as they needed before returning to the experimenter.
This should have left participants with the opportunity to react to our experimental stimulus. The participants passed a bookstore twice – once on the way to the grocer's and once
on the way back to the experimenter.

Participants' approach behavior – a distinct interest in the bookstore – when passing it
while returning to the interviewer was recorded by covert observers. Subjects were interviewed personally upon their return. After the participants set off for the grocer's, the experimenter sent two of the four experimental groups a LA-MMM. One group received a
LA-MMM containing a substantial financial incentive to buy something in the bookshop, in
the form of a code enabling a discount at the checkout – i.e., a coupon LA-MMM. The other
group received a simple special offer LA-MMM advertising special offers at the bookshop.
The LA-MMM arrived on the participants' handsets after they had passed the bookstore the
first time. To investigate the impact of the means of advertising on consumer behavior, a
third group was confronted with a more typical type of store advertising – a 'customer
stopper' that was located directly in front of the bookshop (see **Figure 6.2**).

The customer stopper consisted of the same special offer advertisement as the special offer
LA-MMM. A fourth group – the control group – did not receive any advertising stimulus at
all.

Figure 6.2   Experimental Stimuli in Experiment 1

■ Hypothesis testing and results

To test the manipulation and to sort participants into groups for subsequent analysis, participants were asked whether or not they had received a LA-MMM from the bookstore. 58 of the 114 participants (50.9%) who should have received a LA-MMM stated that they had done so, and that they had also read the message. There was no difference in perception between the special offer and the coupon LA-MMM ($\chi^2 = 1.646$, p = .649).

Table 6.2   Group Configuration

Group	N	Label	Received content
1	70	Control	No stimulus
2	35	Customer stopper	We have a vast selection of SPECIAL OFFERS and current bestsellers located at the front of the bookstore. Enjoy browsing! - Your Bookstore Team
3	29	Special offer LA-MMM	We have a vast selection of SPECIAL OFFERS and current bestsellers located at the front of the bookstore. Enjoy browsing! - Your Bookstore Team
4	29	Coupon LA-MMM	Gift coupon from your campus bookstore: Get a €2 discount on minimum purchases of €5. Simply give the coupon code 'xyz12' at the checkout. Offer valid today only!

Participants who did not read the LA-MMM during the experiment were added to the control group. The coupon LA-MMM group comprised 29 participants and the special offer LA-MMM group also comprised 29 participants. A further 35 participants were confronted with the customer stopper and 70 participants received no stimulus at all or did not read the LA-MMM during the experiment (see **Table 6.2**).

Variables that could introduce bias to the results were controlled for. Participants' involvement in books was measured: an ANOVA with a post-hoc procedure showed no significant difference with respect to involvement between the single groups. Participants' irritation by MMM was tested by means of a semantic differential. This is not employed as a covariate in testing H1, as only those participants who received the LA-MMM in the experimental situation could produce actual reactance to the emitter of the LA-MMM. Irritation of LA-MMM recipients reached medium levels – the participants were only mildly irritated. No significant difference in irritation by MMM could be detected between groups 3 and 4. Moreover, none of the participants expressed concern about the origin of the LA-MMM in the interview. No significant difference was found between the four groups with regard to gender, age or disposable income.

Cross-tabulation demonstrates that, for participants who were confronted with an advertising stimulus, 6 of the 29 subjects (20.7%) who received and read the coupon LA-MMM and 7 of the 29 subjects (24.1%) who received and read the special offer LA-MMM stimulus looked closely at the bookstore, showing distinct approach behavior. Only 2 of the 34 participants (5.9%) from the customer stopper group showed similar approach behavior. H1 suggests that the approach behavior of participants who received the LA-MMM should be more frequent than that of participants who were confronted with the customer stopper. However, no significant difference in approach behavior between the groups customer stopper, special-offer- and coupon-LA-MMM could be detected (χ^2 = 4.397, p = .127). Comparing just the customer stopper and special-offer-LA-MMM groups, which both featured the same text, gives a slightly better result (χ^2 = 4.065, p = .070, Fisher's exact test p = .070). H1 is therefore rejected. The faint tendency seen here changes to significance if the control group, from which 1 of 67 participants (1.5%) showed approach behavior, is included and all four groups are tested in a cross tabulation (χ^2 = 16.493, p = .001). To conclude, LA-MMM induce approach-behavior more often than no stimulus.

Only those participants who received a LA-MMM during experimentation were questioned about whether the LA-MMM was received at an appropriate time and place, since only these individuals could provide a substantial answer. In a confirmatory factor analysis with satisfactory measures of fit (χ^2 = 22.65, df = 24, p = .541, GFI = .95, AGFI = .90, CFI = 1.00, RMSEA = .000, χ^2/df = .944), the factors' 'relevance to the content of the LA-MMM' and 'match of location and time of reception of the LA-MMM' are confirmed. The statements of these two factors were first summarized to two 'compute variables', standardized and then used as independent variables in two multiple linear regression analyses for testing H2A and H2B.

Table 6.3   Regression Analysis of Participants' Willingness to Visit the Bookstore

Dependent variable: Willingness to visit the bookstore

R: .352; R²: .124; Corr. R²: .103; Standard error: 1.280; Durbin-Watson-Statistics: 1.991

	Sum of squares	Df	Mean square	F	Significance
Regression	19.275	2	9.637	5.884	.004
Residual	135.946	83	1.638		
Total	155.221	85			

Independ. variable	B	Stand.err.	Beta	T	Significance	VIF
(Constant)	2.343	.138		16.963	.000	
Content	. .319	.140	.234	2.274	.026	1.003
Time and location	.348	.143	.251	2.437	.017	1.003

In the first regression, willingness to visit the bookstore served as a dependent variable. The corrected R^2 = .103 (p = .004) (see **Table 6.3**) is rather small, but clearly significant. The match of the time and location of reception (β = .251, p = .017) is slightly stronger than relevance of the content of the LA-MMM (β = .231, p = .024).

In the second regression, willingness to buy something in the bookstore served as a dependent variable. Again, the corrected R^2 = .080 (p = .011; see Table 4) is small, but clearly significant. However, this time, the relevance of the content of the LA-MMM (β = .250, p = .017) is stronger than the match of the time and location of its receipt (β = .197, p = .059), which is not significant in itself.

No difference with regard to the dependent variables could be detected between the group that received the financially attractive LA-MMM with the coupon and the group that received the LA-MMM advertising special offers with no coupon. All items were measured on a five-point scale (5 = maximum). Results were as follows: willingness to visit: M_{Coupon} = 2.33, $M_{NoCoupon}$ = 2.66, t = .882, p = .382; willingness to buy: M_{Coupon} = 2.24, $M_{NoCoupon}$ = 2.34, t = .308, p = .760. H2A and H2B cannot therefore be rejected. The location awareness of an MMM has a small but significant influence on consumers' stated willingness to visit a store and their stated buying intention, regardless of whether or not a financial incentive is included.

Table 6.4   Regression Analysis of Participants' Willingness to Buy in the Bookstore

Dependent variable: Willingness to buy something in the bookstore

R: .319; R²: .101; Corr. R²: .080; Standard error: 1.229; Durbin-Watson-Statistics: 2.125

	Sum of squares	Df	Mean square	F	Significance
Regression	14.496	2	7.248	4.798	.011
Residual	128.401	85	1.511		
Total	142.898	87			

Independent variable	B	Stand. err.	Beta	T	Significance	VIF
(Constant)	2.216	.131		16.913	.000	
Content	.321	.132	.250	2.434	.017	1.000
Time and location	.253	.132	.197	1.917	.059	1.000

■ Further findings

In Experiment 1, only 9 of the 35 participants (25.7%) consciously noticed the customer stopper, while 61 of the 94 participants (64.9%) noticed the incoming LA-MMM ($\chi^2 = 15.744$, p = .000). Furthermore, a count of the number of coupons for books and other merchandise used in the bookstore in the first experiment showed that 6 of the 44 coupons sent by LA-MMM (13.63%) were actually redeemed. However, this number cannot be compared with the other experimental groups (the 'customer stopper' and 'special offer' groups) since it was not possible to find out how many of them actually entered the store at a later date.

■ Discussion of Experiment 1

Consumers are not easily convinced to approach a store while they are busy doing something else. It was shown that LA-MMM are noticed but are not able to improve significantly consumers' approach behavior towards stores compared to traditional outdoor advertising. An indicator that LA-MMM might work under certain circumstances is that participants' stated willingness to visit a store and to buy something there could be significantly enhanced if the perceived match of the time and location of receiving the MMM is high. However, a financially attractive coupon does not influence consumers' visiting and buying intentions.

6.6 Experiment 2

■ Methodology

Experiment 2 tests the third, fourth, and fifth hypotheses. In Experiment 2, we tested whether consumers that are already in a store and willing to shop there can be influenced by LA-MMM to buy particular products (highly congruent context). Participants were recruited from among the customers of a suburban hypermarket. A convenience sample totaling 100 persons participated (49 females, 51 males, M_{age} = 36.7, SD = 13.847). From the starting point in the hypermarket, participants were equipped with a PDA displaying a short electronic shopping list. As a distracting task, participants were asked to find the designated products on the list in the hypermarket and to tick off on the PDA those they found. When they ticked off one of two particular items, one of two different experimental advertisements popped up on the PDA's screen, accompanied by a ringtone. The advertisements made the consumers aware of interesting products that were located close to the product they had just ticked off the list. As in Experiment 1, pricing information was included in this pop-up advertisement (see **Figure 6.3**).

Figure 6.3   Shopping-List (Left) & Experimental Stimuli from Experiment 2 (Middle, Right)

After completing their shopping task, participants were questioned about their willingness to buy the advertised products. In addition, their shopping carts were checked for the products in question. Since actual buying intentions and buying behavior were being tested, the first experimental group received an advertisement for the well-known Milka brand of chocolate. The second experimental group received an advertisement for the similarly well-known Weihenstephan brand of milk. No significant difference with regard to gender, age or disposable income was detected between the two experimental groups. Due to limited funding, participants could not be provided with money to spend; however, the products advertised cost just $0.99 and $1.29 respectively, so all participants, who were there to buy groceries anyway, should have been in a position to afford these products (net income/month in $: M = 1,627; SD = 1,034).

- Hypothesis testing and results

For a manipulation check, all participants were asked whether they had received an advertising pop-up while shopping, and if so, what it was about. A remarkable 100% of participants had noticed the pop-up, and all but one remembered the message's contents correctly. Attitude towards the brands was also controlled for in both groups. No significant differences were found (attitude towards Milka: $M_{group\ 1}$ = 3.98, $M_{group\ 2}$ = 4.04, t = -.350, p = .727; attitude towards Weihenstephan: $M_{group\ 1}$ = 3.94, $M_{group\ 2}$ = 3.79, t = .875, p = .384). In group 1, the test persons were only exposed to the Milka pop-up; in group 2 only to the Weihenstephan pop-up. Thus we will now refer to the groups as 'Milka', and 'Weihenstephan' respectively.

In Experiment 2, participants' irritation was controlled for by asking how annoyed they were by the LA-MMM. Both groups were annoyed by MMM to a similar extent – around four on a five-point scale, where 1 means 'not annoyed at all' and 5 means 'very annoyed' (M_{Milka} = 4.16, $M_{Weihenstephan}$ = 3.94, t = 1.022, p = .309). The standard deviations were similar and small (SD_{Milka} = 1.017, $SD_{Weihenstephan}$ = 1.132). A regression analysis of annoyance on willingness to buy the advertised product had no significant results (R^2 = .016, $F_{(1,\ 96)}$ = 1.551, p = .216; $T_{Annoyance}$ = -1.245, β = -.126, p = .216).

To test H3, a t-test to compare the willingness to buy Milka between the group that received the pop-up for Milka and the group that did not (M_{Milka} = 2.82, $M_{Weihenstephan}$ = 2.88, t = -.220, p = .827) was run. In another t-test, the stated willingness to buy Weihenstephan milk between the group that received the pop-up for Weihenstephan and the group that did not was compared ($M_{Weihenstephan}$ = 2.08, M_{Milka} = 2.44, t = 1.666, p = .099).

H3 is therefore rejected: consumers' stated willingness to buy the advertised product could be enhanced for neither Milka nor Weihenstephan via LA-MMM. Indeed, their willingness to buy Weihenstephan milk was in fact slightly lower if they received the Weihenstephan LA-MMM.

Using a cluster analysis, consumers' types of buying decisions for chocolate and milk were determined. For chocolate, all but six cases showed very high values for the item 'I am enthusiastic about chocolate when I notice it and buy it on impulse' (M = 4.73, SD = .494) and low to medium values for items signifying other types of buying decisions. The 94 participants who buy chocolate impulsively were used for further analysis. For milk, a cluster analysis found that all but three cases out of 100 showed high approval for the items 'I buy milk regularly' (M = 4.69, SD = .549) and 'I buy milk automatically'

(M = 4.58, SD = .536), but scored low on items signifying other buying decisions. The 97 participants who buy milk habitually were included in the further analysis.

A cross-tabulation of participants' actual buying behavior of Milka for recipients of the Milka LA-MMM with that of recipients of the Weihenstephan LA-MMM is used to test H4 (see **Table 6.5**). Overall, participants bought 13 Milka products. No significant differences in consumers' buying behavior could be detected between the experimental groups (χ^2 = .803, Fisher's p = .552). H4 is therefore rejected.

Table 6.5   Cross-Tabulation of the Milka Message Received and Sales of Milka

Received message: Milka	Yes	No	Sum
Bought Milka	8	5	13
Did not buy Milka	39	42	81
Sum	47	47	94

To test H5, we cross-tabulated participants' actual buying behavior for Weihenstephan milk for recipients of the Weihenstephan LA-MMM with that of recipients of the Milka LA-MMM (see **Table 6.6**). Due to small numbers in some cells, the exact Fisher-Yates-Test is calculated (Bortz and Lienert 2002). As for Milka, no significant advantage was found in the number of items sold to the group that received the pop-up for Weihenstephan milk compared to the control group receiving the Milka LA-MMM (4 versus 2 products; Fisher's exact test p = .436). H5 is therefore also rejected.

Table 6.6   Cross-Tabulation of Receiving the Weihenstephan Message and Sales of Weihenstephan

Received message: Weihenstephan	Yes	No	Sum
Bought Weihenstephan	4	2	6
Did not buy Weihenstephan	44	47	91
Sum	48	49	97

- Discussion of Experiment 2

The results of Experiment 2 are disappointing for brand management. Even when consumers are already in a store and in the mood for shopping (Dhar/Huber/Khan 2007), they are still not easily encouraged to buy specially advertised products. Context-sensitive MMM had no significant effect either on consumers' stated willingness or their actual buying behavior for the advertised brands. Although most participants were somewhat or even highly annoyed by the LA-MMM, their behavioral intentions were not influenced by this.

- Further findings

In Experiment 2, all participants noticed the LA-MMM. It is therefore safe to say that LA-MMM still attract great attention from recipients. Finally, although there were no significant differences in consumers' actual buying behavior for Milka chocolate and Weihenstephan milk, an enormous improvement in overall sales for products in the category 'milk' was found in the experimental groups (see **Table 6.7**). This effect was not found for the category 'chocolate' (see **Table 6.8**).

Table 6.7   Cross-Tabulation of Receiving the Weihenstephan Message and Sales of Any Brand of Milk

Received message: Weihenstephan	Yes	No	Sum
Bought milk	26 (54%)	11 (24%)	37
Did not buy milk	22 (46%)	38 (76%)	60
Sum	48	49	97

Table 6.8   Cross-Tabulation of Receiving the Milka Message and Sales of Any Brand of Chocolate

Received message: Milka	Yes	No	SUM
Bought chocolate	19 (40.4%)	20 (42.6%)	39
Did not buy chocolate	28 (59.6%)	27 (57.4%)	55
Sum	47	47	94

Of the 48 participants who received the Weihenstephan pop-up, 26 (54%) bought a carton of milk, while only 11 of the 49 (22%) who received the chocolate pop-up bought chocolate (χ^2 = 10.339, Fisher's p = .002). This effect could not be detected for sales of all chocolate brands (χ^2 = .044, Fisher's p = 1.000). It is possible that the LA-MMM stimulus induced memory-based spontaneous buying decisions for the whole category 'milk'; however, this finding requires further testing. Thus, advertising a whole category of goods by LA-MMM at the point of sale could remind consumers that they need to buy frequently bought goods. However, it would be necessary to ascertain whether LA-MMM are more efficient than in-store radio or similar advertising for milk and other product categories.

6.7   Implications

The results of the study contradict much of what has been claimed for MMM and LA-MMM. Firstly, LA-MMM are only slightly more effective than traditional advertising at arousing consumers' interest in a store. Thus, the approach behavior of consumers receiving a LA-MMM (with or without a financial incentive) is not much more pronounced than that of consumers confronted with traditional outdoor advertising, even though LA-MMM are better than no advertising stimulus at all.

Secondly, consumers' stated willingness to visit a store and to buy something there is, again, only slightly enhanced if a coupon or special-offer LA-MMM supports them in this aim.

Thirdly, the second experiment did not find any effect on consumers' impulse buying behavior for chocolate where a LA-MMM made them aware of the availability of Milka chocolate. This applied both to Milka (i.e., the advertised brand) and to the category 'chocolate' in general. Sales of the advertised brand of milk were also not significantly improved by using LA-MMM. It was only possible to increase overall sales in the category 'milk', not the sales of the particular brand that was advertised. Further testing is required in order to clarify the reasons for this.

Irritation with the LA-MMM in Experiment 1 was on average at a medium level, while reactance to the context-aware advertisement in Experiment 2 was quite high. However, there was no significant negative correlation between perceived irritation and approach respective to buying behavior.

In conclusion, our study shows that consumers are only mildly influenced by LA-MMM. Consumers do not feel a strong urge to buy the products or visit the stores advertised.

■ Limitations

The limitations of the study include a lack of accountability for long-term effects (Vakratsas/Ma 2005) of the LA-MMM, and for positive effects of the LA-MMM on brand equity, which are thought to be positive (Palazón-Vidal/Delgado-Ballester 2005). Further limitations include the small sample size, the use of a student sample in Experiment 1 and a convenience sample in Experiment 2, the fact that only three products from two stores were tested, and the fact that the LA-MMM was accompanied by a ringtone while the customer stopper did not make an acoustic signal. It could be interesting to repeat Experiment 1 with a person in front of the store handing out flyers instead of the advertising board.

There were a number of reasons underlying these drawbacks. Sample sizes were restricted as it was very difficult to secure the cellphone numbers of a larger number of participants in Experiment 1 without revealing the experimental manipulation. In Experiment 2, pop-up advertisements had to be programmed onto the PDAs – thus our test persons could not use their own personal mobile devices. In addition, the second experiment was conducted in a real supermarket and it took some time for the participants to complete the tasks. It was not easy to find many test persons who were willing to spend the extra time required for our experiment during their normal shopping trip. Despite these limitations, we believe that our studies provide some useful initial insights into the (non-)efficiency of MMM.

Literature

[1]   Aalto, L./Göthlin, N./Korhonen, J./Ojala, T. (2004): Bluetooth and WAP Push Based Location-aware Mobile Advertising System. Proceedings of the 2nd International Conference on Mobile Systems, Applications, and Services, Boston, MA, pp. 49-58.

[2]   Bagozzi, R. P./Baumgartner, H./Pieters, R. (1998): Goal-directed Emotions. Cognition and Emotion, Vol. 12, 1, pp. 1-26.

[3]   Barnes, S. J. (2002): Wireless Digital Advertising: Nature and Implications. International Journal of Advertising, Vol. 21, pp. 399-420.

[4]   Barnes, S. J./Scornavacca, E. (2004): Mobile Marketing: The Role of Permission and Acceptance. International Journal of Mobile Communication, Vol. 2, 2, pp. 128-139.

[5]   Barutçu, S. (2007): Attitudes towards Mobile Marketing Tools: A Study of Turkish Consumers. Journal of Targeting, Measurement, and Analysis for Marketing, Vol. 16, 1, pp. 26-38.

[6]   Barwise, P./Strong, C. (2002): Permission-based Mobile Advertising. Journal of Interactive Marketing, Vol. 16, 1, pp. 14-24.

[7]   Bauer, H. H./Barnes, S. J./Reichardt, T./Neumann, M. M. (2005): Driving Consumer Acceptance of Mobile Marketing: A Theoretical Framework and Empirical Study. Journal of Electronic Commerce Research, Vol. 6, 3, pp. 181-192.

[8]   Berlyne, D. E. (1960): Conflict, Arousal and Curiosity. New York: McGraw-Hill.

[9]   Bhargava, M./Donthu, N. (1999): Sales Response to Outdoor Advertising. Journal of Advertising Research, Vol. 39, 4, pp. 7-18.

[10] Bortz, J./Lienert, G. A. (2002): Concise Statistics for Clinical Research (Kurzgefasste Statistik für die Klinische Forschung). Heidelberg: Springer.

[11] Brehm, J. (1989): Psychological Reactance: Theory and Applications. Advances in Consumer Research, Vol. 16, pp. 72-75.

[12] Cleff, E. B. (2007): Privacy Issues in Mobile Advertising. International Review of Law Computers & Technology, Vol. 21, 3, pp. 225-236.

[13] Cleff, E. B. (2008): Regulating Mobile Advertising in the European Union and the United States. Computer Law & Security Report, Vol. 24, 5, pp. 421-436.

[14] Choi, Y. K./Hwang J.-S./McMillan, S. J. (2008): Gearing Up for Mobile Advertising: A Cross-Cultural Examination of Key Factors That Drive Mobile Messages Home to Consumers. Psychology & Marketing, Vol. 25, 8, pp. 756-768.

[15] De Reyck, B./Degraeve, Z. (2003): Broadcast Scheduling for Mobile Advertising. Operations Research, Vol. 51, 4, pp. 509-517.

[16] Dey, A. K. (2001): Understanding and Using Context. Personal and Ubiquitous Computing, Vol. 5, 1, pp. 4-7.

[17] Dickinger, A./Haghirian, P./Murphy, J./Scharl, A. (2004): An Investigation and Conceptual Model of SMS Marketing. Proceedings of the 37th Hawaii International Conference on Systems Sciences, Hawaii, HI.

[18] Dhar, R./Huber, J./Khan, U. (2007): The Shopping Momentum Effect. Journal of Marketing Research, Vol. 44, 3, pp. 370-378.

[19] Donoghue, S. (2000): Projective Techniques in Consumer Research. Journal of Family Ecology and Consumer Sciences, Vol. 28, pp. 47-53.

[20] Donovan, R. J./Rossiter, J. R. (1982): Store atmosphere: An Experimental Psychology Approach. Journal of Retailing, Vol. 58, pp. 34-57.

[21] Donthu, N./Cherian, J./Bhargava, M. (1993): Factors Influencing Recall of Outdoor Advertising. Journal of Advertising Research, Vol. 33, 3, pp. 64-72.

[22] Dourish, P. (2004): What We Talk About When We Talk About Context. Personal and Ubiquitous Computing, Vol. 8, 1, pp. 19-30.

[23] Ducoffe, R. H. (1996): Advertising Value and Advertising on the Web. Journal of Advertising Research, Vol. 36, 5, pp. 21-35.

[24] Edwards, S. M./Li, H./Lee, J.–H. (2002): Forced Exposure and Psychological Reactance: Antecedents and Consequences of the Perceived Intrusiveness of Pop-Up-Ads. Journal of Advertising, Vol. 31, 3, pp. 83-95.

[25] Foxall, G. R./Yani-de-Soriano, M. (2005): Situational Influences on Consumers' Attitudes and Behavior. Journal of Business Research, Vol. 58, 4, pp. 518-525.

[26] Gröppel-Klein, A. (2005): Arousal and Consumer In-store Behavior. Brain Research Bulletin, Vol. 67, pp. 428-437.

[27] Ha, L. (1996): Advertising Clutter in Consumer Magazines: Dimensions and Effects. Journal of Advertising Research, Vol. 136, 4, pp. 76-84.

[28] Haghirian, P./Madlberger, M. (2005): Consumer Attitude toward Advertising via Mobile Devices – An Empirical Investigation Among Austrian Users. Proceedings of the 13th Conference on Information Systems, Regensburg.

[29] Haugtvedt, C. P./Schumann, D. W./Schneier, W. L./Warren, W. L. (1994): Advertising Repetition and Variation Strategies: Implications for Understanding Attitude Strength. Journal of Consumer Research, Vol. 21, 1, pp. 176-189.

[30] Heilman, C. M./Nakamoto, K./Rao, A. (2002): Pleasant Surprises: Consumer Response to Unexpected In-store Coupons. Journal of Marketing Research, Vol. 39, 2, pp. 242-52.

[31] Hinde, S. (2003): Spam: The Evolution of a Nuisance. Computers and Security, Vol. 22, 6, pp. 474-478.

[32] Hoyer, W. D. (1984): An Examination of Consumer Decision Making for a Common Repeat Purchase Product. Journal of Consumer Research, Vol. 11, 3, pp. 822-829.

[33] Hristova, N./O'Hare, G. M. P. (2004): Ad-Me: Wireless Advertising Adapted to the User Location, Device and Emotions. Proceedings of the 37th Hawaii International Conference on Systems Sciences, Hawaii, HI.

[34] Informa Telecoms & Media (2009): World Cellular Subscriptions March 2009. www.3gamericas.org/index.cfm?fuseaction = page&pageid = 565.

[35] Kaasinen, E. (2003): User Needs for Location-Aware Mobile Services. Personal and Ubiquitous Computing, Vol. 7, 1, pp. 70-79.

[36] Kannan, P. K./Chang, A.–M./Whinston, A. B. (2001): Wireless Commerce: Marketing Issues and Possibilities. Proceedings of the 34th Hawaii International Conference on System Sciences, Hawaii, HI, pp. 1-6.

[37] Karp, G. (2007): Mobile Marketing and Interactive Promotions on Mobile Devices: Navigating Legal Hurdles. International Journal of Mobile Marketing, Vol. 2, 2, pp. 78-85.

[38] Kassarjian, H. H. (1977): Content Analysis in Consumer Research. Journal of Consumer Research, Vol. 4, 1, pp. 8-18.

[39] Kim, G. S./Park, S.-B./Oh, J. (2008): An Examination of Factors Influencing Consumer Adoption of Short Message Service (SMS). Psychology & Marketing, Vol. 25, 8, pp. 769-786.

[40] Kroeber-Riel, W./Weinberg, P./Gröppel-Klein, A. (2009): Konsumentenverhalten, München.

[41] Kurkovsky, S./Harihar, K. (2006): Using Ubiquitous Computing in Interactive Mobile Marketing. Personal and Ubiquitous Computing, Vol. 10, 4, pp. 227-240.

[42] Leppäniemi, M./Karjaluoto, H./Salo, J. (2004): The Success Factors of Mobile Advertising Value Chain. E-Business Review, Vol. 4, pp. 93-97.

[43] Mahmoud, Q. H./Yu, L. (2006): Havana Agents for Comparison Shopping and Location-Aware Advertising in Wireless Mobile Environments. Electronic Commerce Research and Applications, Vol. 5, 3, pp. 220-228.

[44] Martin, B. A. S./van Durme, J./Raulas, M./Merisavo, M. (2002): Email Advertising: Exploratory Insights from Finland. Journal of Advertising Research, Vol. 43, 3, pp. 293-300.

[45] McGoldrick, P. J./Betts, E. J./Keeling, K. A. (1999): Antecedents of Spontaneous Buying Behavior During Temporary Markdowns. Advances in Consumer Research, Vol. 26, pp. 26-33.

[46] Mehrabian, A./Russell, J. A. (1974): An Approach to Environmental Psychology. Cambridge, MA: MIT Press.

[47] Mises, L. von (1949): Human Action – A Treatise on Economics. New Haven: Yale University Press.

[48] Natter, M./Mild, A./Wagner, U./Taudes, A. (2008): Planning new tariffs at tele.ring – the application and impact of an integrated segmentation, targeting and positioning tool, in: Marketing Science, Vol. 27, 4, pp. 600-609.

[49] Newell, J./Meier, M. (2007): Desperately Seeking Opt-in: A Field Report from a Student-led Mobile Marketing Initiative. International Journal of Mobile Marketing, Vol. 2, 2, pp. 53-57.

[50] Okazaki, S. (2004): How do Japanese Consumers Perceive Wireless Ads? A Multivariate Analysis. International Journal of Advertising, Vol. 23, 4, pp. 429-454.

[51] Okazaki, S. (2008): Determinant Factors of Mobile-Based Word-of-Mouth Campaign Referral among Japanese Adolescents. Psychology & Marketing, Vol. 25, 8, pp. 714-731.

[52] Palazón-Vidal, M./Delgado-Ballester, E. (2005): Sales Promotion Effects on Consumer-Based Brand Equity. International Journal of Market Research, Vol. 47, 2, pp. 179-204.

[53] Plant, S. (2000): On the Mobile – The Effects of Mobile Telephones on Social and Individual Life. Schaumburg, IL: Motorola.

[54] Petty, R. D. (2000): Marketing without Consent: Consumer Choice and Costs, Privacy, and Public Policy. Journal of Public Policy and Marketing, Vol. 19, 1, pp. 42-53.

[55] Petty, R. D. (2003): Wireless Advertising Messaging: Legal Analysis and Public Policy Issues. Journal of Public Policy & Marketing, Vol. 22, 1, pp. 71-82.

[56] Petty, R. E./Haugtvedt, C. P./Smith, S. M. (1995): Elaboration as a Determinant of Attitude Strength: Creating Attitudes That Are Persistent, Resistant, and Predictive of Behavior. In R. E. Petty and J. A. Krosnick (Eds.), Attitude Strength: Antecedents and Consequences (pp. 93-130), Mahwah, NJ: Lawrence Erlbaum.

[57] Quelch, J./Cannon-Bonventre, K (1983): Better Marketing at the Point of Purchase. Harvard Business Review, Vol. 61, 6, pp. 162-169.

[58] Ramsey, E./Ibbotson, P./Bell, J./Gray, B. (2004): A Projectives Perspective of International 'E'-services. Qualitative Market Research: An International Journal, Vol. 7, 1, pp. 34-47.

[59] Rettie, R./Grandcolas, U./Deakins, B. (2005): Text Message Advertising: Response Rates and Branding Effects. Journal of Targeting, Measurement and Analysis for Marketing, Vol. 13, 4, pp. 304-312.

[60] Rook, D. W. (1988): Researching Consumer Fantasy. In: E. C. Hirschman and J. N. Sheth (Eds.), Research in Consumer Behavior, 3, (pp. 247-270), Greenwich, CT: Jai Press.

[61] Rook, D. W. (1987): The Buying Impulse. Journal of Consumer Research, Vol. 14, 2, pp. 189-199.

[62] Rust, L. (1993): Observations: How to Reach Children in Stores: Marketing Tactics Grounded in Observational Research. Journal of Advertising Research, Vol. 33, 6, pp. 67-72.

[63] Speck, P. S./Elliott, M. T. (1997): The Antecedents and Consequences of Perceived Advertising Clutter. Journal of Current Issues and Research in Advertising, Vol. 19, 2, pp. 39-54.

[64] Spira, J. S. (2002): Attitude Strength and Resistance to Persuasion. Advances in Consumer Research, Vol. 29, pp. 180-181.

[65] Staats, A. W. (1996): Behavior and Personality: Psychological Behaviorism. New York, NY: Springer.

[66] Tezinde, T./Smith, B./Murphy, J. (2002): Getting Permission: Factors Affecting Permission Marketing. Journal of Interactive Marketing, Vol. 16, 4, pp. 28-36.

[67] Tsang, M. M./Ho, S.-C./Liang, T.-P. (2004): Consumer Attitudes toward Mobile Advertising: An Empirical Study. International Journal of Electronic Commerce, Vol. 8, 3, pp. 65-78.

[68] Tseng, Y.-C./Wu, S.-L./Liao, W.–H./Chao, C.–M. (2001): Location Awareness in Ad Hoc Wireless Mobile Networks. Computer, Vol. 34, 6, pp. 46-52.

[69] Vatanparast, R. (2007): Piercing the Fog of Mobile Advertising. Proceedings of the International Conference on the Management of Mobile Business, 19.

[70] Vakratsas, D./Ma, Z. (2005): A Look at the Long-run Effectiveness of Multimedia Advertising and Its Implications for Budget Allocation Decisions. Journal of Advertising Research, Vol. 45, 2, pp. 241-254.

[71] White, T. B./Zahay, D. L./Thorbjørnsen, H./Shavitt, S. (2008): Getting too Personal: Reactance to Highly Personalized Email Solicitations. Marketing Letters, Vol. 19, 1, pp. 39-50.

[72] Will, V./Eadie, D./McAskill, S. (1996): Projective and Enabling Techniques Explored. Marketing Intelligence & Planning, Vol. 14, 6, pp. 38-43.

[73] Wolin, L. D./Korgaonkar, P./Lund, D. (2002): Beliefs, Attitudes and Behavior towards Web Advertising. International Journal of Advertising, Vol. 21, 1, pp. 87-113.

[74] Woodside, A. G./Waddle, G. L. (1975): Sales Effects of In-store-advertising. Journal of Advertising Research, Vol. 15, 3, pp. 29-33.

[75] Zeimpekis, V./Giaglis, G. M./Lekakos, G. (2003): A Taxonomy of Indoor and Outdoor Positioning Techniques for Mobile Location Services. SIGecom Exchanges, Vol. 3, 4, pp. 19-27.

[76] Zhang, J./Mao, E. (2008): Understanding the Acceptance of Mobile SMS Advertising among Young Chinese Consumers. Psychology & Marketing, Vol. 25, 8, pp. 787-805.

[77] Zineddin, A./Garvey, P. M./Pietrucha, M. T. (2005): Impact of Sign Orientation on On-Premise Commercial Signs. Journal of Transportation Engineering, Vol. 131, 1, pp. 11-17.

7 Combining Micro and Macro Data to Study Retailer Pricing in the Presence of State Dependence

Daniel Klapper, Humboldt University of Berlin, Germany

German Zenetti, Goethe University Frankfurt, Germany

Abstract

Consumers of repeat-purchase goods have a higher probability of choosing products that they have purchased in the past. This form of persistence or state dependence has emerged in scanner panel data for many product categories. Considering the existence of state dependence by firms is important for the better understanding of consumer purchase behavior and pricing. If state dependence is a function of loyalty, then firms may want to engage in strategic pricing to control the evolution of preferences. However, manufacturers and retailers have limited access to scanner panel data. In addition, scanner panel data are often not suitable for use in pricing decisions because they provide price information only for those items that a consumer has purchased in a particular store and on a certain day. In this paper, we will show how firms can use readily available store-level scanner data in combination with tracking data, which firms routinely collect, to estimate the impact of state dependence on consumer purchase behavior and determine the resulting effect on the pricing decisions of firms. We model demand using a flexible, random coefficient logit model for aggregated data that takes into account the heterogeneity of brand perceptions and customer responses to pricing and promotions. This model also accounts for the possibility that competing brands exhibit flexible substitution patterns. The results indicate that consumers may change their purchase behavior if they have recently purchased a particular brand. We then use the demand side estimates on the supply side to show how retailer pricing and profitability are affected if a retailer does or does not anticipate state dependence in predicting consumer purchase behavior.

Keywords

State Dependence, Aggregate Random Coefficient Logit Model (BLP), Micro and Macro Data.

7.1   Introduction

Consumers of repeat-purchase consumer goods have a higher probability of choosing products that they have purchased in the past. This form of persistence in consumer choice data has been labeled state dependence or inertia in choice data and was first documented by Frank (1962) and Massy (1966). In their seminal paper, Guadagni/Little (1983) showed that past purchase behavior helps explain and forecast purchase behavior using consumer panel data. Since 1983, numerous papers have included the effect of state dependence in brand choice models (e.g., Keane 1997; Seetharaman/Ainslie/Chintagunta 1999; Horsky/Misra/Nelson 2006; Dubé/Hitsch/Rossi/Vitorino 2008; Dubé/Hitsch/Rossi 2010).

The observation that past purchases and current choice probabilities are linked has also been criticized (e.g., Hausman/Taylor 1981); this relationship has been characterized as the result of unobserved heterogeneity in consumer preferences. However, Dubé et al. (2010) established state dependence in their data by comparing a variety of flexible model specifications that allow for heterogeneity patterns. In particular, these authors used a flexible, semiparametric heterogeneity specification that included a mixture of multivariate normal distributions. These authors estimated their choice model using a Bayesian Markov chain Monte Carlo algorithm to differentiate between state dependence and heterogeneity. These results, drawn from different choice data, indicate the influence of state dependence.

As indicated in Dubé et al. (2010), one common explanation for the empirical finding that past purchases or consumption alters the current utility of product consumption is that consumers face psychological switching costs when changing brands (additionally see Farrell/Klemperer 2007). This type of switching cost may encourage loyalty in the context of brand choice. An alternative explanation is that consumers may face search costs if they consider brands whose products they have not bought in the past. However, Dubé et al. (2010) show that display advertising, which reduces search costs, does not moderate the loyalty effect. Another explanation for state dependence is that consumer learning creates changes in choice probabilities over time. However, this explanation was not confirmed by Dubé et al. (2010).

Loyalty is a significant factor in both consumer purchase behavior and pricing by firms. If state dependence is due to loyalty, then firms may wish to engage in strategic pricing to control the evolution of preferences (additionally see Farrell/Klemperer 2007). A major factor that has limited the development of pricing strategies based on state dependence is that this procedure requires the access to consumer panel data. Firms or cooperative retailers cannot collect these data; rather, these data must be bought from independent market research companies. In addition, consumer panel data are now collected via in-home scanning from a large number of households. These households are typically scattered throughout the entire country and not clustered around certain stores. This scattering limits the value of consumer panel data with regard to pricing issues because the prices of the purchased products are reported by the panelists. Such self-reporting leads to possible reporting bias and does not indicate competitors' prices (additionally see Einav/Leitag/Nevo 2010). Because many retailers employ micro marketing, i.e. setting prices according to local factors such as disposable income, inferring competitors' prices from consumer panel data is not possible. Firms therefore prefer to use store-level scanner data. These data are often provided by retailers to their suppliers (manufacturers). One example is the Extranet for the drugstore "dm," which provides manufacturers access to information about the sales and marketing mix of dm's stores. A disadvantage of store-level scanner data is that they are aggregated across individual purchases. However, manufacturers and retailers typically collect additional information from representative samples of consumers on a regular basis. These data are often called tracking data and provide information about recent consumer purchases as well as consumer preferences and attitudes towards brands or advertising.

In this paper, we show how to use these two distinct data sources. We combine macro data (store-level scanner data) with micro data (tracking data) to study the impact of past purchases (state dependence) on consumer purchase behavior. Furthermore, we also study the implications of our findings for the pricing strategies of firms, examining the example of a retailer that maximizes its category profits. We model demand using a flexible, random-coefficient logit model for aggregated data that considers the heterogeneity of brand perceptions and responses to pricing and promotions. This model accounts for the possibility that competing brands exhibit flexible substitution patterns. These findings also indicate that consumers may change their purchase behavior if they have recently purchased a product of a particular brand.

The remainder of this paper is structured as follows. After presenting our modeling approach, we describe the data in detail. We then analyze the estimation results and impact of state dependence on pricing strategies. In particular, we show how retailer pricing and profitability are affected if the retailer accounts for state dependence as a factor in consumer purchase behavior.

7.2 Modeling Framework

Market

In this section, we outline our modeling framework. First, we introduce a demand model that explains the observed sales data. We then examine the supply side, which enables us to estimate marginal costs and compute equilibrium prices for an a priori defined form of competitive interaction among manufacturers and retailers.

Demand Side

Our demand model relies on the random coefficient choice model for aggregated data. This model was introduced by Berry/Levinsohn/Pakes (1995) and is commonly called the BLP model. Although the BLP model is estimated using aggregate data, it allows for heterogeneity in consumer preferences.

Berry et al. (1995) also showed how to address the endogeneity problem that arises when firms base their marketing decisions on expectations regarding consumer responses to these decisions.

In the BLP model consumers are assumed to be utility maximizers. Therefore, this model begins with a consumer utility function. The utility that consumer i, $i=1,...,I$, obtains from product j, $j=1,...,J_t$, at market t, $t=1,...,T$, can be expressed as the following (Nevo 2000b):

$$u_{ijt} = \alpha_i p_{jt} + x'_{jt}\beta_i + \xi_{jt} + \varepsilon_{ijt}$$

$$= [p_{jt}, x'_{jt}][\alpha, \beta']' + \xi_{jt} + [p_{jt}, x'_{jt}](\Pi D_i + \Lambda v_i) + \varepsilon_{ijt}$$

$$= \delta_{jt} + \mu_{ijt} + \varepsilon_{ijt},$$

where p_{jt} denotes the price, and x_{jt} represents the vector of all variables except for price (e.g., promotions). The market is defined with reference to the purchase occasion (i.e., the timing of the observation) and/or the geographical area or retailer. α and β measure the mean influence of price and non-price factors on the utility for consumer i. ξ_{jt} is an unobserved characteristic of product j in market t (ξ is also called demand shock), and ε_{ijt} is an extreme value error.

Unobserved, v_i, and observed, D_i, heterogeneity are included in the utility function. Under the assumption of a linear relationship, we can write the vector of random coefficients as the sum of a mean component and the deviation from the mean, measured using observed individual specific variables and a vector of error terms, $[\alpha_i, \beta'_i]' = [\alpha, \beta']' + (\Pi D_i + \Lambda v_i)$. Π contains the matrix parameters of observed individual specific variables D_i and is distributed according to $D_i \sim P_D(D)$. For the original BLP model (see Berry et al. 1995), the elements of the matrix D_i were obtained from the U.S. Current Population Survey (CPS). However, we possess access to tracking data for representative consumers in the ground coffee category for each period and can draw directly from this set of consumers.

Therefore, matrix D_i contains the micro data, which may generally vary not only by consumer, but also by market and/or brand. For example, D_i may contain information regarding which products were purchased recently by a consumer. For the sake of simplicity, the unobserved individual specific deviation from the mean parameter v_i is assumed to be independent of D_i (Nevo 2000b). In general, v_i could be distributed according to any distribution, but most often, the multivariate normal distribution is chosen (e.g., Nevo 2001, Sovinsky Goeree 2008; Albuquerque/Bronnenberg 2008; Gowrisankaran/Rysman 2009) Therefore, $v_i \sim N(0, I_K)$, so that the random coefficients are multivariate normal distributed with mean $[\alpha, \beta']$ and covariance matrix Σ. Thus, Λ denotes the lower triangular Cholesky factor of the covariance matrix (i.e., $\Sigma = \Lambda \cdot \Lambda'$). Next to the maximum extreme value-distributed error term ε_{ijt} of the logit model, which is usually independently and identically distributed, ξ_{jt} represents an unobserved demand shock. Unobserved product characteristics are considered by this variable; they are usually assumed to be known by consumers and used by firms to set prices.

Thus, the utility of product j in market t can be decomposed into the mean value, $\delta_{jt} \equiv [p_{jt}, x'_{jt}][\alpha, \beta']' + \xi_{jt}$, and the consumer-specific deviation from the mean, which is $\mu_{ijt} \equiv [p_{jt}, x'_{jt}](\Pi D_i + \Lambda v_i)$.

Given consumer utility and distributional assumptions, we can write the expected market share s_{jt} as

$$s_{jt} = E_{D,v}(s_{ijt}) = \int_D \int_v \frac{exp(\delta_{jt} + \mu_{ijt}(D_i, v_i))}{1 + \sum_{l=1}^{J_t} exp(\delta_{lt} + \mu_{ilt}(D_i, v_i))} \phi(v) dv \, dP_D(D), \qquad (7.1)$$

where $\phi(v)$ is the density of the standard normal distribution. In our estimation, we approximate the expected market shares in equation (7.1) using numerical integration. Therefore, we use draws from Halton sequences (e.g., Train 2000, Bhat 2000).

The price elasticity of demand can be derived in a straightforward manner. The price elasticity of the demand for product j with respect to the price of product k in market t is given as the following:

$$\eta_{jkt} = \frac{p_{kt}}{s_{jt}} \int_D \int_v \alpha_i s_{ijt}(1_{\{k=j\}} - s_{ikt}) \phi(v) dv \, dP_D(D), \qquad (7.2)$$

where $1_{\{A\}}$ denotes the indicator function, which is one if argument A is true and otherwise zero. Equation (7.2) shows that computing price elasticities is equivalent to averaging individual price sensitivities and weighing them using individual choice probabilities. In this manner, the model captures how individual consumer preferences influence individual choices and create more flexible substitution patterns than in the homogenous aggregate logit model (Nevo 2000b). For example, the model reflects that a price-sensitive consumer will substitute higher-priced products for lower-priced ones.

As is commonly performed (Berry et al. 1995), we used the generalized method of moment (GMM) technique to estimate the model. This estimation method does not require a distributional assumption regarding demand shock and will easily allow additional moment conditions to be considered (e.g., additional supply side moment conditions) (Nevo 2000a; Nevo 2000b; Sovinsky Goeree 2008).

If product prices are dependent on market shares, those prices are correlated with demand shock (ξ), and an endogeneity problem arises. To correct for endogeneity, many researchers use a set of valid instrumental variables in the estimation. These instrumental variables should be correlated with the endogenous variables and uncorrelated with the error term (ξ). For instance, the manufacturer costs associated with production can be used as instrumental variables for prices. (For a detailed discussion of the correct usage of instrumental variables in the BLP model, see Berry et al. 1995; Nevo 2001.)

If the error terms (ξ) are autocorrelated and/or exhibit heteroscedasticity and if the process is stationary, which indicates that the degree of autocorrelation is reasonable small, we can use a weighting matrix according to Newey/West (1987) in the estimation process.

The error terms are used to estimate a heteroscedasticity and autocorrelation correction term with a predefined lag. In general, practicing to set the lag to the smallest integer larger than or equal to $T^{1/4}$ is common (Greene 2003).

Supply Side

The goal of this research is not only to characterize demand and price elasticities but also to develop optimal pricing strategies given an a priori defined form of competitive interaction among firms. Therefore, a stance regarding the supply side must be taken. Using the BLP model in a repeat-purchase consumer goods market, we must make an explicit assumption regarding how manufacturers and retailers interact. We assume a manufacturer Stackelberg game in which the manufacturers sell their products to the retailers at wholesale prices. The manufacturers face Bertrand competition among one another and maximize their profits based on wholesale prices. The retailers act as local monopolists and maximize their category profits given wholesale prices. Manufacturers foresee what pricing retailers will select and include this information in their price setting mechanism. To facilitate the following discussion, we eliminate the index for markets t, $t=1,...,T$.

The profits of retailer r, $r=1,..,R$, that offers product set F^r is (see e.g., Villas-Boas 2007)

$$\Pi^r = \sum_{k \in F^r} (p_k - w_k - c_k^r) \cdot M \cdot s_k ,$$

where M is the total market size, p_k is the price that the consumer pays to retailer r, w_k represents the wholesale price and c_k^r denotes the marginal costs for the retailer. To determine the retailer profit-maximizing price, one must derive the first-order condition (FOC) of retailer r for product j. Detailed mathematical descriptions of the first-order conditions for retailers can be found in Villas-Boas/Zhao (2005) for cases in which the retailer acts as a local monopolist and in Villas-Boas (2007) for cases in which the retailer has competitors in that product category.

Manufacturer b, $b=1,...,B$, produces product set $F^{r,b}$ with marginal costs c_j^b and makes the following profit when the products are sold through retailer r:

$$\Pi^b = \sum_{k \in F^{b,r}} (w_k - c_j^b) \cdot M \cdot s_k$$

A manufacturer considers the effect of wholesale price w_k on each retail price (Villas-Boas 2007). Accounting for double marginalization (e.g., Cabral 2000), the FOC of the product j manufacturer can be used to determine the optimal wholesale price and manufacturer markup. Again, details can be found in Villas-Boas/Zhao (2005) or Villas-Boas (2007).

Given our assumptions about the competitive interactions among retailers and manufacturers, the optimal prices of product j can be expressed as the following:

$$p_j = m_j^b + m_j^r + c_j^b + c_j^r , \tag{7.3}$$

m_j^b is the manufacturer markup and m_j^r is the retailer markup for product j. Note that wholesale prices do not need to be observed; rather, they can be determined from cost estimates and from the manufacturer markup given the assumptions about the competitive interactions among retailers and manufacturers.

The marginal costs for manufacturers and retailers are not separately identified and must be subsumed into one measure of marginal costs. We then regress the prices minus the markup by manufacturers and retailers on a matrix ω of cost shifters,

$$p_j - m_j^b - m_j^r = \omega\gamma + \eta, \qquad (7.4)$$

where γ represents a parameter vector and η a mean zero error term. Again, the use of instrumental variables may be necessary because the prices included on the left hand side of the regression equation are likely to be set dependent on the error term η. Estimates of marginal cost are then obtained from $\omega\gamma$.

Equation (7.4) can be jointly estimated with the demand side estimation process, which creates parameter estimates with lower variance if both the demand side and the supply side are correctly specified (Wooldridge 2002). However, we follow Chintagunta/Nair (2011), who strongly recommend estimating demand without imposing parametric supply-side assumptions on the parameter estimation.

7.3   Data Description: Ground Coffee

We estimate the demand model using data from the ground coffee industry in Germany from the years 2000 and 2001. Our scanner data provide information about national representative weekly product sales at the store level in six major retail chains (i.e., Edeka, Markant, Metro, Rewe, Spar and Tengelmann). In the analyses, we focus on coffee from the seven largest ground coffee brands that sell 500-gram packages (i.e., Jacobs, Melitta, Dallmayr, Tchibo, Eduscho, Onko and Idee), which together represent approximately 95% of the ground coffee market. The sales of private labels (1.7 % market share) and minor brands (2.6% market share) are not considered in the analyses (Draganska/Klapper 2007). We define a market (i.e., a purchase occasion) as a particular retailer in a particular week and assume that retailers act as local monopolists.

The market share for each brand at each retailer is computed based on the potential customers who visit a retailer in a certain week (i.e., the market size). We therefore use weekly retailer revenues. Based on industry reports, total store revenues can be divided by the average checkout sum per outlet to compute the size of the market for a particular retailer in a particular week.

Table 7.1 provides an overview of average product prices, the percentage sold on sale and the inside-good market share and also indicates the market share of each brand.

An anonymous market research company conducted monthly face-to-face interviews with approximately 320 persons who constitute a representative sample of the target group of coffee consumers. From this tracking data, we use the information regarding whether the respondents recently purchased a product by a particular brand. This variable is denoted as *PurchRecent*. To match the monthly tracking data with the weekly information culled from the scanner data, we use exponential smoothing.

Table 7.1   Descriptive Overview

Brand	Inside Share	Market Share	Price	Promotion	PurchRecent
Jacobs	28.4	1.35	7.25	20.67	35.19
	(6)	(0.44)	(0.71)	(18.2)	(4)
Melitta	18.54	0.87	6.66	19.53	17.81
	(6)	(0.36)	(0.66)	(20)	(4.2)
Dallmayr	11.15	0.55	8.02	15.33	19.4
	(4.6)	(0.29)	(0.72)	(19.6)	(4.8)
Tchibo	19.46	0.76	8.36	11.6	24.4
	(4.1)	(0.33)	(0.79)	(0.1)	(0)
Eduscho	14.03	0.57	7.04	16.32	12.69
	(4.5)	(0.41)	(0.86)	(0.1)	(0)
Onko	6.26	0.36	6.53	17.89	4.38
	(3.8)	(0.62)	(1.65)	(0.2)	(0)
Idee	2.13	0.09	8.15	11.54	1.35
	(1.4)	(0.1)	(1.22)	(0.2)	(0)

Average inside shares, market shares, prices, percentage sold on sale
and recent purchases per brand. The standard deviations are in parentheses.

7.4 Demand Side Estimation Results

This section presents the estimation results for the demand side and indicates how including state dependence improves the model estimation. The results obtained using an aggregate random coefficient model without micro data are compared to those obtained when we include information about consumers' recent purchases.

The demand model incorporates the information from the MADAKOM store-level scanner data, the information from the tracking data and our assumption of a manufacturer Stackelberg game. Based on these assumptions, we conduct the demand estimation using pooled data; we assume that the marginal effect of prices and promotions is identical for consumers across the six retailers. However, we also include specific effects in the utility function to allow for brand and retailer influences on choice behavior. For example, buying Tchibo coffee at Edeka may be a very different experience from buying Tchibo coffee at Metro because of shelf allocation, display, etc. In addition, we include a dummy variable for the second year of our data to account for the general decrease in ground coffee consumption and for possible unobserved discrepancies between the two years. To account for the heterogenous responses of consumers to prices and promotions, we include random coefficients for the two parameters. Furthermore, we allow for random variation in the preference for inside goods (i.e., the ground coffee brands) versus outside goods. Because the joint influence of prices and promotions may trigger differential consumer responses, we also include an interaction effect for the random coefficients of prices and promotions.

To estimate the impact of state dependence on consumer purchase behavior, we use the tracking data and draw consumers from that data. Our measure of individual state dependence is the stated information for each period indicating whether a consumer recently purchased a product by a particular brand. Hence, combining the store-level scanner data (i.e., the macro data) with the tracking data (i.e., the micro data) allows us not only to account for unobserved heterogeneity in the data but also to account for observed heterogeneity. In our model setup, we interact the state dependence variable with an overall brand constant (in the first model), with prices (in the second model) and with promotions (in the third model). Comparing the values of the GMM objectives shows that the model in which state dependence is interacted with prices outperforms the other two models. Hence, only the results for this model are reported in the following.

Given our model setup, the utility that an individual customer, i, $i=1,...,I$, obtains from product j, $j=1,...,J_t$, in market t, $t=1,...,T$, at retailer h_t, $h_l=1,...,H$, is

$$u_{ijt} = \delta_{jt} + \mu_{ijt} + \varepsilon_{ijt} ,$$

where the mean influence is defined by

$$\delta_{jt} = \beta_{jh_t}\left(Brand_j \cdot Retailer_{h_t}\right) + \beta_{Year}(Year_t) + \beta(Promotion) + \alpha\left(Price_{jt}\right) + \xi_{jt}.$$

When we only account for unobserved heterogeneity (i.e., when we do not use the micro data), the deviation from the mean is defined as

$$\mu_{ijt} = \gamma_1 v_{1,i} + \gamma_2 v_{2,i}(Promotion_{jt}) + [\gamma_3 v_{3,i} + \gamma_4 v_{4,i}(Promotion_{jt})](Price_{jt})$$

When we do use the micro data, the deviation from the mean is defined as

$$\mu_{ijt} = \gamma_1 v_{1,i} + \gamma_2 v_{2,i}(Promotion_{jt})$$

$$+ [\gamma_3 v_{3,i} + \gamma_4 v_{4,i}(Promotion_{jt}) + \pi(PurchRecent_{ijt})](Price_{jt}).$$

Because of the endogeneity of prices, we must use instrumental variables. For this purpose, we use raw coffee cost data from the New York Stock Exchange[4]. Raw coffee costs can be regarded as almost exogenous for the German coffee industry given that the prices are set worldwide at the stock exchange. At the same time, raw coffee is the main ingredient of ground coffee products and is therefore the main driver of product prices. The instrumental variable is interacted with the dummy variables for the combinations of retailers and brands.

Table 7.2 shows the results obtained using the two models (i.e., the one without observed heterogeneity, the "Only Macro Data" model) and the one that considers state dependence, the "Micro and Macro Data" model. The results of the over-identification test (Hansen 1982) show that both models satisfy the orthogonality condition with respect to their instrumental variables and error terms (ξ). The model that employs the micro data outperforms the model that only accounts for unobserved heterogeneity; the former has a lower GMM objective value, and the difference between the objective values is significant according to the GMM distance test (e.g., Baum, Schaffer/Stillman 2002).

Table 7.2   Demand Side Parameter Estimates

Variable	Only Macro Data		Mirco and Macro Data	
	par	se	par	se
Manufacturer retailer constants				
Jacobs / Edeka	2.84	0.41	2.03	0.23
Melitta / Edeka	1.32	0.39	0.85	0.21
Dallmayr / Edeka	2.41	0.42	1.85	0.24
Tchibo / Edeka	3.59	0.44	2.85	0.26
Eduscho / Edeka	1.94	0.41	1.55	0.22
Onko / Edeka	0.53	0.38	0.31	0.20

[4] There are different contract prices available and they are highly correlated. Thus, we employ only the contract price that is most strongly correlated with price. Furthermore, the raw prices are adjusted using the exchange rate as well as the tax rate (i.e., 2.213 Euro/kilogram) and are corrected for a decrease in weight of 15% that occurs during the roasting process.

Variable	Only Macro Data		Mirco and Macro Data	
	par	se	par	se
Idee / Edeka	0.89	0.43	0.79	0.25
Jacobs / Markant	2.22	0.39	1.46	0.22
Melitta / Markant	1.03	0.38	0.57	0.20
Dallmayr / Markant	1.74	0.41	1.20	0.24
Tchibo / Markant	3.04	0.42	2.33	0.26
Eduscho / Markant	1.63	0.39	1.27	0.22
Onko / Markant	-0.08	0.37	-0.29	0.20
Idee / Markant	0.10	0.41	0.01	0.24
Jacobs / Metro	2.13	0.40	1.30	0.24
Melitta / Metro	0.98	0.39	0.50	0.22
Dallmayr / Metro	1.37	0.41	0.81	0.25
Tchibo / Metro	2.50	0.41	1.79	0.25
Eduscho / Metro	1.54	0.39	1.17	0.22
Onko / Metro	-0.37	0.38	-0.57	0.21
Idee / Metro	-0.17	0.40	-0.23	0.25
Jacobs / Rewe	1.76	0.38	0.96	0.23
Melitta / Rewe	0.76	0.38	0.29	0.22
Dallmayr / Rewe	1.03	0.40	0.47	0.25
Tchibo / Rewe	2.99	0.41	2.27	0.26
Eduscho / Rewe	1.20	0.38	0.84	0.22
Onko / Rewe	-0.33	0.36	-0.52	0.20
Idee / Rewe	-0.06	0.40	-0.09	0.25
Jacobs / Spar	1.32	0.38	0.49	0.24
Melitta / Spar	0.09	0.37	-0.39	0.22
Dallmayr / Spar	1.23	0.39	0.64	0.26
Tchibo / Spar	2.11	0.39	1.42	0.26
Eduscho / Spar	0.38	0.37	0.03	0.22
Onko / Spar	-1.34	0.36	-1.53	0.21
Idee / Spar	-0.31	0.39	-0.30	0.26

Variable	Only Macro Data		Mirco and Macro Data	
	par	se	par	se
Jacobs / Tengelmann	2.81	0.40	1.99	0.23
Melitta / Tengelmann	2.09	0.38	1.62	0.21
Dallmayr / Tengelmann	2.50	0.41	1.95	0.25
Tchibo / Tengelmann	3.18	0.43	2.44	0.26
Eduscho / Tengelmann	1.48	0.40	1.10	0.22
Onko / Tengelmann	-2.18	0.40	-2.36	0.23
Idee / Tengelmann	0.58	0.42	0.51	0.25
Year Dummy	-0.30	0.02	-0.29	0.02
Promotion	1.82	0.24	1.85	0.19
Price	-1.03	0.08	-0.99	0.04
Unobserved heterogeneity				
STD Constant	0.03	0.64	0.07	0.16
STD Promotion	1.92	0.07	1.94	0.07
Cov Promotion and Price	-0.25	0.02	-0.23	0.02
STD Price	0.17	0.01	0.12	0.01
Past behavior				
Purchased recently * Price			0.20	0.02
Over id test	114.85		108.11	
Chisq	144.35		143.25	

Parameter estimates and standard errors for the model
with micro and macro data and for the model with only macro data.

The interpretation of the parameter estimates uses only the best fitting model; however, to analyze the price elasticities, we use both models. The brand constants across the six retailers show that consumers value Tchibo the most on average, followed by Jacobs and Dallmayr. Across all retailers, the valuation of Onko and Idee is lower than that of the other five brands. This observation is consistent with the mean market shares and prices of the brands. The comparison of the retailer constants reveals that these brands are also valued differently across retailers.

Hence, it seems that consumers have a different purchase experience when they buy a particular brand at a particular retailer. The retailer constants also indicate that Tengelmann and Edeka seem to be more capable in selling ground coffee.

The estimate of the year dummy shows that the overall preference for ground coffee is declining. These results are consistent with the store-level scanner data. Consumers react positively to promotions and negatively to prices. The parameter estimates for observed and unobserved heterogeneity indicate that consumer valuations of inside goods do not vary significantly. We include brand- and retailer-specific constants in our model that absorb a significant amount of the heterogeneity in the data. However, valuations of promotions and prices significantly vary across consumers. There are some consumers who are more promotion sensitive than others and some who are more price sensitive than others. The parameter estimate for the covariance effect of prices and promotions shows that consumers are more price sensitive during promotional periods.

The effect of prices on consumer utility and market shares is reflected in the price elasticity estimates. We now compare the price elasticities obtained from the model using only macro data to those obtained from the model that uses micro and macro data. **Table 7.3** and **Table 7.4** show the direct price elasticities and cross-price elasticities derived from the two model specifications. The price elasticities are significantly different. The inclusion of state dependence in the utility function reduces the parameter estimate for the price coefficient. These estimation results are consistent with findings reported in other research (e.g., Dubé et al. 2010, Horsky et al. 2006, Fader 1993, Erdem/Keane 1996). The smaller price coefficient obtained using the "Micro and Macro Data" model leads to larger direct price elasticities and smaller cross-price elasticities. Accounting for state dependence shows that the response of consumers to prices and price changes is less pronounced. This makes sense because current purchases are driven not only by general brand preferences and brand prices, but also by consumer experience with recently purchased products by particular brands. However, cross price elasticity estimates also decline, indicating that consumers with experience with a particular brand respond less to the prices of competing brands. The estimation results show that manufacturers and retailers can benefit from consumers' tendency to continue to purchase items by a particular brand. However, the cross-price elasticities also reveal that it is more difficult to attract consumers who have recently purchased an item by a competing brand. In addition, the differences in direct price elasticities and cross-price elasticities also reveal that firms' pricing strategies are affected even if they do not take into account the dynamic effect of state dependence in making their pricing decision. Firms that base their pricing strategies on elasticity data derived from the "Micro and Macro Data" model will set higher prices than will firms relying solely on macro data.

Table 7.3   Price Elasticities of Demand From the Model "Only Macro Data"

Brand	Jacobs	Melitta	Dallmayr	Tchibo	Eduscho	Onko	Idee
Jacobs	-6.292	0.134	0.149	0.152	0.139	0.133	0.149
	(0.452)	(0.093)	(0.089)	(0.084)	(0.088)	(0.101)	(0.084)
Melitta	0.071	-5.916	0.076	0.077	0.071	0.062	0.077
	(0.053)	(0.362)	(0.055)	(0.051)	(0.051)	(0.052)	(0.054)
Dallmayr	0.058	0.055	-6.785	0.066	0.058	0.053	0.066
	(0.045)	(0.041)	(0.364)	(0.044)	(0.042)	(0.044)	(0.047)
Tchibo	0.116	0.109	0.133	-6.887	0.118	0.109	0.141
	(0.055)	(0.052)	(0.059)	(0.304)	(0.055)	(0.055)	(0.062)
Eduscho	0.060	0.057	0.065	0.070	-6.184	0.059	0.068
	(0.030)	(0.030)	(0.030)	(0.033)	(0.310)	(0.032)	(0.032)
Onko	0.023	0.021	0.023	0.022	0.021	-5.846	0.022
	(0.022)	(0.020)	(0.020)	(0.017)	(0.020)	(0.474)	(0.017)
Idee	0.010	0.010	0.012	0.012	0.010	0.010	-6.871
	(0.010)	(0.010)	(0.010)	(0.010)	(0.010)	(0.010)	(0.285)

Direct price elasticity and cross-price elasticity of demand. The empirical standard
errors are in parentheses. The cells contain the percentage change in the market share
of the brand in a particular row according to a one percent change in the price of the brand
in a particular column.

Table 7.4   Price Elasticities of Demand From the Model "Only Macro Data"

Brand	Jacobs	Melitta	Dallmayr	Tchibo	Eduscho	Onko	Idee
Jacobs	-5.520	0.083	0.087	0.077	0.087	0.093	0.100
	(0.405)	(0.062)	(0.059)	(0.046)	(0.058)	(0.076)	(0.060)
Melitta	0.042	-5.472	0.048	0.043	0.048	0.046	0.055
	(0.032)	(0.418)	(0.037)	(0.032)	(0.036)	(0.040)	(0.040)
Dallmayr	0.033	0.035	-6.282	0.034	0.037	0.036	0.044
	(0.026)	(0.028)	(0.416)	(0.024)	(0.028)	(0.032)	(0.033)

Brand	Jacobs	Melitta	Dallmayr	Tchibo	Eduscho	Onko	Idee
Tchibo	0.056	0.063	0.069	-6.223	0.072	0.071	0.087
	(0.026)	(0.030)	(0.032)	(0.333)	(0.035)	(0.036)	(0.040)
Eduscho	0.034	0.037	0.039	0.040	-5.901	0.042	0.046
	(0.017)	(0.020)	(0.020)	(0.020)	(0.322)	(0.022)	(0.022)
Onko	0.015	0.015	0.015	0.013	0.015	-5.794	0.016
	(0.017)	(0.014)	(0.014)	(0.010)	(0.014)	(0.566)	(0.014)
Idee	0.006	0.006	0.007	0.007	0.007	0.007	-7.160
	(0.000)	(0.000)	(0.000)	(0.000)	(0.000)	(0.000)	(0.339)

See the description for the table above.

7.5   The Impact of State Dependence on Retailer Pricing

The effect of state dependence on retailer pricing is studied in a two-period dynamic game. In one case, the retailer does not include the dynamic effect of prices in its pricing decision; in the other case, the retailer accounts for the cross-period effect of prices via state dependence. Because of the cross-period effects, we have to endogenize *PurchRecent*. That is, we must assess how consumer recent purchases, as indicated by the tracking data, are related to the market shares of particular brands in an equilibrium model in which prices and purchase behavior are the outcome of the underlying preferences of the consumers and of the equilibrium assumptions regarding competition. To do this, we regress the average weekly values for recent purchases on the one-period-lagged average market shares using logistic regression. To capture the non-linear effects of the lagged market shares on recent purchases, we also include the squared lagged market shares and the semi-log of the lagged market shares as regressors. The adjusted R^2 of the logistic regression is approximately 0.75, and the corresponding parameter estimates are significant and show how recent consumer purchases can be linked to observed market shares. These parameter estimates are used to update the recent purchase information in our equilibrium model. Hence, we simultaneously compute the equilibrium prices, market shares and recent purchases given the demand and supply model and the model that relates recent purchases to market shares.

In addition, we require an estimate of marginal costs. We use the demand parameter estimates from the "Only Macro Data" model and simultaneously solve equations (7.1) and (7.3) using the predictions of equation (7.4) to estimate the marginal costs. When we estimate marginal costs, we account for the fact that Jacobs and Onko are owned by the same manufacturer and that Tchibo and Eduscho are owned by the same manufacturer. Our cost shifters are retailer-brand interactions and a linear trend variable for the different weeks in our data sample. The dependent variable in the regression (7.4) is log transformed to ensure positive marginal costs.

Table 7.5   Average Equilibrium Results Without Consideration of State Dependence

Brand	Jacobs	Melitta	Dallmayr	Tchibo	Eduscho	Onko	Idee
Ret markup in t1	1.07	1.12	1.18	1.17	1.16	1.07	1.31
Ret markup in t2	1.07	1.12	1.18	1.17	1.16	1.07	1.31
Price in t1	7.25	6.66	8.02	8.36	7.04	6.47	8.15
Price in t2	7.25	6.66	8.02	8.36	7.04	6.47	8.15
Market share in t1	0.85	0.48	0.29	0.53	0.42	0.17	0.05
Market share in t2	0.78	0.45	0.27	0.45	0.38	0.19	0.05
Profit in t1	121.46	65.09	41.93	89.57	70.76	32.67	9.34
Profit in t2	110.71	60.48	39.37	76.63	63.17	35.07	9.31

Average equilibrium results across retailers who do not include the effect of state-dependence in their pricing shown for the retailer markups, prices, market shares and retailer profits (in tsd. Euros).

The equilibrium results obtained using the procedure outlined above for the case in which the retailer does not include the effect of state dependence in its pricing are shown in **Table 7.5**. This table reports average market shares, prices, retailer markups and estimated profits for each of the seven brands across the six retailers for the two consecutive periods. Hence, we only report the average outcome across retailers for each brand. Based on our equilibrium assumptions, it is possible to verify that the retailer sets an identical margin between 1.07 and 1.31 Euros for each brand in the two periods. This results in weekly prices between 6.66 and 8.36. The corresponding market shares range from 0.05 to 0.85, and the average per-period profits are between 8,480 and 104,770 Euros. It is important to note that these equilibrium results are based on the assumption that the retailer does not include the dynamic effect of prices on consumer purchase behavior or the effect of state dependence in its pricing. Hence, a retailer optimizes its profit using the demand parameters from the model that does not include observed heterogeneity (i.e., that does not use the "Micro and

Macro Data" model). However, true demand is determined under the correct model, which includes the cross-period effects of state dependence on utility.

We now contrast the results achieved assuming myopic price setting by retailers with those achieved when the retailer includes the effect of state dependence in its pricing using the parameter estimates from the "Micro and Macro Data" model. The estimation results from the previous section reveal that consumers are less price sensitive when evaluating brands that they have recently purchased. The retailer now includes the cross-period effect of prices and past purchases in setting prices. The dynamic game for the two periods can be solved using a very simple version of finite horizon dynamic programming in which optimal prices are calculated via backward induction (Rust 1996). For a given new market share in period one, we predict the new mean values of *PurchRecent* using the parameter estimates from the logistic regression as outlined above. Then we randomly sample consumers for period two and assign stated purchases and stated non-purchases until the new mean values are close to the predicted new mean values.

Table 7.6   Average Equilibrium Results with Consideration of State Dependence

Brand	Jacobs	Melitta	Dallmayr	Tchibo	Eduscho	Onko	Idee
Ret markup in t1	1.21	1.14	1.15	1.25	1.15	1.09	1.25
Ret markup in t2	1.25	1.16	1.23	1.26	1.17	1.17	1.19
Price in t1	7.39	6.67	7.98	8.44	7.03	6.37	8.09
Price in t2	7.42	6.69	8.06	8.45	7.04	6.63	8.03
Market share in t1	0.77	0.47	0.3	0.5	0.43	0.19	0.06
Market share in t2	0.67	0.43	0.26	0.43	0.38	0.19	0.06
Profit in t1	122.5	65.15	41.92	89.79	70.85	32.83	9.38
Profit in t2	110.78	60.53	39.64	79.53	63.48	35.66	9.42

Average equilibrium results across retailers who include the effect of state dependence in their pricing; retailer markup, prices, market share and retailer profits (in tsd. Euros).

In general, we expect prices in the dynamic case to be higher because the true price sensitivities are smaller, but we also expect that the prices in period one will be lower than those in period two. Because retailers may 'invest' in loyalty in the first period (state dependence) by lowering retail prices, they should charge higher prices in the second period, as this will allow them to profit from less price-elastic consumers during that period.

The equilibrium outcomes for the two-period case are presented in **Table 7.6**. The results show that the retailers adjust their pricing according to the cross-period effect of state dependence. Now a retailer sets different markup levels in the two periods; they range from 1.09 to 1.26 Euros for each brand. The differences between the markup levels in the two consecutive periods are generally small across all brands. However, they yield different prices in both periods, which again create different market shares. The estimation results also show that the retailers exploit the cross-period effect of prices. Retailers earn higher profits in both periods than when acting myopically. The differences in profits shown in **Table 7.5** extend as high as 3.78 percent for Tchibo in the second period. These are small differences; however, they translate to large absolute profit differences if we look not only at the two periods but also at a longer time horizon. Even in this simple setting in which retailers optimize prices only across two consecutive periods, taking into account state dependence can increase retailer profits.

7.6   Conclusions

In this paper, we have shown how the effect of state dependence can be included in the estimation of an aggregate random coefficient logit model. The existence of state dependence is important not only to consumer purchase behavior but also to pricing by firms. Our modeling approach combines macro and micro data. Macro data provide information about a brand's sales, prices and promotions. We extract the micro data from tracking data for monthly repeated samples of consumers. These consumers have been interviewed regarding their product experiences, images and preferences. Using both data sources enables us to investigate the impact of state dependence on sales via aggregate data and to identify the consequences for pricing strategies. Our empirical estimation results show that accounting for state dependence yields lower estimated price elasticities. Consumers are less price sensitive but also respond less to competitor prices. This finding has implications for firms' pricing strategies. To illustrate the retailer pricing problem, we use a manufacturer Stackelberg game to show that retailers should charge higher prices if they account for the cross-period effect of state dependence. Our example over two periods also shows that to ensure optimal pricing, a retailer should charge lower prices in the first period than in the second period. Considering state dependence leads retailers to invest in market share by offering lower prices; using these tactics pays off in future periods. In further research, we will investigate the effects of state dependence on firm pricing and consumer purchase decisions in an infinite horizon game. We will thereby study the impact of state dependence on manufacturer and retailer pricing and the interaction between manufacturer and retailer prices.

Literature

[1] Albuquerque, P./Bronnenberg, B. J. (2008): Market Areas of Car Dealerships.

[2] Baum, C. F./Schaffer, M. E./Stillman, S. (2002): Instrumental Variables and GMM: Estimation and Testing, Boston College Economics Working Paper 545.

[3] Berry, S. T./Levinsohn, J./Pakes, A. (1995): Automobile Prices in Market Equilibrium, Econometrica, Vol. 63, 4, pp. 841-890.

[4] Bhat, C. R. (2000): Quasi-random Maximum Simulated Likelihood Estimation of the Mixed Logit Model, Transportation Research Part B, 35, pp. 677-693.

[5] Cabral, L. M. B. (2000): Introduction to Industrial Organization, MIT Press, Cambridge.

[6] Chintagunta, P. K./Nair, H. S. (2011): Discrete-choice Models of Consumer Demand in Marketing.

[7] Draganska, M./Klapper, D. (2007): Retail Environment and Manufacturer Competitive Intensity, Journal of Retailing, Vol. 83, 2, pp. 183-198.

[8] Dubé, J.-P./Hitsch, G. J./Rossi, P. E. (2010): State Dependence and Alternative Explanations for Consumer Inertia, RAND Journal of Economics, Vol. 41, 3, pp. 417-445.

[9] Dubé, J.-P./Hitsch, G. J./Rossi, P. E./Vitorino, M. A. (2008): Category Pricing with State-dependent Utility, Marketing Science, Vol. 27, 3, pp. 417-429.

[10] Einav, L./Leitag, E./Nevo, A. (2010): Recording Discrepancies in Nielsen Homescan Data, Are they present and do they matter?, Quantitative Marketing and Economics, Vol. 8, 2, pp. 207-239. 25

[11] Erdem, T./Keane, M. P. (1996): Decision-making under Uncertainty: Capturing Dynamic Brand Choice Processes in turbulent Consumer Goods Markets, Marketing Science, Vol. 15, 1, pp. 1-20.

[12] Fader, P. S. (1993): Integrating the Dirichlet-multinomial and Multinomial Logit Models of Brand Choice, Marketing Letters, Vol. 4, 2, pp. 99-112.

[13] Farrell, J./Klemperer, P. (2007): Chapter 31 Coordination and Lock-in: Competition with Switching Costs and Network Effects, Vol. 3 of Handbook of Industrial Organization, Elsevier, pp. 1967 - 2072.

[14] Frank, R. E. (1962): Brand Choice as a Probability Process, The Journal of Business, Vol. 35, 1, pp. 43-56.

[15] Gowrisankaran, G./Rysman, M. (2009): Dynamics of Consumer Demand for New Durable Goods. Working Paper.

[16] Greene, W. H. (2003): Econometric analysis, Prentice Hall, Upper Saddle River.

[17] Guadagni, P. M./Little, J. D. C. (1983): A Logit Model of Brand Choice Calibrated on Scanner Data, Marketing Science, Vol. 2, 3, pp. 203-238.

[18] Hansen, L. (1982): Large Sample Properties of Generalized Method of Moments Estimators, Econometrica, Vol. 50, 3, pp. 1029-1054.

[19] Hausman, J. A./Taylor, W. E. (1981): Panel Data and unobservable individual Effects, Journal of Marketing Research, Vol. 49, 6, pp. 1377-1398.

[20] Horsky, D./Misra, S./Nelson, P. (2006): Observed and unobserved Preference Heterogeneity in Brand-choice Models, Marketing Science, Vol. 25, 4, pp. 322-335.

[21] Keane, M. P. (1997): Modeling Heterogeneity and State Dependence in Consumer Choice Behavior, Journal of Business and Economic Statistics, Vol. 15, 3, pp. 310-327.

[22] Massy, W. F. (1966): Order and Homogeneity of Family specific Brand-switching Processes, Journal of Marketing Research, Vol. 3, 1, pp. 48-54.

[23] Nevo, A. (2000a): Mergers with Differentiated Products: The Case of the Ready-to-eat Cereal Industry, RAND Journal of Economics, Vol. 31, 3, pp. 395-421.

[24] Nevo, A. (2000b): A practitioner's Guide to Estimation of Random Coefficients Logit Models of demand, Journal of Economics & Management Strategy, Vol. 9, 4, pp. 513-538.

[25] Nevo, A. (2001): Measuring Market Power in the Ready-to-eat Cereal Industry, Econometrica, Vol. 69, 2, pp. 307-342.

[26] Newey, W. K./West, K. D. (1987): A Simple, Positive Semi-definite, Heteroskedasticity and Autocorrelation Consistent Covariance Matrix, Econometrica, Vol. 55, 3, pp. 703-708.

[27] Rust, J. (1996): Handbook of economics - chapter 14: Numerical Dynamic Programming in Economics, in H. M. Amman, D. A. Kendrick & J. Rust (eds), Handbook of Computational Economics, Vol. 1, Elsevier Science B.V., pp. 619-729.

[28] Seetharaman, P. B./Ainslie, A./Chintagunta, P. K. (1999): Investigating Household State Dependence Effects across Categories, Journal of Marketing Research, Vol. 36, 4, pp. 488-500.

[29] Sovinsky Goeree, M. (2008): Limited Information and Advertising in the U.S. Personal Computer Industry, Econometrica, Vol. 76, 5, pp. 1017-1074.

[30] Train, K. E. (2000). Halton Sequences for Mixed Logit, Working paper, Department of Economics, University of California, Berkley 27.

[31] Villas-Boas, J. M./Zhao, Y. (2005): Retailer, Manufacturers, and individual Customers: Modeling the Supply-side in the Ketchup Marketplace, Journal of Marketing Research 42, pp. 83-95.

[32] Villas-Boas, S. B. (2007): Vertical Relationships between Manufacturers and Retailers: Inference with Limited Data, Review of Economic Studies 74, pp. 625-652.

[33] Wooldridge, J. M. (2002): Econometric Analysis of Cross Section and Panel Pata, MIT Press.

8 Service Satisfaction With Premium Durables: A Cross-Cultural Investigation

Michael Löffler, Dr. Ing. h. c. F. Porsche AG, Germany

Reinhold Decker, University of Bielefeld, Germany

Abstract

In premium durable markets post-purchase contacts between customers and dealers are typically sparse, making each after sales contact a valuable opportunity to build-up and ensure customer satisfaction and loyalty. Customer loyalization becomes increasingly difficult due to extended service intervals and increasing price competition in basic technical support. The identification of cross-culturally mattering drivers of customer service satisfaction in after sales business is therefore an issue of increasing importance.

Based on a sophisticated customer survey differences of service quality perception and underlying triggers are analyzed. The study contrasts individualistic with collectivistic cultural contexts and empirically substantiates nonlinearity of satisfaction triggers in the case of premium durables. We show that individualistic and collectivistic backgrounds may reveal significant differences regarding important triggers of service satisfaction (e.g. explanation of work done), whereas brand sympathy over-proportionally triggers service satisfaction across cultures. The knowledge of internationally counting after sales service satisfaction triggers and nonlinearity of effects allows for optimizing global process standards, focusing the training of service personnel on aspects that really count, as well as planning of effective marketing activities.

Keywords

Service Satisfaction, Brand Sympathy, Cross-Cultural Study, Premium Durables, Nonlinear Brand Effect.

8.1   Introduction

8.1.1   Ongoing Interest in Satisfaction Research and Existing Gaps

Already decades ago, Churchill/Surprenant (1982, p. 491) reported that "since the early 1970s the volume of consumer satisfaction research has been impressive". Since then, customer satisfaction has developed into a pivotal issue of modern marketing literature and represents a key element of today's marketing theory and practice. Comprehensive overviews of current research results on customer satisfaction are, among others, provided by Zhang et al. (2008) as well as Homburg and Luo (2007). Or to put it in the words of Fournier and Mick (1999, p. 5): "Thorough summaries and critiques of the marketing satisfaction literature exist [...] and need not be duplicated here".

However, highlighting some of the remaining research directions provides an opportunity to ignite further discussions. Particularly thorough and more systematic approaches in cross-cultural service satisfaction research are a common suggestion. Zhang et al. (2008), for instance, focus on aspects like country selection, the comparability of questionnaires and survey instruments as well as the service context.

Regarding multi-cultural studies, focusing on countries with more distinct dissimilarities are a further requirement. Johnsson et al. (2002, p. 767) compare customer satisfaction among different industries, but limit themselves to Sweden, Germany and the USA which are considered "relatively similar". Accordingly, they suggest that research should be directed to more dissimilar countries.

Identifying satisfaction drivers that matter internationally is a frequent suggestion for empirical research. To "understand the relevant service quality dimensions [...] that could reinforce positive customer satisfaction assessments" and, therefore, identifying relevant triggers of service satisfaction was also highlighted by Olorunniwo et al. (2006, p. 68). A related facet is the empirical coverage of other, i.e. still under-researched service areas and the identification of specific quality issues usually affecting other service sectors (Sultan and Simpson, 2000).

8.1.2   After Sales Services as a Challenge to Customer Satisfaction With Premium Durables

According to the research suggestions above, premium durables in an international context are an area which is still less thoroughly investigated but proves to be highly interesting for several reasons:

First, during the ownership period of durables, main service interactions and customers' brand/product experiences typically arise after the purchase or sales act. For durables like homes, cars or premium watches the ownership period typically exceeds the period of product evaluation and purchase by far. Focusing on after sales services therefore puts a spotlight on the predominant type of customer/dealer and/or manufacturer touch points. However, empirical research on consumer experiences is still limited in the area of luxury or premium brands according to the extensive literature review by Bauer et al. (2011, p. 59).

Second, after sales services are developing more and more into a main source of revenues in many product categories. Wise/Baumgartner (1999) and, more recently, Cohen et al. (2006) illustrate this for industries like automotive, consumer electronics and home appliances. Here, the after sales service market has become four to five times the size of the corresponding original equipment business. This clearly supports Loomba (1996, p. 4) who argues that "after-sales customer service […] is now being recognized as an important research priority".

Third, premium brands typically harmonize international sales, service and architectural standards. This standardized environment allows focusing on cultural context effects of service satisfaction while limiting (potentially) biasing differences in the service context. Just to mention an example in the field of premium electronic durables: Apple stores in New York, Munich and Tokyo echo in the exterior (e.g., shiny logo, facade with large-scale glass elements) as well as in the interior (e.g., furnishing with wooden tables).

Last but not least, technological changes and developing customer trends have changed and will further influence the after sales services sector. So, for example, the shift towards digital photography has changed the corresponding business model of after sales services fundamentally (developing photos, offering online photo albums, etc.). The trend towards electric cars and e-mobility heavily affects after sales services in the car industry (e.g., to change oil, clutches or spark plugs becomes obsolete for electric vehicles, severely impacting the main sources of after sales revenues).

8.1.3   Focus of This Study

The article empirically analyzes international differences in satisfaction drivers and puts special emphasis on those triggers that count internationally: What are the core aspects of service satisfaction, irrespective of cultural dissimilarities? What makes the difference between satisfied and unsatisfied customers beyond country-specific characteristics?

The underlying study is based on a sophisticated large scale survey in the USA and Japan. Design and implementation of the study followed the above mentioned research suggestions, while the focus was broadened by including the impact of brand sympathy. To the best of our knowledge, this is the first cross-cultural study for high-end premium durables based on real customer data and real service occasions. Furthermore, it explicitly studies the context effects of individualistic and collectivistic countries. Discriminating between these two types of cultures enables more general implications regarding existing response patterns and directly corresponds with the relevant discussions in international marketing (e.g., Oyserman et al. (2002) for a comprehensive discussion of individualism and collectivism and their implications for cross-cultural research).

Based on behavioral theories, the nonlinear influence of brand sympathy on service satisfaction is investigated by means of regression analysis. A comprehensive understanding of intercultural differences of satisfaction drivers is enabled by a systematic selection of variables that potentially affect consumers' overall service satisfaction.

8.2   Development of Research Hypotheses

Following the comprehensive review by Zhang et al. (2008) culture influences customers' perception of service. While not intending to paraphrase the research already existing, selected studies are briefly recapitulated to illustrate the rationale behind our hypotheses for the less thoroughly researched area of premium durables.

8.2.1   Hypotheses on Cultural Contexts and Their Impact on Customer Satisfaction

Customers judge services differently depending on the cultural context. Japan and the USA are typically rated very dissimilar in this respect: Japan is a prototypically collectivistic and high-context country: meaning is more implicit and assessments are mostly less extreme. The USA is usually classified as an individualistic, low-context country: communication is more direct, less related to social contexts and response to products and services is more explicit (Ueltschy et al., 2007; Sultan/Simpson, 2000). The special relevance of comparisons between America and Japan has already been emphasized by Oyserman et al. (2002) and hence reflected in an intensive discussion of this pair of countries.

In a recent study on the role of total quality management (TQM) regarding the enhancement of customer satisfaction Mehra/Ranganathan (2008, p. 918) investigated the hypothesis "The impact of a TQM program on customer satisfaction will be the same across individualistic and collectivistic cultures." The validity of this assumption was confirmed by means of a comprehensive meta-analytical study.

Satisfaction levels are found to be higher in the "individualistic" USA (Johnson et al., 2002). Lewis (1991) also found that US customers rate more extremely than European customers. Different service perceptions of US and European customers are also empirically confirmed by Sultan/Simpson (2000). However, none of these studies consider the case of premium durables. Therefore the following hypothesis for premium durables is worth testing:

H1: Customer satisfaction concerning internationally standardized services significantly differs across countries, where satisfaction levels are

- higher in individualistic countries (like the USA) and
- lower in collectivistic countries (like Japan).

Basically, what really counts with respect to the fulfillment of customer service expectations presumably differs across borders. However, similar triggers of service satisfaction may exist internationally: for durables the brief review of international studies in the automotive area in **Table 8.1** highlights some of them. "Personal interaction" and "thoroughness of work performed" are among the aspects being mentioned in nearly every study.

Accordingly, our second hypothesis focuses on the existence of global performance triggers of premium durables, irrespective of differing cultural contexts:

H2: There is a core set of satisfaction triggers that impacts overall satisfaction perception internationally both in individualistic and collectivistic countries.

Although **Table 8.1** would allow hypothesizing on international satisfaction triggers, we are going to develop the gross set of triggers more thoroughly in Subsection 8.3.2 (see "item selection"). This more properly reflects the premium segment focused on in this article, as **Table 8.1** is based on general studies that potentially do not reveal the characteristics of the premium segment.

Hypothesis 2 directly continues the recent research by Bauer et al. (2011, p. 66) and follows their research suggestions ("How do consumers, for instance, perceive luxurious services [...]? What characterizes them, what are the common denominators?"). The empirical confirmation or rejection of H2 also corresponds with the research recommendation by Zhang et al. (2008, p. 222) requiring the enrichment of "our current understanding of variations, as well as commonalities of consumers' service experiences across cultures."

8.2.2   Hypotheses on Brand Sympathy and Its Impact on Customer Satisfaction

Brand and associated expectations are reported as important antecedents of customer service perception and evaluation (Vargo et al., 2007). According to the theoretical considerations by Burmann et al. (2009, p. 394) brand sympathy is "a measure of the level of positive brand perception" and "highly relevant, since it indicates the interaction between brand identity and brand image". Büschken (2007) points out that brand sympathy captures elements of the potential buyer's affective reaction to a brand and, with a view to the empirical study reported in this paper, he explicitly rates the relevance of brand sympathy in the car industry as obvious.

Löffler (2002) shows that variations of this feature across countries particularly emerges in the automotive sector. But cultural differences may also moderate the impact of brand names on service quality evaluation (Malai and Speece, 2005). The respective effects may be nonlinear as indicated by Vargo et al. (2007) or inversely s-shaped according to Homburg et al. (2005). This leads us to the last pair of hypotheses:

H3: Brand sympathy is one of the most important factors of cross-national service satisfaction, where importance levels are

- higher in individualistic countries (like the USA) and
- lower in collectivistic countries (like Japan).

H4: The impact of brand sympathy on overall satisfaction is nonlinear and country-specific in its magnitude and the type of nonlinearity.

Table 8.1   Selected Service Satisfaction Triggers in International Studies in the Automotive Area

Author(s)	Selected Key Triggers of Service Satisfaction	Country	Sample Size
Andaleeb/Basu (1994)	– Personal interaction – Value for money of service	USA	133
Bei/Chiao (2001)	– Product quality	Taiwan	495
Burmann (1991)	– Thoroughness of work performed – Empathy with the customer	Germany	6,000
Martilla/James (1977)	– Thoroughness of work performed – Personal interaction, complaint handling	USA	284

Author(s)	Selected Key Triggers of Service Satisfaction	Country	Sample Size
Mittal/Kumar/Tsiros (1999)	– Thoroughness of work performed – Perceived fairness	USA	100,040
Oliver/Swan (1989)	– Value for money of service – Personal interaction – Product quality	USA	184
Verhoef et al. (2007)	– Brand/make (studies differentiate between volume and premium brands) – Value for money of service	Nether-lands	922
Wöllenstein (1996)	– Handling of appointment booking – Flexibility to accommodate customer's schedule	Germany	n. a.

8.3   Methodology

8.3.1   The Premium Car Market as a Proxy for Premium Durable Markets

The after sales service sector in the premium car industry can serve as a prototype for many premium durable goods markets. The premium car industry is "one of the most advanced [industries] among the durable goods" (Gaiardelli et al., 2007, p. 702). The importance of this industry from a consumer's perspective is also reflected by its high share of personal consumption expenditures. So, in the after sales area, according to the U.S. Bureau of Economic Analysis (August 2008), expenditures on vehicle repairs totaled 224.2 billion US-\$ in 2007 and significantly exceeded corresponding figures for new vehicle (102.0 billion US-\$) and used vehicle purchases (56.5 billion US-\$). An extensive discussion of the premium car market as topic of marketing research and consumer behavior analysis can be found in Shcheglova (2009). Last but not least, and in line with Odekerken-Schröder et al. (2010, p. 373), this research focuses on premium cars since "consumers typically maintain strong relationships with premium cars", which, among others, makes after sales service an important component of overall brand perception.

8.3.2   Research Design

The research design considers recent suggestions by Zhang et al. (2008) as well as Smith/Reynolds (2001) on cross-cultural customer service research. These include, among others, (1) to carefully select the countries researched, (2) to address the problems related to selection of items questioned in different countries and (3) to control the service context.

■ Country selection

Customer satisfaction may be affected by a country's stage of economic development (Johnson et al., 2002). As this has not been the study's primary objective, the focus is on mature automotive markets. Within them, the largest markets have been selected that represent a prototypically individualistic and collectivistic culture, namely the USA and Japan respectively. These countries are well-suited for cross-cultural comparisons due to their cultural diversity (Ueltschy et al., 2007, p. 412). Focusing on a durable with internationally standardized processes and product/service offerings results in (close to) identical service context conditions across borders. Therefore, customers of a European manufacturer of sporty premium cars have been selected for the empirical investigation (details are provided below).

■ Item selection

In a first step, the gross set of items was derived by carefully collecting main triggers of service satisfaction based on a broad variety of related studies (see **Table 8.1**). A total of about 40 attributes proved potentially relevant, namely

- first contact (including "flexibility to accommodate your schedule", "handling of appointment booking", etc.),
- service initiation (including "waiting time when you dropped off the vehicle", "appearance of the dealership", etc.),
- vehicle pick-up (including "value for money of service", "explanation of work done", etc.),
- service delivery (including "thoroughness of maintenance/repair work performed", etc.) and
- experience with service personnel (including "courtesy/friendliness of the service personnel", "responsiveness of the service personnel to your requests/wishes", etc.).

In-depth discussions with market experts from the USA and Japan of the participating premium car manufacturer assured that "the construct is valid in all of the nations/cultures being considered" (Smith/Reynolds, 2001, p. 454).

In a second step the gross set of attributes was surveyed among customers in the USA and Japan in a pre-study. Additionally, correlation and factor analyses led to the final set of variables used in the main study: "handling of appointment booking", "flexibility to accommodate customer's schedule", "explanation of work done", "value for money", "thoroughness of work performed". In addition, ratings of "personal interaction" and "brand sympathy" were elicited as well as overall service satisfaction. As the manufacturer considered had implemented strict corporate identity guidelines in all mature markets and the dealerships are nearly all CI-compliant (including facilities, furnishing, etc. and encompassing the whole service area), attributes like "appearance of dealership" had not been included in the final set of attributes.

In a third step, the attributes finally selected had been cross-checked with established service satisfaction measurement approaches. Cross-checking was done in accordance with the contributions by Grönroos (1984) as well as Parasuraman et al. (1988). The model suggested by Philip/Hazlett (1997) was included for cross-checking due to its interesting hierarchical structure.

Table 8.2   Correspondence of Attributes Selected and Empirical Satisfaction Concepts

Attribute	... corresponds to ... in the study by ...		
	Grönroos (1984)	Parasuraman et al. (1988)	Philip/Hazlett (1997)
Brand sympathy	image	assurance	peripheral attributes
Handling of appointment booking	functional quality	responsiveness	core attribute
Flexibility to accommodate customer's schedule	functional quality	responsiveness	core attribute
Explanation of work done	technical quality, functional quality	responsiveness	pivotal attribute
Value for money of service	technical quality, functional quality	reliability	pivotal attribute
Thoroughness of work performed	technical quality	reliability	pivotal attribute
Personal interaction	functional quality	empathy	core attribute

Table 8.2 shows that the key dimensions typically used for measuring service quality are reflected in the study at hand (left column). The correspondence of some attributes selected to the attributes of the concepts referred to is not necessarily unambiguous and serves as an illustration only (cf. the original definition of SERVQUAL dimensions in Parasuraman et al. (1988, p. 23) and Philip/Hazlet (1997, p. 274)). The identifiers used in the subsequent analyses are underlined.

■ Control of context variables

Context variables can be controlled for the manufacturer and the product category surveyed: The ambience and processes of servicing are standardized and should not bias service satisfaction ratings. (Non-cultural) context variables are very similar, following the methodological suggestions by Winsted (1999) and Zhang et al. (2008).

■ Data collection

Customers who purchased a vehicle in the past 12 to 24 months prior to 2009 were surveyed during 2009. This reflects typical service patterns (the first main service not later than 12 months after purchase) and covers customers with at least one service occasion due to standard service intervals. The approach is similar to the one by Mittal/Kamakura (2001, p. 135) and also utilizes a 5-point Likert scale, ranging from 1 = "poor" to 5 = "excellent".[5] In total, 729 respondents participated in the survey (USA: 402; Japan: 327).

■ Reliability of data

Internal consistency was checked by means of Cronbach's alpha. The respective values are provided in **Table 8.3** and in line with figures reported, e.g., by Parasuraman et al. (1988) ($\alpha = 0.92$) as well as Cronin/Taylor (1992) ($\alpha = 0.90$). Furthermore, the Spearman-Brown split-half reliability coefficient is above 0.85 for all countries and thus further supports the impression of high reliability.

Table 8.3   Reliability Analysis of the Empirical Data

	USA	Japan
Cronbach's alpha	0.90	0.88
Spearman-Brown split-half reliability coefficient	0.88	0.87

8.4   Empirical Findings

8.4.1   Hypothesis H1 — Customer Satisfaction Rating

To empirically test our first hypothesis average satisfaction levels between countries have been checked by means of t-tests, revealing significant differences between the average satisfaction ratings in the USA and Japan ($p < 0.05$).

The result extends previous findings in the field of premium durables. Ueltschy et al. (2007[41]), e.g., report on different satisfaction levels depending on customers' cultural context and Sultan/Simpson (2000) empirically confirmed differences in satisfaction ratings of airline groups among US and European passengers. The product surveyed in our study (premium automobile) is close to identical across countries and the related service processes are highly standardized.

---

[5] Likert scales are "the dominant measurement method in both mono- and cross-cultural studies" (Smith/Reynolds, 2001, p. 451).

However, standardized services resulted in internationally significant different satisfaction ratings. Insofar our findings further support recent studies on related topics like the one by Mehra/Ranganathan (2008).

8.4.2 Hypothesis H2 — Global Satisfaction Triggers in Different Cultural Contexts

For assessing the influence of the selected variables linear regression (with variables according to **Table 8.2** and error term ε) was used. We define

$$satisfaction = const + b_{bra} \times brand + b_{app} \times appointment + b_{fle} \times flexibility + b_{exp} \times$$
$$explanation + b_{val} \times value + b_{tho} \times thoroughness + b_{int} \times interaction + \varepsilon.$$

(8.1)

In order to check for multicollinearity, variance inflation factors (VIF) are used. The VIF values are below 3.0 for both countries. Although there is no common recommendation on "critical" cutoffs, the VIF values seem tolerable against the practical hints by Cohen (1983) and O'Brien (2007).The resulting parameter estimates are given in **Table 8.4**.

Three variables are worth being mentioned explicitly, namely "brand sympathy", "handling of appointment booking" and "personal interaction" (referred to as "brand", "appointment" and "interaction"). These variables prove to be important for both countries and, therewith, both cultural contexts.

Table 8.4 Regression Parameters and Rankings by Parameter Values (Limited to Significant Parameters)

	USA			Japan		
	Parameter	Sign. Level	Rank	Parameter	Sign. level	Rank
Brand	0.384	1%	1	0.185	1%	2
Appointment	0.254	1%	3	0.216	1%	1
Flexibility				0.157	1%	3
Explanation	0.130	1%	5			
Value						
Thoroughness	0.255	1%	2			
Interaction	0.243	1%	4	0.137	< 5%	4
R²		0.719			0.422	

This clearly supports hypothesis H2. The remaining ("local") variables, on the other hand, reveal simply that the intuitive plausibility of a factor does not necessarily make it matter across borders and cultural contexts. This is also illustrated by the variable "value" (value for money of service, see **Table 8.2**) which would be intuitively rated as an important trigger of service satisfaction. However, for the researched premium durable it proved not to be of relevance for satisfaction perception. Underlying reasons might be that customers of premium automotive brands are rating time and flexibility over cost advantages (supporting findings by Verhoef et al., 2007).

8.4.3   Hypothesis H3 — Importance of "Brand Sympathy"

The results presented in **Table 8.4** already mark brand sympathy as an important trigger of service satisfaction. The corresponding parameter ranks highest for the USA. The predominant importance of brand sympathy is statistically significant for the USA: the parameter value for "brand sympathy" is significantly higher than the second highest parameter "thoroughness of work performed" (see **Table 8.4**, $p < 0.01$ regarding parameter differences). As already mentioned in connection with H1 the importance of "brand sympathy" follows a clear ordering (higher value for individualistic countries): $b_{bra,USA} > b_{bra,JAP}$. The difference is statistically significant at the 1% level using the approach by Cohen (1983[10]). The sample sizes $n_{USA}/n_{JAP} = 402/327$ are remarkably above the value $n = 100$ recommended by Cohen (1983, p. 80). Therefore, we conclude, that hypothesis H3 can be confirmed.

Our findings extend the results of Verhoef et al. (2007), not only to the premium car market, but also to low- as well as high-context countries (USA vs. Japan): brand sympathy strongly moderates the evaluation of service satisfaction triggers and, hereby, becomes part of service quality evaluation itself.

The results of Bloemer/Pauwels (1998) on triggers of after sales loyalty already indicate differences among volume and premium automobile brands. The present findings extend their work on high- vs. low context countries and mark brand sympathy as a key after sales satisfaction trigger for premium automobiles. This is also supported by Grönroos (2000) who illustrates the moderating effect of brand images on service quality perception, but without addressing the context-dependent component of individualistic and/or collectivistic cultures.

8.4.4 Hypothesis H4 — Nonlinear Impact of "Brand Sympathy"

Nonlinearity of brand sympathy with respect to service satisfaction can be hypothesized based on different behavioral theories. A detailed review in the context of pricing has been provided, e.g., by Kalyanaram/Winer (1995). The nonlinear response may be formulated as a part-wise convex or concave function f, following assimilation contrast theory by Sherif et al. (1958) or prospect theory by Tversky/Kahneman (1991), to mention just two of them.

■ Basic findings

Function f is assumed to be accessible by Taylor series development (at least piecewise) and to be realizable by a polynomial function. To allow for convex as well as concave (nonlinear) polynomial approximations, the order has to be 3 at least. With the variables above denoted by x_i (except for "brand sympathy"; for abbreviations of variables see **Table 8.2**), corresponding coefficients b_i (and c_τ for "brand [sympathy]", $\tau = 1, 2, 3$) and an error term ε the above response function can be rewritten as (where index i refers to variables "appointment", …, "interaction":

$$satisfaction = const + f(brand) + \sum_{i=2}^{7} b_i \times x_i = const + \sum_{\tau=1}^{3} c_\tau \times brand^\tau + \sum_{i=2}^{7} b_i \times x_i + \varepsilon \tag{8.2}$$

We tested for nonlinearity of the brand sympathy effect on the overall satisfaction by checking for statistical significance of the parameters c_τ ($\tau = 1, 2, 3$) in the equation above. The results are reported in **Table 8.5**. All values displayed are significant at the 5% level, c_2^{Japan} at the 10% level. The percentages in the last line of the table represent the increase of R^2 compared to the corresponding values in **Table 8.4**.

Table 8.5   Polynomial Approximation of the Brand Sympathy Effect

	USA	Japan
c_1	3.301	-0.177
c_2	-0.981	0.048
c_3	0.095	n. s.
Increase in R²	+4.3%	+1.0%

(n. s. = not significant)

For the USA, the coefficients of a cubic polynomial approximation, for Japan the coefficients of a quadratic approximation prove significant, which supports hypothesis H4. Polynomial approximations of response function f (values standardized for comparison purposes) according to **Table 8.5** are presented in **Figure 8.1**. Different cultural contexts are echoed by nearly convex and concave effects. Practical implications of this finding will be discussed in Subsection 8.5.1.

Figure 8.1   Polynomial Approximation of Brand Sympathy's Effect on Service Satisfaction

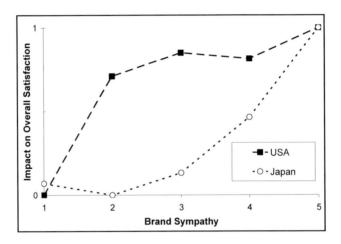

■ Robustness of the nonlinear model in practical applications

For the U.S. sample the nonlinear effect proved predominant. To evaluate the robustness for practical applications a posteriori segments of "completely unsatisfied" (rating levels 1 and 2 on the 5-point Likert scale), "unsatisfied" (levels 2 and 3), "satisfied" (levels 3 and 4) and "completely satisfied" (levels 4 and 5) customers have been checked separately for the USA. These groupings realistically reflect practical usage patterns of service satisfaction ratings according to commercial studies. NOP World Automotive, for example, groups top levels of a Likert scale to define "intenders" in their purchase funnel methodology and J. D. Power calculates customer segments "pleased" and "indifferent" on two neighbouring levels of a 10-point Likert scale in their sales satisfaction index study.

The sample was randomly divided into two groups: 90% of the participants were used to estimate the linear and cubic effect of "brand sympathy" on "service satisfaction". The holdout sample (10%) was used for testing predictive validity. This procedure was repeated 10 times. The corresponding hit rates are displayed in **Table 8.6** (As these segments overlap, the segment sizes sum up to more than 100%.).

If a respondent was "unsatisfied" (represented by levels 2 and 3 on the Likert scale), the linear response function assigns about half (53.3%), the cubic response function however assigns about two third (64.7%) of these customers correctly.

Table 8.6   Predictive Validity of the Linear and the Nonlinear (Cubic) Effect of "Brand Sympathy" by Segments

	Segments Based on Grouped Likert Ratings			
	Levels 1 & 2 ("completely unsatisfied")	Levels 2 & 3 ("unsatisfied")	Levels 3 & 4 ("satisfied")	Levels 4 & 5 ("completely satisfied")
Segment size	9.1%	9.8%	21.5%	85.0%
Linear response	67.8%	53.3%	67.4%	97.0%
Cubic response	69.9%	64.7%	67.6%	96.1%
Differences in hit rates	+3.1%	+21.4%	+0.3%	-0.9%

For three out of four segments the cubic response pattern provides better hit rates. Most important is the remarkable advantage in the segment of "unsatisfied" customers, where the nonlinear response function increases the corresponding hit rates by 21.4%: The cubic approach allows for a much clearer identification of those customers who potentially need additional effort to compensate for service shortcomings and to avoid negative effects of unfulfilled service expectations. In premium durable markets, customers, for obvious reasons, are typically characterized by high customer values. The systematic avoidance of customer losses and implementation of churn activities for unsatisfied customers needs techniques to clearly identify this specific segment. The nonlinear approach as suggested in this study implicates remarkable advantages in this respect.

8.5   Discussion and Implications

Service satisfaction in connection with premium durables and its international diversity is still a less researched area. Taking premium cars as a study object, the empirical part started from a sophisticated survey on service satisfaction of real customers with different cultural backgrounds. Internationally identical as well as country-specific drivers of service satisfaction have been identified. The USA and Japan served as prototypical individualistic and collectivistic countries respectively. Aspects of personal interaction proved important for both countries and brand sympathy, throughout, exhibits a strong, nonlinear effect on overall service satisfaction.

8.5.1   Managerial Implications

Country-specific satisfaction levels are not only the sheer outcome of professional custom-er-oriented after sales services, but also reflect cultural diversity. The present study also revealed that global brands may have a core set of attributes that trigger service satisfac-tion. This result is not imperative as cultural diversity and contexts are reflected in custom-ers' individual service expectations. The knowledge of internationally counting service satisfaction triggers allows for taking advantage of global process standardizations in the after sales sector. This includes the training of service personnel, the planning of marketing activities and the implementation of service improvements for areas that are relevant on an international scale. Similar implications regarding the necessity of multicultural training of business personnel were also drawn by Mehra/Ranganathan (2008, p. 922).

The significant effect of brand sympathy on service satisfaction underscores the long-term importance of brand-related activities beyond the point of purchase. According to the pre-sented findings, brand-oriented communication not only pays off in the pre-purchase phase but is also a promising investment in the post-purchase period to maintain or even strengthen brand sympathy. Hence, excluding the post-purchase period in service-oriented product markets may result in suboptimal marketing budget allocations and incorrect measurements of effectiveness.

The detected nonlinearity regarding brand sympathy reinforces recommendations for pul-sating communication strategies. This would result in over-proportional effects (satisfaction ratings) due to concentration. Furthermore, the risk of remaining in the "flat mid part" of the response function is eliminated by more concentrated campaigns, where efforts do not result in proportionally higher responses. Pulsating brand campaigns using all channels should be preferred in countries with response patterns as detected for the USA. The avail-able results also contribute to the general knowledge about nonlinear response patterns in customer satisfaction research. Homburg et al. (2005), for example, could prove a nonlinear effect of customer satisfaction on willingness to pay, whereas Wang et al. (2010) empirically illustrate the nonlinear effects of standardization on service satisfaction.

Furthermore, the detected nonlinearity of response patterns allows for a better identifica-tion of "unsatisfied" customers, resulting in a superior starting point for customer retention activities. This provides additional opportunities to increase customer retention in markets that are highly competitive and where customer values are comparably high.

8.5.2   Limitations and Future Research

The implications of this study are characterized by two main limitations, namely the focus of the empirical considerations on one product category (premium cars) and one prototypi-cal individualistic and collectivistic country each (USA and Japan, respectively). On the other hand, this limitation enabled the collection of meaningful customer data related to real service occasions which increases the managerial significance of our results.

Future research should be devoted to the replication of the measurements concerned, e.g., by focusing on service-oriented premium consumer electronics, in order to verify the presented findings or uncover product-related differences. Furthermore, from a more theoretical point of view, in-depth investigations of the nonlinear effect of brand sympathy on service satisfaction bear great potential regarding the motivation of pulsating advertising campaigns in the after sales sector. It can be assumed that the extent of nonlinearity not only depends on the product category but also on the culture considered. Last but not least further analyses are required in order to separate the interesting cross-cultural differences from the effects resulting from different response styles in individualistic and collectivistic countries respectively. In a study on cross-cultural comparisons of rating scales among East Asian and North American students, Chen et al. (1995, p. 175) detected a relation between culture and response style, but their study did not offer evidence for the suggestion that a response style in which extreme values are avoided and the midpoint is preferred provides a meaningful explanation for the cross-cultural differences obtained for the East Asian and the North American respondents. This supports the conclusions drawn in the previous sections but also leaves room for further research.

Literature

[1] Andaleeb, S./Basu, A. (1994): Technical Complexity and Consumer Knowledge as Moderator of Service Quality Evaluation in the Automobile Industry, Journal of Retailing, Vol. 70, 4, pp. 367-381.

[2] Bauer, M./von Wallpach, S./Hemetsberger, A. (2011): My Little Luxury – A Consumer-centred, experiential View, Marketing ZFP, Vol. 33, 1, pp. 57-67.

[3] Bei, L.-T./Chiao, Y.-C. (2001): An Integrated Model for the Effect of Perceived Product Quality, Perceived Service Quality, and Perceived Price Fairness on Consumer Satisfaction and Loyalty, Journal of Consumer Satisfaction, Dissatisfaction and Complaining Behavior, Vol. 14, pp. 125-50.

[4] Bloemer, J./Pauwels, K. (1998): Explaining Brand Loyalty, Dealer Sales Loyalty and Dealer After-sales Loyalty: The Influence of Satisfaction with the Car, Satisfaction with the Sales Service and Satisfaction with the After-sales Service, Journal of Consumer Satisfaction, Dissatisfaction and Complaining Behaviour, Vol. 11, pp. 78-90.

[5] Büschken, J. (2007): Determinants of Brand Advertising Efficiency: Evidence from the German Car Market, Journal of Advertising, Vol. 36, 3, pp. 51-73.

[6] Burmann, C. (1991): Konsumentenzufriedenheit als Determinante der Marken- und Händlerloyalität: Das Beispiel der Automobilindustrie, Marketing ZfP, Vol. 13, 4, pp. 249-258.

[7] Burmann, C./Jost-Benz M./Riley, N. (2009): Towards an Identity-based Brand Equity Model, Journal of Business Research, Vol. 62, pp. 390-397.

[8] Chen, C./Lee, S.-Y./Stevenson, H. W. (1995): Response Style and Cross-cultural Comparisons of Rating Scales Among East Asian and North American Students, Psychological Science, Vol. 6, 3, pp. 170-175.

[9] Churchill, G./Surprenant, C. (1982): An Investigation into the Determinant of Customer Satisfaction, Journal of Marketing Research, Vol. 19, 11, pp. 491-504.

[10] Cohen, A. (1983): Comparing Regression Coefficients Across Subsamples: A Study of the Statistical Test, Sociological Methods & Research, Vol. 12, 1, pp. 77-94.

[11] Cohen, M. A./Narendra, A./Vipul, A. (2006): Winning the Aftermarket, Harvard Business Review, May, pp. 2-13.

[12] Cronin, J.-J./Taylor, S. A. (1992): Measuring Service Quality: A Reexamination and Extension, Journal of Marketing, Vol. 55, 3, pp. 55-68.

[13] Fournier, S./Mick, D. G. (1999): Rediscovering Satisfaction, Journal of Marketing, Vol. 63, 4, pp. 5-23.

[14] Gaiardelli, P./Saccani, N./Songini, L. (2007): Performance Measurement of the After-sales Service Network – Evidence from the Automotive Industry, Computers in Industry, Vol. 58, pp. 698-708.

[15] Grönroos, C. (1984): A Service Quality Model and its Marketing Implications, European Journal of Marketing, Vol. 18, 4, pp. 36-44.

[16] Grönroos, C. (2000): Service Management and Marketing: A Customer Relationship Management Approach, Wiley, New York.

[17] Homburg, C./Koschate, N./Hoyer, W. D. (2005): Do Satisfied Customers Really Pay More? A Study of the Relationship between Customer Satisfaction and Willingness to Pay, Journal of Marketing, Vol. 69, April, pp. 84-96.

[18] Homburg, C./Luo, X. (2007): Neglected Outcomes of Customer Satisfaction, Journal of Marketing, Vol. 71, 4, pp. 133-49.

[19] Johnson, M./Herrmann, A./Gustafsson, A. (2002): Comparing Customer Satisfaction Across Industries and Countries, Journal of Economic Psychology, Vol. 23, pp. 749-769.

[20] Kalyanaram, G./Winer, R. (1995): Empirical Generalizations from Reference Price Research, Marketing Science, Vol. 14, 3, G161-G169.

[21] Lewis, B. (1991): Service Quality: An International Comparison of Bank Customers' Expectations and Perception, Journal of Marketing Management, Vol. 7, pp. 47-62.

[22] Löffler, M. (2002): A Multinational Examination of the '(Non-) Domestic Product' Effect, International Marketing Review, Vol. 19, 5, pp. 482-498.

[23] Loomba, A. P. S. (1996): Linkages between Product Distribution and Service Support Functions, International Journal of Physical Distribution & Logistics Management, Vol. 26, 4, pp. 4-22.

[24] Malai, V./Speece, M. (2005): Cultural Impact on the Relationship Among Perceived Service Quality, Brand Name Value, and Customer Loyalty, Journal of International Consumer Marketing, Vol. 17, 4, pp. 7-39.

[25] Martilla, J./James, J. (1977): Importance-Performance Analysis, Journal of Marketing, Vol. 39, 1, pp. 77-79.

[26] Mehra, S./Ranganathan, S. (2008): Implementing Total Quality Management with a Focus on Enhancing Customer Satisfaction, International Journal of Quality & Reliability Management, Vol. 25, 9, pp. 913-927.

[27] Mittal, V./Kamakura, W. A. (2001): Satisfaction, Repurchase Intent, and Repurchase Behavior: Investigating the Moderating Effect of Customer Characteristics, Journal of Marketing Research, Vol. 38, 2, pp. 131-42.

[28] Mittal, V./Kumar, P./Tsiros, M. (1999): Attribute-level Performance, Satisfaction, and Behavioral Intentions over Time: A Consumption System Approach, Journal of Marketing, Vol. 63, 4, pp. 88-101.

[29] O'Brien, R. M. (2007): A Caution Regarding Rules of Thumb for Variance Inflation Factors, Quality & Quantity, Vol. 41, 5, pp. 673-690.

[30] Odekerken-Schröder, G./Hennig-Thurau, T./Knaevelsrud, A. B. (2010): Exploring the Post-termination Stage of Consumer-brand Relationships: An Empirical Investigation of the Premium Car Market, Journal of Retailing, Vol. 86, 4, pp. 372-385.

[31] Oliver, R./Swan, J. (1989): Equity and Disconfirmation Perception as Influences on Merchant and Product Satisfaction, Journal of Consumer Research, Vol. 16, December, pp. 372-383.

[32] Olorunniwo, F./Hsu, M./Godwin, U. (2006): Service Quality, Customer Satisfaction, and Behavioral Intentions in the Service Factory, Journal of Services Marketing, Vol. 20, 1, pp. 59-72.

[33] Oyserman, D./Heather M. C./Kemmelmeier, M. (2002): Rethinking Individualism and Collectivism: Evaluation of Theoretical Assumptions and Meta-analyses, Psychological Bulletin, Vol. 128, 1, pp. 3-72.

[34] Parasuraman, A./Zeithaml, V. A./Berry, L. L. (1988): SERVQUAL: A Multiple Item Scale for Measuring Consumer Perception of Service Quality, Journal of Retailing, Vol. 64, 1, pp. 12-37.

[35] Philip, G./Hazlett, S. A. (1997): The Measurement of Service Quality: A New P-C-P Attributes Model, International Journal of Quality & Reliability Management, Vol. 14, 3, pp. 260-286.

[36] Shcheglova, M. (2009): An Integrated Method to Assess Consumer Motivation in Difficult Market Niches: A Case of the Premium Car Segment in Russia, unpublished PhD thesis, TU Berlin.

[37] Sherif, M./Taub, D./Hovland, C. (1958): Assimilation and Contrast Effects of Anchoring Stimuli on Judgements, Journal of Experimental Psychology, Vol. 55, pp. 150-155.

[38] Smith, A./Reynolds, N. (2001): Measuring Cross-cultural Service Quality: A Framework for Assessment, International Marketing Review, Vol. 19, 5, pp. 450-481.

[39] Sultan, F./Simpson, M. C. (2000): International Service Variants: Airline Passenger Expectations and Perceptions of Service Quality, Journal of Services Marketing, Vol. 14, 3, pp. 188-216.

[40] Tversky, A./Kahneman, D. (1991): Loss Aversion and Riskless Choice: A Reference Dependent Model, Quarterly Journal of Economics, Vol. 11, pp. 1039-1061.

[41] Ueltschy, L./Laroche, M./Eggert, A./Bindl, U. (2007): Service Quality and Satisfaction: An International Comparison of Professional Services Perceptions, Journal of Services Marketing, Vol. 21, 6, pp. 410-423.

[42] Vargo, S. L./Nagao, K./He, Y./Morgan, F. W. (2007): Satisfiers, Dissatisfiers, Criticals, and Neutrals: A Review of Their Relative Effects on Customer (Dis)Satisfaction, Academy of Marketing Science Review, Vol. 11, 2.

[43] Verhoef, P. C./Langerak, F./Donkers, B. (2007): Understanding Brand and Dealer Retention in the New Car Market: The Moderating Role of Brand Tier, Journal of Retailing, Vol. 83, 1, pp. 97-113.

[44] Wang, G./Wang, J./Ma, X./Qiu, R. G. (2010): The Effect of Standardization and Customization on Service Satisfaction, Journal of Service Science, Vol. 2, pp. 1-23.

[45] Winsted, K. F. (1999): Evaluating Service Encounters: A Cross-cultural and Cross-industry Exploration, Journal of Marketing Theory & Practice, Vol. 7, 2, pp. 106-123.

[46] Wöllenstein, S. (1996): Betriebstypenprofilierung in vertraglichen Vertriebssystemen, Lang, Frankfurt.

[47] Wise, R./Baumgartner, P. (1999): Go Downstream: The New Profit Imperative in Manufacturing, Harvard Business Review, Vol. 77, 5, pp. 133-41.

[48] Zhang, J./Beatty, S./Walsh, G. (2008): Review and Future Directions of Cross-cultural Consumer Services Research, Journal of Business Research, Vol. 61, 3, pp. 211-224.

9 Brand Loyalty vs. Loyalty to Product Attributes

Cam Rungie, University of South Australia, South Australia

Gilles Laurent, HEC Paris, France

Abstract

Typically, in a specific category, a product or service can be defined not only by the brand it bears but also by multiple other attributes (e.g., pack size, price level, product formulation): a total of ten attributes for our example, detergents. While many papers have been devoted to brand loyalty, very few have been devoted to loyalty to other attributes: Is a household loyal to a certain pack size? To a certain price level? To a certain product formulation? These questions have important managerial implications in terms of the design and management of a brand's product line. In this paper, we propose a systematic comparison of brand loyalty against loyalty to other attributes. We show that the two common measures of behavioural loyalty, share of category requirements and repeat rate, have problematic validity, due to the confounding influence of market share and purchase rate. In contrast, we argue that the Polarization index avoids these confounds and is therefore a better measure of loyalty. On the example of detergents, we show how to use Polarization to compare behavioural loyalty across attributes (e.g., are households more loyal to brands or to price levels?) and across different levels of one attribute (e.g., are consumers more loyal to high price levels than to low price levels?).

Keywords

Loyalty, Attributes, Polarization, Repeat Rate, SCR.

9.1   Introduction

In many product or service categories, each brand does not market a single item but rather a range of items that offer varying combinations of attributes: different product formulations, different perfumes, different pack sizes, different price levels, etc. The brand manager must first design this range: how many items? Offering which attribute combinations? And, second, manage this range: Should it be marketed as a single entity with a unique marketing mix? Or with specific marketing actions for specific items? (Specific distribution channels? Specific merchandising? Specific ads? Specific promotional offers?) Should certain attributes be emphasized? In which manner?

The detergents category offers an interesting example of high managerial importance. We identify ten attributes of each item: the specific brand it bears; whether this is a national brand or a private brand; product formulation; ingredients; pack type; pack size; price per unit of pack size; perfume; the type of fabric it can handle; whether it is designed for hand- or machine-washing. Each attribute can take multiple levels: from two levels (hand-washing vs. machine-washing) to 32 levels (32 brands), with many intermediate values (e.g., 8 pack types, 7 pack sizes, 17 perfumes, 4 types of fabric).

In this paper we address these questions. Our approach is to focus on loyalty in the category. How loyal are consumers to each attribute, and to each level of the attribute? How loyal are they to a brand? How loyal are they to a product formulation? to a pack size? to a price level? Which attribute benefits from the highest degree of loyalty? From the lowest degree? What is the level of brand loyalty in the category compared to the levels of loyalty to the other attributes?

How to evaluate loyalty? We show that two well-established measures of behavioral loyalty, share of category requirements (SCR) and repeat rate (RR), are not suited to comparisons across attributes because of confounding with the market shares and the category purchase rates of attribute levels. We argue that one should rather use the Polarization index of each attribute level to assess the degree of loyalty to that level. We demonstrate how to proceed using the detergent example.

The paper is organized as follows. We describe Polarization as a measure of consumer behavioral loyalty, contrasting it with RR and SCR. We then analyze the empirical example of loyalty to different attributes for the detergent category. We first present average results for each attribute, then detailed results for each attribute level. On this basis, we discuss successively niche and change-of-pace; segmentation and targeting; very high and very low polarizations; variations in loyalty across brands and across price levels; and the link between loyalty and amount of choice. The paper ends with a technical appendix.

9.2   Polarization Is a Measure of Loyalty

Two measures of behavioral loyalty are used very frequently: Repeat Rate and Share of Category Requirements. We describe them using the traditional example of brand loyalty, and extend them to the case of loyalty to other attributes, before discussing the Polarization index.

■ Repeat Rate (RR)

Consider two consecutive purchases from the category by a consumer. Repeat Rate for brand B is the proportion, among consumers who bought B on their first purchase, of those who purchase it again on the second occasion. The greater RR, the greater the loyalty. RR is comprised between 0% and 100% but usually Market Share ≤ RR ≤ 100%. Similarly, we can compute a repeat rate for a pack size: the proportion, among consumers who bought pack size P on their first purchase, of those who purchase it again on the second occasion; and we can compute RRs for all attributes.

■ Share of Category Requirements (SCR)

Consider purchases over a period of time, e.g. one year. SCR is the purchases of brand B by all consumers as a proportion of the purchases of the category made by those consumers who buy the brand at least once. The greater the SCR the greater the loyalty. SCR is comprised between 0% and 100% but usually Market Share ≤ SCR ≤ 100%. Similarly, we can compute a SCR for a pack size: the purchases of pack size P by all consumers as a proportion of the purchases of the category made by those consumers who buy the pack size at least once; and we can compute SCRs for all attributes.

■ Polarization Index

Polarization has been discussed by multiple authors in previous literature (Jacoby/Chestnut 1978; Sabavala/Morrison 1977; Kalwani 1980; Fader/Schmittlein 1993; Uncles/Ehrenberg/Hammond 1995; Ehrenberg/Uncles/Goodhardt 2004; Jarvis/Rungie/Goodman/Lockshin 2006; Jarvis/Rungie/Lockshin 2007). We begin by a formal definition of the Polarization index for a brand (we summarize here the technical appendix). When consumer i makes a purchase from the category let p_{ji} be the probability he will select brand j. Then, summing over j, $\sum p_{ji} = 1$ and $0 \leq p_{ji} \leq 1$. We model each purchase in the category as a Bernoulli trial based on the probability p_{ji}. Consider now the population of consumers. Over this population, let the probability of selecting level j when a purchase is made be the random variable P_j: each consumer i has a probability p_{ji}, and P_j describes the distribution of these individual probabilities across consumers. The mean of this probability is the market share: $\pi_j = E[P_j]$. Polarization is defined as:

$\phi_j = Var(P_j)/\{E[P_j](1-E[P_j])\}$,

i.e. the variance $Var(P_j)$ of P_j, standardized by dividing it by its maximum possible value $\{E[P_j](1-E[P_j])\}$, so that Polarization can only take values between 0 and 1 (or 0% and 100%). The greater the polarization then the greater the variance of P_j across consumers (for a particular market share $E[P_j]$).

The lowest possible value of Polarization, zero, occurs if $Var(P_j)$ equals zero, i.e. if all consumers have the same probability of choosing brand j. This means there is no loyalty for brand j because, whether or not the previous purchase was of brand j, the probability of purchasing j on the next occasion is exactly P_j for all consumers. In contrast, the highest possible value of Polarization, one, occurs if $Var(P_j)$ equals $\{E[P_j](1-E[P_j])\}$, i.e. if consumers can be divided in two groups: a group of consumers who always purchase brand j, and a group of consumers who never purchase brand j (the proportion of the first group in the population of consumers being $\pi_j = E[P_j]$). Here, loyalty is absolute: all consumers who bought j on the first purchase re-buy it on the second purchase, while consumers who did not buy j on the first purchase will never purchase it on the second purchase.

It can be shown (see appendix) that Polarization can be defined in another manner as a standardized index: a standardized RR. Consider the possible values of RR for brand j. The maximum value of RR is always one, corresponding to cases where consumers are perfectly loyal (if a consumer buys j on one purchase, he will buy j on all subsequent purchases). The minimum value of RR, however, is equal to the market share $\pi_j = E[P_j]$ of brand j. It occurs when all consumers have the same value of P_j : whatever the choice on the first purchase, the probability of choosing it on the second purchase is π_j . Thus, given the minimum value of RR varies, it makes sense to develop a standardized measure of RR, such as its minimum is zero and its maximum is one. This leads to the following formula, which can be shown to be identical to the previous definition of Polarization:

$\phi_j=(\rho_j-\pi_j)/(1-\pi_j)$

where π_j is brand j's market share and ρ_j is the RR.

The formal definition of Polarization given above:

$\phi_j = Var(P_j)/\{E[P_j](1-E[P_j])\}$

leads to another interpretation of Polarization as the reliability of consumer behaviour as a measure of consumer preferences. When polarization is zero, this implies that the choice made by a consumer on the first purchase (brand j or another brand) provides no indication whatsoever on the consumer's preferences, since the probability of purchasing j on the next purchase is always P_j. When polarization is one, the choice made on the first purchase provides a perfect diagnostic of the consumer's preference: if the consumer has chosen j, he will always choose j on later purchases; if he has not chosen j on the first purchase, he will never choose it on later purchases.

Thus, the Polarization index of brand j can have three interpretations: the standardized variance of P_j across consumers, the standardized Repeat Rate (RR) of brand j, the reliability of a consumer's choice as an indicator of the consumer's true preference for brand j. All three interpretations relate to the same concept: the degree of loyalty to brand j.

The discussion above about the Polarization for brand j generalizes easily to the Polarization index of any level of any attribute.

9.3   The Data

The data was provided by MarketingScan. It recorded purchases by 7768 households over all supermarkets in two regional cities in France in 2005. There were 50275 purchase transactions recording a total of 52135 items purchased in the detergent category. The authors wish to thank MarketingScan and GfK, and specially Laurent Battais, Raimund Wildner, and Gérard Hermet, for providing the data and for their assistance in this study.

Table 9.1   Attributes in the Detergent Category (Five Attributes Have Loyalty Greater Than Brand (See Polarization)

Attribute		Average Level of Loyalty		
Name	# of Levels	Share of Category Requirements%	Repeat Rate %	Polarization %
Type of Brand (National/Private)	3	71.7	81.0	50.8
Product Formulation	7	56.3	69.7	49.4
Price per Unit of Pack Size	4			39.1
Ingredients	3	92.2	93.9	37.2
Pack Type	8	37.2	49.1	36.0
Brand	32	30.5	42.0	34.3
Pack Size	7	42.4	52.2	32.3
Perfume	17	54.0	60.4	26.6
Fabric	4	74.8	78.5	25.9
Type of Washing (Machine/Hand)	2	87.4	88.4	16.8

Table 9.1 shows the results for the ten attributes of detergents. For each measure in the table a higher score indicates greater loyalty. We display the three measures of loyalty discussed above: share of category requirements (SCR), repeat rate (RR) and Polarization.

For each measure, the loyalty measure is averaged over the levels of the attribute, weighted by market share. **Table 9.1** ranks the attributes according to their Polarization: At the top, type-of-brand, has the highest loyalty and at the bottom, type-of-washing, has the lowest.

The table shows that there are five attributes where the loyalty is higher than for brands. For type of brand and product formulation the loyalty is much higher. While our comments are based on polarization (which in this paper we argue is the most valid measure of loyalty), the two other measures (SCR and RR) lead to conclude that all attributes have higher levels of loyalty than brand.

These results demonstrate the extent to which consumers base their purchase decisions on specific attributes rather than specific brands. The management of a brand line is not just a matter of developing the individual consumer's preference for the brand so he becomes more loyal to it. Managing a brand is more about ensuring that it provides, through its range of EANs, the attributes which really drive consumer choice and loyalty. Consumers buy the brand which gives them the attributes and EANs they want. Brand management is about much more than managing the brand itself.

A loyal consumer can be expected to be deal resistant. The consumer is loyal, despite being exposed to a constant bombardment of competitors' advertising and promotions. This may reflect an 'active' motivation, like he has a high preference which is hard to shift, or it may be a more 'passive' motivation, such as he ignores advertising and promotions. Either way he is resistant, and so has lower elasticity and is easier to keep. And, as they are deal resistant, there is every reason to believe that these loyal consumers can generate higher margins.

The degree of loyalty, as assessed by the Polarization index, helps determine the nature of marketing actions directed towards communications with the consumer. When loyalty is low there is high switching. The product is likely to be already in the consumers' repertoire. Small things will make a difference. Sales are easier to win but there again they will also be easier to lose. Marketing should emphasise regular, low cost activities and will be short term and somewhat tactical. Where there is high loyalty selling more to existing customers can be difficult as they are already loyal. The customers of other brands are deal resistant so winning new customers can require more effort and will be expensive. However, once won new customers may stay longer, and marketing with a higher cost for each consumer targeted can be justified. Marketing, and in particular promotions, can be longer term and strategic.

When loyalty is low, the critical issue is why is it low? This cannot be determined directly from the repeat purchase loyalty measures, but it can possibly be determined from other background product knowledge or from market research. When an attribute has low loyalty it might be because (i) the consumer has a definite requirement for multiple levels of the attribute due to variety seeking, multiple uses for the product, different usage situations, multiple users in the household, in which case the attribute is still relatively important, or (ii) the consumer is indifferent and is choosing 'as if' randomly, in which case the attribute is unimportant. These consumer motivations should have a major impact on marketing actions.

For the ten attributes in **Table 9.1** there are over 80 different attribute levels. The three measures of loyalty (RR, SCR, and Polarization), and the market shares, for each of these appear in **Table 9.2** to **Table 9.11**. These should be interpreted in much the same manner as above. If a specific attribute level has high loyalty then it should be emphasised. If it has low loyalty then further evaluation is required to determine the consumer motivations. And again loyalty, as measured by Polarization, should influence the manner of emphasis and style of communication with consumers for the individual attribute levels.

As the sample size and repeat purchases in the data are large the sampling variation will be small relative to the results in the tables. The standard errors for the polarizations are all less than 1, range from 0.3 to 0.7 (Rungie/Brown/Laurent/Rudrapatna 2005).

Table 9.2   Type of Brand (National/Private)

Attribute Level	Market Share	SCR	RR	Polarization
National brand	75.0	80.7	87.8	51.2
Retail brand	23.2	46.1	62.0	50.5
Other	1.7	27.8	41.3	40.3
Total	100.0	71.7	81.0	50.8

Table 9.3   Product Formulation

Attribute Level	Market Share	SCR	RR	Polarization
Powder	25.2	51.8	68.3	57.6
Pearls	0.6	39.6	55.7	55.5
Liquid	52.5	66.0	77.9	53.4
Paste	16.5	43.9	59.7	51.7
Capsule	1.9	33.1	46.4	45.4
Flakes	0.2	17.1	19.3	19.1
Gel	3.1	17.1	16.7	14.1
Total	100.0	56.4	69.7	49.4

Table 9.4 Price per Unit of Pack Size (Quartiles)

Attribute Level	Market Share	Polarization
Q1 (low price)	24.9	49.1
Q2	24.8	35.9
Q3	25.3	34.5
Q4 (high price)	24.9	39.9
Attribute Average	100.0	39.1

Table 9.5 Ingredients

Attribute Level	Market Share	SCR	RR	Polarization
Compact	4.2	30.3	45.3	42.9
Standard	94.9	95.6	96.8	37.4
NA	0.9	18.1	18.1	17.4
Total	100.0	92.2	93.9	37.2

Table 9.6 Pack Type

Attribute Level	Market Share	SCR	RR	Polarization
Barrel	18.6	44.9	61.5	52.8
Box	18.2	44.5	60.2	51.4
Ecological refill	2.7	34.6	50.3	48.9
Bottle	15.7	35.6	47.1	37.3
Pack	5.9	29.3	37.9	34.0
Flask	17.5	33.0	42.6	30.4
Drum/metal	18.5	33.5	42.0	28.8
Tube	2.9	17.0	16.8	14.3
Refill	0.0	9.5	6.3	6.3
Total	100.0	37.2	49.1	36.0

Table 9.7 Brand

Attribute Level	Market Share	SCR	RR	Polarization
NET NET	0.8	40.6	56.9	56.6
CARREFOUR	10.5	43.6	59.0	54.2
EPSIL	4.1	37.3	51.0	49.0
MAISON VERTE	1.4	31.3	47.3	46.5
LE CHAT	4.8	32.1	48.4	45.8
ARIEL	11.7	35.9	51.8	45.4
BIEN VU	0.7	36.2	45.4	45.0
NUCLEAR	0.0	34.1	45.0	45.0
U	2.9	31.8	45.8	44.2
CASINO	1.5	30.7	44.6	43.7
CHAMPION	1.2	29.9	43.1	42.4
DASH	5.9	29.4	44.0	40.5
AUCHAN	1.2	29.0	41.1	40.4
N1	0.4	26.9	39.4	39.2
X-TRA	6.5	28.8	40.2	36.1
JEAN REGNIER	0.0	31.1	35.3	35.3
SKIP	12.3	31.2	42.9	34.9
ANTARTICS	0.2	22.4	33.5	33.3
VIZIR	1.2	23.1	32.8	31.9
PERSIL	4.4	24.9	34.2	31.2
APTA	0.7	24.7	31.4	30.9
SUPER CROIX	3.6	24.4	32.9	30.4
CHANTE CLAIR	0.4	20.0	30.0	29.7
GAMA	3.8	25.2	32.2	29.6
OMO	4.6	23.1	32.2	28.9
MELIOR	0.1	21.2	28.2	28.2
BONUX	2.0	21.9	29.4	28.0
MIR BLACK	7.9	27.0	33.6	27.9

Attribute Level	Market Share	SCR	RR	Polarization
AXION	0.2	17.1	19.1	19.0
PERSAVON	0.3	17.6	18.2	17.9
GENIE	2.0	17.8	17.6	15.9
BOY	0.0	20.3	15.1	15.0
WOOLITE	1.1	16.8	15.9	15.0
NETTY	0.0	23.3	14.3	14.3
BLANDIS	0.0	13.9	13.0	13.0
MR PROPRE	0.5	14.5	12.7	12.2
PAIC BLANC	1.0	15.2	11.9	11.0
RAINETTE	0.0	15.2	8.2	8.2
BIOLANE	0.0	12.9	7.5	7.5
Total	100.0	30.5	42.0	34.3

Table 9.8   Pack Size

Attribute Level	Market Share	SCR	RR	Polarization
<=1	20.2	34.2	44.9	31.0
>1 & <=2	22.3	41.0	53.1	39.6
>2 & <=3	43.2	53.8	64.3	37.1
>3 & <=4	1.6	17.0	15.0	13.6
>4 & <=5	7.0	24.9	32.2	27.1
>5 & <=6	3.0	17.6	16.7	14.1
>6	2.6	20.9	23.3	21.2

Table 9.9 Perfume

Attribute Level	Market Share	SCR	RR	Polarization
Pure	0.1	25.2	34.7	34.7
Fleur bleue	2.4	25.7	34.1	32.5
No perfume	65.9	69.2	76.2	30.1
Fresh	0.4	21.4	27.4	27.1
Floral	5.2	24.4	30.9	27.1
Source	2.5	21.2	26.2	24.3
Other	15.0	28.5	35.0	23.6
Sun	0.3	21.2	22.9	22.7
Alpine	3.2	20.8	24.5	22.1
Aloe vera	2.4	19.6	22.9	21.0
Air	0.2	17.1	19.1	19.0
Fr-in	0.1	15.4	14.9	14.8
Lemon	0.0	18.4	13.7	13.7
Orange blossom	0.4	17.8	13.7	13.4
Spring	0.9	15.5	12.4	11.6
Fr-vi	0.5	14.7	10.7	10.3
Peach	0.3	14.4	9.5	9.2
Citrus fruits	0.2	11.1	4.2	4.0
Lemon peel	0.0	16.7	1.0	1.0
Fl-ci	0.0	14.9	1.0	1.0
Total	100.0	54.0	60.4	26.6

Table 9.10   Fabric

Attribute Level	Market Share	SCR	RR	Polarization
Colored fabric	8.4	29.4	35.3	29.4
All-purpose	83.8	84.4	88.2	27.1
Wool	6.7	21.1	21.8	16.2
Other	1.1	16.6	15.7	14.8
Total	100.0	74.8	78.5	25.9

Table 9.11   Type of Washing (Machine/Hand)

Attribute Level	Market Share	SCR	RR	Polarization
Hand-wash	7.5	20.9	23.2	16.9
Washing machine	92.5	92.8	93.7	16.8
NA	0.0	7.0	0.8	0.7
Total	100.0	87.4	88.4	16.8

9.4   Results and Discussion

Niche and Change-of-Pace

In some of these tables the Polarizations for the different levels of an attribute are approximately equal to the attribute average. What is of interest are the exceptions where there are attribute levels with noticeably higher or lower loyalty. This approach to calculating loyalty provides a formal method for identifying "niche" and "change-of-pace" levels (Kahn/Kalwani/Morrison 1988). A niche is a level with a polarization much in excess of the attribute average. A change-of-pace is a level with a polarization much less than that attribute average. For pack-type in **Table 9.6** e.g., Barrel is niche and Drum/metal is change-of-pace.

The implications of niche and change-of-pace levels are much as has already been discussed for attributes. A niche level has high loyalty. Customers will be deal resistant and less elastic. For a change-of-pace level there will be high switching. Market research should be undertaken to determine the nature of the consumer motivations which generate the low loyalty. We are not suggesting that there is necessarily an advantage of niche over change-of-pace. We are stating that marketing managers need to know the loyalty patterns for attribute levels so appropriate strategies can be developed, as the strategies for niche and change-of-pace will be different.

In this analysis we are emphasising loyalty but the tables also report market share. The importance of attribute levels with low market share is influenced by loyalty. If market share is low but loyalty is high then there is an opportunity. This is discussed further in the next section. Low market share for an attribute level does not imply it is unimportant in the marketing mix.

Segmentation and Targeting

If direct marketing is possible, then in general, promotions for a product would be targeted at those consumers who purchase the same products before. This is a standard strategic platform of direct marketing. But how is the 'same product' defined? Who should be targeted, those consumers who bought the same brand, those who bought the same product formulation, the same pack type, the same perfume, etc.? The answer is in loyalty. Direct marketing should be targeted on the basis of those attributes, and attribute levels, with high loyalty. If the polarization for an attribute level is high then target those consumers who have previously purchased it. An excellent example is in product formulation. There are two levels of this attribute, capsules and paste, which have low market share but high loyalty. Direct marketing should include campaigns which target just those who have bought these formulations before. Sales will not be high as the market shares are low, but a targeted campaign offering these formulations back to those who have bought them before will be effective in generating higher strike rates, lower promotional costs and greater margins. Targeting and segmentation should be planned around consistent purchase behavior and those attributes and levels with high loyalty. This form of 'loyalty segmentation' is not in use in marketing and yet it is implicit in the marketing's concept of segmentation. What could be more relevant than past loyal purchase behavior? What could be more relevant than the attributes to which there has been past loyal purchase behavior?

Very High and Very Low Polarization

Particular attention can be focused on any attribute level with high loyalty, e.g. above 50% which is a quite high level of loyalty. Two brands have loyalty above this threshold. So too is the loyalty for national versus store brands. The highest loyalty over all attribute levels is for powder (57%) and there are a total of four product formulations above the threshold of which one, Pearls, has very low market share. Also there are two pack types, Barrel and Box, with loyalty above the threshold. Marketing should emphasise these attribute levels, with the possible exception of Pearls which should be analyzed separately. These attribute levels should be well represented in the product range. Promotions in particular should focus individually on each of these attribute levels. In the decision between advertising the brand as a single consumer concept or advertising specific attributes there should be at least some emphasis and specific focus on each of these attribute levels.

Conversely, it is also useful to analyse cases of low loyalty, e.g. below 30%. There are many loyalties below this level. Further analysis, possible involving market research, is required to determine the consumer motivation driving these low loyalties.

If they reflect variety seeking, multiple uses, which is most likely the case for type-of-washing (**Table 1.11**), multiple usage situations, or multiple users in the household, then the attribute and its levels are still important. However, if they reflect consumer indifference and 'as if' random purchase choice behavior then the attribute level has less importance.

Variation in Loyalty Across Brands

As shown in **Table 9.1** and **Figure 9.1**, there is considerable variation in loyalty across brands. There are many brands which can be considered niche (with excess loyalty and at the top of the graph) and conversely many which can be considered change-of-pace (at the bottom of the graph). An often observed pattern is that big brands have higher behavioral loyalty (Fader/Schmittlein 1993). The three brands with the highest market shares all have polarizations equal to or above average, see **Figure 9.1**.

Figure 9.1   Variations in Loyalty for Brands as a Function of Market Share

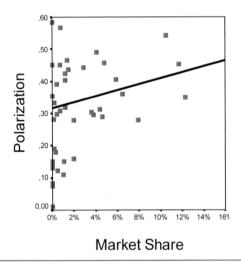

By contrast, a niche brand, which has smaller market share but higher behavioral loyalty, may have restricted availability over the market; it can have high market share within a small segment and so in that segment has the loyalty of a big brand. As mentioned earlier the communications strategies differ between niche and change of pace.

Variation in Loyalty Across Price Levels

Price, like pack size, is quite different from the other attributes. Price takes on a continuous range of values, while the other attributes take on discrete levels (e.g., liquid, powder, etc.). Thus, price has been grouped into classes. Bigger packs are more expensive, of course, so **Table 9.1** analyzes the average price per unit of volume, with four levels being the four quartiles. The results show that the lower price classes have excess loyalty and form a niche.

Loyalty and Amount of Choice

As a more academic point, there is a suggestion in the literature that loyalty levels may be driven by the amount of choice available to the consumer. If there is a greater array of alternatives there will be less loyalty (Driesener 2005). Of course, the argument could be in reverse. If there is less loyalty then brand managers may make more alternatives available to the consumer as it is easier to create adopters of a new product in the category. However, **Table 9.1** shows the relationship between the number of levels and loyalty over the ten attributes. There is not a strong relationship.

Variation in Loyalty With Market Share and Purchase Rate

SCR and RR are, by their definitions, functions of Market Shares, but Polarization is not, see the technical appendix. A simple and important example of the impact of market share on SCR and RR is given in **Table 9.1**. Brands have low average market shares because there are many levels, i.e. there are many brands. Conversely, ingredients and fabric are attributes with only a few levels and in each there is one level with very high market share. This has a gross impact on SCR and RR which are both much higher than for brands. Often SCR and RR are only used to analyse brands and often the range of market shares for brands is relatively small. By extending the analysis here to other attributes where market shares are much higher and vary more the limitations of these measures are quite clear. It is not valid to use SCR and RR to compare loyalties across attributes.

Finally we consider how SCR is also a function of the Average Category Purchase Rate, but Polarization is not, see the technical appendix and Corsi/Rungie (2011). **Figure 9.2** presents an empirical example of how SCR is influenced by the category purchase rate. It shows the SCR for the brands of detergent for data aggregated over different lengths of time. Length varies from 6 months to 12 months. The data aggregated months selected from over the full year thus removing the impact of any potential trend effects and allowing the analysis to focus solely on impact of the number of purchases. As the total purchases analysed increases, the purchase rate increases and the SCRs all decline steadily. This is because SCR is influenced by purchase rates: The larger the purchase rate the larger the consumers' repertoires and the smaller the SCRs for each of the brands. Variations in SCR can be due to nothing more than changes in the purchase rate.

By comparison **Figure 9.3** shows the same results for polarization. There is no influence of the length of the period of analysis, which leads to an increase in the purchase rate. Thus,

Polarization is more valid than SCR for comparing loyalty between data sets with different purchase rates, such as comparisons between time periods, product categories and markets.

Figure 9.2   As the Quantity of Data Analysed Increases the SCRs for the Brands of Detergent All Reduce. Thus SCR Is Not a Valid Measure of Behavioral Loyalty As It Also Reflects Purchase Rate.

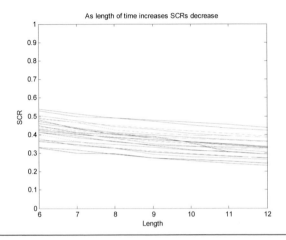

Figure 9.3   Polarization Is Not Influenced by Changes in the Purchase Rate

---

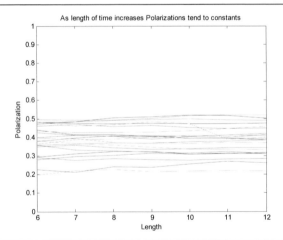

9.5   Summary

This paper has presented an approach to analysing behavioral loyalty to product and service attributes in a specific category, and for comparing it to brand loyalty. It is based on computing the Polarization index of each level of each attribute. We argue that Polarization levels are of importance to the selection of the marketing mix and product ranges and is of relevance to marketing. Over the ten attributes we consider in the empirical example the variations in the levels of Polarization are substantial and certainly large enough to be an important marketing consideration. While some marketing literature emphasizes brands the empirical results show that consumer behavior does not. Five of the ten attributes have loyalty levels greater than for brands. It might be argued that this is because there are more brands - market shares are typically lower than for the levels of the other attributes - but this is not the case. The argument that loyalty is driven by number of items from which consumers choose is not supported. The Polarizations of the levels within each attribute also vary considerably leading to the identification of niche and change-of-pace levels such as a particular pack type or price point. We discuss how marketers should consider the role, and Polarizations, of attributes other than brand in the design and management of the range of items to be presented within a product category and the brand's product line. The paper provides theoretical and empirical evidence that some measures of loyalty are confounded with other important market characteristics; i.e. with average purchase rate and market shares. When comparing loyalty between attributes, categories or markets, Polarization is a valid measure, whereas Share of Category Requirements and Repeat Rate are not.

Appendix

Consider an attribute with h levels. This might be, for example, product formulation where h=7, in our example (see **Table 9.3**). Consider purchases over a period of time, e.g. over a year. Consider the purchases made by consumer i.

Let his purchases of the category be k_i and his purchases of level j of the attribute be r_{ji}. Then $\Sigma\ r_{ji} = k_i$.

When he makes a purchase from the category let p_{ji} be the probability he will select level j. Then $\Sigma\ p_{ji} = 1$ and $0 \le p_{ji} \le 1$.

In any one purchase the selection of the level is a Bernoulli trial based on the probabilities $p_{1i}, p_{2i}, \ldots, p_{hi}$.

Consider now the population of consumers. Over this population, let the purchases of the category be the random variable K, let the purchases of level j of the attribute be the random variable R_j and let the probability of selecting level j when a purchase is made be P_j.

Here K and R_j are integer and not negative and $\Sigma R_j = K$.

Also, P_j is continuous, $\Sigma\ P_j = 1$ and $0 \le P_j \le 1$.

These three random variables give formal definitions for the measures used above (Rungie/ Goodhardt 2004). These definitions assume K is independent of P_j.

Market Share for level j, $\pi_j = E[P_j]$

SCR for level j $\varsigma_j = E[R_j]/E[K\,|\,R_j>0]$

Repeat Rate for level j, $\rho_j = E[P_{j2}]/E[P_j]$

Polarization for level j, $\phi_j = Var(P_j)/\{E[P_j](1-E[P_j])$

Also

Average Category Purchase Rate, $v = E[K]$

It can be shown that:

$0 \le \pi_j \le 1$

$0 \le \phi_j \le 1$

$0 \le \rho_j \le 1$

$0 \le \varsigma_j \le 1$

It can be shown that RR is a function of the market share and the polarization.

$\rho_j = \pi_j + \phi_j - \pi_j\phi_j$

It can also be shown that SCR is a function of the average category purchase rate, the market share and the polarization. The functional form is complex but the graphical relationship is simple. If distributions are assumed then the relationship can be demonstrated using simulations. Depending on the distributions the relationship can have closed forms. Assume P_j has a beta distribution. The beta distribution has two parameters α_1 and α_2. Mean, $\pi_j = \alpha_1/(\alpha_1+\alpha_2)$, variance $= \pi_j(1- \pi_j)/(1+\alpha_1+\alpha_2)$ and polarization, $\phi_j =1/(1+\alpha_1+\alpha_2)$. If the probability density function for K is $f(k)$ then (Rungie/Goodhardt 2004):

SCR for j,

$$
\varsigma_j = \frac{\pi_j \sum_{k=1}^{\infty} f(k)k}{\sum_{k=1}^{\infty} f(k)k \left(1 - \frac{\Gamma\left(\dfrac{1-\varphi_j}{\varphi_j}\right)\Gamma\left(\left(\dfrac{1-\varphi_j}{\varphi_j}\right)(1-\pi_j)+k\right)}{\Gamma\left(\dfrac{1-\varphi_j}{\varphi_j}+k\right)\Gamma\left(\left(\dfrac{1-\varphi_j}{\varphi_j}\right)(1-\pi_j)\right)} \right)}
$$

It can be shown that this mathematical analysis implies that (i) if the average category purchase rate increases then the SCR will decrease and (ii) if market share increases then SCR and repeat rate increase. In the results section of the paper we discuss the empirical evidence for these claims.

Literature

[1] Corsi, A. M./Rungie, C. M. (2011): Is the polarization index a valid measure of loyalty for evaluating changes over time?. Journal of Product and Brand Management, Vol. 20, 2, pp. 111-120.

[2] Driesener, C. (2005): Empirical generalisations in the parameter values of the Dirichlet model: an examination across 50 categories. Ehrenberg Bass Institute. Adelaide, University of South Australia. PhD.

[3] Ehrenberg, A. S. C./Uncles, M.D./Goodhardt, G. G. (2004): Understanding brand performance measures: Using Dirichlet benchmarks. Journal of Business Research, Vol. 57, 12, pp. 1307-1325.

[4] Fader, P. S./ Schmittlein, D. C. (1993): Excess Behavioral Loyalty for High-Share Brands: Deviations from the Dirichlet Model for Repeat Purchasing. Journal of Marketing Research, Vol. 30, 4 November.

[5] Jacoby, J./ Chestnut, R. W. (1978): Brand Loyalty Measurement and Management. New York, NY, John Wiley & Sons.

[6] Jarvis, W./ Rungie, C. M./Goodman, S./Lockshin, L. (2006): Using Polarization to Identify Variations in Behavioral Loyalty to Price Tiers. Journal of Product and Brand Management, Vol. 15, 4, pp. 257-264.

[7] Jarvis, W./Rungie, C. M./Lockshin, L. (2007): The polarisation method for merging data files and analysing loyalty to product attributes, price and brands in revealed preference. International Journal of Marketing Research 49 (4 Data Integration Special Issue).

[8] Kahn, B./ Kalwani, M. U./Morrison, D. G. (1988): Niching Versus Change-of-Pace Brands: Using Purchase Frequencies and Penetration Rates to Infer Brand Positionings. Journal of Marketing Research, Vol. 25, November, pp. 384-390.

[9] Kalwani, M. U. (1980): Maximum Likelihood Estimation of Zero-Order Models Given Variable Numbers of Purchases per Household. Journal of Marketing Research XVII, pp. 547-551.

[10] Rungie, C. M./Brown, B./Laurent, G./Rudrapatna, S (2005): A Standard Error Estimator for the Polarization Index: Assessing the Uncertainty in Loyalty. Marketing Bulletin 16.

[11] Rungie, C. M./Goodhardt, G. J. (2004): Calculation of theoretical brand performance measures from the parameters of the Dirichlet model. Marketing Bulletin 15.

[12] Sabavala, D. J./ Morrison, D. G. (1977): A model of TV show loyalty. Journal of Advertising Research, Vol. 17, 6, pp. 35-43.

[13] Uncles, M. D./Ehrenberg, A. S. C./Hammond K. (1995): Patterns of buyer behavior: Regularities, models and extensions. Marketing Science, Vol. 14, 3, 2 of 2, G71-G78.

Marketing Management

1 Market Shaping Orientation and Firm Performance

Markus Blut, Technische Universität Dortmund, Germany

Hartmut H. Holzmüller[1], Technische Universität Dortmund, Germany

Markus Stolper, ARDEX GmbH, Germany

[1] Contact author
The authors would like to thank Abbie Griffin, Andreas Eggert and Stefanie Paluch for helpful comments on an earlier draft of this paper.

Abstract

Marketing theory suggests market orientation as an effective strategy for achieving and maintaining competitive advantage (Kohli/Jaworski 1990; Narver/Slater 1990). Reviewing the literature, Jaworski et al. (2000) criticize most conceptualizations of the construct to be too narrow and to neglect a proactive understanding of shaping customers and/or the market. Against this background, we discuss two approaches to being market oriented: the first can be described as a *'market driven'* and the second as a *'market shaping'* approach. We develop new measures for the latter construct and empirically test its antecedents and consequences. Moreover, we examine moderator variables affecting the market shaping orientation-performance linkage, using a sample of 181 firms.

Keywords

Marketing Strategy, Market Orientation, Market Shaping Orientation.

1.1   Introduction

Since the late 1980's marketing theory suggests market orientation as an effective strategy for achieving and maintaining competitive advantage (Jaworski/Kohli/Sahay 2000; Narver/Slater 1990). Current understanding of market orientation relates to the organization-wide generation and dissemination of customer and competitor information and is associated with a firm's ability to learn and respond to the market (Kohli/Jaworski 1990). It has been conceptualized from both a behavioral and a cultural perspective (Homburg/Pflesser 2000; Kirca/Jayachandran/Bearden 2005). Reviewing prior research on market orientation, Jaworski et al. (2000) criticize most conceptualizations of the construct as being too narrow. They extend the understanding of market orientation through distinguishing between two complementary approaches: The first approach which is characterized as 'market driven', describes market orientation as a reactive concept, where companies intend to keep the status quo by focusing mainly on existing customers and their current needs. The second 'market driving'-approach is a more proactive understanding of the concept, where companies shape not only customers' but also other market participants' behaviors and/or market structure in a direction that enhances the competitive position of a firm (Jaworski et al. 2000). In our research, we focus on the latter approach and coin it 'market shaping orientation'.

To our best knowledge the relevance of this approach has not been investigated empirically. The importance of this perspective is underlined by a recent meta-analysis supporting that the market orientation-performance linkage does not always hold (Kirca et al. 2005). Against this background Jaworski et al. (2000) highlight the potential of market shaping orientation as a complementary approach to being market driven. Unfortunately, most prior research on this construct is qualitative in nature. Several propositions to the antecedents of market shaping orientation have been pointed out (Carrillat/Jaramillo/Locander 2004; Harris/Cai 2003; Kumar et al. 2000), but these propositions still need empirical validation. Furthermore, although market shaping orientation is discussed to lead to higher organizational performance, this relationship and factors affecting the market shaping orientation-performance linkage have not been tested empirically. Hence, the understanding of the market shaping orientation construct, its relevance and strategies to strengthen a firm's market position is hampered.

A better understanding of the construct, gives managers guidance on how to improve their organizations' market shaping efforts and under what circumstances they should implement a market shaping strategy (Jaworski et al. 2000; Kumar et al. 2000). Our study fills a research gap by (1) developing a measurement instrument of the market shaping orientation construct based on the recent conceptualization developed by Jaworski et al. (2000), (2) discussing and empirically testing antecedents and performance outcomes of the market shaping orientation construct, and finally, (3) examining the moderating effects of market turbulence and technological change on the market shaping orientation-performance linkage.

In accordance with these research objectives, the paper is organized as follows: First, we give a brief overview of prior research on the concept under study and introduce the conceptualization developed by Jaworski et al. (2000) to capture a firm's market driving activities. As suggested by these scholars, we employ their conceptualization to develop our measures. Second, we set up our conceptual framework capturing antecedents, consequences and moderators and discuss our research hypotheses. Third, we present the results of the empirical analysis, based on a sample of 181 managers from electrical industry. We close with a summary of our findings, a discussion about its limitations and further research needed.

1.2   Market Shaping Orientation: The Construct

The conceptual roots of the market shaping orientation concept can be traced back to scholars such as Zeithaml/Zeithaml (1984), Clark/Varadarajan/Pride (1994) and Hamel (1996) and their research on environmental management. This stream of research examines when environmental change should be taken into strategic consideration and how companies proactively manage "the rules of the game". The term market driving was mentioned for the first time by Kumar (1997) in a case study about changes in the retail industry. Later Kumar and colleagues (2000) note that this approach is already being adopted by several established firms, e.g., Body Shop, IKEA, and Dell. A first definition of the construct was given by Jaworski et al. (2000), who describe market driving orientation as "changing the composition and/or roles of players in a market and/or the behavior(s) of players in the market." It seems that it is almost impossible for a company to drive a market, therefore we prefer a somewhat modest signifier, namely market shaping.

Jaworski et al. (2000) argue that firms which influence market players and/or affect market structure more often can be viewed as being more market shaping. In contrast to being market driven, the market shaping orientation approach is not only a more proactive approach, it also includes every stakeholder of the company not only customers and/or competitors. Although the idea of market shaping orientation is not entirely new and has been partially discussed in concepts like customer leading (also known as proactive market orientation) and pioneering, but change of competitor behavior and market structure is not included in these approaches (Hills/Sarin 2003).

Following Jaworski's et al. (2000) conceptualization of market driving, we distinguish between two sets of activities: (1) activities that shape the market structure and (2) activities that shape market behavior (see **Figure 1.1**).

1.2.1 Shaping Market Structure

Regarding the first set of activities, the structure of a market can be shaped by applying three generic strategies (Jaworski et al. 2000): (1) eliminating players in the market; (2) creating a new market structure through setting and/or modifying the current set of players; (3) changing the functions of the players in the market. While the first approach captures those activities that address a reengineering of the value chain to eliminate players which add only little value from the customer perspective (e.g., players in the channel of distribution, competitors, suppliers), the second captures activities that develop a different set of players to better meet customer needs (build a new web of players, add complementary players). Finally, the last strategy captures activities that involve forward or backward integration of a firm within the value chain.

Figure 1.1 Conceptualization of Market Shaping Orientation

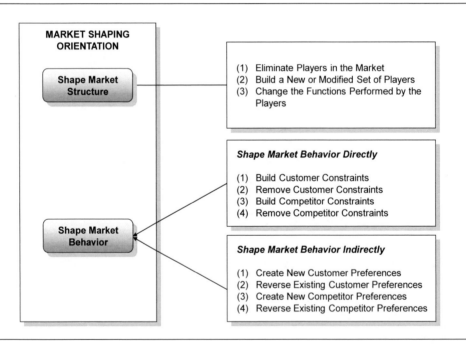

1.2.2   Shaping Market Behavior

Regarding the second set of activities, Jaworski et al. (2000) distinguish between activities that directly shape market behavior and those having an indirect effect. Market behavior can be shaped directly through: (1) building or (2) removing customer constraints as well as through (3) building or (4) removing competitor constraints. This does not only refer to influencing real constraints, but also includes management of imagined constraints. Additionally to activities influencing customer behavior directly, companies can shape preferences of customers or competitors and thereby, indirectly influence market behavior; these activities include: (1) creating new or (2) reversing existing customer preferences and (3) creating new or (4) reversing existing competitor preferences. By introducing new offerings and/or new benefits, the customers' preferences can be changed and customers' behavior is influenced. Similarly, competitors' preferences can be influenced depending on the direction that enhances the competitive position of the firm.

1.3   Conceptual Framework and Hypothesis Development

To develop our conceptual framework, we reviewed literature on market orientation, resource based view, capability approach, and marketing strategy that is relevant to our research focus. Based on this review, we define the key constructs and their interrelationships within our framework and describe their theoretical foundations. The framework comprises four sets of factors: (1) antecedents that increase or decrease a market shaping orientation, (2) the market shaping orientation construct, (3) consequences of a market shaping orientation, and (4) moderator variables influencing the relationship between market shaping orientation and performance (see **Figure 1.2**).

Functional Capabilities. Functional capabilities are based on competencies like expertise and skills and therefore they dependent on people within the value chain (Hall 1993). In our research, we identified the strength of a firm's vision (Carrillat et al. 2004; Hamel/Prahalad 1991; Kumar et al. 2000) and its sensitivity to the market place (Kumar et al. 2000; Harris/Cai 2003) to be discussed when implementing market shaping orientation. A firm's vision represents an ideological goal that organizational members picture as a brighter future (MacKenzie/Podsakoff/Rich 2001). It is crucial for proactive management because without having a vision, organizations have no chance to influence their future proactively (Carrillat et al. 2004). A clear vision helps companies to focus on activities and offerings that are not only derived from customers' current needs. Employees throughout all departments receive orientation when planning new activities and projects following this vision (Jaworski et al. 2000). Thus, we propose that a firm's strength of vision leads to higher market shaping orientation. Formally,

> H_1: The greater a firm's strength of vision, the greater is its market shaping orientation.

A firm's sensitivity for change can be defined as its ability to see opportunities and constraints in the environment (Conger/Kanungo 1994). Companies being able to detect small changes in their market environment can react proactively to market changes they are confronted with. Through investments on market research and interviews regarding future preferences of every stakeholder, these changes were barely detected (Hamel/Prahalad 1991; Kumar et al. 2000). Hence, we assume that a firm's sensitivity for change leads to higher market shaping orientation. Thus,

> H₂: The greater a firm's sensitivity for change, the greater is its market shaping orientation.

Figure 1.2   Conceptual Framework

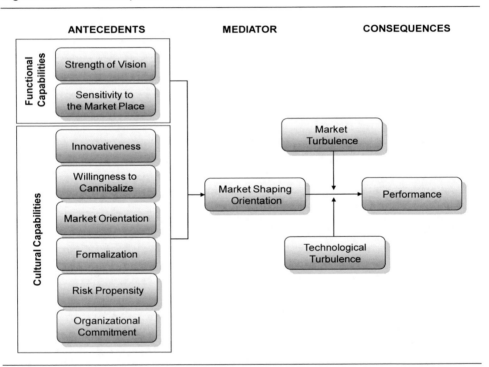

Cultural Capabilities. Like functional capabilities, cultural capabilities are based on competencies and apply to the organization as a whole. They include habits, attitudes, beliefs and values, and permeate individuals or groups across the organization (Hall 1993). We identified innovativeness (Hills/Sarin 2003; Jaworski et al. 2000), willingness to cannibalize (Chandy/Tellis 1998; Kumar et al. 2000), market orientation (Jaworski et al. 2000; Kumar et al. 2000), degree of formalization (Kumar et al. 2000), risk taking (Clark et al. 1994; Hamel/Prahalad 1991), and organizational commitment to be potential antecedents that enhance or impede market shaping orientation.

Innovativeness refers to the openness to new ideas as an aspect of a firm's culture (Hurley/Hult 1998). Shaping markets is related to establishment of new ideas within the market (e.g., process, products or structure of the value chain). These ideas can only be established, when having a strong innovation orientation within a firm (Hills/Sarin 2003; Jaworski et al. 2000). Hence, we propose that innovativeness of a firm leads to higher market shaping orientation. Formally,

> **H3:** The greater a firm's innovativeness, the greater is its market shaping orientation.

Market orientation is described as the organization-wide generation of market intelligence and is associated with a firm's ability to learn and respond to the market (Kohli/Jaworski 1990). Jaworski et al. (2000) argue market driven orientation and market shaping orientation to be complementary approaches. Kumar et al. (2000) extend this discussion by assuming market orientation to be the basis for market shaping orientation. Only when exactly knowing current market conditions, companies can shape markets in a direction that is favorable. Hence we propose that market orientation of a firm leads to higher market shaping orientation. Thus,

> **H4:** The greater a firm's market orientation, the greater is its market shaping orientation.

A firm's degree of formalization refers to employees' degree of freedom, when performing activities (Aiken/Hage 1968). The more flexible the corporate culture, the better employees can react to environmental uncertainties (Hall/Haas/Johnson 1967). For the generation of new ideas and their implementation, a flexible corporate culture has been shown to be highly relevant (Aiken/Hage 1968; Pierce/Delbecq 1977). Therefore, we propose that a lower degree of formalization leads to higher market shaping orientation. Hence,

> **H5:** The lower a firm's degree of formalization, the greater is its market shaping orientation.

Risk taking of a firm captures its managers' tendency or preference for taking risks or being adventurous (Raju 1980). Changing the status quo is always associated with certain risks and potential losses. If management is willing to take risks and accept failures, changing the marketplace and introducing new ideas will become more likely (Clark et al. 1994; Hamel/Prahalad 1991; Jaworski/Kohli 1993; Kumar et al. 2000). Thus, we propose that a firm's risk taking leads to higher market shaping orientation. Formally,

> **H6:** The greater a firm's risk taking, the greater is its market shaping orientation.

The willingness of a company to cannibalize refers to the extent to which a firm is accepts to reduce actual or potential value of its investments (Chandy/Tellis 1998). The literature discusses market shaping orientation activities to be related to introduction of innovations into a market. When a firm is not willing to accept innovation due to potential cannibalization effects, market shaping orientation activities will be less likely (Chandy/Tellis 1998; Kumar et al. 2000).

Therefore, we propose that a firm's willingness to cannibalize leads to higher market shaping orientation. Hence,

> **H7:** The greater a firm's willingness to cannibalize, the greater is its market shaping orientation.

A firm's organizational commitment refers to the relative strength of an individual's identification with and involvement in a particular organization (Mowday/Porter/Steers 1979). Driving markets requires commitment from employees, due to this strategies' riskiness and its need for employees' innovation generation and diffusion. Hence, we propose that a firm's organizational commitment leads to higher market shaping orientation. Thus,

> **H8:** The greater a firm's organizational commitment, the greater is its market shaping orientation.

1.3.1 The Consequences of Market Shaping Orientation

The impact of market orientation, in terms of being driven by the market, on firm performance has been tested in several empirical studies (Kirca et al. 2005). Arguing that long term profitability could not be achieved by only being market driven, Jaworski et al. (2000) assume that a firm's market shaping orientation has to be assessed. Kumar et al. (2000) refer to strategies being conducted by successful companies when analyzing the concept of market shaping orientation. Hence, it is logical to examine whether firms that show a high market shaping orientation exhibit superior performance. Thus, we propose that a market shaping orientation leads to superior firm performance. Formally,

> **H9:** The greater the market shaping orientation of a firm, the greater is its performance.

1.3.2 Moderators: Market Turbulence and Technological Change

Little attention has been paid to contextual factors determining the appropriateness of a market shaping orientation strategy (Jaworski et al. 2000). Turbulence of the market might be one of these conditions, which is defined as changes in the composition of customers and their preferences (Kohli/Jaworski 1990). Under stable market conditions, companies do not have to find new ways of satisfying customer needs – incremental innovations derive from the customer and radical innovation is less effective. Companies' effort on changing markets should be more effective when being confronted with turbulent market conditions. Following this argumentation, it is assumed that market shaping orientation has no effect on performance in a stable market. Specifically, we assume that the market shaping orientation–performance linkage is likely to increase, when market turbulence increases. Hence,

> **H10:** The higher the market turbulence, the greater is the positive effect of a firm's market shaping orientation on its performance.

Supplementary to market turbulence, Kohli/Jaworski (1990) discuss technological turbulence to be an environmental condition of high relevance, because of its influence on a firm's strategy effectiveness. Technological turbulence describes the degree of technological change within the industry. In many industries technological innovations are developed outside the industry under question (Kohli/Jaworski 1990). Under these conditions, a firm's capability to change market structure by gathering ideas and innovations outside the boundaries of the industry becomes more crucial for being successful.

Therefore, it is assumed that the market shaping orientation–performance linkage is likely to increase, when technological turbulence increases. Thus,

> H_{11}: The higher the technological change, the greater is the positive effect of a firm's market shaping orientation on its performance.

1.4 Research Methodology

1.4.1 Measurement

The designed questionnaire consists mainly of measures based on well-established scales. They were selected on the basis of their extent of use in previous research and the reported reliability and validity. We made some adaptations to meet the specific characteristics of the industry under study and the research setting. To ensure face validity, a number of marketing researchers and specialists were consulted. For our research, we used reflective scales for most of our constructs except for the market shaping orientation construct, which is operationalized as a formative scale. All items were measured using a 7-point Likert scale anchored by "7" ("strongly agree") and "1" ("strongly disagree"). Functional capabilities, a firm's strength of vision and its sensitivity to the market place were measured with scales adapted from Conger/Kanungo (1994). Regarding cultural capabilities, again measures for the latent variables were adapted from prior research, specifically for innovativeness (Hurt/Joseph/Cook 1977), willingness to cannibalize (Chandy/Tellis 1998), market orientation (Deshpande/Farley 1998), degree of formalization (Ferrell/Skinner 1998), risk taking (Jaworski/Kohli 1993), and organizational commitment (Meyer/Allen 1991). Performance measures were taken from Deshpande/Farley/Webster (1993), while for the two environmental moderators, market turbulence and technological turbulence measures were adapted from Jaworski/Kohli (1993).

Since an established measurement instrument for market shaping orientation is not available in the literature, we developed a measure based on Jaworski's et al. (2000) conceptualization. We followed the approach suggested by Diamantopoulos/Winklhofer (2001) and generated a large pool of items, considering all facets of the conceptualized construct. As market shaping orientation is conceptualized as an index of strategies and activities, which are not necessary related to each other, we decided to use a formative measurement.

The items were tested by asking marketing experts to check the items with regard to ambiguity or other difficulties first. Second we carried out the test suggested by Anderson/Gerbing (1991) with 22 marketing experts in order to check content validity. This was followed by another pre-test among 25 top managers, which showed no problems concerning multicollinearity (tested by condition index and VIF values) and indicator weights.

1.4.2   Sample Characteristics and Data Collection

The targeted sample includes executives of all members of the central association of the German electrical industry (N = 1,162). A package containing a cover letter, a standardized questionnaire, and a prepaid envelope was sent to each respondent. To encourage response, the cover letter explained nature and relevance of the study and promised a small amount of donation to a charity organization for each completed questionnaire. We received a total of 181 responses at a response rate of about 15.6 percent. In detail, we collected 130 questionnaires from managing directors and chief executive officers (72%), 15 from assistant managing directors (8%), 27 from head of marketing and business development (15%), and 9 from head of research and development (5%). The respondents had significant amounts of work experience and were able to evaluate their firm's strategy appropriately. The responding firms' number of employees ranges from 50 employees to 1,000 with an average of 372 employees per company. In terms of size and company focus (e.g., automation, consumer electronics) the collected sample is representative for the German electronic industry. We tested for nonresponse bias and found no significant differences between early and late respondents. Since the data for dependent and independent variables were obtained from the same informant, there is a possibility of common method bias (CMB). Applying the methods suggested by Podsakoff and colleagues (2003) to test for CMB, particularly the "single-method-factor approach", we can conclude that CMB is not a significant issue in our study.

1.5   Analysis and Results

1.5.1   Measurement Model

Measurement reliability was examined through confirmatory factor analysis and the calculation of Cronbach alpha coefficient (see **Table 1.1**, Panel A). It can be noted that the coefficient alpha is larger than .7, the threshold generally proposed in the literature (Nunnally 1978). Also, composite reliabilities are larger than .6 for all constructs (Bagozzi/Yi 1988). Discriminant validity of the constructs was assessed using the criterion proposed by Fornell/Larcker (1981). Again, the criterion was met (see **Table 1.1**, Panel B). Therefore, reliability and validity of the constructs in this study are acceptable.

1.5.2   The Structural Model

To test the antecedents and consequences of market shaping orientation, we applied a component-based SEM approach. Specifically, we use PLS because it does not require multivariate normal distributed data, is more suitable for small samples and is recommended when calculating a research models with formative indicators (Chin 1998; Fornell/Bookstein 1982; Hulland 1999; Tenenhaus et al. 2005).

Table 1.1   Reliability and Validity of the Constructs

A: Scale Properties			
	Coefficient Alpha	**Composite Reliability**	**Average Variance Extracted**
Strength of Vision	.84	.90	.76
Sensitivity for Change	.85	.85	.50
Innovativeness	.74	.83	.56
Cannibalize	.79	.79	.52
Market Orientation	.76	.76	.52
Formalization	.76	.84	.58
Risk Taking	.72	.84	.63
Commitment	.90	.92	.65
Market Turbulence	.80	.91	.83
Technological Change	.78	.84	.58
Performance	.79	.87	.62

B: Correlations Between Variables

	1.	2.	3.	4.	5.	6.	7.	8.	9.	10.	11.
Strength of Vision	-										
Sensitivity for Change	.63	-									
Innovativeness	.61	.46	-								
Cannibalize	.42	.43	.51	-							
Market Orientation	.17	.27	.63	.17	-						
Formalization	.28	.27	.20	.26	.16	-					
Risk Taking	.24	.18	.36	.28	.03	.22	-				
Commitment	.60	.51	.48	.40	.27	.23	.24	-			
Market Turbulence	.28	.20	.21	.32	.10	.02	.08	.28	-		
Technological Change	.36	.28	.35	.22	.12	.13	.16	.37	.46	-	
Performance	.24	.21	.21	.15	.17	.12	.17	.34	.13	.17	-
Average Variance Extracted	.76	.50	.56	.52	.52	.58	.63	.65	.83	.58	.62

As suggested by Chin (1998), we use PLS to estimate the main and interaction effects in our model. We first examine direct effects only and in a second step we include interaction terms in our model (Baron/Kenny 1986; Chin et al. 2003). Overall, our predictors offer a good explanation for the focal construct. Our model explains 32.4% of the variance in the market shaping orientation construct and the applied Stone-Geisser test supports our model's predictive relevance (Fornell/Cha 1994). The results of hypotheses testing for H_1–H_9 are summarized in **Table 1.2**, Panel A.

H_1, which predicted that a firm's visionary power is positively associated with its market shaping orientation, was not supported ($\beta = -.180$, p < .10). Contrary to our expectations, a negative effect was found. H_2, which predicted that a higher sensitivity for change would lead to greater market shaping orientation, was not supported either ($\beta = -.066$, p > .10).

In support of H_3, a firm's innovativeness was positively associated with its market shaping orientation ($\beta = .404$, p < .01).

H_4, which assumed a positive association between a firm's willingness to cannibalize and market shaping orientation, was not supported ($\beta = -.035$, p > .10). Supporting H_5, marketing orientation was positively linked to market shaping orientation ($\beta = .227$, p < .01). No support was found for H_6, assuming a positive impact of a firm's degree of formalization and market shaping orientation ($\beta = .081$, p > .10) H_7, which predicted a positive impact of risk taking on market shaping orientation was supported ($\beta = .242$, p < .01) and H_8 has to be rejected, organizational commitment had no impact on market shaping orientation ($\beta = -.022$, p > .10).

Finally, market shaping orientation was found to have a positive effect on performance, therefore H9 was supported by our findings (β = .319, p < .01). Overall, four out of nine hypotheses were supported by these findings.

Table 1.2   Results of Structural Equation Model

A: Results of Hypothesis Testing: H1-H9

Construct	Direction	Construct	Est.	t-value	f²	p	Hyp.	Result
Market shaping orientation	←	Strength of Vision	-.180	1.739	.022	.10	H1	Rejected
	←	Sensitivity	-.066	.858	.004	-	H2	Rejected
	←	Innovativeness	.404	3.937	.126	.01	H3	Confirmed
	←	Cannibalize	.035	.636	.001	-	H4	Rejected
	←	Market Orientation	.227	3.270	.061	.01	H5	Confirmed
	←	Formalization	.081	1.368	.010	-	H6	Rejected
	←	Risk Taking	.242	2.915	.074	.01	H7	Confirmed
	←	Commitment	-.022	.343	.001	-	H8	Rejected
Performance	←	Market shaping orientation	.319	4.701	.114	.01	H9	Confirmed

B: Results of Hypothesis Testing: H10-H11

Construct	Direction	Construct	Est.	t-value	f²	p	Hyp.	Result
Performance	←	Market shaping orientation X Market Turbulence	.145	1.744	.120	.10	H10	Confirmed
	←	Market shaping orientation X Technological Turbulence	.117	1.438	.120	-	H11	Rejected

Regarding potential direct effects of the firm's capabilities on performance, the mediating effect of market shaping orientation was tested applying the method proposed by Baron/Kenny (1986). Examining only those capabilities that have a significant impact on market shaping orientation, we have to summarize, that innovativeness and risk taking have no direct effect on business performance. Market orientation is the only capability found to have a direct effect on business performance beside its indirect effect.

To determine under which conditions market shaping orientation strategies should be established, moderators of the link between market shaping orientation and firm performance are tested, using structural equation modeling (see **Table 1.2**, Panel B). The results indicate, that H_{10}, which predicted that higher levels of market turbulence are associated with stronger effects of a firm's market shaping orientation on its firm performance, was supported by our findings ($\beta = .145$, $p < .10$) and H_{11}, assuming that technological turbulence influences the link between market shaping orientation and performance, has to be rejected ($\beta = .117$, $p > .10$).

1.6 Discussion

1.6.1 Core Findings

Examining the contribution of this research, we refer to Jaworski's et al. (2000) initial article and the discussed research agenda. First, the authors underline the need for developing clear measurement to focus on market shaping orientation activities in contrast to activities of being driven by the market. These measures were developed in this study and relevance of market shaping orientation strategy has proven that several of a firm's capabilities influence performance only indirectly through market shaping orientation. In detail, market shaping orientation was found to be a fully mediator between capabilities and firm performance with the exception of market orientation. Thus, we could provide insight into the relationship between the two complementary approaches of market shaping orientation and market orientation. Second, Jaworski et al. (2000) recommended the investigation of conditions under which a market shaping approach works. In our research market turbulence was found to be a moderator enhancing the effectiveness of market shaping orientation strategies. Third, the authors discussed the extent to which a market can be shaped, to be of further interest. We investigated electrical industry and gave insight into market shaping orientation effectiveness within this industry. By testing antecedents of market shaping orientation, managers of this industry receive guidance on how to implement a market shaping strategy. Specifically, a firm's innovation orientation, market orientation, and top management's risk taking were identified as influencing market shaping orientation.

1.6.2 Managerial Implications

Over the past decades most companies have turned from product orientation to market orientation, realizing that a few companies within each industry are one step ahead by shaping markets instead of only reacting to markets. Hence, managers have to learn how to become more proactive in managing market behavior and/or structure besides being market driven to ensure future firm performance. The findings of our study give several insights for managers how to ensure market shaping orientation capabilities.

Establishment of Market Shaping Orientation. Results of our analysis suggest that a firm's market shaping orientation depends on three factors: (1) innovativeness, (2) manager's risk taking and (3) market orientation. A firm's innovativeness was found to have the strongest impact on a firm's market shaping orientation activities; hence, we recommend enhancing capabilities to innovate. Besides budget allocation, implementation of innovative culture should influence innovation capabilities. When having an adhocracy-type of culture, employees will be encouraged to think about change and give suggestions about potential actions revolutionizing industries. Furthermore, managers' risk taking may foster products and/or services that not necessarily meet customers' current needs (Kumar et al. 2000). Managers often face risk and uncertainty when changing and/or re-structuring markets. Through implementation of a risk taking culture these managers become more willing to embark on risks and find new solutions for current problems. Not only should employees be willing to change, they should also be granted head space for making mistakes and these potential failures as well as the associated losses have to be tolerated by top management. Hence, employee rewards and incentives could further enhance a market shaping orientation. Finally, market shaping orientation has been discussed to be a complementary strategy to being market driven. Our findings support this assumption; hence, companies should foster their market orientation to learn about current market structures and current needs and by doing so they could also learn about opportunities for successful market change.

Different Context, Different Impact. One environmental factor was found influencing market shaping orientation effectiveness. Since managers want to know when to implement market shaping orientation strategies, we especially suggest this strategy for industries being confronted with high market turbulence. Under these circumstances, firms only have limited opportunities to learn from current customer needs. Hence, increasing activities to improve business as opposed to solely relying on customers and markets should be more successful.

1.6.3   Limitations and Directions for Future Research

Although our study establishes that market shaping firms achieve higher performance, longitudinal studies would deepen our understanding of the long-term effects of market shaping strategies. As the variables examined in our study were gathered from a single source, there is a clear possibility of biases; hence, we encourage replication of our study combining data from multiple sources. Hills/Sarin (2003) assume the effectiveness of market shaping orientation to depend on industry characteristics. Therefore, further insights might be gathered through conducting studies across several industries, because of the specific focus of this research. The overall fit of our research model indicates that there may be further antecedents of market shaping orientation to be identified in future studies. Additional company characteristics such as size, age or brand strength should be tested with regard to their impact on market shaping orientation (Jaworski et al. 2000). We examined two of many environmental variables being discussed to influence strategies' effectiveness. Hence, further moderators like price pressure or competitors' behavior could be tested empirically in future studies.

Literature

[1] Aiken, M./Hage, J. (1968): Organizational Interdependence and Intra-Organizational Structure, American Sociological Review, Vol. 33, 6, pp. 912-930.

[2] Anderson, J. C./Gerbing, D. W. (1991): Predicting the Performance of Measures in a Confirmatory Factor Analysis with a Pretest Assessment of Their Substantive Validities, Journal of Applied Psychology, Vol. 76, 5, pp. 732-740.

[3] Bagozzi, R. P./Yi, Y. (1988): On Evaluation of Structural Equation Models, Journal of the Academy of Marketing Science, Vol. 16, 2, pp. 74-94.

[4] Baron, R./Kenny, D. A. (1986): The Moderator-Mediator Variable Distinction in Social Psychological Research: Conceptual, Strategic, and Statistical Considerations, Journal of Personality and Social Psychology, Vol. 51, 6, pp. 1173-1182.

[5] Carrillat, F. A./Jaramillo, F./Locander, W. B. (2004): Market-Driving Organizations: A Framework, Academy of Marketing Science Review, 2004, 5, pp. 1-14.

[6] Chin, W. (1998): Issues and opinion on structural equation modeling, MIS Quarterly, Vol. 22, 1, pp. 7-16.

[7] Carrillat, F. A./Marcolin, B. L./Newsted, P. N. (2003): A partial leastsquares latent variable modeling approach for measuring interaction effects: Results from a monte carlo simulation study and an electronic-mail emotion/adoption study, Information Systems Research, Vol. 14, 2, pp. 189-217.

[8] Chandy, R. K./Tellis, G. J. (1998): Organizing for Radical Product Innovation: The Overlooked Role of Willingness to Cannibalize, Journal of Marketing Research, Vol. 35, 4, pp. 474-487.

[9] Clark, T./Varadarajan, P. R./Pride, W. M. (1994): Environmental Management: The Construct and Research Propositions, Journal of Business Research, Vol. 29, 1, pp. 23-36.

[10] Collins, J. C./Porras, J. I. (1991): Organizational Vision and Visionary Organizations, California Management Review, Vol. 34, 1, pp. 30-53.

[11] Conger, J. A./Kanungo, R. N. (1994): Charismatic Leadership in Organizations: Perceived Behavioral Attributes and Their Measurement, Journal of Organizational Behavior, Vol. 15, 5, pp. 439-452.

[12] Day, G. S. (1994): The Capabilities of Market-Driven Organizations, Journal of Marketing, Vol. 58, 4, pp. 37-53.

[13] Deshpande, R./Farley, J. U. (1998): Measuring Market Orientation: Generalization and Synthesis, Journal of Market-Focused Management, Vol. 2, 3, pp. 213-232.

[14] Deshpande, R./Farley, J. U./Webster, F. E. Jr. (1993): Corporate Culture, Customer. Orientation and Innovativeness in Japanese Firms: A Quadrad Analysis, Journal of Marketing, Vol. 57, 1, pp. 3-15.

[15] Diamantopoulos, A./Winklhofer, H. M. (2001): Index Construction With Formative Indicators: An Alternative to Scale Development, Journal of Marketing Research, Vol. 38, 2, pp. 269-277.

[16] Ferrell, O. C./Skinner, S. J. (1988): Ethical Behaviour and Bureaucratic Structure in Marketing Research Organizations, Journal of Marketing Research, Vol. 25, 1, pp. 103-109.

[17] Fornell, C./Bookstein, F. L. (1982): Two Structural Equation Models: LISREL and PLS applied to Consumer Exit-Voice Theory, Journal of Marketing Research, Vol. 19, 4, pp. 440-453.

[18] Fornell, C./Larcker, D. F. (1981): Evaluating Structural Equation Models with Unobservable Variables and Measurement Error, Journal of Marketing Research, Vol. 18, 1, pp. 39-50.

[19] Fornell, C./Cha, J. (1994): Partial Least Squares, in: Bagozzi, R. (ed.), Advanced Methods of Marketing Research, Oxford: Blackwell.

[20] Hall, R. (1993): A Framework Linking Intangible Resources and Capabilities to Sustainable Competitive Advantage, Strategic Management Journal, Vol. 14, 8, pp. 607-618.

[21] Hall, R./Haas, J. E./Johnson, N. J. (1967): Organizational Size, Complexity, and Formalization, American Sociological Review, Vol. 32, 6, pp. 903-911.

[22] Hamel, G. (1996): Strategy as Revolution, Harvard Business Review, Vol. 74, 4, pp. 69-81.

[23] Hamel, C./Prahalad, C. K. (1991): Corporate Imagination and Expeditionary Marketing, Harvard Business Review, Vol. 69, 4, pp. 81-93.

[24] Harris, L. C./Cai, K. Y. (2003): Exploring Market shaping orientation: A Case Study of De Beers in China, Journal of Market-Focused Management, Vol. 5, 3, pp. 171-196.

[25] Hills, S. B./Sarin, S. (2003): From Market Driven to Market shaping orientation: An Alternative Paradigm for Marketing in High Technology Industries, Journal of Marketing Theory and Practice, Vol. 11, 3, pp. 13-25.

[26] Homburg, C./Pflesser, C. (2000): A Multiple-Layer Model of Market-Oriented Organizational Culture: Measurement Issues and Performance Outcomes, Journal of Marketing Research, Vol. 37, 4, pp. 449-462.

[27] Hulland, J. (1999): Use of Partial Least Squares (PLS) in Strategic Management Research: A Review of four recent studies, Strategic Management Journal, Vol. 20, 2, pp. 195-204.

[28] Hurley, R. F./Hult, G. T. (1998): Innovation, Market Orientation, and Organizational Learning: An Integration and Empirical Examination, Journal of Marketing, Vol. 62, 3, pp. 42-54.

[29] Hurt, T. H./Joseph, K./Cook, C. D. (1977): Scales for the Measurement of Innovativeness, Human Communication Research, Vol. 4, 1, pp. 58-65.

[30] Jaworski, B. J./Kohli, A. K. (1993): Market Orientation: Antecedents and Consequences, Journal of Marketing, Vol. 57, 3, pp. 53-70.

[31] Jaworski, B. J./Kohli, A. K./Sahay A. (2000): Market-driven versus driving-markets, Journal of the Academy of Marketing Science, Vol. 28, 1, pp. 45-54.

[32] Kirca, A. H./Jayachandran, S./Bearden, W. O. (2005): Market Orientation: A Meta-Analytic Review and Assessment of Its Antecedents and Impact on Performance, Journal of Marketing, Vol. 69, 2, pp. 24-41.

[33] Kohli, A. K./Jaworski, B. J. (1990): Market Orientation: The Construct, Research Propositions, and Managerial Implications, Journal of Marketing, Vol. 54, 2, pp. 1-18.

[34] Kumar, N. (1997): The Revolution in Retailing: from Market Driven to Market shaping orientation, Long Range Planning, Vol. 30, 6, pp. 830-836.

[35] Kumar, N./Scheer, L./Kotler, P. (2000): From Market Driven to Market shaping orientation, European Management Journal, Vol. 18, 2, pp. 129-142.

[36] Lado, A. A./Wilson, M. C. (1994): Human Resource Systems and Sustained Competitive Advantage: A Competency-Based Perspective, Academy of Management Review, Vol. 19, 4, pp. 699-727.

[37] Lipton, M. (1996): Opinion: Demystifying the Development of an Organizational Vision, Sloan Management Review, Vol. 37, 4, pp. 83-92.

[38] MacKenzie, Scott B./Podsakoff, Phillip M./Rich, Gregory A. (2001): Transformational Leadership and Transactional Leadership and Salesperson Performance, Journal of the Academy of Marketing Science, Vol. 29, 2, pp. 115-134.

[39] Markides, C. C. (1999): A Dynamic View of Strategy, Sloan Management Review, Vol. 40, 3, pp. 55-63.

[40] Narver, J./Slater, S. (1990): The Effect of a Market Orientation on Business Profitability, Journal of Marketing, Vol. 54, 4, pp. 20-35.

[41] Meyer, J. P./Allen, N. J. (1991): A Three-Component Conceptualisation of Organizational Commitment, Human Resources Management Review, Vol. 1, 1, pp. 61-89.

[42] Mowday, R. T./Porter, L. W./Steers, R. M. (1982): Employee-Organizational Linkages: The Psychology of Commitment, Absenteeism and Turnover, New York: Academic Press.

[43] Nunnally, J. C. (1978): Psychometric Theory (2nd ed.), New York: McGraw-Hill.

[44] Pierce, J./Delbecq, A. L. (1977): Organization Structure, Individual Attitudes, and Innovation, Academy of Management Review, Vol. 2, 1, pp. 26-37.

[45] Pil, F. K./Cohen, S. K. (2006): Modularity: Implications for Imitation, Innovation, and Sustained Advantage, Academy of Management Review, Vol. 31, 4, pp. 995-1011.

[46] Podsakoff, P. M./MacKenzie, S. B./Lee, J.-Y./Podsakoff, N. P. (2003): Common Method Biases in Behavioral Research: A Critical Review of the Literature and Recommended Remedies, Journal of Applied Psychology, Vol. 88, 5, pp. 879-903.

[47] Raju, P. S. (1980): Optimum Stimulation Level: Its Relationship to Personality, Demographics, and Exploratory Behavior, Journal of Consumer Research, Vol. 7, 3, pp. 272-282.

2 Sponsorship of Televised Sport Events

An Analysis of Mediating Effects on Sponsor Image

Reinhard Grohs[2], Innsbruck University, Austria

Heribert Reisinger, University of Vienna, Austria

---

[2] Contact author.

The authors would like to thank Bettina Cornwell for helpful comments on an earlier draft of this article. We also thank Sabine Vsetecka and Matthias Steffen for providing the data sets for the Alpine Ski World Championship and Soccer Euro study, respectively.

Abstract

The present study contributes to our understanding of brand image formation in sport sponsorship. The authors propose that event image, event-sponsor fit and sponsorship exposure mediate the effect of interest in the sponsored event on sponsor image in two ways. First, high interest in the sponsored event increases perceived event image which in turn benefits sponsor image. Second, high event interest increases spectatorship of the event, and hence exposure to the sponsors of the event. High sponsorship exposure positively impacts on perceived event-sponsor fit and further on sponsor image. Empirical tests at two large televised sport events confirm the proposed hypotheses. Sponsorship managers and event organizers need to be cautious, however, that high levels of exposure can be a nuisance for spectators and might have a direct negative impact on perceived sponsor image.

Keywords

Sport Sponsorship, Sponsor Image, Event Image, Event-Sponsor Fit, Event Interest, Sponsorship Exposure.

2.1   Introduction

Sponsorship of televised sport events has become an important communication tool for companies (e.g., Meenaghan 1996; Sandler/Shani 1989). For hallmark events such as the Beijing Olympics 2008, costs for sponsorship rights reached 1.5 billion US dollar (The Wall Street Journal 2008). At the FIFA Soccer World Cup sponsors like Adidas and Budweiser spent tens of millions of dollars each on sponsorship fees to be official sponsors of the event (Johar et al. 2006). Reasons for companies to engage in special-event (sport) sponsorship are manifold: First, sponsors achieve media exposure to an international, often truly global audience, increasing sponsor prominence and awareness (Lardinoit/Derbaix 2001; Otker/Hayes 1987). Second, hospitality packages allow sponsors to invite key clients and provide them with unique and outstanding experiences (Cornwell/Maignan 1998; Cornwell et al. 2001a). Third, and probably most important, sponsorships are particularly successful in improving the image of the sponsor (Cornwell et al. 2001b; Grohs et al. 2004).

Given the large sums invested in sponsorship of sport events, companies increasingly demand a return on their sponsorship investment and have been eager to measure sponsorship effects. Research on image effects provides evidence that two major conditions drive sponsor image. The meaning transfer model suggests that positive meaning that is ascribed to a sponsored activity will rub off to a sponsor of that event (e.g., Gwinner 1997, based on McCracken 1989). Additionally, congruence theory posits that a better a priori fit between the event and the sponsor benefits perceptions of sponsor image (e.g., Speed/Thompson 2000, based on Kamins 1990).

Other drivers impacting on the goal of image improvement are less understood. Of particular interest for the current investigation are factors that are an integral component of (televised) sport events. A considerable amount of research investigated how interest in the event and sponsorship exposure relate to sponsor image. Event interest is of paramount importance, as sport events convey strong emotional experiences, and attachment to sports, events, teams or athletes is high (e.g., Burnett et al. 1993). Sponsorship exposure is another important issue for sponsors, as sponsorship of sport events allows for a continuous presentation of the sponsor brand during the broadcast of the event (e.g., through perimeter advertising or on athletes' shirts). Some empirical investigations support a direct impact of event interest (e.g., Gwinner/Swanson 2003) and sponsorship exposure (e.g., Cornwell et al. 2001b) on sponsor image, while other studies find no such effect (e.g., Olson 2010; Quester/Farrelly 1998).

The present study argues that these mixed results are a consequence of omitted mediators. In detail, we propose a conceptual framework suggesting that event interest and sponsorship exposure impact on sponsor image on two routes via the mediating variables event image and event-sponsor fit. The model is tested at two large televised sport events for several different sponsors using structural equation modeling. The findings contribute to our understanding of how sponsorship works and provide insights for companies as well as event organizers on the antecedents of sponsor image, thereby providing means for enhancing sponsorship effectiveness.

2.2 Theoretical Foundations of Sponsor Image Formation

2.2.1 Sponsor Image

The Elaboration Likelihood Model posits that two routes to persuasion exist, the central and the peripheral route (Petty/Cacioppo 1986). The central route comprises thoughtful processing of the presented information, while the peripheral route relies on contextual effects that influence persuasion. In a sponsorship context, improvement of sponsor image also happens along these two paths. Consumers' perceptions of a sponsor can benefit from the perception of the event, constituting the peripheral route. Consumers might, however, also evaluate the sponsor, in particular the fit between the event and the sponsor. Such an evaluation relates to the central route of information processing and impacts on sponsor image, too.

The study proposes that event interest and sponsorship exposure are two important antecedents influencing both the perception of the event as well as the thoughtful processing of sponsor information. Consequently, event image and event-sponsor fit are expected to mediate the relationships between event interest and sponsor image as well as between sponsorship exposure and sponsor image. It is argued that, on the one hand, event interest positively affects sponsor image via event image. On the other hand, event interest positively affects sponsorship exposure which in turn increases sponsor image via event-sponsor fit. **Figure 2.1** depicts the comprehensive structural model of sponsorship effects of event image, event-sponsor fit, event interest, and sponsorship exposure on sponsor image in televised sport events. The following subsections outline the theoretical rationale for the proposed relationships in the model.

2.2.2 Event Image

The positive effect of event image on sponsor image is discussed in the meaning transfer model (McCracken 1989). Gwinner (1997) uses McCracken's (1989) model in a sponsorship context and argues that meaning and associations attached with the event will transfer to the sponsor brand when the brand is linked with the event through sponsorship. Empirical support for the image transfer concept comes from Otker/Hayes (1987, FIFA Soccer World Cup) and Stipp/Schiavone (1996, Summer Olympics). Consequently, hypothesis H1 states:

H1: Event image positively affects sponsor image.

2.2.3   Event-Sponsor Fit

The match-up hypothesis supports the proposition that a thoughtful assessment of the fit between a liked object (e.g., celebrity, sport event) and a brand associated with the object (e.g., endorsed brand, sponsor) influences the perceived brand image (e.g., Gwinner/Eaton 1999). Research in advertising demonstrates that matching a celebrity spokesperson with perceived product characteristics leads to more positive consumer attitudes toward the endorsed brand (e.g., Till/Busler 2000). In sponsorship research, empirical studies by Gwinner/Eaton (1999) and Simmons/Becker-Olsen (2006) report a better sponsor image for consumers who perceive a high event-sponsor fit. Hypothesis H2 therefore states:

>   H2: Event-sponsor fit positively affects sponsor image.

In a similar manner, cognitive perceptions of event-sponsor fit might be linked to the image of the sponsored event. Event image consists of all objects, activities and associations related to the event, including the sponsor brands and the match-up between event and sponsor. If a sponsor is perceived to match the event this can positively impact not only on perceived sponsor image (cf. H2) but also on event image. Such effects have not yet been investigated in sponsorship research but are found in brand extension studies where consumer evaluations of the fit between parent brand (i.e., event image) and extension (i.e., sponsor image) affected both the brand extension and the parent brand (e.g., Czellar 2003). In a sponsorship context these findings suggest hypothesis H3:

>   H3: Event-sponsor fit positively affects event image.

2.3   Development of Mediating Hypotheses

2.3.1   Event Interest

Social identity theory states that high identification with an entity leads to more positive perceptions of the entity (e.g., Ashforth/Mael 1989). Consequently, consumers highly interested in a sport event will have better perceptions of this event. The concept of social identity provides a powerful explanation of attitudes and behaviors toward particular leisure activities. The relationship between social identification with events, teams, or rock stars and positive evaluations of these entities is confirmed in a large number of studies (e.g., Madrigal 2001; Meenaghan 2001; Wann/Branscombe 1993). Hypothesis H4 therefore states:

>   H4: Event image mediates the positive effect of event interest on sponsor image.

Social identity theory also predicts behavior with regard to the entity people identify with. High social identification leads to activities congruent with the entity, such as the quest for a greater association with the entity (e.g., Ashforth/Mael 1989). In a sport event context highly interested consumers will aim for a greater association with the sport event, resulting in increased spectatorship of or participation in the event.

Increased participation invariably causes higher levels of sponsorship exposure. Wann/Branscombe (1993) indeed find that persons who strongly identify with a sports team exhibit greater willingness to invest larger amounts of time in order to watch the team play. Consequently, hypothesis H5 states:

> **H5:** Sponsorship exposure mediates the positive effect of event interest on event-sponsor fit.

2.3.2 Sponsorship Exposure

Cognitive learning theory posits that repetition increases message learning, albeit at a diminishing rate (Hawkins et al. 2001). Cornwell et al. (2001b, 49) argue that repetition in sponsorship functions like repetition in advertising by linking and strengthening brand associations in consumers' memory. The link between a sponsor and the sponsored event created by the sponsorship is strengthened by higher levels of sponsorship exposure. As event and sponsor share a larger amount of associations and nodes, recipients of the sponsor message can be expected to experience a greater perceived fit between event and sponsor. Although empirical sponsorship research with regard to this relationship is scarce, Till/Shimp (1998) explain a similar effect in their study on celebrity endorsements suggesting a positive impact of repeated pairings of celebrity endorser and endorsed brand on the fit between the two. Hypothesis H6 therefore states:

> **H6:** Event-sponsor fit mediates the positive effect of sponsorship exposure on sponsor image.

Figure 2.1 Model of Sponsor Image Formation

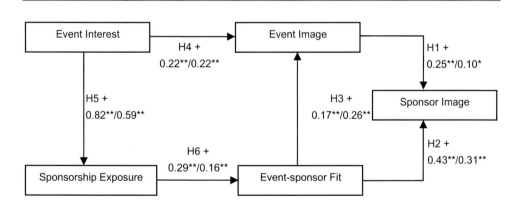

Alpine Ski World Championship / UEFA Soccer European Championship
** p<0.01, * p<0.05

2.4   Empirical Study

2.4.1   Study Design and Data Collection

Two large televised sport events were used to empirically test the relationships, the Alpine Ski World Championship (Ski WCH) and the UEFA Soccer European Championship (Soccer Euro). The Ski WCH lasted for two weeks, the Soccer Euro for three weeks, and both events experienced high levels of TV coverage in the countries the studies were conducted (i.e., Austria for the Ski WCH; Germany and the Netherlands for the Soccer Euro). Four top-tier sponsors were selected for each study – a car brand (BMW), chocolate manufacturer (Milka), beer brand (Carlsberg), and watch manufacturer (Tag Heuer) at the Ski WCH, and a soft drink producer (Coca-Cola), fast food chain (McDonalds), mobile telecommunications provider (T-Mobile) and credit card company (MasterCard) at the Soccer Euro. These sponsors received equivalent standardized sponsorship packages allowing for a simultaneous analysis in order to reduce sponsor-specific effects and increase generalizability of the results across sponsors.

Data was collected within three weeks after the events had finished using standardized questionnaires. Exploratory interviews with sponsorship managers of four sponsors revealed that these companies were predominantly aiming at a younger male target audience. Prior empirical studies also suggested that sport sponsorship usually targets young audiences that are difficult to reach by traditional marketing tools (Nufer 2002; Quester/Thompson 2001). Consequently, respondents were selected to reflect the target population of the events and the sponsors in terms of age and gender using a convenience sampling approach.

Potential respondents were contacted through mail, email, or personally. Respondents who indicated that they were following the respective event were provided with a standardized questionnaire. Non-response was rather low (around 30 percent) probably because of the high level of interest that the two events generated in the countries where the data collection took place. In the Ski WCH study 143 respondents filled out the questionnaires. Eliminating respondents who did not complete all questions resulted in between 89 (Tag Heuer) and 121 (Milka) responses per sponsor. Different numbers of responses per sponsor are caused by the fact that some respondents were not familiar with all sponsors in the study. The Soccer Euro study produced 151 questionnaires, and elimination of respondents who failed to completely fill out the questionnaire resulted in 122 responses for each sponsor. Familiarity of sponsors was not an issue in this case, because all four sponsors were highly prominent and market leaders in their respective product categories.

2.4.2 Constructs and Measures

In order to test the proposed structural model, respondents had to rate a) the event image, b) the sponsor images, c) event-sponsor fit, d) event interest, and e) sponsorship exposure. To assess the image transfer from the event to the sponsor, three conditions need to be satisfied. First, the image dimensions that should transfer to the sponsor have to be essential characteristics of the event (e.g., "sporty" is associated with the Soccer Euro, whereas "classy" is not). Second, the image dimensions conveyed by the event have to be a reasonable addition to the sponsor image (e.g., "healthy" is a welcome image dimension for a fast food company, but not for a credit card brand). Third, event and sponsor image must be measured with the same image items to ensure that specific event image dimensions influence the corresponding sponsor image dimensions.

In line with these suggestions image dimensions were identified for the two televised sport events. For both events a three-step approach was used to generate valid and suitable image items. First, a literature review provided the basis for possible image dimensions (e.g., Aaker 1997; Gwinner/Eaton 1999; Malhotra 1981). Second, personal interviews with sponsor representatives indicated relevant image dimensions for specific brands. Finally, an exploratory study with selected individuals produced additional meaningful image items for both events and all sponsor brands.

For the Ski WCH the pretest generated ten image items associated with the event, i.e., sport, dynamic, health, success, Austria, youth, precision, sociableness, enthusiasm and winter. For specific sponsors some image items were eliminated as they did not fit with the product category. The final list of image items used to measure event image plus the four sponsor images is depicted in **Table 2.1**. Respondents were asked to rate on five-point scales how they perceived the Alpine Ski World Championship and the four sponsors on the relevant image dimensions (1 ... no relation, 5 ... very strong relation; higher numbers indicate a more positive image).

A similar procedure generated ten bipolar image items related to the Soccer Euro, i.e., unathletic/sporty, static/dynamic, unhealthy/healthy, traditional/innovative, lame/energetic, mature/youthful, unemotional/emotional, boring/exciting, monotonous/cheerful, and colorless/colorful. Using the repertory grid method (e.g., Marsden/Littler 2000) specific items were selected to measure sponsor and event images for the four sponsors (cf. **Table 2.1**). Respondents indicated on seven-point semantic differential scales how the image items related to the UEFA Soccer Euro and the sponsoring companies (e.g., 1 ... unathletic, 7 ... sporty; higher numbers indicate the preferred image). Single-item scales were used to measure event-sponsor fit, event interest, and sponsorship exposure. The theoretical rationale for using single-item measures is that all three constructs have a "concrete singular" object (i.e., an object that is easily and uniformly imagined), and respondents have no problem in agreeing as to what the attributes of the three constructs are (e.g., Rossiter 2002). Additionally, previous research also employed single-item indicators to measure the respective constructs (e.g., Cornwell et al. 2006; Hansen/Scotwin 1995; Johar et al. 2006; Wakefield et al. 2007).

Table 2.1   Event and Sponsor Image Dimensions

Alpine Ski World Championship

Event Image	Sponsor Image			
	BMW	**Milka**	**Carlsberg**	**Tag Heuer**
Sport	Sport	Sport	Sport	Sport
Dynamic	Dynamic	Dynamic	–	Dynamic
Health	–	Health	Health	–
Success	Success	Success	Success	Success
Austria	Austria	Austria	Austria	Austria
Youth	Youth	Youth	Youth	Youth
Precision	Precision	–	–	Precision
Sociableness	–	Sociableness	Sociableness	Sociableness
Enthusiasm	Enthusiasm	Enthusiasm	Enthusiasm	Enthusiasm
Winter	Winter	Winter	Winter	Winter

UEFA Soccer European Championship

Event Image	Sponsor Image			
	Coca-Cola	**McDonalds**	**T-Mobile**	**MasterCard**
Sporty	–	Sporty	–	Sporty
Dynamic	Dynamic	Dynamic	Dynamic	Dynamic
Healthy	–	Healthy	–	–
Innovative	Innovative	–	Innovative	–
Energetic	–	–	Energetic	–
Youthful	Youthful	Youthful	Youthful	–
Emotional	Emotional	Emotional	Emotional	Emotional
Exciting	Exciting	Exciting	–	Exciting
Cheerful	Cheerful	–	–	Cheerful
Colorful	Colorful	–	–	–

In the Ski WCH study event-sponsor fit was measured on a five-point scale asking respondents to rate whether they perceived a strong link between event and sponsor (1 … not at all, 5 … certainly). To measure event interest, respondents indicated how interested they were in the Alpine Ski World Championship on a five-point rating scale (1 … no interest, 5 … very high interest). Sponsorship exposure was assessed by asking how often respondents watched TV broadcasts from the Ski WCH (1 … not at all, 5 … daily).

The Soccer Euro study used similar measures. Respondents stated their level of agreement with the statement "There is a strong link between the event and the sponsor" on a seven-point rating scale to measure event-sponsor fit (1 … strongly disagree, 7 … strongly agree). Next, they stated how interested they were in the UEFA Soccer Euro on a seven-point rating scale (1 … not interested at all, 7 … very interested). Finally, respondents confirmed their sponsorship exposure by indicating how many matches they had watched during the Soccer Euro on a six-point rating scale (1 … less than five, 6 … more than 25).

2.4.3   Model Estimation and Results

Demographic characteristics of the samples complied with the target audiences of the events. The Ski WCH sample consisted of 58 percent males and 42 percent females. 28 percent of the respondents were younger than 26 years old, 36 percent from 26 to 35 years old, and 36 percent older. In the Soccer Euro sample 67 percent of the respondents were male and 33 percent female. Overall, spectators at the Soccer Euro were younger than at the Ski WCH with 68 percent of the respondents aged younger than 26 and the remaining 32 percent aged between 26 and 35 years.

To estimate the model in **Figure 2.1** average scores were formed for all sponsor and event images resulting in four sponsor images and four corresponding event images in each study. The data was pooled across all four sponsors in both studies. This procedure led to 434 observations in the Ski WCH study (120 BMW, 121 Milka, 104 Carlsberg, 89 Tag Heuer) and 488 observations in the Soccer Euro study (122 per sponsor). Means, standard deviations, and correlations among the constructs are shown in **Table 2.2**.

AMOS 7 was used to estimate the model in **Figure 2.1** based on the correlations among the constructs in the model. For both data sets the model provided a good fit with the data (Ski WCH: $\chi^2_{(4)}=8.65$, p=0.07, AGFI=0.97, RMR=0.028, CFI=0.99; Soccer Euro: $\chi^2_{(4)}=7.94$, p=0.09, AGFI=0.98, RMR=0.035, CFI=0.99). With regard to the structural relationships H1 to H6, all proposed paths were significant at a level of p<0.05 in both studies. In agreement with the proposed hypotheses all standardized path coefficients were positive (cf. **Figure 2.1**).

Table 2.2   Means, Standard Deviations, and Correlations Among Constructs

Construct	Sponsor Image	Event Image	Event-sponsor Fit	Event Interest	Sponsorship Exposure
Mean	2.75 / 3.98	4.31 / 5.87	2.96 / 3.93	3.27 / 5.75	3.29 / 3.83
SD	0.79 / 1.15	0.41 / 0.61	1.56 / 1.55	1.28 / 1.38	1.37 / 1.59
Sponsor Image		0.35 / 0.18	0.49 / 0.34	0.14 / 0.03	0.17 / -0.01
Event Image			0.23 / 0.28	0.27 / 0.25	0.27 / 0.24
Event-Sponsor Fit				0.29 / 0.08	0.29 / 0.16
Event Interest					0.82 / 0.59

Alpine Ski World Championship / UEFA Soccer European Championship

Not surprisingly, the relationship between event interest and sponsorship exposure showed the largest effect in both studies (H5; Ski WCH: standardized coefficient=0.82, $p<0.01$; Soccer Euro: standardized coefficient=0.59, $p<0.01$). These results provide strong evidence for the hypothesis that people attached to a sport event are indeed willing to spend more time following the event. The second strongest effect in both studies was found for the relationship between event-sponsor fit and sponsor image (H2; Ski WCH: standardized coefficient=0.43, $p<0.01$; Soccer Euro: standardized coefficient=0.31, $p<0.01$). This finding supports the hypothesis that matching event and sponsor benefits perceptions of sponsor image. All other path coefficients were of slightly lower magnitude, nevertheless providing unambiguous support for the remaining hypotheses. Sponsorship exposure exerted a significant positive influence on event-sponsor fit (H6; Ski WCH: standardized coefficient=0.29, $p<0.01$; Soccer Euro: standardized coefficient=0.16, $p<0.01$); both event-sponsor fit (H3; Ski WCH: standardized coefficient=0.17, $p<0.01$; Soccer Euro: standardized coefficient=0.26, $p<0.01$) and event interest (H4; Ski WCH: standardized coefficient=0.22, $p<0.01$; Soccer Euro: standardized coefficient=0.22, $p<0.01$) had a significant positive impact on event image; and event image had a significant positive impact on sponsor image (H1; Ski WCH: standardized coefficient=0.25, $p<0.01$; Soccer Euro: standardized coefficient=0.10, $p<0.05$).

In a next step, modification indexes were examined to confirm the mediating effect, that is, that the proposed model covered all significant empirical relationships among the constructs. Modification indexes indicated only one significant relationship not predicted by the model, namely between sponsorship exposure and sponsor image for the Soccer Euro sample. For exploratory purposes the model in **Figure 2.1** was altered to include a direct path from sponsorship exposure to sponsor image. Estimating the new model for the Soccer

Euro data improved the model fit significantly ($\chi^2_{(3)}$=3.90, p=0.27, AGFI=0.98, RMR=0.017, CFI=1.00; $\Delta\chi^2_{(1)}$=4.04, p<0.05). While all other effects remained stable, the additional path coefficient exhibited a significant negative impact of sponsorship exposure on sponsor image (standardized coefficient=-0.09, p<0.05) suggesting that higher exposure to event sponsorship reduces perceived sponsor image. Adding the same path for the Ski WCH data did not improve the fit of the model ($\chi^2_{(3)}$=8.38, p=0.04, AGFI=0.96, RMR=0.028, CFI=0.99; $\Delta\chi^2_{(1)}$=0.27, p>0.1). The relationship between sponsorship exposure and sponsor image was negative but not significant (standardized coefficient=-0.02, p=0.60) indicating that sponsorship exposure has no direct effect on sponsor image. From these analyses it can be concluded that the existing model is a parsimonious representation of the empirical reality. A discussion of the findings is presented in the next section.

2.5 Implications and Further Research

2.5.1 Theoretical Implications

Two independent empirical studies of large sport events confirm the proposed model of sponsor image formation in televised sport events. The stability of the results is a strong indicator that the model is a valid and reliable representation of how event image, event-sponsor fit, event interest and sponsorship exposure impact on sponsor image.

The study demonstrates that event image and event-sponsor fit exert a strong positive effect on brand image for sponsors of televised sport events. These results support the conceptual idea of the Elaboration Likelihood Model that sponsor image is formed via two routes; the perceptions of the event (peripheral route), and the processing of information related to the link between sport event and sponsor (central route). Furthermore, the findings show that event interest impacts directly on event image and indirectly via sponsorship exposure on perceived event-sponsor fit. No significant direct path between event interest and sponsor image provides evidence that event image, event-sponsor fit and sponsorship exposure completely mediate the effect of event interest on sponsor image (e.g., Baron/Kenny 1986; Iacobucci et al. 2007).

The role sponsorship exposure plays is somewhat ambiguous. In line with the proposed model, sponsorship exposure has a positive impact on sponsor image via event-sponsor fit and event image. Further exploratory analyses revealed that sponsorship exposure also has a significant negative direct effect on sponsor image in the Soccer Euro study. It seems that with increased exposure to the Soccer Euro sponsors are seen as a nuisance. No significant direct negative effect was found in the Ski WCH study. A reason for this finding might be that concerted sponsorship activities were more prevalent during the UEFA Soccer Euro than during the Alpine Ski World Championship leading to a higher perceived commercialization of the event. Commercialization can counteract the positive features of sponsorship (i.e., that it is subtle, credible, and therefore capable of creating goodwill) and breed negative feelings toward the sponsors (e.g., Lee et al. 1997).

Additional research investigating boundary conditions of the observed effect and its relationship with the commercialization of sport events will be of interest to both researchers and practitioners.

2.5.2   Managerial Implications

Sponsors as well as organizers of large sport events learn from this study that televised sport events are indeed capable of transferring specific image components from the sponsored activity to the sponsor. Hence, sponsorship managers should carefully choose events that carry image components they want to be associated with the company. Moreover, sponsor image is perceived to be better if the sponsor fits well with the event. This effect is particularly strong, and it obviously benefits a sponsor's image if an a priori fit between the company and the event exists. Even if preexisting fit is low, research has shown that using marketing tools to communicate the sponsorship (such as advertising, packaging, etc.) increases event-sponsor fit and thereby perceived sponsor image (e.g., Cornwell et al. 2006; Simmons/Becker-Olsen 2006).

Another important aspect for sponsors is that persons attached to a particular event are more likely to hold positive views of this source of identification as well as of companies supporting the event. The pivotal role of event interest is a distinguishing feature and unique advantage of sport sponsorships. Contrary to most other communications tools (with the exception of event marketing), sponsored sport events are particularly capable of generating emotionally laden experiences, which, in turn, create vivid imagery of the sponsoring brand for the consumer (e.g., Cliffe/Motion 2005). Companies should, therefore, identify sports and events that are important for their target audiences and focus their sponsorship activities on creating lasting experiences to strengthen the relationships between brands and consumers.

Obtaining maximum sponsorship exposure (for example, by negotiating contracts that guarantee high levels of sponsor exposure) is often a goal for companies signing sponsorship contracts. From the viewpoint of image improvement (notwithstanding the positive effects of higher exposure on media coverage and sponsor awareness) this is a double-edged sword. Positive effects of increased sponsorship exposure on sponsor image are likely because sponsorship exposure increases perceived fit. In cases of high sponsorship activity and extensive media coverage, yet sponsorship exposure seems to become a nuisance and reduces sponsor image by transferring the negative evaluations of an overly commercialized event onto the sponsors.

2.5.3   Limitations and Further Research

Almost identical results for two different sport events provide evidence of stability of the findings and indicate a high level of external validity. Also, the sample populations reflect the target audiences for the events and sponsors. Nevertheless, using convenience samples is a limitation of the study, as the findings might not generalize to other populations. Further research could use random sampling techniques to investigate the applicability of the results to other data sets.

The empirical test of the proposed model used two different sports (one winter sport focusing on individual athletes and one summer sport focusing on national teams) and eight sponsors in various product categories. Hence, the research covered a breadth of different applications of sport sponsorship, an important tool for brands trying to communicate with their audiences. It remains, however, limited to large televised sport events. Other studies might want to assess the proposed model for other kinds of sponsorship, such as arts or socio-sponsorship, to point out similarities and differences in the ways different sponsorships are processed.

The study provides a comprehensive structural model of how brand image is formed in sponsorships. While the research addresses mechanisms of how event image, event-sponsor fit, event interest and sponsorship exposure impact on sponsor image, the data does not provide proof of causality. To support the direction of the paths in the model an experimental design would be more appropriate, as some authors suggest (e.g., Cornwell et al. 2005). Such a methodology would also allow for investigating more elaborate relationships like possible interactions between the variables in the model. Finally, researchers identified other important antecedents of brand image in sponsorships. Future research could examine the effects of these variables on sponsor image and explore how they fit into the nomological network proposed in the present study.

Literature

[1]   Aaker, J. (1997): Dimensions of brand personality. Journal of Marketing Research, Vol. 34, August, pp. 347-356.

[2]   Ashforth, B. E./Mael, F. (1989): Social identity theory and the organization. Academy of Management Review, Vol. 14, 1, pp. 20-39.

[3]   Baron, R. M./Kenny, D. A. (1986): The moderator-mediator variable distinction in social psychological research: conceptual, strategic, and statistical considerations. Journal of Personality and Social Psychology, Vol. 51, 6, pp. 1173-1182.

[4]   Burnett, J./Menon, A./Smart, D. T. (1993): Sports marketing: a new ball game with new rules. Journal of Advertising Research, Vol. 33, 5, pp. 21-35.

[5]   Cliffe, S. J./Motion, J. (2005): Building contemporary brands: a sponsorship-based strategy. Journal of Business Research, Vol. 58, 8, pp. 1068-1077.

[6]   Cornwell, T. B./Humphreys, M. S./Maguire, A. M./Weeks, C. S./Tellegen, C. L. (2006): Sponsorship-linked marketing: the role of articulation in memory. Journal of Consumer Research, Vol. 33, December, pp. 312-321.

[7]   Cornwell, T. B./Maignan, I. (1998): An international review of sponsorship research. Journal of Advertising, Vol. 27, 1, pp. 1-21.

[8]   Cornwell, T. B./Pruitt, S. W./Van Ness, R. (2001a): The value of winning in motorsports: sponsorship-linked marketing. Journal of Advertising Research, Vol. 41 (January/February), pp. 17-31.

[9]   Cornwell, T. B./Roy, D. P./Steinard, E. A. II (2001b): Exploring managers' perceptions of the impact of sponsorship on brand equity. Journal of Advertising, Vol. 30, 2, pp. 41-51.

[10] Cornwell, T. B./Weeks, C. S./Roy, D. P. (2005): Sponsorship-linked marketing: opening the black box. Journal of Advertising, Vol. 34, 2, pp. 21-42.

[11] Czellar, S. (2003): Consumer attitude toward brand extensions: an integrative model and research propositions. International Journal of Research in Marketing, Vol. 20, 1, pp. 97-115.

[12] Grohs, R./Wagner, U./Vsetecka, S. (2004): Assessing the effectiveness of sports sponsorships – an empirical examination. Schmalenbach Business Review, Vol. 56, 2, pp. 119-138.

[13] Gwinner, K. P. (1997): A model of image creation and image transfer in event sponsorship. International Marketing Review, Vol. 14, 3, pp. 145-158.

[14] Gwinner, K. P./Eaton, J. P. (1999): Building brand image through event sponsorship: the role of image transfer. Journal of Advertising, Vol. 28, 4, pp. 47-57.

[15] Gwinner, K. P./Swanson, S. R. (2003): A model of fan identification: antecedents and sponsorship outcomes. Journal of Services Marketing, Vol. 17, 3, pp. 275-294.

[16] Hansen, F./Scotwin, L. (1995): An experimental enquiry into sponsoring: what effects can be measured? Marketing and Research Today, Vol. 23, 3, pp. 173-181.

[17] Hawkins, S. A./Hoch, S. J./Meyers-Levy, J. (2001): Low-involvement learning: repetition and coherence in familiarity and belief. Journal of Consumer Psychology, Vol. 11, 1, pp. 1-11.

[18] Iacobucci, D./Saldanha, N./Deng, X. (2007): A mediation on mediation: evidence that structural equations models perform better than regressions. Journal of Consumer Psychology, Vol. 17, 2, pp. 140-154.

[19] Johar, G. V./Pham, M. T./Wakefield, K. L. (2006): How event sponsors are really identified: a (baseball) field analysis. Journal of Advertising Research, Vol. 46 (June), pp. 183-198.

[20] Kamins, M. A. (1990): An investigation into the "match-up" hypothesis in celebrity advertising: when beauty may be only skin deep. Journal of Advertising, Vol. 19, 1, pp. 4-13.

[21] Lardinoit, T./Derbaix, C. (2001): Sponsorship and recall of sponsors. Psychology & Marketing, Vol. 18, 2, pp. 167-190.

[22] Lee, M.-S./Sandler, D. M./Shani, D. (1997): Attitudinal construct toward sponsorship: scale development using three global sporting events. International Marketing Review, Vol. 14, 3, pp. 159-169.

[23] Madrigal, R. (2001): Social identity effects in a belief-attitude-intentions hierarchy: implications for corporate sponsorship. Psychology & Marketing, Vol. 18, 2, pp. 145-165.

[24] Malhotra, N. K. (1981): A scale to measure self-concepts, person concepts, and product concepts. Journal of Marketing Research, Vol. 18, November, pp. 456-464.

[25] Marsden, D./Littler, D. (2000): Exploring consumer product construct systems with the repertory grid technique. Qualitative Market Research, Vol. 3, 3, pp. 127-144.

[26] McCracken, G. (1989): Who is the celebrity endorser? Cultural foundations of the endorsement process. Journal of Consumer Research, Vol. 16, December, pp. 310-321.

[27] Meenaghan, T. (1996): Ambush marketing – a threat to corporate sponsorship. Sloan Management Review, Vol. 38, 1, pp. 103-113.

[28] Meenaghan, T. (2001): Understanding sponsorship effects. Psychology & Marketing, Vol. 18, 2, pp. 95-122.

[29] Nufer, G. (2002): Wirkungen von Sportsponsoring: Empirische Analyse am Beispiel der Fußball-Weltmeisterschaft 1998 in Frankreich unter besonderer Berücksichtigung von Erinnerungswirkungen bei jugendlichen Rezipienten. Berlin: Mensch-und-Buch-Verlag.

[30] Olson, E. L. (2010): Does sponsorship work in the same way in different sponsorship contexts? European Journal of Marketing, Vol. 44, 1/2, pp. 180-199.

[31] Otker, T./Hayes, P. (1987): Judging the efficiency of sponsorship: experience from the 1986 Soccer World Cup. European Research, Vol. 15, 4, pp. 3-8.

[32] Petty, R. E./Cacioppo, J. T. (1986): Communication and persuasion. Central and peripheral routes to attitude change. New York: Springer Verlag.

[33] Quester, P. G./Farrelly, F. (1998): Brand association and memory decay effects of sponsorship: the case of the Australian Formula One Grand Prix. Journal of Product & Brand Management, Vol. 7, 6, pp. 539-556.

[34] Quester, P. G./Thompson, B. (2001): Advertising and promotion leverage on arts sponsorship effectiveness. Journal of Advertising Research, Vol. 41, January/February, pp. 33-47.

[35] Rossiter, J. R. (2002): The C-OAR-SE procedure for scale development in marketing. International Journal of Research in Marketing, Vol. 19, 4, pp. 305-335.

[36] Sandler, D. M./Shani, D. (1989): Olympic sponsorship vs. "ambush" marketing: who gets the Gold? Journal of Advertising Research, Vol. 29, August/September, pp. 9-14.

[37] Simmons, C. J./Becker-Olsen, K. L. (2006): Achieving marketing objectives through social sponsorships. Journal of Marketing, Vol. 70, October, pp. 154-169.

[38] Speed, R./Thompson, P. (2000): Determinants of sport sponsorship response. Journal of the Academy of Marketing Science, Vol. 28, 2, pp. 226-238.

[39] Stipp, H./Schiavone, N. P. (1996): Modeling the impact of Olympic sponsorship on corporate image. Journal of Advertising Research, Vol. 36, July/August, pp. 22-27.

[40] The Wall Street Journal (2008): Athletic-wear firm's Olympic dream fades: China's Li Ning ends unofficial bid to capture spotlight. Vol. 25, June, 2008, B1.

[41] Till, B. D./Busler, M. (2000): The match-up hypothesis: physical attractiveness, expertise, and the role of fit on brand attitude, purchase intent, and brand beliefs. Journal of Advertising, Vol. 29, 3, pp. 1-13.

[42] Till, B. D./Shimp, T. A. (1998): Endorsers in advertising: the case of negative celebrity information. Journal of Advertising, Vol. 27, 1, pp. 67-82.

[43] Wakefield, K. L./Becker-Olsen, K. L./Cornwell, T. B. (2007): I spy a sponsor: the effects of sponsorship level, prominence, relatedness, and cueing on recall accuracy. Journal of Advertising, Vol. 36, 4, pp. 61-74.

[44] Wann, D. L./Branscombe, N. R. (1993): Sports fans: measuring degree of identification with their team. International Journal of Sport Psychology, Vol. 24, pp. 1-17.

3   The Countenance of Marketing: A View From the 21st Century Ivory Tower

Rajan Nataraajan, Auburn University, United States of America

Abstract

In this "thought piece", as a marketing academic, the author reflects on what truly matters in terms of research into marketing in this century. Based upon a careful scan of the "goings on" in the world, he first offers a configuration that may aid in research idea or specific topic generation and then culls out broad areas that are worthy of academic enquiry by marketers of this new millennium.

Keywords

New Millennium Marketing, 21st Century Marketing, Aging, Culture, Leisure, Environment, Happiness.

3.1 Introduction

This "thought piece" is an extension of my forthcoming article in the *Journal of Research for Consumers [JRC]* and this is also partially based on elements of invited talks that I gave to largely academic audiences at several locations on the globe during the 2007-2011 period.[3] Following my style in the above JRC article, again purely in the interest of not marring the flow or readability, I shall refrain from cluttering this piece up with citations save for what must be cited for the sake of clarity. The interested reader can always contact me for further information on anything, be it a term or a name, mentioned in this paper. Having said that, I will, in all humility, readily and willingly admit that my thoughts have been triggered, influenced and even shaped by the minds of the academic communities around the world and their collective body of work reflected in extant literatures, and I thank all of them.

The last millennium ended with two notable events. One was the "dot.com" crash which actually occurred, much to the shock of the newly minted "dot.com" moguls of Silicon Valley, and the other was the "Y2K" scare which turned out to be just a "scare" and did not come to pass. The new millennium was ushered in eleven years ago and we have already witnessed enough calamitous events including the terrible 9/11 tragedy, devastating Tsunami(s), housing market collapse in the world's leading economy, mid-east turmoil, and the worldwide economic crises, to name the most salient ones. However, we have also seen the cautious recovery of the "dot.com" industry and are seeing a more widespread understanding of environmental issues and the need for substantial reduction in carbon footprints, as well as the need for more balanced approaches in world affairs (e.g., the need for a level-playing field in international business, "outsourcing", achievement of peace etc.).

Against this backdrop, while all evidence points to the fact that marketing continues to be the dynamic pidgin discipline that it has been since its inception as a field worthy of serious academic enquiry at the beginning of the last century, one cannot help but wonder if marketing continues to be Drucker's Economic Engine of a society (Nataraajan/Bagozzi, 1999). More aptly perhaps, one ought to wonder if marketing should continue to be purely an economic engine or should it change form in cognizance of the new realities that characterize this century. In any case, the fact remains that the new realities of this century have already begun to and will continue to impact consumers around the globe. Since "C" is at the center of the marketing mix around which the 4Ps (or the 5Ps including "politics", or the 6Ps including "public opinion", or the 7Ps of services marketing) revolve within the constellation of the environmental factors, it follows that any impact of the new realities of this century on "C" will influence all aspects of marketing. Consequently, focusing on these realities will aid us in seeing how marketing is likely to change in this century and possibly beyond. This is what this paper ponders.

---

[3] "Hot Topics for the New Millennium Marketer": Talk given in 2007 at Yonsei University, Seoul National University, and Sookmyung Women's University, all in Seoul, Korea. Updated versions of this talk was given at Peking University, China, in 2008 and at the Vienna School of Business & Economics, Vienna, Austria, in 2011.

3.2   The Base Realities

Nataraajan (2012) points out that if one were to shine the 21st century light on marketing, then three key areas covering the realities of this century become visible. These are Aging, Culture, and Leisure. Clearly, the area that stands out most is "aging" as people are living longer, and the resulting increase in longevity has a profound impact on all aspects of marketing, especially consumer behavior. "Culture" emerges next as most societies around the world are morphing into multicultural ones with swiftly evolving subsets. These cultural subsets are changing the very foci of marketing. Finally, "leisure" emerges as the third area on the broad reality tapestry. Nataraajan further points out that, by and large, "leisure" goes hand in hand with "aging" and that whereas the retired folk obviously have more leisure, the non-retired folk see it in rather severe short supply. In other words, in recent decades, leisure has become a precious commodity for the latter segment. The important consequence of this trend is that people have become far more selective than they have ever been in how they use this valuable resource. Nataraajan further opines that such selectiveness has direct and significant implications for the transportation, travel, tourism, & hospitality sectors, and indirect but clear implications for the rest of the sectors. Overall, these base realities form platforms both severally and jointly for the birth of research projects in marketing that would be meaningful in the 21st century. **Figure 3.1** depicts these base realities.

3.3   The All Pervading Realities

Nataraajan (2012) also sensitizes the reader to two other global realities that envelop and pervade the aforementioned base realities. They are, "terrestrial environment" and "human happiness". Terrestrial environment automatically and heavily impacts all three key areas of aging, culture, and leisure and to say, "If you don't care about the environment, then you are on the verge of losing it all" would be a cliché. The implications for marketing in this regard are self-evident and there is little need to dwell on them. The all pervasive impact of the environment increases the complexity in potential research projects in all areas of marketing. This no doubt renders them more challenging but, by the same token, such challenge makes the research process that much more exciting.

Happiness or bliss, or eudaimonia as the ancient Greeks referred to it (Bagozzi/Nataraa-jan, 2000), has been the intangible object of relentless human pursuit since time immemorial. While one may not always be cognizant of its soothing presence, one will readily feel its absence! A wise philosopher once advised that if you are not hungry, you have protection against the elements, and you have no bodily pain, then you are at "100% happiness". The implication of this advice is that any time you try to get more than this "100%", you will pay a price!

Figure 3.1   The 21st Century Key Areas

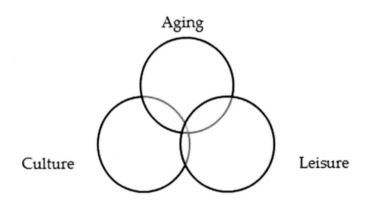

Based on Nataraajan (2012).

Unfortunately however, the vast majority of humans have always gone against the above advice. They have always wanted more than the "happiness" contained in its dictum as evidenced by their desires, attitudes, intentions, opinions, expectations, and actions exhibited since time immemorial, and human history is riddled with the "price" paid.

Be that as it may, this pursuit of happiness continues and the hope is that the people of the 21st century will endeavor to achieve happiness by pursuing it more intelligently than has been done in the past. Rationally, there is a dire need for it now if a potential doom is to be avoided. In fact, just as the "C" drives the marketing mix, human happiness is at the very core of it all and has the potential to influence the entire 21st century scene. It would be wise to realize that a conscious consideration of "Are you happy?" and "Are others happy?" will open up connections to the "not for profit" sector, "corporate sponsorship", "emotions", and facets of "altruism", all of which can lead to potential research projects for marketers.

The inclusion of the roles of terrestrial environment and happiness results in a configuration called the 21st century research smorgasbord (Nataraajan, 2012). **Figure 3.2** depicts this configuration. It shows the three key areas of aging, culture, and leisure as intersecting circles but perhaps, more realistically, they could be viewed as intersecting spheres. As mentioned earlier, while each of these three key areas is a fertile research ground by itself, the sub-areas formed by the intersections of these areas may be of even greater importance as they cover all other aspects of the 21st century realities. Consequently, they will likely be even richer in potential research projects.

Further, a consideration of the pervasive influence of the environment will add to the reality, the richness, and the complexity of potential projects. Finally, if the achievement -and sustenance of- human happiness is seen as the ultimate goal in what we do in marketing, then that realization will cast any research project in new light.

Figure 3.2   The 21st Century Research Smorgasbord

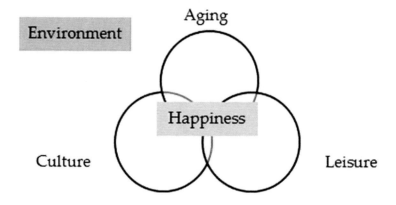

Based on Nataraajan (2012).

It is important to emphasize that each of these five elements encompasses other smaller elements and they, in turn, subsume even smaller ones, and so on. For example, the area of "environment" covers "greening", "sustainability" etc. and they can be broken down to "pollution", "solar power", "water resources" etc., which can be further split into "solar powered cars", "solar powered homes", "bottled water versus faucet water purifiers", and the like. Similarly, "aging" encompasses a huge portion of "medical marketing" and all its ramifications including the online ethical drug business.

If the 21st century marketer projects pretty much any topic on the configuration in **Figure 3.2** and then contemplates on just one section or one intersecting section, then specific research ideas will spring forth in his/her mind. While not all of them may be feasible from a practical standpoint, many of them may be worthy of academic pursuit. As Nataraajan (2012) quips, the only impediment that can come into play to thwart this possibility is a bridled imagination!

3.4   Broad Topic Areas for the 21ˢᵗ Century Marketer

According to the Great Confucius, there are three methods by which we may acquire wisdom. To do this by reflection is the noblest of the three, gaining it by imitation is the easiest of the three, and acquiring it by experience is the bitterest of the three. In line with his sage counsel, by reflecting on what has been happening in the world and on my own direct and indirect (sometimes vicarious) experiences in academia and elsewhere, I have come up with several broad topic areas that strike me as particularly relevant for research into marketing in this century. These are e-commerce, green marketing, healthcare, altruism, relationship marketing, new perspectives and techniques, brand aspects, celebrities, and last but definitely not the least, the government! These will be discussed in varying detail in the rest of the paper.

- E-Commerce

Also known as electronic marketing, internet marketing, or online marketing, the area of e-commerce is gaining importance everyday as it becomes more and more ubiquitous and significantly facilitates and adds strength to global marketing. In the process, it is rapidly changing the predominant "Brick & Mortar" [B&M] based practice of marketing into one that is increasingly becoming cyber-based through "mixed-mode" operation. It is not inconceivable that one day the practice of marketing or business itself will be totally cyber-based.

E-commerce had its reality check after the many myths surrounding it were debunked following the "dot.com" crash (Rosenbloom, 2002) and all the players in this vast and spread out arena began to develop a more down to earth perspective of their roles in it.[4] In particular, the salience of the human element (which had been relegated to a state of unimportance in the hype of "pure play" mode of operation) vis a vis the technological element appears to have been re-established (Nataraajan, 2006). Further, the intensity of the Techno-Hyperopia that characterized e-commerce appears to have mellowed out. Most importantly, the morphing of the image of internet marketing as a Terrible Terminator (of B&M establishments) to that of a Terrific Augmenter (of B&M establishments through "mixed-mode" operation) has occurred. Consequently, internet marketing has gained new respect in the business world and the number of players is increasing by the day around the world. In short, e-commerce is here to stay, period.

---

[4] Rosenbloom pointed out these ten deadly myths of e-commerce. They are the myth of disintermediation, the myth of lower costs, the myth of real time product flow, the myth of profits don't count, the myth of first mover advantage, the myth of market cap worship, the myth of convenience and efficiency are everything, the myth of pure play, the myth of valuation by publicity, and the myth of a whole new culture.

The simplest way to describe the research potential in the e-commerce area for marketers (and particularly for consumer behaviorists) is by pointing out that they can endeavor to replicate whatever research has occurred or occurring in the B&M setup in the online context. In short, all cognitive school specifics including Belief, Attitude both explicit and implicit, Opinion, Intention, Expectation, Behavior, Control both perceived and actual, Involvement, Risk, Knowledge, Framing, Priming, Desire, Memory, Pleasure, Arousal, Personality, Emotion, Self-Concept, Regulatory Focus, Dissonance, Confusion, Anger, Love, Happiness, Impulse behavior, and Aberrant consumer behavior (e.g., compulsive behavior) are topics worthy of academic enquiry in the online context. Further, even some aspects of evolutionary psychology [EP] may be amenable for application in the online context.

Further, specific consumer behavior topics include Shopping & shopper types, Buying, Satisfaction-Dissatisfaction, Complaint Behavior, Switching Cost, Brand Loyalty, Compulsive Buying, Ethical Aspects, Search Behavior, Cultural Aspects, Cross-Cultural Aspects, Corporate Culture, Information Overload, Credence Qualities, Experiential Qualities, Vicarious Learning, Psychographics, Pharmaceutical Marketing, Marketing of Religion, Marketing of Education, Scarcity Theory, Not-for-Profit Sector, Philanthropy, Marketing of Professionals, Entertainment Marketing, Sports Marketing, Effects of the Various New Cyber-Laws, and Behavior in CME, among others.

In fact, researchers have already begun to investigate everything from segmentation potential to e-satisfaction & e-loyalty to the role of emotions in online retail setting to the state of "flow" on the internet and all the way to "atmospherics" potential in the online context. "Travel & tourism", "online auctions", "pharmaceutical marketing", "marketing to young adults & kids [teens & tweens]", "banking and investing", and "trust toward e-tailers" are other specific areas that are being investigated in the online context. Further, the phenomenon of "co-production" (the concept of "prosumers" which refers to consumers also participating in production of offerings) also seems ripe for investigation in the online context.

Furthermore, there have already been attempts to look at the online context from the EP perspective (e.g., the use of "herding", "hunter-gatherers", "optimal foraging" etc.). Finally, researchers, in this mocial[5] era, are increasingly turning to online data collection. All such efforts are commendable but the fact remains that we have barely scratched the surface of the enormous research potential in the area of e-commerce. Take for instance, "atmospherics" in the online context. Images (static and dynamic) and background music have been tackled via screen and banner designs. Bringing in "smell" in the online context also seems to be a distinct possibility. However, the sense of "taste" and the even more difficult sense of "touch" which are taken for granted in the B&M context continue to be only in our imagination as we are not –yet- in the Star Trek era!

---

[5] This term refers to the mobile, social and local forms of communication mix and underscores the worldwide phenomenon of billions of people performing some combination of logging onto social networks and downloading mobile applications.

Be that as it may, think of the realistic possibilities in research topics when e-commerce is viewed in its individual intersection with "aging", "culture", or "leisure" or in its combinatorial forms. First, the advantage of the lack of "location" constraint coupled with aspects of "aging" (e.g., longevity and the desire to be employed if in god health) and "leisure" (e.g., the desire to make an extra buck) could mean more people entering the online business (both "for profit" and "not for profit"). Second, online marketing to the older consumers, the elderly, or those in their golden years opens up newer vistas in research potential as aspects and issues of "delivery", "delay", "complexity", and "trust" in terms of "security" and "privacy" take on deeper if not newer meanings.

In sum, while rapid progress is being made in understanding online marketing (and online consumer behavior), the area of e-commerce is still wide open for more research and this is what we are likely to see in this century.

■ Green Marketing

While "green marketing", also known as environmentally conscious marketing or ecologically conscious marketing, has been receiving mixed reactions owing to global politics of the negative kind as well as the increased costs of "green offerings" vis a vis "non-green offerings", it is expected that such myopia in this regard will slowly wane if not vanish altogether in this century once the negative impact of carbon footprints of nations is felt more intensely around the globe. It is expected that there will be a resurgence of conservation measures like recycling and re-forestation and a more vigorous pursuit of environmentally friendly solar power, wind power, tidal power, and bio-fuels from natural sources like corn and sugarcane. It is also expected that the escalating demand for fresh water with dwindling water resources will have an impact on marketing and consumer behavior around the world.

In short, green marketing will become a "must be done" task in this century. While a good volume of research touching many aspects of ecological consciousness (e.g., organic foods, environmentally friendly attitudes and behaviors [e.g., recycling, safe disposal of chemicals etc.], connections to health care etc.) already exists, definitely more can be done in all aspects including even marketing education in this regard. Further, viewing topics in green marketing in the light of the research Smorgasbord will open up a myriad other new research topics in this area.

■ Health Care

Health care marketing is already a well established sub-field of marketing. Economic (e.g., rising costs), social (e.g., health insurance), political (e.g., type of health care, aspects of the AMA, alternative medicine etc.), moral (e.g., the use of marijuana for medical reasons, alcohol consumption etc.), and ethical (pertaining to the practice of medicine like unneeded procedures, false prescriptions, false medical notes, fudged research etc.) factors as well as aspects of green marketing and food marketing (including relatively newer aspects like genetically modified foods, new cookware etc.) will ensure that this sub-field will rise in importance in this century.

While all five elements of the Smorgasbord will significantly influence this area, "aging" in particular will heavily impact it in this century. It will be beyond the scope of this paper to indulge in further discussion of this area but it would be in order to emphasize the importance of this area in no uncertain terms.

- Altruism

Marketers may have to play a greater role in this area in this century as the world continues to see social and societal misery in a variety of forms. Examples include "hunger", "child abuse" (e.g., "sweat shops"), and "the state of the elderly", among many others. There can be no real eudaimonia in the world until these abate. As mentioned earlier in this paper, viewing this area in the light of the Smorgasbord will open up connections to the "not for profit" sector, "corporate sponsorship", "emotions" etc., all of which can lead to potential research projects for marketers.

- Relationship Marketing

This area will likely become more important in this century as it will be increasingly more difficult to practice it. Reasons include the ever increasing global competition, the pressure to "think globally and act locally", the current state of the online context (e.g., the lack of FTF interaction), political and social aspects of green marketing, and rising costs of operation in general, among others. While some may see the rise of "outsourcing" beyond national borders as somewhat altruistic, it plausibly adds to difficulties in the practice of relationship marketing as it renders it even more multi-layered and introduces political and social factors (e.g., the resulting domestic unemployment and resentment).[6]

- Newer Perspectives & Techniques

Marketing has become and is likely to become even more complex owing to the realities of this century. This warrants a need for fresh perspectives and techniques that can deal with the complexities in marketing practice. Efforts are already underway and some of them are considered here.

Evolutionary Psychology [EP]

Relatively recently, aspects of evolutionary psychology have figured in the collective research interest of consumer behaviorists. Examples include "an evolutionary perspective on gift-giving among young adults", "the behavioral ecology of brand choice", and "birth order effects", among others. The modus-operandi here seems to be one of first viewing broad business/marketing topics from an EP perspective to facilitate shedding light on specific consumer behavior topics. Researchers have already researched "hip-to-waist ratio" to fathom if there is a natural beauty scale which can have implications for the apparel or more broadly the fashion sector. It does not seem farfetched to think that research into

---

[6] "The best and the brightest of the rich world must increasingly compete with the best and the brightest from poorer countries who are willing to work harder for less money." http://www.economist.com/node/21528226.

why human females developed (evolved) breasts could have implications for designing a better brassiere. Who knows what research into why human females, by and large, seem to have a fascination for well-toned male buttocks will lead to as an implication for consumer behavior?

In any case, the use of EP concepts in consumer behavior research has begun to spread to the online context. Examples include "herding in online product choice", "hunter-gatherers in online search", and "optimal foraging online as a response to increasing sensitivity to delay", among others.

Biomarketing

Even more recently, research in neurology, neuroendocrinology, and genetics appear to be aiding the formation of what is now termed "biomarketing". Researchers are investigating the potential of biomarketing in understanding concepts like "self-interest", Machiavellianism, and human empathy. One can readily see the connection to "customer orientation" as well as to "altruism" in general.

New Techniques

All disciplines in the social sciences have been using mathematics and statistics albeit in varying degrees for decades. However, marketing has also seen an influx of concepts from biology and physics (e.g., models from epidemiology, moment of inertia in sales-call scheduling, concomitant measurement [which gave rise to conjoint measurement which led to conjoint analysis] etc.). In current times, business networks have not only grown substantially larger but also are becoming increasingly complex owing to enhanced C-to-C content (via blogging, Facebook, Twitter etc.). Neural networks, probably the most recent entry into marketing, are showing considerable promise in dealing with the complexities in marketing practice. However, there appear to be other possibilities particularly for determining the stability of such networks. Here is an example.

Example: The measurement of stability of electrical networks comes to mind as a possibility. **Figure 3.3** shows a basic electrical circuit consisting of a resistance, an inductance and a capacitance. The Laplace transfer function of the impedance here would be [R + sL +1/sC]. Typically a Bode plot or a Nyquist plot could be used to determine the stability of this extremely simple and rudimentary electrical network. Perhaps, a similar technique could be developed for determining the stability of marketing networks. Of course, it may be a giant of a leap from the ratio scaled (or at least truly interval-scaled environment in engineering) to the mostly pseudo-interval scaled environment of marketing or consumer behavior in particular but if what was fiction yesterday can become reality today, such possibilities may be worth exploring.[7]

---

[7] It is hoped that Prof. Udo Wagner will take an interest in this regard!

Figure 3.3   New Techniques/Models

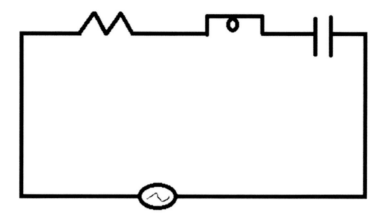

■ Brand Aspects

The realities of the 21st century will affect well known concepts surrounding "brands". The proliferation in brands and brand features coupled with the widespread monopolistic competitive structures in markets characterized by the three key areas of "aging", "culture" and "leisure" within the interplay of environmental factors and the human quest for happiness will likely enhance brand confusion thereby impacting brand personality, brand loyalty and brand equity and/or the newer concept of customer equity. Consequently, all these aspects may have to be recast conceptually in the light of **Figure 3.2**.

■ Celebrities

The perspective on celebrities will also alter when cast against the background in **Figure 3.2**. First, there will be more celebrities emerging from the so called "golden years" segment! It will not be just isolated cases like Ray Kroc of McDonald's fame who became a celebrity in his senior years. Public perceptions of sports marketing will also alter as there will be more of the older participants. It will not be just isolated cases like George Foreman winning back his heavyweight boxing title when he was well into his forties! Second, regardless of the field in which someone makes a mark, the standards for attaining and maintaining the celebrity status will likely become even more stringent than it is now because the public may wish to see a more "comprehensive contribution" to the world before heaping accolades on the candidate and according such status.

■ The Government

I shall end this paper by proclaiming that no organizational entity needs marketing more than a government at any level anywhere on earth. Government needs marketing! A government can be the best fuel for the economic engine called marketing. It can be a symbiotic relationship. Marketing can help the government in taking sound economic decisions and in turn, the government can help in feeding the marketing engine!

Literature

[1] Bagozzi, R.P./Nataraajan, R. (2000): The year 2000: Looking forward. Psychology & Marketing, Vol. 17, pp. 1-11.

[2] Nataraajan, R. (2012): To the young and the restless marketing academic aspirant: Musings on the publishing game. Journal of Research for Consumers [forthcoming]

[3] Nataraajan, R. (2006): Marketing on the internet: Looking back & looking forward. International Journal of Advanced Media and Communication, Vol. 1, 2, pp. 103-110.

[4] Nataraajan, R./Bagozzi, R.P. (1999): The year 2000: Looking back. Psychology & Marketing, Vol. 16, pp. 631-642.

[5] Rosenbloom, B. (2002): The ten deadly myths of e-commerce. Business Horizons, Vol. 45, 2, pp. 61-66.

4   Profiting From Uncertainty

Kalyan Raman, Northwestern University and University of Michigan, United States of America

Hubert Gatignon, INSEAD, France

Abstract

We show that market response uncertainty can be judiciously harnessed in determining the optimal advertising budget and spending pattern to improve the expected profitability of a firm. Using stochastic optimal control, we derive the optimal feedback advertising policy to accomplish this objective, and establish that the optimal advertising policy increases profitability at a rate directly proportional to the error variance.

Keywords

Advertising Budget Allocation, Sales Response to Advertising, Uncertainty.

4.1   Introduction

Market response uncertainty is typically regarded as a nuisance that impedes the researcher's objectives, especially those pertaining to estimation and optimization. Yet, carefully harnessed, uncertainty is a source of enhanced profitability! The profitability gain is realized by rigorous mathematical construction of the marketing policy, achieved through stochastic optimal control. We will demonstrate this in the context of a classic model of sales response to advertising—a model empirically well-established and extensively used for profit maximization.

The main result is that, relative to a policy that ignores uncertainty when maximizing profit, the optimal advertising policy increases profitability at a rate directly proportional to the error variance. The proportionality factor is a function of the model parameters and is a by-product of the analytical form of the optimal advertising policy. A secondary result is that uncertainty changes the optimal policy both quantitatively and qualitatively. The key theoretical contribution is the counter-intuitive insight that profitability can be significantly increased by exploiting uncertainty, and the central methodological contribution is a systematic algorithm for doing so. The key managerial output is an easily implementable methodology for turning uncertainty into enhanced profits.

4.2   Literature Review

4.2.1   Allocation of Marketing Resources and Uncertainty

Uncertainty in market response and in marketing effectiveness parameters was first recognized to analyze the question of experimentation with advertising budget over time. Using an adaptive control approach, Little (1966) established the value of experimentation with subsequent expansions by Pekelman/Tse (1980) or Nguyen (1985). The trade offs between short term profit maximization and long term benefits from better estimates of marketing effectiveness have clearly been identified by these authors. However, this literature does not concern the issue of allocation of resources across marketing mix, market segments or territories.

The extent marketing literature that explicitly recognizes market response uncertainty is relatively sparse. The Dorfman-Steiner (1954) theorem provide rules for the allocation of a marketing budget across marketing mix instruments. However, these rules assume that the elasticities are estimated without error, even if they can have deterministic variations based on exogenous factors or due to interaction among the marketing mix variables (Gatignon/Hanssens 1987).

We first identify the aspects of uncertainty which have been considered and how this uncertainty is taken into account. Then, we review the conclusions that can be derived from taking these uncertainties into account. We finally draw conclusions from the evolution of the literature on optimal marketing resource allocation.

4.2.2   Uncertainty in Marketing Resource Allocation Models

We can identify three aspects regarding the inclusion of uncertainty in marketing resource allocation models:

1. uncertainty in response function and in marketing parameter estimates,
2. allocation decision with uncertainty without expected value/risk trade-offs,
3. allocation decision under risk.

Morey/McCann (1983) use the information about the estimation error of the elasticity to derive a confidence interval for the ratio of elasticities that correspond to the optimal allocation rule of the Dorfman/Steiner rule.

Another approach consists in considering the uncertainty in the demand function to derive the risk adjusted sales. Jagpal/Brick (1982) derive the risk adjusted elasticities for each of the marketing instruments and use these to apply the Dorfman-Steiner ratio of elasticities. The allocation of resources (including coordination in pricing) is considered in Reibstein/Gatignon (1984). Using a multiplicative response function, where the error term is linearized after a logarithmic transformation, the expected value of sales quantities is a function of the variance of the sales regression equation. This variance, which corresponds to the uncertainty in the response function, is part of the expression determining the optimal allocation. In this case, it is not the elasticity which is risk-adjusted but the decision rule based on maximizing the expected profits contains the variance of unexplained demand. The expected value takes the uncertainty estimates into account but does not adjust for risk. In a decision about which market test should be conducted, Chatterjee et al. (1988) consider the risk adjusted profits to be expected by calculating the certainty equivalent payoff. This constant absolute risk-aversion utility function is also assumed by Mantrala/Sinha/Zoltners (1992). Adding flexibility in the allocation of advertising across market segments (or territories) when the advertising response function contains noise, Holthausen/Assmus (1982) offer the possibility to a manager to choose their risk aversion preference function, each proposing an optimal allocation under an expected profit and variance tradeoffs "efficient frontier." Two patterns of noise are considered by Holthausen/Assmus (1982): (1) the first model follows the typical multiplicative sales response function where the sales variance increases with advertising levels and (2) an alternative uncertainty specification where the uncertainty increases as the advertising level deviates from a level that management is more familiar with (e.g., past and current advertising spending levels). Similarly to Reibstein/Gatignon (1984) or Gatignon/Hanssens (1987), the advertising sales response noises can be correlated across markets.

Mantrala/Sinha/Zoltners (1992) consider uncertainty in a similar way by taking into account the random term of the sales response function as well as the uncertainty in the estimated parameters, and the correlated errors across submarkets.

4.2.3 Extent of Evidence Regarding the Impact of Considering Uncertainty for Allocation of Resources

Three basic conclusions can be drawn from the literature:

1. Uncertainty affects allocation decisions, although the way in which decisions are affected depends on the response function specification and the risk aversion extent of the decision maker,
2. More resources get allocated to uncertain markets (mix, product or area),
3. Taking risk into account can improve overall profit under some conditions.

Jagpal/Brick (1982) show that the role of uncertainty depends on how the response function is specified. When specified as a multiplicative response function and maximizing the expected value of profits, Reibstein/Gatignon (1984) show that taking into consideration the estimated regression error variances leads to different optimal prices within a product line allocation decision problem. More specifically, in their Bayesian model to optimal market testing strategies, Eliashberg et al. (1988) find that it is optimal to invest in market tests for which there is greater uncertainty. This follows also from the generalizations of the Dorfman-Steiner theorem which recognize uncertainty.

Aykac et al. (1989) provide a first evidence about the difference between the optimal allocation by a risk neutral versus a risk averse manager in the context of advertising budgeting decisions. Mantrala/Sinha/Zoltners (1992) combine the budget level decision and the allocation decision and analyze the interactions of one on the other. They compare the investments when managers of submarkets and the aggregate spending allocator have different risk aversion preferences. It follows logically that when both managers are risk averse, the optimal investment is less than if they are both risk neutral. More interestingly, when the two decision makers' attitude towards risk differs, they both under-invest. It is in particular intriguing that the model leads to the result that a risk-averse investor invests more heavily when faced to a risk averse allocator than with a risk neutral one. The explanation comes from the fact that the risk averse allocator will allocate resources in a way that reduces the demand uncertainty which leads to investor to spend more.

4.2.4   Recent Trends in Research on Marketing Resource Allocation

Recent research on marketing resource allocation have prioritized the specification of models that correspond better to the complexity of market response, especially in terms of interactions among mix variables and competitive dynamics. Gatignon/Hanssens (1987) show how the allocation of resources across marketing mix is affected by the synergies (or interactions) among the mix instruments. However, if they mention that the parameter estimates used for calculating the optimal allocation are subject to uncertainty, they do not incorporate that uncertainty into the allocation optimization. Also, the allocation decision across marketing mix instruments is calculated, given that the total advertising budget is set. While corresponding to the situation of the Navy considered in Gatignon/Hanssens (1987), this is not typically the case. Naik/Raman (2003) expand this approach to a dynamic process of the marketing mix effects (through a Kalman filtering process) and by deriving the optimal budget across the mix variables. The dynamic process specified for the response function requires the use of optimal control theory but the uncertainty is not considered, just as in Gatignon/Hanssens (1987). Their empirical analysis of the synergistic effects of television and print advertisements leads to the conclusion that increases in synergy leads to larger overall budgets, but this leads to a greater proportion of the budget that is spent to the more effective mix variable. This approach is expanded to markets with competition in Naik, Raman/Winer (2005) where synergies between advertising and promotional spending are considered as well as the strategic foresight of decision makers who anticipate what competitors' future decisions will be. This analysis applied to a detergents market, leads to the interesting conclusion that large brands under-advertise and over-promote while the reverse is true of smaller brands (although the authors do caution the reader that these specific conclusions may not hold across model specifications). Therefore, while the literature has moved towards recognizing the importance of considering the allocation of marketing resources across marketing mix elements that interact, their dynamics and the strategic foresight of competitive decisions, the role of uncertainty in the process which was identified in earlier research has been ignored in these more complex models. Given that earlier investigations of the effects of taking uncertainty into account shows significant differences between models that recognize the uncertainty versus those that do not, it is critical to also assess the role of uncertainty in these more complex marketing resource allocation problems.

4.3   Model Formulation

We assume that sales is related to aggregate advertising through a Nerlove-Arrow model, an assumption enjoying wide-spread empirical support (Naik/Raman 2003, Raman, Mantrala, Sridhar, & Tang 2011) in the marketing mix literature (see Gatignon 1993 for a review). Nerlove/Arrow (1962) proposed the intermediate construct of goodwill to capture the cumulative effect of advertising—however the model shown below is equivalent to assuming a linear relationship between goodwill and sales and has been empirically validated in various sources (Naik/Raman 2003, Raman et al. 2011). Let S(t) denote sales and u(t) denote advertising, both at time 't.' Then,

$$\frac{ds}{dt} = -\delta S(t) + \beta u(t) \tag{4.1}$$

Uncertainty causes deviations of the predicted sales from the actual sales level. One source of noise is the omission of other influencers of sales from the mathematical model. First we introduce noise into equation (1) through a white noise process $\varepsilon(t)$ with intensity parameter σ, which by definition satisfies the following properties: $E[\varepsilon(t)] = 0$, and $E[\varepsilon(t)\,\varepsilon(s)] = 0$, whenever $t \neq s$. Thus $E[\varepsilon(t)] = 0$ signifies that the average value or mean of the random error at time "t" is zero, and this is a standard assumption in the literature on modeling noisy phenomena. The term $E[\varepsilon(t)\,\varepsilon(s)]$ is the expectation operator applied to the product of random errors at two different times 's' and 't;' technically it denotes the covariance between the errors at two different times. In this case, because of the zero-mean assumption, it also denotes the correlation between $\varepsilon(t)$ and $\varepsilon(s)$; and so the property $E[\varepsilon(t)\,\varepsilon(s)] = 0$ means that the errors at two different times are *uncorrelated*, which substantively means that an error at one point in time does not influence the error at another point in time. This too is a standard assumption in the dynamic modeling literature (see Hanssens/Parsons/Schultz 2003 for a review).

Next we exploit the fundamental relationship between a white noise process $\varepsilon(t)$ and a Brownian Motion process W(t): $W(t) = \int_{s=0}^{s=t} \varepsilon(s)\,ds$ (Øksendal 2003).

Thus the result of smoothing a white noise process is a Brownian Motion process—a relationship, which, when written in differential notation, yields dW = $\varepsilon(t)$ dt. Therefore,

$$\frac{ds}{dt} = -\delta S(t) + \beta u(t) + \sigma \frac{dW}{dt} \tag{4.2}$$

Dropping the 't' for convenience, and rearranging the above terms yields our final model, which we will call the stochastic Nerlove-Arrow model.

$$dS = (-\delta S + \beta u)dt + \sigma dW \tag{4.3}$$

4.4   The Optimization Problem

The firm's decision problem is to allocate u(t) over its planning horizon [0, ∞] to maximize discounted long-term profits. Maximize

$$J(u) = \int_0^\infty e^{-\rho t}\, \pi\big(S(t), u(t)\big)\, dt \tag{4.4}$$

where,

$$\pi\,(S, u) = mS - u^2 \tag{4.5}$$

subject to the dynamics in Eqn. 4.3.

The value function V(s) is defined as

$$V(s) = \max_u \left[\int_t^\infty e^{-\rho w}\, \pi(S(w))\, dw \right] \tag{4.6}$$

where S(t) = s at time 't.' The quadratic cost function (4.5) finds precedence in a number of prior papers (Raman 2006, Raman/Naik 2004, Naik/Raman 2003, Fruchter/Kalish 1996, Erickson 1991).

4.5   Results

The value function V(s, t, T) satisfies the Hamilton-Jacobi-Bellman (HJB) equation (Fleming/Rishel 1975),

$$\rho V + \max_U \left[e^{-\rho t}\pi(s, u) + V_s f(s, u) + \frac{\sigma^2 V_{ss}}{2} \right] = 0 \tag{4.7}$$

where $V_s = \dfrac{\partial V}{\partial s}$, $V_{ss} = \dfrac{\partial^2 V}{\partial s^2}$ and $f(s, u) = -\delta s + \beta u$.

We will prove all the mathematical assertions below in the Appendix. Solving the second-order nonlinear differential equation (4.7) for V(s) yields the following expression:

$$V(s) = -\frac{m\,s}{\delta} + \frac{s^2\,(2\,\delta + \rho)}{\beta^2} + \frac{m^2\,\beta^4 + 4\,\delta^2\,(2\,\delta + \rho)\,\sigma^2}{4\,\beta^2\,\delta^2\,\rho} \tag{4.8}$$

The optimal feedback advertising policy u(s), where the notation indicates its dependence on sales 's,' is: $u\,(s) = \dfrac{\beta\,V_s}{2}$. Computing V_s from (4.8).

$$u(s) = \frac{1}{2}\,\beta\left(-\frac{m}{\delta} + \frac{2\,s\,(2\,\delta + \rho)}{\beta^2}\right) \tag{4.9}$$

u(s) is feasible (i.e. u (s) > 0) for $s > \frac{\beta^2 m}{2(2\delta + \rho)}$.

$$\text{Deterministic } u(s) = \frac{m\beta}{2(\delta + \rho)}$$

(4.10)

4.6   Remarks

- Remark 1:

  Equation (4.10) is the classic deterministically optimal advertising policy and is a special case of the results in Naik/Raman (2003). Sasieni (1989, 1975) established the optimality of constant spending rate policies such as (4.10), called Even policies, for a large class of deterministic response functions. Sasieni's results assume absence of market response uncertainty—our analysis recognizes that uncertainty will influence the market response function.

- Remark 2:

  Neither the (stochastic) optimal policy (4.9) nor the deterministic optimal policy (4.10) is an explicit function of the error variance σ^2, but there is a fundamental difference between the two. Equation (4.9) is a *feedback* policy and depends upon the sales level 's' at time 't.' Although it appears as though uncertainty plays no role in the feedback structure, it in fact influences the expected profit (value function)—a consequence of the dependence of optimal advertising on sales which is influenced by uncertainty. Remark 3 elaborates this point.

- Remark 3:

  Equation (4.8) shows that the expected profit increases with the variance level σ^2, but the gain due to variance is realizable only through implementation of the *stochastic* optimal policy (4.9). Implementation of the classic Even policy (4.10) would leave money on the table because it ignores error variance.

- Remark 4:

  We offer a simple example to illuminate the content of Remarks 2 and 3. Suppose that $S = \beta u$ is the response function and u is the constant spending level prescribed by the Even policy, say u = K. The Even policy realizes the profit $\beta u - K^2$. Next suppose that $S = \beta u + \varepsilon$ is the response function, $E(\varepsilon) = 0$, $E(\varepsilon^2) = \sigma^2$, and u is the feedback policy prescribed by u = θS, where θ is a function of model parameters, usually less than one (otherwise the firm would spend more than its sales on advertising). The feedback policy realizes the profit $E[S - (\theta S)^2] = (1 - \theta^2)(\beta^2 u^2 + \sigma^2)$. In other words, the feedback policy realizes a gain proportional to the error variance, of magnitude $(1 - \theta^2)\sigma^2$, a gain that would be zero when uncertainty is ignored because in that case $\sigma^2 = 0$. This simple example ignores the dynamics of advertising but makes the point that the structure of the feedback policy exploits error variance to improve profitability.

Because our stochastic Nerlove-Arrow model incorporates dynamics and uncertainty, and the objective is the maximization of expected discounted profit over $[0, \infty)$, our calculations are more elaborate and require stochastic optimal control.

- Remark 5:

  It is often thought that uncertainty analysis is important only when the decision maker is risk-averse (References needed—perhaps Horowitz et al. in Management Science?). Here we see that, even under expected profit maximization—which presumes risk-neutrality—the analysis of uncertainty creates non-trivial benefits in the form of enhanced profit.

4.7   Analysis

$$\text{Gain} = \frac{(2\delta + \rho)\left(m^2\beta^4\rho - 4m\,s\,\beta^2\,\delta\rho\,(\delta + \rho) + 4\delta^2\,(\delta + \rho)^2\,(s^2\rho + \sigma^2)\right)}{4\beta^2\delta^2\rho\,(\delta + \rho)^2} \qquad (4.11)$$

$$\text{Noise Contribution To Gain} = \frac{(2\delta + \rho)\,\sigma^2}{\beta^2\rho} \qquad (4.12)$$

$$\text{Coefficient of } \sigma^2 \text{ in Noise Contribution} = \frac{1}{\beta^2} + \frac{2\delta}{\beta^2\rho} \qquad (4.13)$$

Expression (4.13) shows that uncertainty increases expected profit more when: (1) the response coefficient β is smaller, the discount rate ϱ is smaller, and the decay δ is larger.

4.8   Conclusions

Advertising budgeting and its temporal allocation are important problems in integrated marketing communications and within a broader context, they are an important part of the marketing mix optimization problem. The combination of market response dynamics and market response noise makes profit maximization of a firm's marketing communications process a complex stochastic control problem. Market response is noisy because it is influenced by many factors over which the firm lacks control such as the state of the economy or technological developments. The optimal amount to spend on marketing communications requires careful mathematical analysis because it depends on the interaction of many factors. Answers to even simple questions are far from obvious. The issues here are: How much should the firm spend, given a profit maximization objective, and how should it spread the optimal amount over time? The first is an optimal budgeting issue and the second an optimal scheduling (or timing) issue.

Is it better to spread the budget evenly over time, to decrease spending over time, to increase spending over time, or to do something more complicated? The issue is important because large sums of money are at stake and suboptimal spending patterns significantly reduce profitability.

We provide a rigorous analysis of the joint influence of market response dynamics and market response uncertainty upon the structure and pattern of dynamic spending of a key marketing communications instrument. The topic of uncertainty is subtle because, contrary to intuition, noise is *not* always a hindrance. Our analysis shows that, by using stochastic optimal control, uncertainty, as measured by the error variance, can be incorporated into the structure of the optimal advertising policy to improve the expected profitability compared to the profit attainable through a dynamically optimal advertising policy that ignores uncertainty.

Appendix

Perform the maximization in the HJB equation (4.7 in text), where ,

$$V_s = \frac{\partial V}{\partial s}, \quad V_{ss} = \frac{\partial^2 V}{\partial s^2} \quad \text{and} \quad f(s,u) = -\delta s + \beta u :$$

$$\rho V + \max_u \left[e^{-\rho t} \pi(s,u) + V_s f(s,u) + \frac{\sigma^2 V_{ss}}{2} \right] = 0 \tag{A1}$$

The result is the nonlinear second-order ordinary differential equation (ODE):

$$4ms - 4V\rho - 4s\delta V_s + \beta^2 V_s^2 + 2\sigma^2 V_{ss} = 0 \tag{A2}$$

Conjecture that,

$$V(s) = v_0 + v_1 s + v_2 s^2 \tag{A3}$$

where v_0, v_1 and v_2 are unknown coefficients determined by computing V_s and V_{ss} from (A3) and substituting them into (A2).

There are two solutions for v_2:

$$v_2 = 0 \tag{A4a}$$

$$v_2 = \frac{2\delta + \rho}{\beta^2} \tag{A4b}$$

There are two solutions for v_1, corresponding to (A4a) and (A4b) respectively:

$$v_1 = \frac{m}{\delta + \rho} \tag{A5a}$$

$$v_1 = -\frac{m}{\delta} \tag{A5b}$$

There are two solutions for v_0, corresponding to (A4a, A5a) and (A4b, A5b) respectively:

$$v_0 = \frac{m^2 \beta^2}{4\rho(\delta + \rho)^2} \tag{A6a}$$

$$v_0 = \frac{m^2 \beta^4 + 4\delta^2(2\delta + \rho)\sigma^2}{4\beta^2 \delta^2 \rho} \tag{A6b}$$

There are two value functions V(s), corresponding to (A4a, A5a, A6a) and (A4b, A5b, A6b) respectively:

$$V(s) = \frac{m^2 \beta^2}{4\rho(\delta + \rho)^2} + \frac{ms}{\delta + \rho} \tag{A7a}$$

$$V(s) = -\frac{ms}{\delta} + \frac{s^2(2\delta+\rho)}{\beta^2} + \frac{m^2\beta^4+4\delta^2(2\delta+\rho)\sigma^2}{4\beta^2\delta^2\rho} \tag{A7b}$$

(A7a) corresponds to ignoring uncertainty and yields the classic Nerlove-Arrow optimal policy—this is a special case of Naik/Raman (2003) obtained by specializing their results to one communications instrument; (A7b) yields the stochastic optimal policy:

$$\text{Deterministic } u(s) = \frac{m\beta}{2(\delta+\rho)} \tag{A8a}$$

$$u(s) = \frac{1}{2}\beta\left(-\frac{m}{\delta} + \frac{2s(2\delta+\rho)}{\beta^2}\right) \tag{A8b}$$

Finally, we will prove, that (A7b) dominates (A7a), *uniformly* in 's,' and for *all* values of all the parameters. The difference (A7b) – (A7a) is:

$$\text{Difference} = \frac{(2\delta+\rho)(m^2\beta^4\rho-4ms\beta^2\delta\rho(\delta+\rho)+4\delta^2(\delta+\rho)^2(s^2\rho+\sigma^2))}{4\beta^2\delta^2\rho(\delta+\rho)^2} \tag{A9}$$

Since the denominator is positive, we focus on the numerator:

$$\text{Numerator of Difference} = m^2\beta^4\rho - 4ms\beta^2\delta^2\rho + 4s^2\delta^4\rho - 4ms\beta^2\delta\rho^2 + 8s^2\delta^3\rho^2 + 4s^2\delta^2\rho^3 + 4\delta^4\sigma^2 + 8\delta^3\rho\sigma^2 + 4\delta^2\rho^2\sigma^2 \tag{A10}$$

(A10) is minimized at the value shown in (A11):

$$\text{Minimizing Value Of } s = \frac{m\beta^2}{2\delta(\delta+\rho)} \tag{A11}$$

Substituting (A11) in (A10),

$$(A7b) - (A7a) = 4\delta^2(\delta+\rho)^2\sigma^2 \tag{A12}$$

The right hand side of (A12) is positive for all values of all the parameters and because it is the minimum value of (A10), it follows that, uniformly for *all* s, so long as $\sigma > 0$:

$$(A7b) > (A7a) \tag{A13}$$

Literature

[1] Aykac, A./Corstjens, M./Gautschi, D./Horowitz, I. (1989): Estimation Uncertainty and Optimal Advertising Decisions, Management Science, Vol. 35, 1, pp. 42-50.

[2] Chatterjee, R./Eliashberg, J./Gatignon, H./Lodish, Leonard M. (1988): A Practical Bayesian Approach to Selection of Optimal Market Testing Strategies, Journal of Marketing Research, Vol. 25, 4, pp. 363.

[3] Dorfman, R./Steiner, P. O. (1954): Optimal Advertising and Optimal Quality, American Economic Review, Vol. 44, 5, pp. 826-836.

[4] Erickson, G. M. (1991): Dynamic Models of Advertising Competition. Boston, MA: Kluwer Academic Publishers.

[5] Fleming, W. H./Rishel, R. (1975): Deterministic and Stochastic Optimal Control. Springer-Verlag: New York.

[6] Fruchter, G. E./Kalish, S. (1998): Dynamic Promotional Budgeting and Media Allocation, European Journal of Operational Research, Vol. 111, pp. 15-27.

[7] Gatignon, H. (1993): Marketing Mix Models, In Handbook of OR and MS, Eds. J. Eliashberg and G. L. Lilien, Vol. 5, pp. 697-732.

[8] Gatignon, H./Hanssens, D. M. (1987): Modeling Marketing Interactions with Application to Salesforce Effectiveness, Journal of Marketing Research, Vol. 24, 3, pp. 247-257.

[9] Hanssens, D. M./Parsons, L. J./Schultz, R. L. (2003): Market Response Models: Econometric and Time Series Analysis, Boston, MA: Kluwer.

[10] Holthausen, D. M., Jr./Assmus, G. (1982): Advertising Budget Allocation Under Uncertainty, Management Science, Vol. 28, 5, pp. 487-499.

[11] Jagpal, H. S./Brick, I. E. (1982): The Marketing Mix Decision Under Uncertainty, Marketing Science, Vol. 1, 1, pp. 79-92.

[12] Little, J. D. C. (1966): A Model of Adaptive Control of Promotional Spending, Operations Research, Vol. 14, 6, pp. 1075-1097.

[13] Mantrala, M. K./Sinha, P./Zoltners, A. A. (1992): Impact of Resource Allocation Rules on Marketing Investment-Level Decisions and Profitability, Journal of Marketing, Vol. 29, 2, pp. 162-175.

[14] Morey, R. C./McCann, J. M. (1983): Estimating the Confidence Interval for the Optimal Marketing Mix: An Application to Lead Generation, Marketing Science, Vol. 2, 2, pp. 193-202.

[15] Naik, P. A./Raman, K./Winer, R. S. (2005): Planning Marketing-Mix Strategies in the Presence of Interaction Effects, Marketing Science, Vol. 24, 1, pp. 25-34.

[16] Nerlove, M./Arrow, K. J. (1962): Optimal Advertising Policy under Dynamic Conditions. Economica, Vol. 29, 114, pp. 129-142.

[17] Dung, N. (1985): An Analysis of Optimal Advertising Under Uncertainty, Management Science, Vol. 31, 5, pp. 622-633.

[18] Øksendal, B. (2003): Stochastic Differential Equations: An Introduction with Applications, Berlin et al.: Springer.

[19] Pekelman, D./Tse, E. (1980): Experimentation and Budgeting in Advertising: An Adaptive Control Approach, Operations Research, Vol. 28, 2, pp. 321-347.

[20] Raman, K./Sridhar, S./Mantrala, M. K./Tang, E. (2011): Optimal Resource Allocation with Time-Varying Marketing Effectiveness, Margins and Costs, Journal of Interactive Marketing, Forthcoming.

[21] Raman, K. (2006): Boundary Value Problems in Stochastic Optimal Control of Advertising. Automatica, Vol. 42, 8, pp. 1357-1362.

[22] Raman, K./Naik, P. A. (2004): Long-term Profit Impact of Integrated Marketing Communications Program, Review of Marketing Science, Vol. 2, Article 8.

[23] Reibstein, D. J./Gatignon, H. (1984): Optimal Product Line Pricing: The Influence of Elasticities and Cross-Elasticities, Journal of Marketing Research, Vol. 21, 3, p. 259.

[24] Sasieni, M. W. (1989): Optimal advertising strategies, Marketing Science, Vol. 8, 4, pp. 358–370.

[25] Sasieni, M. W. (1971): Optimal advertising expenditure, Management Science, Vol. 18, 4, pp.64–72.

5   An Empirical Analysis of Brand Image Transfer in Multiple Sports Sponsorships

Henrik Sattler[8], University of Hamburg, Germany

Oliver Schnittka, University of Hamburg, Germany

Franziska Völckner, University of Cologne, Germany

---

[8] Contact author.

Abstract

Multiple sponsorships, which refer to sponsees that are sponsored by two or more brands, are gaining managerial relevance. Surprisingly, prior research has focused on single sponsorships, i.e., sponsees with only one sponsoring brand. This study is first to analyze image transfer effects within multiple sponsorships. Specifically, this research investigates image transfer effects (1) from the sponsee (e.g., FIFA World Cup) to the sponsoring brands and (2) between the sponsoring brands as well as the influence of the fit between the participating entities and brand familiarity on these transfer effects. The findings indicate that a familiar sponsoring brand primarily benefits from the sponsee, whereas an unfamiliar sponsoring brand mainly benefits from a connection with a familiar sponsoring brand.

Keywords

Multiple Sponsorships, Brand Image Transfer, Image-Based Fit.

5.1   Introduction

Worldwide sponsorship spending has increased significantly in recent years (Poon/Prendergast 2006). In 2008, $16.6 billion was spent on sponsorships in North America, an increase of 23.9% compared to 2006 (IEG 2008). Sports sponsorships dominate these expenditures. For instance, 69.0% of North American sponsorship expenditures in 2008 focused on sports sponsorships (IEG 2008). Moreover, sports sponsorship remains one of the fastest growing areas of promotion (Koo et al. 2006). Sponsorship growth results mainly from an increasing disillusionment with traditional media, government restrictions (e.g., on tobacco or alcohol advertising), and the heightened popularity of sponsored mega-events (e.g., FIFA World Cup, Olympic Games) (Grimes/Meenaghan 1998; Quester/Thompson 2001).

Brand image enhancement represents the most common goal of corporate sponsorships (Grohs et al. 2004; pilot checkpoint 2007). A unique and distinctive brand image gives firms the ability to differentiate their products and generate a competitive advantage (Aaker 1991; Keller 1993). Thus, sponsors primarily aim to build positive associations for the sponsoring brand through sponsorships. According to the associative network memory model of brand knowledge (Keller 1993) some favorable associations invoked by the sponsee (i.e., the sponsored institution) may become indirectly associated with the sponsoring brand since the sponsor creates a link with that sponsee (Grohs et al. 2004). That is, associations transfer to consumers' perceptions of the sponsor's brand image through the established linkage between the sponsee and sponsoring brand in consumers' memory (Cornwell/Maignan 1998). Such transferred associations might strengthen already existing connotations or add novel sponsee-specific connotations to the sponsor's brand image (Gwinner 1997).

Nearly all major sports teams and events are sponsored by more than one brand (i.e., multiple sponsorships). For instance, twelve different sponsoring brands (e.g., adidas, Coca Cola, and Deutsche Post) simultaneously sponsored the FIFA Women's World Cup 2011 in Germany. The prevalence of multiple sponsorship arrangements in practice results primarily from the great costs associated with running a major event and thus the overly expensive fees for exclusive, single sponsorship rights. Although the presence of multiple sponsorships is well-established in practice, previous literature has focused on the brand image effects of single sponsorships (i.e., sports teams and events which are sponsored by only one brand). Therefore, prior research solely provides evidence of a positive image transfer for sponsors through such single sponsorships (e.g., Grohs et al. 2004; Pope et al. 2009; Speed/Thompson 2000).

To the best of our knowledge, only three previous studies consider *multiple* sponsorships but merely analyze whether the sponsoring brands influence consumers' attitudes toward the sponsee (Ruth/Simonin 2003) or directly compare consumers' attitudes toward the sponsoring brand across single and multiple sponsorship conditions (Carrillat et al. 2005; Ruth/Simonin 2006).

Most importantly, prior research has not addressed brand image *transfer* effects since such an investigation requires quantifying the change in brand image caused by single versus multiple sponsorships using a no sponsorship condition as the baseline.

Moreover, Carrillat et al. (2005) and Ruth/Simonin (2006) only investigate an *overall effect* of sponsorship alliances on the participating brands (a limitation that also appears in related studies on co-branding; e.g. Simonin/Ruth, 1998). However, because multiple sponsorships consist of more than two participating entities (i.e., the sponsee and sponsoring brands), the overall effect of multiple sponsorships on a sponsor's brand image should consist of two different sub-components: an image transfer from the sponsee (e.g., a sponsored event) to the sponsoring brands (see β_1 and β_2 in **Figure 5.1**) and an image transfer between the sponsoring brands (see β_{3a} and β_{3b}). Yet no existing study analyzes these subcomponents of image transfer effects for sponsors associated with multiple sponsorships.

Figure 5.1   Different Subcomponents of Brand Image Transfer in
                     Multiple Sponsorships

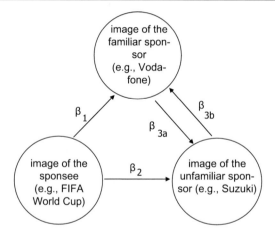

Against this background, we empirically analyze, for the first time, the overall effects of multiple sponsorships compared with single sponsorships using a no sponsorship condition as the baseline. Furthermore, we intend to explain the overall effects of multiple sponsorships by isolating the image transfer effects (1) from the sponsee (e.g., a sponsored event) to the sponsoring brands and (2) between the sponsoring brands. By considering the different sub-components of the overall brand image effects in multiple sponsorship arrangements, rather than simply analyzing overall effects, we provide a more detailed performance analysis of multiple sponsorships that should also be relevant for analyses of other brand alliances, such as co-branding.

In addition, we investigate the moderating impact of image-based fit between the participating entities (i.e., the sponsee and the sponsoring brands), as well as the influence of brand familiarity on the brand image transfer effects caused by multiple sponsorships.

5.2 Hypotheses

5.2.1 Overall Brand Image Transfer Effects Triggered by Single and Multiple Sponsorships

Multiple sponsorships typically include sponsoring brands with different levels of brand familiarity (or brand strength), such as a highly familiar global brand and a rather unfamiliar local brand. Thus, we particularly consider brands with different levels of familiarity. Furthermore, as we stated before, multiple sponsorships may trigger brand image transfer effects (1) from the sponsee (e.g., a sponsored event) to the sponsoring brands as well as (2) between the sponsoring brands.

According to brand anchoring theory, a positive image transfer should emanate from the familiar brand (e.g., Vodafone) to the unfamiliar brand (e.g., Suzuki) within multiple sponsorships but not vice versa (β_{3b}=0 in **Figure 5.1**); the more familiar a brand is the more likely it is to influence other (unfamiliar) brands, whereas the less likely it is that this brand will be influenced by other entities (i.e., the sponsee or the unfamiliar sponsoring brand) (Esch et al. 2009). Thus, we posit that the overall effect of multiple sponsorships on the familiar sponsoring brand does not include an image transfer from the unfamiliar co-sponsoring brand, but rather consists solely of the image transfer that emanates from the sponsee to the familiar sponsoring brand. Furthermore, following Alba/Hutchinson's (1987) reasoning that an increasing number of presented brands increases the cognitive load of consumers and thereby constrains their information processing, we also assume that image transfer effects from the sponsee to each sponsoring brand are weaker in multiple sponsorships compared with single sponsorships. Therefore, the overall brand image transfer effects should be weaker for multiple sponsorships compared to single sponsorships as well:

> H_{1a}: The overall brand image transfer from the sponsoring arrangement to the familiar sponsoring brand decreases for multiple sponsorships compared with single sponsorships.

Whereas the unfamiliar brand should not affect the image of the familiar brand, the image of the unfamiliar sponsoring brand should be affected by the familiar sponsoring brand (β_{3a}≠0, **Figure 5.1**). Thus, we posit that the overall effect of multiple sponsorships on the unfamiliar sponsoring brand consists of two different image transfers: the image transfer that emanates from the sponsee as well as the image transfer that emanates from the familiar sponsoring brand. According to H_{1a}, we assume that image transfer effects from the sponsee to the sponsoring brands (β_1 and β_2 in **Figure 5.1**) are weaker in multiple sponsorships compared with single sponsorships. Depending on whether the additional image transfer from the familiar to the unfamiliar brand (β_{3a} in **Figure 5.1**) outweighs this lower transfer from the sponsee (Alba/Hutchinson 1987), overall brand image transfer to the unfamiliar brand might be smaller, equivalent to, or even larger in the context of multiple sponsorships compared with single sponsorships.

We assume that the additional image transfer from the familiar to the unfamiliar brand compensates for the lower image transfer from the sponsee to the unfamiliar brand in multiple sponsorships and hypothesize:

> **H$_{1b}$:** The overall brand image transfer from the sponsoring arrangement to the unfamiliar sponsoring brand in multiple sponsorships is equivalent to that in single sponsorships.

5.2.2   Isolating Brand Image Transfer Effects in Multiple Sponsorships

The assumption that sponsorships induce favorable brand image transfers largely reflects Heider's (1958) balance theory, which posits that people want the relations among cognitive elements linked in a triangular relationship (i.e., sponsor, sponsee, and consumer) to be harmonious or balanced (Dean 1999; 2002). Consumers may even change their attitudes to achieve consistency if an imbalance exists (Dalakas/Levin 2005). Because consumers tend to value the sponsee (e.g., sports events or teams) more than the sponsoring brand and because highly valued objects are generally more resistant to change, any adjustment should affect the less valued sponsoring brand. That is, consumers engage in a positive image transfer from the sponsee to the sponsoring brand (see β_1 and β_2 in **Figure 5.1**) resulting in a more favorable image of the sponsoring brand(s) through multiple sponsorships (Crimmins/Horn 1996).

Epstein et al. (2007) investigate the influence of familiar and unfamiliar locations on neural responses and show that the simultaneous presentation of familiar and unfamiliar stimuli leads consumers to perceive the familiar stimulus first. In the context of multiple sponsorships, the familiar sponsoring brand may represent a visual anchor for consumers' attention and thus should be the primary beneficiary of the image transfer that emanates from the sponsee. In contrast, the unfamiliar sponsoring brand lacks a strong link to the sponsee, because consumers do not pay attention to the brand. As a consequence, few (positive) features associated with the sponsee transfer to the unfamiliar sponsoring brand. Thus, we hypothesize:

> **H$_{2a}$:** In multiple sponsorships, brand image transfer from the sponsee to the familiar sponsoring brand is greater than brand image transfer from the sponsee to the unfamiliar sponsoring brand (i.e., $\beta_1 > \beta_2$, **Figure 5.1**).

In addition, multiple sponsorships consist of an image transfer between the sponsoring brands. Brand anchoring theory asserts that familiar brands are more likely to influence other unfamiliar brands but are less likely to be influenced by other entities (Esch et al. 2009). Consumers tend to adjust their attitudes toward unfamiliar entities positively when they appear with familiar entities, because the latter provide a stimulus anchor. In a similar vein, prior research into the halo effect indicates that consumers tend to evaluate a stimulus on the basis of a few core associations and superimpose the properties of a brand's image (Nisbett/Wilson 1977; Rosenzweig 2007; Thorndike 1920). The superimposition of the favorable, familiar sponsoring brand image on the less favorable, unfamiliar image of the co-sponsor should induce a positive image transfer from the familiar to the unfamiliar sponsoring brand (β_{3a} in **Figure 5.1**), but not vice versa. Therefore, we hypothesize:

> **H2b:** In multiple sponsorships, brand image transfer emanates from the familiar sponsoring brand to the unfamiliar sponsoring brand (i.e., $\beta_{3a} \neq 0$, **Figure 5.1**).

Finally, schema theory suggests that the degree to which consumers transfer their associations from one object to another depends on the level of perceived image-based fit or match between these objects (Misra/Beatty 1990). When they receive new information (e.g., announcement of a multiple sponsorship), consumers tend to use their existing association schemas about the participating entities (i.e., the sponsee and sponsoring brands) to process the information. A high degree of image congruence between the two entities therefore should facilitate information processing and lead to a more favorable image transfer from one entity to the other (Meyers-Levy/Tybout 1989; Roy/Cornwell 2003). Several studies indicate a moderating impact of image-based fit on the image transfer effects between the sponsee and the sponsoring brand in single sponsorships (e.g., Gwinner/Eaton 1999; Koo et al. 2006); we similarly hypothesize:

> **H3a:** The greater the image-based fit between the sponsee and the sponsoring brands in multiple sponsorships, the greater is the positive image transfer that emanates from the sponsee to the respective sponsoring brand.

> **H3b:** The greater the image-based fit between the sponsoring brands in multiple sponsorships, the greater is the positive image transfer that emanates from the familiar sponsoring brand to the unfamiliar sponsoring brand.

5.3 Empirical Study

5.3.1 Research Design

We selected automobiles and telecommunication as the sponsoring brands' product categories since they are among the top three sponsoring categories worldwide (Sports Marketing Surveys Ltd. 2004). A pre-test with 69 participants identified Vodafone as a rather familiar brand in the telecommunication industry ($M_{Familiarity\ Vodafone}=3.64$, SD=2.10) and Suzuki as a rather unfamiliar brand in the automobile industry ($M_{Familiarity\ Suzuki}=1.79$, SD=1.10), each measured on a seven-point, three-item Likert scale. Further, participants perceived Vodafone as significantly more familiar than Suzuki (t=7.35, p<0.01). The FIFA World Cup 2010 in South Africa served as the sponsored event, because it is one of the largest sports events worldwide and entails high involvement ($M_{\text{Involvement World Cup}}$=5.83, SD=1.32) and favorable attitudes ($M_{\text{Image World Cup}}$=6.03, SD=1.37) by consumers. We implemented a *hypothetical* sponsorship to avoid respondent information biases; neither Vodafone nor Suzuki has been a sponsor of the FIFA World Cup so far.

The study had a 2 (sponsoring brand's familiarity: high vs. low) × 3 (sponsorship: no sponsorship vs. single sponsorship vs. multiple sponsorship) between-subjects design. We recruited 667 adults (average age: 34.68 years; 58.4 percent female) through an online access panel in summer 2008. Respondents could enter the study through an individual link contained in the e-mail. Upon entry to the study, respondents were randomly assigned to one of the six experimental conditions. Each respondent saw a (hypothetical) press release stating that either Vodafone or Suzuki, or both brands together will sponsor the forthcoming FIFA World Cup 2010. The final sample consisted of 649 respondents, as we had to eliminate 18 subjects who completed the questionnaire in an unreasonably short time.

We measured all constructs on seven-point, multi-item Likert scales with higher scores indicating more favorable ratings. The measures of respondents' images of the FIFA World Cup and the sponsoring brands used five items adopted from Huber/Matthes (2007): *good, likeable, positive, benevolent,* and *favorable.* To measure familiarity with the entities and image-based fit between the FIFA World Cup and the sponsoring brands, we used three items from Kent/Allen (1994) and Gwinner/Eaton (1999): *familiar, experienced,* and *knowledgeable* for familiarity and *similar image, related associations,* and *similar attitude* for image-based fit. The measure of image-based fit between the two sponsoring brands used two items from Bhat/Reddy (2001): *similar* and *is like.* All measures achieved an acceptable level of reliability (Cronbach's alphas ranging from 0.79 to 0.97). Furthermore, we subjected each scale to an exploratory factor analysis and found an acceptable level of convergent validity; for all scales, the variation in an item explained by its factor exceeded 80 percent.

5.3.2   Results

The manipulation check result confirmed our intended manipulation of the sponsoring brands' familiarity levels. Respondents perceived Vodafone as significantly more familiar than Suzuki ($M_{\text{Familiarity Vodafone}}$=2.91, SD=1.73 vs. $M_{\text{Familiarity Suzuki}}$=1.71, SD=0.97; t=14.08, p<0.01). Thus, different effects of the single and multiple sponsorships on the brand images of Vodafone and Suzuki can be attributed to perceived differences in brand familiarity.

We used multiple t-tests to test the overall effects of single and multiple sponsorships on the sponsor's brand image (H_{1a} and H_{1b}), and a structural equation model to isolate the different image transfer effects in the multiple sponsorship condition (H_{2a} - H_{3b}).

5.3.2.1   Overall Brand Image Transfer Effects

We tested H_{1a} by comparing the image enhancement of the familiar sponsoring brand Vodafone in the single sponsorship condition with the image enhancement in the multiple sponsorship condition. A marginally significant image effect occurred in the single sponsorship condition ($M_{Image No Sponsorship}$=3.13, SD=1.31; $M_{Image Single Sponsorship}$=3.54, SD=1.24; t=-1.68, p<0.1), but the image effect in the multiple sponsorship condition was not significant ($M_{Image Multiple Sponsorship}$=3.37, SD=1.39; t=-1.28, p>0.1).

Thus, the single sponsorship condition affected the brand image of Vodafone more than the multiple sponsorship condition, in support of H_{1a}.

As we postulated in H_{1b}, the image of the unfamiliar sponsoring brand should improve to the same extent in both the single and multiple sponsorship conditions. Image transfer from the sponsorship to Suzuki was significant in both the single ($M_{Image No Sponsorship}$=2.73, SD=0.98; $M_{Image Single Sponsorship}$=3.11, SD=1.01; t=-2.03, p<0.05) and the multiple ($M_{Image Multiple Sponsorship}$=3.04, SD=1.18; t=-2.16, p<0.05) sponsorship conditions, but effect sizes revealed minor differences between the image transfer effects ($d_{No Sponsorship / Single Sponsorship}$=0.39 vs. $d_{No Sponsorship / Multiple Sponsorship}$=0.29). Although both values reflect "small" effect sizes (0.2<d<0.5) according to Cohen (1988), effect size in the single sponsorship condition was 1.35 times larger than in the multiple sponsorship condition indicating an unequal image transfer for single and multiple sponsorships for the unfamiliar sponsoring brand Suzuki. Therefore, H_{1b} received no support.

5.3.2.2 Isolated Brand Image Transfer Effects in Multiple Sponsorships

We used a covariance-based structural equation modeling approach to test the model in **Figure 5.1** (β_{3b}=0) with maximum likelihood estimation (software package AMOS 5.0). The model fit was satisfactory (CFI=0.95, NFI=0.94, GFI=0.86; Homburg/Baumgartner 1995). Furthermore, all standard errors were smaller than 0.05, which indicated that the estimates of the structural model's parameters were reliable.

While consumers' image of the FIFA World Cup positively affected consumers' image of Vodafone (β_1=0.17, t=3.59, p<0.01), we did not find a significant effect for Suzuki (β_2=0.04, t=1.04, p>0.05). That is, as we postulated in H_{2a}, in the multiple sponsorship condition the image transfer emanating from the sponsee to the sponsoring brands was greater for the familiar brand than for the unfamiliar brand. Regarding the image transfer between the sponsoring brands, the image of Vodafone significantly affected the image of Suzuki (β_{3a}=0.24, t=5.70, p<0.01), in support of H_{2b}.

To assess the moderating effect of image-based fit within multiple sponsorships we divided our sample into two groups of cases according to different levels of image-based fit (i.e., low and high; split-half procedure) and then estimated the model in each subgroup without coefficient equality constraints. Consistent with H_{3a}, the image of the FIFA World Cup had a greater positive impact on the image of the familiar sponsoring brand (Vodafone) for respondents who perceived a high image-based fit between the two entities

($\beta_{1 \text{ high fit}}=0.33$, t=5.07, p<0.01) compared with respondents who perceived a low image-based fit ($\beta_{1 \text{ low fit}}=0.05$, t=0.97, p>0.05). To determine whether this difference was significant, we constrained the model coefficient to be equal across subgroups and re-estimated the model. The Chi-square difference test revealed a statistically significant moderating effect of image-based fit ($\Delta\chi^2=10.87$, df=1, p<0.01). In addition, the image transfer from the FIFA World Cup to the unfamiliar sponsoring brand Suzuki was significantly moderated by image-based fit between both entities ($\beta_{2 \text{ high fit}}=0.22$, t=3.67, p<0.01; $\beta_{2 \text{ low fit}}=0.07$, t=1.44, p>0.05; $\Delta\chi^2=3.90$, df=1, p<0.05), in further support of H3a.

Finally, the image of Vodafone had a greater impact on the image of Suzuki when image-based fit between these sponsoring brands was high ($\beta_{3a \text{ high fit}}=0.59$, t=10.25, p<0.01) compared with when it was low ($\beta_{3a \text{ low fit}}=0.04$, t=0.81, p>0.05; $\Delta\chi^2=48.03$, df=1, p<0.01). Thus, H3b received support as well.

5.4 Discussion

Although the presence of multiple sponsorships is well-established in practice, no prior study has analyzed the potential image transfer effects on the sponsoring brands in multiple sponsorships. These image transfer effects may emanate from the sponsee to the sponsoring brands and between the sponsoring brands. Against this background, we empirically analyze and isolate, for the first time, image transfer effects in multiple sponsorships. Specifically, we isolate image transfer effects (1) from the sponsee (e.g., a sponsored event) to the sponsoring brands and (2) between the sponsoring brands to explain the overall effects of multiple sponsorships compared with single sponsorships and thereby provide a more detailed performance analysis of multiple sponsorships.

Our results show that within multiple sponsorships familiar sponsoring brands primarily receive a positive brand image transfer from the sponsee, whereas unfamiliar brands mainly benefit from the familiar sponsoring brand. Furthermore, image-based fit favorably moderates these image transfer effects. Thus to achieve high levels of image transfer through multiple sponsorships, familiar sponsoring brands should focus primarily on high image-based fit with regard to the sponsee while unfamiliar sponsoring brands should focus primarily on high image-based fit with regard to the familiar co-sponsoring brand.

However, positive overall brand image transfer effects through multiple sponsorships only occur for unfamiliar sponsoring brands. This finding might indicate that a negative image effect from the unfamiliar to the familiar sponsoring brand exists and decreases the overall benefit of the familiar brand in multiple sponsorships. Analyzing this proposition in detail could be an interesting avenue for further research.

We only considered two sponsoring brands within our multiple sponsorship scenario. However, nearly all major sports teams and events are sponsored by more than two sponsoring brands (e.g., the FIFA Women`s World Cup 2011, which was sponsored by twelve different sponsoring brands). An increasing number of co-sponsoring brands might increase the cognitive load of consumers and thereby constrain their information processing (Alba/Hutchinson 1987). This should diminish the image transfer effects from the familiar co-sponsoring brands to the less familiar or unfamiliar co-sponsoring brands. Thus, similarly to the familiar sponsoring brand in this study, multiple sponsorships with a high number of co-sponsors could be an ineffective communication tool for unfamiliar sponsoring brands as well.

Literature

[1] Aaker, D. A. (1991): Managing brand equity. Capitalizing on the value of a brand name. New York.

[2] Alba, J. W./Hutchinson, J. W. (1987): Dimensions of consumer expertise. Journal of Consumer Research, Vol. 13, 4, pp. 411-454.

[3] Bhat, S./Reddy, S. K. (2001): The impact of parent brand attribute associations and affect on brand extension evaluation. Journal of Business Research, Vol. 53, 3, pp. 111-122.

[4] Carrillat, F. A./Lafferty, B. A./Harris, E. G. (2005): Investigating sponsorship effectiveness: Do less familiar brands have an advantage over more familiar brands in single and multiple sponsorship arrangements? Journal of Brand Management, Vol. 13, 1, pp. 50-64.

[5] Cohen, J. (1988): Statistical power analysis for the behavioral sciences. 2nd ed. Hillsdale, NJ.

[6] Cornwell, T. B./Maignan, I. (1998): An international review of sponsorship research. Journal of Advertising, Vol. 27, 1, pp. 1-21.

[7] Crimmins, J./Horn, M. (1996): Sponsorship: From management ego trip to marketing success. Journal of Advertising Research, Vol. 36, 4, pp. 11-21.

[8] Dalakas, V./Levin, A. M. (2005): The balance theory domino: How sponsorships may elicit negative consumer attitudes. Advances in Consumer Research, Vol. 32, 1, pp. 91-97.

[9] Dean, D. H. (1999): Brand endorsement, popularity, and event sponsorship as advertising cues affecting consumer pre-purchase attitudes. Journal of Advertising, Vol. 28, 3, pp. 1-12.

[10] Dean, D. H. (2002): Associating the corporation with a charitable event through sponsorship: Measuring the effects on corporate community relations. Journal of Advertising, Vol. 31, 4, pp. 77-87.

[11] Epstein, R. A./Higgins, J. S./Jablonski, K./Feiler, A. M. (2007): Visual scene processing in familiar and unfamiliar environments. Journal of Neurophysiology, Vol. 97, 5, pp. 3670-3683.

[12] Esch, F.-R./Schmitt, B. H./Redler, J./Langner, T. (2009): The brand anchoring effect: A judgement bias resulting from brand awareness and temporary accessibility. Psychology & Marketing, Vol. 26, 4, pp. 383-395.

[13] Grimes, E./Meenaghan, T. (1998): Focusing commercial sponsorship on the internal corporate audience. International Journal of Advertising, Vol. 17, 1, pp. 51-74.

[14] Grohs, R./Wagner, U./Vsetecka, S. (2004): Assessing the effectiveness of sports sponsorships – an empirical examination. Schmalenbach Business Review, Vol. 56, 2, pp. 119-138.

[15] Gwinner, K. P. (1997): A model of image creation and image transfer in event sponsorship. International Marketing Review, Vol. 14, 3, pp. 145-158.

[16] Gwinner, K. P./Eaton, J. P. (1999): Building brand image through event sponsorship: the role of image transfer. Journal of Advertising, Vol. 28, 4, pp. 47-57.

[17] Heider, F. (1958): The Psychology of Interpersonal Relations. New York.

[18] Homburg, C./Baumgartner, H. (1995): Beurteilung von Kausalmodellen. Marketing ZFP, Vol. 17, 3, pp. 162-176.

[19] Huber, F./Matthes, I. (2007): Sponsoringwirkung auf Einstellung und Kaufabsicht - Theoretische Grundlagen und Ergebnisse einer empirischen Studie. Marketing ZFP, Vol. 29, 2, pp. 90-104.

[20] IEG (2008): Sponsorship spending to total $16.78 billion in 2008. IEG Press Release, Vol. January, No. 18, http://www.sponsorship.com/About-IEG/Press-Room/Sponsorship-Spending-To-Total-$16.78-Billion-In-20.aspx.

[21] Keller, K. L. (1993): Conceptualizing, measuring, managing customer-based brand equity. Journal of Marketing, Vol. 57, 1, pp. 1-22.

[22] Kent, R. J./Allen, C. T. (1994): Competitive interference in consumer memory for advertising: The role of brand familiarity. Journal of Marketing, Vol. 58, 3, pp. 97-105.

[23] Koo, G. Y./Quarterman, J./Flynn, L. (2006): Effect of perceived sport event and sponsor image fit on consumers' cognition, affect, and behavorial intentions. Sport Marketing Quarterly, Vol. 15, 2, pp. 80-90.

[24] Meyers-Levy, J./Tybout, A. (1989): Schema congruity as a basis for product evaluation. Journal of Consumer Research, Vol. 16, 1, pp. 39-54.

[25] Misra, S./Beatty, S. E. (1990): Celebrity spokesperson and brand congruence: An assessment of recall and affect. Journal of Business Research, Vol. 21, 2, pp. 159-171.

[26] Nisbett, R. E./Wilson, T. D. (1977): The halo effect: Evidence for unconscious alteration of judgments. Journal of Personality and Social Psychology, Vol. 35, 4, pp. 250-256.

[27] Pilot checkpoint (2007): Sponsor Visions 2007. Hamburg.

[28] Pope, N./Voges, K. E./Brown, M. (2009): Winning ways—Immediate and long-term-effects of sponsorship on perceptions of brand quality and corporate image. Journal of Advertising, Vol. 38, 2, pp. 5-20.

[29] Quester, P. G./Thompson, B. (2001): Advertising and promotion leverage on arts sponsorship effectiveness. Journal of Advertising Research, Vol. 41, 1, pp. 33-47.

[30] Rosenzweig, P. (2007): The halo effect: ... and the eight other business delusions that deceive managers. New York.

[31] Roy, D. P./Cornwell, T. B. (2003): Brand equity's influence on responses to event sponsorships. Journal of Product & Brand Management, Vol. 12, 6, pp. 377-393.

[32] Ruth, J. A./Simonin, B. L. (2003): Brought to you by brand A and brand B—Investigating multiple sponsors' influence on consumers' attitudes toward sponsored events. Journal of Advertising, Vol. 32, 3, pp. 19-30.

[33] Ruth, J. A./Simonin, B. L. (2006): The power of numbers – Investigating the impact of event roster size in consumer response to sponsorship. Journal of Advertising, Vol. 35, 4, pp. 7-20.

[34] Simonin, B. L./Ruth, J. A. (1998): Is a company known by the company it keeps? Assessing the spillover effects of brand alliances on consumer brand attitudes. Journal of Marketing Research, Vol. 35, 1, pp. 30-42.

[35] Speed, R./ Thompson, P. (2000): Determinants of sport sponsorship response. Journal of the Academy of Marketing Science, Vol. 28, 2, pp. 227-238.

[36] Sports Marketing Surveys Ltd. (2004): The World Sponsorship Monitor 2004 Annual Review.

[37] Thorndike, E. L. (1920): A constant error on psychological rating. Journal of Applied Psychology, Vol. 4, pp. 25-29.

6   Effects of Money-Back and Low-Price Guarantees on Consumer Behavior

State of the Art and Future Research Perspectives

Thomas Suwelack[9], University of Münster, Germany

Manfred Krafft, University of Münster, Germany

---

[9] Contact author.

Abstract

Money-back guarantees (MBGs) and low-price guarantees (LPGs) are frequently implemented in retailing practice to positively influence consumer behavior. In this literature review 28 MBG and 30 LPG studies are systemized and discussed. While both a behavioral and an economic research stream exist, the focus of this review is on the effects of MBGs and LPGs on consumer behavior. Furthermore, this literature review provides some avenues for future MBG and LPG research and offers implications for retailing practice.

Keywords

Money-Back Guarantees, Low-Price Guarantees, Literature Review, Consumer Behavior, Retailing.

6.1   Introduction

In recent times of economic pressure money-back guarantees (MBGs) and low-price guarantees (LPGs) offer increasingly powerful tools for attracting consumers and gaining competitive edges in the marketplace (Ho/Ganesan/Oppewal 2011; Sullivan 2009). By offering an MBG, a retailer or manufacturer promises that any customer who is not satisfied with a purchase can return the item within a certain time period and receive a full refund (Davis/Gerstner/Hagerty 1995). Already in 1907, Henkel introduced an MBG for its detergent brand Persil (Henkel 2010). To stimulate sales during the last economic downturn, General Motors (GM) advertised a 60-day "no-questions-asked" return policy on its cars (Healey 2009). As these century-apart examples indicate, MBGs are ubiquitous in marketing practice (Mann/Wissink 1988), primarily because of their potential positive impact on business success (Davis/Gerstner/Hagerty 1995).

In contrast, by offering an LPG a retailer promises to match or beat competitors' prices (Chatterjee/Heath/Basuroy 2003). If a customer finds the same product at a different store for a lower price, the seller will refund the price difference. Unlike other price signals, such as reference prices, special offers, or coupons, an LPG is a strategic, store-level policy applied to all merchandise in the store, rather than single items (Kukar-Kinney/Walters 2003). They also are gaining popularity across stores from a wide range of industries (e.g., electronics, furniture, appliances, grocery, department stores), of different sizes (small and large), and in distinct channels (offline and online) (Kukar-Kinney 2006).

By signaling certain attributes of a product or retailer both LPGs and MBGs serve as tools to address the problem of asymmetric information between buyers and sellers. Specifically, research has demonstrated that an MBG signals high quality (e.g., Moorthy/Srinivasan 1995; Wood 2001), whereas an LPG signals low price (e.g., Dutta/Bhowmick 2009; Srivastava/Lurie 2001). Moreover, these guarantees decrease consumers' risk perceptions (e.g., Biswas/Dutta/Pullig 2006; Grewal et al. 2003) and increase their value perceptions and purchase intentions (e.g., Biswas/Dutta/Pullig 2006; Vieth 2008).

Considering the many MBG and LPG studies available, as well as the prominent use of these tools in marketing practice, this manuscript aims primarily to systemize and discuss the relevant studies (as in Chapter 6.3), according to two research streams: behavioral and economic. The focus of this article is on the effects of MBGs and LPGs on consumer behavior, which usually are investigated empirically, whereas effects on sellers' profits or consumer welfare tend to be demonstrated using theoretical or mathematical approaches. Thus, this manuscript emphasizes studies that adopt a behavioral perspective and presents the research that uses economic approaches rather briefly. To support the main discussion in Chapter 6.3, Chapter 6.2 characterizes MBGs and LPGs and describes their implementation. After suggesting some directions for MBG and LPG research in Chapter 6.4, this manuscript concludes with a summary and final implications in Chapter 6.5.

6.2 Characterization of MBGs and LPGs and Their Implementation

6.2.1 Characterization of MBGs and LPGs

Guarantee serves two functions: (1) risk sharing and (2) information signaling (Shie 1996). By compensating buyers if the seller fails on its specific promise, guarantees reduce consumer risk. Kaplan/Szybillo/Jacoby (1974) identify five risk dimensions: performance, financial, social, physical, and psychological risk. By promising the lowest market price, LPGs mainly address consumers' financial risk (Biswas/Dutta/Pullig 2006). An MBG instead can also reduce other forms of risk because it is more general in terms of what justifies a product return (i.e., any form of dissatisfaction). Vanhamme/de Bont (2008) argue that an MBG effectively reduces social and financial risk for surprise gifts. Furthermore, psychological risk should be lower in the presence of an MBG, because it reduces cognitive conflict by offering the option to postpone the final purchase decision and increasing the flexibility of the choice task. That is, purchase irreversibility does not occur at the time of purchase but rather at the end of the MBG period. Finally, an MBG should reduce perceived performance risk by signaling high product quality.

Table 6.1 Characterization of MBGs and LPGs

	Promise	Compensation for Failure	Type of Risk Addressed	Signaling Effect
MBG	Product satisfaction	Money back	Financial, social, performance, and psychological	Increase quality perceptions
LPG	Lowest price	Refund of price difference	Financial	Reduce price perceptions

Signaling theory is frequently applied in guarantee-oriented research to explain the information signaling function of guarantees. This theory pertains particularly to situations characterized by information asymmetry about an unobservable attribute (e.g., product quality, retailer's price level) (Kirmani/Rao 2000). Signaling with an observable attribute (e.g., reputation, advertising, MBG, LPG) can resolve some uncertainties about the unobservable attribute (Srivastava/Lurie 2004). Specifically, sellers might offer MBGs to signal high product quality, whereas LPGs signal low prices. These tools are effective in signaling quality or price when only a high quality/low price seller would benefit from the MBG/LPG offer (separating equilibrium) (Boulding/Kirmani 1993). In contrast, a retailer's LPG, for example, is unconvincing if its nearest competitor is 50 miles away, because the search costs are too high for the consumer to compare prices and request a refund.

In this case, also a high price seller might benefit from the offer (pooling equilibrium) and therefore consumers might not trust the signal the LPG is intended to send. Table 6.1 summarizes the above mentioned elements of the two guarantees.

6.2.1.1   Implementation of MBGs and LPGs

Whereas LPGs only makes sense when issued by a retailer, MBGs can be offered by retailers or manufacturers. However, Davis/Gerstner/Hagerty (1995) assume that an MBG is more effective when issued by a retailer rather than by a manufacturer, because retailer MBGs offer the retailer the potential for additional sales when customers return items, reduce the need for in-store demonstrations by allowing consumers to test products at home, and help to share the burden, because some manufacturers take back returned items for at least a partial refund. **Table 6.2** provides a recent overview of the types of retailers that offer MBGs and/or LPGs, emphasizing the importance of MBGs and LPGs in practice.

Table 6.2   Frequencies of MBGs and LPGs by Retail Type

	Retail type															
	Automobile	Books	Clothing	Electronics	Entertainment	Flooring	Home	Marine	Music	Office	Perishables	Pets	Shoes	Sports	Toys	All Stores
Stores Investigated	4	2	6	5	5	1	8	1	1	3	1	2	4	2	2	47
MBG	4	2	6	2	5	0	8	1	0	3	1	2	4	2	2	41 87%
LPG	3	0	1	4	0	1	4	1	1	2	1	2	0	1	1	22 47%

Source: Adapted from McWilliams/Gerstner (2006).

Both MBGs and LPGs strongly vary in their designs, depending on the specifications of the guarantee terms (Kukar-Kinney/Walters 2003; Posselt/Gerstner/Radic 2008). Referring to MBGs, a seller may impose policy restrictions through strict conditions for returning a product and limited test durations. For example, Olympus offers a 30-day test period on its digital cameras, but imposes high return conditions, in that consumers have to fill out long forms and pay parcel assurance and postal charges on product return (Olympus 2011). The longer the MBG's duration, the greater the opportunity for a consumer to test the product and therefore reduce uncertainties related to its characteristics (Heiman/McWilliams/Zilberman 2001a). Low return conditions facilitate product returns and reduce consumer transaction costs (e.g., time spent to return the product), so offering an MBG with a long duration and low return conditions (i.e., less restrictive MBG) should have a strong positive effect on sales. Regarding the cost side of an MBG offer, some researchers propose greater "hurdles" for returning the product, through more restrictive guarantee designs (e.g., Chu/Gerstner/Hess 1998). Such designs decrease consumers' moral hazard, which occurs when consumers opportunistically return products after consuming some of their value. Despite credibility concerns that might arise, sellers frequently offer MBGs with short durations and/or strict return conditions. According to Fruchter/Gerstner (1999), they should do so especially when product maintenance demands significant effort by the consumer, such as for skis. Moorthy/Srinivasan (1995) propose that the extent of product value depreciation and the amount of total product value that can be consumed during the test period represent the key criteria for determining MBG design.

The type of product is less of a concern for LPGs; even department stores, with their wide variety of products, offer them. Yet various LPG designs appear in marketing practice, which Kukar-Kinney/Walters/MacKenzie (2007) classify according to three criteria: refund depth, policy scope, and time period. Refund depth refers to the amount of money a customer receives if he or she finds a lower price elsewhere. There are two basic forms of LPGs: price matching and price beating. When a retailer issues a price-matching guarantee, it promises to provide exactly the price difference between its own price and the lower competitor's price (e.g., "If you find a lower price elsewhere, we will refund the difference"). To enhance the signaling quality of an LPG, some retailers go a step further and issue a price-beating guarantee, such that they pay an additional compensation, beyond the price difference (e.g., "If you find a lower price elsewhere, we promise to refund the price difference plus an additional 10%"). The policy scope determines how many and which type of competitors are eligible for price comparisons. Most LPGs specify a certain radius within which competitors must be located (e.g., 10 miles) and exclude online stores, whose lower operating costs enable them to offer lower prices than bricks-and-mortar stores (Grewal et al. 2003). Finally, the time period specifies the number of days or weeks within which the lower-priced offer must be identified.

6.3   Review of MBG and LPG Research

The literature review in this chapter is based on a search for MBG and LPG studies in marketing journals with A or B rankings (according to VHB-JOURQUAL 2.1 ranking) that regularly publish articles about marketing signals, consumer behavior, and retailing. Thus, the sample included issues of *Journal of Marketing, Journal of Consumer Research, Journal of Marketing Research, Marketing Science, International Journal of Research in Marketing, Journal of Retailing, Marketing Letters, Journal of Consumer Psychology,* and *Psychology & Marketing,* dating from 1980 until summer 2011. Additional searches in online databases (e.g., Ebsco, Google Scholar) used the following keywords as input: low-price guarantee, price-matching guarantee, price-beating guarantee, money-back guarantee, retailer return policy, and guarantee. Finally, reference lists of matching articles were screened to identify additional articles. This search resulted in the identification of 28 MBG and 30 LPG studies.

6.3.1   Systematization of MBG and LPG Research

Both MBGs and LPGs have been researched from consumer behavior and economic perspectives (see **Figure 6.1**; summation of studies in parentheses does not correspond with the
absolute number of existing MBG and LPG studies because some studies analyze several
consumer effects). Behavioral studies offer pre- and postpurchase investigations; they also
can be distinguished according to the consumer decision-making process analyzed, such as
consumer evaluations or intentions. The consumer effect that results from an MBG or LPG
provides the final criterion for systemizing behavioral research. In contrast, economic studies can be classified by four (MBG) or two (LPG) main topics.

In MBG literature, researchers have examined consumers' prepurchase evaluations with
regard to quality perceptions, value perceptions, risk perceptions, and other effects. MBG
effects on consumers' intentions entail two variables, namely search and purchase intentions. In the postpurchase stage, studies focus on quality perceptions and deliberation time
(evaluative outcomes) or search and loyalty intentions (intentional outcomes). Considering
the focus of this article, these behavioral studies are the subject of an in-depth discussion in
Chapter 6.3.2.1, whereas Chapter 6.3.2.2 offers an overview of studies applying economic
approaches to analyze MBGs' effects on profits and product quality signaling, examine
optimal MBG designs, and investigate multiple cue effects.

In LPG literature, researchers have analyzed consumers' prepurchase evaluations related to
price perceptions, value perceptions, quality perceptions, and other effects (Chapter 6.3.3.1).
Intentions studied in the context of an LPG include search and purchase intentions. In the
postpurchase stage, inferred retailer motives and other evaluative effects as well as search
and repurchase intentions have been studied. Another focus of LPG research involves economic effects of an LPG offer, with studies that examine effects on either price competition
or price discrimination (Chapter 6.3.3.2).

Figure 6.1   Classification of MBG and LPG Studies

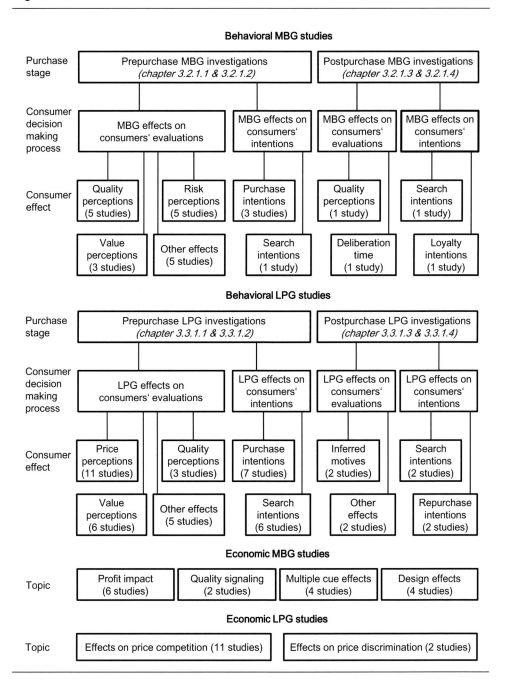

6.3.2   Literature Review of MGB Studies

6.3.2.1   MBG Studies Using a Behavioral Approach

MBG Effects on Consumers' Prepurchase Evaluations

Behavioral MBG studies include both prepurchase and postpurchase investigations (a complete overview of these studies is available from the authors upon request). An important evaluative outcome variable analyzed in prepurchase studies is consumers' *quality perceptions*. Based on signaling theory, Wood (2001) shows that an MBG increases product quality perceptions in a catalog purchasing context. This is because the offer implies a self-imposed penalty for poor performance, meaning that it would be economically unwise for sellers of low-quality products to provide MBGs (Kirmani/Rao 2000). Götting (2008) extends the analysis of Wood (2001) as he considers company reputation as a moderator variable and demonstrates that the effect of an MBG on quality perceptions in a catalog purchasing context is stronger for low reputation companies (i.e., the firm is rather unknown) than for high reputation companies. In contrast, without specifying the purchase environment, Vieth (2008) shows that effects on quality perceptions are stronger for high reputation companies. From a theoretical point though, both effects can be explained. According to Purohit/Srivastava (2001), the credibility of a low-scope cue, which can be offered instantly, can be increased by a high-scope cue, whose valence is established over time and cannot be changed in the short term. Thus Vieth (2008) finds an enforcing impact of high company reputation (high-scope cue) on the effect of an MBG (low-scope cue) on quality perceptions. In Götting's (2008) catalog purchasing context, with its high purchase uncertainty, consumers actively search for cues to evaluate products (Bonifield/Cole/Schultz 2010). The low company reputation is not a diagnostic cue, so in this case consumers rely more on the MBG to assess the product characteristics. Consistently, Bonifield/Cole/Schultz (2010) reveals positive effects of an MBG on quality perceptions in an e-tailing context, though the relation holds only when the MBG is not restrictively designed.

Vieth (2008) also analyzes the type of product as a moderating variable; an MBG increases quality perceptions for experience goods but not for search goods, because search goods can be evaluated solely with intrinsic product information. In contrast, d'Astous/Guèvremont (2008) find no quality effect of an MBG, despite their use of two moderator variables, namely product risk and product complexity. These authors admit that their experimental design might have contributed to this lack of effect, in that they used branded products that could have reduced the signaling effects of the MBG. However, the majority of MBG studies indicate a positive effect on quality perceptions, yet they are highly heterogeneous with respect to the type of product, retailer, or purchase context analyzed. The researchers do not control for variables analyzed in previous MBG studies, which makes their studies difficult to compare.

Götting (2008), Vieth (2008), and Grewal et al. (2003) analyze MBG effects on consumers' *value perceptions*. Value perceptions consist of a trade-off between quality and price perceptions, so we might expect that an MBG that has a positive effect on quality perceptions also

increases value perceptions. However, according to Fruchter/Gerstner (1999), an MBG enables the firm to translate added consumer value into higher prices. Furthermore, Grewal et
al. (2003) empirically demonstrate that consumers expect higher prices when an MBG is
offered. These counterbalancing effects on value perceptions make it seem less surprising
that we find diverging results in the three studies that have focused on value perceptions.
That is, whereas Götting (2008) and Vieth (2008) find a positive effect of an MBG on value
perceptions, Grewal et al. (2003), who also consider price effects, do not.

Grewal et al. (2003) confirm that an MBG reduces *risk perceptions*. Furthermore, they reveal
that this effect occurs to a greater degree for low reputation versus high reputation online
sellers, which corresponds to the results obtained for quality perceptions. Vanhamme/de
Bont (2008) investigate how an MBG influences purchase decisions for surprise gifts, when
givers are unsure of the receiver's reactions. In this scenario, MBGs serve as important risk
relievers, especially by reducing social and financial risk perceptions. Other studies investigate different risk relievers, including MBGs, in a remote purchase context. A simple comparison of different tools, such as brand name, price, or reputation, shows that an MBG
ranks highest in terms of reducing risk perceptions (Akaah/Korgaonkar 1988; Van den
Poel/Leunis 1999). Hawes/Lumpkin (1986) investigate which risk handling tactic is most
important for the selection of a patronage mode. Price/quality perceptions are most important, personal experience ranks second, and MBG is third, which indicates it is a commonly used means to choose a certain purchase environment.

Finally, some other and diverse MBG effects with respect to consumers' prepurchase evaluations are briefly outlined. Wood (2001) shows that an MBG reduces consumers' *deliberation
time* for the decision to order products in a remote purchase context, because it provides the
consumer with more flexibility and postpones the point of irreversibility. As research has
predominantly focused on cognitive variables, Vieth (2008) also investigates an affective
variable in an MBG context. Using items such as "Accepting this offer would give me
pleasure" or "Purchasing this product would make me feel good," Vieth assesses the perceived *emotional value of the offer*. The results show that MBGs strongly affect the emotional
value and also reveal the importance of this construct in the proposed framework in relation to the cognitive ones. On a more aggregate level, d'Astous/Guèvremont (2008) show
that an MBG positively affects consumer evaluations by increasing a *retailer's image*, especially if the return policy has a long duration and money-back compensation (instead of
store credit only). These characteristics provide more flexibility and signal the confidence of
the seller in its products. Finally, in an early study Schmidt/Kernan (1985) examine what
consumers expect when a retailer offers an MBG. Results show that an MBG not only positively affects expectations about a retailer's merchandise but also its *service level*, in that
consumers expect a store atmosphere to be better and the sales personnel to be more friendly.

MBG Effects on Consumers' Prepurchase Intentions

Some studies investigate the effects of an MBG on consumers' prepurchase intentions by focusing on their search and purchase behavior. D'Astous/Guèvremont (2008) find that a longer test duration reduces *search intentions*, or the need for additional information about product alternatives in the competitive environment, because consumers can better assess a product's characteristics after purchase. However, they also find a three-way interaction between test duration, product complexity, and financial product risk affecting search intentions. With a short test duration, consumers need more information before purchase if the product is financially risky and complex. Thus, sellers should offer long test durations for such products to reduce consumers' search intentions.

Three studies show that an MBG increases *purchase intentions*. Vieth (2008) reveals an indirect effect of an MBG on purchase intentions, through consumer emotions (see **Figure 6.2**). Another indirect path appears for MBG → quality perceptions → perceived economic value → purchase intentions, though this path explains less variance of purchase intentions than the indirect effect through perceived emotional value.

Figure 6.2   MBG Outcomes Suggested by Vieth (2008)

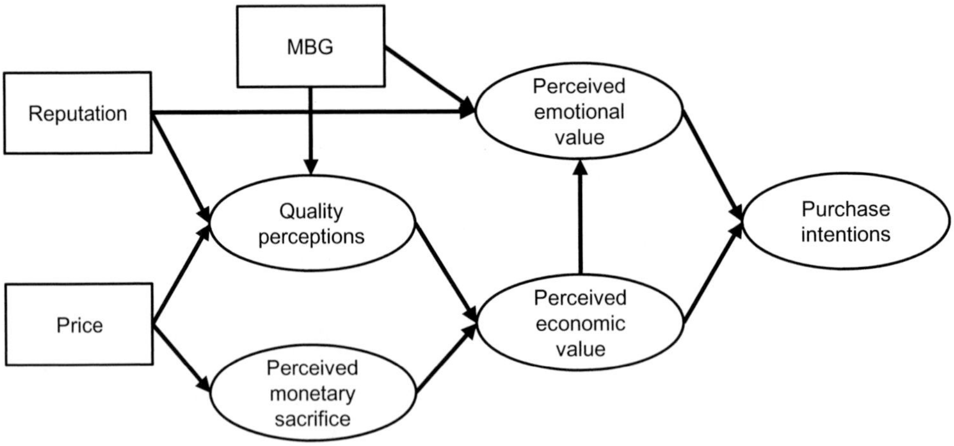

Source: Vieth (2008).

Götting (2008) shows that an MBG increases purchase intentions in a catalog context, though without providing a detailed analysis of the consumer inferences that lead to this result. Finally, Lee/Ang/Dubelaar (2005) investigate the effects of an MBG on purchase probability in online versus offline buying contexts. The greater degree of information asymmetry for internet sellers compared with bricks-and-mortar sellers, means that an MBG increases purchase probabilities more for a web merchant than for a store merchant.

MBG Effects on Consumers' Postpurchase Evaluations

In only one study, consumers' postpurchase evaluations resulting from an MBG are analyzed. Focusing on catalog purchases, Wood (2001) not only investigates how an MBG affects the decision to order a product (see Chapter 6.3.2.1), but also whether it influences the subsequent decision to keep or return the product. Specifically, based on signaling theory the author hypothesizes that higher prepurchase *product quality perceptions* persist after product receipt. Even with tactile experience, many product attributes are difficult to assess, so an MBG can positively affect product quality perceptions in the postpurchase stage. The empirical results confirm this proposition. Furthermore, Wood investigates *deliberation time* for the postpurchase decision to keep or return the product, which seemingly should increase, because with an MBG, the consumer has an opportunity to reconsider the purchase decision. However, the author acknowledges the endowment principle, which holds that consumers perceive more value for products they own (Kahneman/Knetsch/Thaler 1990), even without actual possession of the product (Sen/Johnson 1997). Notable implications arise from this effect for remote purchasing contexts; after deciding to order and while waiting for delivery, the consumer may feel a sense of ownership already, which increases the personal value of the product. Wood's results support this theoretical argument, because deliberation time did not increase for the postpurchase decision to keep or return the product, which in turn implies that the overall amount of decision conflict in a catalog purchasing context decreases when an MBG is present.

MBG Effects on Consumers' Postpurchase Intentions

In two publications, consumers' postpurchase intentions are analyzed. Wood (2001) investigates *search intentions* between the period consumers order a product from a catalog and receive it. Higher quality perceptions resulting from an MBG should increase the likelihood of discontinuing search for product alternatives, which is supported by the data. Götting (2008) shows that an MBG increases consumers' *loyalty intentions* as consumers are more likely to recommend a store that offers an MBG compared to a store that does not. According to the author, consumer loyalty is a direct response to company loyalty. An MBG can be interpreted as a signal of company loyalty because it is associated with up-front and potential future costs providing a consumer with more flexibility in a purchase context.

6.3.2.2 MBG Studies Using an Economic Approach

In studies that use an economic approach, MBGs are analyzed whether they influence profits and quality signaling, as well as how they interact with other marketing tools and which MBG designs are optimal (a complete overview of these studies is available from the authors upon request). Davis/Gerstner/Hagerty (1995) integrate four variables in their *profit* analysis of MBGs: the probability of a product not meeting consumer needs, salvage value of returned merchandise, transaction costs of returning the product, and the value of product trial. An MBG emerges as most profitable when two conditions are met: First, the salvage value of the merchandise must be greater than the transaction costs of the consumer and, second, the transaction costs of the consumer must be sufficiently high to limit moral hazard problems. Fruchter/Gerstner (1999) show that an MBG is most profitable when sellers charge a price premium for the MBG offer but generously compensate unsatisfied consumers for the full purchase price plus some or all of their transaction costs. However, the price premium associated with an MBG also can be detrimental to consumers who are easy to satisfy. For this consumer segment, the same product purchase without an MBG is a better option. Thus Heiman/McWilliams/Zilberman (2002) account for different bundle options, such that a retailer allows consumers to choose between buying the product with an MBG at a higher price or buying without the MBG at a lower price (unbundled MBG policy). A bundled MBG policy cannot provide this flexibility. A comparison of unbundled and bundled policies using option theory shows that unbundled policies are most profitable if consumers' need-fit probabilities are highly heterogeneous. If return costs and need-fit likelihood are high, it is more profitable to the retailer not to offer an MBG. A bundled MBG policy is optimal if variations in product valuations are small across consumers.

Moorthy/Srinivasan (1995) investigate whether an MBG can signal product *quality* in a direct marketing context, when product quality is not observable before purchase. They consider different parameters, such as seller and consumer transaction costs and consumer moral hazard. Consistent with signaling theory, Moorthy/Srinivasan (1995) find that the MBG can signal product quality if the consumers' transaction costs are low. Furthermore, when consumer moral hazard is small, the company should absorb some of these costs to enhance signaling strength. Shieh (1996) states that a monopolist can fully reveal its quality characteristics using price and MBG information. Applying a mathematical approach, this author shows that such information comes with no costs; while signaling with price alone would be costly. Furthermore, full reimbursement of the purchase price is optimal.

Other studies analyze *multiple cue effects*. Heiman/McWilliams/Zilberman (2001a and 2001b) analyze product demonstrations and MBGs and argue that a retailer's decision to offer demonstrations, an MBG, or both largely depends on the type of product offered and the level of consumer purchase uncertainty. For example, when a product's characteristics are difficult to comprehend before purchase, an MBG seems more appropriate than in-store demonstrations. Because MBGs usually entail higher costs relative to demonstrations, their use should be considered carefully. McWilliams/Gerstner (2006) analytically investigate both MBGs and LPGs and show that by offering an LPG in addition to an MBG, a retailer can increase sales and improve customer retention. If the retailer solely provides an MBG and the consumer finds a lower price at a different retailer, the consumer incurs transaction costs for returning the product and buys the product at the cheaper store. Moreover, the retailer must pay out the full purchase price and loses the consumer to the competitor. Also, the retailer incurs additional transaction costs to restock a product that has lost value through product depreciation. Adding an LPG to an MBG would resolve these problems, because the consumer would receive (only) the price difference and would not have to buy the same item from the lower-priced competitor. Nor would the retailer lose the customer or need to restock the product.

Finally, a few economic MBG publications deal with *optimal MBG designs*. According to Anderson/Hansen/Simester (2009), a generous policy offers more flexibility for the consumer and therefore increases MBG value and sales. A more restrictive MBG policy reduces the signaling qualities of an MBG and has a negative impact on consumer responses, but also reduces customer cheating. Davis/Hagerty/Gerstner (1998) analytically investigate the optimal level of consumer hassle (i.e., policy restrictions). A low-hassle policy is optimal when the product's benefits cannot be consumed quickly, cross-selling is possible, a high salvage value for returned merchandise can be obtained, and the moral hazard problem is minimal. When moral hazard problem is large, Hess/Chu/Gerstner (1996) find that partial refunds are optimal, and that the nonrefundable part should increase with the value of the merchandise. Noting the large variance of MBG designs offered in practice, Posselt/Gerstner/Radic (2008) develop an MBG index that can help consumers and sellers assess the quality of an MBG. Three empirically tested "MBGQual" indices measure the insurance protection, costs, and attractiveness to consumers for each specific MBG.

6.3.3 Literature Review of LPG Studies

6.3.3.1 LPG Studies Using a Behavioral Approach

LPG Effects on Consumers' Prepurchase Evaluations

With regard to prepurchase investigations, most researchers study price effects resulting from an LPG (a complete overview of these studies is available from the authors upon request). Signaling theory serves to explain these price effects, in that an LPG signal effectively reduces consumers' *store price perceptions* only in the case of a separating equilibrium, that is, when the signal benefits a low-priced retailer but not a high-priced one. Assuming an efficient market in which consumers claim price refunds when they are eligible, a high-priced retailer does not benefit from this offer, because it would constantly have to refund consumers. In these conditions, a low-priced retailer can credibly communicate its low store prices by offering an LPG. Simple main effects of an LPG on price perceptions emerge in two studies. Jain/Srivastava (2000) demonstrate that LPGs reduce consumers' price expectations and increase their confidence about finding low prices at the LPG-issuing store. Lurie/Srivastava (2005) show that LPGs change consumers' price evaluations by increasing their estimates of the lowest and average prices in the market. In turn, they perceive that an LPG-issuing seller offers lower prices than the competition.

Other researchers find that an analysis of simple main effects is not sufficient, because the relation of an LPG to price perceptions depends on several moderator variables that can be classified as market, consumer, and company variables. In reference to market variables, Srivastava/Lurie (2004) investigate market-level search costs; specifically, they manipulate search costs commonly known to all consumers, such that people can infer the degree to which other consumers engage in price search. Using signaling theory, the authors demonstrate that perceptions of store prices are lower in the presence of an LPG if search costs are low but not if search costs are high.

When search costs are low, the market mechanism is strong, because expectations about consumers engaging in price search are high. Only in this case are LPGs an effective tool for reducing store price perceptions.

Some authors show that consumer heterogeneity needs to be considered. Biswas/Dutta/Pullig (2006) investigate perceived price dispersion as an important consumer moderator variable. When perceived price dispersion is high, the perceived risk of losing out a better priced option increases, and consumers consider the LPG as any other price cue, i.e. paying little attention to it. In contrast, when price dispersion is low, consumers interpret the LPG as a signal of low prices, because doing so creates little risk. As results support these suggestions, the authors analyze whether a higher refund depth in the form of a price-beating guarantee may resolve the problems of price signaling when perceived price dispersion is high; results again confirm their proposition. Investigating a similar consumer moderator variable, namely consumers' price range knowledge, Lurie/Srivastava (2005) show that an LPG reduces store price perceptions only if consumers do not know the range of prices in the market—even though Biswas/Dutta/Pullig's (2006) finding, that price evaluations are not affected when perceived price dispersion is high, implies the opposite. However, Lurie/Srivastava (2005) argue that consumers with limited knowledge have no internal reference prices available, so they have a strong need to process price cues in the external store environment. These empirical results and theoretical considerations show that perceived price dispersion and price range knowledge are conceptually distinct constructs with different moderating effects on the relation of an LPG to price perceptions.

Two studies investigate company variables as moderators of the relation of LPGs and prepurchase price perceptions. First, Kukar-Kinney/Xia/Monroe (2007) investigate assortment uniqueness, which refers to the proportion of retailer brands to national brands that a retailer offers, as a moderator between LPG depth and price fairness perceptions. Because an LPG applies only to identical brands, retailer brands are excluded from price comparison. Thus, a negative effect of high assortment uniqueness on price fairness perceptions receives support from their data, though the results also show that greater refund depth can be used to compensate for negative effects resulting from an assortment that mainly consists of retail brands. Second, because consumer behavior differs contingent to the purchase environment, Kukar-Kinney/Grewal (2007) investigate the moderating effects of the purchase channel (internet versus bricks-and-mortar) on price perceptions, and they consider store reputation as an additional moderator variable. The lack of personal interaction in the online channel makes it more difficult for consumers to enforce an LPG. In line with signaling theory, this reduced opportunity to enforce the LPG and the resulting higher hassle costs diminish the credibility of the signal online. Therefore, results show that an LPG leads to lower price perceptions in the bricks-and-mortar environment but not in the internet environment (**Figure 6.3**).

Moreover, the authors hypothesize that an LPG affects store price perceptions more strongly when issued by a reputed retailer, because credibility gets enhanced when the retailer previously has incurred costs to improve its reputation (see also Vieth's (2008) analysis of an MBG's impact on quality perceptions when reputation is high). **Figure 6.3** confirms that the effects of an LPG are (slightly) stronger for reputed retailers than for retailers with low reputation.

Considering an LPG's negative effects on price perceptions and consumers' price–quality inferences (see Rao/Monroe (1989) and Völckner/Hofmann (2007) for meta-analyses on the price-quality relationship), some researchers study *quality effects* of an LPG. Neither Jain/Srivastava (2000) nor Lurie/Srivastava (2005) find significant effects of an LPG on quality perceptions, but Chatterjee/Heath/Basuroy (2003) provide deeper insights into this relation by investigating the type of product and consumers' need for cognition as moderators. Thus they find a negative effect of an LPG on quality perceptions when high need for cognition consumers evaluate an experience good. These consumers process LPG information more deeply and are therefore more likely to draw price–quality inferences. Furthermore, compared with search goods that are easy to evaluate before purchase using intrinsic cues, experience goods are more difficult to evaluate, and consumers are more likely to rely on extrinsic cues such as an LPG.

Figure 6.3　　　Interaction of LPG and Purchase Channel (Left) and LPG and Reputation (Right) on Price Perceptions

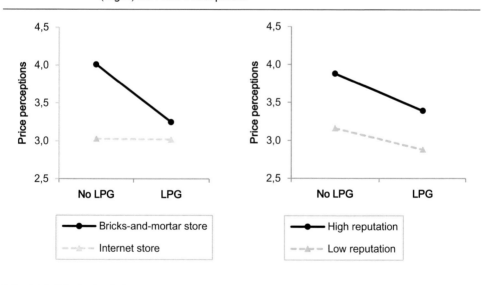

Source: Kukar-Kinney/Grewal (2007).

According to Dutta/Biswas/Grewal (2007), an LPG incorporates informational and protective functions. The informational function addresses the mechanism of signaling the lowest prices in the market; the protective function means the LPG can be a tool to protect consumers from fluctuating market prices. Both functions should reduce consumers' *risk perceptions*. Biswas/Dutta/Pullig (2006) argue that an LPG fixes the lower bound of the market price continuum and therefore price uncertainty declines. Considering this informational function of an LPG financial risk perceptions decrease—especially when consumers know that they will receive compensation after a purchase if they find a lower price at another retail store (protective function). Dutta/Bhowmick (2009) analyze the impact of an LPG on overpayment risk in an online versus offline context. Similar to Chatterjee/Heath/Basuroy (2003), they consider cognitive elaboration as a further moderator variable. According to their results, independent of the purchase context, an LPG reduces overpayment risk when cognitive elaboration is low, but when elaboration is high, consumers become more skeptical of online compared with offline signals, thereby reducing the efficacy of the former.

With regard to the relationship of an LPG and consumers' *value perceptions* Kukar-Kinney/Walters (2003) show that higher refunds and a larger scope of the policy both positively affect value perceptions, because they offer larger savings and provide more opportunities to find lower prices. Biswas et al. (2002) analyze advertised reference price as a moderator variable of the relation of an LPG and value perceptions; an LPG more strongly increases value perceptions for low or absent reference prices compared with high advertised reference prices, because only a high reference price provides adequate price information to the consumer and reduces the need to elaborate on the message of an LPG. Moreover, a retailer's price image moderates the LPG's effects on value perceptions: The effect is stronger for high price image retailers compared with low price image retailers, because the value perceptions of the latter are already high without the LPG offer. Similarly, Lurie/Srivastava (2005) find an interaction effect of an LPG and price level on value perceptions, such that the LPG increases value perceptions for high priced goods but not for low priced goods. Price range knowledge affects this interaction effect though, so it only occurs when price range knowledge is low. Finally, Biswas/Dutta/Pullig (2006) show that the effect of an LPG on value perceptions is mediated by price and risk perceptions; Kukar-Kinney/Xia/Monroe (2007) confirm a mediating effect via price fairness perceptions.

Additionally, some other effects of an LPG on consumers' evaluations have been analyzed. For example, Kukar-Kinney/Walters (2003) investigate *LPG believability* by manipulating refund depth and refund scope. They find that refund scope does not affect LPG believability, but a higher refund depth reduces it. As noted previously, refund depth correlates positively with value perceptions, such that the retailer faces a trade-off: Higher refunds increase value perceptions but also reduce LPG believability. A strong company reputation might help avoid any negative consequences resulting from deeper refunds. Consumers' inferences about a *retailer's motives* represents another interesting variable studied in an LPG context; according to Kukar-Kinney/Xia/Monroe (2007), a consumer suspects negative seller motives if the retailer offers few national brands on which LPGs apply. Comparing LPGs with always-low-price strategies, Ho/Ganesan/Oppewal (2011) show that LPGs are associated with better seller motives. They appear superior in terms of both perceived store integrity and perceived store intention to protect the consumer against price variations in the market. This is due to the obligatory promise to compensate the consumer for a lower price found at a competitor, signaling greater commitment.

LPG Effects on Consumers' Prepurchase Intentions

Regarding LPG effects on consumers' prepurchase intentions, research shows a direct negative effect on search intentions (e.g., Srivastava/Lurie 2001) and a direct positive effect on purchase intentions (e.g., Jain/Srivastava 2000). Biswas/Dutta/Pullig (2006) also identify indirect effects of an LPG, through price and risk perceptions (see **Figure 6.4**); that is, by reducing perceptions of financial risk and store prices, an LPG reduces search intentions and increases purchase intentions. Moderation analyses show that these results hold only in the case of low price dispersion.

Figure 6.4 LPG Outcomes Suggested by Biswas/Dutta/Pullig (2006)

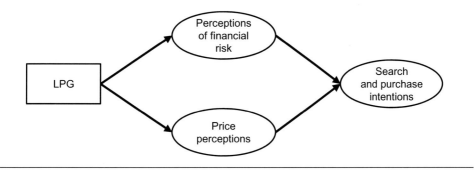

Source: Adapted from Biswas/Dutta/Pullig (2006).

The results support the general assumption that search and purchase intentions correlate negatively (e.g., Eschweiler 2006). However, not all studies support this assumption. For example, Kukar-Kinney/Walters/MacKenzie (2007) investigate price consciousness as a moderator of the relationship between LPG refund depth and intentions. With respect to search intentions, they find that consumers with low price consciousness limit their price search, whereas those with high price consciousness extend their price search in response to an increase in refund depth. For purchase intentions, the authors find that consumers with high price consciousness increase their purchase intentions in the presence of high refund depth, more so than consumers with low price consciousness, because they are motivated to search for lower prices after purchase and thus are more likely to benefit from the LPG. In other words, the negative correlation between search intentions and purchase intentions does not exist at high levels of refund depth and price consciousness. Biswas et al. (2002) demonstrate that the effect of an LPG on consumers' intentions is moderated by a retailer's price image. Because it becomes a more distinctive cue in the case of a high price image store, an LPG enhances purchase intentions more in this condition.

However, search intentions also increase, because the refund amount tends to be higher for high price image stores. In contrast, if a store's price image is low, the LPG reduces search intentions. Similarly, Srivastava/Lurie (2001) show that search intentions decline more strongly when the base price for a product is low.

Focusing on purchase intentions as the final outcome variable, Kukar-Kinney/Walters (2003) show that the effect of refund depth and competitive scope on purchase intentions is mediated by LPG believability and LPG value. Specifically, a higher refund depth and a larger competitive scope both positively affect LPG value, though a higher refund depth has a negative effect on LPG believability. LPG believability and LPG value, in turn, positively influence purchase intentions. Kukar-Kinney/Xia/Monroe (2007) show that refund depth and assortment uniqueness affect shopping intentions indirectly through fairness perceptions (see **Figure 6.5**). More precisely, a greater uniqueness of assortment negatively affects fairness perceptions, both directly and indirectly (through inferred motives). However, greater refund depth can compensate for negative effects resulting from an assortment that mainly consists of retail brands. Finally, higher fairness perceptions are effective in positively influencing shopping intentions directly and indirectly (through value perceptions).

Figure 6.5   LPG Outcomes Suggested by Kukar-Kinney/Xia/Monroe (2007)

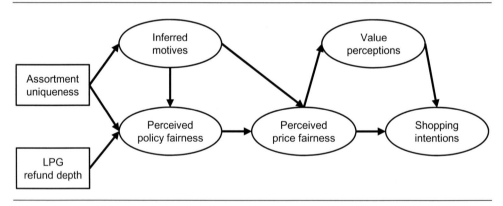

Source: Adapted from Kukar-Kinney/Xia/Monroe (2007).

LPG Effects on Consumers' Postpurchase Evaluations

To explore how consumers evaluate the retailer when finding a lower price after purchase, Kukar-Kinney (2006) and Xia/Kukar-Kinney/Monroe (2010) investigate an LPG's effects on *perceived seller motives*. Kukar-Kinney (2006) shows that consumers are less likely to suspect negative motives in offering an LPG when they receive a refund after detecting a lower competitor price than when they never detect a lower price. This interesting finding indicates that as long as a retailer does not deny its consumers a price refund, its motives appear innocent. Xia/Kukar-Kinney/Monroe (2010) show that denying a price refund causes consumers to infer negative seller motives, especially if the effort invested to achieve the advantages of an LPG has been high. Thus, both studies confirm that retailers should always refund consumers, to avoid negative consumer inferences about the motives for offering an LGP. However, policy restrictions may prevent the retailer from issuing a refund to the consumer. Estelami/Grewal/Roggeveen (2007) account for responses to a refusal of an LPG request by analyzing postpurchase *store price perceptions* and *service quality perceptions*. Consumers' reactions to the refusal depend on the locus of causality (Folkes 1988): If the retailer is to blame, consumer effects should be more negative than if it is the consumer's fault. However, the results show that price perceptions do not vary with causality; indicating that consumers do not self-attribute refund refusals. Service quality evaluations instead are more positive when the consumer is the cause, rather than the seller.

Dutta/Biswas/Grewal (2007) investigate the effects of a low price signal default (i.e., lower price detected after purchase) on *perceptions of retailer credibility*. A large default (i.e., large price difference between price paid and lower price detected) leads to significantly lower credibility perceptions when a competitor offers the lower price, but not when the same seller offers a lower price, such as in a subsequent sale. This is because in the former case, the default gets attributed to the seller's opportunism, whereas in the latter case, consumers generally believe that the seller merely is attempting to remain price competitive. Moreover, the authors investigate whether unfavorable LPG default effects persist even after the consumer has been compensated according to the LPG promise. The authors show that if consumers conceptualize an LPG primarily as a signal of lowest prices (informational function), negative retailer credibility perceptions due to an LPG default will persist. In contrast, when consumers interpret an LPG as a tool protecting the consumer from fluctuating market prices (protective function), a retailer may restore its credibility by issuing the refund.

LPG Effects on Consumers' Postpurchase Intentions

In terms of postpurchase intentions, LPG research has addressed two variables: search intentions and repurchase intentions. An LPG lowers *pre*purchase search intentions (Biswas/Dutta/Pullig 2006), especially when search costs are low (Srivastava/Lurie 2004), but may increase consumers' *post*purchase *search intentions*, depending on certain moderating variables. Kukar-Kinney/Grewal (2007) analyze effects of an LPG on postpurchase search intentions for both internet and bricks-and-mortar store environments. The LPG appears more enforceable in the offline environment, so the perceived benefits of postpurchase search are higher there, resulting in higher postpurchase search intentions offline compared with online. Dutta/Biswas (2005) consider value consciousness and penalty level as moderators and find that the effect of an LPG on postpurchase search intentions is stronger for consumers with high value consciousness. Moreover, a price-beating guarantee results in higher postpurchase search intentions than does a price-matching guarantee. This effect is not significant for less value conscious consumers, but it is significant for high value conscious consumers, which again confirms the moderating role of value consciousness.

Finally, in two studies the effect of an LPG on *repurchase intentions* is investigated. Dutta/Biswas/Grewal (2007) show that repurchase intentions generally decrease when a retailer defaults on its low price promise, though the effect depends on specific LPG default conditions. Repurchase intentions are lowest in response to a large default detected at another retailer. They are less affected when the lower price is detected at the same seller. In addition, Kukar-Kinney (2006) analyzes the relative effect of refund depth and policy scope on repurchase intentions. She finds no effects of refund depth on repurchase intentions, but policy scope exerts a positive effect. The integration of consumer variables reveals that this effect is strongest for consumers who are highly skeptical and price conscious.

6.3.3.2   LPG Studies Using an Economic Approach

Studies using an economic approach investigate LPG effects on firm profits and consumer welfare and focus on two main topics: price competition and price discrimination (a complete overview of these studies is available from the authors upon request). With regard to price competition, the question is whether LPGs lead to higher prices. The promise implicit in an LPG indicates that the price of an issuing seller must be lower than a competitor's. From a game theory perspective, LPGs thus decrease competitors' incentives to reduce their prices, so price competition diminishes, resulting in higher prices (Arbatskaya 2001; Hviid/Shaffer 1999; Logan/Lutter 1989; Salop 1986; Zhang 1995). According to Salop (1986), companies use LPGs to increase prices up to a level that maximizes profits of the companies that participate in this price strategy. Hess/Gerstner (1991) therefore define LPGs as collusive devices that help oligopolists charge monopoly prices. Because of this negative effect on consumer welfare, some authors propose that LPGs should be prohibited by law (e.g., Edlin/Emch 1999).

However, some studies question this negative effect and assert that LPGs actually may increase price competition. For example, Chen/Narasimhan/Zhang (2001) state that an LPG causes stores to price more aggressively through their effect on motivating consumers to search harder for lower prices. Chatterjee/Heath/Basuroy (2003) explicitly show that consumers perceive markets with one or more LPG-issuing firms as more competitive, rather than collusive. Furthermore, the economic press postulates that LPG policies initiate price competition. The Financial Times (1996), for example, ran the headline "Tesco Launches a New Price War" to report on Tesco's introduction of an LPG. Therefore, retailers with a cost advantage appear to use this policy to convince customers of their low price level (Hess/Gerstner 1991). Overall, LPGs' effects on price competition and consumer welfare remain controversial.

According to Png/Hirshleifer (1987), an LPG also can be used for price discrimination as it allows retailers to screen consumers according to their search costs. Invoking an LPG requires the consumer to search for lower prices and return to the LPG retailer. Therefore, only consumers with low search costs invoke an LPG. This information can be used to discriminate among consumers with high versus low search costs.

Then, because consumers with high search costs do not invoke LPGs and tend to be less price sensitive, an LPG-issuing retailer can charge higher prices for this customer segment (McWilliams/Gerstner 2006). Finally, assigning responsibility for invoking an LPG to consumers, Corts (1996) argues LPGs should be used to segment consumers according to their knowledge of competitors' prices.

6.4 Implications for Future MBG and LPG Research

6.4.1 Research Perspectives for MBG Effects on Consumers

Consumer effects resulting from an MBG have been less frequently investigated than those resulting from an LPG. In addition to this overarching distinction, other important gaps in literature remain. First, previous research offers only contradictory findings regarding the potential effects of an MBG on quality perceptions. Götting (2008) and Wood (2001) provide evidence for a quality effect in a catalog purchase context; Vieth (2008) finds a quality effect for experience but not for search goods; and d'Astous/Guèvremont (2008) find no quality effect, not even for financially risky and complex products characterized by high purchase uncertainties. These divergent findings are surprising, in that the signaling argument used to explain the MBG quality effect is strong. Future MBG research should integrate additional consumer theories that account for consumer irrationality if it is to understand the guarantee's actual impact on consumer behavior. Moreover, the setting of prior studies remains highly heterogeneous in terms of moderator variables and samples, so future studies should build on past MBG research and control for a more comprehensive list of variables to identify the conditions in which an MBG does affect quality perceptions.

Second, research on MBGs solely investigated cognitive variables, such as quality or risk perceptions, though Chandon/Wansink/Laurent (2000) show that promotions have both cognitive and emotional effects. Furthermore, Yoo/Park/MacInnis (1998) recommend to study the role of emotions in a retail context, the retail factors that affect them, and their effects on outcome variables. Vieth (2008) finds strong mediating effects of emotions evoked by an MBG on consumer behavior, though his study is somewhat limited, in that he investigates only a single emotional construct (emotional value of the offer) and measures it rather broadly (i.e., the construct's items are very close to indicators of general liking scales). Considering this limitation, future studies should focus on analyzing specific consumer emotions to explain consumer behavior more precisely (Bagozzi/Gopinath/Nyer 1999). Ramanathan/Williams (2007) distinguish between negative and positive emotions, which consumers can feel simultaneously. As a start, researchers should consider anticipated disappointment (negative emotion) and contentment (positive emotion), two emotions that strongly affect consumer behavior (Griskevicius/Shiota/Nowlis 2010; Simonson 1992).

Third, Hogreve/Gremler (2009) recommend research on the effectiveness of different MBG designs, which vary in their conditions for returning a product and test duration. Although Heiman et al. (2002) argue that both these design elements are very important for consumer behavior, research has not examined consumer responses to variations of MBG designs empirically. Restrictive MBG designs might have negative effects on prepurchase consumer evaluations. Specifically, prior literature on LPGs reveals that the credibility of a guarantee decreases when it is restrictive and should therefore be examined as a key mediator of MBG design effects on consumers' prepurchase behavior. In contrast, in the postpurchase period, restrictive MBG designs may have positive effects for a retailer, in that they reduce the $100 billion product return costs that sellers face each year (Anderson/Hansen/Simester 2009). As Harris (2008) finds evidence of opportunistic consumer behavior in the form of "retail borrowing", further research should determine which MBG terms facilitate such opportunistic behavior or how it might be repressed.

Finally, using a mathematical approach McWilliams/Gerstner (2006) show that offering an LPG in addition to an MBG increases customer retention and thereby positively affects profits. Their study also reveals that retailers regularly offer both an MBG and LPG. From a behavioral perspective this offer might be very effective, since it could result in low price and high quality perceptions at the same time. However, it is also possible that negative effects of an LPG on quality perceptions as well as positive effects of an MBG on price perceptions diminish the combined offer's effectiveness. Therefore, it would be interesting to analyze how MBGs and LPGs interact to impact on consumer behavior.

6.4.2   Research Perspectives for LPG Effects on Consumers

The LPG effects on consumer behavior have been more extensively researched than MBG effects, though some promising academic voids remain that future research might address. First, considering the many empirical LPG studies that use experimental data to represent subjects' evaluations and intentions, researchers should conduct more field studies to gather data that reflect real shopping behavior. Such data are more difficult to obtain, but after 10 years of intensive behavioral LPG research, academics need to investigate whether their empirical results are valid in real-world situations. Ho/Ganesan/Oppewal (2011) suggest a combination of laboratory experiments and field studies to assess consumers' cognitive responses and actual store behavior. Furthermore, previous research often relies on convenience samples, such as students who participate for course credit. Future LPG studies should use representative samples to enhance generalizability since evaluations of advertising claims clearly vary across consumer segments (Friestad/Wright 1994). Also, the type of LPG manipulation may be a concern. In practice, some retailers highlight the LPG refund conditions, rather than claiming low store prices, which may have important consequences for consumers' interpretations of LPGs (Dutta/Biswas/Grewal 2007). While refund conditions refer to the protective function, claiming low prices emphasize an LPG's informational role. The different effects of these framing conditions should lead researchers to analyze the effects of semantic variations of an LPG on consumer behavior (Dutta/Biswas 2005).

Second, LPG studies focus predominantly on signaling theory, which assumes rational market actors. Consumer responses to an LPG offer can never be fully understood if researchers do not apply appropriate consumer theories.

In particular, emotions have been found to strongly affect consumer behavior, especially in a retailing context (Puccinelli et al. 2009). For example, consumers may feel betrayed or disappointed in case of an LPG default (Dutta/Biswas 2005). These emotional responses may have a stronger impact on consumer behavior than price or service quality perceptions, two variables that have been analyzed by Estelami/Grewal/Roggeveen (2007) in this context. Other emotions, such as pleasure at finding lower prices, especially for deal-prone consumers (Lichtenstein/Netemeyer/Burton 1990), or feeling of relaxation when buying with an LPG, especially for risk-averse consumers, might be relevant too. Strong effects of emotions in turn would challenge previous (cognitive) LPG models as incomplete.

Third, retailers usually use several pricing tactics to convince consumers of the attractiveness of its prices (e.g., references prices, coupons, special offers, LPGs), but the field is missing investigations of multiple price cues (Ho/Ganesan/Oppewal 2011). Ho, Ganesan, and Oppewal (2011) compare the effectiveness of an LPG with an always-low-price strategy, but no study analyzes the interdependencies of various pricing tactics. Experimental settings may be used to address this issue, as they better cope with multiple stimuli and their effects on behavioral measures compared to analytical models (Srivastava/Lurie 2004). Ho/Ganesan/Oppewal (2011) also suggest investigating consumer responses when multiple retailers offer an LPG, which is an important topic because previous researchers have not integrated competing LPGs by more than one seller in their consumer behavior models (Biswas/Dutta/Pullig 2006), though in practice, several competitors offer LPGs simultaneously.

Finally, LPG research should investigate other moderators that affect the relation of an LPG to consumer responses. Specifically, academics should analyze the effectiveness of this tool for different types of products. In most empirical LPG studies, high-priced items and search goods (e.g., DVD players, digital cameras) serve to test the theoretical predictions. Only two studies consider price level as a moderator variable for the relation of an LPG with consumer behavior (Srivastava/Lurie 2001; Lurie/Srivastava 2005). In terms of a broader generalization of LPG findings though, analyses should include high versus low financial risk products, search versus experience products, hedonic versus utilitarian products, high versus low involvement products, and products purchased frequently versus infrequently. Additional moderators of interest include consumer characteristics, such as their tendency to use a price–quality schema, consumer skepticism, involvement, risk aversion, or promotion proneness. Integrating these variables in existing LPG models may produce different results and help managers to target specific consumer segments appropriately.

6.5   Conclusion

As prominent tools used widely in marketing practice, MBGs and LPGs have been studied extensively in marketing research. This review of 58 articles published in marketing, business, and economic journals applies a consistent classification to both MBG and LPG research. First, literature can be classified as behavioral or economic. Second, behavioral MBG and LPG studies can be grouped according to the purchase stage (prepurchase versus postpurchase), the decision-making process (evaluation versus intention), and the consumer effect (e.g., value perception, search intention) analyzed. Third, economic MBG studies comprise four topics: profit impact, quality signaling, multiple cue effects, and optimal guarantee design, whereas economic LPG studies consist of either price competition or price discrimination investigations.

This article has focused mainly on the consumer effects of these guarantees and therefore on behavioral studies. Regarding prepurchase evaluations of MBGs, some authors demonstrate that MBGs increase perceptions of product quality, reduce consumers' perceived risk, and enhance price expectations, emotional responses, value perceptions, and the retailer's image. In terms of prepurchase intentions, an MBG reduces search intentions and increases purchase intentions. However, the results are not always straightforward as MBG effects often depend on moderator variables, such as reputation or purchase channel. For example, an MBG may have the strongest impact on prepurchase behavior when provided by a remote seller with a low reputation because consumer purchase uncertainty is highest. However, results are controversial as Vieth (2008) finds that a strong company reputation increases its signaling qualities. Only two studies examine postpurchase effects of an MBG and indicate that an MBG increases loyalty intentions and enhances quality perceptions even after product usage.

Despite these various contributions, substantial gaps remain. Empirical research provides controversial findings regarding the quality effect of an MBG in the prepurchase stage, and thus, future research needs to investigate the conditions in which an MBG serves as a signal of high quality, by controlling for previously studied variables and integrating new ones (i.e., market, company, and consumer variables). Considering some countervailing effects of MBGs and LPGs on quality and price perceptions, namely an MBG potentially increases quality and price perceptions whereas and LPG might reduce quality and price perceptions, researchers should also analyze how these tools interact to influence consumer behavior. Furthermore, previous research has focused on cognitive MBG effects, though Vieth (2008) claims that consumer emotions better explain relevant consumer behaviors. Additional research is needed to analyze specific emotional responses that might mediate MBG effects on consumer behavior. Finally, MBG research should analyze consumer behavior after the purchase to discern how many consumers return an item and whether these costs balance out any additional revenues generated from an MBG. In this context, MBG researchers should study design effects, because although restrictive designs might limit customer cheating, they also may decrease MBG credibility and negatively affect consumer behavior. Studying this trade-off is an interesting area for future MBG research.

Academics studying evaluations resulting from LPGs in the prepurchase stage have shown that these tools lower price perceptions and risk perceptions, but increase value perceptions. As for MBG research, the inclusion of moderator variables sheds more light into the outcomes. For example, LPG effects on price perceptions depend on market-level search costs, consumers' perceived price dispersion, and the purchase channel. Consumers' prepurchase intentions also are influenced by an LPG that reduces search intentions and increases patronage intentions. Other studies reveal that LPGs have carry-over effects and thus influence postpurchase behavior: They increase price perceptions when a retailer defaults on its promise to offer the lowest price, but their effects on service quality evaluations are positive if the retailer adequately refunds the consumer. In terms of postpurchase intentions, an LPG appears to increase search intentions, especially for value-conscious consumers. Repurchase intentions decrease when a retailer fails on its promise to offer the lowest prices.

Despite these many findings, there are several avenues to extend LPG research. Researchers should conduct field experiments to gain access to real shopping behavior, not just evaluations and intentions. Although consumer decision-making processes are important influences on behavior, it would be interesting to determine how an LPG actually pays off, a question that has not been answered satisfactorily yet. Moreover, as in MBG research, the analysis of consumer emotions has been largely ignored. Further research should focus on prepurchase emotions such as liking or feeling of relaxation when offered an LPG and postpurchase emotions such as pleasure at finding lower prices. Also, feelings of betrayal or disappointment could be particularly relevant in an LPG default context and mediate consumers' responses. Finally, retailers rarely communicate single price cues. Therefore, the incremental effect of an LPG on a consumer's purchase decision, compared with other price cues such as reference prices, needs to be investigated.

Overall, this effort to systematize and summarize MBG and LPG research clearly shows that both guarantees can be powerful tools in a seller's marketing mix, though ongoing MBG and LPG research should integrate various market variables (e.g., competitive versus noncompetitive markets), company variables (e.g., internet versus bricks-and-mortar seller), and consumer variables (e.g., less versus more skeptical consumers) to analyze the conditions in which these guarantees are most effective. In other words, which companies acting in which markets serving which customers benefit from these offers? Considering the ubiquity of MBGs and LPGs in marketing practice, behavioral and economic researchers should work in interdisciplinary teams to provide additional insights into this question.

Literature

[1] Akaah, I. P./Korgaonkar, P. K. (1988): A Conjoint Investigation of the Relative Importance of Risk Relievers in Direct Marketing. Journal of Advertising Research, Vol. 28, 4, pp. 38-44.

[2] Anderson, E. T./Hansen, K./Simester, D. (2009): The Option Value of Returns: Theory and Empirical Evidence. Marketing Science, Vol. 28, 3, pp. 405-423.

[3] Arbatskaya, M. (2001): Can Low-Price Guarantees Deter Entry? International Journal of Industrial Organization, Vol. 19, 9, pp. 1387-1406.

[4] Bagozzi, R. P./Gopinath, M./Nyer, P. U. (1999): The Role of Emotions in Marketing. Journal of the Academy of Marketing Science, Vol. 27, 2, pp. 184-206.

[5] Biswas, A./Dutta, S./Pullig, C. (2006): Low Price Guarantees as Signals of Lowest Price: The Moderating Role of Perceived Price Dispersion. Journal of Retailing, Vol. 82, 3, pp. 245-257.

[6] Biswas, A./Pullig, C./Yagci, M. I./Dean, D. H. (2002): Consumer Evaluation of Low Price Guarantees: The Moderating Role of Reference Price and Store Image. Journal of Consumer Psychology, Vol. 12, 2, pp. 107-118.

[7] Bonifield, C./Cole, C./Schultz, R. L. (2010): Product Returns on the Internet: A Case of Mixed Signals? Journal of Business Research, Vol. 63, 9-10, pp. 1058-1065.

[8] Boulding, W./Kirmani, A. (1993): A Consumer-Side Experimental Examination of Signaling Theory: Do Consumers Perceive Warranties as Signals of Quality? Journal of Consumer Research, Vol. 20, 1, pp. 111-123.

[9] Chandon, P./Wansink, B./Laurent, G. (2000): A Benefit Congruency Framework of Sales Promotion Effectiveness. Journal of Marketing, Vol. 64, 4, pp. 65-81.

[10] Chatterjee, S./Timothy, H. B./Basuroy S. (2003): Failing to Suspect Collusion in Price-Matching Guarantees: Consumer Limitations in Game-Theoretic Reasoning. Journal of Consumer Psychology, Vol. 13, 3, pp. 225-267.

[11] Chen, Y./Narasimhan, C./Zhang, Z. J. (2001): Consumer Heterogeneity and Competitive Price-Matching Guarantees. Marketing Science, Vol. 20, 3, pp. 300-314.

[12] Chu, W./Gerstner, E./Hess, J. D. (1998): Managing Dissatisfaction. Journal of Service Research, Vol. 1, 2, pp. 140-155.

[13] Corts, K. S. (1996): On the Competitive Effects of Price-Matching Policies. International Journal of Industrial Organization Vol. 15, 3, pp. 283-299.

[14] d'Astous, A./Guèvremont, A. (2008): Effects of Retailer Post-Purchase Guarantee Policies on Consumer Perceptions with the Moderating Influence of Financial Risk and Product Complexity. Journal of Retailing and Consumer Services, Vol. 15, 4, pp. 306-314.

[15] Davis, S./Gerstner, E./Hagerty, M. (1995): Money Back Guarantees in Retailing: Matching Products to Consumer Tastes. Journal of Retailing, Vol. 71, 1, pp. 7-22.

[16] Davis, S./Hagerty, M./Gerstner, E. (1998): Return Policies and the Optimal Level of "Hassle". Journal of Economics and Business, Vol. 50, pp. 445–460.

[17] Dutta, S./Bhowmick, S. (2009): Consumer Responses to Offline and Online Low Price Signals: The Role of Cognitive Elaboration. Journal of Business Research, Vol. 62, 6, pp. 629-635.

[18] Dutta, S./Biswas, A. (2005): Effects of Low Price Guarantees on Consumer Post-Purchase Search Intention: The Moderating Roles of Value Consciousness and Penalty Level. Journal of Retailing, Vol. 81, 4, pp. 283-291.

[19] Dutta, S./Biswas, A./Grewal, D. (2007): Low Price Signal Default: An Empirical Investigation of Its Consequences. Journal of the Academy of Marketing Science, Vol. 35, 1, pp. 76-88.

[20] Edlin, A. S./Emch, E. R. (1999): The Welfare Losses from Price-Matching Policies. Journal of Industrial Economics, Vol. 47, 2, pp. 145-167.

[21] Eschweiler, M. (2006): Externe Referenzpreise. Wiesbaden: Gabler.

[22] Estelami, H./Grewal, D./Roggeveen, A. (2007): The Negative Effects of Policy Restrictions on Consumers' Post-Purchase Reactions to Price-Matching Guarantees. Journal of the Academy of Marketing Science, Vol. 35, 2, pp. 208-219.

[23] Financial Times (1996): Tesco Launches a New Price War, September 5, p. 1.

[24] Folkes, V. S. (1988): Recent Attribution Research in Consumer Behavior: A Review and New Directions. Journal of Consumer Research, Vol. 14, 4, pp. 548-565.

[25] Friestad, M./Wright, P. (1994): The Persuasion Knowledge Model: How People Cope with Persuasion Attempts. The Journal of Consumer Research, Vol. 21, 1, pp. 1-31.

[26] Fruchter, G. E./Gerstner, E. (1999): Selling with "Satisfaction Guaranteed". Journal of Service Research, Vol. 1, 4, pp. 313-323.

[27] Götting, P. (2008): Anbieterloyalität - Strategie Und Instrument Zur Gewinnung Von Kunden Und Kundenloyalität - Theoretische Diskussion Und Empirische Befunde Im B2C Marketing. Oestrich-Winkel: European Business School.

[28] Grewal, D./Munger, J. L./Iyer, G. R./Levy, M. (2003): The Influence of Internet-Retailing Factors on Price Expectations. Psychology and Marketing, Vol. 20, 6, pp. 477-493.

[29] Griskevicius, V./Shiota, M. N./Nowlis, S. M. (2010): The Many Shades of Rose-Colored Glasses: An Evolutionary Approach to the Influence of Different Positive Emotions. Journal of Consumer Research, Vol. 37, 2, pp. 238–250.

[30] Harris, L. C. (2008): Fraudulent Return Proclivity: An Empirical Analysis. Journal of Retailing, Vol. 84, 4, pp. 461-476.

[31] Hawes, J./Lumpkin, J. (1986): Perceived Risk and the Selection of a Retail Patronage Mode. Journal of the Academy of Marketing Science, Vol. 14, 4, pp. 37-42.

[32] Healey, J. R. (2009): GM Will Offer 60-Day, Money-Back Guarantee on New Cars. in USA TODAY.

[33] Heiman, A./McWilliams, B./Zhao, J./Zilberman, D. (2002): Valuation and Management of Money-Back Guarantee Options. Journal of Retailing, Vol. 78, 3, pp. 193-205.

[34] Heiman, A./McWilliams, B./Zilberman, D. (2001a): Demonstrations and Money-Back Guarantees: Market Mechanisms to Reduce Uncertainty Journal of Business Research, Vol. 54, 1, pp. 71-84.

[35] Heiman, A./McWilliams, B./Zilberman, D. (2001b): Reducing Purchasing Risk with Demonstrations and Money-Back Guarantees. The Marketing Management Journal, Vol. 11, 4, pp. 58-72.

[36] Henkel (2010): Innovationsgeschichte.
http://web.archive.org/web/20080321163437/www.henkel.de/cps/rde/xchg/henkel_de/hs.xsl/10105_DED_HTML.htm (accessed June 21 2010).

[37] Hess, J. D./Chu, W./Gerstner, E. (1996): Controlling Product Returns in Direct Marketing. Marketing Letters, Vol. 7, 4, pp. 307-317.

[38] Hess, J. D./Gerstner, E. (1991): Price-Matching Policies: An Empirical Case. Managerial and Decision Economics, Vol. 12, 4, pp. 305-315.

[39] Ho, H./Ganesan, S./Oppewal, H. (2011): The Impact of Store-Price Signals on Consumer Search and Store Evaluation. Journal of Retailing, Vol. 87, 2, pp. 127-141.

[40] Hogreve, J./Gremler, D. D. (2009): Twenty Years of Service Guarantee Research. Journal of Service Research, Vol. 11, 4, pp. 322-343.

[41] Hviid, M./Shaffer, G. (1999): Hassle Costs: The Achilles' Heel of Price-Matching Guarantees. Journal of Economics & Management Strategy, Vol. 8, 4, pp. 489-521.

[42] Jain, S./Srivastava, J. (2000): An Experimental and Theoretical Analysis of Price-Matching Refund Policies. Journal of Marketing Research, Vol. 37, 3, pp. 351-362.

[43] Kahneman, D./Knetsch, J. L./Thaler, R. H. (1990): Experimental Tests of the Endowment Effect and the Coase Theorem. Journal of Political Economy, Vol. 98, 6, pp. 1325-1348.

[44] Kaplan, L. B./Szybillo, G. J./Jacoby, J. (1974): Components of Perceived Risk in Product Purchase: A Cross-Validation. Journal of Applied Psychology, Vol. 59, 3, pp. 287-291.

[45] Kirmani, A./Rao, A. R. (2000): No Pain, No Gain: A Critical Review of the Literature on Signaling Unobservable Product Quality. Journal of Marketing, Vol. 64, 2, pp. 66-79.

[46] Kukar-Kinney, M. (2006): The Role of Price-Matching Characteristics in Influencing Store Loyalty. Journal of Business Research, Vol. 59, 4, pp. 475-482.

[47] Kukar-Kinney, M./Grewal, D. (2007): Comparison of Consumer Reactions to Price-Matching Guarantees in internet and Bricks-and-Mortar Retail Environments. Journal of the Academy of Marketing Science, Vol. 35, 2, pp. 197-207.

[48] Kukar-Kinney, M./Walters, R. G. (2003): Consumer Perceptions of Refund Depth and Competitive Scrope in Price-Matching Guarantees: Effects on Store Patronage. Journal of Retailing, Vol. 79, 3, pp. 153-160.

[49] Kukar-Kinney, M./Walters, R. G./MacKenzie, S. B. (2007): Consumer Response to Characteristics of Price-Matching Guarantees: The Moderating Role of Price Consciousness. Journal of Retailing, Vol. 83, 2, pp. 211-221.

[50] Kukar-Kinney, M./Xia, L./Monroe, K. B. (2007): Consumers' Perceptions of the Fairness of Price-Matching Refund Policies. Journal of Retailing, Vol. 83, 3, pp. 325-337.

[51] Lee, B.-C./Ang, L./Dubelaar, C. (2005): Lemons on the Web: A Signaling Approach to the Problem of Trust in internet Commerce. Journal of Economic Psychology, Vol. 26, 5, pp. 607-623.

[52] Lichtenstein, D. R./Netemeyer, R. G./Burton, S. (1990): Distinguishing Coupon Proneness from Value Consciousness: An Acquisition-Transaction Utility Theory Perspective. Journal of Marketing, Vol. 54, 3, pp. 54-67.

[53] Logan, J. W./Lutter, R. W. (1989): Guaranteed Lowest Prices: Do They Facilitate Collusion? Economics Letters, Vol. 31, 2, pp. 189-192.

[54] Lurie, N. H./Srivastava, J. (2005): Price-Matching Guarantees and Consumer Evaluations of Price Information. Journal of Consumer Psychology, Vol. 15, 2, pp. 149-158.

[55] McWilliams, B./Gerstner, E. (2006): Offering Low Price Guarantees to Improve Customer Retention. Journal of Retailing, Vol. 82, 2, pp. 105-113.

[56] Moorthy, S./Srinivasan, K. (1995): Signaling Quality with a Money-Back Guarantee: The Role of Transaction Costs. Marketing Science, Vol. 14, 4, pp. 442-466.

[57] Olympus (2011): 30 Tage testen mit Geld-zurück-Garantie.
http://www.olympus.de/digitalkamera/images/dyw/pdf/PEN_Geld-Zurueck-Garantie_Flyer.pdf (accessed July 15 2011).

[58] Png, I. P. L./Hirshleifer, D. (1987): Price Discrimination through Offers to Match Price. Journal of Business, Vol. 60, 3, pp. 365-383.

[59] Posselt, T./Gerstner, E./Radic, D. (2008): Rating E-Tailers' Money-Back Guarantees. Journal of Service Research, Vol. 10, 3, pp. 207-219.

[60] Puccinelli, N. M./Goodstein, R. C./ Grewal, D./Price, R./Raghubir, R./Stewart, D. (2009): Customer Experience Management in Retailing: Understanding the Buying Process. Journal of Retailing, Vol. 85, 1, pp. 15-30.

[61] Purohit, D./Srivastava, J. (2001): Effect of Manufacturer Reputation, Retailer Reputation, and Product Warranty on Consumer Judgments of Product Quality: A Cue Diagnosticity Framework. Journal of Consumer Psychology, Vol. 10, 3, pp. 123-134.

[62] Ramanathan, S./Williams, P. (2007): Immediate and Delayed Emotional Consequences of Indulgence: The Moderating Influence of Personality Type on Mixed Emotions. Journal of Consumer Research, Vol. 34, 2, pp. 212-223.

[63] Rao, A. R./Monroe, K. B. (1989): The Effect of Price, Brand Name, and Store Name on Buyers' Perceptions of Product Quality: An Integrative Review. Journal of Marketing Research, Vol. 26, 3, pp. 351-357.

[64] Salop, S. C. (1986): Practices That (Credibly) Facilitate Oligopoly Coordination. in New Developments in the Analysis of Market Structure, J. E. Stiglitz and G. F. Matthewson (eds). Cambridge: MA: MIT Press.

[65] Schmidt, S. L./Kernan, J. B. (1985): The Many Meanings (and Implications) of 'Satisfaction Guaranteed'. Journal of Retailing, Vol. 61, 4, pp. 89-108.

[66] Sen, S./Johnson, E. J. (1997): Mere-Possession Effects without Possession in Consumer Choice. Journal of Consumer Research, Vol. 24, 1, pp. 105-117.

[67] Shieh, S. (1996): Price and Money-Back Guarantees as Signals of Product Quality. Journal of Economics & Management Strategy, Vol. 5, 3, pp. 361-377.

[68] Simonson, I. (1992): The Influence of Anticipating Regret and Responsibility on Purchase Decisions. Journal of Consumer Research, pp. 105-118.

[69] Srivastava, J./Lurie, N. (2001): A Consumer Perspective on Price-Matching Refund Policies: Effect on Price Perceptions and Search Behavior. Journal of Consumer Research, Vol. 28, 2, pp. 296-307.

[70] Srivastava, J./Lurie, N. (2004): Price-Matching Guarantees as Signals of Low Stores Prices: Survey and Experimental Evidence. Journal of Retailing, Vol. 80, 2, pp. 117-128.

[71] Sullivan, E. A. (2009): Guaranteeing Success. Marketing News, p. 20.

[72] Van den Poel, D./Leunis, J. (1999): Consumer Acceptance of the Internet as a Channel of Distribution. Journal of Business Research, Vol. 45, 3, pp. 249-256.

[73] Vanhamme, J./de Bont, C. J. P. M. (2008): "Surprise Gift" Purchases: Customer Insights from the Small Electrical Appliances Market. Journal of Retailing, Vol. 84, 3, pp. 354-369.

[74] Vieth, M. (2008): Geld-zurück-Garantien - eine Empirische Wirkungsanalyse aus Konsumentensicht. Wiesbaden: Gabler.

[75] Völckner, F./Hofmann, J. (2007): The Price-Perceived Quality Relationship: A Meta-Analytic Revew and Assessment of Its Determinants. Marketing Letters, Vol. 18, 3, pp. 181-196.

[76] Wood, S. L. (2001): Remote Purchase Environments: The Influence of Return Policy Leniency on Two-Stage Decision Processes. Journal of Marketing Research, Vol. 38, 2, pp. 157-169.

[77] Xia, L./Kukar-Kinney, M./Monroe, K. B. (2010): Effects of Consumers' Efforts on Price and Promotion Fairness Perceptions. Journal of Retailing, Vol. 86, 1, pp. 1-10.

[78] Yoo, C./Park, J./MacInnis, D. J. (1998): Effects of Store Characteristics and In-Store Emotional Experiences on Store Attitude. Journal of Business Research, Vol. 42, 3, pp. 253-263.

[79] Zhang, Z. J. (1995): Price-Matching Policy and the Principle of Minimum Differentiation. Journal of Industrial Economics, Vol. 43, 3, pp. 287-299.

7   The Perceived Value of Brand Heritage and Brand Luxury

Managing the Effect on Brand Strength

Klaus-Peter Wiedmann, Leibniz University Hannover, Germany

Nadine Hennigs, Leibniz University Hannover, Germany

Steffen Schmidt, Leibniz University Hannover, Germany

Thomas Wüstefeld, Leibniz University Hannover, Germany

Abstract

The heritage aspect is a crucial part of a luxury brand as it has to appear both perfectly modern to the society of the day and at the same time laden with history. Heritage adds the association of depth, authenticity and credibility to the brand's perceived value and can result in an intensified brand loyalty and the willingness to accept higher prices. Incorporating relevant theoretical and empirical findings, the aim of the present study is to examine the antecedents and outcomes of luxury value and brand heritage as perceived by consumers and effects resulting on brand strength. Based on a structural modeling approach, results reveal the most important effects of the perceived luxury and heritage of a brand on consumer perceived value in terms of the customer's economic, functional, affective, and social evaluation of a brand and its related effects on the affective, cognitive and intentional brand strength.

Keywords

Brand Heritage, Brand Luxury, Brand Management, Structural Equation Modeling, Partial Least Squares.

7.1   Introduction

Marketing managers need to constantly improve their understanding of the complexity and dynamics of a customer's value perceptions. As the highest level of prestigious brands encompassing several physical and psychological values (Vigneron/Johnson 1999), the management of luxury brands addresses various aspects of customer perceived value. Therefore, it is critical for luxury researchers and marketers to understand the reasons why consumers buy genuine luxury brands, what they believe real luxury is, and how their perception of luxury value affects their buying behavior.

Apart from the luxury aspect especially during turbulent times of dynamics or economical crisis, characterized by uncertainty and consumer disorientation, consumers tend to prefer strong brands with a heritage that indicate their reliability and authenticity (Leigh et al. 2006). The heritage aspect is a crucial part of a luxury brand as it has to appear both perfectly modern to the society of the day and at the same time laden with history (Kapferer/Bastien 2009). Heritage adds the association of depth, authenticity and credibility to the brand's perceived value and can result in an intensified brand loyalty and the willingness to accept higher prices (e.g., Urde/Greyser/Balmer 2007). Thus, if and to what extent consumers assign value to the heritage and luxury aspect of brands is the research focus of this study.

Incorporating relevant theoretical and empirical findings, the aim of the present study is to examine the antecedents and outcomes of luxury value and brand heritage as perceived by consumers and effects resulting on brand strength. Our paper is structured as follows: first, we analyze existing literature on the luxury concept and its elements; second, we develop a conceptual model focusing on the value-based key drivers of luxury perception and brand heritage; and third, to explore the various dimensions and effects underlying the perceived values of luxury brands and brands with a heritage, we present the methodology and results of our empirical study. Based on a structural modeling approach, we identify the most important effects of the perceived luxury and heritage of a brand on consumer perceived value in terms of the customer's economic, functional, affective, and social evaluation of a brand and its related effects on the affective, cognitive and intentional brand strength. Finally, the results of our study are discussed with regard to future research and managerial implications.

7.2   Construct Definition and Literature Review

7.2.1   The Concept of Brand Heritage

Urde/Greyser,/Balmer define the brand heritage construct as part of a corporate brand identity: "a dimension of a brand's identity found in its track record, longevity, core values, use of symbols and particularly in an organisational belief that its history is important" (2007, pp. 4–5). In contrast to a historical overview that is grounded only in the past, traditions and brand heritage embrace not only the time frame "the past" but also "the present" and "the future" (Wiedmann et al. 2011a). The heritage aspect represents longevity and sustainability as a promise to the stakeholders that the core values and performance of the brand are authentic and true (Urde 2003). Especially in a tumultuous global economy characterized by uncertainty and consumer disorientation or in times of economic crisis and dynamics consumers tend to prefer brands with a heritage that indicates their credibility, reliability and authenticity (Leigh et al. 2006). Moreover, such brands use their longevity and sustainability to indicate that their stated core values and performance level are reliable. Hence, heritage creates value and leverage for a brand, especially in a turbulent global market (Aaker 1996). In sum, the heritage of a brand adds the association of depth, authenticity, and credibility to the brand's perceived value. In referring to an integrated understanding of the brand heritage construct and its elements, this research follows the work of Buß (2007) as well as Wiedmann et al. (2011a und 2011b) and the formative elements bonding, continuity, credibility, cultural meaning, cultural value, differentiation, familiarity, identity meaning, identity value, imagination, knowledge, myth, orientation, prestige and success images.

7.2.2   The Concept of Brand Luxury

Seen as goods for which the simple use or display of a particular branded product brings esteem for its owner, luxury brands enable consumers to satisfy psychological and functional needs. The psychological benefits are considered the main factor distinguishing luxury from non-luxury products (Nia/Zaichkowsky 2000). In the literature, a concept of exclusivity or rarity is well documented: Luxury brands are those whose price and quality ratios are the highest in the market (McKinsey 1990), and even though the ratio of functionality to price might be low with regard to certain luxury goods, the ratio of intangible and situational utility to price is comparatively high (Nueno/Quelch 1998). Therefore, luxury brands compete based on the ability to evoke exclusivity, brand identity, brand awareness, and perceived quality from the consumer's perspective (Phau/Prendergast 2000). Because luxury is a subjective and multidimensional construct, a definition of the concept should follow an integrative understanding. This paper uses the luxury brand definition of Vigneron/Johnson (1999) as the highest level of prestigious brands encompassing several physical and psychological values.

For the purposes of our study, we follow the insights of Wiedmann, Hennigs, Siebels (2007, 2009) who developed and investigated an integrated conceptual framework of consumers' luxury brand perception based on the following key elements: price, usability, utility, uniqueness, quality, self-identity value, hedonism, materialism, conspicuousness and recognition value.

7.2.3   The Concept of Customer Perceived Value (CPV)

As a context-dependent (Holbrook 1994; Parasuraman 1997), highly personal and multi-dimensional concept, customer perceived value can be defined as "an interactive relativistic consumption preference experience" (Holbrook 1994, p. 27), "a tradeoff between the quality or benefits they perceive in the product relative to the sacrifice they perceive by paying the price" (Monroe 1990, p. 46), "a customer's perceived preference for and evaluation of those product attributes, attribute performances, and consequences arising from use that facilitate (or block) achieving the customer's goal and purposes in use situations" (Woodruff 1997, p. 142), or "a consumer's overall assessment of the utility of a product based on perceptions of what is received and what is given" (Zeithaml 1988, p. 14). In accordance to the insights of Smith/Colgate (2007), we focus on the following four dimensions of customer perceived value: (1) the economic value as the monetary aspect of customer value, (2) the functional value, which represents the core benefit and basic utilities for the perceived value, (3) the affective value as representative for a more emotional perceived value based on feelings and (4) the social value, which stands for customer's personal orientation and personal matters.

7.2.4   The Concept of Brand Strength

For defining the brand strength construct we follow the insights of Wiedmann et al. (2011a, pp. 4-5): Understood as the differential impact of brand knowledge on consumer responses to marketing efforts (Keller 2007), brand strength reflects a brand's ability to differentiate its offerings from those of the competition and to create customer value through meaningful associations. To examine the strength of a brand in terms of the consumer's overall attraction to it, for the purposes of this paper, we consider brand strength to be the set of associations and behaviors displayed by a brand's customers (Srivastava/Shocker 1991). The constitutive elements of perceived brand strength are manifold, and they include the category in which the brand operates, the culture and attitudes of the target audience, the competitive positioning and functional product attributes (Aaker/Biel 1993). Taking into account the breadth of this range of considerations, we decided to concentrate on one of the most significant components of overall brand strength: the strength of consumer attitudes toward the brand (Aaker/Keller 1990). As evaluations stored in the memory of consumers (Judd et al. 1991) and important guides for behavior, attitudes play a crucial role in influencing consumer choices.

Based on a tripartite model including belief-based (cognitive), emotion-based (affective) and intention-based (behavioral) components (Rosenberg et al. 1969), attitudes are "tendencies to evaluate an entity [attitude object] into some degree of favour or disfavour, ordinarily expressed in cognitive, affective and behavioural responses" (Eagly/Chaiken 1993, p. 155).

7.3 The Conceptual Model and Related Hypotheses

The proposed conceptual model for investigating the relationship between brand heritage, brand luxury, customer perceived value and brand strength is shown in **Figure 7.1**.

Figure 7.1 Conceptual Model

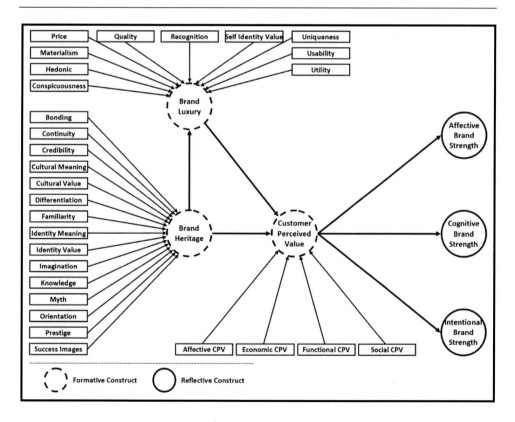

■ Brand Heritage → Customer Perceived Value

Particularly in turbulent times and purchase decisions that are associated with certain risks, the heritage aspect provides consumers with a feeling of security and well-being. Furthermore, in a tumultuous global economy, consumers tend to prefer brands with a heritage because these brands are perceived to be more credible, trustworthy and reliable. For this reason, the brand heritage construct can minimize consumers' buying risk and can add consumer perceived value (e.g., Muehling/Sprott 2004; Stewart-Allen 2002):

> **H1:** Brand heritage has a positive effect on customer perceived value.

■ Brand Luxury → Customer Perceived Value

In order to analyze the impact of brand luxury on customer perceived value, in our empirical study, we conceptualize luxury brand perception as being caused by the aforementioned constructs as formative indicators (cf., methodology section). Besides functional needs, luxury brands satisfy psychological needs as a main factor in differentiating luxury from non-luxury products (Nia/Zaichkowsky 2000). Moreover, the ratio of experienced intangible and tangible utility to paid price of luxury brands reaches a high level compared to non-luxury brands (Nueno/Quelch 1998). Hence, with reference to the key dimensions of customer perceived value, we hypothesize:

> **H2:** Brand luxury has a positive effect on brand's customer perceived value.

■ Brand Heritage → Brand Luxury

Brands with a heritage can benefit from going back to its roots and identifying what made it special (Aaker 2004). Heritage brands stand for longevity and sustainability, as proof that the core values and performance of the given products are reliable and true (Urde 2003). Especially those values strengthen and consolidate the luxury brand perception (for example such brand like Cerutti 1881 or Chanel):

> **H3:** Brand heritage has a positive effect on luxury brand perception.

■ Customer Perceived Value → Brand Strength

Delivering value is an ongoing and important concern in management (Ulaga/Chacour 2001). Concerning the question of how consumers perceive and evaluate brands especially the value of a brand can increase the brand equity in general. Concretely, this is also true for enhancing the brand strength with regard to the attitude-based apperception of a brand (Leone et al. 2006; Lassar et al. 1995; Keller 1993). Suggesting that customer perceived value performs as an accumulator in which the perceived heritage and luxury values are saved, we hypothesize the following:

> **H4:** Customer Perceived Value has a positive effect on a) affective brand strength, b) cognitive brand strength, c) intentional brand strength.

7.4   Methodology

7.4.1   The Questionnaire

To measure the constructs as conceptualized in our model this study used already existing and tested measures (i.e., Wiedmann et al. 2011a and 2011b; Dubois/Laurent 1994; Richins/Dawson 1992; Tsai 2005) and generated further items resulting from exploratory interviews with luxury consumers. The questionnaire items were rated on a five-point Likert scale (1=strongly disagree, 5=strongly agree) and specified to the brand CHANEL, one of the world's leading luxury brands with a strong heritage.

7.4.2   Index Construction With Formative Indicators

The construct for which we generated a measurement instrument based on formative indicators are brand heritage, brand luxury and customer perceived value. In contrast to the development and validation of multi-item scales based on reflective measures, the index construction using formative measures has received little attention. Following Diamantopoulos/Winklhofer (2001), there are four steps for constructing indexes based on a formative indicator: content specification, indicator specification, indicator collinearity and external validity. Because the latent variable is determined by its formative indicators, the specification of the domain of content is extremely important. Failure to consider all facets of the construct will lead to an exclusion of relevant indicators and parts of the construct itself. Our understanding of brand heritage relies on the theoretical derived and empirical checked core elements as proposed by Buß (2007) and Wiedmann et al. (2011a and 2011b), focusing on brand luxury we refer to the key elements of luxury value as proposed by Wiedmann, Hennigs/Siebels (2009), and with regard to the customer perceived value, we follow Smith/Colgate (2007). In addition, the generation of the items followed the guidelines of clarity, length, directionality, lack of ambiguity and avoidance of jargon (e.g., DeVellis 1991; Spector 1992).

7.4.3   The Sample

To investigate the research model, an Internet survey with a snowball sampling method was developed in Germany. It was organized using an Internet form sent to selected web pages and private customers via personalized emails with the invitation to actively contribute to the survey. In winter 2010, a total of 333 valid questionnaires were received. **Table 7.1** describes the sample characteristics.

Table 7.1   Demographic Profile of the Sample

Variable		n	%
Age	16 – 24 years	153	45.9
	25 – 29 years	106	31.8
	30 – 39 years	28	8.4
	40 years +	46	13.8
Gender	Male	94	28.2
	Female	239	71.8
Marital status	Single	269	80.8
	Married	48	14.4
	Widowed	0	0.0
	Divorced	11	3.3
	No answer	5	1.5
Education	Not graduated from high school	4	1.2
	Lower secondary school	2	0.6
	Intermediate secondary school	24	7.2
	A-Levels	187	56.2
	University Degree	115	34.5
	No answer	1	0.3
Occupation	Full time	84	25.2
	Part-time	24	7.2
	Pensioner / retiree	5	1.5
	House wife / husband	1	0.3
	Job training	11	3.3
	Student	193	58.0
	Scholar	9	2.7
	Seeking work	3	0.9
	No answer	3	0.9

Respondents were mainly aged 16 to 29 years with higher education. Those who are female and single were over-represented, which is indicative of the fact that many female students are particularly interested in a luxury brand like CHANEL. The higher percentage of young to middle-aged and female consumers in the sample may also be attributed to the greater Internet usage of young to middle-aged people.

7.5   Results and Discussion

7.5.1   PLS Path Modeling and Related Evaluation Criteria

In our exploratory study context, PLS (Partial Least Squares) path modeling was considered as the appropriate method for the empirical tests of our hypotheses. We used the analysis software SmartPLS 2.0 (Ringle et al. 2005) with no replacement and a bootstrapping procedure (probing individual sign changes). We followed the suggestions of Chin (1998) and his catalogue of non-parametric criteria for assessing the reliability and validity of the measures in the PLS estimation model. In general the assessment of the structural model's properties is only worthwhile if the measurement models exhibits a satisfactory degree of validity (Henseler, Ringle/Sinkovics 2009).

7.5.2   Evaluation of the Formative Measurement Model

Table 7.2 presents the variables defined as formative indicators for the constructs of brand heritage, brand luxury and customer perceived value. In respect of the question of multicollinearity for our formative measurement models, the maximum variance inflation factors (VIF) for brand heritage, brand luxury and customer perceived value are 2.80, 3.04 and 2.09, as shown in **Table 7.3**, and lies below the common threshold of 10 (Diamantopoulos/Winklhofer 2001). Thus, multicollinearity does not pose a problem in our study. With regard to the assessment of external validity of each formative indicator, we examined whether they were significantly correlated with any global items that summarize the corresponding essence of brand luxury, brand heritage and customer perceived value. For that reason, appropriate seven-point semantic differentials for (i) the perceived extent of brand's tradition (1=not at all traditional, 7=very traditional), (ii) the perceived extent of brand's luxury (1=not at all luxury, 7=very luxury) and (iii) the perceived extent of brand's usefulness (1=very negative, 7=very positive) were applied. All formative indicators are significantly correlated with this adequate item in supporting their external validity (cf. **Table 7.3**). As shown in **Table 7.4,** not all formative indicator's weights are significant and above .1, but none of the indicators could be excluded from a theory-driven view without losing information to cover all facets of the corresponding construct (Cenfetelli/Bassellier 2009).

Table 7.2   Manifest Variables of the Formative Measurement Models

Brand Heritage	
BH_Continuity	*"This brand is very continuous."*
BH_Success_Images	*"This brand is related to images of success."*
BH_Bonding	*"I am bonded to this brand."*
BH_Orientation	*"This brand sets the valuation standard for other brands."*
BH_Cultural_Value	*"The products of this brand are a part of national treasure."*
BH_Cultural_Meaning	*"The products of this brand promote a certain way of living."*
BH_Imagination	*"I have an absolutely clear imagination of this brand."*
BH_Familiarity	*"My familiarity with this brand is very high."*
BH_Myth	*"This brand has a strong cultural meaning."*
BH_Credibility	*"This Brand represents honesty and truthfulness."*
BH_Knowledge	*"This brand is highly known in the society."*
BH_Identity_Value	*"This Brand has a strong brand identity."*
BH_Identity_Meaning	*"If somebody praises this brand, to me, it is a personal compliment."*
BH_Differentiation	*"This brand is unique compared to other brands."*
BH_Prestige	*"This brand has a very good reputation."*
Brand Luxury	
LX_Price	*"This brand is worth its price."*
LX_Usability	*"This brand makes life more attractive."*
LX_Uniqueness	*"This brand is very exclusive."*
LX_Quality	*"This brand is very valuable."*
LX_Self_Identity	*"This brand emphasizes the personality of its owner."*
LX_Utility	*"This brand stands for usefulness."*
LX_Hedonism	*"This brand stands for sensuality."*
LX_Materialism	*"This brand evokes the desire to possess it."*
LX_Conspicuousness	*"This brand gives its owner a social recognition."*
LX_Recognition	*"This brand stands for people who succeeded in their life."*

Customer Perceived Value	
CPV_affective	*"This brands evokes positive perceptions."*
CPV_economic	*"This brand offers a lot for its price."*
CPV_functional	*"The products of this brand are very suitable."*
CPV_social	*"People who own this brand will be seen in a positive light."*

Table 7.3   Test for Multicollinearity and External Validity

Formative Indicators	VIF	Spearman's Rank Correlation Coefficient
BH_Continuity	1.58	0.441 ***
BH_Success_Images	1.78	0.330 ***
BH_Bonding	1.30	0.436 ***
BH_Orientation	1.63	0.509 ***
BH_Cultural_Value	1.45	0.285 ***
BH_Cultural_Meaning	1.23	0.103 ***
BH_Imagination	1.75	0.302 ***
BH_Familiarity	1.73	0.459 ***
BH_Myth	1.95	0.444 ***
BH_Credibility	1.70	0.448 ***
BH_Knowledge	1.69	0.323 ***
BH_Identity_Value	1.82	0.152 ***
BH_Identity_Meaning	2.80	0.100 ***
BH_Differentiation	2.00	0.254 ***
BH_Prestige	1.80	0.164 ***
LX_Price	1.81	0.281 ***
LX_Usability	1.84	0.317 ***
LX_Uniqueness	3.04	0.170 ***
LX_Quality	1.49	0.329 ***
LX_Self_Identity	1.75	0.236 ***
LX_Utility	1.24	0.170 ***

Formative Indicators	VIF	Spearman's Rank Correlation Coefficient
LX_Hedonism	2.35	0.333 ***
LX_Materialism	1.58	0.181 ***
LX_Conspicuousness	2.11	0.230 ***
LX_Recognition	2.01	0.314 ***
CPV_affective	2.09	0.621 ***
CPV_economic	1.76	0.506 ***
CPV_functional	1.39	0.321 ***
CPV_social	2.03	0.479 ***

Significance: *** p = 0.01; ** p = 0.05; * p = 0.10

Table 7.4 Bootstrapping Results for the Outer Weights

Formative Indicator → LV	Original Sample	Sample Mean	Standard Deviation	Standard Error	T Statistics
BH_Bonding → Brand Heritage	0.151	0.152	0.053	0.053	2.861***
BH_Continuity → Brand Heritage	0.018	0.043	0.032	0.032	0.569***
BH_Credibility → Brand Heritage	0.214	0.211	0.047	0.047	4.527***
BH_Cultural_Meaning → Brand Heritage	0.199	0.196	0.056	0.056	3.559***
BH_Cultural_Value → Brand Heritage	0.055	0.059	0.038	0.038	1.455***
BH_Differentiation → Brand Heritage	0.130	0.132	0.047	0.047	2.788***
BH_Familiarity → Brand Heritage	0.118	0.117	0.054	0.054	2.164***
BH_Identity_Meaning → Brand Heritage	0.158	0.158	0.042	0.042	3.737***
BH_Identity_Value → Brand Heritage	0.007	0.049	0.036	0.036	0.196***
BH_Imagination → Brand Heritage	0.005	0.041	0.033	0.033	0.157***
BH_Knowledge → Brand Heritage	-0.060	-0.062	0.037	0.037	1.601***
BH_Myth → Brand Heritage	-0.039	-0.049	0.037	0.037	1.054***
BH_Orientation → Brand Heritage	0.078	0.080	0.043	0.043	1.814***
BH_Prestige → Brand Heritage	0.254	0.250	0.053	0.053	4.767***
BH_Success_Images → Brand Heritage	0.129	0.124	0.053	0.053	2.436***

Formative Indicator → LV	Original Sample	Sample Mean	Standard Deviation	Standard Error	T Statistics
LX_Conspicuousness → Brand Luxury	0.165	0.159	0.053	0.053	3.128***
LX_Hedonism→ Brand Luxury	0.249	0.247	0.043	0.043	5.824***
LX_ Materialism → Brand Luxury	0.435	0.435	0.044	0.044	10.000***
LX_Price → Brand Luxury	0.068	0.068	0.038	0.038	1.781***
LX_Quality → Brand Luxury	0.117	0.116	0.042	0.042	2.773***
LX_Recognition → Brand Luxury	0.103	0.102	0.048	0.048	2.131***
LX_Self_Identity_Value → Brand Luxury	0.037	0.047	0.034	0.034	1.089***
LX_Uniqueness → Brand Luxury	0.047	0.053	0.031	0.031	1.520***
LX_Usability → Brand Luxury	0.139	0.139	0.046	0.046	3.009***
LX_Utility → Brand Luxury	0.088	0.092	0.045	0.045	1.963***
CPV_affective → Customer Perceived Value	0.595	0.593	0.050	0.050	11.848***
CPV_economic → Customer Perceived Value	0.351	0.353	0.053	0.053	6.665***
CPV_functional → Customer Perceived Value	0.103	0.106	0.044	0.044	2.320***
CPV_social → Customer Perceived Value	0.143	0.139	0.054	0.054	2.675***

Significance: *** $p = 0.01$; ** $p = 0.05$; * $p = 0.10$

7.5.3 Evaluation of the Reflective Measurement Models

With regard to evaluate our reflective measurement models, Table 7.5 presents the manifest variables that are reflective indicators for the three measurement models of brand strength. The results show sufficiently high factor loadings for all factors, with .66 being the smallest loading (cf. Table 7.6). This is evidence of indicator reliability. In addition, the PLS model estimation reveals that all reflective model constructs exhibit satisfactory results in terms of internal consistency (Bagozzi/Yi 1988). As shown in Table 7.6, the average variance extracted (AVE) estimates range from 60% to 74%, the Cronbach's alphas range from .68 to .88 and the composite reliability values range from .82 to .92. To assess discriminant validity, we used the Fornell-Larcker criterion: the AVE of each latent variable should be higher than the latent variable's highest squared correlation with any other latent variable (Fornell/Larcker 1981). Each of the tested latent variables satisfies the criterion requirements, suggesting discriminant validity.

Table 7.5   Manifest Variables of the Reflective Measurement Models

Affective Brand Strength	
BS_affective_01	*"This brand suits me completely."*
BS_affective_02	*"This brand keeps to its promise."*
BS_affective_03	*"I find this brand very pleasant."*
Cognitive Brand Strength	
BS_cognitive_01	*"This brand is very famous."*
BS_cognitive_02	*"In my opinion the quality of this brand is very high."*
BS_cognitive_03	*"This brand is very distinctive."*
Intentional Brand Strength	
BS_intentional_01	*"I intend to buy brand XY in the future."*
BS_intentional_02	*"I am very faithful to brand XY."*
BS_intentional_03	*"The products of brand XY are worth a higher price than other products."*
BS_intentional_04	*"I would recommend brand XY to my friends."*

Table 7.6   Assessing the Reflective Measurement Models

	Factor Loadings	Average Variance Explained (AVE)	Cronbachs Alpha	Composite Reliability	Fornell-Larcker-Criterion (AVE > Corr²)
Affective Brand Strength	0.82 – 0.90	74%	0.829	0.897	0.74 > 0.73
Cognitive Brand Strength	0.66 – 0.84	60%	0.676	0.819	0.60 > 0.54
Intentional Brand Strength	0.82 – 0.90	74%	0.882	0.919	0.74 > 0.73

7.5.4   Evaluation and Discussion of the Structural Model

As shown in **Table 7.7**, the coefficients of determination of the endogenous latent variables (R-square) for brand luxury, customer perceived value and affective, cognitive plus intentional brand strength are high at .70, .68, .57, .45 and .57 respectively. All Stone-Geisser Q-square values are higher than .26, which indicates that our introduced model has high predictive relevance. In order to test our research hypotheses, we applied a nonparametric bootstrapping procedure (individual sign changes) to assess the significance of the path coefficients as presented in **Table 7.8**. We postulate in hypotheses 1 to 4 a positive effect on related constructs. The results reveal a positive and highly significant (p < .01) impact of brand heritage and brand luxury on the customer perceived value (H1 and H2), a significant impact of customer perceived value on all aspects of brand strength (H4) and a positive impact of brand heritage on the brand luxury (H3) with path coefficients ranging from .43 to .84. Thus, our empirical results provide full support for all four hypotheses.

Understood as the indicators' relative importance in respect to forming the summed scale that represents the latent variables brand heritage, brand luxury and customer perceived value; the outer weights explain the latent variables with small to high impact. In our study (cf. **Table 7.4**), first, the outer weights with the highest impact of brand luxury are materialism (.44) and hedonism (.25). Second, the highest outer weights of brand heritage are prestige (.25) and credibility (.21). And third, the outer weights with the highest impact of customer perceived value are the affective (.60) and economic (.35) dimension of customer perceived value. These results suggest that our investigation brand CHANEL has to address functional (tangible aspects like materialism or economic values) as well as psychological (intangible aspects like hedonism and affective values) needs to increase their brand strength in terms of a positive customer behavior.

Table 7.7   Assessing the Structural Model

Endogenous LV	R²	Q²
Brand Luxury	0.701	0.270
Customer Perceived Value	0.679	0.417
Affective Brand Strength	0.569	0.418
Cognitive Brand Strength	0.445	0.263
Intentional Brand Strength	0.567	0.411

Table 7.8   Bootstrapping Results for the Structural Relations

Exogenous LV → Endogenous LV	Original Sample	Sample Mean	Standard Deviation	Standard Error	T Statistics
Brand Heritage → Brand Luxury	0.837	0.845	0.017	0.017	50.251***
Brand Heritage → Customer Perceived Value	0.431	0.442	0.059	0.059	7.328***
Brand Luxury → Customer Perceived Value	0.428	0.420	0.059	0.059	7.212***
Customer Perceived Value → Affective Brand Strength	0.754	0.756	0.026	0.026	28.854***

Exogenous LV → Endogenous LV	Original Sample	Sample Mean	Standard Deviation	Standard Error	T Statis-tics
Customer Perceived Value → Cognitive Brand Strength	0.667	0.668	0.036	0.036	18.373***
Customer Perceived Value → Intentional Brand Strength	0.753	0.755	0.025	0.025	30.404***

Significance: *** p = 0.01; ** p = 0.05; * p = 0.10

In sum, the overall model assessment shows that the PLS estimation model is reliable and valid according to the criteria associated with the formative and reflective outer model as well as the inner path model. Our empirical results suggest the following implications for further research and managerial practice, as described in the next paragraph.

7.6   Next Research Steps and Managerial Implications

7.6.1   Theoretical Contribution and Research Implications

The primary goal of this paper was to establish and explore a multidimensional framework of value-based drivers and consequences of brand heritage and brand luxury. A better understanding of the drivers of brand heritage, brand luxury and related effects in the eyes of consumers is valuable for both researchers and marketers. Even though our results are only initial empirical hints, they should be explored in further research and implemented in managerial practice in different ways. In comparing differences and similarities in the perception of a given heritage brand or luxury brand, a study focusing on diverse cross-cultural groups may lead to interesting results. More specifically, it can be assumed that consumers in different parts of the world buy, or wish to buy, products for apparently varied reasons; however, regardless of their nationality, the basic motivational drivers are expected to be the same among the economic, functional, affective, and social dimensions of value perception. Besides, the importance of the formative indicators of brand heritage and brand luxury may vary with regard to the product category (e.g., fashion vs. technology). Therefore, a study could compare the causal relationship of brand heritage and brand luxury to consumer perceived value with reference to different products or even brands.

Furthermore, a comparison of the evaluation of genuine and fake luxury products or brands with or without a strong aspect of heritage could enhance the conceptualization, measurement and management of brand heritage and brand luxury in the light of their effect on customer perceived value and brand strength.

7.6.2 Implications for Brand Management

For marketing managers, our study may form the basis of a structured understanding of the perceived value of the heritage and luxury aspect associated with their brand. With regard to economic, functional, affective, and social value dimensions, marketers might be able to address and improve purchase value for consumers, who may differ in their value orientations and prefer that a certain brand satisfy either their cognitive or emotional needs. Based on deeper insights related to the question of why consumers buy their brands, marketing managers may elicit more sales from their target consumers by adequately addressing their value perception. Thus, marketers should first explore the core values expressed by their brands, products, and market communications, and then compare them to their customers' value systems. This is useful from both a market segmentation point of view and a market positioning point of view, and will enhance the efficiency of marketing efforts for brands with a high degree of heritage and/or luxury.

In a global economy, where competitive products or counterfeits are easily available, brand managers should identify and concentrate on the specific value dimension that is regarded as the most important driver of consumption for their brand. Based on this, the market communication should stress the perceived values and emphasize the benefits of the given brand over competing brands or fake products. Even if low-cost counterfeit luxuries allow their buyers to be in tune with fashion without spending an exorbitant amount of money, a counterfeit product will never be able to provide the same pleasure or satisfy the individual need for sensory gratification. Consumers who place importance on the heritage aspect or hedonistic and materialistic product features might have a negative attitude towards a counterfeit purchase because they are aware of the self-deceiving aspect of this behaviour.

In order to be successful and to obtain a high perceived value in their customers' eye, luxury brand managers will have to address all relevant value dimensions: To be considered as a luxury brand in the eyes of the customers, it's about understanding the customers' evaluation and accentuating the brand appropriately to appeal to both their cognitive needs and affective desires. In sum, successful luxury brands balance the timelessness of brand heritage with innovative market communication and brand positioning to address contemporary consumers' needs and value perception.

Literature

[1]   Aaker, D. A. (1996): Building Strong Brands. New York: Free Press.
[2]   Aaker, D. A. (2004): Leveraging the corporate brand. California Management Review, Vol. 46, 3, pp. 6–18.
[3]   Aaker, D. A./Biel, A. L. (1993): Brand Equity and Advertising: Advertising's Role in Building Strong Brands. Hillsdale, NJ: Lawrence Erlbaum Associates.
[4]   Aaker, D. A./Keller, K. L. (1990): Consumer evaluations of brand extensions. Journal of Marketing, Vol. 54, 1, pp. 27–41.
[5]   Bagozzi, R. P./Yi, Y. (1988): On the evaluation of structural equation models. Journal of the Academy of Marketing Science, Vol. 16, 1, pp. 74–94.
[6]   Buß, E. (2007): Geschichte und Tradition – die Eckpfeiler der Unternehmensreputation. Archiv und Wirtschaft, Vol. 40, 2, pp. 72–85.
[7]   Cenfetelli, R./Bassellier, G. (2009): Interpretation of Formative Measurement in IS Research. MIS Quarterly, Vol. 33, 4, pp. 689-707.
[8]   Chin, W. W. (1998): The partial least squares approach to structural equation modeling. In: G.A. Marcoulides (Ed.), Modern Methods for Business Research. Mahwah, NJ: Lawrence Erlbaum Associates, pp. 295–358.
[9]   DeVellis, R. F. (1991): Scale Development: Theory and Applications. Newbury Park, CA: Sage Publications.
[10] Diamantopoulus, A./Winklhofer, H. M. (2001): Index construction with formative indicators: An alternative to scale development. Journal of Marketing Research, Vol. 38, 2, pp. 269–277.
[11] Dubois, B./Laurent, G. (1994): Attitudes toward the concept of luxury: An exploratory analysis. In S. Leong & J. Cote (Eds.), Asia Pacific advances in consumer research, Vol. 1. Provo, UT: Association for Consumer Research, pp. 273–278.
[12] Eagly, A. H./Chaiken, S. (1993): The Psychology of Attitudes. Fort Worth, TX: Harcourt Brace Jovanovich.
[13] Fornell, C./Larcker, D. F. (1981): Evaluating structural equation models with unobservable variables and measurement error. Journal of Marketing Research, Vol. 18, 2, pp. 39-50.
[14] Henseler, J./Ringle, C. M./Sinkovics, R. R. (2009): The use of partial least squares path modeling in international marketing. Advances in International Marketing, Vol. 20, pp. 277–319.
[15] Holbrook, M. B. (1994): The Nature of Customer Value: An Axiology of Services in the Consumption Experience. In Rust and R. L. Oliver, (Eds.), Service Quality: New Directions in Theory and Practice, Thousand Oaks, CA: Sage.
[16] Judd, C. M./Downing, J. W./Drake, R. A./Krosnick, J. A. (1991): Some dynamics properties of attitude structures: Context-induced response facilitation and polarization. Journal of Personality and Social Psychology, Vol. 60, 2, pp. 193–202.
[17] Kapferer, J.-N./Bastien, V. (2009): The Luxury Strategy: Break the Rules of Marketing to Build Luxury Brands. Kogan Page Ltd.
[18] Keller, K. L. (1993): Conceptualising, measuring and managing customer based brand equity. Journal of Marketing, Vol. 57, 1, pp. 1–22.
[19] Keller, K. L. (2007): Strategic Brand Management: Building, Measuring and Managing Brand Equity. Upper Saddle River, NJ: Prentice-Hall.
[20] Lassar, W./Mittal, B./Sharma, A. (1995): Measuring customer-based brand equity. The Journal of Consumer Marketing, Vol. 12, pp. 11-19.
[21] Leigh, T. W./Peter, C./Shelton, J. (2006): The consumer quest for authenticity: The multiplicity of meanings within the MG subculture of consumption. Journal of the Academy of Marketing Science, Vol. 34, 4, pp. 481–493.
[22] Leone, R. P./Rao, V. R./Keller, K. L./Luo, A. M./McAlister, L./Srivastava, R. (2006): Linking Brand Equity to Customer Equity. Journal of Service Research, Vol. 9, 2, pp. 125-138.
[23] McKinsey (1990): The luxury industry: An asset for France. Paris: McKinsey.

[24] Monroe, K. B. (1990): Pricing: Making Profitable Decisions. New York: McGraw-Hill Book Company.

[25] Muehling, D. D./Sprott D. E. (2004). The Power of Reflection: An Empirical Examination of Nostalgia Advertising Effects. Journal of Advertising, Vol. 33, 3, pp. 25–35.

[26] Nia, A./Zaichkowsky, J. L. (2000): Do counterfeits devalue the ownership of luxury brands? Journal of Product & Brand Management, Vol. 9, pp. 485–497.

[27] Nueno, J. L./Quelch, J. A. (1998): The mass marketing of luxury. Business Horizons, Vol. 41, pp. 61–68.

[28] Parasuraman, A. (1997): Reflections on Gaining Competitive Advantage Through Customer Value. Journal of the Academy of Marketing Science, Vol. 25, 2, pp. 154-161.

[29] Phau, I./Prendergast, G. (2000): Consuming luxury brands: The relevance of the "rarity principle." Journal of Brand Management, Vol. 8, pp. 122–138.

[30] Richins, M./Dawson, S. (1992): A consumer values orientation for materialism and its measurement: Scale development and validation. Journal of Consumer Research, Vol. 19, pp. 303–316.

[31] Ringle, C. M./Wende, S./Will, A. (2005): SmartPLS 2.0 M3, http://www.smartpls.de.

[32] Rosenberg, M. J./Hovland, C. I./McGuire, W. J./Abelson, R. P./Brehm, J. W. (1969): Attitude Organization and Change: An Analysis of Consistency among Attitude Components. New Haven, CT: Yale University Press.

[33] Smith, J. B./Colgate, M. (2007): Customer Value Creation: A Practical Framework. Journal of Marketing Theory and Practice, Vol. 15, 1, pp. 7-23.

[34] Spector, P. E. (1992): Summated Ratings Scales Construction: An Introduction. Newbury Park, CA: Sage Publications.

[35] Srivastava, R. K./Shocker, A. D. (1991): Brand Equity: A Perspective on its Meaning and Measurement. Boston, MA: Marketing Science Institute, Report no., pp. 91–124.

[36] Stewart-Allen, Allyson L. (2002). Heritage Branding Helps in Global Markets. Marketing News, Vol. 36, 16, August 5, p. 7.

[37] Tsai, S. (2005): Impact of personal orientation on luxury-brand purchase value. International Journal of Market Research, Vol. 47, pp. 429–454.

[38] Ulaga, W./Chacour, S. (2001): Measuring Customer-Perceived Value in Business Markets - A Prerequisite for Marketing Strategy Development and Implementation. Industrial Marketing Management, Vol. 30, pp. 525–540.

[39] Urde, M./Greyser, S. A./Balmer, J. M. T. (2007): Corporate brands with a heritage. Journal of Brand Management, Vol. 15, 1, pp. 4–19.

[40] Urde, M., (2003): Core Value-Based Corporate Brand Building. European Journal of Marketing, Vol. 37, 7–8, pp. 1017–1040.

[41] Vigneron, F. and Johnson, L. W. (1999). A review and a conceptual framework of prestige-seeking consumer behavior. Academy of Marketing Science Review, Vol. 1, pp. 1–15.

[42] Wiedmann, K.-P./Hennigs, N./Schmidt, S./Wuestefeld, T. (2011a): The importance of brand heritage as a key performance driver in marketing management. Journal of Brand Management, online, pp. 1-13.

[43] Wiedmann, K.-P./Hennigs, N./Schmidt, S./Wuestefeld, T. (2011b): Drivers and Outcomes of Brand Heritage: Consumers' Perception of Heritage Brands in the Automotive Industry. Journal of Marketing Theory and Practice, Vol. 19, 2, pp. 205–220.

[44] Wiedmann, K.-P./Hennigs, N./Siebels, A. (2007): Measuring consumers' luxury value perception: A cross-cultural framework. Academy of Marketing Science, Vol. 11, pp. 1–21.

[45] Wiedmann, K.-P./Hennigs, N./Siebels, A. (2009): Value-Based Segmentation of Luxury Consumption Behavior. Psychology & Marketing, Vol. 26, 7, pp. 625–651.

[46] Woodruff, R. (1997): Customer Value: The Next Source for Competitive Advantage. Journal of the Academy of Marketing Science, Vol. 25, 2, pp. 139–153.

[47] Zeithaml, V. A. (1988): Consumer Perceptions of Price, Quality, and Value: A Means-End Model and Synthesis of Evidence. Journal of Marketing, Vol. 52, 3, pp. 2-22.

Business Administration in Vienna

1 Studying Business Administration in Vienna

The Perception of Alternative Educational Institutions by Freshman Now and Then

Claus Ebster, University of Vienna, Austria

Heribert Reisinger, University of Vienna, Austria

Abstract

The goal of this study was to investigate how students at the Center for Business Studies at the University of Vienna and the Vienna University of Economics and Business differ with respect to their personality traits and their expectations of their respective universities. To this aim, 816 students at the University of Vienna and the Vienna University of Economics and Business were surveyed using face-to-face interviews. Results indicate that students at the two institutions differ in a variety of ways. Students at the University of Vienna evaluate broad course offerings, support services by lecturers, and a good climate between students as being more important than do students at Vienna University of Economics and Business. Respondents in the two samples also differ with respect to their self-assessed verbal and quantitative skills. The implications of these results are discussed and findings are compared with those of an earlier study investigating students at the two universities.

Keywords

Business Studies, Vienna, Students Profile.

Introductory Remark

While most higher education in Austria is controlled by public universities, understanding the wants and needs of each university's main stakeholder group, i.e., its students, has recently become of paramount importance. The advent of private universities, semi-private universities of applied sciences as well as increased competition among the traditional Austrian research universities has made student-centered marketing research a valuable tool in the arsenal of recruiting tools now available to university administrators. It is a trend that is also reflected internationally (Newman, 2002). This article presents the results of a marketing research study carried out to aid the positioning and targeting of the Center for Business Studies at the University of Vienna, an institution shaped by the leadership of Udo Wagner, to whom this volume and article are also dedicated. Not only does this study reveal the general image that students have of business education at the University and its main competitor, the Vienna University of Economics and Business, but the study is also a useful replication of a study carried out by Wagner and colleagues in 1996 (Reisinger/Wagner/Endlich, 1997). This restudy thus allows for a longitudinal analysis of students' perceptions of their alma maters through a comparison of now and then.

1.1   The Center for Business Studies and Its Main Competitor

Founded in 1365, the University of Vienna is one of the oldest universities worldwide and the oldest in the German speaking world. For centuries, Philosophy, Theology, Medicine, and Law have been researched and taught at the University, which with nearly 90,000 students and 9,400 employees is one of Europe's largest institutions of higher learning. It is also the home of nine Nobel laureates.

In spite of the University's long history, Business Administration was only fairly recently introduced as a field of study and scholarly research. That journey began in 1971, when for the first time in the history of the University, a Chair in Business Administration was created (Wagner, 1995, 37). Twenty years later in 1991, the Center for Business Studies was opened. At that time, there were 653 students. When Wagner and colleagues conducted their study in 1996, 3,761 students were studying at the Center for Business Studies. As seen in **Table 1.1**, in the last five years the number of students at the Center for Business Studies has increased steadily. In Fall semester 2010, there were 3,507 active students.

Table 1.1   Number of Active Students Studying at the Center for Business Studies

Degrees	2006 Spring	2006 Fall	2007 Spring	2007 Fall	2008 Spring	2008 Fall	2009 Spring	2009 Fall	2010 Spring	2010 Fall
Bachelor	724	1088	1037	1271	1199	1527	1522	1917	1711	2219
Master	107	136	161	221	255	312	335	439	510	601
Diploma	1539	1237	1063	932	815	661	598	523	472	380
Doctorate	200	232	250	299	276	257	276	304	304	307
Total	2570	2693	2511	2723	2545	2757	2731	3183	2997	3507

Source: Department of Quality Assurance, University of Vienna (2011)

The following programs of study are currently offered at the Center for Business Studies:

■ Bachelor of Business Administration and Bachelor of International Business Administration

■ Magister/Master of Business Administration, Magister/Master of International Business Administration and Master of Quantitative Economics, Management, and Finance

■ PhD in Management, PhD in Logistics and Operations Management, PhD in Finance, and a Doctorate in Business and Law.

In addition, the Faculty of Business, Economics, and Statistics offers degree programs in Economics, Statistics, and Operations Research at the Bachelor's, Master's and PhD levels.

The self-conception of the Department of Business Administration as well as the entire Faculty for Business, Economics and Statistics is that of a strongly research-based institution with an emphasis placed on quantitative methods. This self-image is echoed by the media as well. In 2009, the German Business Magazine *Handelsblatt* ranked the Department of Business Administration as the #1 Department of Business in Germany, Austria, and Switzerland, based on the research output of its faculty (Handelsblatt, 2009).

The main competitor for the Center for Business Studies is the Vienna University of Economics and Business (WU), founded in 1898 as the Imperial Export Academy and renamed the University of Economics and Business in 1975. The University's student population has significantly increased in the past two decades, from 8,000 in 1981 to its current 26,800 (WU Website, n.d.).

The Vienna University of Economics and Business offers the following degree programs:

■ Bachelors in Business, Economics and Social Sciences. Students enrolled in the University's most popular program can choose between majors in Business Administration, International Business Administration, Economics and Socio-Economics, as well as Information Systems.

- English-language Master's programs in International Management, Quantitative Finance, Strategy, Innovation and Management Control, and Supply Chain Management are offered.

- German-language Master's programs in Management, Business Education, Business Informatics, Business Law, Economics, Finance and Accounting, Taxation and Accounting, and Socio-Economics are available.

- Doctorate in Social and Economic Sciences, Doctorate in Business Law, and a PhD in Finance are also offered.

The Center for Business Studies at the University of Vienna and the Vienna University of Economics and Business have both made concrete plans to relocate their premises in the near future. In the case of the Center for Business Studies, this decision was made for two reasons: a) To unite the various departments and faculty for Business, Economics and Statistics, which currently resides in different locations, under one roof; b) To move the Center for Business Studies, currently housed in a suburb of Vienna, to a more desirable location in downtown Vienna, close to the main campus of the University of Vienna. The Center will relocate in the Fall of 2013.

The Vienna University of Economics and Business will relocate at the end of 2012. This decision was motivated by a desire to move to a larger, more modern campus. Unlike the Center for Business Studies, the Vienna University of Economics and Business will move from its current, central location in Vienna's 9th district to a suburban campus that is close to the Vienna Fairground.

1.2   Research Goals

The goal of this empirical study was to investigate how students at the Center for Business Studies and the Vienna University of Economics and Business differ with respect to their personality traits and their expectations of their respective universities. In other words, the aim was to identify the "typical" student at each institution. More specifically, the research goal was threefold:

1. To determine the differences in the expectations and personality profiles of students at the University of Vienna's Center for Business Studies compared to the Vienna University of Economics and Business.

2. To investigate how students' expectations and their personality profiles have changed over time.

3. To discover how students are responding to the planned relocation of the two institutions.

1.3   Method

The respondents to this study were 816 freshmen and sophomores studying at the Center for Business Studies ('Betriebswirtschaftszentrum' – BWZ) and the Vienna University of Economics and Business ('Wirtschaftsuniversität Wien' – WU). Of these, 344 respondents were students at the Center for Business Studies and 472 were studying at the Vienna University of Economics and Business. The sampling method used was a convenience sample. To ensure the integrity of the data and minimize (item) non-response, face-to-face interviews were conducted by 6 trained research assistants. The interviews took place from May to June 2011.

The questionnaire employed for the study had four sections as follows:

a. Items related to a respondent's decision to study at one of the two institutions (Course offerings, Lecturer's support service, Climate between students, Studying abroad, Size of Vienna University of Economics and Business, and Job prospects)

b. Items related to the respondent's personality (Mathematical skills, Linguistic skills, Extraversion, Risk taking, Self-confidence, Up-to-dateness)

c. Items related to the current and prospective locations of the two institutions (Evaluation of both locations)

d. Socio-demographic questions (Gender, Citizenship, Employment in addition to studying).

Most of the items used were closed questions (7-point rating scales and multiple-choice questions). One open format question was employed. It asked students for the most important reason for why they had decided to study Business Administration. A coding scheme was subsequently developed to quantify the responses to this unstructured question.

1.4   Results

1.4.1   Socio-Demographics and Reason to Study Business Administration

Female respondents accounted for 55.4% of the sample, and 67.1% of the students were Austrian citizens. 37.3% of the respondents are employed (for at least 10 hours per week) in addition to their academic studies. **Table 1.2** shows the relative frequencies of the most important reason that BWZ and WU students decided to study Business Administration. The two items 'Interest in the subject' and 'Good job prospects' together accounted for more than 60% of the stated reasons (for WU students more than 70%).

BWZ students very seldom stated as the main reason that they held a diploma from a business-oriented senior high school ('Handelsakademie' – HAK); they mentioned business study as a supplement to other studies three times more often than WU students. Other reasons for studying Business Administration were frequently stated by BWZ students (more than 20% of the responses to the open format question).

Table 1.2   Student Reasons for Studying Business Administration

Reason	Students at the Center for Business Studies (in %)	Students at the Vienna University of Economics and Business (in %)
Interest in the subject	36.2	43.9
Good job prospects	26.0	28.5
Money	3.2	5.0
Fun	0.9	1.2
Business high school diploma	0.9	7.1
Studying a semester abroad	0.3	0.3
Supplement to other studies	8.3	2.7
International focus	1.3	2.7
Other	22.9	8.6
	100.0	100.0

1.4.2   Student Profiles for the Center for Business Studies and the Vienna University of Economics and Business

Figure 1.1 compares the student profiles of the Center for Business Studies at the University of Vienna to those for the Vienna University of Economics and Business in a snake diagram. The diagram connects the average responses to the items measured on a 7-point rating scale. **Figure 1.1** also provides information on whether BWZ and WU mean responses are statistically different (employing a series of *t*-tests).

Figure 1.1   Snake Diagramm BWZ vs. WU

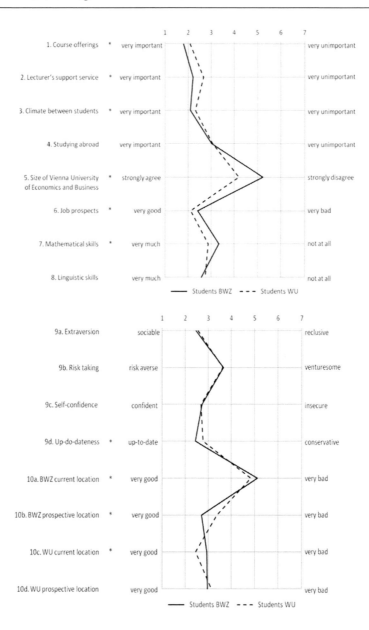

Asterisks (*) indicate the statistically significant differences at an α-level of .05.

In terms of tendency, the profiles of BWZ and WU students are related, but exhibit some distinctive features. BWZ students significantly evaluate broad course offerings, support services by lecturers, and a good climate between students as being more important than do WU students. The possibility to study abroad is seen as equally important by both groups of students. In absolute terms, the enormous size of the Vienna University of Economics and Business compared to the size of the Center for Business Studies is not seen as an advantage in studying at the WU. However, WU students rather agreed with the statement (Item 5) more than did BWZ students (significant difference). Significantly better job prospects are expected by WU students.

Items related to the respondent's personality showed few significant differences between the two profiles. WU students significantly assess their mathematical skills as being higher than BWZ students. BWZ students assessed their linguistic skills as higher (yet this difference was not statistically significant). Self-evaluations concerning extraversion, risk taking, and self-confidence were almost similar between the two student groups. BWZ students significantly consider themselves as more up to date and less conservative than WU students.

1.4.3   Current and Prospective Locations

WU students evaluated the current location of the BWZ as significantly better than did BWZ students (cf., **Figure 1.1**). BWZ students, however, evaluated the prospective BWZ location significantly better than did the WU students. WU students evaluated the current location of the WU significantly better than did BWZ students. Concerning the prospective WU location, no significant difference appears to exist (BWZ students evaluated this new WU location slightly better).

In addition to the profile of specific differences it is interesting to review and analyze how a specific group of students evaluated the current against the future location of an institution. **Table 1.3** shows these relevant figures (mean differences were tested with dependent samples t-tests). BWZ students as well as WU students evaluated the prospective BWZ location better than the current BWZ location (p<0.01). These differences are high in absolute terms, especially for BWZ students (5.1 vs. 2.7). BWZ students view both WU locations as equal (p=0.88). WU students, however, rate the prospective WU location worse than the current WU location (p<0.01).

Table 1.3   Evaluation of the Location

Location	BWZ students	WU students
BWZ current location	5.1	4.8
BWZ prospective location	2.7	3.4
WU current location	2.9	2.5
WU prospective location	3.0	3.1

Note: 1 ... very good, 7 ... very bad

1.5   Discussion

1.5.1   The Current Perspective (Research Goal 1)

BWZ students as well as WU students are business oriented, but the business focus is stronger for WU students. More often than the BWZ students, WU students stated as a reason for studying Business Administration that they are interested in this field of study and that they hold a diploma from a business-oriented high school. BWZ students mentioned more often that Business Administration is a supplement to another major. These students take their main study with another faculty at the University of Vienna, but then do choose the so-called 'Erweiterungscurriculum' Business Administration (an Erweiterungscurriculum is a structured combination of elective courses). In addition, BWZ students have many additional reasons for studying Business Administration that did not fit as easily into the coding scheme for the open format question on the study.

When evaluating the BWZ and WU profile, it is apparent that BWZ students appear to be more demanding than WU students. Broad course offerings, support service by lecturers, and a good climate between students is more important to them. They also expect worse job prospects than do WU students. However, a question does remain. Are these results basically rooted in the personalities of the students, or does the educational institution shape student needs and wants to a greater extent?

1.5.2   A Now and Then Perspective (Research Goal 2)

The present study is a replication of the Wagner and colleagues study carried out in 1996. Two decades later, the results changed noticeably in two respects. The founding of the Center for Business Studies was aimed especially to attract students with an interest in international business affairs. This target was met in the early years of BWZ. Today, many international students study at BWZ, and internationality is directly experienced in the classrooms. This international focus, however, is very seldom stated by students as the main reason for their studying Business Administration (at both the BWZ and the WU). Courses on international matters belong now to the standard repertoire of a business faculty, and they are no longer seen as innovative in and of themselves. The propensity of BWZ students to study abroad also decreased by approximately one scale point (WU students' propensities for foreign studies decreased only slightly). This result might also reflect a saturation level concerning student interest in international business studies.

Probably the most striking divergence between the two studies is that BWZ students assess their mathematical skills as being lower than for WU students. The reverse was the case two decades ago. This finding is surprising, as the University of Vienna's Faculty of Business, Economics, and Statistics as well as the Center for Business Studies emphasize their analytical/quantitative approach in research and teaching as a "Unique Selling Proposition". This approach is seen as a distinguishing feature via comparable faculties and business schools; hence, students with an interest in quantitative methods and analytical abilities are still an important target group for the Center for Business Studies. On the supply side, it is thus advisable to offer courses with analytical/quantitative content that is both understandable and motivates students to apply the techniques (Wagner/Reisinger, 1999). It is well known that the gap between the availability of quantitative methods and the use of those methods in practice is large, especially in the field of marketing research (Wagner/Reisinger, 2007; Wagner/Reisinger, 1997). Recognizing methodology as a valuable tool should be a basis for attracting the right targeted group and also for developing practical applications of such methods during students' later careers.

1.5.3   The Future Perspective (Research Goal 3)

While the WU's prospective location is considered to be slightly worse than its current location, the BWZ's prospective location is evaluated as being considerably better than its current location. Hence, the Center for Business Studies at the University of Vienna is expected to increase its market share to the detriment of the Vienna University of Economics and Business in the medium term.

In light of the never-ending discussion in Austria about restricted admission to academic studies and enrollment fees, it is doubtful whether increasing market share is desirable. Hopefully the prospective new BWZ location will not only attract a higher number of students, but also attract those of a high academic caliber.

Literature

[1] Department of Quality Assurance, University of Vienna (2011): University Statistics.

[2] Handelsblatt (2009): Handelsblatt Ranking Betriebswirtschaftslehre 2009. http://tool.handelsblatt.com/ tabelle/?id=29. Accessed on Sept. 19, 2011.

[3] Newman, C. M. (2002): The current state of marketing activity among higher education institutions. Journal of Marketing for Higher Education, Vol. 12, 1, pp. 15-24.

[4] Reisinger, H./Wagner, U./Endlich, E. (1997): Wirtschaftsuniversität und Betriebswirtschaftszentrum der Universität Wien im Vergleich: Die Wahrnehmung alternativer Bildungseinrichtungen aus der Sicht von Studienanfängern. Forschungsberichte des Instituts für Betriebswirtschaftslehre der Universität Wien.

[5] Wagner, U. (1995): Tätigkeitsbericht des Instituts für Betriebswirtschaftslehre der Universität Wien. Institut für BWL der Universität Wien.

[6] Wagner, U./Reisinger, H. (2007): Einsatzmöglichkeiten für statistische Methoden in der Marktforschung. In: VMÖ. Verband der Marktforscher Österreichs (Eds.): Handbuch der Marktforschung, 2nd. ed., facultas.wuv, Vienna, pp. 217-222.

[7] Wagner, U./Reisinger, H. (1999): Die Vermittlung quantitativer Inhalte im betriebswirtschaftlichen Unterricht. In: Gaul, W., Schader, M. (Eds.): Mathematische Methoden der Wirtschaftswissenschaften. Physika-Verlag, Heidelberg, pp. 455-463.

[8] Wagner, U./Reisinger, H. (1997): Die Anwendung statistischer Methoden in der Markt- und Meinungsforschung in Österreich. Österreichische Zeitschrift für Statistik, Vol. 26, pp. 59-70.

[9] WU Website (n.d.): Website of the Vienna University of Economics and Business. http://www.wu.ac.at. Accessed on July 25, 2011.

Udo Wagner

1 The Marketing Scientist

1.1 Stations of His Life

1. Personal Information	
Date of birth	July 19, 1952, Klagenfurt, Austria
Current position	Full Professor and Chair of Business Administration / Marketing at the University of Vienna, Austria
2. Education	
1970-1976	(Masters) in Mathematics, Vienna University of Technology, Austria
1984	Doctorate in Econometrics, Vienna University of Technology, Austria
1991	Habilitation, Venia docendi in Business Administration and Operations Research, Vienna University of Economics and Business, Austria
3. Appointments	
1976-1988	Assistant Professor, Department of Management, Vienna University of Economics and Business, Austria
1987	Visiting Professor, Department of Marketing, Ecole Supérieure des Sciences Economiques et Commerciales (ESSEC), Cergy-Pontoise, and Université de Droit, d'Economie et des Sciences d'Aix-Marseilles, France
1989	Visiting Professor, Department of Marketing, Graduate School of Management, Purdue University, West Lafayette USA
1990	Fixed-term Professor, Institute of Decision Theory and Operations Research, University of Karlsruhe, Germany
1990-1991	Tenure track Professor, Department of Marketing, Graduate School of Management, Purdue University, West Lafayette, USA
1991	Offer for a chaired professorship of Business Administration from the University of Karlsruhe, Germany (rejected), Associate Professor of Business Administration, Vienna University of Economics and Business, Austria
Since 1991	Full Professor and Chair of Business Administration / Marketing, University of Vienna, Austria 1992-2004 Head of the Department of Business Administration, University of Vienna, Austria 2004-2006 Dean of the Faculty of Business, Economics and Statistics, University of Vienna, Austria 2006 Visiting Professor, Babes-Bolyai University, Cluj-Napoca, Romania 2007 Visiting Professor, National Chiao Tung University, Hsinchu, Taiwan and Paris Dauphine University, France

1.2   Professional Activities

Research Focuses and Publications	Empirical market research and market modeling, consumer behaviour; applications of quantitative procedures and methods of OR, statistics, and econometrics in management and marketing; corporate social responsibility of firms; more than 200 publications (see chapter 2).
European Marketing Academy (EMAC)	2005-2011 Vice-president of the European Marketing Academy – Development; 2011 President-elect; 2012 President (2012-2014).
Korean Scholars of Marketing Science (KSMS)	Since 2006 Member of the Board of Directors of the Korean Scholars (formerly: Academy) of Marketing Science (KSMS)
Conference Chair	2008 Global Marketing Conference at Shanghai, People's Republic of China, Conference Co-Chair; 2010 Fourth German-French-Austrian Conference on Quantitative Marketing at Vienna, Austria, Conference Chair; 2012 Global Marketing Conference at Seoul, Republic of Korea, Conference Co-Chair.
Editorial Activities	Editor of Marketing ZFP – Journal of Research and Management (since 2011); guest editor of a special issue on "Stochastic Models of Consumer Behaviour", European Journal of Operational Research 76 (2), 1994; guest editor of a special issue on „Operations Research in Marketing", Operations Research Spektrum 22 (1), 2000; guest editor of a special issue of Journal of Business Research (2011).
Editorial Board Member	International Journal of Research in Marketing; Journal für Betriebswirtschaft; Marketing – Journal of Research and Management; Marketing ZFP; Journal of Business Research; Journal of Korean / Global Academy of Marketing Science; Business Research; Akademija MM; der markt – Journal für Marketing.
Scientific Reviewing (selection)	Central European Journal for Operations Research and Economics; Decision Support Systems; Die Betriebswirtschaft; International Journal of Forecasting; Journal of Marketing Research; Management Science; Mathematical Reviews; Zeitschrift für Betriebswirtschaft; Zeitschrift für betriebswirtschaftliche Forschung. Fonds zur Förderung der wissenschaftlichen Forschung; Jubiläumsfonds der ÖNB; Österreichische Akademie der Wissenschaften; National Science Foundation; Rudolf Sallinger-Fonds.
Research Projects (grants/third-party funds; selection)	„Preiswahrnehmung in Tankstellenshops"(2009). Funding: BP Austria; „Gehverhalten von Kunden in Interspar-Filialen"(2009). Funding: Interspar Austria; „Spotlight Viewer – Entwicklung eines neuen Verfahrens zur Messung der visuellen Aufmerksamkeit von Konsumenten beim Betrachten von Werbeanzeigen" (2005). Funding: Hochschuljubiläumsstiftung der Stadt Wien; „Zukunftsorientierte Positionierung des Pflegemanagements" (2003). Funding: Jubiläumsfonds der österreichischen Nationalbank; „Combined Internet based Market and Engineering System for Laser Job Shops – CIMELAS" (2001). Funding: European Commission: Information Society Technologies Programme;

	"Self-Tuning and User-Independent Laser Material Processing Units – SLAPS" (1999). Funding: European Commission: Brite Euram III – Science, Research and Development; "Die Schätzung von Markenpräferenzen auf Grund von Produktbewertungen" (1997). Funding: Universitätspreis der Wiener Wirtschaft; „Aussagekraft von Kaufabsichten" (1996). Funding: Jubiläumsfonds der österreichischen Nationalbank; „Wertanalyse im Dienstleistungsmarketing" (1995). Funding: Stiftung der Bank Austria zur Förderung der Wissenschaft und Forschung an der Universität Wien; „Strategische Gruppen und Wettbewerbsvorteile" (1994). Funding: Bundesministerium für Wissenschaft und Forschung; „Möglichkeiten und Grenzen des Bundling als Markenstrategie" (1993). Funding: Universitätspreis der Wiener Wirtschaft.
Other Activities (selection)	Lecturer resp. director of studies in International Business and other fields e. g. at the University of Applied Sciences at Eisenstadt, Austria (since 1991); Member of the supervisory board of the "Innovationszentrum Universität Wien GmbH" (since 2000).

1.3   Awards and Honors

1989	Senator-Wilhelm-Wilfing Research Award, Vienna University of Economics and Business, Austria.
1991	"Milestone of Business Administration", Zeitschrift für Betriebswirtschaft / Journal of Business Economics, Germany
1995	Verdienstkreuz in Gold, awarded by the state capital of Burgenland, Freistadt Eisenstadt, Austria.
2000	Komturkreuz, awarded by the federal state Burgenland, Austria.
2006	Dr. h.c., honorary doctorate, awarded in acknowledgement of outstanding contributions to Marketing Science by the Technische Universität Braunschweig, Germany.
2007	"Top Publikation 2007" Award, Vienna University of Economics and Business, Austria, "Excellent Service Award 2007", Korean Academy of Marketing Science.
2008	Premier Award, Best Paper Award of the Journal of the Korean Academy of Marketing Science, "Excellent Service Award 2008", Korean Academy of Marketing Science.
2009	Rank No. 9 of all German-speaking researchers in the field of Marketing according to the Handelsblatt Betriebswirte-Ranking 2009, Best Paper Award, German Academic Association for Business Research (VHB)., Germany.
2011	Member of the EMAC Fellows.

2 List of Publications

2.1   Articles

(Classification of journals according to JOURQUAL/JOURQUAL2 rankings, German Academic Association for Business Research (VHB))

■ A+ Journals

Natter, M./Mild, A./Wagner, U./Taudes, A. (2008): Planning New Tariffs at tele.ring – The Application and Impact of an Integrated Segmentation, Targeting and Positioning Tool, in: Marketing Science, 27 (4), pp. 600-609.

Bemmaor, A. C./Wagner, U. (2000): A Multiple-Item Model of Paired Comparisons - Separating Chance from Latent Preference, in: Journal of Marketing Research, 37 (4), pp. 514-524.

Wagner, U./Taudes, A. (1986): A Multivariate Polya Model of Brand Choice and Purchase Incidence, in: Marketing Science, 5 (3), pp. 219-244.

Taudes, A./Wagner, U. (1985): EXORB - A Program System to Examine to Order of Individual Brand Choice Processes, in: Journal of Marketing Research, 22 (2), pp. 218-219.

Wagner, U. (1979): COLLDICO - A Program System for Performing Regression Analysis in the Presence of Collinearity, Diagnosis and Correction, in: Journal of Marketing Research, 16 (4), p. 561.

■ A Journals

Wagner, U./Hoppe, D. (2008): Erratum on the MBG/NBD Model, in: International Journal of Research in Marketing, 25 (3), pp. 225-226.

Hildebrandt, L./Wagner, U. (2000): Marketing and Operations Research - a Literature Survey, in: OR Spektrum 22 (1), pp. 5-18.

Wagner, U./Taudes, A. (1991): Microdynamics of New Product Purchase - a Model Incorporating both Marketing and Consumer-Specific Variables, in: International Journal of Research in Marketing, 8 (3), pp. 223-249.

Wagner, U./Taudes, A. (1987): Stochastic Models of Consumer Behaviour, in: European Journal of Operational Research, 29 (1), pp. 1-23.

■ B Journals

Berger, S./Wagner, U./Schwand, Ch. (2012): Assessing Advertising Effectiveness: The Potential of Goal-Directed Behavior, in: Psychology and Marketing, 29, forthcoming.

Ko E./Taylor, Ch./Sung, H./Lee, J./Wagner, U./Navarro, D./Wang, F. (2012): Global Marketing Segmentation Usefulness in the Sportswear Industry, in: Journal of Business Research, in press; available online March 11, 2011.

Grohs, R./Wagner, U. (2011): Erkennen und verstehen Kinder kontextgebundene Markenpräsentationen? in: Marketing - Zeitschrift für Forschung und Praxis, 33 (1), pp. 7-18.

Ebster, C./Wagner, U./Bumberger, C. (2007): Die Wirkung der kontextbezogenen Verbundpräsentation auf die emotionale Produktbeurteilung, in: Marketing - Zeitschrift für Forschung und Praxis, 29 (1), pp. 40-53.

Hoppe, D./Wagner, U. (2007): Customer Base Analysis: The Case for a Central Variant of the Betageometric/NBD Model, in: Marketing - Journal of Research and Management, 3 (2), pp. 75-90.

Natter, M./Mild, A./Wagner, U./Taudes, A. (2007): Die Planung neuer Tarife bei tele.ring mittels eines integrierten Segmentierungs-, Zielmarktfestlegungs- und Positionierungstools, in: Marketing - Zeitschrift für Forschung und Praxis, 29 (3), pp. 195-210.

Grohs, R./Wagner, U./Vsetecka, S. (2004): Assessing the Effectiveness of Sport Sponsorships - An Empirical Examination, in: Zeitschrift für betriebswirtschaftliche Forschung / Schmalenbach Business Review 56 (2), pp. 119-138.

Wagner, U./Reisinger, H./Gausterer, K. (2001): Die Bestimmung des Markenwechselverhaltens mit Hilfe von Querschnittsdaten, in: Zeitschrift für Betriebswirtschaft/ Journal of Business Economics, 71 (10), pp. 1113-1130.

Baldauf, A./Cravens, D./Wagner, U. (2000): Examining Determinants of Export Performance in Small Open Economies, in: Journal of World Business, 35 (1), pp. 61-79.

Decker, R./Röhle, M./Wagner, U. (1997): Modellgestützte Marketing-Mix-Planung unter Berücksichtigung von Konkurrenzeffekten, in: Zeitschrift für Betriebswirtschaft/ Journal of Business Economics, 67 (11), pp. 1167-1187.

Wagner, U./Geyer, A. (1995): A Maximum Entropy Method for Inverting Laplace Transforms of Probability Density Functions, in: Biometrika, 82 (4), pp. 887-892.

Nenning, M./Topritzhofer, E./Wagner, U. (1991): Empirische Befunde zum Verhältnis zwischen Marktführer und Zweitmarke, in: Meilensteine der Betriebswirtschaftslehre, 60 Jahre Zeitschrift für Betriebswirtschaft/ Journal of Business Economics, Ergänzungsheft 2, pp. 110-121.

Wagner, U./Taudes, A. (1989): Erfahrungen bei der empirischen Marktmodellierung, in: Marketing - Zeitschrift für Forschung und Praxis, 11 (1), pp. 59-65.

Wagner, U. (1980): Reaktionsfunktionen mit zeitvariablen Koeffizienten und dynamische Interaktionsmessung zwischen absatzpolitischen Instrumenten, in: Zeitschrift für Betriebswirtschaft/ Journal of Business Economics, 50 (4), pp. 416-485.

Nenning, M./Topritzhofer, E./Wagner, U. (1979): Multikollinearität im Marketing-Mix - Ridge Regression und andere Diagnose- und Korrekturverfahren aus der Sicht des Anwenders, in: Marketing - Zeitschrift für Forschung und Praxis, 1 (2), pp. 101-114.

Nenning, M./Topritzhofer, E./Wagner, U. (1979): Zur empirischen Überprüfung behaupteter Produkt-Relaunch-Effekte - Ein interventionsanalytischer Ansatz, in: Zeitschrift für betriebswirtschaftliche Forschung, 31 (12), pp. 926-932.

Nenning, M./Topritzhofer, E./Wagner, U. (1979): Zur Kompatibilität alternativer kommerziell verfügbarer Datenquellen für die Marktreaktionsmodellierung - Die Verwendung von Prewhitening-filtern und Kreuzspektralanalyse sowie ihre Konsequenzen für die Analyse betriebswirtschaftlicher Daten, in: Zeitschrift für Betriebswirtschaft/ Journal of Business Economics, 49 (4), pp. 281-297.

Nenning, M./Topritzhofer, E./Wagner, U. (1979): Zur Modellierung und Diagnose struktureller Zusammenhänge in Oligopolsituationen - Seemingly Unrelated Regressions und Zeitreihenanalyse der Residuen, in: Zeitschrift für Operations Research, 23 (2), pp. 45-56.

Nenning, M./Topritzhofer, E./Wagner, U. (1978): Empirische Befunde zum Verhältnis zwischen Marktführer und Zweitmarke, in: Zeitschrift für Betriebswirtschaft/ Journal of Business Economics, 48 (12), pp. 1025-1036.

Nenning, M./Topritzhofer, E./Wagner, U. (1978): Markengoodwill, Lebenszyklus und Wettbewerbsintensität - Meß- und Interpretationsprobleme empirischer Marktdiagnostik, in: Zeitschrift für betriebswirtschaftliche Forschung, 30 (8), pp. 535-543.

- C Journals

Kleinsasser, S./Wagner, U. (2011): Price endings and the tourism consumers' price perceptions, in: Journal of Retailing and Consumer Services, 18 (1), pp. 58-63.

Cornelius, B./Wagner, U./Natter, M. (2010): Managerial Applicability of Graphical Formats Supporting Positioning Decisions, in: Journal für Betriebswirtschaft, 60 (3), pp. 167-201.

Hoppe, D./Wagner, U. (2010): Small Sample Properties of the Pareto/Negative Binomial Distribution Model, in: Marketing - Journal of Research and Management, 6 (1), pp. 39-50.

Diamantopoulos, A./Wagner, U. (2009): Research Productivity in Business Economics: The Case of Marketing, in: German Economic Review, 10 (2), pp. 243-248.

Ebster, C./Wagner, U./Neumüller, D. (2009): Children's Influence on In-store Purchases, in: Journal of Retailing and Consumer Services, 16 (2), pp. 145-154.

Ebster, C./Wagner, U./Richter, V./Prenner, M. (2009): Context Effects of Erotic Television Advertising, in: Marketing - Journal of Research and Management, 5 (2), pp. 61-70.

Ebster, C./Wagner, U./Valis, S. (2006): The Effectiveness of Verbal Prompts on Sales. in: Journal of Retailing and Consumer Services, 13 (3), pp. 169-176.

Krycha, K./Wagner, U. (1999): Applications of Artificial Neural Networks in Management Science - a Survey, in: Journal of Retailing and Consumer Services, 6, pp. 185-203.

■ D Journals

Ebster, C./Wagner, U./Auzinger, C. (2007): The Effect of Displaying Products in their Usage Context – A Field Experimental Investigation, in: Journal of Global Academy of Marketing Science, 17 (2), pp. 99-110.

Loitlsberger, E./Wagner, U. (2003): Zum Selbstverständnis der Betriebswirtschaftslehre als normative Wissenschaft, in: Journal für Betriebswirtschaft, 53 (4), pp. 128-147.

Wagner, U./Reisinger, H. (1997): Die Anwendung statistischer Methoden in der Markt- und Meinungsforschung in Österreich, in: Österreichische Zeitschrift für Statistik, 26 (1), pp. 59-70.

Wagner, U./Taudes, A. (1982): Tagungsbericht zum 7. Symposium über Operations Research, in: Journal für Betriebswirtschaft, 32 (3), pp. 224-225.

■ E Journals

Wagner, U./Jamsawang, J. (2011): Several Aspects of Psychological Pricing: Empirical Evidence from some Austrian Retailers, in: European Retail Research, 25 (2), pp. 1-9.

Ebster, C./Wagner, U. (2009): Geheime Verführer: Der Einfluss von Kindern auf Spontankäufe im Supermarkt, in: Planung & Analyse, 37 (4), pp. 2-4.

Fritz, W./Wagner, U. (2001): Preismanagement im Electronic Commerce, in: WiSt, 12, pp. 648-652.

Wagner, U./Grohs, R./Stadler, E. (2001): Einige Überlegungen zur Preisbildung im österreichischen Lebensmitteleinzelhandel im Zuge der Umstellung auf den Euro, in: der markt 40 (2+3), pp. 110-120.

Baldauf, A./Srnka, K. J./Wagner, U. (1997): Untersuchung eines neuartigen Shopkonzeptes mittels Kundenlaufstudie, in: der markt, 36 (3+4), pp. 103-111.

Wagner, U. (1997): Ausgewählte Diplomarbeiten und Dissertationen des Instituts für Betriebswirtschaftlehre - Lehrstuhl für Marketing an der Universität Wien aus dem Studienjahr 1996/97, in: der markt, 36 (2), pp. 103-111.

Srnka, K. J./Wagner, U. (1996): Ethik im Management österreichischer Unternehmen - Verknüpfung von Theorie und Praxis, in: der markt, 35 (4), pp. 199-207.

Wagner, U. (1995): Institut für Betriebswirtschaftslehre, Lehrstuhl für Marketing, in: der markt, 34 (3), pp. 111-115.

Wagner, U./Gemeinböck, G. (1993): Rechtliche Aspekte des Product Placement in Österreich, in: Werbeforschung & Praxis, 4, pp. 145-149.

Wagner, U. (1988): Vollstochastische Kaufverhaltensmodelle, in: der markt, 27 (1), pp. 36-45.

Wagner, U./Hohenecker, J. (1983): Überprüfung der absatzwirtschaftlichen Auswirkungen einer Produktdiversifikation auf dem Frischmilchmarkt mit Hilfe der Interventionsanalyse, in: Die Bodenkultur, 34 (1), pp. 74-86.

2.2   Books

Wagner, U. (1985): Vollstochastische Kaufverhaltensmodelle - Ihr Beitrag zur Analyse realer Märkte Wien, Athenäum Verlag.

Nenning, M./Topritzhofer, E./Wagner, U. (1981): Empirische Marktmodellierung, Würzburg/Wien Physica-Verlag.

2.3   Editor

Wagner, U./Wiedmann, K.-P./von der Oelsnitz, D. (2011): Das Internet der Zukunft. Bewährte Erfolgstreiber und neue Chancen, Wiesbaden, Gabler Verlag.

Wagner, U./Reisinger, H./Schwand, C. (2009): Fallstudien aus der österreichischen Marketingpraxis 5, Wien, WUV-Universitätsverlag.

Taylor, C./Schmitt, B./Wagner, U./Jia, J. (2008): Proceedings of the Global Marketing Conference at Shanghai, CD-Rom, KAMS.

Wagner, U./Reisinger, H./Schwand, C./Hoppe, D. (2006): Fallstudien aus der österreichischen Marketingpraxis 4, Wien, WUV-Universitätsverlag.

Wagner, U./Reisinger, H./Baldauf, A. (2003): Fallstudien aus der österreichischen Marketingpraxis 3, Wien, WUV-Universitätsverlag.

Wagner, U. (2001): Zum Erkenntnisstand der Betriebswirtschaftslehre am Beginn des 21. Jahrhunderts, Wien, Duncker & Humblot.

Wagner, U./Reisinger, H./Baldauf, A. (1998): Fallstudien aus der österreichischen Marketingpraxis 2, 2. überarb. Aufl. (1. Aufl. 1997), Wien, WUV-Universitätsverlag.

Wagner, U./Reisinger, H. (1996): Fallstudien aus der österreichischen Marketingpraxis, 2. überarb. Aufl. (1. Aufl. 1994), Wien, WUV-Universitätsverlag.

2.4   Book Chapters

Wagner, U./Jamsawang, J./Hinteregger, L. M. (2011): Haben ausgewählte Zahlen eine kulturspezifische Bedeutung für die Preissetzung? Eine internetbasierte Analyse, in: Wagner, U., Wiedmann, K.-P. und von der Oelsnitz, D., Das Internet der Zukunft, Wiesbaden, Gabler, pp. 245-266.

Wagner, U./Baldauf, A. (2007): Marktabgrenzung und Marktstrukturierung, in: Albers, S. and Herrmann, A., Handbuch Produktmanagement, 3. Aufl., (1. Aufl. 2000), pp. 252-272.

Wagner, U./Reisinger, H. (2007): Einsatzmöglichkeiten für statistische Methoden in der Marktforschung, in: VMÖ, Handbuch der Marktforschung, pp. 217-222.

Wagner, U./Reisinger, H. (2005): The Option of No-Purchase in the Empirical Description of Brand Choice Behaviour, in: Baier, D., Decker, R. und Schmidt-Thieme, L., Data Analysis and Decision Support, Festschrift für Wolfgang Gaul, Berlin, Springer, pp. 323-334.

Fritz, W./Wagner, U. (2004): Soziale Verantwortung als Leitidee der Unternehmensführung und Gegenstand der akademischen Ausbildung, in: Wiedmann, K., Fritz, W. und Abel, B., Management mit Vision und Verantwortung, pp. 425-449.

Wagner, U./Grohs, R./Leisch, M. (2003): Zur Entwicklung der Beziehungen zwischen Hersteller und Handel auf dem Neuwagenmarkt, in: Ahlert, D., Olbrich, R., Schröder, H., Jahrbuch Vertriebs- und Handelsmanagement 2003 - Marktstrategische Veränderungen in der Hersteller-Handels-Dyade, Frankfurt am Main, Deutscher Fachverlag, pp. 252-261

Wagner, U./Srnka, K. J. (2003): Zur Bedeutung von Information im Marketing, in: Dosoudil, I., Information und Wirtschaft - Aspekte einer komplexen Beziehung, Wien, WUV, pp. 25-52.

Bemmaor, A. C./Wagner, U. (2002): Estimating Market-Level Multiplicative Models of Promotion Effects with Linearly Aggregated Data - A Parametric Approach, in: Franses, P. H. und Montgomery, A. L., Econometric Models in Marketing, Elsevier Science, (Advances in Econometrics, 16), pp. 165-189.

Wagner, U./Fritz, W. (2001): Tendenzen marktorientierter Preispolitik im ‚Electronic Commerce‘, in: Wagner, U., Zum Erkenntnisstand der Betriebswirtschaftslehre am Beginn des 21. Jahrhunderts, pp. 451-474.

Wagner, U./Reisinger, H./Russ, R. (2001): Der Einsatz von Methoden des Data Mining zur Unterstützung kommunikationspolitischer Aktivitäten der Lauda Air, in: Hippner, H., Küsters, U., Meyer, M. und Wilde, K. D., Handbuch Data Mining im Marketing, Viehweg, Braunschweig, Wiesbaden, pp. 875-888.

Wagner, U./Boyer, C. (2000): Measuring Brand Loyalty on the Individual Level - a Comparative Study, in: Decker, R. und Gaul, W., Classification and Information Processing at the Turn of the Millennium, pp. 275-287.

Wagner, U./Reisinger, H. (1999): Die Vermittlung quantitativer Inhalte im betriebswirtschaftlichen Unterricht, in: Gaul, W. und Schader, M., Mathematische Methoden der Wirtschaftswissenschaften, Heidelberg Physica, pp. 455-463.

Wagner, U./Baldauf, A. (1998): The Austrian Consumer within the European Community - A Cross-Cultural Comparison, in: Backhaus, K., Contemporary Developments in Marketing, pp. 469-487.

Decker, R./Röhle, M./Wagner, U. (1995): Kaufverhaltensmodelle im praktischen Einsatz für Analyse und Optimierung, in: Baier, D. und Decker, R., Marketingprobleme - Innovative Lösungsansätze aus Forschung und Praxis, pp. 63-72.

Wagner, U./Geyer-Schulz, A./Taudes, A. (1988): Exploring the Possibilities of an Improvement of Stochastic Market Models by Rule-Based Systems, in: Gaul, W. und Schader, M., Data, Expert Knowledge and Decisions, pp. 54-66.

Wagner, U./Pichler, M. (1987): Mathematische Grundausbildung für Studenten der Wirtschaftswissenschaften, in: Dörfler, W., Fischer, R. und Peschek, W., Wirtschaftsmathematik in Beruf und Ausbildung, pp. 275-306.

Wagner, U./Taudes, A. (1985): The Multivariate Polya Process as a Model of Consumer Behaviour, in: Beckmann, M., Methods of Operations Research, (54), pp. 573-574.

Wagner, U. and Taudes, A. (1985): Brand Choice as a Heterogeneous Nonstationary Zero Order Process, in: Henn, R., Methods of Operations Research, (55), pp. 331-349.

Wagner, U./Taudes, A. (1983): Entwicklung und empirische Validierung eines heterogenen Kaufverhaltensmodells, in: Henn, R., Methods of Operations Research, (46), pp. 653-666.

Wagner, U./Taudes, A. (1983): On a Generalized Zero Order Model of Consumer Behavior, in: Zufryden, F. S., Advances and Practices of Marketing Science, pp. 240-254.

Nenning, M./Topritzhofer, E./Wagner, U. (1982): Preisreaktion, Markengoodwill, Lebenszyklus und Wettbewerbsintensität, in: Böcker, F., Preistheorie und Preisverhalten, pp. 90-100.

Wagner, U. (1982): On Discriminating among Stochastic Models - a Survey, in: Feichtinger, G. und Kall, P., Operations Research in Progress, pp. 367-379.

Nenning, M./Topritzhofer, E./Wagner, U. (1979): On the Reliability of Alternative Commercially Available Data Sources for the Measurement of Market Response - The Use of Prewhitening and Cross-Spectral Analysis, in: Montgomery, D. B. und Wittink, D. R., Market Measurement and Analysis, pp. 502-514.

2.5   Conference Proceedings

Berger, S./Wagner, U. (2010): Implicit Measurement of Advertising Effectiveness by Recording Goal-Directed Behavior, Marketing Theory Challenges in Emerging Societies. 1st EMAC Regional Conference.

Berger, S./Wagner, U. (2010): Implicit Measurment of Advertising Effectiveness by Reccording Goal-Directed Behavior, New Directions - New Insights. 4th GFA-Conference.

Grohs, R./Wagner, U./Steiner, R. (2010): Children's Sponsorship Perceptions and Sponsor Awareness, 5th International Research Days on Marketing Communications, Nancy.

Grohs, R./Wagner, U./Steiner, R. (2010): Child's Play? An Investigation into Children's Ability to Identify Sponsors and Understand Sponsorship Intentions, New Directions - New Insights. 4th GFA-Conference, Vienna.

Grohs, R./Wagner, U./Steiner, R. (2010): Drivers of Correct Sponsor Identification for Children, The Essentials of Marketing. 39th EMAC Conference.

Hoppe, D./Wagner, U. (2010): A Monte Carlo Study on Sampling Properties of the Pareto/NBD Model, 32nd Annual INFORMS Marketing Science Conference, Cologne.

Hoppe, D./Wagner, U. (2010): The Role of Lifetime Activity Cues in Customer Base Analysis, New Directions - New Insights. 4th GFA-Conference, Vienna.

Hoppe, D./Wagner, U. (2010): Small Samples Properties of the Pareto/NBD Model, The sic Senses - The Essentials of Marketing. 39th EMAC Conference.

Wagner, U./Ebster, C./Kulnig, A. (2010): Increasing Advertising Awareness in Freesheets, New Directions - New Insights. 4th GFA-Conference, Vienna.

Wagner, U./Jamsawang, J. (2010): Einige empirische Ergebnisse zur psychologischen Preissetzung im österreichischen Handel, Tagungsprogramm Handelsforschung Berlin.

Wagner, U./Reisinger, H./Schuster, M. (2009): Modelling Concepts of Non-purchase Behaviour for Low-Involvement Goods, Cheng Kong GSB Marketing Research Forum, Beijing.

Ebster, C./Wagner, U./Geider, B. (2008): The Effect of Floor Texture on Consumer Behaviour at the Point of Sale, SMA Proceedings.

Ebster, C./Wagner, U./Geider, B. (2008): Floor Covering as a Means to Influence the Duration of Shopping? 2008 Korean Academy of Marketing Science International Conference and Fashion Marketing Symposium.

Ebster, C./Wagner, U./Prenner, M./Richter, V. (2008): Carry-Over Effects of Television Commercials, Marketing landscapes: A Pause for Thought - Proceedings from the 37th EMAC Conference.

Ebster, C./Wagner, U./Richter, V./Prenner, M. (2008): Contest Effects of Television Advertising, in: Proceedings of the Global Marketing Conference at Shanghai, Shanghai (CD-Rom).

Ko, E./Wagner, U./Kim, K./Sung, H./Kim, E./Taylor, C./Lee, J. (2008): Segmentation and Targeting Sportswear Consumers in Global Markets, in: Proceedings of the Global Marketing Conference at Shanghai, Shanghai (CD-Rom).

Wagner, U. (2008): Branding for Food Products - The Austrian Case, Proceedings from the Symposium Launching Strategy for Productive National Food Cluster in Korea".

Hoppe, D./Wagner, U. (2007): Customer Base Analysis: The Case for a Central Variant of the Betageometric/NBD Model, Third German French Austrian Conference on Quantitative Marketing, Cergy Pontoise.

Ko, E./Wagner, U./Kim, E. Y./Choi, S. M./Lee, J. (2007): A Global Segmentation by Lifestyle and Nationality Focused on Sportswear Consumers, in: Flexible Marketing in an Unpredictable World - Proceedings from the 36th EMAC Conference, (CD-Rom).

Natter, M./Mild, A./Taudes, A./Wagner, U. (2007): Planning New Tariffs at tele.ring – An Integrated Segmentation, Targeting and Positioning Tool Designed for Managerial Applicability, in: Flexible Marketing in an Unpredictable World - Proceedings from the 36th EMAC Conference, (CD-Rom).

Wagner, U./Hoppe, D. (2007): Customer Base Analysis: The Case for a Central Variant of the Betageometric/NBD Model, XXIX Informs Marketing Science Conference, Singapore.

Wagner, U./Lee, S. (2007): A Cross-cultural Comparison of Counterfeit Products Between Austrian, Korean and Rumanian Customers, in: Flexible Marketing in an Unpredictable World - Proceedings from the 36th EMAC Conference, (CD-Rom).

Wagner, U./Lee, S. (2007): A Cross-cultural Comparison of Counterfeit Products Between Austrian, Korean and Rumanian Customers, in: Proceedings of the '2007 Korean Academy of Marketing Science Spring International Conference', p. 11.

Ebster, C./Wagner, U./Bumberger, C. (2006): Bundled Product Presentations in a Retailing Environment, in: Résumé des Communications, XXIIème Congrès International de l'Association Francaise du Marketing 2006, pp. 75-77.

Ebster, C./Wagner, U./Bumberger, C. (2006): The Effects of Presenting Products in their Usage Context, in: Moon, J., Proceedings of the '2006 Academy of Marketing Science / Korean Academy of Marketing Science Cultural Perspectives in Marketing Conference', (CD-Rom).

Ebster, C./Wagner, U./Neumüller, D. (2006): Mommy, I Want That! - Spontaneous Purchases Triggered by Children, in: Andreani, J. C., Proceedings of the 5th International Congress Marketing Trends", Venice, pp. 1-28.

Natter, M./Mild, A./Taudes, A./Wagner, U. (2006): Planning New Tariffs at tele.ring – The Application and Impact of an Integrated Segmentation, Targeting and Positioning Tool, in: Proceedings of the XXVIII Informs Marketing Science Conference, Pittsburgh.

Wagner, U. (2006): Harmonization of the Educational System at University Level within the European Union - Experiences from Austria, in: Vestnik finansovoj akademii, Moskau, (1-2) pp. 37-38.

Ebster, C./Wagner, U./Neumüller, D. (2005): Impulsive Buying Triggered by Children, in: Proceedings of the '2005 Korean Academy of Marketing Science Fall Conference'.

Wagner, U./Ebster, C./Valis, S. (2005): The Effect of Suggestive Selling on Sales, in: Troilo, G., Rejuvenating Marketing: Contamination, Innovation, Integration. Proceedings from the 34th EMAC Conference, Milan, p. 147.

Grohs, R./Wagner, U./Vsetecka, S. (2003): Assessing the Effectiveness of Sport Sponsorships - An Empirical Examination, 2nd International Conference on Research in Advertising, Amsterdam.

Reisinger, H./Wagner, U./Schuster, M. (2003): Die Schätzung von Markentreue, Nichtkäuferanteil und Marktpotenzial aus Handelspaneldaten, in: Leopold-Wildburger, U., Rendl, F. und Wäscher, G., Operations Research Proceedings 2002, pp. 127-132.

Wagner, U./Reisinger, H./Schuster, M. (2001): Extracting Brand Switching Behaviour from Cross-Sectional Information - Further Results, in: Breivik, E., Falkenberg, A. W. und Gronhaug, K., Rethinking European Marketing, Proceedings from the 30th EMAC Conference, Bergen, (CD-Rom).

Hildebrandt, L./Wagner, U. (2000): Marketing and Operations Research - a Literature Survey, Proceedings of the XXII Informs Marketing Science Conference, Los Angeles.

Wagner, U./Reisinger, H./Platter, S. (1999): Extracting Brand Switching Behaviour from Cross-Sectional Information, in: Hildebrandt, L., Annacker, D. und Klapper, D., Marketing and Competition in the Information Age, Proceedings of the 28th EMAC Conference, Berlin, (CD-Rom).

Wagner, U./Baldauf, A./Cravens, D. (1998): Differences in Perceived Environment, Firm Characteristics, and Strategies Between Higher and Lower Export Performers - An Austrian Study, in: Pelton, L. E. und Schnedlitz, P., Proceedings of the American Marketing Association Exchange Colloqium, p. 16.

Baldauf, A./Wagner, U./Grasserbauer, B./Puffer, M. (1996): The Assessment of Strategic Marketing Heterogeneity within Three Austrian Industries, in: Beracs, J., Proceedings from the 25th EMAC Conference, pp. 1405-1410.

Bemmaor, A./Wagner, U. (1996): Estimating Preferences from Ratings in Single and Multiple Paired Comparison Product Tests, in: Hildebrandt, L. und Laurent, G., First French-German Workshop on Quantitative Methods in Marketing.

Wagner, U./Bemmaor, A. (1989): Zur Prognose des Kaufverhaltens aus Kaufabsichtsdaten mit Hilfe des Betabinomial-Modells, in: Pressmar, E., Operations Research Proceedings, pp. 418-425.

Geyer-Schulz, A./Taudes, A./Wagner, U. (1987): Zur Integration von Stochastischen Kaufverhaltensmodellen und regelbasierten Systemen, in: Frank, H., Plaschka, G. und Rössl, D., Wirtschaftliches Handeln unter dynamischen Umweltbedingungen, pp. 49-67.

2.6 Working Papers and Research Reports

Wagner, U./Eske, U./Weitzel, W./Ebster, C. (2011): Shadowing Consumers at the Point of Sale, Forschungsbericht des Instituts für Betriebswirtschaftslehre der Universität Wien.

Wagner, U./Lee, S./Kleinsasser, S./Jamsawang, J. (2011): Luxury Goods vs. Counterfeits – An Intercultural Study, Forschungsbericht des Instituts für Betriebswirtschaftslehre der Universität Wien.

Wagner, U./Weitzel, W. (2011): A Note on Measuring Competition for FMCG Markets, Forschungsbericht des Instituts für Betriebswirtschaftslehre der Universität Wien.

Garaus, M./Wagner, U./Kummer, C. (2011): Causes of Store Environmental Confusion: Empirical Investigation, Forschungsbericht des Instituts für Betriebswirtschaftslehre der Universität Wien.

Wolfsteiner, E./Grohs, R./Wagner, U. (2011): The Effect of Multiple Response Options on Sponsor and Ambush Marketer Identification, Forschungsbericht des Instituts für Betriebswirtschaftslehre der Universität Wien.

Wagner, U./Diamantopoulos, A. (2010): Research Productivity in Business Economics: The Case of Marketing, Internes Arbeitspapier.

Hoppe, D./Wagner, U. (2008): Supplementary Appendix to Customer Bases Analysis: The Case of a Central Variant of the Betageometric INBD Model, Forschungsberichte des Instituts für Betriebswirtschaftslehre der Universität Wien.

Keber, C./Wagner, U./Leitner, M.-L. (2005): Absolventenanalyse, Arbeitspapier der Fakultät für Wirtschaftswissenschaften der Universität Wien, Dezember.

Wagner, U./Zulauf, K. G./Lachhammer, H./Pfisterer-Pollhammer, J./Lehmann, A. (2005): Zukunftsorientierte Positionierung des Pflegemanagements, Schlussbericht des Projekts Nr. 10.757, gefördert durch den Jubiläumsfonds der Österreichischen Nationalbank.

Fritz, W./Wagner, U. (2005): Soziale Verantwortung als Leitidee der Unternehmensführung und Gegenstand der akademischen Ausbildung, Forschungsberichte des Instituts für Betriebswirtschaftslehre der Universität Wien sowie AP 04/03 des Instituts für Marketing, Technische Universität Braunschweig.

Wagner, U./Fritz, W. (2000): Tendenzen marktorientierter Preispolitik im Electronic Commerce, Forschungsberichte des Instituts für Betriebswirtschaftslehre der Universität Wien sowie AP 01/01 des Instituts für Marketing, Technische Universität Braunschweig.

Röhle, M./Wagner, U./Decker, R. (1998): Zur methodengestützten Validierung stochastischer Kaufverhaltensmodelle, Diskussionspapier, Nr. 394, Universität Bielefeld, Fakultät für Wirtschaftswissenschaften.

Wagner, U./Reisinger, H./Sautner, J. (1998): Market Research in Practice - Demand Forecasting for a New Brand, Forschungsberichte des Instituts für Betriebswirtschaftslehre der Universität Wien.

Reisinger, H./Wagner, U./Endlich, E. (1997): Wirtschaftsuniversität Wien und Betriebswirtschaftszentrum der Universität Wien im Vergleich - Die Wahrnehmung alternativer Bildungseinrichtungen aus der Sicht von Studienanfängern, Forschungsberichte des Instituts für Betriebswirtschaftslehre der Universität Wien.

Wagner, U./Baldauf, A. (1997): Economic Integration and Cultural Diversity within the European Union - The Austrian Case from a Consumer Behavior Perspective, Forschungsberichte des Instituts für Betriebswirtschaftslehre der Universität Wien.

Wagner, U./Baldauf, A. (1996): Strategische Gruppen und Wettbewerbsvorteile - Empirische Überprüfung anhand der Textil-, Bau-, Maschinen- und Stahlbauindustrie, Forschungsbericht.

Wagner, U./Krycha, K. (1996): Consumer Behaviour, in: Mazanec, J. und Otruba, H. (Hrsg.), Antragsdokument des Spezialforschungsbereichs (SFB) 'Selbstlernende Modelle in den Sozial- und Wirtschaftswissenschaften' an den Fonds zur Förderung der wissenschaftlichen Forschung (FWF).

Wagner, U./Moser, R. (1993): Study on the Economic Aspects of the Use of Vanadium and Related Metals in the Steel Industry, Working Paper.

Wagner, U. (1989): Maßnahmen zur Optimierung der Hörsaalvergabe - Dokumentation des Zuteilungsalgorithmus und Grobspezifikation der verschiedenen Programme: Bericht über das Projekt 'Optimale Hörsaalvergabe' im Rahmen der Umsetzung der WU-2000 Strategie, Arbeitspapier der Wirtschaftsuniversität Wien, Oktober.

Wagner, U. (1988): Maßnahmen zur Optimierung der Hörsaalvergabe - Pilotphase: Bericht über das Projekt 'Optimale Hörsaalvergabe' im Rahmen der Umsetzung der WU-2000 Strategie, Arbeitspapier der Wirtschaftsuniversität Wien, Oktober.

Wagner, U./Geyer, A. (1988): On the Dynamics of Interpurchase Times, Marketing-Arbeitspapiere der Wirtschaftsuniversität Wien, Nr. 5.

2.7   Case Studies

Wagner, U./Pötz, D. (2003): Strategische Planung bei MLP - Finanzdienstleistungen, in: Wagner, U., Reisinger, H. und Baldauf, A., Fallstudien aus der österreichischen Marketingpraxis 3, Wien, WUV, pp. 49-62.

Wagner, M./Wagner, U. (1998): Universitäts-Bräu - Preispolitische Überlegungen bei der Einführung eines neuen Bieres, in: Wagner, U., Reisinger, H. und Baldauf, A., Fallstudien aus der österreichischen Marketingpraxis 2, Wien, WUV, pp. 225-242.

Wagner, U./Baldauf, A. (1993): Metzgerei Anton Baumgartners Witwe und Co. - Informationsgrundlagen für die Preispolitik, in: Aigner, W., Meyer, M. und Rössl, D., Marketing - Fallstudien für Klein- und Mittelbetriebe, pp. 231-255.

2.8   Reviews

Wagner, U. (1993): Sunspots and Incomplete Financial Markets - the General Case - David Cass, Econom. Theory 2 (3), in: Mathematical Reviews.

Wagner, U. (1992): Market Equilibria under Increasing Returns - Claus Weddepohl, Nieuw Arch. Wisk. (4) 8, 3, in: Mathematical Reviews.

Wagner, U. (1992): The Transactions Cost of Money (A Strategic Market Game Analysis) - Martin Shubik, Shuntian Yao, Mathematical Social Sciences 20, 2, in: Mathematical Reviews.

Wagner, U. (1992): Zur Bedeutung der Concurrency-Theorie für den Aufbau hochverteilter Systeme - Einar Smith, GMD-Bericht Nr. 180, in: Mathematical Reviews.

Wagner, U. (1991): Optimality Conditions for Utility Maximization in an incomplete Market - Ioannis Karatzas, John P. Lehoczky, Gan-Lin Xu, Analysis and optimization of systems 3-23, in: Mathematical Reviews.

Wagner, U. (1991): Perceptual Position and Competitive Brand Strategy in a Two- Dimensional, Two-Brand Market - Gregory S. Carpenter, Management Science 35 (9), in: Mathematical Reviews.

Wagner, U. (1985): Contributions to Operations Research and Mathematical Economics, Volumes 1 and 2 - Gerald Hammer, Diethard Pallaschke (Ed.), in: Österreichische Zeitschrift für Statistik und Informatik, 15 (2-3), pp. 249-251.

Wagner, U. (1984): On the Determination of Advertising Effectiveness - An Empirical Study of the German Cigarette Market - Jan C. Reuijl, in: International Journal of Research in Marketing, 1 (2), pp. 164-166.

Wagner, U. (1982): Die Dynamisierung komplexer Marktmodelle mit Hilfe von Verfahren der Mehrdimensionalen Skalierung - Rudolf Schobert, in: Zeitschrift für Betriebswirtschaft/ Journal of Business Economics, 52 (7).

2.9　　Miscellaneous

Wagner, U. (2012): Editorial, in: Marketing ZFP – Journal of Research and Management, 34 (1).

Wagner, U. (2011): Editorial, in: Marketing ZFP – Journal of Research and Management, 33 (4).

Wagner, U. (2011): Editorial, in: Marketing ZFP – Journal of Research and Management, 33 (3).

Wagner, U. (2011): EMAC on the Go, in: The EMAC Chronicle, 10.

Wagner, U. (2011): Editorial, in: Marketing ZFP – Journal of Research and Management, 33 (2).

Wagner, U. (2011): Management v etické perspective, in: Manazerská Etika, X dil.

Wagner, U. (2011): Conference Attendance as a Prerequisite for EMAC Membership?, in: The EMAC Chronicle, 9.

Wagner, U. (2010): Does the Loyalty of EMAC Members depend on their Country of Origin? in: The EMAC Chronicle, 7, pp. 24-25.

Wagner, U./Avlonitis, G. (2010): Marketing Department Heads Forum, in: The EMAC Chronicle, 8.

Wagner, U. (2009): Preferred Publication Outlets of EMAC Members, in: The EMAC Chronicle, 5, p. 6.

Wagner, U. (2008): EMAC Membership Situation 2008, in: The EMAC Chronicle, 3, pp. 10-12.

Wagner, U. (2008): Pannonia Research Award, Kommentar, in: Campus Burgenland, 1.

Wagner, U. (2007): Cooperation with the Korean Academy of Marketing Science, in: The EMAC Chronicle, 2, p. 9.

Wagner, U. (2007): EMAC Membership Situation, in: The EMAC Chronicle, 1, pp. 6–7.

Fritz, W./Wagner, U. (2006): Soziale Verantwortung und Unternehmenserfolg, in: bdvb-aktuell (Bundesverband Deutscher Volks- und Betriebswirte e.V.), 92, pp. 6-8.

Wagner, U. (2006): Danksagung und Vortrag zur Stellung des Faches Marketing, in: Festreden anlässlich der Verleihung der Ehrendoktorwürde an Herrn o. Univ. Prof. Dipl.-Ing. Dr. techn. Udo Wagner am 9. Dezember 2006 an der Technischen Universität Braunschweig, pp. 43-62.

Matosic, T./Wagner, U. (2000): Nachholbedarf, in: Cash.

Wagner, U./Baldauf, A. (1998): Erfolgsfaktoren österreichischer Exporteure - Ergebnisse einer empirischen Studie, in: Internationale Wirtschaft, 35, pp. 32-39.

Wagner, U./Reisinger, H. (1996): Erfolgreicher Einsatz von Operations Research in Österreich - Ein heuristischer Algorithmus zur Organisation von Servicearbeiten, in: ÖGOR-NEWS 2, pp. 10-11.

Wagner, U. (1990): Eindrücke über den Studienbetrieb an einer amerikanischen Universität, in: wu-memo, 35.

Wagner, U./Geyer, A. (1988): Vorstellung der Forschungsprojekte: Über die Dynamik von Erneuerungsprozessen mit besonderer Berücksichtigung der Dynamik im Kaufverhalten von einzelnen Haushalten; Computergestützte Kaufverhaltensanalyse - quantitative Techniken zur Entscheidungsunterstützung im Marketing, in: Österreichische Hochschulzeitung, 40 (10), pp. 16-19.

2.10 Lecture Scripts

Wagner, U. (2011): Forschung & Entwicklung, Arbeitsunterlagen zur gleichnamigen Lehrveranstaltung.

Wagner, U. (2011): Management Science – Marketing, Arbeitsunterlagen zur gleichnamigen Lehrveranstaltung.

Wagner, U. (2010): Kaufverhalten, Arbeitsunterlagen zur gleichnamigen Lehrveranstaltung.

Wagner, U. (2010): Marketing Management - Preispolitik, Arbeitsunterlagen zur gleichnamigen Lehrveranstaltung.

Wagner, U. (2010): Marketing Modelle, Arbeitsunterlagen zur gleichnamigen Lehrveranstaltung.

Wagner, U. (2010): Marketing Research, Arbeitsunterlagen zur gleichnamigen Lehrveranstaltung.

Wagner, U. (2010): Multivariate Verfahren, Arbeitsunterlagen zur gleichnamigen Lehrveranstaltung.

Wagner, U./Hoppe, D. (2010): Stochastic Models, Arbeitsunterlagen zur gleichnamigen Lehrveranstaltung für Doktoranden.

Wagner, U. (2009): Marketing Management - Preispolitik, Arbeitsunterlagen zur gleichnamigen Lehrveranstaltung.

Wagner, U. (2009): Mathematik & Statistik, Arbeitsunterlagen zur gleichnamigen Lehrveranstaltung.

Wagner, U. (2008): Empirische Sozialforschung, Arbeitsunterlagen zur gleichnamigen MBA-Lehrveranstaltung.

Wagner, U. (2008): Empirische Sozialforschung, Arbeitsunterlagen zur gleichnamigen MBA-Lehrveranstaltung.

Wagner, U. (2008): Kaufverhalten, Arbeitsunterlagen zur gleichnamigen Lehrveranstaltung.

Wagner, U. (2008): Marketing Modelle, Arbeitsunterlagen zur gleichnamigen Lehrveranstaltung.

Wagner, U. (2008): Marketing Research, Arbeitsunterlagen zur gleichnamigen Lehrveranstaltung.

Wagner, U./Hoppe, D. (2008): Stochastic Models, Arbeitsunterlagen zur gleichnamigen Lehrveranstaltung für Doktoranden.

Wagner, U. (2000): Ausgewählte Teilgebiete der Allgemeinen Betriebswirtschaftslehre - Marketing für Fortgeschrittene, Arbeitsunterlagen zur gleichnamigen Lehrveranstaltung.

Wagner, U. (1999): Modellgestützte Unternehmensführung, Arbeitsunterlagen zur gleichnamigen Lehrveranstaltung.

Wagner, U./Reisinger, H./Baldauf, A. (1994): Lösungsvorschläge zu den Problemstellungen aus: Wagner, Udo, Reisinger, Heribert (Hrsg.), Fallstudien aus der österreichischen Marketingpraxis, Skriptum.

Wagner, U. (1991): Stochastische Prozesse in der Betriebswirtschaftslehre II, Skriptum zur gleichnamigen Lehrveranstaltung.

Wagner, U. (1990): Stochastische Prozesse in der Betriebswirtschaftslehre I, Skriptum zur gleichnamigen Lehrveranstaltung.

Wagner, U. (1986): Operations Research am Computer I + II, Skriptum zur Lehrveranstaltung über Operations Research am Computer.

Wagner, U. (1986): Optimierung - Theorie und Praxis II, Skriptum zur Lehrveranstaltung über Optimierung.

Wagner, U. (1985): Optimierung - Theorie und Praxis I, Skriptum zur Lehrveranstaltung über Optimierung.

Nenning, M./Topritzhofer, E./Wagner, U. (1978): Methoden der Marktmodellierung - ein Handbuch, gestützt auf Ergebnisse eines empirischen Forschungsprojektes, Skriptum über quantitative Methoden der Marktmodellierung.

Subject Index

Printed by Books on Demand, Germany